PUBLIC COMPANIES AND EQUITY FINANCE

PUBLIC COMPANIES AND EQUITY FINANCE

Alexis Mavrikakis MA (Cantab), Solicitor (non-practising)

CLP

Published by
The University of Law
2 Bunhill Row, London EC1Y 8HQ

British Library Cataloguing-in-Publication Data

A catalogue record for this book is available from the British Library.

ISBN 978 1 80502 153 7

Typeset by Style Photosetting Ltd, Mayfield, East Sussex

Tables and index by Moira Greenhalgh, Arnside, Cumbria

Preface

This book traces the life of a public company from birth (and its planned conception too), through adolescence and its growth into maturity until its demise, or at least the possibility of its demise, for immortality of course may beckon for this legal form of person. In doing so it concentrates on the public company listed on the London Stock Exchange. It is the mightiest of all companies, the biggest and the most high-profile. As such it operates subject to a whole raft of additional rules and regulations (advice on which provides many a fat cheque for lawyers and other advisers), and is required to expose itself to unparalled public scrutiny (providing rich pickings for newspaper and television journalists with unending column inches or minutes to fill).

This book has been written to explain the issues a lawyer may encounter when advising a public company. It seeks in particular to explain the principles behind the rules and to decipher the jargon which lawyers like to use in relation to those rules.

This book should be useful to law students and trainees in corporate seats, as an overview of public company work and as a guide to using the primary sources more effectively. It may also be of interest to the other professionals who work alongside public company lawyers, such as lawyers who undertake corporate support work, accountants and stockbrokers, as an insight into just what public company lawyers do.

To achieve an overview of public company issues, the best way to read this book is to start at Chapter 1 and read through to Chapter 24. This will guide you in a logical manner through the issues which face a public company, from registration, through flotation, to complying with continuing obligations, raising funds and entering into transactions. However, the book is also suitably cross-referenced to enable it to be used in practice as a reference book.

Brexit has brought with it great challenges for the City and its financial markets, and for the corporate lawyer as well. So much of the law affecting listed companies originated from the EU, and although the UK Government initially preserved as much of the existing EU law as possible, a series of reviews and consultations have kickstarted the process of tailoring the EU's regulatory regime for financial services to reflect the needs and the interests of the UK alone. Indeed, these legislative changes are now making their way into the rulebooks and are being reflected in the law as set out in this book.

I am most grateful to Alistair MacQueen, Robert Nisbet-Smith, Catherine Shephard, David Stott and Peter Watson for variously their bequest, forbearance in the face of deadlines stretched, scrupulous attention to detail and lawyerly insight.

This book should not be relied upon for the provision of, or as a substitute for, legal advice.

Please feel free to e-mail any comments to alexis.mavrikakis@gov.ky.

The law is stated as at 1 September 2024.

Alexis Mavrikakis
Truman Bodden Law School
George Town, Grand Cayman

For Robert and Waffle

and in memoriam

Alistair MacQueen

Suzanne Lowe

and Daisy

Contents

Table of Cases

Table of Statutes

Table of Secondary Legislation

Guidelines

Glossary

ABI	Association of British Insurers (which represents the interests of the UK's insurance industry)
accounting reference date	The date on which the financial year of a company ends
Admission and Disclosure Standards	Rules made by the Stock Exchange in relation to admission to trading and disclosure of information (see **2.9**). Available at the Stock Exchange's website
ADS	Admission and Disclosure Standard
AGM	An Annual General Meeting of shareholders and directors held pursuant to s 336 of the CA 2006
AIM	The Alternative Investment Market of the London Stock Exchange: a global market for smaller and growing companies
AIM Rules	Rules published by the Stock Exchange for AIM-quoted companies. Available at the Stock Exchange's website
AIM Rules for Nominated Advisers	Rules published by the Stock Exchange for Nomads of AIM-quoted companies. Available at the Stock Exchange's website
analyst	Person employed by an investment bank or stockbroking firm to study a company or sector's performance
analyst's report	Report produced by an analyst, rating a company's shares as a buy, sell or hold. Often the report will coincide with the release of the company's results, and can influence the decision of investors as to whether to buy or sell shares in that company
ARGA	Audit, Reporting and Governance Authority (due to replace the FRC)
audit committee	A committee of the board of directors, concerned with matters relating to the company's accounts and auditing (see **8.3.7.3**)
bonus issue	See capitalisation of reserves
bookbuilding	See **4.4.2.1**
BVCA	British Private Equity and Venture Capital Association (the industry body for the private equity and venture capital industry in the UK)
CA 2006	Companies Act 2006
Cadbury Report	The 1992 report of the Committee on the Financial Aspects of Corporate Governance under the chair of Sir Adrian Cadbury (see **8.3.2.1**)
capitalisation of reserves	An issue of securities, credited as fully paid, out of the issuer's reserves, to existing shareholders in proportion to their existing shareholdings (also known as a 'bonus' or 'scrip' issue) (see **13.5.5**)
CARD	Consolidated Admissions and Reporting Directive 2001/34/EC
CBI	The Confederation of British Industry (the UK's leading employers' organisation)

certificate of approval	See **6.11**
CGI	The Chartered Governance Institute
CJA 1993	Criminal Justice Act 1993
CMA	Competition and Markets Authority (see **23.5.1**)
Company Reporting Directive	Directive 2006/46/EC (on accounts and the need for a corporate governance statement)
Conduct of Business Sourcebook	An FCA sourcebook which forms part of the FCA Handbook
continuing obligations	Obligations set out primarily in the Prospectus Regulation Rules, the UK Listing Rules, the Transparency Rules, the Corporate Governance Rules and UK MAR to which a company becomes subject when its securities are admitted to the Official List (see **Chapter 7**)
contract for differences	See **21.8.10.5**
Corporate Governance Rules	Rules published by the FCA relating to the establishment of an audit committee and the inclusion of a corporate governance statement in a listed company's annual report
CREST	The electronic settlement system for uncertificated securities trading (see **2.5.3.1**)
CSMAD	Directive on Criminal Sanctions for Market Abuse 2014/57/EU
DBT	Department for Business and Trade
dematerialisation	The process of replacing paper share certificates and stock transfer forms with an electronic system (see **2.10.1**)
derivative	A financial instrument the value of which depends on the performance of an underlying asset or security. Examples include futures, options and swaps (see **21.8.10.5**)
Disclosure Guidance	Guidance published by the FCA on the interpretation of UK MAR requirements in relation to the public disclosure of inside information
DTR	Disclosure Guidance and Transparency Rule
EA 2002	Enterprise Act 2002
EC Merger Regulation	Council Regulation 139/2004/EC
EEA	European Economic Area, a trading area comprising the Member States and Iceland, Liechtenstein and Norway
EFTA	European Free Trade Association: a free trade area established in 1960. Its current members are Iceland, Liechtenstein, Norway and Switzerland
equity securities	As defined in s 560 of the CA 2006, ordinary shares in a company or rights to subscribe for or to convert securities into, ordinary shares in the company
equity shares	As defined in s 548 of the CA 2006 and the UK Listing Rules, shares comprised in a company's equity share capital, that is, the issued share capital excluding any part of that capital which, neither as respects dividends nor as respects capital, carries any right to participate beyond a specified amount in a distribution
ESA	European Supervisory Authority, of which ESMA is one

ESCC	The equity shares (commercial company) listing category on the Main Market of the Stock Exchange
ESMA	European Securities and Markets Authority, the EU regulatory body overseeing the financial markets including stock exchanges in the EU
Euroclear UK & International Limited	The operator of CREST, owned by Euroclear Holding SA/NV
European Union (EU)	An economic and political union of European Member States created on 1 November 1993 by the Treaty on European Union (the 'Maastricht Treaty')
FCA	Financial Conduct Authority
FCA Handbook	A handbook published by the FCA, and updated monthly, of the rules and guidance issued by the FCA under the FSMA 2000, including the Part 6 Rules and the Code of Market Conduct
financial instrument	Instruments set out in Article 2(1)(24) of MiFIR (see below) including shares in companies
flotation	See IPO
FPO 2005	Financial Services and Markets Act 2000 (Financial Promotion) Order 2005 (SI 2005/1529)
FRC	Financial Reporting Council. An independent regulator which has responsibility for accounting standards in the UK and promotes high standards of corporate governance. Produces the UK Corporate Governance Code and The Stewardship Code (due to be replaced by ARGA)
financial year	The period for which a company must prepare statutory accounts pursuant to the CA 2006
FSA	Financial Services Authority
FSA 2012	Financial Services Act 2012
FSAP	The European Commission's Financial Services Action Plan
FSMA 2000	Financial Services and Markets Act 2000
FTSE 100	A Stock Exchange index of the largest (by market capitalisation) 100 companies admitted to trading on the Stock Exchange
GAP	general accounting practice
GC100	The Association of General Counsel and Company Secretaries of the FTSE 100, which produces guidelines to assist its members in complying with the Part 6 Rules
gearing	The ratio of a company's debt to its equity (see **18.9.1**)
GM	General Meeting of the company
IFRS International Financial Reporting Standards	Accounting standards adopted for use in the UK for companies with securities admitted to trading on the LSE
inside information	See **7.5.2.1**
Investment Association	The representative of the UK's asset management industry

Investment Association Share Capital Management Guidelines	See **14.5.7** and reproduced in **Appendix 2**
Investment Association Transaction Guidelines	Reproduced in **Appendix 1**
IPCs	Investment Protection Committees (representative bodies of major institutional investors)
IPO	Initial public offering (of shares), also known as flotation. This refers to the company's first offer of shares on a stock market
irrevocable undertaking	See **21.10**
ISS	Information Society Service. See **7.5.2.6**
leverage	The opportunity to create profit by financing a business through debt which is entitled to only a finite return (see **18.2.2**)
liquidity	The ease with which a security can be traded on a market
listing particulars	A marketing document published, in terms acceptable to the FCA, as a condition of admission of certain specialist securities to listing (see **6.3**)
Listing Regulations 2001	Financial Services and Markets Act 2000 (Official Listing of Securities) Regulations 2001(SI 2001/2956)
long-form articles	See **1.9.3.1**
Main Market	The Stock Exchange's principal market for listed securities
MAR	Market Abuse Regulation (EU) 596/2014
MAR Regulations 2016	Financial Services and Markets Act 2000 (Market Abuse) Regulations 2016 (SI 2016/680)
market capitalisation	See **13.3.6**
Markets in Financial Instruments Directive II	Directive 2014/65/EU (together with MiFIR sets the legislative framework for investment firms and securities markets in the EU)
Markets in Financial Instruments Regulation	Regulation (EU) 600/2014 (together with MiFID II sets the legislative framework for investment firms and securities markets in the EU)
market-makers	A member of the Stock Exchange offering the market a two-way price (ie, buying and selling) in particular securities (see **2.5.2**)
member firms	See **2.5.1**

Member States	The 27 Member States of the European Union, namely Austria, Belgium, Bulgaria, Croatia, Cyprus, Czechia, Denmark, Estonia, Finland, France, Germany, Greece, Hungary, Ireland, Italy, Latvia, Lithuania, Luxembourg, Malta, the Netherlands, Poland, Portugal, Romania, Slovak Republic, Slovenia, Spain and Sweden. Currently nine applications for membership from North Macedonia, Montenegro, Serbia, Turkey, Albania, Bosnia and Herzegovina, Moldova, Georgia and Ukraine are under consideration
MiFID II	See Markets in Financial Instruments Directive II
MiFIR	See Markets in Financial Instruments Regulation
Misleading Statements Order 2001	Financial Services and Markets Act 2000 (Misleading Statements and Practices) Order 2001 (SI 2001/3645)
NED	non-executive director
Nomad	The nominated adviser of an AIM Company (see **24.4.1**)
NSM	National Storage Mechanism (the UK's online facility for storing regulated information)
offer period	See **22.3.4**
PAL	Provisional allotment letter, which is a negotiable document issued by a company which notifies the recipient that securities have been allotted to them on a provisional basis (see **17.7.3.1**)
Panel	Panel on Takeovers and Mergers (which regulates public company takeovers in the UK and issues the Takeover Code)
Part 6 Rules	The UK Listing Rules, the Prospectus Regulation Rules, the Transparency Rules and the Corporate Governance Rules
Perimeter Guidance Manual	A regulatory guide, forming part of the FCA Handbook, about the circumstances in which authorisation is required under FSMA 2000
PDMR	Person discharging managerial responsibility. See **7.8.2.1**
PERG	Perimeter Guidance Manual
PIP	Primary Information Provider
PIRC	Pensions & Investment Research Consultants (the UK's leading independent research and advisory consultancy, providing services to institutional investors on corporate governance)
PLSA	Pensions and Lifetime Savings Association (the UK representative body for organisations providing pensions)
PMQI Order 2001	Financial Services and Markets Act (Prescribed Markets and Qualifying Investments) Order 2001 (SI 2001/1996)
poison pills	See **22.4.9**
PRA	Prudential Regulation Authority
Practice Statements	Informal guidance issued by the Panel Executive (see **20.5.6.1**)
Pre-Emption Group Statement of Principles	See **14.6.16** and reproduced in **Appendix 3**

Primary Information Provider	See **7.5.2.7**
private equity house	See venture capital company
Professional Securities Market	The Stock Exchange's market for listing debt, convertibles and depositary receipts. Debt securities can be listed on either the Main Market or on the Professional Securities Market
profit forecast	See **22.4.5.1**
prospectus	A marketing document for the offer of securities, published in terms acceptable to the FCA. See **Chapter 6**
Prospectus Regulation	Regulation (EU) 2017/1129
PRR	Prospectus Regulation Rule
Prospectus Regulations 2019	SI 2019/1043
Prospectus Rules	Rules published by the FCA setting out the form, content and approval requirements for a prospectus
QCA	The Quoted Companies Alliance (a UK representative body established to protect the interests of the smaller quoted company (that is, outside the FTSE 350))
QCA Code	The corporate governance guidelines for Small and Mid-sized Quoted companies by the Quoted Companies Alliance (see **24.7**)
Regulated Activities Order 2001	Financial Services and Markets Act 2000 (Regulated Activities) Order 2001 (SI 2001/544)
Regulatory Information Service	See **7.5.2.6**
remuneration committee	A committee of the board of directors with responsibility primarily for determining or recommending the remuneration of the executive directors (see **8.3.7.4**)
responsibility statement	See **6.5.2.1** and **22.4.5.2**
RIE	Recognised Investment Exchange (includes the Stock Exchange)
rights issue	An issue to existing holders of securities of rights to subscribe or purchase further securities pro rata their existing holdings made by means of the issue of a PAL or other negotiable document (see **17.7.1**)
RIS	Regulatory Information Service (includes RNS)
RNS	Company news service of the Stock Exchange (an RIS and PIP)
rump	Those shares not taken up by the shareholders on a rights issue which it is sought to place in the market (see **17.7.5**)
scrip issue	See capitalisation of reserves
SEAQ	The Stock Exchange Automated Quotations System, a computer screen system enabling Stock Exchange members to advertise share prices for AIM-quoted securities that are not traded on SETS (see **2.5.2**)

Secondary Information Provider	See **7.4.2.2**
Second Company Law Directive	Directive 77/91/EC
settlement	See **2.5.3**
SETS	The Stock Exchange Electronic Trading Service, an order-driven electronic trading system for FTSE 100 securities and for the most traded AIM-quoted securities (see **2.5.2**)
SETSqx	The Stock Exchange Electronic Trading Service – quotes and crosses. A trading system for securities less liquid than those traded on SETS
short-form articles	See **1.9.3.1**
SIP	Secondary Information Provider
SLC	substantial lessening of competition
SMEs	small and medium-sized enterprises
Smith Report	The report of an independent group chaired by Sir Robert Smith, to clarify the role and responsibility of audit committees (see **8.3.2.2**)
sponsor	A person approved by the FCA to sponsor an application for an ESCC category listing of securities and to assist the issuer in fulfilling its continuing obligations
stamp duty reserve tax	A tax introduced by the Finance Act 1986 to cover paperless share transactions (which fall outside the ambit of stamp duty)
Statutory Audit Directive	Directive 2006/43/EC (on statutory audits of annual accounts)
stick	Those shares not taken up by shareholders on a rights issue, nor subsequently placed in the market, and which, therefore, fall to the underwriters or sub-underwriters (see **17.7.5**)
Stock Exchange	The London Stock Exchange Group plc
sub-underwriter	A person to whom the underwriters have laid off some or all of the underwriting risk on a marketing of securities
Takeover Code	City Code on Takeovers and Mergers, issued by the Panel (see above)
Takeovers Directive	Directive 2004/25/EC (regulating the takeovers of companies trading on a regulated market in the EU)
Transparency Directive	Directive 2004/109/EC (to enhance transparency on EU financial markets by requiring disclosure of periodic financial reports and of major shareholdings for companies trading on a regulated market in the EU)
Transparency Rules	Rules published by the FCA setting out the requirements for periodic financial reporting for listed companies and the disclosure of major shareholdings
UK Corporate Governance Code	A set of corporate governance standards for ESCC-listed companies drawn up by the FRC
UK GAAP	Generally Accepted Accounting Principles in the UK
UK Listing Rules	Rules published by the FCA, relating to the admission of securities to listing on the Official List and the continuing obligations of listed companies

UKLR	UK Listing Rule
UK MAR	UK version of MAR applicable from 1 January 2021 following the UK's withdrawal from the EU
UK MiFIR	UK version of MiFIR applicable from 1 January 2021 following the UK's withdrawal from the EU
UK Prospectus Regulation	UK version of Prospectus Regulation applicable from 1 January 2021 following the UK's withdrawal from the EU
UK Stewardship Code	A good practice guide for institutional investors when engaging with listed companies in which they invest, drawn up by the FRC
underwriter	In insurance terms, a person who takes on an insurance risk; in terms of the marketing of securities, a person who agrees to take up shares not purchased or subscribed for
venture capital company	A company which specialises in investing, typically, in unlisted, high-risk businesses. The venture capital company helps to develop the business, often with a view to listing, with the aim of achieving significant return on its investment

PART I

BECOMING A LISTED COMPANY

CHAPTER 1

PUBLIC COMPANIES

1.1 INTRODUCTION

There are more than 5.25 million companies registered in England and Wales. Approximately 5,600 are public companies. Of those public companies, approximately 1,300 have floated on the London Stock Exchange. Around 750 are listed on the London Stock Exchange's principal market for larger, more established companies (the 'Main Market'), with approximately a further 550 UK companies quoted on the Stock Exchange's international market for smaller, growing companies (the Alternative Investment Market or 'AIM').

This book is concerned with the small minority of companies which are public, and with that even smaller minority of public companies which have floated on the London Stock Exchange.

1.2 WHAT IS A PUBLIC COMPANY?

A public company is defined by s 4(2) of the Companies Act 2006 (CA 2006). It is a company limited by shares or by guarantee and having a share capital, which has complied with the requirements of the CA 2006 (or former Companies Acts) to enable it to be registered or re-registered as such.

How a company can achieve public company status is explained at **1.9**.

1.3 WHAT IS A LISTED COMPANY?

There are several specific definitions of a listed company in company law legislation, some of which are explored in more depth elsewhere in this book. However, broadly, a listed company is a public company any of the shares in which are officially listed and trade on a stock market.

The stock market which is the focus of this book is the London Stock Exchange's 'Main Market' which is the largest market in the UK. The London Stock Exchange's other market, AIM, is considered in more detail at **2.4** and in **Chapter 24**. In the UK there are two competitor stock markets to the London Stock Exchange: Aquis Stock Exchange (AQSE) and Cboe Europe Equities. For example, the brewer, Adnams plc has joined AQSE rather than the London Stock Exchange. Companies may also be listed on stock markets based overseas, such as the Deutsche Börse in Germany, NASDAQ and the New York Stock Exchange in the USA, Euronext in Amsterdam, Brussels, Dublin, Lisbon, Milan, Oslo and Paris, NASDAQ OMX Nordic covering Denmark, Finland, Iceland and Sweden, and NASDAQ OMX Baltic covering the Baltic countries.

Obviously, when working with specific legislation, care must be taken to analyse the specific definition of 'listed'. For example, under some legislation a company which has its shares quoted on AIM rather than the Main Market will be a listed company, while under other legislation the same company will fall outside the definition of a listed company.

The words 'quoted' and 'listed' are usually used interchangeably, both by the layperson and by the practitioner. However, again, care should be taken to use appropriate terminology in relation to specific markets; the London Stock Exchange, for example, defines shares listed on the Main Market as listed (but not quoted) and shares listed on AIM as quoted but unlisted. Furthermore, the CA 2006 definition of 'quoted company' in s 385 refers to companies listed on 'regulated markets' including the Main Market but not AIM!

This can, of course lead to confusion. The key is to not take for granted the meaning of the terms 'listed' and 'quoted', but to examine (if interpreting such terms) or explain (if using such terms) the context in which they are used, taking account of the differing definitions.

For the purposes of this book, 'listed' is used to mean ordinary shares of an English company admitted to listing on the Official List of the Financial Conduct Authority (FCA) and admitted to trading on the Main Market of the London Stock Exchange.

1.4 THE DISTINCTION BETWEEN 'PUBLIC' AND 'LISTED'

Just because a company is a *public* company, it does not automatically follow that it is a *listed* company. There is some correlation between public companies and listed companies, in that a company must be a public company to become a listed company (private companies cannot become listed companies). However, we already know that only about 20% of public companies are listed.

The distinction between the terms is important, because a company's status will determine how that company is regulated. Public companies are more heavily regulated than private companies; listed public companies are significantly more heavily regulated than unlisted public companies. The question therefore arises, why would investors wish to put their money in a company which is subject to additional restrictions and cost, imposed as a result of greater regulation? The answer rests on a consideration of the advantages (**1.5** and **1.7** below) and disadvantages (**1.6** and **1.8** below) of becoming a public company and a listed company.

1.5 ADVANTAGES OF PUBLIC COMPANY STATUS

1.5.1 Ability to offer shares to the public

It is prohibited for a private company to offer its shares to the public under s 755 of the CA 2006. The main reason for registering or re-registering as a public company, therefore, is to enable a company to offer its shares to the public. The ability to offer shares to the public is an advantage, as it provides a company with a new source of finance (the consideration received for the shares) and opens up new opportunities for raising finance which otherwise may be unavailable to the company.

If s 755 is breached the court has the power to re-register the offending private company as a public one under s 758 of the CA 2006. If, though, the company does not meet the requirements to become a public company then the court either may order that the company is wound up (s 758), or it may make a remedial order under s 759 of the CA 2006. The remedial order seeks to put a person affected by a breach of s 755 back in the position they were in before the breach. The court has wide-ranging powers to achieve this. The application to court for a s 758 or s 759 order can be made by a shareholder or creditor of the offending company, or by the Secretary of State for Business and Trade (DBT).

1.5.2 Prestige

A secondary reason for a company to register or re-register as a public company is to benefit from the prestige conferred by the letters 'plc' ('public limited company'). Some companies therefore opt for public company status even if they have no immediate plans to offer shares to the public. Subsidiaries of public companies are often public companies too, for this reason.

1.6 POTENTIAL DISADVANTAGES OF PUBLIC COMPANY STATUS

As noted at **1.5.1** and **1.5.2** above, public company status brings with it the financial advantage of being able to offer shares to the public, and a certain element of commercial respectability. However, these advantages mean (in theory at least) that any public company, even if unlisted, can be owned by members of the public who have little day to day involvement in the company's business, and who therefore require greater statutory protection than the owners of a private company, who typically are more involved in the running of their companies, often as directors. For this reason, public companies are much more strictly regulated than private companies. This will add to the cost of running the company, and may restrict what it wishes to do and how it seeks to operate. **Table 1.1** below summarises the main differences between the regulation of public companies and private companies.

Table 1.1: Public companies compared to private companies

	Public company	**Private company**
Accounts	Must file with Companies House within 6 months after end of accounting reference period (CA 2006, s 442(2)(b)).	Must file within 9 months after end of accounting reference period (CA 2006, s 442(2)(a)).
	Must file full accounts with Companies House (CA 2006, ss 446 and 447 and ss 384 and 467).	Requirements to file full accounts can be relaxed for small and medium-sized companies (CA 2006, ss 444 and 445).
	Accounts must be laid before a General Meeting no later than 6 months after end of accounting reference period (CA 2006, s 437).	No requirement to do so.
Administration	Must hold an Annual General Meeting (AGM) (CA 2006, s 336).	No requirement to hold an AGM unless articles require it (SI 2007/2194, Sch 3, para 32(1)).
	The requisite percentage for holding a General Meeting on short notice is 95% (CA 2006, s 307(6)(b)).	The requisite percentage for holding a General Meeting on short notice is 90% (CA 2006, s 307(6)(a)).
	Cannot use the written resolution procedure (CA 2006, s 288).	Can use the written resolution procedure (CA 2006, s 288).
Directors	Minimum of 2 (CA 2006, s 154(2)).	Minimum of 1 (CA 2006, s 154(1)).

	Public company	Private company
	Restrictions apply on voting for the appointment of more than one director in just one resolution (CA 2006, s 160).	No equivalent restriction applies.
	A public company can only make a quasi-loan and a credit transaction with one of its directors provided prior shareholder approval has been obtained (CA 2006, ss 198 and 201).	The need for shareholder approval for quasi-loans and credit transactions with a director will be required only if the private company is 'associated with a public company', as defined in CA 2006, s 256 (CA 2006, ss 198(1) and 201(1)).
Financial assistance	Prohibited (CA 2006, s 678), subject to CA 2006, ss 681 and 682. See **Chapter 16**.	Generally permitted. Restrictions apply to private companies which are subsidiaries of public companies.
Secretary	A company secretary is required (CA 2006, s 271). Section 273 sets out qualifications required.	A company secretary is not compulsory (CA 2006, s 270(1)). If a company chooses to have one, there are no qualification requirements.
Share capital	The company must have allotted share capital at least up to the value of the authorised minimum (currently £50,000 – CA 2006, s 763 permits a euro equivalent to this amount, set at €57,100 (SI 2009/2425)) to register (CA 2006, s 761) or re-register (CA 2006, s 91(1)). The company must maintain this as its minimum share capital (CA 2006, ss 650 and 662).	No restriction on allotted share capital.
	Each share allotted must be paid up to at least one-quarter of its nominal value together with the whole of any premium on it (CA 2006, s 586).	No equivalent restriction applies. Can allot shares nil paid, partly paid or fully paid.
	Section 561 pre-emption rights on allotment can be disapplied under s 570 or 571 by special resolution or excluded and replaced by articles conferring a corresponding right under s 568.	Section 561 pre-emption rights on allotment can be disapplied under s 569 (by special resolution or provision in the articles), under s 570 or 571 by special resolution or excluded under s 567 (by provision in the articles).
	Restrictions apply on consideration for allotment of shares (ss 585, 587 and 598).	These sections do not apply.

	Public company	Private company
	Valuer's report required to value non-cash consideration for the allotment of shares (s 593).	No equivalent requirement applies.
	GM required in the event of a serious loss of capital (s 656).	No equivalent requirement applies.
	Charges on own shares are void, subject to certain exceptions (s 670).	Subject to certain requirements in s 670(2), charges on own shares are permitted.
	Can redeem and purchase shares out of distributable profits or the proceeds of a fresh issue, but not out of capital (ss 687 and 692).	Can redeem and purchase shares out of distributable profits, the proceeds of a fresh issue, or out of capital (ss 687 and 692).
Shareholders	Has disclosure obligations under DTR 5 and CA 2006, Pt 22 (see **Chapter 15**).	No equivalent restrictions apply.
Takeovers	Subject to the City Code on Takeovers and Mergers.	Typically not subject to the City Code on Takeovers and Mergers (but see exceptions at **20.5**).

1.7 ADVANTAGES OF LISTING

If obtaining public company status enables a company to offer shares to the public, what further advantage is there in listing?

1.7.1 Providing a market for the company's shares

A listing will provide access to a market on which members of the public and financial institutions can buy and sell shares in the company. As the shares can be bought at a pre-agreed price and sold relatively easily (the shares are said to be 'liquid'), they will be an attractive investment, particularly for members of the public who may not be familiar with the (usually more complicated) methods of buying and selling shares off the stock market. This market also enables the original owners of the company or private equity or venture capitalist investors to sell their shares and exit from the company, thereby reaping the rewards of their investment (although they may be restricted from exiting for a period of time immediately following the listing, to promote confidence in the company).

Frasers Group plc, formerly Sports Direct International plc, the retail empire, gives an example of what this can mean in practice (whilst at the same time making you question your choice of career ...). The company was originally 100% owned by the entrepreneur, Mike Ashley. He sold 43% of his shares on the company's listing in 2007, netting him £929 million. In June 2024 Mike Ashley still owns 73% of the company, worth a tidy £2.9 billion.

As we know from **1.5** above, those same members of the public and financial institutions can buy and sell shares in an unlisted public company if that company chooses to offer them its shares. Although both unlisted and listed companies need to take account of the same rules regarding how the shares are offered to the public (see **Chapter 6**), the shares in an unlisted company will not be listed or trading on a stock market. Therefore, the process of buying the shares, and subsequently finding people to sell them to, will not be as easy (the shares are not as 'liquid') and so members of the public, in particular, will be less inclined to invest in them.

1.7.2 Easier access to capital

A listing enables the company to raise finance through issuing new shares ('equity finance'), both at the same time as the initial listing and afterwards, from the huge supply of capital available through the stock market. See **4.4** and **Chapter 17**. A large number of listed companies take advantage of this equity finance to raise money as an alternative or in addition to money raised through debt finance (ie, lending). For example, one of the reasons given by the board of directors of CAB Payments Holdings plc (which provides cross-border payments and foreign exchange services) for its £850 million listing on the London Stock Exchange in July 2023 was to support the company's 'growth by giving the company access to a wider range of capital-raising options which may be of use in the future'.

1.7.3 Access to acquisition opportunities

As a result of its access to the stock market and to its ready supply of capital, a listed company can often more easily raise cash or offer new shares in itself as consideration, thereby generally affording it the opportunity to expand through acquisition of other companies or businesses. Unlisted companies do not have the same access to this capital, not being part of a stock market, and, as explained in **1.7.1** above, unlisted company shares are not as attractive a form of consideration from a seller's perspective.

1.7.4 Prestige

The prestige attached to public company status (see **1.5.2**) can be enhanced further if the company lists successfully. In order to list, a company has to receive regulatory approval following considerable investigation into the company's suitability for listing. As listed companies have had their affairs scrutinised yet still obtained this approval, potential customers and suppliers may perceive listed companies to have greater financial standing than unlisted companies. This may help a listed company to negotiate better terms on which to conduct its business.

1.7.5 Profile

The press usually focuses its coverage on listed rather than unlisted companies, and listed companies will also be the subject of analysts' reports (produced by investment banks which rate a company's shares as a buy, sell or hold in order to assist investors with their investment decisions), so the profile of the company and its products will be raised. This can help create and sustain demand for, and therefore liquidity in, its shares. Enhancing the company's profile and creating a liquid market in its shares were additional reasons given by the board of directors of CAB Payments Holdings plc for its listing on the London Stock Exchange in July 2023.

1.7.6 Employee incentives

Listed companies can offer share ownership schemes to employees. While share ownership schemes are available to private companies, and are commonly used to motivate senior staff, listed companies have the additional advantage of being able to offer employees shares which have an identifiable value (as they are listed on a stock market). If employees own part of the company, the hope is that their commitment to the business will increase. The company should, therefore, benefit from being able to recruit and retain key employees. Again, this was a reason given by the board of directors of CAB Payments Holdings plc for its listing on the London Stock Exchange in July 2023.

1.7.7 Increased efficiency

Listed companies are strictly regulated (see **1.8.1** below). To comply with regulatory requirements, listed companies often have to improve their existing internal regulatory checks and controls. These improvements can, in turn, improve the operating efficiency of the company as a whole.

1.8 POTENTIAL DISADVANTAGES OF LISTING

1.8.1 Increased regulatory regime

As **Table 1.1** above shows, even an unlisted public company's regulatory regime is much stricter than that of a private company, to reflect the fact that any public company can offer shares to the public at large. However, once a public company is listed, the regime becomes even stricter than that set out in **Table 1.1**. This is because, as noted in **1.7.1** above, the ready market in listed company shares means that, in practice, members of the public tend to invest in listed companies, rather than in unlisted public companies, and therefore it is the shareholders of listed companies who require the most protection. The increased level of regulation involves higher costs for the company, a greater administrative burden, and places restrictions on what the company and its directors can do and how they do it. So what extra rules, over and above those summarised in **Table 1.1**, are imposed on a listed company?

1.8.1.1 Prospectus Regulation Rules, UK Listing Rules, Transparency Rules, Corporate Governance Rules, UK Market Abuse Regulation and UK Prospectus Regulation

The Prospectus Regulation Rules, the UK Listing Rules, the Transparency Rules and the Corporate Governance Rules apply to any listed company, as do UK MAR and the UK Prospectus Regulation. Such companies must consider the FSMA 2000, the UK Prospectus Regulation, the Prospectus Regulation Rules and the UK Listing Rules when first seeking a listing and subsequently when raising equity finance, and the UK Prospectus Regulation, the Prospectus Regulation Rules, the UK Listing Rules, the Transparency Rules, the Corporate Governance Rules and UK MAR for their continuing obligations while listed on the Stock Exchange. **Chapters 5** and **6** consider the listing process; **Chapter 17** examines equity finance. **Chapter 7** looks at continuing obligations in more detail.

1.8.1.2 Statutory provisions

Certain statutory provisions apply to listed companies only:

(a) *The CA 2006*. For example, pursuant to s 420, the directors of a listed company are required to prepare a remuneration report on their pay, bonuses, share options and other related matters for inclusion in the company's Annual Report. It is a criminal offence for a director to fail to do so.

(b) *The FSMA 2000*. The penalties for market abuse committed in breach of UK MAR are set out in Pt VIII of the Financial Services and Markets Act 2000 (FSMA 2000). These only apply to shares listed on various markets, including the Main Market. **Chapter 10** explores the market abuse provisions in more detail.

(c) *The CJA 1993*. Part V of the Criminal Justice Act 1993 (CJA 1993) provides that it is a criminal offence for a person who holds knowledge as an insider to deal, or encourage someone else to deal, in shares listed on a regulated market (which includes the Main Market). This is known as 'insider dealing'. **Chapter 11** considers insider dealing in more detail.

1.8.2 External forces

External forces beyond the control of a listed company, such as market conditions, rumour or developments in a certain market sector, can affect the company's value. The Covid pandemic initially caused sharp drops in the value of companies listed on the Main Market, even where their market sector was not directly affected by lockdowns, as investors sought what they perceived to be safer assets than shares for their money. Sometimes external forces can have a positive effect on share price, such as a cut in interest rates which may push up the share price of a heavily indebted company if its interest payments are reduced as a result; but on other occasions external forces work to depress the share price (consider, for example, the effect of the pandemic on the share price of companies in the travel, leisure and hospitality industries). The fact that the value of the company can be so affected by forces outside its control can be a source of frustration to management.

1.8.3 Increased shareholder power

A large number of outsiders will become shareholders in the company when it lists. An extreme example is BT plc, which has approximately 700,000 shareholders. Not only will any equity held by management be diluted by the influx of these shareholders, but listed companies are required to obtain shareholder approval of certain transactions and decisions which, in unlisted companies, would fall to management alone. The inevitable consequence is a decrease in management's level of control over the company. Furthermore, the pressure to keep shareholders happy with, for example, continually increasing dividend payments can cause management to focus on short-term rather than long-term performance. There is also the risk that shareholders will sell to unwelcome buyers seeking to take over the company.

1.8.4 Loss of privacy

The listing process under the FSMA 2000, the UK Prospectus Regulation, the Prospectus Regulation Rules and the UK Listing Rules, and the continuing obligations of the UK Prospectus Regulation, the Prospectus Regulation Rules, the UK Listing Rules, the Transparency Rules, the Corporate Governance Rules and UK MAR (referred to at **1.8.1.1** above), the higher profile of the company (referred to at **1.7.5** above), and the greater accountability to shareholders (referred to at **1.8.3** above) mean that decisions of the management of a listed company are subject to much greater scrutiny than an unlisted company. If the company is underperforming, this loss of privacy can be very unwelcome.

Even on a personal level, the scrutiny can be both intense and undesirable. Matthew Moulding, the founder, chair and CEO of THG plc floated his company in London in September 2020, valuing it at £5.4 billion. After the IPO had successfully concluded, he remarked with great frankness, 'Since I announced the IPO it's been in the press a lot, which I've struggled with. I don't like it. I don't want it. I don't seek it. Pre-IPO it just blew up.'

1.8.5 Cost and time

The cost and time spent on the listing process, raising equity finance, complying with the continuing obligations of a listed company and maintaining good relations with investors can be onerous, and the company must decide before listing whether this time and money would be better directed towards running the business. The former co-founder and chair of Betfair plc, which floated in 2010, in discussing mistakes which ultimately led to him resigning as chair, said that the IPO 'was more of a distraction than we realised at the time. It took us 12 months at least to fully digest the process and that knocked us out of our stride for a bit.'

1.8.6 De-listing

The balance of advantages over disadvantages of a listing may shift over time for companies already trading on the Stock Exchange. Since the Covid pandemic started and Brexit came fully into force, a number of companies have decided to de-list from the Stock Exchange. In other words they left the Main Market and transferred to the lesser regulated AIM or they left the Stock Exchange and reverted to being unlisted public companies. An example is Ryanair Holdings plc, the owner of the low cost airline Ryanair, which announced its intention to de-list in November 2021 as a result of legal issues arising from Brexit. Its board of directors argued that the low trading volume in the company's shares could no longer justify the costs of listing on the Stock Exchange. The company continues to maintain a listing within the EU in Dublin. Superdry plc (the clothing retailer) announced it was de-listing from the Main Market in July 2024, explaining that this action was being taken to avoid entering insolvency, to allow the company to return to a more stable footing and to accelerate its turnaround plan and drive it towards a viable and sustainable future.

A strong example of these disadvantages can be seen with THG, which joined the stock market in September 2020 with a value of £5.4 billion. After an impressive start, the share price has collapsed to about 20% of its IPO value, with THG plc worth just £900 million in June 2024. In a sobering assessment of the IPO experience, the founder, chair and CEO, Matthew Moulding, when asked if he would do the IPO again, said, 'S***, no. No. I wouldn't ... it's just sucked from start to finish.' He added, 'Genuinely I can say, from the moment I even announced on my Insta the IPO, from that day forward has been the worst period ever. Ever. And there hasn't been a positive day since the IPO ... the obvious lesson is: don't IPO in the UK.'

1.9 ACHIEVING PUBLIC COMPANY STATUS

A company can achieve public company status in two ways:

(a) registering as a public company on original incorporation; or

(b) registering as a private company on original incorporation then re-registering as a public company.

The procedures under (a) and (b) ensure that the resulting public company complies with the CA 2006 requirements relating to a public company's articles, name and share capital.

1.9.1 Incorporation of a company

Under s 9 of the CA 2006, the following must be sent to the Registrar of Companies to incorporate any company, private or public:

(a) memorandum of association (in the form set out in Sch 1 to the Companies (Registration) Regulations 2008 (SI 2008/3014));

(b) an application for registration (Form IN01) containing:

- (i) a statement of share capital and initial shareholding (content requirements set out in s 10);
- (ii) a statement of the proposed first officers of the company (content requirements set out in s 12);
- (iii) a statement of the intended registered office;
- (iv) copy articles of association (unless the new model articles are adopted unamended); and
- (v) a statement of compliance that all requirements of the CA 2006 have been met (further requirements set out in s 13); and

(c) a registration fee.

1.9.2 Registration as a public company on original incorporation

In addition to sending the documents referred to at **1.9.1** above to the Registrar, there are the following extra requirements to register as a public company on original incorporation:

(a) *Articles*. The articles must be in a form suitable for a public company. Under s 20 of the CA 2006, on registration of a public company a default set of model articles will apply, save to the extent that they are excluded or modified. These public company model articles can be found in Sch 3 to the Companies (Model Articles) Regulations 2008 (SI 2008/3229).

(b) *Name*. The company name must end with 'public limited company' or the Welsh equivalent (CA 2006, s 58), or with the abbreviation 'plc' or its Welsh equivalent 'ccc' (CA 2006, s 58(2)).

(c) *Allotted share capital*. The allotted share capital of the company must be not less than the 'authorised minimum' (CA 2006, s 761(2)). Currently the authorised minimum is

£50,000 (CA 2006, s 763). In addition, each share allotted must be paid up to at least one-quarter of its nominal value together with the whole of any premium on it (CA 2006, s 586).

1.9.2.1 Certificate of incorporation

If the company meets all the requirements set out at **1.9.1** and **1.9.2** above, then it will be able to obtain a certificate from the Registrar that the company has been registered as a public company on original incorporation. However, although this certificate of incorporation will prove that the public company exists (CA 2006, s 15(1)), and details of the company will now be recorded at Companies House, the public company needs to obtain one other certificate before it can commence business – a trading certificate.

1.9.2.2 Trading certificate

A company which has been registered as a public company on original incorporation must not begin business or exercise any borrowing powers until it has a trading certificate, issued under s 761 of the CA 2006, confirming that the company has met the *allotted* share capital requirements of the CA 2006 (see **1.9.2** above). The certificate is proof that the company can trade and borrow. To obtain this certificate, an application must be made (accompanied by a statement of compliance) to the Registrar under s 762 of the CA 2006.

The allotted share capital requirements are that the company must have allotted shares at least up to the value of the authorised minimum (CA 2006, s 761), which, as stated in **1.9.2** above, is currently £50,000 (s 763) or the euro equivalent – currently €57,100 (Companies (Authorised Minimum) Regulations 2009 (SI 2009/2425)). Each allotted share must be paid up to at least one-quarter of its nominal value together with the whole of any premium on it (CA 2006, s 568).

What does this mean in practice? Well, if 50,000 shares with a nominal value of £1 each are allotted at nominal value with no premium, the minimum consideration which must be paid to the company is one-quarter of the nominal value of each share, that is 0.25p per share, making a total minimum payment of £12,500 for 50,000 shares.

If, however, the shares are allotted for, say, £3 each, then each share has a premium (the amount by which the price exceeds the nominal value) of £2. This premium must be paid to the company together with a minimum of a quarter of the nominal value of each share, which is £2 plus 0.25p, that is £2.25 per share, making a total minimum payment of £112,500 for 50,000 shares.

1.9.3 Re-registration as a public company

A company which has registered as a private company on original incorporation (by complying with the requirements detailed at **1.9.1** above) can re-register as a public company pursuant to ss 90–96 of the CA 2006. The company must pass a special (or written) resolution, meet the specified conditions and submit an application in a prescribed form to the Registrar (s 90(1)).

1.9.3.1 Resolution

The special (or written) resolution must:

(a) approve the re-registration of the company (CA 2006, s 90(1)(a));

(b) alter the company's name so it is in a form suitable for a public company. Section 58(1) of the CA 2006 requires that the name must end with 'public limited company' or 'plc' (or the Welsh equivalent – s 58(2)); and

(c) alter the articles so that they are in a form suitable for a public company. It is probable that the existing private company articles will require substantial amendment; it is often easier to adopt an entirely new set of articles rather than to amend the existing articles.

If the company is re-registering as a public company as a preliminary step to listing in the immediate future, it may be appropriate to adopt a set of articles suitable not only for a public company but also for a public company which is listed. In this case the articles will probably disapply the model articles in their entirety and will be bespoke. These are known as long-form articles (as opposed to articles which apply the model articles either in their entirety or with some amendment, which are referred to as short-form articles).

1.9.3.2 Share capital requirements

The resolution deals with the requirements as to a public company's articles and name. What about the share capital requirements of a public company? This is dealt with by s 90(2). *At the time the shareholders pass the special resolution* (see **1.9.3.1**) the company must have satisfied certain conditions as to its share capital, namely that the company must have allotted shares at least up to the value of the authorised minimum (s 91(1)(a)), which is currently £50,000 (CA 2006, s 763) or the euro equivalent, currently €57,100, and that each allotted share must be paid up to at least one-quarter of its nominal value together with the whole of any premium on it (s 91(1)(b)).

(These requirements reflect the requirements which must be satisfied when a company originally incorporated as a public company applies for a trading certificate, set out at **1.9.2.2** above. A trading certificate therefore is not required for a private company which re-registers as a public company; the certificate of incorporation is all the company requires.)

Note that s 91(1)(c) and (d) provide some further requirements as to shares which have been allotted in consideration of an undertaking. Note also that some shares can be disregarded for the purposes of satisfying the share capital requirements (see s 91(2), (3) and (4)).

1.9.3.3 Application for re-registration

The special resolution must be delivered to the Registrar together with an application for re-registration on Form RR01, which has been signed by a director, the company secretary or a person authorised by the directors under s 270 or s 274 of the CA 2006. If the existing private company does not have a company secretary, one must be appointed and details included in the application. This is because under s 271 of the CA 2006, a public company must have a company secretary, whereas this is not a requirement for a private company. The application must be accompanied by the fee for re-registration (currently £71, together with £30 for any change of name – this change of name fee is not required if the company simply changes from 'ltd' to 'plc') and the following documents:

(a) the revised articles (s 94(2)(b));

(b) a balance sheet prepared not more than seven months before the application, containing an unqualified report by the company's auditors (s 94(2)(c), s 92(1)). If the company's accounting reference date is within this seven-month period, this requirement can be met by the end of year balance sheet; if not, then an interim balance sheet must be prepared and must be audited, which can prove time-consuming and expensive. The auditors must also provide a written statement regarding the level of the company's net assets (as revealed by the balance sheet) in comparison to the company's called-up share capital and undistributable reserves (s 92(1)(c));

(c) a valuation report on any shares which have been allotted for non-cash consideration between the date of the balance sheet (referred to at (b) above) and the date the special resolution was passed (s 93(1)(a), s 93(2)(a)). This ensures that a private company seeking to re-register is brought into line with the general requirement under s 593 that public companies seeking to allot shares for non-cash consideration must have such consideration valued before allotting the shares; and

(d) a statement of compliance in the prescribed form (s 90(1)(c)(ii)).

1.9.3.4 Certificate of re-registration on incorporation as a public company

If the Registrar is satisfied with the application, they will issue the company with a certificate of re-registration on incorporation as a public company (CA 2006, s 96). The private company becomes a public company, and the revised articles and change of name will take effect on the issue of this certificate, which is proof of public company status.

1.9.3.5 Trading disclosures

The Company, Limited Liability Partnership and Business (Names and Trading Disclosures) Regulations 2015 (SI 2015/17) made under s 82 of the CA 2006 set out the requirements for a company to identify itself, at certain locations (including any place of business), on certain documents (including letters and order forms) and on its websites. The company must state its registered name and certain other registration details depending on the circumstances. Breach of these requirements can result in a fine for the company and any officer of the company who is in default. The company must update its websites and order new signs and company documentation, which will reflect its new identity, in advance of re-registration to ensure that it can meet these requirements with effect from the date the certificate of incorporation on re-registration is issued.

1.10 ACHIEVING LISTED COMPANY STATUS

When a company which does not have any shares listed on the stock market decides to list shares for the first time, the listing process is known as flotation or an IPO. There are different methods of flotation, the main methods for a company new to listing being by a public offer, placing or an introduction. Deciding to float is a serious step for a public company; the process is much more complex (and expensive) than that required for a private company to achieve public company status. **Chapters 4, 5** and **6** examine the complexities of flotation in more detail.

CHAPTER 2

THE LONDON STOCK EXCHANGE

2.1 WHAT IS THE LONDON STOCK EXCHANGE?

London Stock Exchange plc (the Stock Exchange) is a listed company. It has four principal areas of business:

(a) a market place for trading in company securities;

(b) a provider of trading platforms on which brokers can buy and sell securities;

(c) a supplier of market information to the financial community, and

(d) a market place for trading in equity derivatives.

The focus of this book is on the Stock Exchange's role as a market place for trading in a specific type of company securities – shares.

The Stock Exchange is at the centre of one of the world's three main financial centres – London, New York and Tokyo – with around 2,000 companies listed on it worth an estimated £3,500 billion, and is the most international stock market in the world, with companies from over 100 countries and territories, from the USA and China to Malawi, Bangladesh, Papua New Guinea and Kazakhstan, listed on it. It also has one of the world's largest pools (and Europe's largest pool) of capital, with many £ billions available from UK-based sources, such as hedge, pension and insurance funds.

2.2 THE MARKET PLACE

The Stock Exchange has two markets for shares, the Main Market and the Alternative Investment Market (AIM). Both markets serve two main functions. First, they enable companies to raise funds by issuing new shares to the public. This is referred to as the primary market for shares. Secondly, they allow those issued shares to be traded (bought and sold) by the public. This is referred to as the secondary market for shares. The Main Market has both a primary and secondary market, therefore, as does AIM.

2.3 THE MAIN MARKET

The Main Market is the Stock Exchange's principal market for listed companies and is what the layman will think of as 'the stock market'. This is the market on which the shares of many household-name companies, such as Deliveroo, Vodafone, easyJet, BP, HSBC and Marks & Spencer (as well as a host of lesser-known companies), are listed. Within the Main Market, there are specific groupings for certain sectors: techMARK for innovative technology companies; landMARK for UK regional companies.

A Specialist Fund Segment (SFS) was created in 2017 designed for investment companies that wish to target the biggest and most sophisticated investors. We will not be considering the SFS any further in this book. You can find out further details from the LSE's website.

There are currently just over 1,000 companies listed on the Main Market, which includes not only UK companies but also approximately 270 overseas companies.

The 100 largest companies make up the FTSE 100, which is used as a measure for judging the market value of these Main Market companies at any one given time. It is this FTSE 100 value which is used in the press to describe the current market, for example when a news headline states, 'The FTSE 100 has dropped below 7,000'. The 100 largest companies are selected every three months.

2.4 AIM

The AIM is the Stock Exchange's Alternative Investment Market. It is a global market for smaller and growing companies. The AIM is a separate market from the Main Market, and while some companies may choose to move from AIM onto the Main Market at some point (such as ASOS plc, the fashion retailer in February 2022), there is no obligation to do so. In fact, lately, the trend has been for Main Market companies to move to AIM (such as Mothercare plc, the children's retailer in February 2021), where the regulatory burden can be lower and the costs of raising finance cheaper than on the Main Market, or to leave it altogether to avoid the regulatory burden and costs (such as All Leisure Group plc in June 2016 – the company ceased trading six months later due to financial problems).

There are currently approximately 720 companies listed on AIM (such as Boohoo, Fevertree Drinks and Jet2), which includes about 150 overseas companies. The AIM was a rapidly expanding market until the financial crisis of 2007/08, reaching a peak of over 1,700 companies. Since then the total number of AIM companies has dropped dramatically by almost 1,000 companies or well over 50%, most recently as a result of high interest rates caused by inflation and continued worries about the UK economy post-Brexit by international investors.

As stated at **1.3** above, the focus of this book is on companies which are listed on the Main Market. However, **Chapter 24** provides a brief overview of the regulation of AIM companies, compares AIM with the Main Market, and considers the advantages and disadvantages of joining AIM.

2.5 DEALING ON THE MARKETS

Dealing (ie, buying and selling shares) is not an area in which a corporate lawyer typically will have much involvement. The focus of the lawyer's role is to help to bring a client company to the market successfully, and then ensure that the company is advised of the regulatory regime it must follow in order to maintain its listing. However, the corporate lawyer's clients may well have an in-depth knowledge of dealing and the markets, and those clients may be unsettled if the lawyer helping to bring the company to market has no comprehension of how that market works. The following, therefore, is intended to provide some basic information on the mechanics of dealing.

There are two elements to buying and selling shares. The first is usually referred to as 'trading', and this is the process by which a seller is matched with a buyer. The second element is 'settlement', which is the process of paying the purchase price and transferring the shares.

2.5.1 Member firms

Member firms carry out most of the trading on the Stock Exchange's markets. They are investment firms (banks, stockbrokers and fund managers) which trade either on behalf of clients, or on behalf of their firms. Examples of current member firms are Barclays Bank plc, Citigroup Global Markets, Crédit Suisse Securities, Deutsche Bank AG, Goldman Sachs International, Merrill Lynch International and UBS.

2.5.2 Mechanics of trading

The Stock Exchange has fully automated trading systems. This means that you will not see traders shouting and waving on a trading floor as you might in some stock exchanges abroad (eg NYSE in New York).

The Stock Exchange has devised various electronic systems for trading shares. These apply regardless of whether the shares are held in paper form (with a share certificate) or electronically (via CREST, see **2.5.3.1**). For the large Main Market-listed companies, including those on the FTSE 100 index, and for the most highly traded AIM-quoted companies, there is the Stock Exchange Electronic Trading Service (SETS), which is known as the order book. This electronic system matches 'buy' and 'sell' orders for the same shares and executes the trade automatically. A further system, SETSqx, supports the trading of shares in companies with turnover which is insufficient for the SETS system (such as the least liquid Main Market companies and most AIM companies). Finally, there is the Stock Exchange Automated Quotations (SEAQ) system for AIM securities not traded on SETS or SETSqx. With this system certain member firms act as competing 'market makers' in relation to certain shares. They will set the 'buy' and 'sell' prices for these shares, using current news about the company, the market sector and the strength of demand for shares as a guide. Member firms acting as 'brokers' will then buy and sell the shares when they think the price set by the market makers is right.

On average, approximately 615,000 trades a day in shares are executed on the Stock Exchange's equity markets.

2.5.3 Settlement

Once a share has been traded on the market, it needs to be transferred from the seller to the buyer, and the consideration monies need to be transferred from the buyer to the seller. This process is known as 'settlement'. There is a risk during the time between the trade being struck and settlement being made that the transaction will fail (for example, if one of the parties is declared bankrupt).

The settlement system discussed in **2.5.3.1** covers shares held in uncertificated form only, as these represent the vast majority of shares traded on the Stock Exchange.

2.5.3.1 CREST

CREST was introduced in 1996 and is a paperless (that is, the shares are held in electronic form and no share certificates exist, ie they are uncertificated) share settlement system through which trades on the Stock Exchange's markets can be settled. The system has legal backing under the Uncertificated Securities Regulations 2001 (SI 2001/3755). Euroclear UK and Ireland Limited operates this system. As the system is electronic and paperless, settlement can be made swiftly (within two business days of any trade), so the risk period between trade and settlement is reduced. Approximately 88% of the UK share market's value is voluntarily traded through CREST. There are various options for a shareholder wishing to hold shares through CREST.

CREST member

A CREST member must be linked up to CREST by computer network, so typically it is the member firms of the Stock Exchange (see **2.5.1** above) who have this type of membership. CREST members hold shares as nominees for individual clients (institutional or private investors), so the name of the CREST member, rather than the client, will be entered into the company's register of members as legal owner. The client will be the beneficial owner of the shares.

Each CREST member has an identification number for itself ('participant ID') and at least one other identification number for specific accounts it holds, such as an account for shares beneficially held on behalf of a specific institution ('member account ID').

CREST 'sponsored member'

This type of membership is designed to attract private investors (institutions and individuals). The benefit to the private investor is that its name will appear on the company's register of members (in contrast to the position if it holds shares through a CREST member, where the CREST member's name will feature on the register). Sponsored members who are individuals are known as 'personal members' to distinguish them from sponsored members which are corporate bodies. However, one drawback is that the CREST personal member does not have the required computer link-up to CREST. A CREST sponsor, who will be a CREST member, will provide this for the sponsored member, and will charge for the service.

Nominee shareholder

Other investors who are not CREST members or sponsored members, who hold their shares in electronic form, will hold them as nominees. This means that the shareholder will be the beneficial owner of their shares rather than the legal owner, and the name of the nominee (usually a CREST member) will appear on the share register.

The corporate lawyer and CREST

In practice, the impact of CREST for the corporate lawyer is not dramatic. For example it may involve ensuring that some standard wording is drafted into certain documents, such as how CREST shareholders can accept an offer and receive consideration (in a takeover) or take up shares (when raising equity finance), or being aware of CREST shareholders when considering the mechanics of an AGM. Some standard wording is available on the Euroclear website. The lawyer should be aware that Stamp Duty Reserve Tax is collected on paperless share transactions such as the transfer of shares within CREST. CREST itself, however, is responsible for collecting this tax.

2.6 INVESTORS IN THE MARKETS

There are different types of investor in the companies listed on the Stock Exchange. The importance of these have changed over time to reflect the development of financial markets both in the UK and globally. In the 2020s almost 60% of shares on the Stock Exchange are now owned by overseas investors, reflecting economic advances overseas, globalisation and the UK financial markets' openness to international investment. UK-based investors, although in the minority, are still extremely important in funding listed companies on the Stock Exchange. The main types of investors are set out below.

2.6.1 Retail investors

These are individual members of the public. They can invest directly in shares listed on the Main Market or quoted on AIM, either in the primary market (by subscribing for new shares issued by a company or being sold by existing shareholders on an IPO) or in the secondary market (by buying or selling shares on the stock market after the company has floated). More usually, individuals will invest indirectly in shares on the Stock Exchange (because, for example, their pensions, other savings schemes or employment incentive schemes are invested in the Stock Exchange's markets). Obviously, the aim of the retail investor who invests is to realise a healthy profit on the sale of the investment, but of course what is intended and what is achieved can be very different.

Retail investors generally need enhanced protection in their dealings on the Stock Exchange, as they are generally considered to be less well qualified to understand how the markets work and the full extent of the risks involved. As a consequence, the level of regulation imposed on listed companies will be higher where retail investors are involved.

2.6.2 Institutional investors

Institutional investors (also known as institutional shareholders) are large organisations such as banks, insurance companies, pension funds and investment funds (including unit trusts and hedge funds). The huge amount of money they have available to invest means that institutional investors have considerable influence over the companies in which they invest. By way of example, approximately 86% of AstraZeneca plc's (the biotech company) issued share capital is owned by large investors, principally institutional investors. The 18 largest shareholders alone own 50% of the company. By contrast, the more numerous, retail investors in AstraZeneca own only about 14% of the issued shares.

Traditional institutional investors such as pension funds, banks and insurance companies are now eclipsed in the size of their total shareholdings in listed companies by other types of financial institution and investment funds including hedge funds.

As specialist investors, such institutions generally require less protection (and thus regulation) when investing in listed companies. The main institutional investors have, however, formed their own representative bodies called Investment Protection Committees (IPCs). Well known IPCs include the Investment Association and the Pensions and Lifetime Savings Association (PLSA). The IPCs issue guidelines as to how members should exercise their shareholder vote. While these guidelines do not have the force of law, listed companies do generally treat them as binding, such is the influence of the institutional shareholders through their ownership of large numbers of shares in listed companies.

Chapter 14 looks at some of these guidelines in more detail. **Chapter 8** also considers the role of institutional investors in relation to corporate governance.

2.6.3 Sovereign wealth funds

Sovereign wealth funds are investors on behalf of countries that have amassed huge surpluses of money. Often these are mineral rich countries which have profited from the sale of oil, gas and other natural resources, with some of the largest being Abu Dhabi's Investment Authority, Norway's Government Pension Fund, Saudi Arabia's Public Investment Fund, Qatar's Investment Authority and Kuwait's Investment Authority, each having hundreds of billions of investments in Sterling.

Other sovereign wealth funds are owned by countries which have saved their nation's money for investment, such as China's Investment Corporation and Singapore's Investment Corporation. These funds, too, often own investments totalling many billions in Sterling.

Sovereign wealth funds will invest their money in a wide range of different assets, with a small proportion of this being invested on the London Stock Exchange by buying shares in listed companies either directly or indirectly. For example, Saudi Arabia's Public Investment Fund owns a significant minority of the shares in the luxury car manufacturer Aston Martin Lagonda Holdings plc, listed on the Main Market.

2.6.4 High net worth individuals

High net worth investors are, unsurprisingly, very wealthy individuals who may well invest some of their money in listed companies. The difference when compared with retail investors is that these investors are assumed to have a much better understanding of the risks of investment on the Stock Exchange and as such are generally subject to lower levels of regulation, and therefore protection.

2.7 REGULATION OF THE STOCK EXCHANGE

Section 19 of the FSMA 2000 prohibits any person from carrying on any regulated activity in the UK unless that person is either authorised or exempt. This is known as the general prohibition (see **9.4**). The Financial Conduct Authority (FCA) has granted a recognition order to the Stock Exchange under s 290 of the FSMA 2000. This means that the Stock Exchange is a 'recognised investment exchange' and, therefore, under s 285(2) of the 2000 Act, is exempt from the general prohibition. To remain a recognised investment exchange, the Stock Exchange must continue to satisfy various requirements drafted pursuant to s 286 of the FSMA 2000, including the Financial Services and Markets Act 2000 (Recognition Requirements for Investment Exchanges and Clearing Houses) Regulations 2001 (SI 2001/995), as amended, and the rules in the specialist sourcebook, 'Recognised Investment Exchanges', which form part of the FCA Handbook of Rules and Guidance. These requirements include that the Stock Exchange must:

(a) ensure that business conducted by means of its facilities is conducted in an orderly manner and so as to afford proper protection to investors;

(b) make arrangements for the provision of pre-trade and post-trade information about share trading;

(c) make clear and transparent rules concerning the admission of securities to trading on its financial markets; and

(d) be able to promote and maintain high standards of integrity and fair dealing in the carrying on of regulated activities by persons using facilities provided by the Stock Exchange.

2.8 THE ROLE OF THE STOCK EXCHANGE IN THE IPO PROCESS

The Stock Exchange shares responsibility with the FCA for regulating IPOs. The FCA has responsibility for the official listing of securities in the UK. **Chapter 3** considers this role more closely. The Stock Exchange has responsibility for admitting shares to trading on its markets. Any company seeking to be a listed company (as defined in **1.3** above) must seek to have its shares:

(a) admitted to *listing* on the Official List (for which it must liaise with the FCA); and

(b) admitted to *trading* on the Main Market (for which it must liaise with the Stock Exchange).

Chapter 5 considers this process in more detail.

2.9 ADMISSION AND DISCLOSURE STANDARDS

The Stock Exchange has its own set of rules for companies joining the Main Market (they do not apply to companies joining AIM). These rules are called the Admission and Disclosure Standards, and they set out the requirements for companies seeking admission to trading, as well as the continuing obligations for companies already admitted to trading. They apply to both companies incorporated in the UK and overseas. The Admission and Disclosure Standards are available on the Stock Exchange's website.

2.10 FUTURE DEVELOPMENTS

2.10.1 Trading

Under ss 783 to 790 of the CA 2006, there is the power for DBT to make regulations to enable shares to be owned or transferred without written documentation. At the time of writing, no such regulations exist. Replacing paper share certificates and stock transfer forms with an electronic system is known as 'dematerialisation'.

In 2022 the UK Government expressed a desire that all shares in listed companies be dematerialised, with listed company shareholders no longer able to hold shares in paper form. Since then there has been little information on when this change might be implemented.

CHAPTER 3

THE FINANCIAL CONDUCT AUTHORITY

3.1 SOURCES OF REGULATION

The regulatory framework governing the listing of securities (including company shares) on the Stock Exchange in the UK has its origins in EU law. The European Commission has long sought to create a single market in financial services across all Member States of the EU and to strengthen regulatory supervision of financial markets, and the EU institutions have passed many pieces of legislation to further this aim. A key goal of the EU is the completion of the Capital Markets Union. This has, as its aims, to help businesses access more diverse sources of capital from anywhere in the EU, make markets work more efficiently, and offer investors and savers additional opportunities to put their money to work in order to enhance growth and create jobs.

The key EU legislation affecting the listing of securities on the Stock Exchange was contained in five instruments: the Prospectus Regulation ((EU) 2017/1129), the Market Abuse Regulation (MAR) ((EU) 596/2014), the Transparency Directive (2004/109/EC), the Markets in Financial Instruments Directive II (MiFID II) (2014/65/EU) and the Markets in Financial Instruments Regulation (MiFIR) ((EU) 600/2014). MiFID II and MiFIR, although important in practice, are very technical in their subject matter and are of only limited relevance to this book.

The implementation of this EU legislation in the UK during the UK's membership of the EU fundamentally shaped the UK's listing regime, and initially the UK government wanted to keep the law the same after Brexit. In order to do so, on 1 January 2021 when EU law ceased to have effect in the UK, the UK had to 'on-shore' these EU Regulations, so that they would continue to have legal effect in the UK despite Brexit but under UK law rather than EU law (although with some minor changes). This 'on-shoring' (which involved passing a UK law to retain the EU Regulations) was necessary because EU Regulations have legal effect automatically across the EU without the need for implementing legislation by national parliaments. In other words, the main rules affecting the listing of securities on the Stock Exchange only existed in EU law. These would no longer have applied in the UK from 1 January 2021, resulting in a massive hole in the law (and undoubted chaos on the markets). The two EU Directives mentioned were required to be passed into UK law at the time, so these were already a part of UK law.

These 'on-shored' EU Regulations are now commonly referred to with the prefix 'UK', so MAR has become 'UK MAR' (ie the UK version of the EU MAR), the Prospectus Regulation has become the UK Prospectus Regulation (ie the UK version of the EU Prospectus Regulation) and so on. This approach has been adopted in this book.

The European Securities Markets Authority (ESMA) which is based in Paris has overarching responsibility for regulating and supervising financial markets, including stock markets in the EU. The ESMA issues draft technical standards and guidelines applicable across the EU. It also makes recommendations and guidelines on the application of EU law. Some of these technical standards and guidelines continue to have effect in the UK where they have been 'on-shored' into UK law. In addition, some further non-binding resources such as FAQs provided by ESMA are still being relied upon informally even though they have no direct legal effect in the UK. You can find these resources on the ESMA website, http://esma.europa.eu.

The FSMA 2000, as amended, is the other primary piece of UK legislation regulating the listing of securities on the Stock Exchange, with most of the detailed rules being set out in the FCA Handbook (accessible online on the FCA's website). The most important rules for our purposes are three 'sourcebooks' which are grouped together in the Handbook under the heading, 'Listing, Prospectus and Disclosure'. These three sourcebooks contain four sets of rules: the UK Listing Rules, the Prospectus Regulation Rules, the Transparency Rules and the Corporate Governance Rules. The last two are found in the Disclosure sourcebook and are known collectively as the Disclosure Guidance and Transparency Rules or DTRs.

The UK Listing Rules, Prospectus Regulation Rules, Transparency Rules and Corporate Governance Rules are collectively referred to as the 'Part 6 Rules' by s 73A of the FSMA 2000.

3.2 THE REGULATOR FOR LISTING IN THE UK

The FCA has a number of roles including that of financial markets regulator. This includes the regulation of issuers of securities subject to listing, and oversight of trading platforms and Recognised Investment Exchanges (RIEs) such as the Stock Exchange. The FCA therefore has the primary regulatory role over listed companies in the UK (although it will share certain functions with HM Treasury in relation to certain matters). It is the regulator which dominates this book. You should, however, be aware that certain listed companies will also fall under the regulation of the PRA. The PRA authorises, regulates and supervises institutions such as banks, building societies, insurance companies and systemically important investment companies. In other words Barclays Bank plc, which is listed on the Main Market of the Stock Exchange, will be subject to regulation by both the FCA and the PRA, whereas Ocado plc, the supermarket delivery firm, will only be regulated by the FCA. The financial services companies are subject to extra scrutiny due to their special importance to the UK's economy and, frankly, because it was not the non-financial services companies such as Tesco plc, easyJet plc and Marks and Spencer plc which caused the 2007/08 financial crisis, and nor are they likely to cause the next one. You can find out more about the PRA on its website, www.bankofengland.co.uk/prudential-regulation.

3.3 WHAT DOES THE FCA DO AS FINANCIAL MARKETS REGULATOR?

The FCA has responsibility for the official listing of securities under Pt VI of the FSMA 2000. This includes:

(a) maintaining the Official List (s 74(1));

(b) drafting the Prospectus Regulation Rules, the UK Listing Rules, the Transparency Rules and the Corporate Governance Rules (s 73A);

(c) determining applications for admission to listing, which includes reviewing the documentation which a company must produce to have its shares listed (s 75);

(d) ensuring that listed companies comply with their continuing obligations under the UK Listing Rules, the Transparency Rules, the Corporate Governance Rules and the Prospectus Regulation Rules, which includes approving documentation prepared by listed companies, such as circulars; and

(e) having the power to sanction any listed company which does not comply with the Prospectus Regulation Rules, the UK Listing Rules, the Transparency Rules and the Corporate Governance Rules (or any director of such a company) (eg s 91).

Chapter 5 looks at the listing process in more detail and considers how the FCA is involved in that process in practice.

3.4 RELATIONSHIP BETWEEN THE FCA AND THE STOCK EXCHANGE

In its capacity as financial markets regulator under the FSMA 2000, the FCA regulates the Stock Exchange. In an IPO, as stated at **2.8** above, both the FCA and the Stock Exchange are involved in the flotation process and have different roles to play. The FCA oversees the admission of shares to *listing* and the Stock Exchange oversees the admission of shares to *trading*. A listed company needs to have its shares admitted both to listing and to trading. **Chapters 4, 5** and **6** consider how a company can do this.

3.5 UK PROSPECTUS REGULATION, UK LISTING, TRANSPARENCY AND CORPORATE GOVERNANCE RULES

As referred to at **3.3**, the FCA has responsibility for four sets of rules, discussed at **3.5.1** to **3.5.3** below.

References to the Prospectus Regulation Rules and UK Listing Rules are prefaced with 'PRR' and 'UKLR', and the Transparency and Corporate Governance Rules with 'DTR'. The paragraph number is suffixed with 'R' to indicate if this is a rule (and so binding), or 'G' to indicate if this is guidance (non-binding but generally if followed will be acceptable conduct).

3.5.1 The Prospectus Regulation Rules

The Prospectus Regulation Rules (PRR) repeat much of the UK Prospectus Regulation and so to this extent do not add anything to the existing law but there is also some guidance on the application of the UK Prospectus Regulation. The PRR contain provisions about the need for, content of, and approval process for, a marketing document for an IPO called a prospectus.

These Rules apply to companies:

(a) seeking to *offer* transferable securities *to the public in the UK*. This includes offers of shares by companies seeking admission to AIM or the Main Market for the first time, or which are already admitted; and/or

(b) seeking to *admit* transferable securities to *trading on a regulated market in the UK* (which includes the Main Market but not AIM) (even where there is no offer to the public referred to at (a) above).

The Prospectus Regulation Rules will therefore apply on an IPO and after the listed company has joined the Main Market.

Chapters 5 and **6** consider the Prospectus Regulation Rules in more detail.

3.5.1.1 UK Commission Delegated Regulation (EU) 2019/980 (UK PR Regulation)

The UK Prospectus Regulation takes the form of a framework directive. Further necessary detail on the format, content, scrutiny and approval process for a prospectus is contained in an EU Delegated Regulation, the PR Regulation. This has been on-shored and retained in UK law and is known in this book as the UK PR Regulation. Annexes in this law specify in detail the content requirements of the main parts of a prospectus. Helpfully for the practitioner, the

Prospectus Regulation Rules replicate the key contents of the UK PR Regulation (the articles are set out at PRR 2.3.1UK).

3.5.1.2 UK Commission Delegated Regulation (EU) 2019/979 (UK Prospectus RTS Regulation)

A second EU Delegated Regulation supplements the UK Prospectus Regulation and this too has been on-shored and retained in UK law. It is known in this book as the UK Prospectus RTS Regulation. It contains rules on certain aspects of the prospectus, eg the key financial information content requirement, certain technical matters and supplementary prospectuses.

3.5.1.3 The FSMA 2000 (Prospectus) Regulations 2019 (Prospectus Regulations 2019)

The FSMA 2000 (Prospectus) Regulations 2019 (SI 2019/1043) amended the FSMA 2000 to bring it into line with the original EU Prospectus Regulation and are still in force.

3.5.1.4 The Public Offers and Admissions to Trading Regulations 2024 (POAT Regulations)

The current UK Prospectus Regulation is due to be replaced to allow for the introduction of new (non-EU law based) rules for producing prospectuses for an IPO and other transactions in the UK. The POAT Regulations will bring the necessary changes into being once the date for revocation of the UK Prospectus Regulation has been decided by the Government, which is expected in the first half of 2025.

3.5.2 The UK Listing Rules

The UK Listing Rules contain the following key provisions:

(a) Listing Principles (see **3.5.2.1** below);

(b) the requirements for listing;

(c) rules regarding sponsors;

(d) the continuing obligations of a listed company (which are supplemented by some continuing obligations in the DTRs and under UK MAR);

(e) the listing application process; and

(f) the cancellation and suspension of listing.

The UK Listing Rules apply to companies whose shares are admitted to listing on the Official List, so they will apply to companies whose shares trade on the Main Market but *not* to companies whose shares trade on AIM. The UK Listing Rules also apply to companies which are the subject of an application for admission to listing on the Official List but whose shares are not yet trading on the Main Market. This means that a company seeking to float on the Main Market of the Stock Exchange will have to take account of the UK Listing Rules even before its IPO has successfully completed.

The UK Listing Rules are divided into 24 chapters. Chapter 1 sets out preliminary matters applicable to all securities; Chapter 2 contains the listing principles which apply to all listed companies; Chapter 3 sets out the requirements for listing, and Chapter 20 the procedure; Chapters 4 and 24 cover sponsors; Chapters 5 to 10 apply to equity shares (commercial companies); and Chapter 21 deals with suspension and cancellation of listing. These then are the key chapters for this book. The remaining chapters apply to different types of security and investment vehicles, such as investment funds (Chapter 11) and debt securities (Chapter 17), and so are not covered further.

3.5.2.1 The Listing Principles

The Listing Principles apply to every listed company (UKLR 2.1.1R). They are intended to ensure that listed companies pay due regard to the fundamental role they play in maintaining market confidence and ensuring fair and orderly markets (UKLR 2.1.3G). They are designed to assist listed companies in identifying their obligations and responsibilities under the UK Listing Rules and other Part 6 rules (UKLR 2.1.4G).

The Listing Principles, which are set out at 2.2.1R of the UK Listing Rules, are as follows:

Listing Principle 1	A listed company must take reasonable steps to establish and maintain adequate procedures, systems and controls to enable it to comply with its obligations. UKLR 2.2.2–4G make clear that in particular these procedures etc must allow for the identification of certain important transactions regulated by the UKLR and for proper disclosure of information on the listed company to the market, the FCA and its sponsor. The listed company should be able to explain to the FCA where information is held and how it can be accessed (UKLR 2.2.5G).
Listing Principle 2	A listed company must deal with the FCA in an open and co-operative manner.
Listing Principle 3	A listed company must take reasonable steps to enable its directors to understand their responsibilities and obligations as directors.
Listing Principle 4	A listed company must act with integrity towards holders and potential holders of its listed securities.
Listing Principle 5	A listed company must ensure that it treats all holders of the same class of its listed securities that are in the same position equally in respect of the rights attaching to those listed securities.
Listing Principle 6	A listed company must communicate information to holders and potential holders of its listed securities and listed equity securities in such a way as to avoid the creation or continuation of a false market in those listed securities.

The FCA has provided further guidance on the application of the Listing Principles in its Technical Note FCA/TN/203.5 Compliance with the Listing Principles (available in the Knowledge Base section of the FCA's website), which makes it clear that the Principles are enforceable like any other UK Listing Rule, it is prepared to take enforcement action on the basis of a breach of the Principles alone and breach can lead to sanction by the FCA (see **3.6** below). For example, Prudential plc was fined £14 million in January 2011 for breaching (what is now) Listing Principle 2 and other rules, and Carillion plc would have been fined almost £38 million for breaching (what is now) Listing Principle 2 and other rules were it not for the fact that the company was insolvent and in liquidation.

3.5.3 The Transparency and Corporate Governance Rules and the disclosure requirements under UK MAR

The Transparency and Corporate Governance Rules are contained in one FCA sourcebook, the Disclosure Guidance and Transparency Rules (DTRs). DTRs 1A and 4–6 set out the Transparency Rules. DTRs 1B, 4.1.7R and 7 contain the Corporate Governance Rules. UK MAR contains certain disclosure obligations, and guidance on these is provided in DTRs 1–3.

The Transparency Rules (together with amendments made to the FSMA 2000) implemented the Transparency Directive in the UK. They seek principally to improve investors' access to information about companies trading on the UK financial markets, to enable them to invest more efficiently.

The Transparency Rules require more financial information to be revealed publicly about companies listed on the Stock Exchange more regularly than before. They also require the disclosure of significant shareholdings in listed companies, to ensure that these companies are aware of who is building up a significant stake in them, which may be a precursor to a takeover. They are considered in greater detail in **Chapters 7** and **15**.

As with the UK Listing Rules, DTRs 1A, 1B, 4 and 6–7 apply to companies whose shares trade on a regulated market, so they will apply to companies whose shares trade on the Main Market but *not* to companies which are quoted on AIM. Note, however, that DTR 5 applies to both types of company.

The Corporate Governance Rules were made under s 89(O) of the FSMA 2000. The Rules implemented part of the Statutory Audit Directive and the Company Reporting Directive in the UK. Among other provisions, the Statutory Audit Directive requires listed companies to establish an audit committee in compliance with the Directive's terms. Rules relating to the establishment of an audit committee were already in existence for listed companies in the UK but on a non-statutory basis (see **8.3**). The Statutory Audit Directive required, in the UK, the existing rules to be put on a statutory basis. The Company Reporting Directive, in order to help promote credible company financial reporting and to prevent financial malpractice, requires listed companies to include a corporate governance statement in their annual reports. The Corporate Governance Rules are considered in greater detail in **Chapters 7** and **8**.

UK MAR includes rules about a listed company's obligation to:

(a) inform the market about new developments and its financial condition and performance (that is, to disclose 'inside information');
(b) maintain 'insider lists'; and
(c) disclose transactions in shares by directors and senior executives and persons closely associated to them. They are examined in detail in **Chapter 7**.

DTRs 1–3 contain guidance on the application of these disclosure requirements under UK MAR and should therefore be considered alongside the rules contained in UK MAR. Note that the Disclosure Guidance in DTRs 1–3 is not legally binding but purely advisory.

3.6 SANCTIONS FOR BREACH OF THE KEY RULES

The FCA can impose a variety of sanctions under powers granted by the FSMA 2000, depending on the particular set of rules breached. The sanctions may apply to securities other than just shares, such as debt securities, but as these are beyond the scope of this textbook they are not discussed. If necessary, reference should be made to the FSMA 2000 and the relevant definitions.

For breaches of **any of the Part 6 Rules** (UK Listing Rules, Prospectus Regulation Rules, Transparency Rules and Corporate Governance Rules) and the UK Prospectus Regulation, the FCA can:

(a) privately or publicly censure:
    (i) the listed company (FSMA 2000, s 91(3)), and/or
    (ii) a director or former director of the listed company knowingly concerned in the breach (FSMA 2000, s 91(3));

    In October 2020, for example, Aviva plc was publicly censured for breaches of the old listing rules and the DTRs.
(b) impose an unlimited fine on:
    (i) the listed company (FSMA 2000, s 91(1), (1A) and (1B)), and/or
    (ii) a director or former director of the listed company knowingly concerned in the breach (FSMA 2000, s 91(2) and (2A)).

For example, in September 2022 Barclays Bank plc was fined £40 million for breaching the old listing rules for publishing misleading information, not including all necessary information in a circular and not acting with integrity towards its shareholders.

In December 2022 Metro Bank PLC and two former directors were fined £10 million, £223,100 and £134,600 respectively for publishing misleading information in breach of (what is now) UKLR 1.3.3R.

The FCA tends to censure a listed company rather than fine it when it is in severe financial difficulty (eg Carillion plc in June 2022 which had become insolvent). Three former directors of Carillion plc were, however, fined a total of £790,400 for being knowingly concerned in Carillion plc's breaches of the old listing rules.

In addition the FCA can:

(a) suspend the *listing* on the Official List of a listed company's shares (FSMA 2000, s 77(2) and (2A) and UKLR 21.1.1R);

In June 2021, for example, the FCA suspended the listing of Umuthi Healthcare Solutions plc for failure to provide necessary financial information and proper information on the ownership of its shares.

(b) cancel the *listing* on the Official List of a listed company's shares (FSMA 2000, s 77(1) and (2A) and UKLR 21.2.1R);

In July 2022 the FCA ultimately cancelled the listing of Umuthi Healthcare Solutions plc for not rectifying the ongoing issues mentioned above.

(c) impose an unlimited fine, publicly censure, impose conditions on or suspend the sponsor for a breach of its responsibilities (FSMA 2000, s 88A).

In August 2016, for example, the FCA fined Cenkos Securities Plc £530,500 for breach of its responsibilities under the old listing rules in relation to it acting as a sponsor for Mission Capital plc on its Main Market IPO (which ultimately had to be abandoned).

Further, for a breach of the **UK Prospectus Regulation or the Prospectus Regulation Rules**, the FCA can:

(a) suspend or require the withdrawal of the offer of shares to the public (FSMA 2000, s 87K(2) and (3));
(b) suspend *trading* or prohibit *trading* in the listed company's shares (FSMA 2000, s 87L).

In addition, for a breach of the **Transparency Rules**, the FCA can:

(a) suspend or prohibit the *trading* on the Main Market of a listed company's shares (FSMA 2000, s 89L);
(b) impose an unlimited fine on a person subject to the Transparency Rules (FSMA 2000, s 91(1B)). For example, in August 2011 the FSA, forerunner to the FCA, imposed a fine of £210,000 on Sir Ken Morrison (formerly Chair and director of Wm Morrison Supermarkets Plc) for his failure to comply with the Transparency Rules.

In addition, for a breach of the **Corporate Governance Rules**, the FCA can suspend or prohibit the *trading* on the Main Market of a listed company's shares (FSMA 2000, s 87L).

For a breach of the **disclosure requirements of UK MAR** (UK MAR, Articles 17, 18 and 19), the FCA can:

(a) censure or fine any person (including a company) who has contravened any provision of UK MAR (FSMA 2000, s 123(1), (2) and (3));
(b) censure or fine persons discharging managerial responsibility (PDMRs) within a listed company or persons closely associated with PDMRs (DTR 1.5.3G(1));
(c) fine a former director who was knowingly concerned in any breach by the issuer (DTR 1.5.3G(2));

(d) suspend *trading* in the listed company's shares (FSMA 2000, s 122I);

(e) temporarily ban an individual from buying or selling financial instruments (including shares) (FSMA 2000, s 123A); and

(f) require the company, PDMRs and persons closely associated with PDMRs to provide any information the FCA reasonably requires for the protection of investors or the orderly operation of the financial markets (FSMA 2000, s 122A) and require the company to publish such information (FSMA 2000, s 122G).

In December 2020 the FCA fined a PDMR (see (b) above) of Braemar Shipping Services plc £45,000 for failing to make notifications in breach of UK MAR Article 19.

Breaches of the Part 6 Rules, the UK Prospectus Regulation and the disclosure requirements under UK MAR may also give rise to some or all of both the civil liability set out at **6.7.1** and the criminal liability set out at **6.7.2** depending on the provision breached.

The FCA has prepared the Enforcement Guide (EG) and a Decision Procedure and Penalties Manual (DPPM), which can be found in the Regulatory Guides and Regulatory Processes sections respectively of the FCA Handbook on the FCA's website. They provide useful guidance on the approach the FCA will take regarding enforcement of breaches of the Part 6 Rules, the UK Prospectus Regulation, the disclosure requirements under UK MAR and other rules.

3.7 FUTURE DEVELOPMENTS

Financial Services and Markets Act 2023

This Act intends, amongst other things, to revoke EU financial services law that had been retained following Brexit and replace it with UK-sourced rules. The then UK Government's vision was for an open, green, and technologically advanced financial services sector that is globally competitive, with this Act being at its core. The Act will result in fundamental amendments to the FSMA 2000. It will also grant the FCA much wider powers to enable it to draw up legally binding rules which will be included in the FCA's Handbook (eg the UK Listing Rules, new Prospectus Rules and Disclosure Guidance and Transparency Rules) rather than, as is currently the case, in legislation. Laws which will be repealed include the UK version of the Prospectus Directive, the UK version of MAR, the UK version of MiFIR and the related delegated legislation.

In addition, the Act will amend the FSMA 2000 to introduce a principle that all decision making must take account of the UK Government's legal duty under s 1 of the Climate Change Act 2008 to achieve a 'net zero' emissions economy by 2050.

The FCA has already taken the first major step by introducing the new UK Listing Rules which replaced the former Listing Rules on 29 July 2024.

The FCA is consulting on replacing the current prospectus regime with new Prospectus Rules. These are discussed in greater detail at the end of **Chapter 6** below.

Further consultations to take soundings on the future shape of the regulation of the financial services industry in the UK and the detailed rules which should apply to listed companies, including the rules and principles mentioned in this chapter, are expected. You will be able to follow this process via the FCA's website.

Please note that these changes when implemented will have a significant impact on the content of this chapter.

CHAPTER 4

Initial Public Offerings: Preparation

4.1 WHAT IS AN INITIAL PUBLIC OFFERING?

An initial public offering (IPO), also known as a flotation, is the process by which a company becomes a listed company (for our purposes as defined at **1.3** above). The terms 'IPO' and 'flotation' are used interchangeably. As **Chapters 2** and **3** established, any company seeking to become such a listed company must undergo a parallel admission procedure to have its shares:

(a) admitted to *listing* on the Official List (for which it must liaise with the FCA and comply with the Prospectus Regulation Rules and the UK Listing Rules); and

(b) admitted to *trading* on the Main Market (for which it must liaise with the Stock Exchange and comply with the Admission and Disclosure Standards).

While lawyers and other advisers need to be aware of the distinction between admission to listing and admission to trading, in practice the FCA and the Stock Exchange co-operate to ensure that the process is seamless. In fact, the layman would probably not be aware that, technically, an IPO involves two admission procedures. **Chapter 5** considers the actual IPO process in more detail. This chapter looks at the preparatory steps a company should take in the year (or two) preceding the IPO.

4.2 APPOINTING A TEAM OF ADVISERS

An IPO is a very complex transaction and good corporate advisers are vital to a successful outcome. In the year before the IPO the company must consider carefully who to appoint as its advisers. Usually it will seek preliminary advice on this matter from its current advisers (typically its lawyers and accountants). These advisers may not have the necessary expertise to advise in relation to the IPO itself, but they should be able to recommend suitable advisers who can provide guidance to the company. The company will sign engagement letters with some of the key advisers to govern the terms and conditions of their appointment specifically in relation to the IPO.

Any company seeking to float requires professional advice in relation to a wide range of issues. Lawyers advising on the legal aspects of the IPO form just part of a considerably larger team of advisers, who each take responsibility for various aspects of the float. Lawyers advising on an IPO cannot expect to work in isolation. They need excellent communication and project management skills. They also need a good understanding of the roles and responsibilities of the rest of the team. So who does what?

4.2.1 The company and the directors

As set out in **Chapter 6** below, the main marketing document for an IPO is the prospectus, and this must contain a substantial amount of information about the company. It is the directors who have primary responsibility for the accuracy of this information. While the directors cannot delegate this responsibility, practically they cannot supply all the information required in the time provided. Instead they enlist the help of the company secretary and key managers to locate, and provide to the advisers drafting the prospectus, accurate information about the company. Obviously this diverts many of the company's senior employees and directors from their usual role of day-to-day management and ensuring that the company is profitable. Companies need to be made aware of this hidden cost and distraction from their usual roles (see **1.8.5** above).

4.2.2 Sponsor

This is a role required by the FSMA 2000 and the UKLR. UK Listing Rule 4.2 sets outs when a company needs to appoint or consult with a sponsor. UK Listing Rule 4.2.1R(1) provides that any company applying for admission of its equity shares to the ESCC category which requires the publication of a prospectus must have a sponsor (see **4.3.1.2** below). As a prospectus will usually be required on an IPO, the prospective listed company will have to appoint a sponsor.

The sponsor has a crucial role in guiding the company and its management through the flotation process and advising the company on the interpretation of the UK Listing Rules. It will liaise with the FCA and, to a lesser extent, the Stock Exchange on behalf of the company, and will relay any comments back to the company. The sponsor also co-ordinates the team of advisers and will advise them on the timetable for the IPO. The lawyers in particular will have day-to-day contact with the sponsor as the flotation process progresses.

Usually an investment bank, or possibly on smaller IPOs a stockbroker, will adopt the role of sponsor, but it must be approved by the FCA. UK Listing Rule 24.4.5R sets out the criteria for sponsor approval. A list of approved sponsors is on the FCA website (UKLR 24.4.1G). The sponsor must abide by rules in UKLR 24.2.12.R to 24.2.17G to ensure that conflicts of interest which may arise do not adversely affect its ability to perform its functions properly or market confidence in sponsors. On larger IPOs there may be more than one sponsor appointed, 'joint sponsors', who will share the responsibilities of the role between them; however just one of them must be nominated as the contact with the FCA (UKLR 4.4.1R).

Chapter 24 of the UKLR contains the rules relating to the sponsor. UK Listing Rule 24.2 sets out the responsibilities and general principles for a sponsor, including the duty to act with due care and skill (UKLR 24.2.6R) and the duty to act with honesty and integrity (UKLR 24.2.7R). With the exception of UKLR 24.2.9R (requiring sponsors to deal with the FCA in an open and co-operative way and to deal promptly with all FCA enquiries), which applies to sponsors at all times, UKLR 24.2 only applies to sponsors in connection with the provision of 'sponsor services', that is when they have to act under UKLR 4.2. Advice given by a sponsor outside of this definition is not within the UKLR and subject to other legal rules.

UK Listing Rules 24.3.1R to 24.3.4G set out the specific duties of the sponsor in relation to an IPO. The sponsor owes duties to the FCA, and a firm must take up an appointment as sponsor only once it is satisfied of the company's suitability for listing. Of course, no sponsor would want to be associated with an unsuccessful float in any event.

4.2.3 Broker

The broker advises the company with a view to ensuring that there is sufficient demand for the company's shares once the company has floated. The broker will analyse market conditions, liaise with potential investors to market the shares and advise the company on the best method of flotation (see **4.4** below) and other tactical issues, such the price of the shares to be marketed and the timing of the IPO. If the firm appointed as sponsor (see **4.2.2**) has stockbroking capability then it may also take on the role of broker. On larger IPOs there may be more than one broker appointed, 'joint brokers', who will share the role

4.2.4 Financial adviser

The financial adviser will advise on a wide range of tactical issues, such as the timing of the IPO, how the offer should be structured (see **4.4** below) and the offer price. This critical role is usually undertaken by the firm acting as sponsor, although on some IPOs it may be shared with a different firm usually drawn from the same pool of investment banks, etc which act as sponsors. In addition to any requirements under the UKLR, the financial adviser will have to ensure that it complies with onerous responsibilities imposed on it under the FSMA 2000 as an authorised person and other legal rules.

4.2.5 Reporting accountants

The reporting accountants review the company's finances. This is an important role, because whatever the company states in the prospectus about its financial situation will influence potential investors as to whether the company is an attractive investment. The company will want to present as positive a financial picture as possible, but the reporting accountants must ensure that this picture is accurate.

The reporting accountants will produce three main reports. The lawyers will have little involvement in the production of these, but they do need to know what they are (there will be frequent references to them in meetings). The first report is the 'long form' report, which is not published but forms the basis of the financial information required to draft the prospectus. The second report is the 'short form' report. This is based on the long form report, but it is published; it forms part of the prospectus. The third report is the 'working capital' report. The reporting accountants prepare this so that the sponsor can ascertain the company's anticipated working capital position for a period following the IPO.

The reporting accountants may also provide 'comfort letters' to the directors, to enable the directors to make certain statements in the prospectus about the financial status of the company which are required by the UK Listing Rules (the directors cannot, however, delegate responsibility for making such statements to the accountants). The reporting accountants may also advise on taxation issues.

Note that the role of reporting accountants is separate from the role of the company's existing auditors. Often the same accountancy firm does adopt both roles, but allocates a different team to each. The sponsor, however, may prefer that the role of reporting accountant is adopted by an entirely different firm, so that it is seen to be independent.

4.2.6 Lawyers

There are usually two teams of lawyers, from different firms, involved in a flotation. They will be specialists in corporate finance. One team advises the company and one team advises the sponsor. Both teams must work closely together to provide a seamless service. The requirement for two teams reflects the fact that, while both the sponsor/financial adviser and the company have the common aim of a successful IPO, there are issues on which their needs conflict. For example, with an ESCC listing the sponsor owes certain duties to the FCA (see **4.2.2**) which the company does not owe. The sponsor will be highly sensitive about the risks of being involved with an unsuccessful IPO, or one which generates bad publicity, and the impact this will have on its ability to obtain work in the future. It may, therefore, wish to exercise a more cautious approach than the company in certain areas. The company and the sponsor are also likely to have conflicting interests regarding underwriting (see **4.2.7** below).

In addition to the company's lawyers and the sponsor's lawyers, there may also be other lawyers representing any selling shareholders, if there is a conflict of interest between the company and such shareholders. If there is no conflict, the company's lawyers may also act for any selling shareholders.

4.2.6.1 The company's lawyers

The company's lawyers draft all the documentation relating to the IPO. This includes not only the prospectus but also any ancillary documents, including any preparatory documentation required to restructure the company (see **4.5** below), such as changing the articles of association, drafting new service contracts for the directors and re-registering the company as a public company (see **1.9.3** above). The company's lawyers are also responsible for the verification process (see **5.3.5** and **6.8** below) and ensure that the directors are fully aware of their responsibilities in relation to the content of the key marketing document for the IPO, the prospectus. The workload of the lawyers is examined in more detail at **5.3**.

4.2.6.2 The sponsor's lawyers

These lawyers work with the company's lawyers to negotiate the agreements between the sponsor and the company and its shareholders (for example, the underwriting agreement). While the company's lawyers will have primary responsibility for processing the IPO documentation, the sponsor's lawyers will also contribute towards drafting. They will keep a close eye on the company lawyers' progress regarding the legal documentation and the verification exercise (see **5.3.5** and **6.8**), and advise their client accordingly. Remember, the sponsor will not wish to be involved with a failure; if anything is not progressing as planned, the sponsor's lawyers must alert their client.

4.2.7 Underwriters

The underwriters take up any shares left over after the IPO (in the event that the float is 'undersubscribed') in return for a negotiated fee, which is typically around 3 to 4% of the amount underwritten. If the IPO is 'fully subscribed' and there are no shares left over, the underwriter has no liability to take any shares. This arrangement is recorded in an underwriting agreement. The underwriter will usually allocate some or all of the risk of the offer being undersubscribed to sub-underwriters, by way of a sub-underwriting agreement (the company will not be party to any sub-underwriting agreement). Often the sponsor will adopt the role of underwriter. Occasionally the broker (if different from the sponsor) will be the underwriter. Usually the sub-underwriters will be other banks and brokers, and the large institutional investors.

4.2.8 Receiving bank

If the IPO is by way of a public/retail offer (see **4.4.1.1** and **4.4.2.2** below), the receiving bank deals with the application forms (see **5.4.2.2**) and consideration for shares. Often the company's clearing bank fulfils this role.

4.2.9 Registrars

The registrars manage the company's share register. They send the share certificates to the successful applicants. This can be a considerable task if the offer is sizeable, for example a public/retail offer. Often the company's clearing bank takes this role in addition to the role of receiving bank.

4.2.10 Financial public relations consultants

It is important for a company to have a positive public profile before, during and after the IPO. Financial PR consultants liaise with the media and analysts to heighten the profile of the company. They also ensure that the company's communications are effective.

For reasons explained in **Chapter 6**, it is important from a legal perspective that the company's communications are not misleading and can be verified by the company (see **5.3.5** and **6.8** below). The lawyers, therefore, have a role in ensuring that the financial PR consultants take into account these legal requirements. There can, in a process which is ultimately about selling a company and its management to investors, be a tendency towards emphasising exuberant unqualified statements, such as 'we are the biggest/the fastest/the best'; these, while being excellent selling messages, rarely survive the lawyers' red pens.

Good financial PR consultants will be aware of the legal limitations on the company's sales pitch from the outset, and can manage the company's expectations in this regard. It is not just pre-prepared communications which need to be handled cautiously, though. The consultants and the lawyers may also provide the directors with media training, so that when the directors are marketing the IPO they do not say anything ('we are the biggest/the fastest/the best') which might have adverse legal implications because it cannot be verified.

4.2.11 Printers

The IPO documentation will be created initially electronically, but ultimately the final version will also have to be professionally printed. Once each document is in substantially final draft form, it will be taken to print. Thereafter, each draft will be printed rather than take the form of a word-processed document. The printers need to turn around the documentation quickly, accurately and securely. Towards the end of the IPO the lawyers will spend some time, often well into the night, at the printers, checking *in situ* the final amendments to the draft.

4.3 IS THE COMPANY READY TO FLOAT?

The company may consider that it is ready to float, but the advisers, and particularly the sponsor/financial adviser, will need to ensure that the company has taken account of all relevant factors in reaching this conclusion. There are two main considerations, namely:

(a) Will the company meet the regulatory requirements for an IPO laid down by the FCA (in relation to listing) and the Stock Exchange (in relation to trading) (see **4.3.1** below)?

(b) Will investors perceive the company to be an attractive investment opportunity (see **4.3.2** below)?

4.3.1 Regulatory requirements

The company may not have considered any regulatory requirements at the time it appoints its advisers. However, as soon as the advisers are on board they will go through the regulatory requirements with the company and discuss the extent to which the company fulfils them. The company can then take action to remedy any problems.

4.3.1.1 Regulatory requirements for admission to listing

Under s 75(4) of the FSMA 2000, the FCA cannot grant an application for listing unless it is satisfied that the requirements of the UK Listing Rules have been complied with.

Previously there was a two-tier system for companies seeking a listing on the Main Market of the Stock Exchange. Companies had a choice and could seek to be admitted to either the more regulated 'premium' listing segment or the lesser regulated 'standard' listing segment of the Official List. On 29 July 2024 a new, single-tier, system was introduced by the FCA under the UKLR to encourage more companies to seek a listing on the Main Market. Prior to the UKLR being introduced, the number of companies seeking an IPO in London had diminished considerably, with many (including UK companies) preferring to list primarily in the USA in order to maximise the benefits of the company's IPO. By introducing a single listing option, which for most companies will result in a significant reduction in its regulatory burden, the Stock Exchange is hoping that more companies, particularly tech companies (which are seen as becoming increasingly dominant in the IPO market), will list on the Main Market and reverse the decline in size and significance of the Stock Exchange. Put simply, the hope is that less regulation will attract more companies, and indeed more innovative ones, to the Main Market.

Although there is just one listing option, there are 11 different categories of listing, as set out in UKLR 1.5.1R. A company seeking to list on the Main Market will fall into one of these categories dependent on the type of security being listed and, sometimes, the type of company. Other categories include companies that are investment funds and debt securities (such as bonds). It is possible to change listing category in accordance with rules set out in UKLR Chapter 21, but this will usually require a significant change to the running of the business and will not occur often. There is also a 'transition category' for companies which were 'standard' listed companies under the old listing rules, allowing them the time to make the changes necessary to move into another category in the future.

The level of regulation imposed on the listed company will vary according to its category of listing on the Main Market. For most trading companies the 'equity shares (commercial company)' category (ESCC) will apply and, as such, this is what we shall concentrate on in this book.

4.3.1.2 Listing of equity shares (commercial companies) (ESCC)

The FCA has the following requirements which a company must meet before its shares can be admitted to listing in the ESCC category. The IPO team must be aware of these requirements and ensure that by the time the FCA hears the listing application, the company is capable of meeting all of them.

Sponsor

UK Listing Rule 4.2.1R provides that any company seeking a listing in the ESCC category must appoint a sponsor for the IPO. The sponsor's role is discussed in more detail at **4.2.2** above; however, the key role of the sponsor from the FCA's point of view is to ensure that the company is suitable for listing, to act as a link between the FCA and the company, and to advise the company in relation to the application for admission to listing and in relation to the UK Listing Rules.

Requirements for listing

Chapter 3 of the UK Listing Rules sets out the conditions which a company must satisfy before it can admit any type of security to the Official List, including equity shares (such as ordinary shares). Chapter 5 of the UK Listing Rules sets out additional conditions which must be satisfied by commercial companies seeking a listing of their equity shares, such as ordinary shares, in the ESCC category. A commercial company seeking a listing of its equity shares on the Official List therefore must fulfil the conditions for listing in both Chapter 3 and Chapter 5 of the UK Listing Rules (UKLR 5.1.4G). In addition, the FCA may impose additional requirements if it thinks it is necessary to protect investors (UKLR 3.1.4R(1)).

The conditions in Chapters 3 and 5 are discussed below, although the UKLR, and particularly the guidance to the UKLR, should be consulted for further detail.

UKLR Chapter 3

(a) *Incorporation (UKLR 3.2.1R).* The company must be duly incorporated and operate in conformity with its constitution. For UK companies this means being a public company (as referred to at **1.5.1**, a private company cannot offer shares to the public). The methods by which a company can achieve public company status are discussed at **1.9** above.

(b) *Validity of securities (UKLR 3.2.2R).* The securities (for our purposes, shares) of the company must comply with all legal requirements, be authorised under the company's memorandum and articles and all necessary consents must be in place. This means that the company must comply with all the provisions of the CA 2006 relating to the issue of shares, such as ss 551 and 561 (see **14.3** and **Chapters 13** and **14** generally).

(c) *Admission to trading (UKLR 3.2.3R).* Shares must be admitted to trading on a regulated market in order to be admitted to listing. As explained at **4.1**, companies seeking to float must not only apply to have their shares listed on the Official List, they must also apply to have their shares admitted to trading (for our purposes, on the Main Market). It is this requirement for listing which links the two obligations and ensures a company cannot have shares which are admitted to listing but not to trading.

(d) *Transferability (UKLR 3.2.4R).* In order to list successfully, shares must be marketable. Therefore they must be freely transferable. This means that rights attaching to shares which are common in private companies, such as rights of pre-emption on transfer and the right of directors to refuse to register share transfers, generally are not permitted in the articles of any company seeking to list. (Note, for the avoidance of confusion, that s 561 of the CA 2006 provides a right of pre-emption on the *allotment*, not *transfer*, of shares, and so does not affect this requirement in any way.)

(e) *Market capitalisation (UKLR 3.2.7R).* Market capitalisation refers to the number of issued shares in a company multiplied by the current market value of each share. In other words, it represents how much the company is worth. It is a requirement of listing that the expected aggregate market capitalisation of the shares to be listed should be at least £30 million. In practice, given the amount of time and costs a company must invest in an IPO, the market capitalisation of shares to be issued on flotation is usually considerably in excess of this figure (for example, the consumer health company Haleon plc's IPO in July 2024 valued the company's shares at over £30 billion). Nevertheless, the FCA has discretion to accept a lower threshold if it is satisfied that there will be an adequate market for the shares (UKLR 3.2.8G).

(f) *Whole class to be listed (UKLR 3.2.9R).* If a company has different classes of share (eg, ordinary shares and preference shares), it can choose to list one class and not another (eg, list only the ordinary shares), but it cannot choose to list only part of one class (eg, half of the ordinary shares); all shares of that class must be listed.

(g) *Prospectus (UKLR 3.2.10R).* A marketing document for the company's shares, known as a prospectus, must be approved by the FCA and published if Article 3 of the UK Prospectus Regulation and s 85 of the FSMA 2000 apply to the listing (see **Chapter 6**).

UKLR Chapter 5

(a) *Externally managed companies (UKLR 5.2.1R).* The company must show the FCA that its board of directors can take strategic decisions without interference from a person outside the company. This rule was introduced as a result of problems in the past with certain listed companies which in practice were controlled through executive decisions taken by people overseas who were not on the board of directors.

(b) *Controlling shareholders (UKLR 5.3).* Special rules apply to a company with a 'controlling shareholder'. A 'controlling shareholder' is defined in the Glossary to the UKLR to mean a shareholder who alone or with persons acting together with them own 30% or more of the voting rights in the company. An example is Mike Ashley of Frasers Group plc (the high street retailer) who at the time of writing owned 73% of the shares in that company. Obviously, there is a real risk with such a large shareholding that the shareholder, acting in their self-interest, will behave directly or indirectly in a way which goes against the spirit or even letter of the UKLR, which are designed to ensure that investors can have full confidence in investing in a company listed on the Stock Exchange.

In order to prevent this from occurring, the company must demonstrate that, despite having a controlling shareholder, it can carry on the business which is its main activity independently of that controlling shareholder (UKLR 5.3.1R). UKLR 5.3.2G sets out examples of where this test may not be met, for example where the controlling shareholder uses the company's assets as security for loans taken out by the shareholder.

Although no longer a legal requirement under the UKLR, companies with a controlling shareholder may wish to put in place a written and legally binding agreement between the controlling shareholder and the company (known as a 'relationship agreement') which would include terms that seek to ensure the company's independence, for example:

(1) transactions and arrangements between the company and the controlling shareholder (and/or any of its associates – such as their spouse or child) will be conducted at arm's length and on normal commercial terms; and

(2) neither the controlling shareholder nor any of its associates will take any action that would have the effect of preventing the company from complying with its obligations under the UK Listing Rules.

Finally, protection must be included in the company's articles of association as explained in the next paragraph.

(c) *Constitutional arrangements* (UKLR 5.4). The company must have articles of association that allow it to comply with the UKLR, including:

(1) enabling the shareholders of the company's shares admitted to the ESCC category to vote on certain important matters which must be decided by them (as set out in UKLR 6.2.27R); and

(2) where the company has a controlling shareholder, upholding the rules on independent directors.

Independent directors

These are certain non-executive directors of the company who have an important role to play in ensuring that the company follows good corporate practice once it is listed (see **8.3.7.2** below). The election or re-election of independent directors must be approved both by a majority of the shareholders of the company as a whole and also by a majority of the independent shareholders alone (ie not including the controlling shareholder). It is possible to override a vote where the independent shareholders reject the election of an independent director, but additional procedures must be followed (UKLR 6.2.8R and 6.2.9R).

(d) *Shares in public hands* (UKLR 5.5). Following the IPO, at least 10% of the class of equity shares to be listed (ie ordinary shares) should be 'in public hands' (UKLR 5.5.1R and UKLR 5.5.2R). This is to ensure there is a sufficiently liquid market in the company's shares once they begin trading on the Main Market. In other words, this rule ensures that there are enough buyers and sellers of shares at any time for investors to either realise or increase their money invested in the company, because this ease of buying and selling shares is one of the main advantages of a company joining a stock market. UK Listing Rule 5.5.3R explains what are *not* considered to be in 'public hands', including shares owned by the company's directors, by anyone connected with a director and by anyone interested in shares which represent 5% or more of that class of share.

If sufficient shares are not in public hands even after the IPO, then the FCA has the power to cancel the company's listing. An example of this was the cancellation of Simon Group plc's listing on 22 August 2007 because only 5% of its shares were in public hands (when at the time 25% needed to be in public hands under the old listing rules).

4.3.1.3 'Sovereign controlled commercial company' (SCCC)

A SCCC is a sub-category of the equity shares (commercial company) category. These are companies with a shareholder that is a Head of State, government or government department or agency controlling 30% or more of the company's voting rights. This category was originally introduced as part of an attempt to persuade Saudi Aramco, the Saudi Arabian state oil producer, to join the London Stock Exchange. Saudi Aramco was planning to undertake an international IPO and was deciding between a number of different stock exchanges, including London's Main Market. The company was, at the time of writing, worth almost $2 trillion and its presence would therefore result in significant fees for London-based advisers, including lawyers. The move was very controversial as it resulted in a significant reduction in the very stringent rules then applicable. It remains to be seen whether this sub-category will succeed in its aim because Saudi Aramco decided to float only on the Riyadh Stock Exchange and no other SCCCs have ever joined this category of the Stock Exchange.

A SCCC must comply with all of the requirements in Chapter 3 as set out at **4.3.1.2** above (UKLR 3.1.1R). However, it need not comply fully with Chapter 5. The rules set out where an exemption applies. For example, UKLR 5.3.6R makes clear that there is no need to comply with the rules on controlling shareholders set out in UKLR 5.3.

4.3.1.4 Application procedure

Chapter 20 of the UK Listing Rules sets out a detailed application procedure, to which the company must adhere in order to have its shares admitted to listing. In particular, the company and its advisers must publish an important marketing document which gives potential investors information about the company so that they can make an informed decision about whether to invest by buying its shares. The marketing document required for a share issue is called a prospectus. This prospectus must comply with the requirements of the UK Prospectus Regulation and be submitted to the FCA in accordance with the UK Prospectus Regulation and the UK Listing Rules. Before the prospectus can be published, the FCA must approve it. **Chapter 6** below examines the prospectus further.

4.3.1.5 Regulatory requirements for admission to trading

As noted at **4.3.1.2**, UKLR 3.2.3R provides that shares cannot be admitted to listing without also being admitted to trading on the Main Market of the Stock Exchange. There is a parallel provision in the Guidance to ADS 2.1 of the Stock Exchange's Admission and Disclosure Standards, which provides that shares cannot be admitted to trading unless they are listed or proposed to be listed. As the two processes are tied together in this way, there is no need for the Stock Exchange to duplicate the onerous regulatory requirements for listing. Instead, the Stock Exchange can 'piggy-back' onto the requirements for listing, and can proceed safe in the knowledge that any company seeking to have its shares admitted to *trading* will have to fulfil the regulatory requirements for *listing* set out in the UK Listing Rules, and comply with the UK Prospectus Regulation, before its application for admission to trading can succeed.

For this reason there are few formal regulatory requirements for admission to trading. One example is that all shares admitted to trading must be compatible with electronic settlement (see **2.5.3.1** above). Instead, the Stock Exchange's Admission and Disclosure Standards set out a very straightforward set of conditions (Section 2 of the ADS), which state that the company must be in compliance with the Stock Exchange's requirements and that the Stock Exchange has discretion to refuse admission in certain circumstances (including the inability to comply with any bespoke condition the Stock Exchange imposes for admission). In effect, therefore, these conditions simply give the Stock Exchange the flexibility to supplement the requirements for listing should it wish. The Admission and Disclosure Standards also set out a basic procedure for admission of the company's shares to trading which is detailed at **5.3.7** and **5.4.3** below.

4.3.2 Commercial requirements

The regulatory requirements detailed in **4.3.1** above obviously exist to ensure that the company is in good shape for the IPO. However, just because a company meets these criteria does not necessarily mean that investors will think the company is an attractive investment. As part of its preparation, the company needs to take an objective view of its business and consider whether, commercially, it is good enough to meet the expectations of potential investors. The sponsor and broker will be able to guide the company through the relevant considerations, but matters to consider include:

(a) Does the company have a good track record?

(b) Where is the company headed? Does it have a viable business plan?

(c) Does the company have an effective board and management team?

(d) Is there anything about the company which could put off investors? Is the company open to any criticism over corporate governance issues (see **Chapter 8**)? Is there an influential substantial shareholder? Have there been any accounting issues? Will the company be able to withstand the intense scrutiny of the IPO process?

(e) Are the market conditions right for an IPO?

(f) Is this the right time in the company's development for an IPO, or would it be better to wait a couple of years?

(g) Is the Main Market the right market for the company, or would AIM be more suitable (see **Chapter 24**)?

There were just three IPOs of UK companies on the Main Market in 2023 and the first half of 2024, with (exceptionally) none of them raising new money for the company. Existing shareholders in one of the companies took advantage of the IPO to sell their shares for a total of £320 million. There is no doubt that the London IPO market has very much been in the doldrums for the past few years. The reasons for the dramatic decline in IPOs in London is complex but has in part been caused by the continuing uncertainties of the post-Brexit trading environment for the UK, the disastrous IPO of Deliveroo in 2021 (described to the *Financial Times* by one of the company's bankers as 'the worst IPO in history'), the catastrophic 'mini budget' of Liz Truss's short-lived government in 2022, the decreasing desire of the massively well-endowed UK pension funds to take risks investing in London due to better returns obtainable elsewhere, and tech companies complaining that London's institutional investors do not sufficiently understand what their companies do, therefore undervaluing their companies.

4.4 CHOOSING HOW TO FLOAT

The company must choose the most suitable way to float on the Stock Exchange. There are a number of different ways in which a company seeking to float can list its shares, namely by:

(a) a public offer;

(b) a placing;

(c) an intermediaries offer; or

(d) an introduction.

The method, or methods, chosen will depend on a number of factors, including how much money the company is prepared to spend on the float (some methods are generally cheaper than others), how well-known the company seeking to float is (some methods are less suitable for relatively unknown companies), how much money the company wishes to raise both on flotation and afterwards (some methods favour a certain type of investor who may have deeper and more open pockets than others), what type of investor the company wishes to have initially (some methods will result in mainly institutional shareholders, others will involve the general public), how wide the company wishes its shareholder base to be after the float (some methods will result in a wider spread of shareholders than others, which may affect how easy it is to trade in the shares).

Some of the methods above are referred to in the Glossary to the UKLR (containing definitions used in the FCA Handbook) but they do not set out a definitive list of how companies can float. As a consequence, you will find that IPOs are frequently described in terms different from those above. These alternative terms are discussed at **4.4.2** below. It should also be noted that there are further ways to list shares once the company has been through the IPO process and is listed on the Stock Exchange (see **17.6**).

4.4.1 Methods of flotation

4.4.1.1 Public offer

A public offer involves an invitation being made to members of the public to buy shares in the company seeking to float. It is usually structured in one of three different ways: as an offer for subscription; as an offer for sale; or as a combination of the two.

An offer for subscription (defined in the Glossary to the UK Listing Rules) is an invitation to the public to subscribe for (ie buy) shares not yet in issue. In other words, on flotation the company will issue new shares and raise new money for the company. This is one of the key advantages to obtaining a listing (see **1.7.2**).

An offer for sale (defined in the Glossary to the UK Listing Rules) is an invitation to the public to subscribe for (ie buy) shares already in issue. In other words, shareholders currently owning a part of the company before the IPO are using the opportunity afforded by the IPO to sell their shares. No new money is raised for the company in this case – all the money goes to the selling shareholders. This allows shareholders (such as venture capitalists or founder shareholders) to realise their investment in the company and is another common reason for a company seeking an IPO.

As mentioned above, it is perfectly – in fact it is very common – both for existing shareholders to want to offload some of their shares and for the company to issue new shares at the same time as part of the IPO. This would mean that the public offer would entail both an offer for subscription and an offer for sale.

Although an essential element of a public offer is that it involves private investors (also known as 'retail investors') buying shares in the company, it does not preclude institutional investors (such as pension funds, insurance companies and investment banks) from participating in the IPO and buying shares in the company at the same time. In fact, in light of the huge resources available to them, the involvement of institutional investors will be essential. The key distinguishing feature of a public offer then is that it involves private investors, but not exclusively so.

The advantages of a public offer are:

(a) This is usually the most appropriate method to raise large amounts of capital.

(b) Private investors can purchase shares, rather than just institutional investors. This means that the shareholder base will be broader (there will be more investors, holding fewer shares), which in turn facilitates the trading of the shares on the market (that is, the shares are more 'liquid').

The disadvantages are:

(a) This is the most expensive method of flotation, partly because it involves underwriting (see **4.2.7** above).

(b) Due to the involvement of the public, the regulatory burden is more onerous.

An example of a public offer is Deliveroo Holdings plc's (the food delivery company) £7.6 billion IPO in April 2021.

4.4.1.2 Placing

A placing (defined in the Glossary to the Listing Rules) involves the marketing of shares either already in issue or not yet in issue to specified persons, or clients of the sponsor or other securities house assisting the placing. Typically this involves the sponsor offering the shares in the company seeking to float to institutional investors. Those shares may be new (raising more money for the company), or existing ones being sold by the current shareholders (raising money for the selling shareholders). The definition of a placing in the UK Listing Rules goes on to state that it does not involve an offer to the public. Great care must be taken here. All this definition seeks to do is to distinguish a placing from a public offer in **4.4.1.1** above for the purposes of the UK Listing Rules. It will not, therefore, involve a general offer to private investors at large (ie to 'retail investors'). It has no impact on the separate definition of offer to the public under s 85(1) of the FSMA 2000 regarding the need to prepare a prospectus (see **6.4.1.3**).

The advantages of a placing are:

(a) This is usually cheaper than a public offer.

(b) The company has greater discretion to choose its shareholders.

(c) The company can raise large amounts of capital.

The key disadvantage is that the shareholder base will be narrower (there will be fewer shareholders, holding more shares), which can impede trading in the company's shares (the shares have less 'liquidity').

An example of a placing is the tech and greeting card company Moonpig plc's £1.2 billion IPO in February 2021.

4.4.1.3 Intermediaries offer

An intermediaries offer (defined in the Glossary to the UK Listing Rules) is similar to a placing (see **4.4.1.2** above). However, the shares can be marketed only to firms who comply with the definition of an intermediary in the FCA Handbook, which broadly means they are offered to stockbrokers independent of the sponsor and any securities house assisting with the IPO. On receipt of the shares, the stockbroker then acts as intermediary and sells them to clients in exchange for a commission.

The advantage of an intermediaries offer is that this method can achieve a wider spread of professional investors than a placing alone.

The disadvantage of an intermediaries offer is that it involves considerable administration and tends to be suitable only in larger IPOs. For this reason, intermediaries offers are quite rare. The cross-border payments and foreign exchange company, CAB Payments Holdings plc's £850 million IPO in July 2023 involved an intermediaries offer.

4.4.1.4 Introduction

An introduction is not defined in the UK Listing Rules. It involves a company with shares already held by the public or institutional investors being admitted to listing on the Stock Exchange without offering any further shares. As we have seen, most companies seek to use an IPO to raise money which can be put towards acquisitions of other companies or businesses, paying off debt or investment in the current business. The question therefore arises as to why a company would wish to float on the Stock Exchange and not raise more money. When is an introduction useful? It is used mainly in three situations:

(a) By overseas companies which already have a wide spread of shareholders. For example, a company may already be listed on the Amsterdam Stock Exchange and now wishes to list in London to bring it closer to one of the biggest sources of equity investment in the world.

(b) Companies quoted on AIM may wish to transfer to the Main Market and take advantage of the higher profile and greater liquidity in shares that this offers. For example, ASOS plc, the clothing retailer, was introduced to the Main Market from AIM in February 2021.

(c) An existing listed company may decide to 'demerge' part or all of its business. GSK plc (Glaxo Smith Kline, the pharmaceutical behemoth) demerged (ie split) its business by floating its consumer healthcare business as a new company, Haleon Group plc, separately on the Stock Exchange in July 2022. GSK plc continues to run its pharmaceutical and biotechnology business.

Generally such a company will have to show a sufficiently wide spread of shareholders, with usually at least 10% being held in public hands as defined under the UK Listing Rules (see **4.3.1.2**). The theory is that, as the company's shares are already widely held and in public hands, the company has already demonstrated the marketability of its shares.

The advantages of an introduction are:

(a) this is usually the cheapest method of flotation;

(b) as it does not usually involve the issue or marketing of any shares, there is no need for underwriting (as underwriting covers the risk that shares offered are not taken up); and

(c) there is little need for advertising.

The disadvantages of an introduction are:

(a) it does not of itself afford an opportunity to raise capital (as no shares are being issued, the company receives no consideration); and

(b) it does not afford the company the same opportunities for publicity as a public offer or placing. This could affect the marketability of the shares after flotation (although as the shares are already widely held in public hands, and are therefore clearly marketable, often this is not an issue).

4.4.2 Other methods

As stated at **4.4** above, you will often see IPOs described in terms different from those set out in **4.4.1**, and these tend to focus on who the offer is aimed at. These include:

(a) an institutional offer;

(b) a retail offer;

(c) a global or international offer;

(d) an employee offer; or

(e) a 'friends and family' offer.

Frequently the word 'offering' is used in place of 'offer' here.

It is important to note that usually one or other of the terms above overlaps with the methods of floating a company described in **4.4.1**. This often causes unnecessary confusion. The key really is to remember that these are all simply different ways of explaining the same thing, namely how a company floats on the Stock Exchange. The fact that there is more than one way to describe an offer of shares involving the public (public offer, offer for subscription, offer for sale and retail offer (see **4.4.2.2**)) does not change the practical reality common to them all, that the shares of the company seeking to list on the Main Market will be offered to private investors at large rather than just to institutional investors. Some of the terms may be more specific: for example, public offer and retail offer are wide terms (focusing on the fact that shares are offered to private investors), whereas an offer for sale (being both a public offer and a retail offer) provides additional information in that it highlights that some of the shares being offered to the public will be coming from existing shareholders (and therefore the money raised will not be of benefit to the company). An offer for sale is also specifically addressed in the UK Listing Rules.

4.4.2.1 Institutional offer

An institutional offer describes an offering of shares on flotation to institutional investors such as investment banks, pension funds and insurance companies. Typically the offer is made by way of a placing, but this is not essential. The key element is the participation of institutional investors in the offer. The institutional offer can be made on a bookbuilt basis or a fixed price basis.

Bookbuilding

The sponsor sends potential investors an invitation to bid for shares before it sets the share price and the size of the offer. Usually the invitation to bid will set out a range of prices. The institutional investor will then bid, stating the number of shares it is willing to buy and at what price, or range of prices. The bids are not binding. The bank will keep a record ('book') of the bids it receives, which helps it to assess the appropriate share price and the likely level of demand for the shares. The thinking is that this process will ensure the highest possible value for the company's shares.

As the offer is not underwritten until all bids have been received, the underwriting risk is reduced to some extent, as the demand for the shares has already been tested among institutional investors, and the period of risk tends to be shorter. This means that usually the offer can be underwritten at a much lower commission rate than with a fixed price institutional offer, thereby saving the company money.

Fixed price

The sponsor and broker use their knowledge of the market to advise on a suitable fixed price per share, which should be attractive to potential investors but which is not too low. Typically the offer will be fully underwritten.

It is currently much more common for such offers to be made on a bookbuilt basis.

4.4.2.2 Retail offer

A retail offer is when the shares are offered to members of the public. This can increase demand for the shares and can raise the profile of the company, because the media will market the IPO to the public. A retail offer is made by way of offer for subscription and/or sale. It is suitable for larger IPOs.

As the public need more protection than institutional investors, a retail offer is more heavily regulated than an institutional offer. Usually a retail offer is made together with an institutional offer.

4.4.2.3 Employee offer

This is when the shares are offered to employees of the company (and often to employees of other group companies). The employees may be given preferential allocation rights for new shares being issued in the company. As referred to at **1.7.6** above, an employee offer allows the company to reward its employees. It also encourages employees to invest in the company, which then ensures they have a vested interest in the ongoing success of the company.

As with a retail offer, an employee offer can increase demand for the shares. The company will set eligibility criteria, such as length of service, to determine which employees can take up the offer. Usually an employee offer is made together with a retail offer, and will mirror its terms.

4.4.2.4 Friends and family offer

This is when the shares are offered to certain individuals. 'Friends and family' captures the essence of the nature of these individuals, but in practice other people, such as suppliers, customers and initial backers, can be offered shares as part of a friends and family offer.

4.4.2.5 Global or international offer

As the name suggests, this is when the offer of shares in the company seeking to float is made to investors not just in the UK but also abroad. Typically it will comprise an offer for subscription and an offer for sale, but the key element is the involvement of overseas investors. A global offer suits larger companies and those with a significant international presence or aspirations to expand internationally.

Depending on how this offer is structured it may require full compliance with local securities laws, which will make the offer even more costly and time-consuming than a pure UK offer. It is usual, though, to set up the offer to take advantage of exemptions under those local laws, for example by limiting the offer overseas to qualifying institutional investors and thereby reducing the foreign regulatory burden.

4.4.3 Combination of different methods

As explained at **4.4** above, it is possible to combine the different methods when a company floats on the Stock Exchange. You will see in the extract from the announcement by Royal Mail, set out below, how it describes its then forthcoming IPO in October 2013. Note how the IPO is described as an 'Offer', which consists of an 'Institutional Offer' (ie to institutional investors) both in the UK and overseas, and as a 'Retail Offer' (for private investors). There is also a reference to intermediaries becoming involved. Furthermore, the announcement states that the Offer will just consist of existing shares. Although not expressly stated, this of course means that the offer will take the form of an offer for sale to private and institutional investors. Because this was a privatisation of a company with already sufficient resources, there was no need to raise further cash for the company by way of an offer for subscription. Note that there was also an Employee Free Shares Offer and an Employee Priority Offer.

> **Royal Mail**
>
> **Announcement of Intention to Float**
>
> Her Majesty's Government ("HM Government") today announces its intention to proceed with an initial public offering (the "IPO" or the "Offer") of Royal Mail.
>
> ...
>
> HM Government intends to dispose of a majority of the existing Shares, taking into account shares sold and the 10 per cent. of Royal Mail to be made available for free to around 150,000 eligible UK-based Royal Mail employees at the time of listing under an employee free shares offer (the "Employee Free Shares Offer"), which is separate and in addition to the Employee Priority Offer referred to below.
>
> ...
>
> Offer to comprise an offer to institutional investors in qualifying jurisdictions (in the UK and elsewhere outside the United States under Regulation S and to QIBs in the United States in reliance on Rule 144A) (the "Institutional Offer") and an offer to members of the public located in the UK (the "Retail Offer"), which includes a priority offer to eligible Royal Mail employees located in the UK (the "Employee Priority Offer").
>
> Members of the public located in the UK will be able to apply for Royal Mail shares in the Retail Offer:
>
> - through participating Intermediaries, who will apply for Royal Mail shares on behalf of their clients; or
> - through a direct online or postal application to HM Government.
>
> In addition, eligible Royal Mail employees located in the UK will be able to apply to HM Government online or through postal application with priority under the Employee Priority Offer (which is part of the Retail Offer).
>
> Minimum application size in the Retail Offer will be £750 for members of the public and £500 for Royal Mail employees eligible under the Employee Priority Offer.

4.5 RESTRUCTURING THE COMPANY

It is usual to restructure a company before its IPO. It is important that the company seeking to float is in good order when it joins the Stock Exchange, and so in the year or so prior to the IPO the company must consider whether it needs to implement any changes. The following are some of the common areas of concern.

4.5.1 Group structure

In all likelihood the company seeking to float will form part of a wider group of companies. Before the company floats, the lawyers must make sure that this group has a rational structure. The most common structure is for the company seeking the IPO to be the holding company of the group. The other companies will then be subsidiaries, organised in a logical manner. A supermarket chain, for example, might group the companies in its supermarket business together, its banking related companies together and its companies for its mobile phone operations together, as in **Figure 4.1** below.

Figure 4.1: Group structure

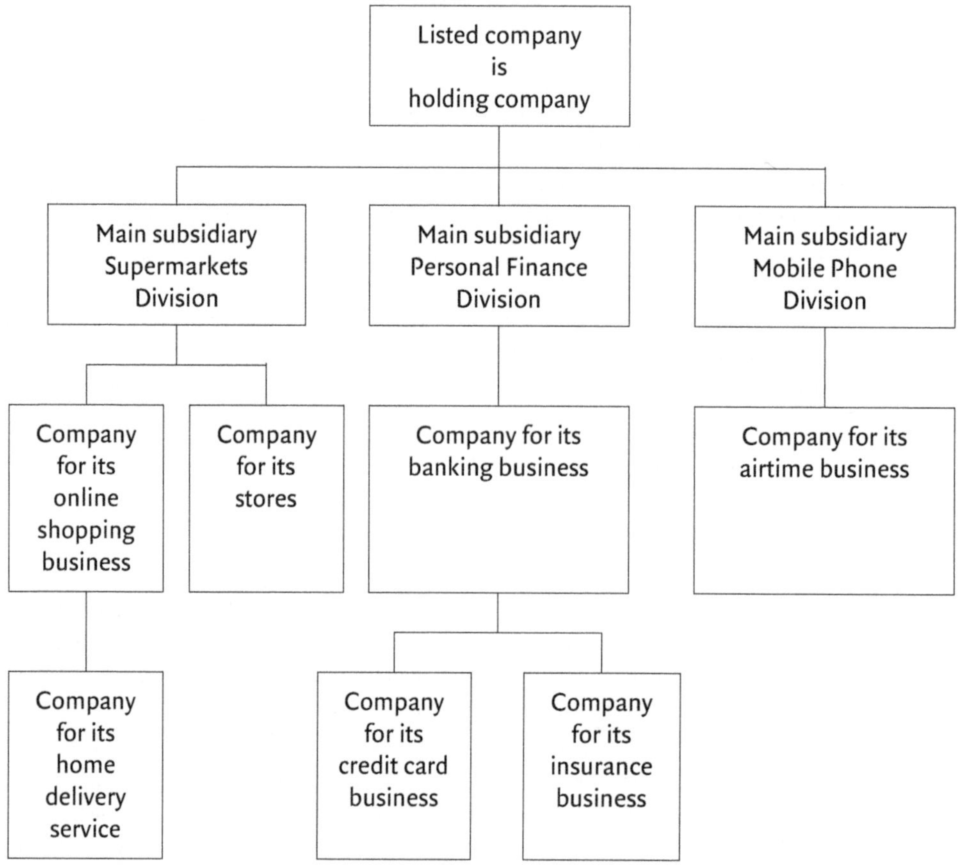

While this seems straightforward, in fact many businesses have grown in an unwieldy fashion through acquisitions and organic growth, with little thought paid to group structure. The company seeking the IPO might be a subsidiary company. Subsidiaries may exist which are now dormant (for example, because all the assets were transferred out of a subsidiary by a previous business sale) and may need to be dissolved. It may be that the company is planning to acquire or dispose of a business or company. If this is the case, the transaction should be completed as soon as possible so that the company structure is stable in the run up to completion. The lawyers need to examine the group structure well in advance of the IPO and effect any necessary changes, possibly by way of share and/or asset sales or purchases, company incorporation and/or dissolution, so that the company forms part of a logical group of companies.

4.5.2 Capital structure

It is of course very important that the offer price of the shares is fixed at the correct level. The share capital of the company may need to be altered to take account of this. For example, imagine that the advisers have stated that the offer price should be between £1.75 and £2.25 per share. However, the company has a current issued share capital of 2,000,000 shares of £1 each (nominal value) and is currently worth £20,000,000. This means that each share has a current value of £10. How could the shares be offered at the advised offer price without the company suffering a huge loss?

There are various solutions which the lawyers can effect. The simplest here would be to subdivide each share of £1 into 5 shares of 20p. This would mean that the company is still worth £20,000,000, but now has an issued share capital of 10,000,000 shares of 20p each, so each share has a current value of £2.00, which is within the acceptable price range.

4.5.3 Company constitution

If the company has not been incorporated as a public company, the lawyers will need to re-register the company as detailed at **1.9.3**. The company's constitution will comprise the articles of association and the memorandum of association. In advance of the IPO, the lawyers need to check these documents to make sure there is nothing in them which is inconsistent with *listed* company status. Usually the company will adopt a completely new set of articles which comply with the requirements for a listed company. Two requirements with which the company's existing articles may not comply are:

(a) there should be no restrictions on the transfer of shares (see **4.3.1.2**, 'Requirements for listing' above); and

(b) provisions need to be included to address certain matters required by UKLR 5.4 (see **4.3.1.2**, 'Constitutional arrangements' above).

4.5.4 The board of directors

As explained in **Chapter 8**, the board of directors of a listed company needs to comply with various principles of corporate governance (best practice). The lawyers need to consider whether any changes should be made to the board well in advance of the IPO, so that the company can make the required appointments and/or dismissals. In addition, it may be that the boards of subsidiary companies could be rationalised further (taking the example in **Figure 4.1** above, it may be logical for Y, a key manager in the Supermarkets Division, to sit on the board of each of the companies in the Supermarkets Division), or perhaps the records of board appointments at Companies House need to be updated.

4.5.5 Legal issues

As **Chapter 6** explores further, the IPO process involves considerable disclosure about the company. Any negative news may discourage potential investors. The lawyers will examine the company's history to identify any breaches of the law and, to the extent possible, remedy them (for example, ensure that all filings at Companies House are up to date). However, when the structure of the IPO is being planned, the lawyer also needs to be alert to any issues which may give rise to legal problems. Two potential problems lawyers need to bear in mind at this stage are:

(a) Might the IPO arrangements give rise to any financial assistance issues (see **Chapter 16**)?

(b) Section 580 of the CA 2006 provides that no share should be issued at a discount to its *nominal* value (see **13.3.1**).

4.6 WHAT NEXT?

This chapter has outlined the preliminary steps a company can take in advance of the IPO process. While it can take a year (or longer) for the company to prepare for an IPO, the actual IPO process itself is much shorter (usually between three to six months). **Chapter 5** considers the IPO process.

4.7 FUTURE DEVELOPMENTS

Financial Services and Markets Act 2023

This Act intends, amongst other things, to revoke EU financial services law that had been retained following Brexit and replace it with UK-sourced rules. The then UK Government's vision was for an open, green, and technologically advanced financial services sector that is globally competitive, with this Act being at its core. The Act will result in fundamental amendments to the FSMA 2000. It will also grant the FCA much wider powers to enable it to draw up legally binding rules which will be included in the FCA's Handbook (eg the UK Listing Rules, new Prospectus Rules and Disclosure Guidance and Transparency Rules) rather than, as is currently the case, in legislation. Laws which will be repealed include the UK version of the Prospectus Directive, the UK version of MAR, the UK version of MiFIR and the related delegated legislation.

In addition, the Act will amend the FSMA 2000 to introduce a principle that all decision making must take account of the UK Government's legal duty under s 1 of the Climate Change Act 2008 to achieve a 'net zero' emissions economy by 2050.

The FCA has already taken the first major step by introducing the new UK Listing Rules which replaced the former Listing Rules on 29 July 2024.

The FCA is consulting on replacing the current prospectus regime with new Prospectus Rules. You will be able to follow this process via the FCA's website. The current regime is discussed in greater detail at the end of **Chapter 6** below.

CHAPTER 5

INITIAL PUBLIC OFFERINGS: THE PROCESS

5.1 INTRODUCTION

This chapter must be read in conjunction with **Chapter 4**, which explains what an IPO is and the preliminary steps a company seeking to float must take, and **Chapter 6**, which examines the content of the vital marketing document, the prospectus. This chapter considers the IPO process itself, that is, the period of between 12 and 24 weeks before flotation when the company applies to the FCA for admission to listing and to the Stock Exchange for admission to trading. The preparation referred to in **Chapter 4**, which takes place in the year or two before the IPO, is generally referred to as 'pre-IPO preparation' rather than as part of the IPO process itself.

5.2 THE IPO PROCESS

A simplified version of the IPO process (other than by way of a bookbuilt offer – see **4.4.2.1**) is set out in **Table 5.1** below. Please note that this sets out the procedure for an ESCC category listing. The procedure for a standard listing is very similar but there is no sponsor involved. The timing of the process is divided into two stages, the private phase and the public phase. The public phase begins on the day when the IPO is announced to the market, and the private phase is the period before this. The day of the announcement of the IPO is not the day the company actually floats. The company floats when the FCA makes an Official List announcement (see **5.4.3.1** below) and the Stock Exchange publishes a London Stock Exchange Notice (see **5.4.3.2** below). Dealing in the company's shares can then begin. This day is known as 'admission day' and occurs a few weeks after the announcement of the IPO.

5.3 THE LAWYERS' PERSPECTIVE

Table 5.1 provides an overview of the IPO process. It includes not just the dual applications for listing and trading but also the advisers' roles. As mentioned previously, it is important that the lawyers appreciate not only who the company's other advisers are, but also what they do and when. Of course, there are some areas where the lawyers will have little or no involvement, and other areas where the lawyers' role will be vital. So where does the lawyers' work lie?

5.3.1 Agreeing the timetable and the list of documents

At the beginning of the IPO process the sponsors will draw up a draft timetable for the IPO. Several factors drive the timetable. The FCA and the Stock Exchange have their own rules about timing, which cannot be changed as they are based on law. The company may have particular requirements as to timing, which may be inflexible (such as a desire to dovetail the IPO with a particular point in the company's financial year) or subject to change (for example, if the company's IPO is dependent on the occurrence of a certain event which has no fixed deadline). There are also practicalities to be taken into account, such as the prevailing sentiment in the stock market and the fact that it is virtually impossible to reduce the IPO procedure to anything less than three months (even on the premise that the advisers require very little sleep). The lawyers will be asked to comment on the draft timetable and agree it. The sponsor will have the task of ensuring that the agreed timetable does not slip. The lawyers need to ensure that:

(a) there are no omissions in the timetable; and

(b) the timetable is viable.

The lawyers will also be involved early in the IPO process in commenting on the list of documents drawn up by the sponsor. The list sets out all the documents required, the parties and who has primary responsibility for producing them. Like the timetable, this will be used as a reference point by all advisers, and so needs to be detailed and accurate.

Table 5.1: The IPO process

24–52 weeks (6–12 months) before announcement of IPO	**Pre-IPO preparation.** Company chooses advisers, considers its suitability for an IPO and the most appropriate method of listing its shares, and effects any necessary restructuring (see **Chapter 4**). Company takes decision to proceed with IPO.
12–24 weeks (3–6 months) before announcement of IPO	**The IPO process begins.** Company appoints advisers and meets sponsor. Sponsor drafts and advisers agree a timetable. Sponsor informs FCA about intended IPO. First marketing meetings with sponsor and broker. Initial planning meetings with advisers take place. Legal and financial due diligence begins (see **5.3.4**).
4–12 weeks (1–3 months) before announcement of IPO	**The process gathers momentum.** Key managers of the company work full-time on the IPO. Accountants produce long-form and draft short-form report (see **4.2.5**). Lawyers produce draft registration document and draft full prospectus and begin the verification process (see **5.3.5** and **6.8**). Initial drafting meetings with advisers. Sponsor submits draft documentation relating to the approval of the registration document and the full prospectus to the FCA (see **5.3.6.1** and **5.3.6.2**). Pay FCA fee for approval of the prospectus (see **5.3.6.2**). Sponsor and company have first meeting with the Stock Exchange. Initial pricing meetings with sponsor, broker, and any underwriters and sub-underwriters. Valuation of any key assets. Meetings with Financial PR consultants (sponsors, brokers and lawyers present).

2–4 weeks (one month) before announcement of the IPO	**The process becomes intense.** Detailed drafting meetings, incorporating FCA's comments. Lawyers complete verification on the registration document. Accountants and sponsors review cash-flow statements and any profit forecasts. Convene completion GM of company. Further PR meetings. Ensure any ancillary documentation (re-registering the company, new memorandum and articles) is prepared. First meeting with registrars. Deadline for submitting draft registration document and draft full prospectus to the FCA is 20 days before approval of registration document and full prospectus respectively (see **5.3.6.1**). Submit draft application for listing to FCA and draft application for trading to LSE.
1–2 weeks before announcement of IPO	Completion GM held. Registration document signed off at board meeting. Registration document approved by FCA and published.
Announcement of IPO	**Announcement and blackout period** Seven-day delay after publication of registration document when no further information on IPO is made public. IPO announced via publication of ITF (intention to float). Directors' marketing roadshows commence.
The day before approval of full prospectus	**All documentation must be signed off:** (a) Verification meeting. (b) Completion board meeting (sometimes known as a pricing meeting). (c) Underwriting agreement signed and held in escrow. (d) Any other agreements (placing, offer for sale) signed and held in escrow. Submit final version of prospectus (and any ancillary documentation referred to in the prospectus) to the FCA. Pricing meeting to agree offer price.
Approval of full prospectus	**FCA approves prospectus.** Offer price is made public. Put prospectus on website and print copies. FCA files prospectus with National Storage Mechanism. Advertise prospectus. Release underwriting agreement from escrow.

1–2 weeks after approval of full prospectus	**Attend to formalities.** Continue to publish prospectus and advertise the IPO. Directors' roadshows continue. Submit '48 hour' documents to the FCA (see **5.3.6.3**) and 'Two day' documents to the Stock Exchange (see **5.3.7.2**) to apply for admission to listing and to trading. Pay FCA admission fee (see **5.3.6.3**). **Day of admissions hearings.** Submit 'on the day' documents to the FCA (see **5.3.6.4**). The FCA hears application for admission to listing. The Stock Exchange hears application for admission to trading. Open application lists and receive applications from investors (see **5.4.2.2**). Close application lists (see **5.4.2.2**).
2–3 weeks after approval of full prospectus	**Admission week.** Announce basis of allotment of shares. Despatch letters of acceptance/regret to investors. **Admission day.** The FCA makes an Official List announcement that shares have been admitted to listing (see **5.4.3.1**) and the Stock Exchange publishes a London Stock Exchange Notice that shares have been admitted to trading (see **5.4.3.2**). Dealing in shares commences. Stock Exchange invoice raised (see **5.3.7.3**).
3–5 weeks after approval of full prospectus	**Formalities.** Receive letters of acceptance. Issue share certificates/credit CREST accounts. Lodge information with the FCA (see **5.3.6.5**) and the Stock Exchange (see **5.3.7.4**). Pay Stock Exchange fee (see **5.3.7.3**).

5.3.2 Drafting documentation

The majority of the lawyers' time will be divided between drafting, meetings (see **5.3.3**) and due diligence (see **5.3.4**). The most important document the lawyers will draft is the prospectus. This is a lengthy, detailed document and **Chapter 6** considers it in more detail.

There will also be ancillary documentation for the lawyers to draft. This will include the ITF announcement. 'ITF' stands for intention to float and is the public announcement that the company intends to launch an IPO. There will also be documents to effect any restructuring (see **4.5** above). These will certainly include board minutes which record the board's progress through the IPO process, and the board's approval of the process and related documentation.

There will also be documentation relating to the method of listing the shares. If it is a public offer by way of an offer for subscription and/or sale (see **4.4.1**), an agreement (between the company, its directors, any selling shareholders and the sponsor) will be required. For a placing (see **4.4.1.2**), a placing agreement is needed (the parties are the same as for an offer for subscription and/or sale agreement).

The lawyers will also produce a sizeable document called a verification note (see **5.3.5** below).

5.3.3 Attending meetings

5.3.3.1 Drafting meetings

So many advisers, as well as the company, need to feed information into the prospectus that it becomes impossible for the adviser with responsibility for the document (the sponsor or the lawyers) to collate and incorporate comments on the draft by e-mail or telephone. Once the draft prospectus is reasonably progressed, there will be numerous drafting meetings, where all the parties can contribute and discuss their comments on the draft. If more than one party has comments on a certain point, those parties can agree revised wording. The meetings are productive, but can be very time-consuming.

5.3.3.2 Completion GM

The completion GM will usually take place a few days before publication of the registration document (which is one part of the prospectus). The IPO itself does not require shareholder approval, but some matters which are vital to the preparation of the company for the IPO often do require such approval. The completion GM is the forum to obtain this consent. Usually, the lawyers will draft the notice to convene this meeting and ensure that it is sent out within the required time limits in the CA 2006 (at least 21 clear days' notice for all resolutions of a public company unless approval is obtained by the shareholders at an AGM to shorten the notice period to 14 clear days – see **8.6.1**). The company's articles of association may extend this notice period. The lawyers will then draft the necessary resolutions and usually will attend the GM to deal with any issues which may arise on the day. There is little scope for error.

The resolutions which may be necessary depend on the particular requirements of the company, but they may include:

(a) if the IPO involves an offer of shares by way of subscription (ie, it involves the company issuing new shares):
  (i) granting authority to allot under s 551 of the CA 2006,
  (ii) disapplying pre-emption rights under s 561 of the CA 2006 on allotment (see **Chapter 14**);

(b) reorganising the share capital (see **4.5.2** above); and/or

(c) adopting new articles of association (see **4.5.3** above).

5.3.3.3 Verification meeting

The key verification meeting takes place just before the completion board meeting. The board sign the verification note at this meeting (see **5.3.5** and **6.8** below).

5.3.3.4 Board meetings

A board meeting will take place the day before the approval of the registration document. The directors will approve all the IPO documentation and the steps required to float the company. In particular, the board will resolve to:

(a) approve the terms of the registration document and intention to float (ITF) announcement;

(b) approve the terms of any ancillary documentation; and

(c) proceed with the IPO.

After this board meeting, the registration document is submitted to the FCA for final approval.

There will be a further board meeting, a completion board meeting, later on to:

(a) approve the terms of the full prospectus for approval by the FCA; and

(b) proceed definitively with the IPO and in particular approve the application for admission to listing and the application for admission to trading.

After this board meeting, the full prospectus is submitted to the FCA for final approval.

5.3.4 Due diligence

Due diligence, often referred to as 'DD' or 'due dil', or sometimes called 'legal review', is a time-consuming exercise that begins early on in the IPO process. The aim of due diligence is to investigate the company thoroughly and collate comprehensive information about it, which can then be used in the prospectus, the financial reports and other IPO documentation. The process also helps the advisers to identify the value of the company (and therefore fix the offer price) and any steps which are necessary to prepare the company for the IPO, such as those outlined at **4.5** above.

Due diligence falls into three main categories:

(a) business due diligence;
(b) financial due diligence; and
(c) legal due diligence.

5.3.4.1 Business due diligence

This is an investigation into the commercial aspects of the company, such as its performance, competitors and strategy. The lawyers do not lead this due diligence, but they do need some of the results of it for the legal due diligence exercise (see **5.3.4.3**).

5.3.4.2 Financial due diligence

This is the investigation carried out by the reporting accountants so that they can produce the long form report, the short form report and the working capital report to which **4.2.5** above refers.

5.3.4.3 Legal due diligence

The lawyers have responsibility for the legal due diligence exercise. Trainees are heavily involved in this process. Basic information about the company will be obtained from public registries, such as Companies House, Land Registry and the Land Charges department, the Patent Office, the Trade Mark Registry and the Designs Registry, and the lawyers will also request copies of the company's statutory books. However, the scope of the legal due diligence exercise is very broad, and the lawyers really need access to the company's management to obtain the level of information required.

As should be clear from the timetable in **Table 5.1** above, the company's management are not time-rich during this stage of the IPO process, and so the lawyers need to make the most of the time that management makes available to them. The usual procedure is for the lawyers to draw up a document called a due diligence questionnaire, which has a heading for each area to be investigated and then lists questions requesting information and documentation relating to each area. The usual areas for investigation are:

(a) corporate – structure and constitution of the company;
(b) business and trading – including requests for all material agreements;
(c) assets;
(d) property;
(e) environmental matters;
(f) insurance;
(g) basic financial information – for example, requests for report and accounts, details of charges and insolvency events (the accountants will request more detailed information as part of the financial due diligence process referred to at **5.3.4.2**);
(h) intellectual property and information technology;
(i) employees;

(j) pensions;
(k) disputes; and
(l) any market-specific regulatory issues.

Each question will be given a number, as will each document requested, so that when the deluge of responses arrive, the lawyers can identify the question to which each response relates. It also means that the responses can be filed in an orderly and logical manner. The company can respond to the due diligence questionnaire in a variety of ways. Some responses can be e-mailed, some need to be discussed face to face. Typically a company will be advised to set up a data room, where all the information provided in response to the questionnaire is kept. A secure virtual data room will usually be set up so that the necessary documents can be accessed and reviewed more easily.

The lawyers must review all the responses very carefully. This involves disseminating the information to specialist teams of lawyers within the firm (for example, all the information will be received by the corporate lawyer who sent out the questionnaire, but when they receive a response relating to pensions, that response will be copied to the pensions department for their comment, and similarly information about employees will be copied to the employment department and so on). The corporate lawyer who co-ordinates the due diligence process must have excellent project management skills.

Once all the information has been reviewed by the appropriate specialists, the corporate lawyer must compile the product of the review into a due diligence report. The level of detail in the report can vary. Some reports focus solely on any problematic issues revealed by the due diligence process, others report in detail on all areas which were reviewed, even if they were problem-free. Either way, the most important part of the due diligence report from the company's point of view is what is known as the 'executive summary'. This is a chapter at the beginning of the report which states succinctly, and in layman's terms, the key issues revealed by due diligence and advises of any steps which are required before or after the IPO in relation to such issues. It is the executive summary which the directors will actually read and act upon. The detail in the rest of the report is still important, however, both for the lawyers (to record that the process was carried out thoroughly and diligently) and for the directors (to record the efforts they have made to ensure that the information in the prospectus complies with the requirements of the UK Prospectus Regulation, the UK PR Regulation and the PRRs and the FSMA 2000 (see **Chapter 6**)). Increasingly, specialist software is being used by law firms to make due diligence a more accurate and efficient process.

5.3.5 Verification

While due diligence is undertaken early in the IPO process, to provide the information which goes into the prospectus, verification does not begin until the first draft of the prospectus is reasonably progressed. Verification is actually part of the due diligence process, but it has evolved into a discrete exercise. Again, trainees are heavily involved in verification. So what is it? Essentially it is a process which produces a written record (called a 'verification note') so that the company can support what it has said in the prospectus. The purpose of verification is to protect those who have responsibility for the prospectus (particularly the directors) from legal liability arising out of its publication (see **6.6** and **6.8** below).

Verification can involve a painstaking line-by-line examination of the prospectus. In the verification note, each statement in the prospectus is phrased as a question, to test that it is true, accurate and not misleading. For example, if there is a line in the prospectus which states, 'We, Cheap as Chips plc, are the largest chain of supermarkets in the world', the verification note would contain a question along the lines of, 'Please confirm that Cheap as Chips plc is the largest chain of supermarkets in the world'. The answer to this question would then be recorded and copies of any supporting documentation would be annexed to the verification note. It may be, of course, that the answer to the question has already been provided as a response to the due diligence questionnaire. If so, management will not appreciate the lawyers asking the same question again. By the time the lawyers carry out verification, therefore, they must be familiar with the responses to the due diligence questionnaire. If the verification process raises questions not dealt with in the due diligence process (which is often not as detailed as the verification process) then the lawyer will send this new list of questions to the company, so management can collate the necessary information before meeting with the lawyers to provide the responses.

Alternatively, the verification process may be limited to ensuring the key selling messages in the prospectus are adequately supported and may ignore the more obvious statements.

The directors and anyone else who has formal responsibility for the prospectus (see **6.5**) cannot be available to all advisers at all times, so in practice they delegate responsibility for answering verification questions to key management (however, they cannot delegate ultimate legal responsibility for the content of the prospectus).

The lawyers must be vigilant in ensuring that the responses the company provides to the due diligence or verification questionnaire really do answer the questions posed. For example, in the example above, a full answer would detail the basis of this pivotal statement: What is the measure of 'largest' – is the company referring to turnover, profits, number of outlets, number of employees? What constitutes a 'chain' – just two shops, or more? How is 'supermarket' defined – is it just a shop that sells predominantly food, or does it include those that sell clothes, books, personal financial products and petrol? What is meant by 'world'? Think of the Baseball World Series involving teams from just the USA and Canada! And so on. The verifier must bear in mind all the elements of the statement and ensure that she covers them adequately when drafting her response.

If the lawyers are not satisfied that the company can support the statement sufficiently, they will feed this information into the drafting meetings and the statement in the prospectus will be amended until the lawyers are satisfied that the statement can be supported. For example, the reference in the statement above to the 'largest' might be amended to 'one of the largest'.

As you might imagine, although this process is ultimately for the benefit of those responsible for the prospectus, including the directors, it is often a source of great frustration to those who have to provide the information, and each lawyer involved in the process (often a junior lawyer or a trainee) must have well-developed social skills, a good sense of humour and a thick skin to survive the process. Each director, and any other person bearing responsibility for the prospectus (see **6.5**), will sign the verification note in the verification meeting (just before the completion board meeting), and it, together with the due diligence report, will provide reassurance to the directors as they accept responsibility for the prospectus in the completion board meeting itself.

As with due diligence, legal tech skills will also be required as, increasingly, specialist software is used to oversee the process of verification in order to both increase accuracy and achieve greater efficiency.

5.3.6 Submission of documentation to the FCA

The sponsor will have the responsibility of ensuring that the documents listed below are submitted to the FCA, and that the documents listed at **5.3.7** below are submitted to the Stock Exchange, in a timely manner. However, each adviser, including the lawyers, needs to be aware of the deadlines.

The documents referred to at **5.3.6.1** (prospectus) and **5.3.6.2** (documents to be submitted with the prospectus) are required by the UK Prospectus Regulation, the UK PR Regulation and the PRRs as part of the prospectus approval process. The documents referred to at **5.3.6.3** to **5.3.6.5** ('48 hour' documents, 'on the day' documents and information to be lodged after admission day) are required by Chapter 20 of the UK Listing Rules as part of the listing application procedure.

5.3.6.1 Prospectus

The FCA must approve the prospectus, pursuant to the procedure set out in the UK Prospectus Regulation, UK PR Regulation and PRRs, before it can be published. In practice, one part of the prospectus, the registration document, will usually be approved first, followed by a full prospectus within a month later. The reasons for doing this are set out at **5.4.1** below. The draft registration document and the draft full prospectus can be submitted separately or together. The company must submit the draft registration document and/or prospectus to the FCA at least 20 working (ie business) days before the date of approval of the document (Art 20(3) of the UK Prospectus Regulation (PRR 3.1.2UK)). The draft must be submitted in searchable electronic format via electronic means via the FCA website (Art 42(1) of the UK PR Regulation).

The FCA will provide its comments on the draft and return the draft to the company's advisers. In practice, 20 working days would not allow much time to deal with any comments the FCA might make. The earlier the draft is submitted the better, and the sponsor will aim to submit the draft some two to three months before the date of approval of the registration document and full prospectus. On receipt of the FCA's comments, the document will be redrafted and resubmitted to the FCA. Subsequent drafts of the prospectus must be marked up ('blacklined') to highlight all changes made to the preceding draft of the prospectus previously submitted to the FCA and be submitted together with a clean copy of the amended draft, a comment sheet containing responses to the FCA's comments and updated lists (see **5.3.6.2** below) (Art 43 of the UK PR Regulation). This process will continue until the FCA confirms it has no further comments. At this point, the registration document or full prospectus can be submitted in final form to the FCA for approval and then printed. The final form prospectus must be submitted before midday on the day approval is to be given (PRR 3.1.6R(3)).

The FCA can approve the prospectus only when it is satisfied that it meets certain criteria set out in Articles 36–38 of the UK PR Regulation (PRR 3.1.1UK) and s 87A of the FSMA 2000, namely that the UK is the home state for the company issuing shares, and the prospectus meets the standards of completeness, comprehensibility and consistency necessary for approval. Once the prospectus has been approved, the FCA uploads the registration document or full prospectus to the NSM (see **5.3.6** above) (PRR 3.2.3UK).

Further information can be obtained from FCA Procedural Primary Market/PN/904.4 Public offer prospectus – drafting and approval (available on the FCA website).

5.3.6.2 Documents to be submitted with the prospectus

As part of the process set out in the UK Prospectus Regulation for approving the prospectus, the draft registration document and draft prospectus, referred to at **5.3.6.1** above, must also be accompanied by the following:

(a) completed Form A (available from the FCA website) which includes the application for approval of the prospectus in final form (PRR 3.1.6R(1)(a)(i));

(b) a completed Publication Form (PRR 3.1.6R(1)(a)(ii)) (available on the FCA website) which provides details of how the prospectus is to be made available to the public;

(c) the relevant fee payable to the FCA (set out in the Fees Manual in the High Level Standards section of the FCA Handbook);

(d) if the order of the items in the prospectus does not follow the order of the Annexes in the UK PR Regulation (see **3.5.1.1** and **6.5.2**), a cross-referenced list setting out where each item can found in the prospectus and a cross-referenced list identifying any items from Annexes to the UK PR Regulation which are not applicable and so have not been included (Art 24(5) of the UK PR Regulation). These lists must be submitted in a searchable electronic format. Lists and instructions for completing them are available from the FCA website. The relevant lists for our IPO are entitled Annex 1, Annex 11 and Annex 20. If there are any items which are not applicable, then these should be identified on these lists;

(e) a copy of any document incorporated into the prospectus by reference in searchable electronic format (Art 19(3) of the UK Prospectus Regulation) (see **6.5.2.2**);

(f) information required by Article 18 of the UK Prospectus Regulation (if requesting permission to omit information from the prospectus – see **6.5.2.3**) (Art 42(2) of the UK PR Regulation);

(g) contact details of a contact point to which the FCA can submit all notifications in writing and by electronic means (Art 42(1) of the UK PR Regulation). This is the Issuer Contact Details Form (available on the FCA website);

(h) eligibility letter prepared by the sponsor to confirm that the company meets the eligibility criteria to join the ESCC category of the Main Market set out in UKLR Chapters 3 and 5 (see **4.3.1.2** above);

(i) eligibility checklist for admission to the Official List under the UK Listing Rules (available on the FCA website);

(j) Sponsor's Declaration on Application for Listing (available on the FCA website); and

(k) any other information the FCA considers, on reasonable grounds, to be necessary.

In addition, UKLR 20.2.2R provides that a fee becomes payable on the date the company makes its application for listing (set out in the Fees Manual in the High Level Standards section of the FCA Handbook).

The submission of the final form of the prospectus (see **5.3.6.1** above) must be accompanied by final form versions of these forms and checklists.

5.3.6.3 '48 hour' documents

No later than midday, at least two business days before the FCA hears the company's application for the admission to listing, the company must submit to the FCA, in final form, the documents set out at UKLR 20.4.2R. These include:

(a) the Application for Admission of Securities to the Official List;

(b) the FCA-approved prospectus;

(c) any circular published in connection with the application;

(d) any FCA-approved supplementary prospectus;

(e) written confirmation of the number of shares to be allotted pursuant to a board resolution allotting the shares (or, if this is not possible, the written confirmation must be provided to the FCA at least one hour before the admission to listing is to become effective); and

(f) written confirmation of the contact details of two executive directors and a person at the company designated to receive documents and deal with enquiries from the FCA.

5.3.6.4 'On the day' documents

By 9 am on the day the FCA hears the company's application for admission to listing (see **5.4.3**), the company must lodge with the FCA, signed by the sponsor, a completed Shareholder Statement and (for certain structures of IPO only) a Pricing Statement (UKLR 20.4.4R). The forms are available from the FCA website.

5.3.6.5 Information to be lodged after admission day

The company must provide to the FCA written confirmation of the number of shares that were allotted if the actual number was lower than that originally announced, as soon as practicable following the hearing of the application for admission to listing (UKLR 20.4.7R).

5.3.6.6 Information to be kept after admission day

The company must keep copies of a number of documents used in the IPO for six years after the date of the IPO and make these available to the FCA at its request. A full list is set out in UKLR 20.4.8R which includes all letters, valuations, contracts, reports and other documents referred to in the prospectus, and the annual report and accounts for the period covered in the prospectus (usually the three prior years).

5.3.7 Submission of documents to the Stock Exchange

5.3.7.1 Provisional application for admission to trading

All companies seeking to float must complete an application form (Form 1, available on the Stock Exchange's website) and submit it, together with a draft copy of the prospectus, to the Stock Exchange no later than 12.00 pm at least 10 business days before the requested date for the hearing of the company's application for admission to trading (ADS 3.2 and para 1.1 of Sch 1). This is treated as a provisional application. A formal application can only be made once the prospectus has been approved by the FCA (see **5.3.7.2**).

5.3.7.2 'Two day' documents

By 12 pm on the day which is at least two business days before the Stock Exchange hears the company's application for admission to trading, the company must submit to the Stock Exchange a copy of the documents listed at ADS Sch 1, Part B, namely:

(a) an application for admission to trading on the finalised Form 1;

(b) an electronic copy of the prospectus;

(c) an electronic copy of any circular, announcement or other document relating to the issue of shares;

(d) an electronic copy of any notice of meeting referred to in any of the documents mentioned above; and

(e) by 4 pm on the day before the expected day of admission, written confirmation of the number of shares to be allotted pursuant to the board resolution (or, if this is not possible, it must be provided to the Stock Exchange by 7 am on the expected day of admission).

This deadline will correspond with that for the submission of the '48 hour' documents to the FCA (see **5.3.6.3**).

5.3.7.3 Fee payable on the day of the application hearing

The Stock Exchange will raise an invoice on admission, which the company must pay within 30 days (ADS 3.7).

5.3.7.4 Information to be lodged after admission day

The company must lodge a statement of the number of shares which were issued (and, where different, the total number of issued shares of that class) as soon as this information is available (ADS 3.10). This corresponds with the requirement of the FCA referred to at **5.3.6.5** above.

5.4 KEY DATES

There are two distinct phases in an IPO – the private phase and the public phase. We will now consider each in turn.

5.4.1 Private phase of the IPO

This is the period prior to the public announcement of the IPO.

Initial marketing activities

Before the finalised FCA-approved prospectus is made available to investors, there is a pre-marketing phase known variously as 'pre-marketing', 'pilot fishing', 'pre-sounding' or 'early investor engagement'. These terms describe the initial exploration by the company and its financial advisers of whether there is sufficient demand for the company's shares to proceed with an IPO.

During this period, the management of the prospective IPO company and the sponsor make themselves available to research analysts working at the sponsor bank and at other banks who will participate in the underwriting of the offer of shares by the company (there is usually a presentation) and give the analysts access to information on the company. The aim of this is to educate the analysts about the company, its management, the proposed IPO and its future plans. The analysts will prepare research reports which will be circulated to prospective investors in the company (principally institutional investors). They contain an abundance of valuable information and assessments by the analysts for the prospective institutional investors aiding a preliminary decision on whether to invest.

These analysts are known as 'connected analysts' because they work for the sponsor and underwriting banks who play a critical role in the success of the IPO. Clearly there is a potential conflict of interest here as the analysts' employers (the sponsor and underwriters) will wish the IPO to be a glittering success. As such the FCA's Conduct of Business Rules (known as the 'COBS Rules' – part of the Business Standards section of the FCA's Handbook, available on the FCA's website) grant so-called 'unconnected analysts' equal access to the management of the company and the sponsor (again usually via a presentation) as well as information on the company. Unconnected analysts work for banks and institutions which are not participating in the IPO and similarly can produce research reports on the IPO if they wish.

Before either the connected or unconnected analysts' reports can be published, the COBS Rules require that an approved disclosure document must first be published. This can be either a full prospectus or just one part of it, the registration document (see **6.5.2.1** below). As this is still an early stage in the IPO process (and therefore before all available necessary information and documentation is ready for a full prospectus), in practice the company will first issue just an FCA-approved registration document (see **5.3.6.1** above). This rule ensures that potential investors should receive FCA-approved information on the IPO before that contained in research reports.

Once the registration document has been published, the COBS Rules impose a minimum time delay before the research reports can be published. The time period depends on whether the company chooses to make the initial presentation to the connected and unconnected analysts, mentioned above, together or separately. If made together then the COBS Rules require a one-day delay, whereas if they were made separately then the delay is a minimum of seven days. In practice the presentations are likely to be made separately because that will help keep the IPO confidential while preparations are under way. In other words, once the registration document has been published, there will usually be at least a seven-day delay before the research reports of the analysts can be published. The presentation to the unconnected analysts will be made at the end of this seven-day period.

5.4.2 Public phase of the IPO

The public announcement of the IPO, which is called the Intention to Float (ITF) announcement, will be on the same day as the publication of the first analysts' reports. We have now entered the public phase of the IPO.

An extract from the ITF for Aston Martin Lagonda Global Holdings plc's £4 billion IPO in October 2018 is set out below. Note that it refers to a 'premium segment listing' under the former listing rules regime. At the time of writing we are still awaiting the first IPO of an ESCC company under the new listing rules.

> **10 September 2018**
>
> **Aston Martin Lagonda Global Holdings plc**
>
> **Intention to Float on the London Stock Exchange and Appointment of New Board Members**
>
> Following its announcement on 29 August 2018 regarding the publication of a registration document, Aston Martin Lagonda, the iconic producer of hand-crafted luxury sports cars, is today confirming its intention to proceed with an initial public offering (the "**IPO**" or the "**Offer**") and details of the Offer. The Company has now become parent of the Group and it is therefore intended that it will apply for admission of its ordinary shares ("**Shares**") to the premium listing segment of the Official List of the FCA (the "**Official List**") and to trading on London Stock Exchange plc's (the "**LSE**") main market for listed securities (together, "**Admission**") ...

As you can see, this is an announcement of an *intention* to float on the Main Market. Investors can already access the registration document, and now the research reports can be circulated to the potential institutional investors as well. We have therefore entered a phase of 'investor education' where institutional investors are contacted with a view to stimulating their interest in participating in the IPO.

5.4.2.1 Approval of prospectus

As explained at **5.3.6.1** above, even though one part of the prospectus, the registration document, will already have been approved by the FCA by this stage, the company, rather than just submitting the remaining two parts for approval as the law allows, will instead submit a full prospectus for approval, updating any information that may have changed in the original registration document.

By the day of approval of the prospectus, all paperwork will have been finalised and the offer price will have been set (at the previous day's completion or pricing board meeting). The prospectus will have been submitted to the FCA at least 20 working days (probably more) before impact day (see **5.3.6.1**). Article 20(3) of the UK Prospectus Regulation (PRR 3.1.2UK) provides that the FCA must notify the company whether it has decided to approve the prospectus before the end of the period of 20 working days beginning with the date of submission of the draft prospectus, although if further drafts have to be submitted, as would be usual, the deadline is 10 working days from the last draft. When the FCA indicates that it has no further comments on the prospectus, it will formally approve the prospectus. It will then notify the company of the formal approval by close of business on the day the decision is taken.

Other ancillary agreements, such as the offer for sale agreement, placing agreement and underwriting agreement, will be dated.

The IPO is live with effect from the day of approval of the prospectus. Investors can now apply to invest in the company. However, the company has not yet floated. Flotation is still conditional upon the FCA admitting the shares to listing and the Stock Exchange admitting the shares to trading, and this will not be done until admission day (see **5.4.3**). The shares in the company are not yet being traded.

5.4.2.2 Publishing the prospectus

Having been approved by the FCA, the prospectus can be published. The company must publish the prospectus at least six working days before the end of the offer period (Art 21(1) of the UK Prospectus Regulation (PRR 3.2.1UK)).

There are three different ways to publish the prospectus, set out in Article 21(2) of the UK Prospectus Regulation (PRR 3.2.2UK), by making it available in electronic form on:

(a) the company's website;

(b) the website of the financial intermediaries placing or selling the shares; or

(c) the Stock Exchange's website.

The company should be aware that, nevertheless, any investor is entitled to demand a free hard copy under Article 21(11) of the UK Prospectus Regulation (PRR 3.2.3UK). Article 21(4) of the UK Prospectus Regulation (PRR 3.2.2UK) states that it is not acceptable to make accessing the document subject to conditions such as completing a registration process or charging for access.

The FCA will upload the prospectus to the NSM (PRR 3.2.6G).

5.4.2.3 Applications for shares

Investors who have been impressed by the prospectus and wish to invest in the company will complete the application form attached to the prospectus and send it to the receiving bank (see **4.2.8**). The application form states the deadline by which the form must reach the receiving bank. This is usually 10.00 am on the day following the FCA's admission hearing. This deadline is known as the time the 'lists open'.

If the offer is popular and over-subscribed, the lists will close at 10.01 am. The board, advised by the sponsor, will then decide on the basis of allotment. If the offer is over-subscribed, clearly not all applicants will receive all the shares they applied for. The basis of allotment is a formula which decides the proportion of shares each applicant will receive. It varies according to the circumstances of the IPO, but it could be, for example, that each applicant receives, say, two-thirds of the number of shares applied for. On the other hand, it could be that the two-thirds ratio is applied only to those investors applying for significant numbers of shares, and those investors applying for small numbers of shares simply enter into a ballot system where they may be allotted their full quota, or none at all. Once the board has decided the basis of allotment, the company will make a formal announcement of the decision to investors.

The £3.3 billion Royal Mail plc IPO in October 2013 comprised a retail offer and an institutional offer. In the retail offer, applicants for up to £10,000 worth of shares all received £750 worth of shares (the minimum allocation) and applicants for over £10,000 received nothing. The retail offer was over-subscribed 7 times. Such was the demand for shares under the institutional offer that it was over-subscribed 20 times.

If the offer is under-subscribed, the lists will remain open longer. The company will then inform the underwriters how many shares they need to take up.

The receiving bank will cash the applicants' cheques and account to the company, and any shareholders who sold existing shares, for the proceeds. The company will then send share certificates, or letters of acceptance (see **5.4.3.4** below), to the successful investors, and (in the event that the IPO is over-subscribed) will send letters of regret to the investors who applied but have not been successful in buying any or all of the shares for which they applied.

5.4.2.4 Admission hearings

The FCA will hear the application for admission to listing on the same day that the Stock Exchange hears the application for admission to trading. The UK Listing Rules provide that the FCA can refuse admission to listing in certain circumstances, such as if it considers the UK Listing Rules not to have been complied with (UKLR 3.1.2G) or if it considers that admission would be detrimental to investors' interests (UKLR 3.1.3G and FSMA 2000, s 75(5)). The Admission and Disclosure Standards (ADS 2.5) also reserve the right for the Stock Exchange to refuse admission to trading if admission might be detrimental to the orderly operation or integrity of the market. However, by the time the hearings take place, all the hard work on the IPO has been completed. The company and its advisers will have been in regular contact with the FCA and the Stock Exchange throughout the IPO process. It is very rare, therefore, for the FCA or the Stock Exchange to refuse admission at this stage.

5.4.3 Admission day

5.4.3.1 The Official List announcement

When the FCA is satisfied that it is prepared to admit the shares to listing, it must announce the admission through a Regulatory Information Service (UKLR 20.2.7G). In practice, the Official List issues an announcement, referred to as an Official List announcement or notice, to the Regulatory News Service (RNS) each day at 8am. This announcement refers to all companies which will list securities that day (both new applicants and companies which are already listed but which are listing further securities). The list does not distinguish the new applicants from the applicants which are already listed but which are listing further shares. Once the announcement is made (often referred to as 'going down the wire') the listing is effective, and dealing in the company's shares can begin. The company has floated.

An excerpt from the Official List announcement dated 8 October 2018 (the date Aston Martin Lagonda Global Holdings plc, a new applicant, floated) follows. Note that it refers to a 'premium' listing under the former listing rules regime. At the time of writing we are still awaiting the first IPO of an ESCC company under the new listing rules.

NOTICE OF ADMISSION TO THE OFFICIAL LIST

08/10/2018 08:00

The Financial Conduct Authority ("FCA") hereby admits the following securities to the Official List with effect from the time and date of this notice:–

Amount	Security Description	Listing Category	ISIN
Issuer Name: Aston Martin Lagonda Global Holdings PLC			
228002890	nominal value to be confirmed on 3-Oct-2018	Premium Equity Commercial Companies	GB00BFXZC448 •

You can see that someone has forgotten to update the security description before publishing this notice. Oops! You will see the correct entry in the notice at **5.4.3.2** below.

5.4.3.2 The London Stock Exchange Notice

Similarly, when the Stock Exchange is satisfied that it wishes to admit the shares to trading, it must announce the admission via a Regulatory Information Service (ADS 2.17). In practice, this will go down the wire at the same time as the Official List announcement.

An excerpt from the London Stock Exchange Notice dated 8 October 2018 is set out below:

NOTICE OF ADMISSION TO TRADING ON THE LONDON STOCK EXCHANGE – XLON

08/10/2018 – 08:00

The following securities are admitted to trading on the LSE with effect from the time and date of this notice

ALBION DEVELOPMENT VCT PLC		
123,285	ORDINARY SHARES OF 1P EACH, FULLY PAID	(0483247)(GB0004832472)
ASTON MARTIN LAGONDA GLOBAL HOLDINGS PLC		
228,002,890	ORDINARY SHARES OF GBP0.00903968713304439 EACH, FULLY PAID	(BFXZC44)(GB00BFXZC448)

5.4.3.3 Dealings in shares

The company and its advisers will watch the market with bated breath on the first day of dealings. Ideally, the market price will rise a little above the offer price, meaning that the shares are trading at a small premium. This can suggest that the company pitched the offer price correctly. If the market price rises significantly, this may suggest that the offer price was something of a giveaway. The shares in Royal Mail plc, which was privatised by the UK Government in October 2013, rose by over 40% on the company's first day's trading on the Main Market. Inevitably this led to commentators complaining that the family silver had been sold on the cheap. Such was the outcry, representatives from investment banks involved in the IPO (such as Goldman Sachs and UBS) were called to give evidence before the House of Commons DBT Select Committee to explain the decisions they took.

If the market price drops below the offer price, the shares are trading at a discount, which may evidence a lack of demand for the shares. Deliveroo Holdings plc, the food delivery company's shares dropped 26% on their first day's trading on the Stock Exchange in March 2021, reflecting initial concerns from investors that the shares in this tech company had been overpriced and doubts over the accuracy of information provided to institutional investors in the marketing of the IPO. The company's share price finally rose above its IPO offer price five months later, but by January 2022 it had plummeted again to below 50% of the IPO price.

5.4.3.4 Letters of acceptance

Sometimes the offer is structured so that initially successful applicants do not receive a share certificate, but a renounceable letter of acceptance. This is a bearer document, and the recipient can transfer title in the shares to someone else simply by handing them the letter (rather than by stock transfer form which is the usual method of transferring shares). Shares can be traded by way of renounceable letter for six weeks from admission day. The company's registrars will enter into the company's register of members whoever holds the letter at the end of that six-week period, and will send them a share certificate.

Letters of acceptance can be a useful method by which shares can be transferred easily at time when there tends to be substantial trading in shares. This also saves the registrars from issuing several new certificates in respect of the same shares.

5.4.4 After admission day

Admission day should not be seen as the end of a process but as the beginning of one. The company is now a listed company. The directors, key managers and the advisers will take the opportunity to celebrate the IPO together, and will then attempt to catch up on the many hours of sleep lost in the previous weeks. Then the company has to get back to business. The directors and management will return to their day-to-day business of running the company. However, life cannot simply return to how it was pre-IPO. There is now a whole new set of rules and regulations for the company to comply with. **Parts II, III** and **IV** of this book consider what life is like for a public company. Before we leave behind the IPO process, however, **Chapter 6** takes a detailed look at the main marketing document for any IPO: the prospectus.

5.5 FUTURE DEVELOPMENTS

Financial Services and Markets Act 2023

This Act intends, amongst other things, to revoke EU financial services law that had been retained following Brexit and replace it with UK-sourced rules. The then UK Government's vision was for an open, green, and technologically advanced financial services sector that is globally competitive, with this Act being at its core. The Act will result in fundamental amendments to the FSMA 2000. It will also grant the FCA much wider powers to enable it to draw up legally binding rules which will be included in the FCA's Handbook (eg the UK Listing Rules, new Prospectus Rules and Disclosure Guidance and Transparency Rules) rather than, as is currently the case, in legislation. Laws which will be repealed include the UK version of the Prospectus Directive, the UK version of MAR, the UK version of MiFIR and the related delegated legislation.

In addition, the Act will amend the FSMA 2000 to introduce:

(i) a secondary objective for the FCA to act in a way that facilitates the long-term growth and international competitiveness of the UK economy, including the financial services sector; and

(ii) a principle that all decision making must take account of the UK Government's legal duty under s 1 of the Climate Change Act 2008 to achieve a 'net zero' emissions economy by 2050.

The FCA has already taken the first major step by introducing the new UK Listing Rules which replaced the former Listing Rules on 29 July 2024.

The FCA is consulting on replacing the current prospectus regime with new Prospectus Rules. These are discussed in greater detail at the end of **Chapter 6** below.

Further consultations to take soundings on the future shape of the regulation of the financial services industry in the UK and the detailed rules which should apply to listed companies, including the rules and principles mentioned in this chapter, are expected. You will be able to follow this process via the FCA's website.

Please note that these changes when implemented are likely to have a significant impact on the content of this chapter.

CHAPTER 6

Initial Public Offerings: The Prospectus

6.1 INTRODUCTION

The lawyer must refer to the UK Prospectus Regulation, the Prospectus Regulation Rules (PRR) and Pt VI of the FSMA 2000 (Official Listing) in order to advise whether a prospectus is required and, if so, to the UK Prospectus Regulation, the UK version of Commission Delegated Regulation (EU) 2019/980 (the UK PR Regulation) and (EU) 2019/979 (the UK Prospectus RTS Regulation) as to what information the document must contain. Assistance is available on interpreting parts of the legislation from the FCA (through its technical and procedural notes, available on its website) and from the ESMA (see **3.1** above) (eg the ESMA Prospectus Regulation FAQs regarding prospectuses which are available on its website: <http://esma.europa.eu>).

6.2 PURPOSE

The prospectus is the main marketing document for the IPO process. Potential investors will read the document and, it is hoped, the information it contains will encourage them to invest in the company. However, the company cannot be selective about what information to include in the document. The UK Prospectus Regulation and the UK PR Regulation prescribe its contents. The lawyers must make sure that the document complies with all of the legal requirements as to content, but that it also retains the style of a marketing document which will attract investors. The prospectus is vital to the success of the IPO and, as is evident from **Chapter 5**, the drafting of this document takes up a large proportion of the IPO process.

6.3 PROSPECTUS OR LISTING PARTICULARS?

The main marketing document for an IPO on the Main Market is called a prospectus. You will see references in the UK Listing Rules (eg UKLR Chapter 23) to another listing document called listing particulars. There is no room for confusion here. Listing particulars are required only for the issue of certain specialist securities, such as debt securities (eg bonds) or depositary receipts (certificates which represent ownership of shares – these are one method by which it is possible to trade in overseas companies). As the focus of this book is on the listing of shares, it makes no further reference to listing particulars and considers only the most important document, the prospectus.

6.4 THE REQUIREMENT FOR A PROSPECTUS

There are two overlapping regimes governing the requirement for a prospectus in the UK. The first originates from the EU-wide regime introduced by the UK Prospectus Regulation. The second is under s 85 of the FSMA 2000. When it was introduced, the original EU Prospectus Regulation did not require implementation in the UK; however, the UK Government chose not to repeal the pre-existing law – s 85 of the FSMA 2000 – but instead to amend it to bring it very closely into line with the new EU law. Post-Brexit the UK Government is maintaining the overlapping system of the UK Prospectus Regulation and s 85 of the FSMA 2000 until fundamental reforms are brought into force via the POAT Regulations (see **3.5.1.4** above), possibly in the first half of 2025 (see **6.12** below).

It is also worth noting that much of the UK Prospectus Regulation is repeated in the Prospectus Regulation Rules (PRR), which form part of the 'Listing, Prospectus and Disclosure' sourcebook in the FCA Handbook. The PRR references are included in this book for completeness where necessary after the UK Prospectus Regulation reference.

Article 3 of the UK Prospectus Regulation (PRR 1.2.1UK) provides that a prospectus, approved by the FCA, is required if the company wishes to do either or both of the following events:

(a) *offer* securities to the *public in the UK* (Art 3(1) of the UK Prospectus Regulation); or

(b) *admit* securities to *trading* on a regulated market situated or operating *in the UK* (even if there is no offer to the public) (Art 3(3) of the UK Prospectus Regulation).

Section 85 of the FSMA 2000 requires a prospectus in similar circumstances, save that:

(a) s 85(1) requires an offer of '*transferable* securities' to the public *in the UK*; and

(b) s 85(2) requires a *request* for admission of '*transferable* securities' to trading on a regulated market *in the UK*.

This book focuses on IPOs which involve the issue and/or sale of ordinary shares which will be listed on the Official List and admitted to trading on the Main Market. This type of IPO involves both (a) and (b) above; both Article 3(1) and Article 3(3) apply, and, subject to any exemptions, a prospectus will be required (one prospectus will suffice). Note that even if the circumstances of an IPO meant that it involved only (a) or (b) above, then, subject to any exemptions, a prospectus would still be required.

The UK Prospectus Regulation includes exemptions to Article 3(1) and Article 3(3). The FSMA 2000 includes exemptions to s 85(1) and s 85(2). If these exemptions apply, a prospectus is not required, so the lawyer must be ready to advise how the float might be structured to avoid the need for this time-consuming and costly document.

It is important to recognise that the exemptions are drafted to apply specifically either to Article 3(1) (offer to the public) or to Article 3(3) (admission to trading) (s 85(1) or s 85(2) of the FSMA 2000). To take the example of our IPO, which involves both an offer to the public and admission to trading, even if it benefits from one of the 'offer to the public' exemptions, it will still require a prospectus unless one of the 'admission to trading' exemptions also applies.

Paragraphs **6.4.1** and **6.4.2** below examine the criteria of Article 3(1) and Article 3(3) (s 85(1) and s 85(2)), and consider the different exemptions which apply to them.

6.4.1 Article 3(1): offer of securities to the public in the UK

Article 3(1) of the UK Prospectus Regulation refers to all public offers of shares, both shares listed on the Official List and shares not listed on the Official List (such as shares listed on AIM).

Article 2 provides guidance on the meaning of the key terms used in Article 3(1).

6.4.1.1 Offer to the public

Article 2(d) of the UK Prospectus Regulation defines 'offer of securities to the public'. There will be an offer if there is a 'communication to persons in any form and by any means, presenting sufficient information on the terms of the offer and the securities to be offered, so as to enable an investor to decide to purchase or subscribe for those securities'. A flotation by way of an offer for subscription and/or sale, placing or intermediaries offer will fulfil this criterion.

Note that the UKLR Glossary defines a placing as *not* constituting a public offer. However, this is unconnected to the definition of a public offer under the UK Prospectus Regulation and so Article 3 and s 85 must still be considered for a placing.

If a communication constitutes an offer to the public, the omission of full terms and conditions or the inclusion of statements that further information may be obtained elsewhere will not affect its status as a public offer (*ADCADA Immobilien AG PCC in Konkurs v the Financial Market Authority (Finanzmarktaufsicht)* (Case E-10/20)).

6.4.1.2 Securities

Article 2(a) of the UK Prospectus Regulation defines 'securities' as 'transferable securities' by reference to Article 2(1)(24) of the Markets in Financial Instruments Regulation (MiFIR). (Certain securities fall outside the scope of the UK Prospectus Regulation. These are set out in Article 1(2) (PRR 1.2.2UK) and are specialist securities, eg Government-issued securities.) For our purposes, it is enough to note that 'securities' includes shares. Therefore our example of an IPO involving the issue or sale of ordinary shares will fulfil this criterion.

6.4.1.3 In the UK

Article 3(1) of the UK Prospectus Regulation requires the offer to the public to take place 'in the UK'.

The list of recipients of any offer for subscription and/or sale, placing or intermediaries offer must be analysed to see if this criterion is fulfilled.

FSMA 2000, s 85(1): offering transferable securities to the public in the UK

Section 85(1) similarly refers to all public offers of shares, including shares not listed on the Official List (such as shares admitted to the AIM).

Section 103 of the FSMA 2000 states that 'offer of transferable securities to the public' has the meaning in s 102B of the FSMA 2000. This in turn provides guidance on the interpretation of some of the key terms used in s 85(1). This is very close to the Article 2(d) definition under the UK Prospectus Regulation.

Offer

There will be an offer if there is a communication to any person which presents sufficient information, on the shares to be offered and the terms on which they are offered, to enable an investor to decide to buy or subscribe for those shares (s 102B(1)). The communication may be made in any form and by any means (s 102B(3)).

A flotation by way of an offer for subscription and/or sale, placing or intermediaries offer will fulfil this criterion.

Transferable securities

Section 102A(3) defines 'transferable security' by reference to Article 2(1)(24) of the Markets in Financial Instruments Regulation (MiFIR). For our purposes it is enough to note that this term includes ordinary shares. Therefore our example of an IPO involving the issue or sale of ordinary shares will fulfil this criterion.

To the public

Section 102B(2) of the FSMA 2000 provides that if the offer is made to 'a person in the United Kingdom' it is made to the public in the UK.

It is likely that an offer for sale or subscription will fulfil this criterion, but that a placing and intermediaries offer will be structured to fall within one of the exemptions, such as the 'only qualified investors' or '150 persons' exemption, so that they do not fulfil this criterion.

In the UK

As referred to above, s 102B(2) of the FSMA 2000 makes clear that this criterion is satisfied if any recipient of the offer is in the UK.

The list of recipients of any offer for subscription and/or sale, placing or intermediaries offer must be analysed to see if this criterion is fulfilled.

6.4.1.4 Exemptions

The exemptions to Article 3(1) of the UK Prospectus Regulation [s 85(1) of the FSMA 2000] (requiring a prospectus for offers to the public) are set out in Article 1(4) (PRR 1.2.3UK) and Article 3(2) of the UK Prospectus Regulation and s 86(1)(e) of the FSMA 2000. The principal exemptions are as follows:

(a) *Offers to qualified investors only (Art 1(4)(a))*. A qualified investor is defined in Article 2(e) of the UK Prospectus Regulation and includes those persons or entities listed in Section I(1)–(4) of Annex II or treated as professional clients under Section II of Annex II to MiFID II. Institutional investors, such as investment banks, insurance companies, investment firms and pension funds, will fall within this definition, as will certain very wealthy individuals.

(b) *Offers to fewer than 150 natural or legal persons (who are not qualified investors) in the UK (Art 1(4)(b))*. HM Treasury has confirmed that there is no need to include the clients of discretionary brokers in calculating the number of persons to whom the offer is made.

(c) *Offers involving significant investment by each investor (Art 1(4)(c) and (d))*. This will apply where each investor invests a minimum total consideration of €100,000 (Art 1(4)(d)) or where the shares being offered are denominated in amounts of at least €100,000 (or equivalent) (Art 1(4)(c)).

(d) *Share swaps (Art 1(4)(e))*. The issue of shares must not involve any increase in the company's issued share capital.

(e) *Offers in conjunction with takeovers (by way of share-for-share exchange) or mergers (Art 1(4)(f) and (g))*. However, a document must be made available to the public which contains information describing the transaction and its impact on the company (referred to as an 'exempted document' – see **22.4.4.2** below).

(f) *Bonus issues and scrip dividends of a class of shares already listed (Art 1(4)(h))*. However, a document must be made available to the public which contains information about the number and type of shares offered, and the reasons for and the detail of the offer.

(g) *Offers by listed companies to employees and/or directors (Art 1(4)(i))*.

(h) *Small offers*. Section 86(1)(e) of the FSMA 2000 exempts offers where the total consideration for the *transferable securities* being offered cannot exceed €8 million.

The exemptions in Article 1(4) above may be combined together (Art 1(6) (PRR 1.2.5UK)). For example, if there was an offer of shares to a total of 160 people, 20 qualified investors and 140 individuals in the UK, this offer would be exempt from the need to prepare a prospectus under Article 1(4)(a) and (b) combined.

6.4.2 Article 3(3): admitting securities to trading on a regulated market in the UK

6.4.2.1 Securities

The definition of securities under Article 3(3) of the UK Prospectus Regulation is the same as for Article 3(1), as discussed at **6.4.1.2** above. Ordinary shares are securities, so our IPO will fulfil this criterion.

6.4.2.2 Admit to trading

The type of IPO which is the focus of this book involves the admission of shares to trading (on the Main Market) and so fulfils this criterion.

6.4.2.3 UK regulated market

This is defined in Article 2(j) of the UK Prospectus Regulation. This refers to Article 4(1)(21) of MiFID II. It will probably pay to be seated before attempting to read it.

> 'Regulated market' means a multilateral system operated and/or managed by a market operator, which brings together or facilitates the bringing together of multiple third-party buying and selling interests in financial instruments – in the system and in accordance with its non-discretionary rules – in a way that results in a contract, in respect of the financial instruments admitted to trading under its rules and/or systems, and which is authorised and functions regularly and in accordance with Title III of this Directive.

Under the Title III referred to, it is up to the FCA to oversee the regulation of such regulated markets, and Article 56 of MiFID II requires a list of regulated markets to be produced. Note that the ECJ has decided that it is not a precondition of being a regulated market that the market be included on the forerunner to the Article 56 list (*Nilas and Others* (Case C-248/11)).

A list of regulated markets can be found on the FCA's website. When you reach the list it merely refers to 'London Stock Exchange'. What is not apparent from this is that the Main Market of the Stock Exchange is a regulated market under MiFID II but AIM is not. Other regulated markets in the UK include Cboe Europe Equities Regulated Market and AQSE Main Market.

Our IPO, being on the Main Market, will therefore involve a regulated market. (Note, however, that an AIM float will require a prospectus only if Article 3(1) applies, ie that shares are being offered to the public as defined and no exemptions apply.)

FSMA 2000, s 85(2): admitting transferable securities to trading on a regulated market

Transferable securities

The definition of transferable securities is discussed at **6.4.1** above. Ordinary shares are transferable securities, so our IPO will fulfil this criterion.

Admit to trading

The type of IPO which is the focus of this book involves the admission of shares to trading (on the Main Market) and so fulfils this criterion.

Regulated market

This is defined in s 103(1) of the FSMA 2000. This refers to the definition contained in Article 4(1)(21) of MiFID II as set out at **6.4.2.3** above.

Our IPO, being on the Main Market, will therefore involve a regulated market.

6.4.2.4 Exemptions

The exemptions to Article 3(3) of the UK Prospectus Regulation [which apply equally to s 85(2) of the FSMA 2000] (requiring a prospectus for shares to be admitted to trading on a regulated market) are set out in Article 1(5) of the UK Prospectus Regulation (PRR 1.2.4UK). The principal exemptions are as follows:

(a) *Admission of shares representing less than 20% of shares of the same class already admitted to trading on the same regulated market (Art 1(5)(a)).* This is a 'de minimis' provision. In calculating the 20% limit, offers of shares for which a prospectus was required in the 12-month period are excluded. In other words the 20% limit only includes shares for which no prospectus is required.

ESMA's Questions and Answers on Prospectuses (available on the ESMA's website) confirm at Q15.1 (although not legally binding these currently still act as guidance post-Brexit) that the 20% limit is applied over a rolling 12-month period. This means that any shares admitted over the previous 12 months, which have not benefited from any other exemption, would count towards the 20%.

EXAMPLE

Imagine a company has 1,000 shares in issue on 28 April 2021. On 5 July 2021 it issued 100 shares to employees under the admission to trading exemption referred to at (f) below. On 5 January 2023 it issues a further 100 shares. The calculation to work out whether the 20% admission to trading exemption applies to this issue of 100 shares is as follows:

$$\frac{\text{Number of shares to be issued (including shares admitted over last 12 months which have not benefited from any other exemption)}}{\text{Number of shares of the same class already admitted to trading on the same market}}$$

that is,

$$\frac{100 \text{ (an issue within the last 12 months which has not benefited from another exemption)}}{1,100}$$

that is, 9.09%. This issue of 100 shares would therefore be covered by the 20% exemption.

One month later, the company issues a further 100 shares. The calculation is now:

$$\frac{100 \text{ (this was covered by the 20\% exemption, not any other exemption, so counts)} + 100}{1,200}$$

that is, 16.67%, so this issue is covered by the 20% exemption.

One month later, the company issues a further 100 shares. The calculation is:

$$\frac{100 + 100 + 100}{1,300}$$

that is, 23.07%, so this issue is outside the 20% exemption and will therefore require a prospectus.

(b) *Shares of a class already listed resulting from the exercise of exchange or conversion rights representing less than 20% of the same class already admitted to trading on the same market (Art 1(5)(b)).*

(c) *Share swaps (Art 1(5)(d)).* As **6.4.1.4(d)** above.

(d) *Offers in conjunction with takeovers (by way of share-for-share exchange) or mergers (Art 1(5)(e) and (f)).* As at **6.4.1.4(e)** an exempted document must be available.

(e) *Bonus issues and scrip dividends of a class of shares already listed (Art 1(5)(g)).* As **6.4.1.4(f)** above.

(f) *Offers to employees and/or directors of a class already listed (Art 1(5)(h)).*

(g) *Shares already admitted to trading on another regulated market (Art 1(5)(j))* subject to the fulfilment of certain conditions.

The exemptions under Article 1(5) may be combined together. However, the exemptions under Article 1(5)(a) and (b) (see **6.4.2.4(a)** and **(b)** above) cannot be used together if this results in the 20% threshold being exceeded (Art 1(6)).

6.4.3 Voluntary prospectus

A company can choose to voluntarily submit a prospectus for approval by the FCA in the UK where its offer to the public of its admission of shares to trading on a regulated market (ie the Main Market) would otherwise fall under one of the exemptions in **6.4.1** or **6.4.2** above (Art 4 of the UK Prospectus Regulation (PRR 1.2.6UK)).

It is not yet clear in what circumstances a company will choose to take advantage of this right.

6.4.4 Conclusion

Having analysed the criteria, we can conclude that:

(a) an IPO;

(b) involving the offer or sale of ordinary shares;

(c) which will be listed on the Official List and admitted to trading on the Main Market,

will require a prospectus, *unless* it benefits from *both*:

(d) an 'offer to the public' exemption; and

(e) an 'admission to trading' exemption.

In practice, as **Table 6.1** below shows, it is unlikely that an IPO can be structured to benefit from the required combination of exemptions.

Table 6.1

Method of flotation	**Public offer under Art 3(1) [s 85(1)]?**	**Admission to trading under Art 3(3) [s 85(2)]?**	**Prospectus required?**
Public offer	Yes. '150 persons' exemption possible but highly unlikely, given size of most retail offers.	Yes. '20%' exemption irrelevant in context of IPO, as no shares currently admitted to trading.	Yes (Art 3(1) [s 85(1)] *and* Art 3(2) [s 85(2)]).
Placing	Yes – however, likely to benefit from 'only qualified investors' or '150 persons' exemption.	Yes. '20%' exemption irrelevant in context of IPO, as no shares currently admitted to trading.	Yes (Art 3(3) [s 85(2)]).
Intermediaries offer	Yes. Likely to benefit from 'only qualified investors' or '150 persons' exemption.	Yes. '20%' exemption irrelevant in context of IPO, as no shares currently admitted to trading.	Yes (Art 3(3) [s 85(2)]).

Method of flotation	Public offer under Art 3(1) [s 85(1)]?	Admission to trading under Art 3(3) [s 85(2)]?	Prospectus required?
Introduction	No. No offer involved.	Yes. '20%' exemption irrelevant in context of IPO, as no shares currently admitted to trading.	Yes (Art 3(3) [s 85(2)]).

6.5 CONTENT

The UK Prospectus Regulation and the UK PR Regulation (PRR Appendix 2) prescribe the content of a prospectus.

Reading about the content requirements of a prospectus is essential, but there is no substitute for having a look at the real thing. It is recommended to check the websites of companies which have recently floated as companies post the prospectus and other documents, such as RNS announcements, on the area of their website aimed at shareholders (usually entitled 'investor relations') or via the NSM.

There are general and specific rules governing the content of a prospectus.

6.5.1 General content requirements

Article 6(1) and Article 6(2) (PRR 2.1.1UK) provide for the general content requirements of a prospectus. These provisions require that any prospectus must:

(a) contain the necessary information which is material to an investor for making an informed assessment of (i) the assets and liabilities, profits and losses, financial position and prospects of the company, (ii) the rights attaching to any securities (for our purposes, shares), and (iii) the reasons for the issue and its impact on the company (Art 6(1)). This information may vary depending on the particular nature of the company, the type of security being issued and the circumstances of the company (in other words there is not an identical format of prospectus for all companies) (Art 6(1)). The FCA must not approve a prospectus unless it is satisfied that such general content requirements have been met (Art 20 of the UK Prospectus Regulation and s 87A(1));

(b) be written and presented in an easily analysable, concise and comprehensible form (Art 6(2)).

6.5.2 Specific content requirements

As explained at **3.5.1.1**, the requirements regarding the content of a prospectus are set out in both the UK Prospectus Regulation and in the annexes of the UK PR Regulation. These requirements are duplicated in the UK Prospectus Regulation Rules (the key rules are set out at PRR 2.1.4UK and PRR 2.3).

The minimum content requirements which apply for a prospectus depend on the type of company issuing shares and the company's circumstances. Not all of the information will be required in every prospectus. It is the lawyer's job to select which minimum content requirements are relevant for the particular transaction.

How can the lawyer find the content requirements required specifically for an IPO?

The starting point is Article 7 of the UK Prospectus Regulation, which sets out the content for the first part of a full prospectus, known as the summary. As the name suggests, this part of the prospectus provides an overview of the key information contained in the document.

For the content of the remainder of the prospectus, it is necessary to turn to the UK PR Regulation. Chapter II of the UK PR Regulation sets out a series of Articles which cover different parts of the prospectus and different types of security issued by a company. The relevant Articles for our IPO of ordinary shares are Articles 2 and 12. The Articles refer to Annexes in the UK PR Regulation which include lists of information which must be included in the prospectus.

For our IPO of ordinary shares, the appropriate annexes are Annexes 1, 11 and 20. (The other annexes are relevant, for example, for the issue of debt securities, derivatives or depositary receipts, or if the issuer falls within a certain category, for example it is a government.)

PRR 3.1.4R requires the company to take all reasonable care to ensure that the prospectus contains the necessary information required by Article 6 and the Annexes of the UK PR Regulation. PRR 3.1.5.R requires the company to take all reasonable care that the prospectus is in accordance with the facts and does not contain any omission likely to affect its import.

Note that under Article 15 of the UK Prospectus Regulation (PRR 2.6), it is possible to produce an abbreviated prospectus for certain smaller companies (known as a UK Growth Prospectus). This applies to:

(a) small and medium-sized enterprises (SMEs); and
(b) companies (other than SMEs whose shares are traded on a UK SME growth market) with reduced market capitalisation.

A SME is defined in Article 2(f) of the UK Prospectus Regulation as:

> companies which, according to their last annual or consolidated accounts, meet at least two of the following three criteria:
>
> 1. an average number of employees during the financial year of less than 250;
> 2. a total balance sheet not exceeding €43 000 000;
> 3. an annual net turnover not exceeding €50 000 000.

A company has reduced market capitalisation in Article 15(1)(b) of the UK Prospectus Regulation if it is a company having had an average market capitalisation of less than €500 000 000 on the basis of end-year quotes during the last three calendar years.

A UK SME growth market is defined in Article 4(1)(12) of MiFID II. AIM is an example of such a market.

Such companies need only provide the lesser information in Annexes 20, 23, 24 and 26 of the UK PR Regulation. It is worth noting that in practice a company which could produce an abbreviated prospectus may still choose to issue a full prospectus if it wishes. Indeed it may have to in order to satisfy overseas securities laws, such as in the US.

6.5.2.1 Format of the prospectus

The company has a choice of how it draws up the prospectus. Either it prepares a single document, or the prospectus may comprise three separate documents (Art 6(3) (PRR 2.2.1UK)):

(a) a summary;
(b) a registration document; and
(c) a securities note.

Article 24 of the UK PR Regulation (PRR 2.2.4UK) sets out requirements as to the basic format of the prospectus.

It is intended that the option to draw up three separate documents will assist companies who are regular issuers of shares in circumstances which require a prospectus (see **6.4** above), as Article 12(2) of the UK Prospectus Regulation provides that any approved registration document remains valid for up to 12 months from the date of approval (subject to the requirement to update). This means that once a registration document has been approved, any further issue of shares will require only a new summary and securities note. As explained at **5.4.1** above, it is now the usual practice for an IPO for a company first to seek approval of just the registration document and then to follow this up with a full prospectus a few weeks later. Why then does the company not just prepare the two outstanding parts to the prospectus given that the registration document has already been approved?

Well, as explained at **6.10**, the registration document will have to be updated if there have been any significant new factors, material mistakes or inaccuracies in the existing registration document. As a result of this, and the fact that a complete and bespoke prospectus tends to have advantages from a marketing perspective, it is expected that companies will continue to use the single document format under the UK Prospectus Regulation, even having already prepared the registration document.

The summary, registration document and securities note are considered in more detail below. Note that even if the company chooses the single document format, the document must include an identifiable summary and the information required by the registration document and securities note.

Article 24(1) of the UK PR Regulation sets out the order of the information in a single document prospectus as follows:

(a) table of contents;
(b) summary;
(c) risk factors; and
(d) information required by the Annexes of the UK PR Regulation (which for an ordinary IPO will be Annexes 1, 11 and 20).

Where there are separate documents, the order is governed by Article 24(2) of the UK PR Regulation.

The summary

Article 7 of the UK Prospectus Regulation provides that the prospectus must include a self-contained summary. This must set out, in no more than seven sides of printed A4 paper, in a way that is easy to read and in clear, non-technical, concise and comprehensible language, the key information that investors need in order to understand the nature and the risks of the company and the securities being offered, and that is to be read together with rest of the prospectus to be an aid to investors considering whether to invest in the shares. The content of the summary must be accurate, fair and clear and must not be misleading. The summary must not cross-refer to other parts of the prospectus or incorporate information by reference. It must therefore be self-contained. It is to be read as an introduction to the prospectus and be consistent with other parts of the prospectus.

Article 7 also sets out the content of the summary. The summary must comprise four sections:

(a) an introduction containing warnings;
(b) key information on the company;
(c) key information on the shares; and
(d) key information on the offer to the public and/or admission to trading on a regulated market (Art 7(4)).

Detailed content information for the introduction can be found in Article 7(5) and includes a series of compulsory warnings. For example, that any decision to invest should be based on the prospectus as a whole, rather than just the summary, and that the investor could lose any money they have invested.

Article 7(6) sets out the required key information on the company under a series of sub-headings which must be used but can be added to:

- 'Who is the issuer of the securities'?
- 'What is the key financial information regarding the issuer'? This must be set out in table format in accordance with Annex I to the UK Prospectus RTS Regulation for an ordinary trading company.
- 'What are the key risks that are specific to the issuer'? The maximum number of risks that can be included is 15 (Art 7(10)).

Article 7(7) sets out the key information which must be included on the shares being offered. Again, this must be set out under compulsory sub-headings which can be added to:

- 'What are the main features of the securities'?
- 'Where will the securities be traded?'
- 'What are the key risks that are specific to the securities'? The maximum of 15 risks mentioned above covers the *whole* summary.

The key information on the offer to the public and for the admission to trading on a regulated market which must be included is set out in Article 7(8). The minimum sub-headings to be used are:

- 'Under which conditions and timetable can I invest in this security'?
- 'Why is this prospectus being produced'?

Note that the summary has particular importance under the passporting procedure (see **6.11** below) as it is the only part of the prospectus which another Member State can request to be translated.

The registration document

The registration document provides information about the company. Article 2 of the UK PR Regulation (PRR 2.3.1UK) requires that it should contain the information set out in Annex 1 to the PR Regulation (accessible via a hyperlink at Appendix 2 to the UK Prospectus Regulation Rules). The main content requirements of Annex 1 are summarised below, but this is intended to provide only a flavour of the content of the prospectus. For comprehensive details of the content requirements, reference must be made to the UK PR Regulation itself. The numerical paragraph references below correspond to the section numbers of Annex 1:

1. *Persons responsible, third party information, experts' reports and competent authority approval*. The document must identify all persons responsible for the information given in the registration document, and those persons must declare in the document that, to the best of their knowledge, the information contained in the registration document is in accordance with the facts and contains no omission likely to affect its import.

   This is referred to as the 'responsibility statement'. (Paragraphs **6.6** and **6.7** below discuss further the issues of responsibility and liability for the document.)

   If the document includes a statement or report attributed to a person as an expert, it must provide information about the expert. If the document contains any information sourced from a third party, the source of that information must be identified, and confirmation must be provided that the information has been reproduced accurately and that, as far as the issuer is aware, no facts have been omitted which would render the information inaccurate or misleading. A statement of approval by the FCA must also be included emphasising that such approval should not be taken as an endorsement of the company involved.
2. *Statutory auditors*. The document must identify the company's auditors.

3. *Risk factors.* A section headed 'Risk Factors' must include the most material risks which are specific to the company.

   This is one of the most important disclosures regarding the company for potential investors. For example, under the law pre-dating the UK Prospectus Regulation, the prospectus issued for Ocado plc's July 2010 IPO contained 49 separate risk factors, including the fact that it is dependent on the specialist skills of its current executive directors, it had never made a profit in its 10 years of existence and anticipates making further losses, its online ordering system may be subject to hacking or vandalism, and there may be a decrease in demand for its services due to health concerns or a pandemic such as mad cow disease or avian flu.

   This section of the prospectus came under close scrutiny in recent years as a result of the global financial crisis and the perceived inadequacy of the then rules in protecting investors. It was noted that there was a tendency towards more generic and standardised risk factors.

   Article 16 of the UK Prospectus Regulation now emphasises that these factors should be specific to the company and its shares and should be material. They should also not be generic (recital 54 of the UK Prospectus Regulation). The limit on 15 risk factors in the summary does not apply to the registration document.

   Each factor should be adequately described, explaining how it affects the company or the shares being offered. They may be assessed as 'low, medium or high' risk. A limited number of categories should be used with the most material risks mentioned first.
4. *Information about the issuer.* This section requires the company to include its name, date of incorporation, the address of its registered office and its website amongst other things.
5. *Business overview.* The company's principal activities and markets must be described. In addition, the important events in the development of the company's business must be included. The document must also contain a description of the company's principal investments, existing and future.
6. *Organisational structure.* The document must detail if the issuer is part of a group, a brief description of the group and the company's position within that group. It must also identify the company's significant subsidiaries.
7. *Operating and financial review.* The document must include a fair review of the development and performance of the company's business and financial condition and the causes of any material changes. The review should also cover the company's likely future development and its research and development activities.
8. *Capital resources.* The document must detail the company's capital resources, including cash flow, borrowing requirements, any restrictions on the use of capital resources and information regarding the anticipated sources of funds for any future investments.
9. *Regulatory environment.* A description of the regulatory environment in which the company operates and that may materially affect its business as well as information on any government, economic, fiscal, monetary or political policy that has or could materially affect the company.
10. *Trend information.* Information is required about the most significant trends in production, sales and inventory, costs and selling prices, and any known trends or uncertainties which are reasonably likely to have a material effect on the company's prospects for the current financial year.
11. *Profit forecasts or estimates.* If a company chooses to include a profit forecast in the prospectus then it must also provide the information set out in section 11 of Annex 1, including a statement setting out the assumptions on which the forecast is based and a report by the company's auditors or independent accountants that the forecast has been properly compiled.

12. *Administrative, management and supervisory bodies and senior management*. The document must provide information about the company's management, particularly the directors, but also potentially any founders (if the company is less than five years' old) and senior managers who are relevant to establishing that the company has appropriate expertise and experience for the management of the company's business. Some of this information could be seen as rather personal, such as details of any convictions in relation to fraudulent offences in the last five years, details of any insolvency events and details of any public sanctions or criticisms of any director by any statutory or regulatory bodies. Ideally there will be no skeletons hiding in the directors' (or, if relevant, senior managers') closets which need to be aired in the prospectus (and if there are not, an appropriate 'negative statement' must be made in the document). However, if there are, then the due diligence process should ensure that they come to light sooner rather than later, so that the financial PR consultants have time to consider how they can manage the issues in a way that will not stop potential investors from investing in the company. Details of any conflict of interest between any of the people covered by section 12 must also be disclosed (and if there are none, an appropriate negative statement must be made).
13. *Remuneration and benefits*. Details of the remuneration (for the last full financial year) and benefits of the directors (and, if relevant, senior managers) must be provided.
14. *Board practices*. Certain information about the running of the board, including periods of service, service contract information and corporate governance compliance (see **Chapter 8**), must be included.
15. *Employees*. The document must include information relating to employees, including the number of employees, information regarding their share or share option ownership, and a description of any arrangements for involving the employees in the company's capital.
16. *Major shareholders*. The document must identify any major shareholder of the company (that is, anyone other than a director who has an interest in the company's capital or voting rights which is notifiable under national law (3% in the UK – see **Chapter 15**), and provide other information as to such shareholders, such as whether or not they have different voting rights.
17. *Related party transactions*. Details of any related party transactions (see **19.5**) must be provided, together with the amount to which such transactions form part of the company's turnover.
18. *Financial information concerning the issuer's assets and liabilities, financial position and profits and losses*. The prospectus must contain a significant amount of financial information, prepared with the help of the reporting accounts. Paragraph **4.2.5** above refers to some of this information. In particular, the short form report, containing information relating to the profits and losses, assets and liabilities, financial record and position of the group for the period of three years before the IPO, must form part of the document. The document must also include a statement as to whether or not there has been any significant change in the financial position of the group since the date to which the last accounts or interim statements were made up. This section also refers to the need for inclusion of the pro forma financial information required by Annex 20 to the UK Prospectus RTS Regulation.

    Information is also required, by item 18.6.1, about any litigation or arbitration (including any pending or threatened) which might have, or has had, a significant effect on the company or the group's financial position. This can be a very sensitive area for the company, which would not usually consider publicising litigation, or the threat of it. However, the UK Prospectus RTS Regulation is very clear that it must do so, subject to the 'significant effect' qualification. If the company does not consider it has anything to disclose in this regard, it must include a 'negative statement' to that effect.

Information about the company's dividend policy must also be included.

19. *Additional information*. The document must include information about the company's share capital, such as the authorised and issued share capital, and certain details of the history of the company's share capital. In addition, various information about the company's memorandum and articles of association must be provided, including a description of the company's objects, a description of the rights attaching to each class of existing shares and a description of any provision in the articles that would delay or prevent a change of control in the company.
20. *Material contracts*. The document should summarise the principal contents of certain contracts referred to as 'material contracts', namely those contracts which have been entered into other than in the ordinary course of business by the company or any member of the company's group:
    (i) in the two-year period preceding the publication of the document (if the contract is material); or
    (ii) at any time (if the contract provides the company or any member of the company's group with any entitlement or obligation which is still material to the company or the group as at the date the registration document is published).

    The lawyers will help the company to identify which documents fall within the definition and draft the summaries of those contracts for inclusion in the document.
21. *Documents available*. The document should include a statement that, for the life of the registration document, certain documents are available for inspection at a named website. These documents include the company's memorandum and articles of association and documents prepared by experts for use in the registration document. The lawyers will assist the company in ensuring the correct documents are made available.

The securities note

The securities note must contain information about the securities (for our purposes, shares) to be offered or admitted. Article 12 of the UK PR Regulation (PRR 2.3.1UK) provides that the securities note should contain the information set out in Annex 11 of the UK PR Regulation. The main content requirements of Annex 11 are summarised below. Again this is intended to provide only a flavour of the content of the prospectus, and for a comprehensive list of the content requirements, you should refer to the UK PR Regulation itself. The numerical paragraph references below correspond to the section numbers of Annex 11.

1. *Persons responsible, third party information, experts' reports and competent authority approval*. As with the registration document, a responsibility statement must be included; this time by all those responsible for the information given in the securities note.

    There is a requirement, to mirror the requirement in Annex 1 relating to the registration document, that if the securities note includes a statement or report attributed to a person as an expert, then it must provide information about the expert. If it contains any information sourced from a third party, the source of that information must be identified, and confirmation must be provided that the information has been reproduced accurately and that, as far as the issuer is aware, no facts have been omitted which would render the information inaccurate or misleading.
2. *Risk factors*. Again, there is a requirement similar to that which exists for the registration document, that the securities note must include, under the section headed 'Risk Factors', risk factors that are material to the shares being offered and/or admitted with the most material set out first. This is to enable investors to assess the market risk associated with the shares. The limit on 15 risk factors in the summary does not apply to the securities note.

3. *Essential information*. The document must include what is referred to as the 'working capital statement', namely a statement that, in the company's opinion, the working capital is sufficient for the issuer's present requirements or, if not, how it proposes to provide the additional working capital it requires. Of course, this ensures the directors address their minds to the ability of the company to thrive, or at least survive, after flotation, and address the likelihood of insolvency problems after the IPO. (The working capital statement is, in effect, a statement that the company is not going to 'go belly up' (ie become insolvent) straight after the IPO.) The document must also include a capitalisation and indebtedness statement. In addition, information must be provided in relation to anyone with any particular interest in the issue/offer of shares (including any conflicting interest), and in relation to the reasons for the offer and how it is intended any proceeds will be used.
4. *Information concerning the securities to be offered/admitted to trading*. Information must be provided about the shares which are to be offered or admitted, including a description of the type and class of shares, the legislation under which the securities were created (since 1 October 2009, the CA 2006), the rights which attach to the shares (such as voting rights, rights to share in capital, dividend rights and pre-emption rights: see **Chapters 13** and **14**). In the case of new issues, the resolutions, authorisations and approvals by virtue of which the shares have been created and/or issued must also be stated (see **Chapter 14**).
5. *Terms and conditions of the offer of securities to the public*. The document must set out detailed terms and conditions of the offer, including the total amount of the offer, the period for which the offer will be open and the circumstances under which the offer can be revoked, the intended categories of investor and distribution amongst them and an indication of the offer price. Details of any underwriters and when the underwriting agreement was or will be reached are also required.
6. *Admission to trading and dealing arrangements*. As a prospectus is required for all public offers (unless an exemption applies), there is a requirement to include a statement as to whether the shares offered will be admitted to trading with a view to their distribution on a regulated market. For our purposes, in the context of an IPO the shares will be admitted to trading on the Main Market, a regulated market.
7. *Selling securities holders*. If the IPO involves an offer for sale of shares (see **4.4.1.1**) then specific details must be provided, including the name and address of the selling shareholders and the number and class of shares being sold by each shareholder.
8. *Expense of the issue/offer*. The securities note must detail the total net proceeds and an estimate of the total expenses of the issue/offer.
9. *Dilution*. The amount and percentage of immediate dilution (see **14.6.2**) resulting from the offer must be included in the document.
10. *Additional information*. Additional information which must be included is a statement of the capacity in which any advisers, referred to in the securities note, have acted, and to identify and reproduce, or summarise, audited information referred to in the document.

6.5.2.2 Incorporation by reference

Under Article 19 of the UK Prospectus Regulation (PRR 2.7.1UK), information can be incorporated by reference into the prospectus, in certain circumstances, without therefore having to be restated in full. This will make the prospectus shorter and more manageable for the reader. To be incorporated, the information must:

(a) be contained in a document listed in Article 19(1) of the UK Prospectus Regulation (PRR 2.7.1UK);
(b) be the most recent available to the company (Art 19(1) (PRR 2.7.1UK));
(c) be accessible using a cross-referenced list in the prospectus and contain hyperlinks to all documents (Art 19(2) (PRR 2.7.1UK)); and

(d) be presented in searchable electronic format when the draft prospectus is being reviewed by the FCA, unless the information has already been approved by or filed with the FCA (Art 19(3) of the UK Prospectus Regulation (PRR 2.7.1UK)).

Examples of information which can be incorporated by reference as set out in Article 19(1) (PRR 2.7.1UK) include information contained in the audited report and accounts of the company, or the company's memorandum and articles of association. As explained at **5.3.6.2** above, the company must submit to the FCA a copy of any information incorporated into the prospectus by reference.

Information cannot be incorporated by reference into the summary section of the prospectus (Art 7(11)).

6.5.2.3 Omission of information

Article 18(1) of the UK Prospectus Regulation (PRR 2.8.1UK) provides that the FCA has the discretion to authorise the omission of any information required by the UK Prospectus Regulation or UK PR Regulation if:

(a) disclosure of the information would be contrary to the public interest; or

(b) disclosure of the information would be seriously detrimental to the company and the omission of the information is not likely to mislead investors in their assessment of the company and the shares being offered; or

(c) the information to be omitted is of minor importance for a specific offer or admission to trading and is unlikely to influence the investors' assessment of the company's financial position and prospects.

Any request to omit information under Article 18(1) must be reasoned (Art 42(2)(d) of the UK PR Regulation). This means it must comply with the FCA's requirements set out in PRR 2.8.2G. It must be in writing, identify the specific information concerned and the reasons for its omission, and state in the company's opinion why Article 18(1) applies by reference to the grounds given in that Article.

The lawyers must make the directors aware of this discretion of the FCA, but they must manage the message carefully. As we have seen, the UK Prospectus Regulation and the UK PR Regulation require significant disclosure in the prospectus. The directors may not want certain information to be included in the prospectus, and will ask the lawyers how they can avoid disclosure of that information. The clear message is that if the UK PR Regulation, or the general disclosure requirement in Article 6(1) of the UK Prospectus Regulation (PRR 2.1.1UK), require such disclosure then the prospectus must contain that information. The FCA will exercise its discretion to omit information only in exceptional circumstances. Indeed, the very fact that directors wish to omit certain information may suggest that they think that such information would deter investors from investing in the company. This means that the information is likely to be highly relevant to investors, and so would not fall within the FCA's discretion in any event. Lawyers need to be firm with directors who may want to conceal facts, because ultimately the directors themselves may be personally liable to investors for inaccuracies in or omissions from the prospectus (see **6.7** below).

6.5.2.4 Checking content

Chapter 5 describes how the prospectus is submitted to the FCA for approval. To help the FCA check that the document complies with its content requirements, checklists must be submitted to the FCA to indicate how the company has complied with the relevant disclosure requirements (Art 42(2) of the UK PR Regulation). Subsequent drafts of the prospectus must be marked up ('blacklined') to highlight all changes made to the preceding draft of the prospectus previously submitted to the FCA to speed up the approval process.

6.6 RESPONSIBILITY

It is all very well requiring the production of a prospectus which will usually run to well in excess of 100 pages (Royal Mail plc's October 2013 IPO prospectus ran to 450 pages!), but what if any of the information included in the prospectus proves to be incorrect, or what if a relevant piece of information has been omitted? This may lead to investors losing money if they have invested as a result in a company which is in reality not what it appears to be from the prospectus. Can the investors be compensated in such circumstances? The answer is yes. Article 11 of the UK Prospectus Regulation and the FSMA 2000 provide the authority to make certain people involved in the preparation of the prospectus take responsibility for the accuracy of its contents. They then make those responsible liable for any mistakes or omissions which cause investors loss.

6.6.1 Who is responsible for the contents of the prospectus?

The answer lies in the Prospectus Regulation Rules as authorised by s 84(1)(d) of the FSMA 2000. Where, as in our case, the prospectus relates to equity shares (ordinary shares), PRR 5.3.2R(2) provides that the following people will be responsible for the prospectus:

(a) the issuer (ie the company) (PRR 5.3.2R(2)(a));

(b) the directors of the company (as at the date the document is published) (PRR 5.3.2R(2)(b)(i));

(c) anyone who has agreed to be named, and is named, in the prospectus as a director, or as having agreed to become a director, either immediately or in the future (after the IPO, for example) (PRR 5.3.2R(2)(b)(ii));

(d) anyone who accepts, and is stated in the prospectus as accepting, responsibility for the prospectus (PRR 5.3.2R(2)(c));

(e) anyone, other than the company, who is offering shares (and if this is another company, the directors of that company at the time the prospectus is published) (PRR 5.3.2R(2)(d));

(f) the person requesting admission to trading of the shares (if not the company) (and if this is another company, the directors of that company at the time the prospectus is published) (PRR 5.3.2R(2)(e)); and

(g) anyone else who authorises the contents of the prospectus (PRR 5.3.2R(2)(f)).

Paragraph (e) above will be of particular concern to any selling shareholders if an offer for sale forms part of the IPO. They may well be individuals who would not be comfortable taking such responsibility. However, comfort is at hand. Prospectus Regulation Rule 5.3.8R provides that a person will not be responsible under PRR 5.3.2R(2)(d) if the shareholder is making the offer in association with the issuer and it is primarily the issuer, or the issuing company's advisers, who draw up the prospectus. This will usually be the case with IPOs, so usually the lawyer will be able to reassure any selling shareholders on the issue of responsibility.

Paragraph (g) above will, for example, cover the accountants (because they have authorised financial information prepared specifically for the prospectus) (Annex 1, section 1 and Annex 11, section 1 – see **6.5.2.1** above). As a result, they must set out a statement in the prospectus that they are responsible for such content. However, they will not be required to give such a statement in respect of financial information incorporated by reference which was not prepared specifically for the prospectus.

The FCA does not consider the sponsor to have authorised the prospectus for the purposes of the responsibility regime, so sponsors do not need to provide such a statement (PRR 5.3.10R).

Lawyers similarly are covered by the exemption in PRR 5.3.10R. They do not have responsibility by reason only of giving advice about the content of the prospectus in a professional capacity.

6.6.2 What does responsibility mean?

The persons with responsibility for the document must ensure that the document complies with the general disclosure obligation imposed by Article 6 of the UK Prospectus Regulation (see **6.5.1** above) and the specific content requirements set out in the UK PR Regulation (see **6.5.2** above). In other words, they must ensure that all relevant information is included in the prospectus. The consequences of this are discussed at **6.7** below.

6.6.3 Responsibility statement

As mentioned at **6.5.2.1** above, a responsibility statement must be included in the prospectus pursuant to item 1.2 of both Annex 1 and Annex 11 of the UK PR Regulation.

6.7 LIABILITY

As stated in **6.6.2** above, those with responsibility for the prospectus must ensure that it meets the content requirements of the UK Prospectus Regulation and the UK PR Regulation. The document must not omit any information or contain information which is incorrect or misleading. The consequence of this is that the persons responsible for the document may incur civil and/or criminal liability in relation to any inaccuracies or misstatements in, or omissions from, the document.

6.7.1 Civil liability

6.7.1.1 Section 91 of the FSMA 2000

A breach of Article 6 of the UK Prospectus Regulation governing the content of the prospectus gives the FCA the power to impose a number of sanctions and measures. These include:

Fines

The FCA can fine the company for breach of the UK Prospectus Regulation, the UK PR Regulation (including the Annexes setting out required content) and the Prospectus Regulation Rules, and if it can prove that any director or former director was knowingly concerned in the breach, it can fine that director.

Censure

The FCA may choose privately or publicly to censure the company, or a director or former director knowingly concerned in the breach, as an alternative to a fine.

6.7.1.2 Section 90 of the FSMA 2000

Section 90 of the FSMA 2000 sets out the liability which a person responsible is most likely to face for problems arising out of the content of the prospectus.

The effect of s 90 of the FSMA 2000 is that those responsible for *listing particulars* must pay compensation to anyone who has acquired shares which are the subject of the listing particulars, and has suffered loss as a result of any inaccurate or misleading statement in the document, or any omission of information which should have been disclosed under s 87A. Section 90(11) provides that this applies equally in relation to a *prospectus*. While it includes specific reference to the general disclosure requirement under s 80 of the FSMA 2000, s 90(11) provides that this applies not only to a failure of the prospectus to meet this requirement, but also to any failure to meet the content requirements of the UK Prospectus Regulation.

Note that s 90(12) provides that a person can be liable solely on the basis of the contents of the summary (see **6.5.2.1**) only if the summary is misleading, inaccurate or inconsistent, or does not include the required 'key information' under Article 7 of the UK Prospectus Regulation (see **6.5.2.1** above) when read together with the rest of the prospectus.

It may help to consider the issue of liability by way of an example.

> **EXAMPLE**
>
> Imagine that an investor, Mr X, encouraged by the positive messages in the prospectus, invests in Company A. In fact, the prospectus failed to include information about a very real risk that a rival's new invention could significantly reduce Company A's sales. Imagine that, after the IPO, the rival's new invention goes terribly wrong. Company A continues to prosper and Mr X makes a good profit. Mr X has suffered no loss and the persons responsible for the inaccurate prospectus, through sheer luck, will incur no liability under s 90.
>
> Consider now what would happen if, in fact, the rival's new invention is a huge success, to the extent that Company A loses significant sales and ultimately goes belly up. Mr X loses his entire investment. He has suffered loss and wants compensation. Section 90 of the FSMA 2000 provides that he should obtain compensation from those persons responsible for the incorrect selling document (that is, mainly, the directors).

What is the scope of s 90? There are two particular phrases in the provision which have caused some debate:

(a) 'who has acquired' – s 90 concerns the loss suffered by a person 'who has acquired' securities. Is this restricted to the original investor, or does it include those who buy the shares from that original investor?

(b) 'as a result of' – for any investor to have a claim to compensation under s 90, she must prove that she suffered loss 'as a result of' the deficiencies in the document. Does this mean that the investor must have relied on the document? Must the investor have read the document?

These phrases leave open the possibility that any aggrieved original investor who had not even read the document, or any subsequent purchaser of the shares from the original investor, could try to run the argument that s 90 is wide enough to afford her a claim for compensation.

There are some exemptions from liability under s 90, which are set out in Sch 10 to the FSMA 2000. These exemptions include:

(a) if, at the time the prospectus was submitted to the FCA, the persons responsible (having made reasonable enquiries) believed the erroneous information was true and not misleading;

(b) where loss arises as a result of a statement by an expert;

(c) where a correction had been published before shares were acquired;

(d) where the erroneous information was reproduced from a public official document; and

(e) where the person seeking compensation acquired the shares knowing the information was deficient.

The first ever case relying on s 90 was commenced in the High Court in 2013. It related to a prospectus prepared for a rights issue (see **17.7** below) rather than an IPO, but it is still instructive for us as s 90 relates to prospectuses used whatever the circumstances. Thousands of investors in Royal Bank of Scotland (RBS) (both institutional, such as the UK Mineworkers' Pension Fund, the Dutch bank ING and the teachers' retirement system of Illinois, USA and private individuals) started the action against RBS and four of its former directors (including the former CEO, Fred Goodwin, who became the public's principal hate figure over the financial crisis in the UK) for what they claim is the loss caused by misleading statements and omissions in RBS's prospectus arising out of its emergency £12 billion share offer in 2008. At the time RBS was desperately trying to raise money from its shareholders to stay afloat, having been caught up in the global financial crisis. The fundraising failed to save RBS, and four months later it announced the second biggest loss ever by a bank in UK. Eventually RBS ended up being taken over by the UK Government to prevent it from collapsing. The investors claimed that if RBS had provided the correct information in the prospectus, they would not have taken up the shares offered at the time, and they claimed the difference between the price paid (£2) and what they say the shares were really worth (in one initial statement by 21 claimants this was said to be just 28 pence).

In June 2017 the last of the approximately 27,000 institutional and individual claimants in a class action seeking around £1.8 billion in compensation settled with RBS, bringing the case to a close in the week the trial was due to start and removing an opportunity to address some of the legal questions around s 90. Legal expenses exceeded well over £100 million.

6.7.1.3 Liability in tort

The persons responsible for the prospectus may also incur tortious liability under the following heads:

(a) *Negligent misstatement.* Those with responsibility for the prospectus owe a duty of care to those investing at the time of the IPO. The publication of a deficient document breaches this duty. If an investor relies on a deficient prospectus and suffers loss because of that reliance then, on the basis of *Hedley Byrne & Co Ltd v Heller & Partners Ltd* [1964] AC 465, those responsible for the prospectus will be liable to that investor. Note that, applying *Caparo Industries v Dickman* [1990] 1 All ER 568, the persons responsible for the document would not owe any duty to any subsequent purchasers of the shares. This, and the fact that the investor must have *relied* on the erroneous information or omission, can be contrasted with the position under s 90 of the FSMA 2000 (see **6.7.1.1**) and therefore makes this a less attractive claim for an aggrieved investor.

(b) *Deceit.* If an investor can prove that any misstatement in the prospectus was made fraudulently, they may have a claim in damages for deceit.

(c) *Misrepresentation Act 1967.* If an investor chooses to invest in the company on the basis of an incorrect or misleading prospectus, they may be able to rescind the contract for the purchase of shares and/or claim damages from the other party to the contract (see also CA 2006, s 655). Note that the other party usually will be the issuer of the shares, ie the company (in the case of an offer for subscription) or the selling shareholder (in the case of an offer for sale), rather than the directors.

6.7.1.4 Liability in contract

The prospectus will form either the whole or part of any contract between an investor buying shares and either the company issuing shares to the investor, or any existing shareholder selling shares to the investor (the circumstances will vary depending on the IPO). If the prospectus is deficient, the investor may be able to rescind the contract, or sue the other party to the contract (the company or the selling shareholder) for damages.

6.7.1.5 Advertisements relating to a prospectus

Article 22 of the UK Prospectus Regulation (PRR 3.3.1UK) lays down a number of requirements relating to advertisements in connection with a prospectus which are supplemented by Articles 13–16 of the UK Prospectus RTS Regulation. Advertisements are defined in Article 2(k) as a communication relating to a specific offer to the public of securities (such as shares) or admission to trading and aiming specifically to promote the possible acquisition of securities. This covers a wide range of communications to investors and the media, including those made via printed matter, the Internet, email, television, text messages, road-shows, briefings, conference calls and presentations to promote the offer. Crucially, the information in each such advertisement must not be inaccurate or misleading. It must also be consistent with the information in an existing prospectus, or one which will be published in due course if the prospectus is not yet finalised. If the information is inaccurate, misleading or inconsistent then liability can also arise for breach of the UK Prospectus

Regulation, and the sanctions in **3.6** above may be applied by the FCA. Care must therefore be taken, particularly by management of a company undertaking a high-profile IPO, when discussing it on television (especially in a live interview) or with a journalist, or if a director feels the urge to tweet about it.

6.7.2 Criminal liability

The threat of paying compensation or damages may be bad enough for the persons responsible, but it could get worse. Reflecting the importance of protecting the investing public, there may even be the possibility of criminal liability. Mentioning this sanction does tend to help any director, who is tiring of the legal due diligence or verification process, to re-focus.

Criminal offences are usually prosecuted by the Crown Prosecution Service, but the FCA has special powers to bring criminal prosecutions, including for the offences set out in ss 401 and 402 of the FSMA 2000.

6.7.2.1 Sections 89 and 90 of the Financial Services Act 2012

A director risks criminal liability under the following provisions of the Financial Services Act 2012:

(a) *Section 89 (misleading statements).* This provision makes it a criminal offence for any person to make a statement which they know to be false or misleading in a material respect, to conceal dishonestly any material facts or recklessly make a statement which is misleading.

(b) *Section 90 (misleading impressions).* This provision catches anything any person does to create a false or misleading impression as to the market in, or price or value of the shares, if they do so deliberately to induce investors to buy investments, sell them, underwrite them or refrain from so doing or, while knowing the impression to be false or misleading makes a gain or causes a loss.

Sections 89 and 90 of the Financial Services Act 2012 are considered in more detail at **9.5** below.

6.7.2.2 Theft Act 1968

Section 19 of the Theft Act 1968 imposes criminal penalties on any director who makes false or misleading statements with intent to deceive shareholders. Clearly this could apply to any director who is responsible for a deficient prospectus, if intent can be proved.

6.7.2.3 Section 85(3) of the FSMA 2000

It is a criminal offence for a person to offer shares to the public or request their admission to trading without providing an approved prospectus to the public.

6.7.2.4 Fraud Act 2006

It is a criminal offence under s 2 of the Fraud Act 2006 dishonestly to make a representation and in doing so intend to make a gain or cause a loss. Under s 3 it is a criminal offence for a person to fail to disclose information which they are legally obliged to do and in doing so make a gain or expose another to the risk of loss. Under s 12, if the offence is committed by a company then a director or other officer of the company is (in addition to the company) liable for that offence if they consent to or connive in that offence. The penalties for these offences under s 1 are a maximum of 10 years' imprisonment and an unlimited fine.

6.8 VERIFICATION

As the range of possible liability set out at **6.7** above makes clear, it is not a good idea for the directors to make incorrect statements in the prospectus, or to omit required material from it.

During the IPO process, therefore, great care is taken to ensure that the prospectus meets the requirements of the UK Prospectus Regulation and the FSMA 2000. As **6.6.1** above explains, directors are not the only people with responsibility for the document, but they do have responsibility, and their responsibility is for the entire document. Accordingly, a process has emerged which aims to ensure that the directors make all reasonable enquiries to satisfy themselves that:

(a) each material statement of fact or opinion in the document is not only true, but also not misleading in the context in which it appears;

(b) the document as a whole gives a true and fair impression of the history, business and prospects of the company; and

(c) the document does not omit any information which makes it misleading or which contravenes the UK Prospectus Regulation and s 87A of the FSMA 2000.

This process is called verification. It protects the directors by providing evidence that they have taken reasonable care to ensure the information required by the UK Prospectus Regulation and s 87A of the FSMA 2000 has been included. It also helps to avoid breaching ss 89 and 90 of the Financial Services Act 2012 (see **9.5**) and the market abuse regime (see **Chapter 10**), and so provides comfort to the sponsor. The verification process is considered in more detail at **5.3.5** above.

6.9 TYPES OF PROSPECTUS

6.9.1 Full/final

So far, this chapter has considered the document which will ultimately be submitted to the FCA for approval as part of the company's application for admission to listing. This is known as the full or final prospectus. However, references to other forms of the prospectus may be made during the IPO process in addition to the abbreviated prospectus under the UK Prospectus Regulation discussed at **6.5.2** above. These references are explained below.

6.9.2 Preliminary/price-range prospectus

This is virtually identical to the full prospectus. It too has to be approved by the FCA before it can be sent out to prospective investors. The key difference is that the price for the shares being offered will not be specified in the document as a fixed amount, instead there will usually be a price range. This type of prospectus is also commonly known as a 'price-range prospectus'. It is even possible to issue the preliminary prospectus without a price or the number of shares being offered being mentioned at all. Approval by the FCA means that this document can be sent out to any potential investor. A pricing statement will subsequently be issued setting out the final price before the offer closes under Article 17(2) of the UK Prospectus Regulation. This statement does not require prior approval by the FCA (possibly with a supplementary prospectus (see **6.9.4** below) if, for example, there has been a material change to the information in the preliminary prospectus).

Note that under Article 21(1) of the UK Prospectus Regulation (PRR 3.2.1UK), an approved prospectus (be it full or preliminary) must be made available to investors at least six working days before the close of the offer (see **5.4.2.2**).

6.9.3 Pathfinder prospectus

Note that, following a recent change to the law (see **5.4.1** above), it is not yet clear whether these will continue to be used.

This is a draft of the prospectus which is sent out to prospective investors to stimulate interest in the IPO. A full prospectus will be sent out once expressions of interest have been received. The crucial difference from the preliminary prospectus (see **6.9.2**) is that it is sent to prospective investors without prior FCA approval. This causes a potential problem in that it could result in a breach of s 21 of the FSMA 2000 (see **Chapter 12**). The impact of s 21 is that it is an offence for a company to send out a pathfinder to induce investors to buy shares. The company can avoid this problem by sending the pathfinder only to persons exempt from s 21 (mainly institutional investors) (see **12.9**). In addition, a pathfinder must comply with the rules relating to advertisements set out in Article 22 of the UK Prospectus Regulation (PRR 3.3.1UK) (see **6.7.1.4**), as clarified in the FCA's Technical Note UKLA/TN/604.1 PD Advertisement regime (available on the FCA's website) (note that this has yet to be updated for the UK Prospectus Regulation).

6.9.4 Factors to take into account

There are a number of factors to weigh up before the company decides whether to issue a preliminary or pathfinder prospectus. (As mentioned above, following a recent change to the law, it is not yet clear whether pathfinder prospectuses will continue to be used.)

A pathfinder can be distributed only to limited categories of person (such as institutional investors) whereas a preliminary prospectus can be sent out to any investor, including a member of the public.

If a preliminary prospectus is used, a supplementary prospectus may have to be prepared which will need to be approved by the FCA before it is distributed (see **6.9.5**). This does not arise with a pathfinder, as no prior prospectus relating to the offer is in existence. The publication of a supplementary prospectus grants investors the right to withdraw their acceptance of the offer (Art 23(2) of the UK Prospectus Regulation (PRR 3.4.1UK)).

Another potential disadvantage of the company choosing to use a preliminary prospectus (which does not arise with a pathfinder) is that investors have the right to withdraw their acceptances of the offer within two working days of the date the company provides the price of the offer to the FCA under Article 17(1)(a) of the UK Prospectus Regulation. However, if the prospectus details the method and conditions for determining the price and amount (or, in relation to the price, states a maximum offer price) then this right to withdraw will not arise (Art 17(1)(b) of the UK Prospectus Regulation).

6.9.5 Supplementary

Article 23(1) of the UK Prospectus Regulation (PRR 3.4.1UK) provides that if, in the period between the approval of the prospectus and the closing of the offer period or the time when dealings in shares commence, there arises or is noted any significant new factor, material mistake or inaccuracy relating to the information included in the approved prospectus which may affect the assessment of the shares, the company must produce a supplementary prospectus without delay. This document must contain details of the new factor, mistake or inaccuracy, and must be approved by the FCA within five working days of submission to it. As mentioned at **6.9.4** above, investors have the right to withdraw their acceptances of the offer during the two working days following publication of the supplementary prospectus (Art 23(2) of the UK Prospectus Regulation (PRR 3.4.1UK)), so this is a situation to be avoided if at all possible and demonstrates another reason for having the thorough due diligence process in the period leading up to the IPO.

6.10 VALIDITY

A prospectus is valid for 12 months after its approval, for any further offers or admissions to trading, provided that it is updated by a supplementary prospectus, approved by the FCA (see **6.9.5**) (Art 12(1) of the UK Prospectus Regulation). As mentioned at **6.5.2.1** above, the registration document is valid for a period of up to 12 months after it has been filed and approved, but this is also subject to updating, using a supplementary registration document, which again requires the approval of the FCA (Article 10(1) of the UK Prospectus Regulation (PRR 5.1UK)).

Given the requirements for FCA approval of any update to either the prospectus (by supplementary prospectus) or the registration document (by a supplementary registration document), any advantage of this extended validity period may be limited, as explained at **6.5.2.1** above.

6.11 PASSPORTING

The EU Prospectus Regulation allows for a 'passporting' procedure under Articles 24–26, whereby a company will not need to produce a prospectus for an offer of shares to the public, or an admission of shares to trading, in one EEA Member State ('MS2') if another EEA Member State ('MS1') has already approved and published a prospectus in the previous 12 months. Subject to updating (see **6.10** above), the company simply must translate the summary (not, interestingly, any other part of the prospectus) into a language acceptable to MS2 and request a 'certificate of approval' from the competent authority in MS1 that the prospectus has been drawn up and approved in accordance with the Prospectus Regulation.

Before Brexit, many companies in the UK took advantage of the passporting procedure for an offer of shares in more than one EEA Member State. However, the passporting procedure is no longer available for UK-based companies from 1 January 2021, the end of the transition period after Brexit. UK companies now need to prepare an additional separate prospectus from the FCA-approved prospectus for an offer of shares into the EEA. This additional prospectus must be approved by the competent authority in a Member State into which the offer is to be made (say France) and then this approved prospectus can be passported into other EEA countries in which the offer is to be made (for example Spain, Germany and Italy).

6.12 FUTURE DEVELOPMENTS

Financial Services and Markets Act 2023

This Act intends, amongst other things, to revoke EU financial services law that had been retained following Brexit and replace it with UK-sourced rules. The then UK Government's vision was for an open, green, and technologically advanced financial services sector that is globally competitive, with this Act being at its core. The Act will result in fundamental amendments to the FSMA 2000. It will also grant the FCA much wider powers to enable it to draw up legally binding rules which will be included in the FCA's Handbook (eg the UK Listing Rules, new Prospectus Rules and Disclosure Guidance and Transparency Rules) rather than, as is currently the case, in legislation. Laws which will be repealed include the UK version of the Prospectus Directive, the UK version of MAR, the UK version of MiFIR and the related delegated legislation.

The FCA has already taken the first major step by introducing the new UK Listing Rules which replaced the former Listing Rules on 29 July 2024.

The FCA is currently consulting on the next stage, replacing the current prospectus regime discussed in this chapter. There will be fundamental reforms introduced when this happens which will have a significant impact on the content of this chapter.

The POAT Regulations (see **3.5.1.4** above) are already in place awaiting full implementation. The UK version of the Prospectus Regulation will be repealed, and the two tests for a prospectus under s 85 of the FSMA 2000 will be replaced by a prohibition on 'offers to the public' with a series of exemptions which are wider than currently is the law. The 'admission to trading' test will be superseded by rules in the FCA's Handbook (new Prospectus Rules replacing the PRRs) governing the need for a prospectus. The detailed content requirements for a prospectus will be drawn up by the FCA and included in its prospectus rules. The FCA will have the power to amend the rules setting out the procedure for approval of a prospectus and those who should take responsibility for it once it is published.

You will be able to follow this process via the FCA's website.

PART II

BEING A LISTED COMPANY

CHAPTER 7

CONTINUING OBLIGATIONS

7.1 INTRODUCTION

Chapter 1 explained that once a company is listed, it becomes subject to continuing obligations. Both the FCA (in UK MAR, the UK Prospectus Regulation and the DTRs, the Prospectus Regulation Rules and the UK Listing Rules) and the Stock Exchange (in the Admission and Disclosure Standards) impose continuing obligations on listed companies. As with the IPO process, however, the FCA and the Stock Exchange have worked together to dovetail their requirements. To what extent the company is subject to continuing obligations depends on the type of security, its listing category on the Main Market and sometimes the type of company. In this chapter we will continue to concentrate on the ESCC-listed company.

7.2 WHY HAVE CONTINUING OBLIGATIONS?

The continuing obligations exist to protect both existing and potential investors. They seek to ensure that there is an orderly market for investments (stability being crucial to investors' confidence in the markets) and that all investors have access to information at the same time (in the interests of fairness).

Put into context, it makes sense that listed companies should bear these obligations. Remember that their shareholder base is diverse, and the vast majority of shareholders will not be involved in the management of the company and may know little about its day-to-day running (see **2.6** above). They therefore require increased protection to ensure that their investment in the company is safe.

At first glance, there may seem to be so many continuing obligations that you might wonder why any company would choose to float. However, the restrictions of an ESCC listing can result in the ability to access sources of funding that may not be available elsewhere. Before embarking on the IPO process, a company should of course consider, as part of its pre-IPO preparation, whether it is capable of meeting the continuing obligations that will be imposed on it after the IPO. If it cannot or does not want to meet the ESCC listing requirements then there is always the option of the less regulated quotation on AIM. However, the obligations are certainly not meant to deter companies from listing. In practice, once companies have put in place the administrative processes to enable them to deal with the obligations, most find that meeting the continuing obligations simply becomes part of the day-to-day running of the business.

The level of regulation imposed on listed companies trading on the Stock Exchange through continuing obligations does vary over time. Controls were strengthened in light of the failure of regulators to prevent the global financial crisis of 2007/08 and the tendency of listed companies, particularly banks, to put themselves in a position which imperilled their very existence and severely damaged the economy. Since then there has been a dramatic drop in the number of companies listing on the Stock Exchange. This has led to occasional significant changes to the rules in an attempt to lure companies back to seek a listing. The latest overhaul was introduced by the FCA on 31 July 2024 with a new set of listing rules, the UK Listing Rules. These have reduced the obligations on listed companies, significantly in part.

The company will, of course, require advice on the continuing obligations from its advisers from time to time. If the company was impressed by the work of its advisers on the IPO, it may well retain those advisers on a permanent basis after flotation. Due to the day-to-day nature of the continuing obligations, the in-house legal department of the listed company will often take responsibility for ensuring that the company meets those obligations. However, where a second opinion is required, or where the in-house solicitors are not available, the company will often call on its external lawyers, who will be expected to know what the continuing obligations are and how to meet them. As is explained below, due to the need to meet the obligations in a timely manner, the company will often require advice on an urgent basis.

7.3 WHERE TO FIND THE CONTINUING OBLIGATIONS

The continuing obligations imposed on listed companies can be found in the CA 2006, Chapters 6–19 of the UK Listing Rules, the DTRs (including the Corporate Governance Rules) and in the Stock Exchange's Admission and Disclosure Standards. Chapters 11, 12 and 15–19 of the UK Listing Rules relate to special types of issuer or security and so fall outside the scope of this textbook. Chapters 7 and 8 of the UK Listing Rules, which deal with certain types of transactions, are discussed at **19.4** and **19.5** respectively. The remainder can be tackled more manageably if they are grouped together as follows:

(a) obligations with continuing application (see **7.4**);
(b) obligations requiring the disclosure and notification of information about the company (see **7.5**);
(c) obligations relating to the shareholders of the company (see **7.6**);
(d) obligations relating to financial information about the company (see **7.7**); and
(e) obligations in the Admission and Disclosure Standards (see **7.10**).

Please note that what follows in this chapter applies only to an ESCC-listed company unless otherwise stated.

The Association of General Counsel and Company Secretaries of the FTSE 100 (GC100) has produced guidelines to assist its members (who are employed by the biggest listed companies) in establishing procedures, systems and controls to ensure that they comply fully with the UK Listing Rules, the DTRs and UK MAR. The two sets of guidelines dated July 2016 cover 'establishing procedures, systems and controls to ensure compliance with Listing Principle 1' and 'MAR: guidelines on the requirement to maintain insider lists'. The guidelines are neither legally binding nor part of the FCA's Handbook, but the corporate lawyer should be aware of their existence.

7.4 OBLIGATIONS WITH CONTINUING APPLICATION

UK Listing Rule 6.2 sets out some of the requirements for an ESCC listing (see **Chapter 4**) which will continue to apply even after the IPO has taken place.

7.4.1 Admission to trading

You will recall that a condition for listing is that the shares are admitted to trading (UKLR 3.2.3R) (see **4.3.1.1**). UK Listing Rule 6.2.1R provides that it is a continuing obligation that the company's shares are admitted to trading at all times. This seeks to ensure that shares in a company are always freely marketable.

7.4.2 Independent business and controlling shareholder

UK Listing Rule 6.2.3R states that an ESCC-listed company must continue to carry on its business independently of any controlling shareholder at all times. This is a requirement for listed companies on first being admitted to the ESCC category of the Main Market under UKLR 5.3.1R (see **4.3.1.2** above). In addition, it must continue to have in place provisions in its articles regarding the election of independent directors (UKLR 6.2.5R).

7.4.3 Compliance with the Transparency and Corporate Governance Rules

Under UKLR 6.2.11G and LR 6.2.12R, an ESCC-listed company must comply with the disclosure requirements under UK MAR (that is, the general obligation of disclosure and related matters discussed at **7.5** below) and the obligations on persons discharging managerial responsibilities (PDMRs) to disclose certain dealings in shares which they own in their listed company (discussed at **7.8** below).

Under UKLR 6.2.13G and LR 6.2.14R, an ESCC-listed company must comply with the Transparency Rules (Chapters 4–6 of the DTRs) and the Corporate Governance Rules (Chapter 7 of the DTRs).

These continuing obligations explicitly reinforce compliance with the DTRs and the UK MAR disclosure obligations under an additional set of rules, the UK Listing Rules.

7.4.4 Contact details

The company must provide to the FCA contact details of at least one person which it nominates to be the first point of contact with the FCA in relation to matters of the company's compliance with the UK Listing Rules and the DTRs and the disclosure requirements under UK MAR (UKLR 6.2.19R). The chosen person must be knowledgeable about the company, the UK Listing Rules and the DTRs, and must be contactable on business days between 7 am and 7 pm (UKLR 6.2.20G). It is advisable for the company to appoint more than one person to perform this role, to ensure that there is always someone available.

7.4.5 Shares in public hands

One of the conditions for listing is that at least 10% of the company's shares are in public hands (UKLR 5.5.1R) (see **4.3.1.1**). UK Listing Rule 6.2.22R provides that the company must comply with this rule at all times. This underpins a fundamental rule of listing on the Stock Exchange. It seeks to ensure a sufficient market is maintained in the shares of the listed company.

7.4.6 Externally managed companies

UK Listing Rule 6.2.25R further requires an ESCC-listed company to ensure that the discretion of its board to make strategic decisions on behalf of the company has not been limited or transferred to a person outside the company's group, as it had to in order to join the Main Market under UKLR 5.2.1R.

7.5 DISCLOSURE AND NOTIFICATION OF INFORMATION ABOUT THE COMPANY

This encompasses one of the most important sets of continuing obligations imposed on listed companies. In order to ensure that shareholders and the market have all the information that they need to decide whether to buy, sell or continue to hold shares in a listed company, all manner of information about the company's activities, management and finances must be publicly disclosed. The rules seek both to protect investors and to maintain confidence in the financial markets. Disclosure of financial information is dealt with at **7.7**.

Some of these disclosure and notification obligations arise under UK MAR and some under the DTRs. As explained at **3.5.3**, the DTRs give effect to the Transparency Directive, introducing the Transparency Rules, and the Statutory Audit Directive and the Company Reporting Directive, introducing the Corporate Governance Rules. In addition, further obligations are set out in UKLR 9.6.

The most important requirement of all is the general obligation to disclose 'inside information' about the company under UK MAR, Article 17(1) (considered at **7.5.1** to **7.5.3**), and this obligation applies to both ESCC-listed companies and to companies quoted on AIM. You should be aware that this obligation under UK MAR applies to issuers of financial instruments (as defined in MiFIR). In other words, it is extremely wide in its application. We will look at it, as in the rest of the book, through the eyes of the listed company only.

7.5.1 The obligation to disclose 'inside information'

The general obligation to disclose inside information reflects Listing Principles 5 and 6, and ensures that the company gives information to the market as a whole (rather than just to a few select investors) and in a timely manner. Remember that there could be many hundreds or thousands of shareholders in the listed company, ranging from an institutional investor based in the City to a retired, civilly-partnered couple in Cleethorpes. The overwhelming majority of them will have no contact with the management who run the listed company on a day-to-day basis. They will therefore be reliant on information provided by the company to assess whether they should continue with their investment in the company. The provision of this information is not left to chance: the company is compelled continually to release important news regarding the company, be it good or bad, under this obligation. The release of this information to the market as quickly as possible will also help ensure that the share price accurately reflects the company's true value, thereby reducing the scope for people with inside knowledge of the company's affairs to profit secretly at the expense of others.

The obligation is set out in UK MAR, Article 17(1) and requires that, subject to UK MAR, Article 17(4) (see **7.5.2.8**), the company must inform the public as soon as possible of inside information that directly concerns the company (UK MAR, Article 17(1)).

The company must also disclose the information on its website and maintain it there for at least five years in accordance with UK MAR, Article 17(1).

7.5.2 Satisfying the requirements of the obligation

To comply with the obligation an understanding of the following issues is required.

7.5.2.1 What is inside information?

UK MAR, Article 7 defines inside information. It is information:

(a) of a *precise nature* (see **7.5.2.2**):

(b) which has not been made public;

(c) which relates, directly or indirectly, to an issuer of a *financial instrument* (see **7.5.2.3**) or to the *financial instrument* itself; and

(d) if generally available, would be likely to have a *significant effect* (see **7.5.2.4**) on the price of the *financial instrument* or the price of related investments.

The FCA believes that the company and its advisers are best placed to make an initial assessment of whether information is 'inside information' which therefore must be disclosed (DTR 2.2.7G). The board must carefully and continuously monitor any changes in the company's circumstances which may mean an announcement is required (DTR 2.2.8G). The criteria referred to in the above definition of 'inside information', which the board must understand in order to decide whether to disclose information, are set out at **7.5.2.2** to **7.5.2.4**.

7.5.2.2 What is information of a 'precise nature'?

UK MAR, Article 7(2) provides that information is of a precise nature if it EITHER:

(a) indicates a set of circumstances that:
   (i) exist; or
   (ii) may reasonably be expected to come into existence; OR
(b) indicates an event that:
   (i) has occurred; or
   (ii) may reasonably be expected to occur; AND
(c) is specific enough to enable a conclusion to be drawn as to the possible effect, on the price of the financial instrument, of that set of circumstances or that event.

It is therefore a two-part test and both parts must be satisfied in order for the information to be precise.

This, of course, is wider than the natural meaning of the words used. It underscores the very wide scope of this general disclosure obligation. In *Geltl v Daimler AG* (Case C-19/11), the ECJ, in considering the definition of inside information, decided that a reasonable expectation that an event will occur means there must be a realistic prospect that the event will occur, not merely a high probability. In addition, the information does not have to be entirely accurate to be precise (Upper Tribunal in *Hannam v Financial Conduct Authority* [2014] UKUT 0233 (TCC)).

In practice this test is interpreted widely and is therefore easy to satisfy.

In addition, under UK MAR, Article 7(2), precise information includes information on:

(a) a protracted process that is intended to bring about, or that results in, particular circumstances or a particular event, those future circumstances or that future event; and
(b) intermediate steps of that process which are connected with bringing about or resulting in those future circumstances or that future event.

This covers events or transactions which occur over a number of stages. Information about an intermediate step will be inside information itself if it satisfies the criteria for inside information (UK MAR, Article 7(3)). Examples of information relating to such intermediate steps are given in UK MAR, recital 17, for example information which relates to the state of contract negotiations, terms provisionally agreed in contract negotiations and the possibility of the placement of financial instruments (eg a listing of shares on the Main Market).

7.5.2.3 What is a financial instrument?

The UK MAR, Article 7 definition of inside information uses the term 'financial instrument'. Financial instruments are defined in UK MAR, Article 3(1)(1), which refers to those instruments specified in Part 1 of Sch 2 to the FSMA 2000 (Regulated Activities) Order 2001 (SI 2001/544), read together with Part 2. This includes 'transferable securities' which are defined in s 102A of the FSMA 2000 by reference to Article 2(1)(24) of MiFIR. Most importantly for our purposes it includes shares, but it also includes other investments such as options to acquire shares, and interest rate, currency and equity swaps.

7.5.2.4 What is a 'significant effect' on a price?

Here we are considering the effect on the listed company's share price of the inside information being made public.

There is no specific figure (percentage or otherwise) which can be set which constitutes a 'significant effect' on the price (DTR 2.2.4G(2)). The test will be satisfied if a reasonable investor would be likely to use the information as part of the basis of their investment decision (UK MAR, Article 7(4)). This is referred to as the 'reasonable investor test'.

Further guidance on how to apply this test is set out at DTR 2.2.5G and DTR 2.2.6G. In particular, DTR 2.2.6G provides that information about the following matters is likely to fulfil the reasonable investor test (and therefore likely to have a 'significant effect' on price):

(a) the company's assets and liabilities;
(b) the performance, or the expectation of the performance, of the company's business;
(c) the company's financial condition;
(d) the course of the company's business;
(e) major new developments in the company's business; or
(f) information previously disclosed to the market.

If a reasonable investor would be likely to use information as part of the basis of their investment decisions, that means it is information which would be likely to have a significant effect on price. There is therefore no need to show that the information is actually price sensitive.

Information which is therefore likely to amount to 'inside information' includes changes in management, acquisitions and disposals, group restructurings, litigation, loss of key customers/contracts, granting of intellectual property rights, development of new products, and receiving a takeover approach (see **22.3.1**). Examples of disclosure of this and other information can be searched for via the RNS section of the Stock Exchange's website.

7.5.2.5 How must the inside information be made public?

Having established that the listed company has inside information which directly concerns it, the listed company must under UK MAR, Article 17(1) inform the public as soon as possible. How is this done?

UK MAR, Article 17(1) sets out various requirements for making sure information is disseminated effectively. The company must ensure that the inside information is made public in a manner which enables fast access and complete, correct and timely assessment of the information by the public. It must not be combined with the company's marketing activities. It must also be posted on the company's website for at least five years.

Further details on the content and method of the required publication of inside information is contained in UK Commission Implementing Regulation (EU) 2016/1055.

In practice, listed companies will satisfy this obligation by making announcements via a Regulatory Information Service (an RIS) and posting it on their website.

7.5.2.6 What is a Regulatory Information Service (RIS)?

An RIS is either a Primary Information Provider (PIP) or an Information Society Service (ISS).

PIP

This is a service which has been approved by the FCA under s 89O of the FSMA 2000 and is on the list of PIPs maintained by the FCA on its website.

ISS

An ISS is an information service which disseminates regulated information and is established in an EEA country outside the UK.

Essentially, a PIP is a UK-based information service regulated by the FCA, and an ISS is a non-UK EEA-based information service regulated by an overseas authority. Listed companies use an RIS to discharge their continuing obligations to make announcements to the public. The best known RIS and PIP (for historical reasons as it used to have a monopoly) is the Stock Exchange's own Regulatory News Service, known as RNS.

In order to be approved as a PIP, the information service must comply with DTR 8.3R which in turn requires compliance with a series of detailed on-going obligations set out in DTR 8.4R. For example, the PIP must use the required 'headline information' in Annex 2 to DTR 8 when releasing information. For example, the release of information about the admission of shares to listing must be headed 'Official List Notice' and (with undisputed accuracy) information about an acquisition must be headed 'Acquisition'. Company announcements made through RNS can be accessed by anyone from the Stock Exchange's website, and all announcements can be accessed from the National Storage Mechanism (see **7.5.2.11** below).

Transparency Rule 6.3.2R requires that all regulated information (which includes information disclosed under UK MAR, Article 17(1)) must be disclosed in accordance with DTRs 6.3.3R to 6.3.8R which set out minimum standards. These are that the information must be:

(a) disseminated in a way ensuring it is capable of being disseminated as widely as possible;

(b) usually communicated in unedited full text;

(c) communicated in a way which ensures the security of the communication and provides certainty as to the source of the information; and

(d) communicated in a way which makes it clear it is regulated information and who the issuer is, and the date, time and subject matter of the communication.

7.5.2.7 What does a Primary Information Provider (PIP) do?

A PIP is an FCA-approved organisation which ensures that information from listed companies (such as regulatory announcements and company news) is disseminated to secondary news sources (Secondary Information Providers, or SIPs), such as Reuters, Bloomberg or Morningstar, at the same time. Due to the electronic nature of these communications, when the information is disseminated by the PIP it is often referred to as being 'sent down the wire'. Most importantly of all, the SIPs then pass on the information to the public at large.

7.5.2.8 Making the disclosure as soon as possible

UK MAR, Article 17(1) requires a company to disclose all inside information 'as soon as possible'. However, where the company is faced with an unexpected and significant event, a short delay may be acceptable if necessary to clarify the situation (DTR 2.2.9G(2)). The company should make what is called a 'holding announcement' where it believes there is a danger that inside information is likely to leak out before the facts and their impact can be confirmed. In such cases, the announcement should contain:

(a) as much detail of the subject matter as possible;

(b) the reasons why a fuller announcement could not be made; and

(c) an undertaking to announce further details as soon as possible (DTR 2.2.9G(2)).

The FCA should be consulted if there are any doubts about the timing of the company's announcements under UK MAR (DTR 2.2.9G(4)).

Obviously, there might be a temptation to delay disclosure of information which would allow the market to determine the true value of the company's shares when the news about the listed company is bad and which would result in a fall in the company's share price. However, a failure to follow the rules can be costly. Lamprell plc was fined over £2.4 million in 2013 for breaches of the forerunner to UK MAR, Article 17 and other provisions as a result of failing to a issue a profit warning for 18 days when senior management had become aware of a deterioration in the financial performance of the company. The delay in the announcement created a false market in the shares, which was demonstrated by a 57% drop in the company's share price once the announcement was made. Another company, JJB Sports plc, was fined £455,000 in January 2011 for breaches of the same rules, for delaying disclosure by over nine months of inside information relating to the price of a company which it bought.

It is also not possible to offset good news against bad news in order to avoid making an announcement. Companies should disclose both types of information and let the market decide whether they cancel each other out. This principle was reaffirmed in a decision to fine Wolfson Microelectronics plc in January 2009 for a breach of the forerunner to both UK MAR, Article 17 and Listing Principle 6. Wolfson had received notification from a customer that it was going to reduce demand for one of Wolfson's products but that it expected to increase demand for another of its products. Wolfson initially failed to make an announcement of the bad news that demand was going to be reduced. Further, in FCA Technical Note UKLA/TN/521.3 Assessing and handling insider information, the FCA emphasises that generally it is not acceptable to 'choreograph' the disclosure of offsetting information which individually meets the test under UK MAR, Article 17.

7.5.2.9 Delaying disclosure

Despite the obligation to disclose inside information as soon as possible, UK MAR, Article 17(4) provides that the company can delay disclosure if the following three conditions are met:

(a) immediate disclosure is likely to prejudice the company's legitimate interests;

(b) delay of disclosure is not likely to mislead the public

(c) the company can ensure the confidentiality of that information.

What are legitimate interests?

ESMA has produced some guidelines, 'MAR Guidelines: Delay in the disclosure of inside information', available on its website, which clarify the meaning of this term. They could include the following circumstances:

(a) the company is conducting negotiations, where the outcome of such negotiations would likely be jeopardised by immediate public disclosure. Examples of such negotiations may be those related to mergers, acquisitions, splits and spin-offs, purchases or disposals of major assets or branches of corporate activity, restructurings and reorganisations;

(b) the financial viability of the company is in grave and imminent danger and immediate public disclosure of the inside information would seriously prejudice the interests of existing and potential shareholders by jeopardising the conclusion of the negotiations designed to ensure the financial recovery of the company;

(c) the company has developed a product or an invention and the immediate public disclosure of that information is likely to jeopardise the intellectual property rights of the company;

(d) the company is planning to buy or sell a major holding in another entity and the disclosure of such an information would likely jeopardise the implementation of such plan; or

(e) a transaction previously announced is subject to a public authority's approval, and such approval is conditional upon additional requirements, where the immediate disclosure of those requirements will likely affect the ability for the company to meet them and therefore prevent the final success of the deal or transaction.

The Guidelines state that these examples are non-exhaustive, so there will be other circumstances where a delay in disclosure of inside information would be justified.

When will disclosure mislead the public?

In the same guidelines mentioned above, ESMA states that this will occur in at least the following circumstances, namely where the inside information whose disclosure the company intends to delay:

(a) is materially different from the previous public announcement of the company on the matter to which the inside information refers to; or

(b) concerns the fact that the issuer's financial objectives are not likely to be met, where such objectives were previously publicly announced; or

(c) is in contrast with the market's expectations, where such expectations are based on signals that the company has previously sent to the market, such as interviews, roadshows or any other type of communication organised by the company or with its approval.

This is not intended to be an exhaustive list.

What happens if the information can no longer be kept confidential?

Under UK MAR, Article 17(7), where disclosure of inside information has been delayed in accordance with UK MAR, Article 17(4) and the confidentiality of that inside information is no longer ensured, the company must disclose that inside information to the public as soon as possible. This includes a situation where a rumour about the inside information is sufficiently accurate. A holding announcement (see above) should be prepared where disclosure of inside information is being delayed so that the announcement can be released swiftly if there is an actual or likely breach of confidentiality (DTR 2.6.3G).

Where there is press speculation or market rumour concerning a company, the listed company should assess whether its general obligation to announce has arisen under UK MAR, Article 17(1). To do this, the company needs to assess carefully whether the speculation or rumour has given rise to a situation where the company has inside information (DTR 2.7.1G).

Knowledge that the press speculation or market rumour is false may not amount to inside information (but there is a possibility that the issuer's knowledge that a particular piece of information or story is false could, in very limited circumstances, amount to inside information). Where it does amount to inside information, the FCA expects that there may be cases where an issuer would be able to delay disclosure in accordance with UK MAR, Article 17(4) (DTR 2.7.3G).

Announcement of delayed inside information

When the delayed disclosure is made to the public, whether planned or because confidentiality could no longer be maintained, the company must notify the FCA immediately, giving specified details of the circumstances of the delay (UK MAR, Article 17(4)). There is an online form available on the FCA's website for this purpose. The FCA has the power to require the company to provide written explanations as to how the conditions in UK MAR, Article 17(4) were met (FSMA 2000 (Market Abuse) Regulations 2016 (SI 2016/680), reg 4).

Disclosure of inside information to third parties in the course of employment, profession or duties

Where a company discloses any inside information to any third party in the normal course of the exercise of an employment, profession or duties, it must make complete and effective public disclosure of that information, simultaneously in the case of an intentional disclosure, and promptly in the case of a non-intentional disclosure. However, this does not apply if the person receiving the information owes a duty of confidentiality, regardless of whether such duty is based on a law, on regulations, on articles of association, or on a contract (UK MAR, Article 17(8)).

The company can therefore disseminate such information to those who owe it a duty of confidentiality in the normal exercise of employment, profession or duties (including its lawyers and other advisers, and the people with whom it is negotiating (eg, the other contracting party)). It is only if there is a leak during these negotiations that the information must be publicly disclosed (see **7.5.1**). The company can, therefore, talk to its lawyers about an impending deal without having to make the information public through an RIS.

The lawyers who receive such information should note two things. First, it would clearly not be very professional to be responsible for any leak of information which would force the company to make an announcement. This means that the lawyers need to make sure that they limit the number of people in their team who have access to such information, and that everyone in their team is aware of the confidential nature of the information. A piece of advice from the Second World War seems pertinent here: 'Loose lips sink ships'. Expecting lawyers to keep quiet presents obvious challenges, but the importance of maintaining confidentiality cannot be over-emphasised. Disclosure Rule 2.5.9G highlights the fact that the wider the group of people to whom information is provided, the greater the risk that there will be a leak, leading to the triggering of the full disclosure obligation. Secondly, the lawyers themselves (and other advisers who receive information) cannot deal in the company's shares until the information has been made public.

An example of what this disclosure obligation under UK MAR, Article 17(1) can mean in practice, and the accompanying effect on share price, is set out below.

SuperGroup issues warning after mix-up

By Andrea Felsted and Adam Jones

Shares in SuperGroup lost more than a third of their value on Friday after the clothing retailer issued its third profit warning in six months, partly because of a mix-up between a plus sign and a minus sign in its forecasting.

The owner of the Superdry brand said that partly as a result of "arithmetic errors" its pre-tax profit would be about £43m for the year to April 29 – a marked reduction from its guidance in a previous profit warning in February, when it had predicted a figure of about £50m.

SuperGroup shares fell 38 per cent to 351.80p, after the fourth profit warning since its float just over two years ago, valuing the group's equity at £283m. The shares now stand about 30 per cent below their 500p float price.

The company said it was "terribly embarrassing to have to come to the market and say we have made a mistake".

It had made an error in its forecast for its wholesale business, where a negative figure had accidentally been treated as a positive during the forecasting process, it said. The adding-up mistake accounted for £2.5m of the profit shortfall.

Julian Dunkerton, chief executive, said the company had been growing fast but recognised that there were weaknesses that it was addressing, citing recent executive appointments that would bring more "formality" to the business.

But John Stevenson, analyst at Peel Hunt said: "This is the latest in a fairly long list of communication errors and problems, and from our point of view it is one too many."

Mr Dunkerton, who owns 32 per cent of the company, said he had no intention of resigning after the latest profit warning.

"I feel that would be a little harsh," he said. "Nobody is more affected than myself if you look at the share register. You must understand that my devotion to this company is 100 per cent, and I have nothing but its progress and its success embedded in my psyche."

SuperGroup said there was a separate profit shortfall of £2m in its wholesale business resulting from demand for stock coming later than expected, although it said most of those sales would fall into its next financial year.

In addition, SuperGroup said its margins had been hit by a greater-than-expected proportion of its sales going through lower-margin channels such as eBay and outlet stores, while an increase in operating costs partly linked to new executive hiring had also been a factor.

Together, these two issues would have a further impact of about £2m on profit, it said. The company said all the problems would have a "minimal impact" on its projections for its next financial year.

SuperGroup is awaiting the arrival of a new chief financial officer, Shaun Wills, who is due to start work at the company on Monday.

Source: *Financial Times*, 20 April 2012

7.5.2.10 Further guidance on handling inside information

There are two FCA Technical Notes which offer guidance on various aspects of inside information: UKLA/TN/521.3 Assessing and handling inside information and UKLA/TN/520.2 Delaying disclosure/dealing with leaks and rumours.

7.5.2.11 National Storage Mechanism

All regulatory announcements made by listed companies are stored in the online National Storage Mechanism (NSM) which is run by the FCA and can be accessed via its website.

7.5.3 Consequences of breaching the general obligation of disclosure under UK MAR, Article 17

7.5.3.1 Breach of UK MAR, Article 17

Any breach of the general obligation of disclosure could lead to the FCA imposing any of the sanctions set out at **3.6** above. Real-life illustrations of sanctions imposed may be found at **7.5.2.8** above and **7.11** below.

7.5.3.2 Criminal offences

Any breach of the general obligation of disclosure under UK MAR, Article 17 may also constitute a criminal offence under s 89 and 90 of the Financial Services Act 2012, which contain provisions relating to misleading statements and misleading impressions. This section is considered in more detail at **9.5**.

It may also give rise to an offence under Pt V of the Criminal Justice Act 1993 relating to insider dealing (see **Chapter 11**).

It is a criminal offence, under s 3 of the Fraud Act 2006, punishable by up to 10 years' imprisonment and/or a fine, fraudulently to fail to disclose information which a person is under a legal duty to disclose in certain circumstances. In extreme cases this could be relevant here.

7.5.3.3 Civil offences

Under s 90A of and Sch 10A to the FSMA 2000, a listed company will be liable to pay compensation to a person who has acquired shares, continues to hold shares or disposes of them and has suffered loss as a result of reliance on any untrue or misleading statement in, or omission from, any published information. This includes all information announced via an RIS, whether required to be so or not. It also covers information disclosed by any other means but whose availability is announced by an RIS. For example, a listed company's announcement via an RIS of the publication of its annual accounts means that liability under s 90A extends to all of the information contained in the accounts.

A company will be liable if a 'person discharging managerial responsibilities' (defined in para 8(5) of Sch 10A and including a director) for the company knew that the statement was wrong or misleading, was reckless as to whether it was, or knew any omission was a dishonest concealment of a material fact.

It is also an offence dishonestly to delay the publication of information which is released through an RIS under s 90A of the FSMA 2000.

Only the company can be directly liable for these offences, but a director could still bear liability to their company for negligence, or could have sanctions imposed on them if they were knowingly concerned in the breach under s 91(2) of the FSMA 2000 (see **3.6** above).

A group of institutional investors filed a claim against Tesco plc in October 2016, claiming compensation under s 90A arising out of an accounting scandal which came to light in 2014 when the company overstated its profits by at least £250 million. Tesco paid a £129 million fine over the matter as part of a deferred prosecution agreement with the Serious Fraud Office. It also agreed with the FCA to pay £85 million in compensation to shareholders.

Another example where such liability might have arisen happened with Currys plc, the retailer. It had to reissue its Christmas trading figures in January 2020 to say sales had gone down by 2% over the period, having previously announced that they had risen by 2%. Following the original announcement, Currys plc's share price rose 6%, and after the mistake was corrected 7 hours later the increase had dropped to 3%. Still, no legal action was taken. This was probably scant consolation for the very bad day in the office for the person who made the 'clerical error'.

The first example of a case based on s 90A/Sch 10A going fully to trial is *ACL Netherlands BV v Lynch* [2022] EWHC 1178 (Ch). The claimants were successful.

Failure to comply with the general obligation of disclosure under UK MAR, Article 17 may well constitute the civil offence of market abuse under UK MAR (see **Chapter 10**).

7.5.4 Insider lists

UK MAR, Article 18(1) provides that the listed company must compile a list of those persons who work for it who have access to inside information relating to the company.

The list should therefore include the company's own employees who have access to inside information. UK MAR, Article 18(2) also requires all persons 'otherwise performing tasks' who have access to inside information about it, such as advisers, accountants or credit rating agencies, to be included on the list. This of course will include the company's lawyers.

In addition, UK MAR, Article 18(1) requires 'any person acting on ... behalf' of the publicly traded company to maintain their own list of those who have access to inside information relating to the company. This means that the company's lawyers themselves (and other advisers and consultants) must draw up their own list setting out those in the firm with access to sensitive information about the company.

Why require these lists? Well, recital 57 to UK MAR states that they are:

> a valuable measure for protecting market integrity. Such lists may serve issuers ... to control the flow of inside information and thereby help manage their confidentiality duties. Moreover, such lists may also constitute a useful tool for competent authorities to identify any person who has access to inside information and the date on which they gained access.

In other words, on the latter point, the lists can help the FCA in its investigations of possible abuse of inside information. If the FCA asks to see the list then the company must provide it as soon as possible (UK MAR, Article 18(1)(c)).

'Access to inside information' is not defined in UK MAR. However, under DTR 2.6.1G, companies should establish effective arrangements to deny access to inside information to persons other than those who require it for the exercise of their functions within the company.

The list should be in the format set out in the templates in Annex 1 to UK Commission Implementing Regulation (EU) 2016/347. It must be kept electronically for at least five years from the date it is drawn up or updated.

The GC100: MAR: guidelines on the requirement to maintain insider lists (see **7.3**) contains guidance for the GC100 member companies on this requirement to maintain insider lists.

An AIM-quoted company does not need to compile such an insider list but it must be able to provide the FCA with one on request. This would need less content than the list for a listed company.

7.5.5 Notifications

In addition to the general obligation to disclose 'inside information' under UK MAR, Article 17, the UK Listing Rules and DTRs set out various specific disclosures, or 'notifications', that a listed company must make.

UK Listing Rule 1.4.8R and Transparency Rule 6.3.2R require that all regulated information (which includes information required to be disclosed under **7.5.5.1** to **7.5.5.10**) must be disclosed in accordance with DTRs 6.3.3R to 6.3.8R which sets out minimum standards of dissemination. The RIS system complies with these rules (see **7.5.2.6** and **7.5.2.7** above). This applies to companies with an ESCC listing.

7.5.5.1 Copies of documents

UK Listing Rules 6.4.1R and 6.4.2R provide that an ESCC-listed company must file a copy of the following documents with the FCA by uploading to the NSM (see **5.3.6** above):

(a) all circulars, notices, reports (at the same time they are issued); and

(b) resolutions, other than resolutions concerning ordinary business at an AGM (as soon as possible after the relevant meeting).

7.5.5.2 Notification relating to capital

Under UKLR 6.4.4R an ESCC-listed company must notify an RIS as soon as possible of the following information in relation to its capital:

(a) proposed changes to capital structure;

(b) any redemption of listed shares ; and

(c) the results of any new issue or offer of listed securities.

Under DTR 6.1.9R, the company must disclose to the public any change in the rights which attach to any class of listed securities.

Transparency Rule 5.5.1R requires the company to disclose the acquisition or disposal of its own shares, and DTR 5.6.1R requires the total number of voting rights and capital for each class of shares to be announced at the end of each month in which there has been an increase (eg, after a rights issue – see **17.7**) or decrease (eg, after a buyback). In addition, under DTR 5.6.1AR, this information must be disclosed at any time after there has been a transaction which produces a material change in the total number of voting rights. A material change is defined in DTR 5.6.1BG as an increase or decrease of 1% or more.

There is also a rule relating to notifications about underwriting.

7.5.5.3 Notification of major interests in shares

Chapter 15 considers Chapter 5 of the DTRs, which requires every shareholder (of a listed company) to notify the company if their or its shareholding:

(a) has fallen from above 3% to below 3%;

(b) has risen from below 3% to above 3%; or

(c) is over 3% and rises or falls to a different percentage level.

The notification referred to at **7.5.5.2** under DTRs 5.6.1R and 5.6.1AR enables shareholders to check whether a change in capital has triggered this requirement.

Transparency Rule 5.8.12R obliges the company to disclose to the public the information it receives under Chapter 5 of the DTRs. The company must make this disclosure in the usual way, that is, by notifying the information to an RIS as soon as possible and no later than the end of the next trading day after receipt of the information. See further at **15.7.1**.

7.5.5.4 Notifications of board charges and directors' details

The company must notify an RIS when a new director is appointed, an existing director resigns, retires or is removed, or there is a change to any important function or executive responsibility of a director (UKLR 6.4.6R).

A search of the RNS archive (available on the Stock Exchange's website) under 'Tesco plc' for the second half of 2014 reveals the turmoil in the board of directors following first a shake-up as a result of poor trading figures and then the revelation of an accounting scandal.

UK Listing Rule 6.4.8R provides that the company must notify an RIS of certain information about new directors, including details of certain current and past directorships, unspent convictions, bankruptcies and any public criticism by a regulatory or statutory body. UK Listing Rule 9.6.9R requires this information to be updated where necessary and to include details of a current director's new directorships in other publicly quoted companies. An example of this type of notification, under the old listing rules, is set out below:

> 18 August 2008
>
> Bradford & Bingley plc
>
> Bradford & Bingley Announces Appointment of New Chief Executive
>
> The Board of Bradford & Bingley plc is delighted to announce that Richard Pym has agreed to join the Board as Chief Executive with immediate effect.
>
> Richard Pym retired as Group Chief Executive of Alliance & Leicester plc (A&L) in July 2007. He joined A&L in 1992 as Group Finance Director, and became Managing Director of Retail Banking in 2001 and Chief Executive in 2002. He was responsible for fundamental changes in A&L's product and channel strategies, including the substantial development of internet capabilities.
>
> He is currently an independent non-executive director of Old Mutual plc, the international asset management group and non-executive Chairman of BrightHouse Group Ltd, an investment of private equity firm Vision Capital. He is also non-executive Chairman of Halfords Group plc, the UK car parts, car accessories and cycle retailer, and will be standing down from this role in due course. He is a qualified Chartered Accountant.
>
> Chairman of Bradford & Bingley, Rod Kent, said: "It has been a key priority for the Board to find a new Chief Executive, and we believe that Richard Pym is ideal for the role."
>
> Richard Pym commented: "Bradford & Bingley has developed strong customer franchises in savings and lending and I am delighted to have been invited to lead the business. I look forward to working with the Board and executive team in building a successful future."
>
> Pursuant to Listing Rule 9.6.13 (1), details of directorships held by Mr Pym in Publicly quoted companies during the past five years are set out below:
>
> Halfords Group plc (current)
> Old Mutual plc (current)
> Alliance & Leicester plc (ceased 2007)
> Selfridges plc (ceased 2003)
>
> Bradford & Bingley also confirms that there are no matters relating to Mr Pym that would require disclosure under Listing Rules 9.6.13 (2) to (6). Mr Pym does not currently have any beneficial interests in Bradford & Bingley shares.

7.5.5.5 Notification of lock-up arrangements

UK Listing Rules 6.4.11R and 6.4.12R provide that the ESCC-listed company must notify an RIS of any lock-up arrangements that have not already been disclosed, or of any changes to any lock-up arrangements previously disclosed. A lock-up arrangement is also known as an irrevocable undertaking (see **21.10**).

7.5.5.6 Notification of shareholder resolutions

The ESCC-listed company must notify an RIS as soon as possible after a general meeting of all resolutions passed (other than resolutions concerning ordinary business passed at an AGM) (UKLR 6.4.13R). Rather unhelpfully, there is no definition of 'ordinary business'. It is for listed companies to determine themselves what is ordinary. It usually includes, eg, the re-appointment of directors and the payment of dividends.

7.5.5.7 Change of name

If the ESCC-listed company changes its name, UKLR 6.4.14R provides that it must, as soon as possible:

(a) notify an RIS (stating the date on which the change has effect);

(b) inform the FCA in writing; and

(c) send the FCA a copy of the revised certificate of incorporation.

For example, on 21 January 2022 Royal Dutch Shell plc announced it had changed its name to Shell plc as part of a restructuring.

7.5.5.8 Change of accounting date

The ESCC-listed company must notify an RIS as soon as possible of any change in its accounting reference date. If the change extends the accounting period to more than 14 months, the company must produce a second interim report (UKLR 6.4.15R to UKLR 6.4.17G).

7.5.5.9 Transactions by persons discharging managerial responsibility

UK MAR, Article 19 requires PDMRs (see **7.8.2.1**) and persons closely associated (PCAs) (see **7.8.2.2**) to disclose certain transactions to their company, including their dealings in the company's shares. This is considered further in **15.7.1**. A listed company must pass on the information it receives to an RIS no later than two working days after the transaction (UK MAR, Article 19(3)).

7.5.5.10 Notification when the RIS is not open for business

It should now be clear that the method prescribed by the DTRs and the UK Listing Rules for making disclosures to the public is through the company's chosen RIS. What happens when the company suddenly discovers it needs to make an announcement, to comply with the 'as soon as possible' requirement, and the RIS is closed? The answer lies in DTR 1.3.6R and UKLR 1.3.4R, which provide that the company must ensure that it distributes the information to at least two national newspapers in the UK and to two newswire services operating in the UK. In addition the information should be notified to an RIS as soon as it re-opens. This is a useful paragraph to know about, as the client may well call its lawyers late at night (when its RIS has closed), needing to know very quickly how to effect the disclosure that same night.

7.6 OBLIGATIONS RELATING TO THE SHAREHOLDERS OF THE COMPANY

There a number of continuing obligations imposed on listed companies which relate specifically to the shareholders of the company.

7.6.1 Equality of treatment

Under Listing Principle 5 (UKLR 2.2.1R) and DTR 6.1.3R, a listed company must ensure equal treatment of all holders of shares who are in the same position.

7.6.2 Prescribed information to shareholders

Under DTR 6.1.4R, a listed company must ensure that all facilities and information necessary to enable shareholders to exercise their rights are available. A company can convey information to shareholders electronically (DTR 6.1.8R) (see **7.9.5**).

Transparency Rule 6.1.12R requires a listed company to inform its shareholders about the time, place and agenda of shareholder meetings, the total number of shares and voting rights, and the rights of shareholders to participate in the meetings. Disclosure and Transparency

Rule 6.1.13R requires a notice or circular to be sent to shareholders regarding the payment of dividends and the allotment of new shares.

7.6.3 Pre-emption rights

UK Listing Rule 9.2.1R provides that if an ESCC-listed company issues equity shares for cash, the company must first offer those shares to the existing equity shareholders pro rata (that is, in proportion to their existing holdings). This right reflects the statutory rights of shareholders under s 561 of the CA 2006. However, the shareholders of a listed company can agree to dispense with their pre-emption rights, and UKLR 9.2.2R makes it clear that any general disapplication by the shareholders of their statutory pre-emption rights will also dispense with the pre-emption rights under UKLR 9.2.1R.

For further information on pre-emption rights, see **Chapter 14**.

7.6.4 Transactions

In order to ensure that the rights of shareholders in ESCC-listed companies are fully protected, the UKLR Chapters 7 and 8 set out obligations on the company in relation to certain key transactions. These require the disclosure of information and, in one case, also the prior approval of the company's shareholders by way of an ordinary resolution. This approval may be necessary even though the CA 2006 or the listed company's articles do not require it.

UK Listing Rule 9.3 requires employee share schemes and long-term management incentive schemes to be approved by ordinary resolution before they are implemented, or alternatively the disclosure of information on the schemes in the annual report, depending on the terms.

UK Listing Rule 9.4 sets out requirements for the issue of further shares after the company has been listed, and these are discussed in more detail in **Chapter 17**.

Chapter 19 deals with further transactions (principally acquisitions and disposals) and related party transactions (UKLR Chapters 7 and 8 respectively).

7.7 FINANCIAL INFORMATION ABOUT THE COMPANY

7.7.1 Transparency Rules

The Transparency Rules, introduced to implement the Transparency Directive, require more information to be disclosed on the finances of the listed company, more often than was previously the case. The aims of the new rules are to increase investor protection and to promote more efficient investment across the EU. They therefore apply to ESCC-listed companies.

7.7.2 Annual financial reports

Chapter 4 of the DTRs requires an issuer whose transferable securities are admitted to trading on a regulated market and whose home Member State is the UK to publish an annual financial report (DTRs 4.1.1R and 4.1.3R) (often described as the Annual Report and Accounts). This includes UK companies whose ordinary shares are trading on the Main Market of the Stock Exchange, and so covers the companies dealt with by this book. It is important to remember that these provisions are in addition to those set out in Part 15 of the CA 2006 dealing with company accounts and reports. Part 15 includes specific provisions for both public companies and quoted companies.

A listed company's annual financial report is required to be published no later than four months after the end of each financial year (DTR 4.1.3R). The forerunner to the FCA, the FSA, issued a warning to listed companies in June 2008 that it would take action in the future against companies that did not comply with this rule. Some listed companies had only been submitting preliminary results rather than a full report by this deadline.

The annual financial report must include:

(a) its audited financial statements (the accounts) prepared in accordance with the applicable accounting standards;

(b) a management report; and

(c) a responsibility statement (DTR 4.1.5) made by the 'persons responsible in the company' (DTR 4.1.12R).

The responsibility statement must certify that, to the best of the persons' knowledge, the financial statements, prepared in accordance with the applicable set of accounting standards, give a true and fair view of the assets, liabilities, financial position and profit and loss of the issuer. It must also certify that the management report includes a fair review of the development and performance of the business and the position of the issuer, together with a description of the principal risks and uncertainties they face (DTR 4.1.12R). The FCA has stated in Technical Note UKLA/TN/501.1 Half-yearly and annual reports (available in the Knowledge Base section of its website) that it would usually be the directors who are the persons responsible.

The annual financial report must be kept publicly available for a period of at least 10 years.

There is a series of additional obligations relating to the annual accounts and reports placed on listed companies under UKLR 6.6. The Financial Reporting Council (FRC) has issued guidance (available on its website) on how this statement should be prepared.

7.7.3 Half-yearly reports

Chapter 4 of the DTRs requires an issuer whose shares are admitted to trading on a regulated market (ie the Main Market) and whose home Member State is the UK to publish a half-yearly financial report covering the first six months of the financial year (DTR 4.2.1R).

The half-yearly report must be made public as soon as possible but no later than three months after the end of the period to which the report relates (DTR 4.2.2R).

The half-yearly financial report must include:

(a) a condensed set of financial statements (ie accounts), which can be, but do not need to be, audited or reviewed by auditors;

(b) an interim management report; and

(c) responsibility statements (DTR 4.2.3R).

The interim management report must include an indication of important events that have occurred and their impact on the accounts, and a description of the main risks and uncertainties for the remaining six months (DTR 4.2.7R). It must also include details of major related party transactions (DTR 4.2.8R) (see **Chapter 19**).

The half-yearly report must be kept publicly available for a period of at least 10 years.

7.7.4 Exemptions

The periodic financial reporting requirements set out at **7.7.2** and **7.7.3** above do not apply in certain circumstances (DTR 4.4). These are not relevant to this book.

7.7.5 Liability

Liability for breaches of UK MAR may arise as set out at **7.5.3** above. Liability may also arise under s 90A of the FSMA 2000 (see **7.5.3.3** above).

Under s 463 of the CA 2006, directors can be liable to their company for any untrue or misleading statement made in or omissions from the directors' report, the directors' remuneration report (see 8.4 below), and summary financial statements taken from them.

A director will be liable only if:

(a) they knew the statement to be untrue or misleading, or were reckless as to whether it was untrue or misleading, or

(b) they knew the omission to be dishonest concealment of a material fact.

If the company fails to publish the required financial information within the prescribed time limits, the FCA may impose any of the sanctions set out at **3.6** above.

7.8 DISCLOSURE OF TRANSACTIONS BY PERSONS DISCHARGING MANAGERIAL RESPONSIBILITIES

UK MAR, Article 19 requires the notification of transactions conducted by persons discharging managerial responsibilities (PDMRs) of listed companies on their own account, or by a person closely associated with them (PCA). PDMRs include directors of the company. The reason for this obligation is that it provides 'not only valuable information for market participants, but also constitutes an additional means for competent authorities to supervise markets' (UK MAR, recital 59). This provision restricts when and how PDMRs can deal in the company's shares. It is in addition to the other rules which apply to dealing by such persons, such as:

(a) the market abuse provisions of UK MAR (see **Chapter 10**);

(b) the insider dealing regime of the CJA 1993 (see **Chapter 11**); and

(c) the statutory duties of directors.

The task of making sure the directors of the listed company comply with UK MAR, Article 19 is usually dealt with in-house, by the company secretary or an in-house lawyer, because the day-to-day nature of compliance means that it would be administratively difficult (and expensive) for external lawyers to police. However, external lawyers will be expected to advise on aspects of UK MAR, Article 19 on occasion, for example if they want a second opinion. As always, recourse should be made to the detail of the rules themselves. However, the following provides a flavour of those parts with which the external lawyer will need to be familiar.

7.8.1 Purpose of UK MAR, Article 19

Why is so much attention paid to the dealings of PDMRs, over and above the dealings of any other shareholder? Well, PDMRs, including directors, manage the day-to-day business of the company. They are best placed to know when they can trade in shares to make a personal profit. For example, say the directors receive an approach from a bidder with a lucrative offer to take over the company. Imagine at this point that the company's shares are worth £1 each and the offer is that bidder will pay £2 for each share. The shareholders do not know it yet, but they are about to double their money. The PDMRs, however, will know it, so what is to stop them from using their advantage over the other shareholders by suddenly investing huge amounts in the company before the offer becomes public knowledge? Answer: UK MAR, Article 19 (or its equivalent). The integrity of the market and the protection of investors require that directors do not abuse their position in this way. UK MAR, Article 19, therefore, restricts the ability of PDMRs to deal in the company's shares.

7.8.2 Applicability of UK MAR, Article 19

UK MAR, Article 19 applies to PDMRs (see **7.8.2.1**) and PCAs (see **7.8.2.2**).

Note that UK MAR, Article 19 will not apply to PDMRs once they leave the company. They will, however, still be caught by the market abuse and insider dealing regimes (see **Chapter 10** and **Chapter 11**). The FCA can also impose a financial penalty on any former director who, while a director, was knowingly concerned in a breach of the UK Listing Rules (FSMA 2000, s 91(2)).

7.8.2.1 Person discharging managerial responsibilities

A PDMR is defined in UK MAR, Article 3(1)(25) as:

(a) a member of the administrative, management or supervisory body [of the listed company]; and

(b) a senior executive who is not a member of the administrative, management or supervisory body of that entity, but who has regular access to inside information relating directly or indirectly to [the listed company] and the power to make managerial decisions affecting the future developments and business prospects of [the listed company].

Practically this will include directors and a few other managers of sufficient seniority to be classified as PDMRs. As regards a senior executive who is not a director, DTR 3.1.2AG(2) makes it clear that the nature, or even absence, of a contractual arrangement between them and the company will not prevent that person being a PDMR if they have regular access to the company's inside information and they can take managerial decisions affecting the company.

See **7.5.2.1** above for the meaning of 'inside information'.

7.8.2.2 Person closely associated (PCA)

A PCA is defined in UK MAR, Article 3(1)(26). Further guidance is given in s 131AC of the FSMA 2000. Note that the wider definition in s 252 of the CA 2006 does not apply here. The definition includes:

(a) certain members of the PDMR's family, that is their:
   - (i) spouse,
   - (ii) civil partner,
   - (iii) child or step-child under 18 (who is not married or civilly partnered),
   - (iv) relative with whom, as at the date of the transaction, they have shared a house for at least one year;

(b) any legal person, trust or partnership, the managerial responsibilities of which are discharged by a PDMR or PCA, which is directly or indirectly controlled by such a person, which is set up for the benefit of such a person or whose economic interests are substantially equivalent to those of such a person.

7.8.3 Obligation to notify

UK MAR, Article 19(1)(a) requires PDMRs and PCAs to notify both the listed company and the FCA of every transaction conducted on their own account relating to shares (and other financial instruments) of that listed company.

The scope of this provision is very wide indeed and further details of what constitutes a transaction can be found principally in Article 10 of UK Commission Delegated Regulation (EU) 2016/522. A limited number of technical examples are given in UK MAR, Article 19(7). At its simplest, it includes buying and selling shares, or agreeing to buy and sell shares.

7.8.4 Exception to the obligation to notify

There is no requirement for a PDMR or PCA to notify a transaction under UK MAR, Article 19 if the total amount of transactions in a calendar year does not exceed 5,000 Euros (UK MAR, Article 19(8)). In other words, transactions only need to be notified once the total has *exceeded* 5,000 Euros.

A PDMR and a PCA are treated separately for this threshold. So, for example, both a director who bought shares worth 4,000 Euros and her husband who bought shares worth 3,000 Euros would not need to make a notification as each of them has not exceeded the 5,000 Euros threshold.

ESMA has confirmed that, where a transaction is conducted in a currency other than the Euro, the exchange rate to be used to determine if the threshold is reached is the official daily foreign exchange rate which is applicable at the end of the business day when the transaction is conducted. Where available, the daily euro foreign exchange reference rate published by the European Central Bank on its website should be used (ESMA Questions and Answers on MAR Section 2 Q1).

The FCA has the power under UK MAR, Article 19(9) to raise the annual limit exempting PDMR and PCA notifications up to 20,000 Euros but has chosen for now to stick to the level of 5,000 Euros.

7.8.5 How and when to make a notification

The notification by the PDMR or PCA to the listed company and the FCA must be made promptly and no later than three working days after the date of the transaction (UK MAR, Article 19(1)). The listed company must make that information public within two working days of receipt of such a notification (UK MAR, Article 19(3)).

A template form for both notifications is annexed to UK Commission Implementing Regulation (EU) 2016/523 and contains the information required by UK MAR, Article 19(6). There is an online version of this form for both PDMRs and their PCAs on the FCA's website for use in the UK.

7.8.6 Transactions during closed periods

A PDMR is not allowed to make a transaction during a 'closed period' (UK MAR, Article 19(11)). In other words, the PDMR cannot, for example, buy or sell shares in their company during this period. However, there is no restriction on a PCA doing so.

7.8.6.1 Definition of closed period

A 'closed period' is defined as the period of 30 calendar days before the announcement of an interim financial report or a year-end report which the listed company is obliged to make public according to the rules of the trading venue where the issuer's shares are admitted to trading or national law. This will be the date of the announcement of preliminary financial results provided the disclosed preliminary financial results contain all the key information relating to the financial figures expected to be included in the final year-end report (ESMA Questions and Answers on MAR Q7.2 (available on its website)).

A company listed on the Main Market of the London Stock Exchange is obliged to produce an annual financial report and a six-monthly report. There will therefore be two 30-day periods in the financial year during which a PDMR cannot buy or sell shares in their company: prior to publication of the preliminary announcement of the company's annual results or the annual financial report (see **7.7.2**); and prior to the publication of the half-yearly report (see **7.7.3**).

7.8.6.2 Exceptions

A PDMR may conduct a transaction during a closed period in the circumstances set out in UK MAR, Article 19(12). This includes, on a case-by-case basis, due to the existence of exceptional circumstances, such as severe financial difficulty which requires the immediate sale of shares.

Further conditions to the use of this exception are set out in UK Commission Delegated Regulation (EU) 2016/522. For example, the PDMR must be able to demonstrate that the particular transaction cannot be executed at another moment in time than during the closed period.

Clarification of what amounts to exceptional circumstances is also given in UK Commission Delegated Regulation (EU) 2016/522. Circumstances shall be considered to be exceptional when they are extremely urgent, unforeseen and compelling and where their cause is external to the PDMR and the PDMR has no control over them.

The PDMR wishing to avail themselves of this exception must provide a reasoned written request to the listed company for obtaining its permission to proceed with immediate sale of shares during a closed period. When examining whether the circumstances described in the written request referred to are exceptional, the listed company shall take into account, among other indicators, whether and to the extent to which the PDMR:

(a) is at the moment of submitting its request facing a legally enforceable financial commitment or claim;

(b) has to fulfil or is in a situation entered into before the beginning of the closed period and requiring the payment of sum to a third party, including tax liability, and cannot reasonably satisfy a financial commitment or claim by means other than immediate sale of shares.

In practice it is likely to be very rare that circumstances will arise permitting the use of this exception.

7.8.7 Sanctions for breach of UK MAR, Article 19

The sanctions for breach of Article 19 are those for breach of the UK MAR disclosure requirements set out at **3.6** above.

7.9 COMMUNICATION WITH SHAREHOLDERS

As we have seen, the UK Listing Rules and DTRs set out many different circumstances when the company must communicate information to its shareholders.

7.9.1 The circular

The usual way of communicating with shareholders is by way of a document known as a circular. The UK Listing Rules define a circular as:

> Any document issued to holders of listed securities including notices of meetings but excluding prospectuses, listing particulars, annual reports and accounts, interim reports, proxy cards and dividend or interest vouchers.

Chapter 10 of the UK Listing Rules, entitled 'Contents of Circulars', prescribes general content requirements for all circulars (UKLR 10.3) (see **7.9.3**) and specific content requirements for particular types of circular (see **7.9.2**). This Chapter applies only to ESCC-listed companies.

7.9.2 When is a circular required?

The UK Listing Rules set out the circumstances when a circular is required. The following are the most commonly encountered by the lawyer. The Chapter 10 UK Listing Rule governing the specific content requirements of the required circular is provided in brackets. This is in addition to the information required by UKLR 10.3.

- Reverse takeover transactions (UKLR 10.4, UKLR 10 Annex 1 and Annex 2) (see **19.4.7.1**)
- Circulars regarding the purchase of own securities ('buyback') (UKLR 10.5)
- Authority to allot shares (UKLR 10.6.1R) (see **14.5.6**)
- Disapplying pre-emption rights (UKLR 10.6.2R) (see **14.6.15**)
- Reduction of capital (UKLR 10.6.3R)
- Capitalisation or bonus issue (UKLR 10.6.4R)
- Scrip dividend alternative (UKLR 10.6.5R)
- Scrip dividend mandate schemes/dividend reinvestment plan (UKLR 10.6.6R)

- Notices of meetings (including business other than ordinary business at an AGM) (UKLR 10.6.7R to 10.6.8G)
- Amendments to the company's constitution (UKLR 10.6.9R)
- Employees' share scheme arrangements (UKLR 10.6.10R to 10.6.13R)
- Discounted option arrangements (UKLR 10.6.14R)
- Reminders of conversion rights (UKLR 10.6.15R)
- Election of independent directors (UKLR 10.6.16R to 10.6.17R)

7.9.3 General content requirements

The basic content requirements of all circulars are prescribed by UKLR 10.3. To provide a flavour of what is in a circular, a sample of the requirements include:

(a) a clear and adequate explanation of the subject matter;

(b) a statement why the shareholder is being asked to vote, or otherwise why the circular is being sent;

(c) if voting or other action is required:

  (i) all information necessary to allow the shareholder to make a properly informed decision; and

  (ii) a heading drawing attention to the importance of the document and advising the shareholder to consult an independent adviser if they are unsure what action to take;

(d) if voting is required, a recommendation from the board as to how shareholders should vote, indicating whether the proposal is, in its opinion, in the shareholders' best interests.

Under UKLR 10.1.7G, the FCA can authorise the omission of information which would otherwise be required to be included if it would be against the public interest or seriously detrimental to the listed company (provided it would not be likely to mislead the public). The procedure in UKLR 10.1.8R must be followed.

7.9.4 FCA approval

Some circulars require prior approval by the FCA before the company can circulate them to shareholders, and others do not. The lawyer will need to be able to advise on whether a circular requires prior approval.

Once published, any circular, approved or otherwise, must be sent to the NSM for publication on its website (see **7.5.2.11**), and an approved circular must be sent to the company's shareholders as soon as practicable after approval.

7.9.4.1 Circulars which do require approval

UK Listing Rule 10.2.1R provides a short list of circulars which require prior approval. These include a 'reverse takeover' circular (see **19.4.7.1** below).

The approval process is detailed in UKLR 10.2.2R to 10.2.7R. The company must submit the draft circular to the FCA at least 10 clear business days before the intended publication date.

7.9.4.2 Circulars which do not require approval

All other circulars which are not listed in UKLR 10.2.1R do not require approval.

7.9.5 Electronic communication

The CA 2006 has introduced provisions in ss 308, 309, 333 and 1143 to 1148 which apply to all companies. They permit (but do not compel) documents or information to be sent from the company to the shareholder or *vice versa* electronically (including via e-mail and on a website), provided the conditions in Schs 4 and 5 are met.

These provisions are supplemented for listed companies by Chapter 6 of the DTRs. Transparency Rule 6.1.7G permits (but does not compel) listed companies to communicate with their shareholders by 'electronic means', provided certain conditions are met, the most important of these being (DTR 6.1.8R) the need for prior approval of the shareholders by ordinary resolution and for identification arrangements to be put in place. This is confirmed by UKLR 1.4.6G.

'Electronic means' is defined in the DTRs as a 'means of electronic equipment for the processing (including digital compression), storage and transmission of data, employing wires, radio optical technologies, or any other electromagnetic means.' A pretty impenetrable definition for most lawyers (except that rarity the lawyer-geek, who will doubtless be salivating at the prospect of explaining the full extent of these terms to their colleagues) – it includes e-mail, websites and a fax.

The CGI has produced a guidance note for electronic communication with shareholders under the CA 2006 and the DTRs (available on its website) setting out recommended best practice.

7.10 THE ADMISSION AND DISCLOSURE STANDARDS

As stated at **7.1** above, the Admission and Disclosure Standards contain continuing obligations which are additional to those set out in the UK Listing Rules. These obligations are set out at ADS Section 4, and they include that the company must comply with the Part 6 Rules. The other continuing obligations are mercifully very brief, compared with the requirements of the UK Listing Rules. They include:

(a) requirements relating to the timetable for what are referred to as 'corporate actions', that is, payment of dividends, open offers, rights issues and the like (ADS 4.7 and Sch 3);

(b) that the Stock Exchange will suspend the admission to trading of any shares which are suspended from admission to listing (ADS 4.12) (this is a mirror image of UKLR 6.2.1R – see **7.4.1** above); and

(c) that the company must pay an annual fee to the Stock Exchange (ADS 4.11).

7.11 SANCTIONS

7.11.1 Sanctions for breach of UK MAR, the UK Prospectus Regulation, the Transparency Rules, the Corporate Governance Rules, the Prospectus Regulation Rules or the UK Listing Rules

Sanctions for breach of these rules are set out at **3.6** above.

7.11.2 Sanctions for breach of the Admission and Disclosure Standards

The sanctions are set out in ADS 4.21. In the event of breach of any continuing obligation, the Stock Exchange may privately or publicly censure a company, fine it, or alternatively cancel the company's admission to trading.

7.12 FUTURE DEVELOPMENTS

Financial Services and Markets Act 2023

This Act intends, amongst other things, to revoke EU financial services law that had been retained following Brexit and replace it with UK-sourced rules. The then UK Government's vision was for an open, green, and technologically advanced financial services sector that is globally competitive, with this Act being at its core. The Act will result in fundamental amendments to the FSMA 2000. It will also grant the FCA much wider powers to enable it to draw up legally binding rules which will be included in the FCA's Handbook (eg the UK Listing Rules, new Prospectus Rules and Disclosure Guidance and Transparency Rules) rather than, as is currently the case, in legislation. Laws which will be repealed include the UK version of the Prospectus Directive, the UK version of MAR, the UK version of MiFIR and the related delegated legislation.

The FCA has already taken the first major step by introducing the new UK Listing Rules which replaced the former Listing Rules on 29 July 2024.

There is no indication at the time of writing that the FCA is considering significant amendments to the provisions currently in the UK version of MAR when it is repealed. These provisions may well be transferred to the FCA's DTRs.

You will be able to follow this process via the FCA's website.

CHAPTER 8

CORPORATE GOVERNANCE

8.1 WHAT IS CORPORATE GOVERNANCE?

Corporate governance refers to how a company is run. This includes not only how a company is directed and controlled, but also how a company is performing, how that performance can be enhanced, and how a company should account to interested parties such as shareholders and employees.

Corporate governance is relevant to all companies, but once a company is listed, those who control the company (directors and controlling shareholders) are not the same as, and therefore may have conflicting interests to, those who own the company (shareholders). This means that corporate governance is a particularly important issue for listed companies.

Corporate governance is periodically at the top of the news agenda. It jumped to the top of politicians' and regulators' concerns worldwide as a result of the global financial crisis in 2007/08 which triggered the deepest recession in the previous 70 years. Listed companies stood at the heart of the crisis, and poor corporate governance of banks and other financial companies has been identified as a major contributory factor. The consequences of these failings continue to reverberate today, and some of the largest UK banks only exist today thanks to government intervention. Although financial services companies were the main focus of many of the subsequent changes to corporate governance rules, it is worth noting that in the UK the rules were amended for listed companies beyond the financial services industry.

8.2 THE UK FRAMEWORK

Common law, the CA 2006, the UK Listing Rules (in particular, the continuing obligations and Listing Principles), the Corporate Governance Rules, the UK Corporate Governance Code, the Stewardship Code, the Large and Medium-sized Companies and Groups (Accounts and Reports) Regulations 2008 (SI 2008/410), the FCA's Code of Market Conduct and various non-legal guidelines produced by representative bodies of institutional shareholders (such as the Investment Association, the PLSA and PIRC) and the accountancy profession all contain provisions which address corporate governance issues. The UK Corporate Governance Code, the Corporate Governance Rules and the 2008 Regulations are discussed further below.

8.3 THE UK CORPORATE GOVERNANCE CODE

8.3.1 Nature

The UK Corporate Governance Code ('UK CGC') is the most prominent part of the UK corporate governance framework. It is a codification of best practice in corporate governance. The UK CGC does not have the force of law. Rather, as **8.3.4** below explains in more detail, companies are required to comply with the UK CGC or, if they do not, to explain their non-compliance. The UK CGC is not included in the UK Listing Rules but instead is available on the FRC's website (www.frc.org.uk).

8.3.2 Background

The UK CGC replaces the previous set of rules known as the Combined Code on Corporate Governance ('Combined Code'). There were four editions of the Combined Code: the original of 1995 and revised versions published in 2003, 2006 and 2008.

8.3.2.1 Background to the original Combined Code of 1995

The provisions of the original Combined Code were based on the findings of three reports, namely the Cadbury, Greenbury and Hampel Reports, which were commissioned in the 1990s to consider corporate governance in detail. The Hampel Committee 'combined' the recommendations of all three reports to produce the original Combined Code. This Combined Code was annexed to the listing rules in 1995, and the listing rules at the time were amended to refer to compliance with it. In 1999 a further report (the Turnbull Report) was commissioned, to provide guidance to listed companies regarding implementation of the requirements in the original Combined Code relating to internal control.

8.3.2.2 Background to the Combined Code of 2003

In 2002, massive financial scandals involving the US companies Enron and WorldCom put corporate governance in the spotlight again. In the UK, two further reports were commissioned immediately. The Financial Reporting Council commissioned the Smith Report (concerning audit issues) and the DTI commissioned the Higgs Report (concerning non-executive directors and remuneration). Those responsible for compiling these reports worked closely together to propose a consolidated revised code. Some of the proposals proved controversial, however, so the Financial Reporting Council set up a working group to revise the code further. The final text of this revised code was published in July 2003.

8.3.2.3 Background to the UK Corporate Governance Code

As part of the UK Government's response to the near collapse of the UK banking system in 2008, the Prime Minister appointed Sir David Walker in February 2009 to conduct a review of the corporate governance of UK banks (later extended to other financial companies) and to make recommendations (the 'Walker Review'). In his report of July 2009 published by HM Treasury, Sir David made 39 recommendations covering board size, composition and qualification; functioning of the board and evaluation of performance; the role of institutional shareholders; remuneration; and risk governance.

As a consequence of the Walker Review, the FRC undertook a further review of the impact and effectiveness of the Combined Code in March 2009, which applied to all listed companies, not just to those in the financial services industry. The FRC also took account of the European Commission's recommendations on the remuneration of executive directors of listed companies and the relevant recommendations of the House of Commons Treasury Committee's third report on the banking crisis.

As a result it replaced the 2008 version of the Combined Code with the UK CGC, which although based on the Combined Code, has been rewritten and contains a number of new provisions. The latest version, dated January 2024, applies to company reporting years beginning on or after 1 January 2025 (except Provision 29 which comes into force a year later).

8.3.3 Application

The UK CGC only applies to companies with an ESCC-listing on the Main Market of the Stock Exchange. These companies have an obligation to 'comply or explain' with the UK CGC under UKLR 6.6.6R (see **8.3.6** below).

In recognition that smaller listed companies can find it difficult to achieve full compliance with all of the demands of the UK CGC, certain provisions do not apply to ESCC-listed companies below the FTSE 350.

8.3.4 Structure

The UK CGC consists of an introduction and 18 principles of good governance. Each principle is supplemented by a set of supporting provisions.

The principles of the UK CGC are divided into five sections. Each section sets out the principles relating to:

1. Board Leadership and Company Purpose (five principles);
2. Division of Responsibilities (four principles);
3. Composition, Succession and Evaluation (three principles);
4. Audit, Risk and Internal Control (three principles);
5. Remuneration (three principles).

8.3.5 Associated guidance

The following guidance on the UK CGC is also available from the FRC website.

8.3.5.1 Corporate Governance Code Guidance

This is available on the FRC's website and provides guidance on the operation of the UK CGC and on certain provisions.

8.3.5.2 The FRC's Guidance on Board Effectiveness

This complements the UK CGC. Companies are not obliged to follow this guide, which offers assistance on how to apply the principles of the UK CGC, but they may find it helpful. The latest version of the guidance, published in July 2018, provides assistance on each of the sections of the UK CGC and suggestions of good practice. The primary purpose of the guidance is to stimulate boards' thinking on how they can carry out their role and encourage them to focus on continually improving their effectiveness.

8.3.5.3 The FRC's Guidance on Risk Management, Internal Control and Related Financial and Business Reporting

This guidance links what was formerly known as the Turnbull Guidance, which set out best practice on internal control, with emerging good practice for risk management.

8.3.5.4 The FRC's Guidance on Audit Committees

The latest version of this guide to best practice in relation to audit committees (formerly known as the Smith Guidance) was published in April 2016. It includes guidance on how to establish a committee, the relationship of the committee with the board, the role and responsibilities of the committee, and how it should communicate with shareholders. As with the Guidance on Board Effectiveness, companies are not obliged to follow this Guidance.

8.3.6 Compliance

8.3.6.1 The principles

While any company can choose to follow the provisions of the UK CGC, the UK Listing Rules provide that, strictly, it applies only to ESCC-listed companies. Even these companies are not subject to any formal requirement to comply with the UK CGC. Instead, the requirement is that any such company must include in its annual financial report (ie the annual report and accounts) a statement, known as a 'disclosure statement', which details:

(a) how it has applied the principles set out in the UK CGC in a way which would enable shareholders to evaluate how the principles have been applied (UKLR 6.6.6R(5)); and

(b) whether it has complied throughout the relevant accounting period with the code provisions set out in the UK CGC and, if it has not, which provisions it has not complied with, the period of non-compliance, and why it has not complied (UKLR 6.6.6R(6)).

The disclosure requirements are therefore referred to as the 'comply or explain' approach. This approach encourages compliance even though strictly it does not require it, because the requirement to disclose any failure to comply carries with it a risk of adverse publicity. The institutional investors have made it clear, however, that they do generally expect compliance and, in practice, companies which do not comply with the UK CGC without good reason are often subject to significant pressure from representative bodies of institutional investors such as the PLSA and PIRC.

In the introductory section to the UK CGC, the FRC acknowledges that an alternative approach to following a specific provision is permissible if good governance can be achieved by that other means. If this applies in a particular company's case then it should set out the background, provide a clear rationale for the action the company is taking and explain the impact that the action has had. The UK CGC goes on to state that shareholders should pay due regard to the company's individual circumstances when considering a company's explanation for a departure from recommended practice. Investors should engage constructively and discuss with the company any departures from the UK CGC's recommendations.

There is no prescribed form of disclosure statement, which, as with other aspects of the corporate governance regime, is intended to afford companies a degree of flexibility.

8.3.6.2 Corporate governance statement

The Corporate Governance Rules (see **3.5.3**) require a listed company to include a corporate governance statement in its directors' report in the company's annual report (DTR 7.2.1R), or in a separate report or on the company's website (DTR 7.2.9R), containing the information set out in DTR 7. It should be noted that there is some overlap with the requirements of DTR 7 and the UK Listing Rules and the UK CGC. This overlap is set out in Appendix B to the FRC's Guidance on Board Effectiveness. For example, DTR 7.2.4G explains that compliance with UKLR 6.6.6R(6) (see **8.3.6.1**) satisfies DTR 7.2.2R and 7.2.3R, which together require information about the corporate governance code followed by the company, how the company applies it in practice and an explanation of any non-compliance with the code. As the UK CGC requires this information to be included anyway, these provisions of the DTRs will usually be superfluous. However, where a listed company chooses to 'explain' rather than 'comply' with the UK CGC, it will have to show that it still meets the minimum requirements in DTR 7.

8.3.7 Key features

As explained at **8.3.4** above, the UK CGC provides guidance for good corporate governance in relation to board leadership and company purpose, division of responsibilities, composition, succession and evaluation, remuneration and audit, risk and internal control. The key features of the provisions relating to each area are discussed below, to provide a flavour of the issues the UK CGC addresses.

The UK CGC does, of course, go into some detail in relation to each of these, and other, issues; therefore any in-depth analysis must involve recourse to the UK CGC itself.

8.3.7.1 Section 1: Board Leadership and Company Purpose

This section comprises five principles (A–E) and eight provisions (1–8). It principally deals with the board's role and engagement with shareholders, workers and other stakeholders. It highlights the overarching role of the board of directors in taking the company forward but also emphasises the importance of shareholders and employees.

Some of the key requirements in this section are as follows:

Principle A A successful company is led by an effective and entrepreneurial board, whose role is to promote the long-term sustainable success of the company, generating value for shareholders and contributing to wider society.

Principle B The board should establish the company's purpose, values and strategy, and satisfy itself that these and its culture are aligned. All directors must act with integrity, lead by example and promote the desired culture.

Principle C Governance reporting should focus on board decisions and their outcomes in the context of the company's strategy and objectives. Where the board reports on departures from the Code's provisions, it should provide a clear explanation.

Principle D In order for the company to meet its responsibilities to shareholders and stakeholders, the board should ensure effective engagement with, and encourage participation from, these parties.

Principle E The board should ensure that workforce policies and practices are consistent with the company's values and support its long-term sustainable success. The workforce should be able to raise matters of concern.

Provision 1 requires the company to disclose in its annual report how opportunities and risks to the future success of the business have been addressed, the sustainability of the company's business and how its governance contributes to the delivery of its strategy.

Provision 2 requires the company to disclose in its annual report how it assesses and monitors the company's culture and how the desired culture has been embedded. It also requires that the management aligns policy, practices or behaviour of the business with the company's purpose, values and strategy.

Provision 3 requires the chair to regularly engage with major shareholders to obtain their views on governance and performance against the company's strategy.

An example of how not to do this was provided by Mike Ashley of Frasers Group plc, the retailer, in 2007. Following the company's IPO (when it was Sports Direct International plc), the share priced almost halved in the following six months. In the face of criticism from investors about the lack of transparency in the company, Ashley gave an interview to the Sunday Times, saying 'I've got balls of steel. Some investors have been great and supportive. But some of these City people act like a bunch of cry babies.'

Provision 4 requires a further disclosure in the company's annual report but only if 20% or more of the votes have been cast against the board's recommendation for a shareholder resolution. After the board has consulted with shareholders to understand the reasons behind the result, the board must explain what impact the shareholders' feedback from the consultation has had on the board and its proposed actions.

Provision 5 requires the company to explain in the company's annual report how employees' and other stakeholders' interests have been considered by the board in its decision making.

Provision 6 requires the board to enable its workforce to raise concerns in confidence and, if they wish, anonymously, together with a procedure to investigate those concerns.

Provision 7 requires the board to ensure conflicts of interest are identified and that third parties do not compromise independent judgement of the directors.

Provision 8 provides that any unresolved concerns of a director on board operation or management should be recorded in the board minutes.

8.3.7.2 Section 2: Division of Responsibilities

This section comprises four principles (F–I) and eight provisions (9–16). It addresses the separation of roles on the board, non-executive directors and the importance of the independence of directors. Some of the key requirements in this section are as follows:

Principle F The chair leads the board and is responsible for its overall effectiveness in directing the company. They should demonstrate objective judgement throughout their tenure and promote a culture of openness and debate. In addition, the chair facilitates constructive board relations and the effective contribution of all non-executive directors, and ensures that directors receive accurate, timely and clear information.

Principle G The board should include an appropriate combination of executive and non-executive (and, in particular, independent non-executive) directors, such that no one individual or small group of individuals dominates the board's decision-making. There should be a clear division of responsibilities between the leadership of the board and the executive leadership of the company's business.

Principle H Non-executive directors should have sufficient time to meet their board responsibilities. They should provide constructive challenge, strategic guidance, offer specialist advice and hold management to account.

Principle I The board, supported by the company secretary, should ensure that it has the policies, processes, information, time and resources it needs in order to function effectively and efficiently

Provision 9 states that the role of the chair and chief executive should be held by separate individuals.

The chair and the chief executive are both responsible for the leadership of the company, but in different ways. While the chief executive is responsible for running the business, the chair must ensure that the board runs effectively.

There has been much discussion over the importance of splitting these roles. It is, for example, less common for this to happen in US listed companies. The debate has, however, now largely been settled in the UK, but sometimes even the bluest of blue-chip listed companies is prepared to run the risk of incurring the wrath of its investors by going against this core principle of the UK CGC. Sir Stuart Rose, former Chair and Chief Executive of M&S, survived a shareholder resolution at its 2009 AGM which was proposed for M&S's breach of this principle: 37.7% of shareholders voted against Sir Stuart Rose's dual role, while 62.3% voted in favour. Sir Stuart had previously noted that it had even resulted in him being described as the 'Robert Mugabe of retail' (after the notorious former President of Zimbabwe). This remains an exceptional step to take, and in M&S's case signified the depth of its worries at the time about its future trading performance in an increasingly tough economic climate.

More recently, Matthew Moulding, the founder of THG plc (formerly The Hut Group) (the health and beauty firm), remained both Chair and CEO of THG plc since its £5.4 billion IPO in September 2020. This resulted in strong push back from its institutional shareholders, particularly as initial enthusiasm about the firm evaporated and the share price plummeted to well below its IPO price. At the time of writing, the company is searching for an individual to become chair instead of the current CEO.

Principle F emphasises the role of the chair as a leader of the board. Provision 3 (see **8.3.7.1** above) explains that the chair has a further important role as a channel of communication between the shareholders and the board.

More detailed guidance on the role of the chair is set out in the FRC's Guidance on Board Effectiveness (see **8.3.5.2**). For example, the chair's responsibilities include drawing up the agenda for board meetings and ensuring that there is sufficient time to discuss the matters. The chair should shape the culture in the boardroom, and they will also be responsible for ensuring contributions, particularly of non-executive directors, and that there are good relations between executive and non-executive directors.

Provision 9 also makes clear that, when appointed, the chair should be independent, measured against criteria set out in Provision 10 of the UK CGC. For example, the chair should not have been an employee in the last five years; not have close family ties with any of the company's advisers, directors or senior employees; not have a material business relationship with the company.

Provision 9 also states that the chief executive should not go on to become the chair. This principle was introduced by the Higgs Report and was controversial, as many listed companies had a tradition of 'sending the chief executive upstairs' to be chair. This provision can be waived in exceptional circumstances if the board consults with major shareholders first, and discloses the reasons behind the decision to all shareholders and on the company's website.

Provision 11 requires that the board should consist of a balance of executive and non-executive directors (commonly referred to as 'NEDs') (in particular *independent* NEDs). At least half of the board should comprise independent NEDs.

The role of the NED is set out at Provision 13. It requires NEDs to scrutinise and hold to account the performance of management and individual executive directors against agreed performance targets. They also have a key role in appointing and removing directors. Under Section 3 of the UK CGC (see **8.3.7.3** below), they must also satisfy themselves that the financial and risk control mechanisms are robust. Section 4 of the UK CGC (see **8.3.7.4** below) further requires NEDs to determine appropriate levels of executive pay.

Provision 12 states that the board should appoint one of the NEDs to be the senior independent director to provide a sounding board for the chair and to act as a go-between for the directors and the shareholders.

Provision 13 also requires that the chair should hold some meetings with the NEDs alone, where the executive directors are not present.

The NEDs must also appraise the performance of the chair at least annually (Provision 12).

Additional guidance on the role of the NED is set out in the FRC's Guidance on Board Effectiveness (see **8.3.5.2**).

The role of the NED is not a particularly easy one in today's climate. Companies need to take care to select a suitable NED who will take the role seriously and be able to meet the dramatically increased expectations of their performance and legal duties in light of the perceived failings of NEDs in preventing the poor decision-making which ultimately led to the global financial crisis.

It is worth remembering that in company law a NED is treated no differently from an executive director and shares the same potential liability. In light of these risks the CGI has produced guidance for prospective directors (both NED and executive), 'Guidance on joining the right board', available on the CGI's website at <www.cgi.org.uk>, to help them to evaluate whether they are joining the board of a listed company which meets their skills and requirements.

Compliance with these requirements of the UK CGC is the reason that companies tend to announce new NED appointments prior to the IPO.

8.3.7.3 Section 3: Composition, Succession and Evaluation

This section comprises three principles (J–L) and seven provisions (17–23). It covers composition of the board, the appointment process for new directors, re-election of existing directors, evaluation of the board's performance and diversity on the board.

Some of the key requirements in this section are as follows:

Principle J Appointments to the board should be subject to a formal, rigorous and transparent procedure, and an effective succession plan should be maintained for board and senior management. Both appointments and succession plans should be based on merit and objective criteria. They should promote diversity, inclusion and equal opportunity.

Principle K The board and its committees should have a combination of skills, experience and knowledge. Consideration should be given to the length of service of the board as a whole and membership regularly refreshed.

Principle L Annual evaluation of the board should consider its composition, diversity and how effectively members work together to achieve objectives. Individual evaluation should demonstrate whether each director continues to contribute effectively.

Appointments to the board

The procedure for appointment of directors should be formal, rigorous and transparent (Principle J). A nomination committee, a majority of which are independent NEDs, should lead the appointment process (Provision 17).

In addition, the UK CGC seeks to encourage listed companies to improve diversity on their boards (Principle J). Principle L and Provision 23 require a special section of the company's Annual Report to include a description of the implementation of the board's policy on diversity and inclusion, and the gender balance in senior management. Although there is currently no suggested or compulsory quota for women on boards as in some other countries, these references represent an acknowledgement of how woefully underrepresented women and minorities are on the boards of UK listed companies (see further **8.7** below).

Evaluation

Directors' performance, both as a board and individually, board committees and the chair, should be evaluated formally and rigorously every year (Provision 21).

The board of a FTSE 350 company should be subject to an external review every three years (Provision 21).

Re-election

Membership of the board should be regularly refreshed (Principle K), and all directors should be subject to annual re-election by the shareholders (Provision 18). The votes will take place at the company's AGM. The hope is that this requirement will encourage directors to engage more with their shareholders, particularly institutional investors.

The chair should not hold office for more than nine years (Provision 19).

8.3.7.4 Section 4: Audit, Risk and Internal Control

This section comprises three principles (M–O) and eight provisions (24–31). It addresses the auditing of the company's finances and risk management within the company.

As explained at **8.3.5.4** above, it is useful to consult the FRC's Guidance on Audit Committees when considering what the UK CGC has to say on this issue. Some of the key requirements in this section are as follows:

Principle M The board should establish formal and transparent policies and procedures to ensure the independence and effectiveness of internal and external audit functions and satisfy itself on the integrity of financial and narrative statements.

Principle N The board should present a fair, balanced and understandable assessment of the company's position and prospects.

Principle O The board should establish and maintain an effective risk management and internal control framework, and determine the nature and extent of the principal risks the company is willing to take in order to achieve its long-term strategic objectives.

There should be an audit committee with at least three members (unless the company is below the FTSE 350, in which case there should be at least two members) who are all independent NEDs. At least one member should have recent and relevant financial experience, and the audit committee as a whole shall have competence relevant to the sector in which the company operates (Provision 24).

The main roles and responsibilities of the audit committee are set out in Provision 25 and include monitoring the integrity of the company's financial statements and overseeing the appointment process for the auditor. A section in the company's annual report should describe the committee's work in discharging those responsibilities (Provision 26). The lawyer may be required to draft the terms of reference for the audit committee. The CGI has published standard form terms of reference for audit committees.

The board should explain in the annual report that they consider the annual report and accounts to be fair, balanced and understandable and provides the necessary information for shareholders to assess the company's position, performance, business model and strategy (Provision 27).

The implementation of the EU's Statutory Audit Directive in the UK through the Corporate Governance Rules introduced a statutory requirement for an Audit Committee for listed companies, including at least one independent member and one member with suitable accounting experience. A statement must be made publicly disclosing which body carries out these functions and how it is comprised. This may be included with the corporate governance statement (see **8.3.6.2**). There is of course an overlap with the provisions of the UK CGC, and the FCA states in DTR 7.1.7G that compliance with the UK CGC's provisions for audit committees will result in compliance with those in the Corporate Governance Rules. It is worth noting that the UK CGC places additional requirements on listed companies beyond those in the EU-inspired Corporate Governance Rules.

8.3.7.5 Section 5: Remuneration

This section comprises three principles (P–R) and 10 provisions (32–41) and covers remuneration of the board and senior management. Some of the key requirements in this section are as follows:

Principle P Remuneration policies and practices should be designed to support strategy and promote long-term sustainable success. Executive remuneration should be aligned to company purpose and values, and be clearly linked to the successful delivery of the company's long-term strategy.

Principle Q A formal and transparent procedure for developing policy on executive remuneration and determining director and senior management remuneration should be established. No director should be involved in deciding their own remuneration outcome.

Principle R Directors should exercise independent judgement and discretion when authorising remuneration outcomes, taking account of company and individual performance, and wider circumstances.

A remuneration committee, of at least three (two in the case of a company below the FTSE 350) independent NEDs, should determine the remuneration of directors and senior management (Provisions 32 and 33).

Executive directors' remuneration should be designed to promote long-term shareholdings by the director (Provision 36).

In designing executive director remuneration policy, the remuneration committee should ensure it is clear, easy to understand, addresses risks of excessive rewards, is predictable, proportionate, not reward poor performance and be aligned to the company's culture (Provision 40).

NEDs' remuneration should be set in accordance with the company's articles or by the board (Provision 34).

Notice periods under service contracts should not exceed one year. The remuneration committee should avoid rewarding poor performance in the event of an early termination of a director's service contract (Provision 40).

Remuneration, and indeed the remuneration committee, has been creating headlines well beyond the financial pages of the press for some years now. The result of the remuneration committees' actions has been a phenomenal rise in the pay and benefits of listed company directors. The average remuneration for FTSE 100 chief executives in 2023 was over 120 times greater than that of the average full-time worker in the UK, standing at over £4.1 million per year (including pay, bonus and awards under share-based performance schemes). In 1998 it was just 45 times greater.

For further information on directors' remuneration, see **8.4**.

8.4 DIRECTORS' REMUNERATION

8.4.1 Background

There are rules governing the remuneration of listed company directors in both the UK Listing Rules and the UK CGC (see **8.3.7.5**). Listed company directors must also comply with the rules set out in Chapters 6 and 9 of Pt 15 of the CA 2006.

In addition, the Large and Medium-sized Companies and Groups (Accounts and Reports) Regulations 2008 (SI 2008/410) supplement the regime regulating the remuneration of directors of listed companies. Finally, the IPCs regularly produce non-binding guidance for their members on directors' remuneration to assist them in deciding whether to vote in favour of or against shareholder resolutions on the matter.

The issue of excessive remuneration for directors of listed companies regularly rises to the top of the political agenda in the UK. Not least because in recent years institutional investors have joined in the criticism. In response to this, there have been changes to the law in the UK introducing a much more rigorous regime of transparency and shareholder control. Some of the changes have been made in response to EU legislation, for example the Shareholders Rights Directive II which had to be implemented by 10 June 2019 in all Member States including the UK.

8.4.2 Nature of the CA 2006 rules and the 2008 Regulations

The latest version of the CA 2006 rules and the 2008 Regulations apply in respect of financial years beginning on or after 1 January 2019.

The CA 2006 rules and the 2008 Regulations (that part which applies to remuneration) apply to 'quoted companies', which are defined by s 385(2) of the CA 2006 as including not only companies admitted to the Official List and the Main Market (referred to as 'listed companies' in this book, see **1.3** above), but also companies listed on a market in an EEA Member State and NYSE and NASDAQ in the USA. The scope of the CA 2006 rules and the 2008 Regulations is therefore wider than the scope of the UK Listing Rules and the UK CGC (see **8.3.5** above). The CA 2006 rules and the 2008 Regulations do not, however, apply to companies quoted on AIM.

8.4.3 Key features

The CA 2006 rules have three key requirements, set out below. Any director of a company which fails to comply with these requirements will be guilty of an offence under the CA 2006 and liable to a fine. A director can also be personally liable to the company for any loss it suffers under s 437 of the CA 2006 for any false or misleading statements in the report, or an omission from it, if they knew or were reckless as to whether the statement was false or misleading, or knew the omission to be a dishonest concealment of a material fact.

8.4.3.1 Directors' remuneration report

Under s 420 of the CA 2006, the company must produce an annual directors' remuneration report (DRR) which contains the information required by Sch 8 to the 2008 Regulations, made under s 421 and s 422A(4) of the CA 2006, in the form prescribed by the Regulations. The information which the report must disclose is considerable, and goes beyond the disclosure requirements of both the UK Listing Rules and the UK CGC. The DRR has two parts, an annual report on remuneration and a directors' remuneration policy.

Annual report on remuneration

This must set out the directors' actual remuneration for the financial year in a specified table form. It must include a single figure for total remuneration for each director together with a breakdown for salary, taxable benefits (eg expenses), annual bonus, long-term performance related awards (eg shares) and pension benefits. Each director's remuneration figures, including the total, are to be listed on a single line in the table for ease of comparison. The preceding year's figures must also be included. The company can use a separate table for the NEDs. Additional comparative graphs and tables must also be included (eg comparing the CEO's remuneration to company performance).

The annual report must also include a statement of how the directors' remuneration policy (see below) is being implemented for the coming year and details of the required shareholder votes (see **8.4.3.3** below) together with the board's response to a significant negative vote.

Directors' remuneration policy

This must be drawn up and included in the annual report when it is to be voted upon by the shareholders, which must be at least once every three years (see **8.4.3.3** below). Again there are rules as to the content and presentation of the information in the policy. For example, for each of the elements of remuneration mentioned in the table in the annual report, the policy must address how that element supports the company's short- and long-term objectives, and the policy must contain details of how termination payments for loss of office will be approached.

There must also be illustrations of how the remuneration policy would affect each executive director if the company's share price rose 50% over the period of performance targets.

The report forms part of the annual report and accounts and must be filed at Companies House (CA 2006, s 439).

8.4.3.2 Audit of DRR

Under s 497 of the CA 2006, the company's auditors must, in addition to auditing the company's accounts and financial information, audit the DRR and state in its report to shareholders whether the information set out in Pt 3 of Sch 8 to the 2008 Regulations relating to the directors' single total remuneration figure, pension benefits, payments for loss of office and other specified matters in the report has been properly prepared in accordance with the CA 2006.

This is of course part of the control mechanism on listed companies to ensure that they reveal all the necessary information correctly.

8.4.3.3 Shareholder approval

Every listed company must send a copy of its annual accounts and reports (including, under CA 2006, s 471(3), the DRR) to every shareholder (CA 2006, s 423). The company must then table the DRR at a general meeting (CA 2006, s 437). Two separate shareholder votes need to be considered, one for each part of the DRR.

Annual report on remuneration

Once a year the company must obtain approval of the annual report on remuneration (by ordinary resolution) of the shareholders (CA 2006, s 439). Note that this requirement does not mean that any specific director's service contract is conditional upon shareholder approval (CA 2006, s 439). If shareholders do not approve the annual report on remuneration, the effect is advisory only. In other words, the board can ignore the vote. One example was the house builder Crest Nicholson plc. In March 2017, 58% of the votes cast were against its remuneration report due to changes to the directors' bonus scheme in order to make it much easier to meet the performance targets. The company paid the bonuses regardless of the vote. Although the board may ignore the vote, such action may have other consequences, both practical and legal, as explained below.

Directors' remuneration policy

Under s 439A of the CA 2006, at least once every three years the shareholders must hold a binding vote by ordinary resolution on the directors' remuneration policy for the company, or sooner if it wishes to alter the policy.

According to DBT, if the ordinary resolution is not passed, the company can either:

(a) continue to use the previously approved policy;

(b) continue with the previous policy and seek shareholder approval of specific remuneration; or

(c) put a revised policy forward for a vote at a later GM (after the AGM).

Once the company has received approval for its new remuneration policy, any obligation to make a payment that would be in contravention of the policy will have no effect under s 226E(1) of the CA 2006. If, however, a payment has already been made, it is deemed to be held by the director on trust for the company, and any director who authorised the payment will be jointly and severally liable to indemnify the company for any loss resulting from the making of the payment under s 226E(2) of the CA 2006.

Note also that under s 439A(2) of the CA 2006, if the ordinary resolution on shareholders approval of the directors' remuneration report is not passed, it will need to put the directors' remuneration policy back to the shareholders the following year for re-approval in a binding vote.

It seems that these powers may be starting to curb the problem of excessive executive pay in some listed companies. This is because institutional investors are becoming much more active in this area in light of a public outcry at the bloated bonuses and remuneration packages of some directors of listed companies even when the companies' share price had dropped sharply.

8.4.3.4 Further measures

There are additional measures which apply to and are being considered for certain financial services companies including banks (some of which are listed on the Main Market). For example, there are a number of Remuneration Codes which require such companies to have in place remuneration policies that are consistent with effective risk management. These codes of practice are designed to ensure that these companies' boards of directors focus more closely both on ensuring that the total amount distributed by a firm is consistent with good risk management and sustainability, and that individual compensation practices provide the right incentives. The codes were introduced in an attempt to try and limit the remuneration policies which encourage excessive risk-taking and which are believed to have played a significant role in provoking the global financial crisis in 2007/08.

8.5 INSTITUTIONAL INVESTORS

As explained at **8.3.6.1** above, it is really the institutional investors (see **2.6.2**) who enforce the UK CGC by making life difficult for those companies who do not comply. Regulators are looking to these investors to assist listed companies in achieving better corporate governance.

8.5.1 UK Stewardship Code

As part of the review of corporate governance in the UK and the subsequent introduction of the UK CGC, the ISC's Code on the Responsibilities of Institutional Investors formed the basis of a new voluntary code published by the FRC, the UK Stewardship Code (see the FRC's website, www.frc.org.uk).

The purpose of the Stewardship Code is to improve corporate governance and long-term returns to shareholders through promoting better dialogue between shareholders and the boards of directors of listed companies. The Stewardship Code defines stewardship as the responsible allocation, management and oversight of capital to create long-term value for clients and beneficiaries leading to sustainable benefits for the economy, the environment and society. The Stewardship Code applies to firms who manage assets on behalf of institutional investors, but the FRC encourages all institutional investors to comply. The Stewardship Code operates on an 'apply and explain' basis. Institutional investors who wish to apply the Stewardship Code must submit an annual compliance report to the FRC. If accepted, the institutional investor becomes a signatory to the Code and the report is made public.

The principles include managing conflicts of interest and monitoring investee companies. The latest version is dated 1 January 2020.

The CGI has published guidance on its website entitled Enhancing Stewardship Dialogue. It is intended to provide practical advice on creating a more meaningful dialogue between companies and institutional investors on strategy and long-term performance.

8.5.2 Investment Protection Committees

The global financial crisis has led to an increased awareness of the importance of good corporate governance. One side-effect has been an increase in shareholder activism, particularly by institutional investors, and greater turnout and voting at listed companies' AGMs. Certain IPCs, such as the PLSA and PIRC, publish their corporate governance expectations and circulate them to shareholders and listed companies. Recent examples include:

(a) 'Stewardship and Voting Guidelines', published in February 2024 by the PLSA, the UK representative body for pension providers, on its website.

(b) 'The Investment Association Principles of Remuneration', published in October 2024.

The Investment Association maintains the Public Register which it describes as the world's first register tracking shareholder dissent at listed companies. The UK Government asked the Investment Association to develop and maintain the Register. It records details of resolutions by UK FTSE All Share companies which have received significant shareholder opposition. You can access the Register on the Investment Association's website.

8.6 SHAREHOLDER RIGHTS DIRECTIVE

As we have seen, better corporate governance can be achieved by greater shareholder involvement in the running of listed companies. To further this aim the EU Shareholder Rights Directive (2007/36/EC) was adopted in June 2007. It was implemented in the UK on 3 August 2009 by the Companies (Shareholders' Rights) Regulations 2009 (SI 2009/1632), which amended Pt 13 of the CA 2006, and seeks to improve the way that companies trade on regulated markets in the EU by improving shareholder information and rights to participate in general meetings. The Directive applies to companies on the Main Market but not to those on AIM. The most important rights are set out below.

8.6.1 Notice period for general meetings

The CA 2006 allowed general meetings of listed companies (not being the AGM) to be held on not less than 14 clear days' notice. Under a new s 307A the notice period must be 21 clear days unless:

(a) the company offers all shareholders the right to vote electronically (which can be met by the company enabling all shareholders to appoint a proxy via a website); and

(b) shareholders pass a special resolution each year at the AGM resolving that only 14 clear days' notice is required for such meetings,

in which case the notice period can be 14 clear days.

Some IPCs have produced guidance on this provision. For example, the Pensions and Lifetime Savings Association (PLSA) has issued guidance on when it will consider the use of a 14-day notice period for listed companies' general meetings to be acceptable, instead of the 21-day period.

Despite the fact that, until this change, general meetings to consider ordinary resolutions only required 14 days' notice, the PLSA has adopted a restrictive position, stating that the 14-day period should only be used in limited circumstances and for time-sensitive matters where its use would be in the interests of shareholders as a whole. The PLSA suggests that shareholders vote against any resolution proposed at a 14-day notice meeting if the use of this shorter notice period has not been adequately justified, or the shareholders need more time to consider their voting decision due to the complexity of the matters proposed. However, it should not prevent a meeting being called on 14 days' notice to approve a transaction with significant time pressures.

When companies propose the resolution to enable meetings to be held on 14 days' notice, the PLSA also requires a statement in the AGM notice of 'the circumstances in which a short notice meeting may be called'. PLSA members should vote in favour of the enabling resolution as long as satisfactory language is included in the AGM circular.

PIRC, in its UK Shareholder Voting Guidelines, also states that it will not support meetings held on the shorter notice period if there is a lack of justification and the proposals are complex.

8.6.2 Contents of notice

The following additional information must now be included in the notice calling a meeting of a listed company (s 337(3) for (f)(ii) and (iii) below and s 311(2) for the remainder):

(a) details of the website containing the information relating to the general meeting (see **8.6.3** below);

(b) a statement that the right to vote is by reference to the Register of Members and the time when the right to vote will be determined;

(c) details of how to attend and vote including deadlines;

(d) details of forms for appointing proxies;

(e) where the company allows voting in advance or electronic voting then the procedure for doing so; and

(f) if the AGM notice is sent out more than six weeks before the meeting it must contain a statement about the shareholders' rights to:

  (i) ask questions at the meeting (see **8.6.4** below);

  (ii) give notice of a resolution at the meeting; and

  (iii) include a matter in the business of the meeting (see **8.6.5** below).

8.6.3 Publication of information on a website

Section 311A requires a listed company to publish certain specified information in advance of the meeting on a website on or before the date on which notice of a meeting is given including the matters set out in the notice itself and details of the company's share capital. The information must be kept on the website for at least two years.

After the meeting s 341(1A) requires additional information about poll votes to be posted on the website, such as the number of votes for and against and abstentions.

8.6.4 Right to ask questions

There is a new right, under s 319A, for shareholders to ask questions at a meeting which the company must cause to be answered unless an exception applies. The exceptions include if it would involve revealing confidential information and if it is undesirable in the interests of the company or good order of the meeting.

8.6.5 Right to requisition a resolution

In addition to the existing right of shareholders (holding either at least 5% of the voting rights of the company or being at least 100 in number owning shares with an average paid-up capital of at least £100 per shareholder) to requisition a resolution at an AGM, they have a new right in s 338A to require the company to include 'a matter' (not being a resolution) in the business of the AGM.

8.6.6 Appointment of proxies

The company must provide an electronic address for the return of proxies (s 333A). Section 327(A1) and s 330(A1) require the appointment and termination respectively of a proxy by a shareholder in a listed company to be in writing. This can be done by electronic means.

8.7 WOMEN ON BOARDS

In 2010, only 12.5% of FTSE 100 directors were female, and 21% of FTSE 100 companies had no women on their boards (producing rather predictable headlines in the UK press about there not being enough women on top). As part of the UK Government's strategy to increase the number of women in the boardrooms of listed companies, the UK Government commissioned Sir Philip Hampton (note the gender) as chair and Dame Helen Alexander as deputy chair to conduct a review. They produced a number of recommendations in their report with the target of improving the gender balance on the boards of FTSE 350 companies to 33% women by 2020 and for FTSE 100 companies to aim for a minimum of 33% women on their executive committees. This is now being built on by the FTSE Women Leaders Review, which is an independent, business-led framework supported by the Government, which sets recommendations to improve the representation of women on boards and in leadership positions of FTSE 350 companies. A new target of 40% has been set to be reached by the end of 2025, with at least one woman in the role of Chair, senior independent NED, CEO or finance director.

As at January 2024, 42.6% of the directors of FTSE 100 largest companies were women. Nearly 75% of the FTSE 100 companies have already reached the 40% threshold, although 7 had not reached 33% of women on their boards. This improvement has been achieved through measures such as the Investment Association altering its voting recommendations to encourage compliance with the targets. It is worth noting that more remains to be done by smaller listed companies. Across all FTSE 350 companies there are only 53 chairs and just 15% of women directors hold an executive position. Some reason to cheer arises in that there are no longer any all-male boards in the FTSE 350, finally overcoming the prejudice that gave rise to recorded reasons given for having no women on their boards in previous years, such as: 'I don't think women fit comfortably into the board environment', 'Most women don't want the hassle or pressure of sitting on a board', and 'All the "good" women have already been snapped up.'

UK Listing Rule 6.6.6R(9) requires listed companies to state in their annual report whether they have reached certain targets including 40% of the board comprising women, set out in the format of UKLR 6 Annex 1R.

The UK CGC requires listed companies to promote equality, diversity and inclusion when considering appointments to the board.

8.8 ETHNIC DIVERSITY

In October 2017, a review headed by Sir John Parker published its final report, 'The Parker Review: A Report into the Ethnic Diversity of UK Boards 2017'. It recommends that FTSE 350 companies should increase the ethnic diversity of their UK boards, in particular that there should be at least one director of colour on every FTSE 100 board by 2021 and on every FTSE 250 board by 2024. By the end of 2023, at least 96 of the FTSE 100 companies had one or more director(s) of colour. In an update to his original report, Sir John said:

> We, as company Chairmen and Chairs of Nominations Committees need to be more assertive – not least by refusing to accept the head-hunter's excuse that 'the candidates just aren't there'. For my part, when I hear this message from my consultants, my next step is to find better consultants who can find the talent either at home or in our world of 7.7 billion people.

Somewhat ironically, the three contributors to the update's introduction – the chair, the Secretary of State for DBT and the chair of Ernst & Young UK – were all white.

UK Listing Rule 6.6.6R(9) requires listed companies to state in their annual report whether they have at least one director from an ethnic minority on the board of directors, set out in the format of UKLR 6 Annex 1.

The UK CGC requires listed companies to promote equality, diversity and inclusion when considering appointments to the board. Furthermore, the corporate governance statement (see **8.3.6.2** above) must include a statement of how the company's diversity policy is applied to the company's board (DTR 7.2.8AR). This provision refers to ethnic diversity and certain other categories such as sexual orientation, disability and socio-economic background.

8.9 FUTURE DEVELOPMENTS

The UK Government announced in March 2019 that the FRC will be replaced by a new regulator, the Audit, Reporting and Governance Authority (ARGA). The new Government announced in its post-election King's Speech 2024 that it would be introducing a bill to Parliament, the Audit Reform and Corporate Governance Bill 2024, to carry out this reform.

CHAPTER 9

THE FINANCIAL SERVICES AND MARKETS ACT 2000 AND THE FINANCIAL SERVICES ACT 2012

9.1 BACKGROUND

The Financial Services and Markets Act 2000 (FSMA 2000) came into force on 1 December 2001. At this point the FSA became the single regulator for the financial services industry. On 1 April 2013 the majority of the Financial Services Act 2012 (FSA 2012) came into force. This resulted in a fundamental overhaul of the system of financial services regulation in the UK. The UK Government introduced the reforms following a thorough post-mortem into the causes of the global financial crisis in 2007/08 which, aside from the deepest recession since World War II, resulted in some of the UK's biggest banks (Lloyds TSB, HBOS (no longer in existence) and Royal Bank of Scotland) being taken into public ownership to prevent them from collapsing.

The single regulator, the FSA, was generally felt to have been 'asleep on its watch' in the years leading up to the crisis. It became known for its light touch regulatory approach. As one senior regulator put it, 'the whole culture of the system fell apart to "anything goes, as long as the compliance officer doesn't say no".' It has been replaced by three new regulators, the Financial Policy Committee (FPC), the Prudential Regulation Authority (PRA) and the Financial Conduct Authority (FCA). The FPC is a committee of the Bank of England and its role is to protect and enhance the stability of the financial system in the UK. The intention is that it spots and neutralises threats to the UK financial system (such as an asset bubble) before they become damaging. Operating at the macro-economic level, the FPC does not therefore regulate individual firms. You can find out more about the FPC at its website <www.bankofengland.co.uk/financial-stability>.

The PRA regulates financial services institutions which are deemed to be systemically important to the UK economy. This covers banks, building societies, insurance companies and certain investment firms such as credit unions. The PRA is currently regulating approximately 1,500 such entities. You can find out more about the PRA at its website <www.bankofengland.co.uk/prudential-regulation>.

The FCA has a multi-faceted role. It is responsible for:

(a) the conduct of business regulation of all regulated firms (including those authorised by the PRA);

(b) the regulation of all non-PRA authorised firms;
(c) the regulation of the UK's financial markets including the Stock Exchange;
(d) fighting financial crime;
(e) the regulation of consumer credit (from 1 April 2014); and
(f) a number of other roles as set out in the FSMA 2000.

The FCA is therefore of most interest to us for the purposes of this book in its role as markets regulator, since it oversees the Stock Exchange and the regulation of listed companies. In practice, a listed bank or insurance company will be regulated by both the FCA and the PRA and subject to the rules in both the FCA and PRA Handbooks. This dual regulation, widely known as 'twin peaks' regulation, aims to minimise the possibility of a financial crisis damaging the UK economy again. In light of their highly specialised nature, the roles and rules of the FPC and the PRA are beyond the remit of this book.

You can access the PRA's rules (the PRA Rulebook) online at <www.prarulebook.co.uk> and the FCA's (the FCA Handbook) online at <https://handbook.fca.org.uk/handbook>.

9.2 THE FCA'S OBJECTIVES

Some of the provisions of the FSMA 2000 are complex. They are easier to understand if you consider them in the context of the objectives set out in the Act. The FCA's strategic objective is ensuring that the relevant markets as defined in s 1F of the FSMA 2000 (including the financial markets) function well (FSMA 2000, s 1B(2)). In addition, the FCA has three operational objectives (FSMA 2000, s 1B(3)):

(a) the consumer protection objective: to secure an appropriate degree of protection for consumers (FSMA 2000, s 1C);
(b) the integrity objective: to protect and enhance the integrity of the UK financial system (FSMA 2000, s 1D) (which includes the Stock Exchange);
(c) the competition objective: to promote effective competition in the interests of consumers in the markets for regulated financial services and services provided by the recognised investment exchanges (RIEs) (which includes the Stock Exchange) (FSMA 2000, s 1E); and
(d) the competitiveness and growth objective: to facilitate, subject to aligning with relevant international standards:
    (i) the international competitiveness of the economy of the UK (including in particular the financial services sector), and
    (ii) its growth in the medium to long term (FSMA 2000, s 1EB).

9.3 RELEVANCE TO PRACTICE

No corporate finance lawyer can avoid the FSMA 2000. Together with the CA 2006, the 2000 Act will be the most thumbed statute on the lawyer's desk. It affects all professional firms which carry on regulated activities, and also affects how companies, particularly listed companies, conduct their day-to-day corporate and trading activities. The lawyer will have most involvement with the following provisions of the FSMA 2000:

(a) the general prohibition on carrying on a regulated activity in the United Kingdom (s 19);
(b) the financial promotion regulatory framework (s 21);
(c) the rules relating to the official listing of securities (Pt VI and in particular ss 85, 86, 87A–87D, 87G, 87J–87P, 90, 90A and 91); and
(d) powers relating to the UK MAR disclosure requirements and the market abuse regime (ss 122A–131AE).

This chapter considers (a) above. **Chapter 12** considers financial promotion; **Chapter 6** explores the rules of the FSMA 2000 relating to the listing of securities; **Chapter 7** deals with the disclosure requirements under UK MAR; and **Chapter 10** considers market abuse.

9.4 THE GENERAL PROHIBITION ON CARRYING ON A REGULATED ACTIVITY

Lawyers must be aware of the general prohibition in s 19 of the FSMA 2000 not only so that they can advise their clients accordingly, but also so that they can ensure that neither they nor their law firm breach that section.

9.4.1 The general prohibition

Section 19 of the FSMA 2000 prohibits any person from carrying on a regulated activity in the United Kingdom unless they are:

(a) an authorised person; or

(b) an exempt person.

This is known as the 'general prohibition'. Contravention of the general prohibition is a criminal offence (s 23). Any agreement which results from a breach of s 19 will be unenforceable (s 26). A company which enters into an agreement in breach of s 19 can be wound up in the public interest by the FCA (*Digital Satellite Warranty Cover Ltd v FSA* [2011] EWCA Civ 1413).

9.4.2 Regulated activities

The general prohibition relates to the carrying on of a 'regulated activity'. What is a regulated activity? The actual definition is provided by s 22 of the FSMA 2000. It is:

> an activity of a specified kind which is carried on by way of business and:
>
> (a) relates to an investment of a specified kind; or
>
> (b) in the case of an activity of a kind which is also specified for the purposes of this paragraph, is carried on in relation to property of any kind.
>
> An activity is also a regulated activity if it is an activity of a specified kind which is carried on by way of business and relates to:
>
> (a) information about a person's financial standing, or
>
> (b) the setting of a specified benchmark.

This is not particularly helpful. Schedule 2 to the Act, together with a number of statutory instruments, including the Financial Services and Markets Act 2000 (Regulated Activities) Order 2001 (SI 2001/544) ('Regulated Activities Order 2001') (as amended over 15 times!), seeks to clarify the definition. Schedule 2 to the FSMA 2000 provides examples of regulated activities, and the Regulated Activities Order 2001 details the meaning of specified activities (Pt II) and specified investments (Pt III). In practice, recourse should be made to these sources. However, for our purposes it is more useful to consider a few of the more common examples of 'regulated activities' which a corporate finance lawyer might encounter, namely those relating to investments (such as shares). The regulated activities include:

(a) dealing in investments (Regulated Activities Order 2001, Chapters IV and V) – this includes dealing as principal or agent;

(b) arranging deals in investments (Regulated Activities Order 2001, Chapter VI) – this includes making arrangements with a view to another person buying or selling shares;

(c) managing investments (Regulated Activities Order 2001, Chapter VII) – this includes managing someone else's shares;

(d) advising on investments (Regulated Activities Order 2001, Chapter XII) – this includes giving advice to someone buying or selling shares. It will not include general advice in relation to an investment, or merely explaining the implications of exercising rights. So, for example, explaining the meaning of technical jargon, or advising how to complete an application form will not amount to advising on investments. (It could, however, still amount to arranging deals in investments – see (b) above.)

The definition of 'regulated activities' is very wide. The prohibition prevents any person carrying on a regulated activity, unless that person is an authorised person or an exempt person. So who are these persons?

9.4.3 Authorised person

Section 31(1) of the FSMA 2000 defines an 'authorised person'. The most common example of an authorised person is someone who has obtained permission from the FCA or PRA (depending on the type of business – see **9.1** above) to carry on regulated activities (under Pt IV of the Act), such as an investment bank seeking to act as a sponsor or broker (see **Chapter 4**). Part IV of the Act contains the detail of how such permission is obtained. From the lawyer's point of view, however, the important issue is that, unless a client is an authorised person or an exempt person, it will be prohibited from carrying out any regulated activity, and the lawyer must advise the client to instruct an authorised person (or, more rarely, an exempt person) to carry out the activity instead.

9.4.4 Exempt person

A person is exempt if they have been granted an exemption order under s 38(1) of the FSMA 2000, or is exempt as an 'appointed representative' under s 39(1) of the Act. In practice, exempt persons are encountered rarely. However, the most common 'exempt person' with which lawyers will be familiar is any RIE or recognised clearing house pursuant to s 285 of the FSMA 2000. For example, in certain circumstances (see s 285(2)) the Stock Exchange as an RIE will be exempt from the general prohibition.

9.5 THE FINANCIAL SERVICES ACT 2012

As stated at **9.1** above, the FSA 2012 implemented the substantial changes to the FSMA 2000. In addition, Pt 7 of the FSA 2012 repealed the former offences of misleading statements under s 397 of the FSMA 2000 and replaced them with new offences in ss 89–91 of the FSA 2012. These are very important as they are criminal offences punishable by imprisonment and directly cover the activities of listed companies and their directors. It is therefore essential that the corporate finance lawyer is able to advise in relation to them. In this book we will only be considering the first two offences of misleading statements (s 89) and misleading impressions (s 90). The third offence (s 91) sets out offences for misleading statements and impressions in relation to benchmarks, which currently only applies to LIBOR, a benchmark for interest rates. As such, it does not relate directly to the content of this book.

9.5.1 Misleading statements

9.5.1.1 The criminal offence

Section 89 of the FSA 2012 provides that it is a criminal offence for a person either to:

(a) make a statement which they *know* to be false or misleading in a material respect; or

(b) make a statement which is false or misleading in a material respect, being reckless as to whether it is; or

(c) dishonestly conceal any material facts whether in connection with a statement made by that person or otherwise (s 89(1))

if the person makes the statement or conceals the facts with the intention of inducing, or is reckless as to whether making it or concealing them may induce, another person to:

(i) enter into, or offer to enter into, or refrain from entering or offering to enter into a *relevant agreement*, or

(ii) exercise, or refrain from exercising, any rights conferred by a *relevant investment* (s 89(2)).

Note that the person who is induced does not have to be the recipient of the statement.

9.5.1.2 'Relevant agreement'

A relevant agreement is defined by s 93(3) of the FSA 2012. The definition refers to 'specified kinds of activity', which are contained in art 2 of the Financial Services Act 2012 (Misleading Statements and Impressions) Order 2013 (SI 2013/637) ('Misleading Statements Order'). An example of a relevant agreement is an agreement to sell (or not sell) shares.

9.5.1.3 'Relevant investment'

A relevant investment is defined by s 93(5) of the FSA 2012. Reference is made to 'specified kinds of investment', which are contained in art 4 of the Misleading Statements Order. Shares and bonds are examples of relevant investments.

9.5.1.4 'Reckless'

'Reckless' includes not only someone not giving any thought to the accuracy of a statement, but also someone making a statement when they are aware that they should first make some enquiries as to the accuracy of the statement yet fail to make such enquiries (provided those enquires would have revealed that the statement was false or misleading).

9.5.1.5 The UK Market Abuse Regulation

Failure to comply with the general obligation of disclosure set out in UK MAR, Article 17(1) (see **7.5.1**) may constitute the dishonest concealment of material facts for the purpose of s 89 (see **9.5.1.1(b)**).

9.5.1.6 Example

The most common s 89 scenario which a corporate finance lawyer will encounter is where a client makes a misleading statement so that shareholders continue to buy, or do not sell, shares, when if the statement was actually truthful, those shareholders might be tempted not to buy, or to sell, their shares.

There have been no cases under the FSA 2012 yet. Under its predecessor, s 397 of the FSMA 2000, the former chief executive and former finance director of a software company called AIT were convicted for publicly issuing a statement on the company's turnover and profits knowing it to be untrue. The former chief executive was sentenced to three and a half years' imprisonment (reduced to 18 months on appeal). The former finance director was sentenced to two years' imprisonment (reduced to 9 months on appeal).

In another case in June 2011, Stuart Pearson, the CEO of an AIM-quoted company, who was found guilty of making misleading statements about the company's assets contrary to s 397, was sentenced to 12 months' imprisonment and disqualified as a director for five years.

9.5.2 Misleading impressions

9.5.2.1 The criminal offence

This is an offence under s 90 of the FSA 2012. Section 90(1) provides that it is a criminal offence to:

(a) do any act, or engage in any course of conduct;
(b) which creates a false or misleading impression;
(c) as to the market in, or the price or value of, any relevant investment (see **9.5.1.3**);
(d) if that person intends to:
   (i) create that impression, and

(ii) by creating the impression, to induce another person to acquire, dispose of, subscribe for or underwrite the investments or to refrain from doing so; and/or

(iii) is misleading or reckless as to whether it is, and the person intends to produce the results in s 90(4) or is aware that creating the impression is likely to produce any of the results in s 90(4).

The results in s 90(4) are the making of a gain for that person or another person, or the causing of loss to another person or the exposing of another person to the risk of loss.

9.5.2.2 Examples

One scenario in which this offence might arise is as follows. Bidder plc plans to make a takeover offer for Target plc. It therefore seeks to build up a stake in Target plc (see **Chapter 21**). Target plc suspects that Bidder plc is going to make a bid for it, and is not pleased. It arranges for its associate companies to buy shares in Target plc, so that the share price of Target plc rises, which makes Bidder plc's stakebuilding exercise more costly. Bidder plc will have to pay more for its stake. This contravenes s 90 of the FSA 2012, because Target plc has deliberately created a misleading impression in the shares of Target plc with the intention of making Bidder plc refrain from dealing in the shares of Target plc.

Two *Daily Mirror* journalists were found guilty of conspiracy to commit a similar offence under a forerunner to s 90 of the FSA 2012. The journalists bought shares in listed companies and then tipped them as a buy in their column in the *Daily Mirror*, 'City Slickers'. The share price rose post-publication and the two men then sold the shares, making a profit. They were aided by a third person (who pleaded guilty to the same charge), who used Internet message boards to stimulate interest in the same companies. As an indication of how serious the offence is, one of the journalists was sentenced to six months' imprisonment, having made approximately £40,000 profit. The second, who co-operated with the investigation, made £15,000 profit and was sentenced to community service. On the steps of the court after sentencing he remarked, 'That was a close one!' The third person was sentenced to three months' imprisonment, having made £17,000.

9.5.2.3 Defence

Section 90(9) provides a defence for a person charged under s 90(1) if they can show that they reasonably believed their conduct would not create a false or misleading impression.

9.5.3 Relationship between s 89 and s 90

The provisions are not mutually exclusive. One act can give rise to charges under both provisions.

9.5.4 Sanctions

Section 92(1) of the FSA 2012 provides that the offences of making a misleading statement or creating a misleading impression are punishable by imprisonment and/or a fine. On summary conviction, the maximum sentence is 12 months and/or a fine up to the statutory maximum, and on conviction on indictment the maximum sentence is 10 years and/or an unlimited fine. As mentioned in **9.5.1.6** above, a CEO was sentenced to 12 months' imprisonment and disqualified as a director for five years in June 2011.

The risk of directors breaching s 89 and s 90 by making a misleading statement in a prospectus was examined at **6.7.2.1** above. As noted in that paragraph, the verification process is used to try to ensure that s 89 and s 90 are not breached during the marketing of an IPO, and the threat of a prison sentence is usually enough to focus the directors' attention on this process.

9.6 FUTURE DEVELOPMENTS

Financial Services and Markets Act 2023

The Act will amend the FSMA 2000 to introduce a principle that all decision making must take account of the UK Government's legal duty under s 1 of the Climate Change Act 2008 to achieve a 'net zero' emissions economy by 2050.

CHAPTER 10

MARKET ABUSE

10.1 INTRODUCTION

Market abuse is a civil offence which was originally created by the FSMA 2000. From 3 July 2016, it had statutory force in the UK via the EU's Market Abuse Regulation (MAR). With effect from 1 January 2021, MAR continues to have effect in the UK post-Brexit but under English law and in the form of UK MAR. It supplements the criminal offences of:

(a) misleading statements and misleading impressions under the FSA 2012 (see **9.5** above); and

(b) insider dealing under the CJA 1993 (see **Chapter 11**),

which target the same kind of behaviour covered by the market abuse regime.

It is one of the FCA's statutory objectives, the integrity objective (ss 1B(3) and 1D of the FSMA 2000), to protect and enhance the integrity of the UK financial system. Section 1D(2)(c) defines 'integrity' to include 'its not being affected by behaviour that amounts to market abuse'.

The enforcement of market abuse has increased significantly in recent times. During the financial crisis in 2007/08 we saw some of the world's and the UK's biggest banks driven to failure, nationalisation or a rescue takeover in the space of days by a loss of confidence expressed in part through a collapsing share price. Rumours abounded as to which institution might be next to be in trouble, and this resulted in breathtaking falls and rises in share prices as panic spread and confidence ebbed and flowed depending on the latest developments.

This presents opportunities to make huge amounts of money, not just legitimately (however morally questionable this may be) but also for the unscrupulous at a potentially devastating cost to the companies, investors, employees and ultimately economies involved. Now that the financial crisis has passed, it remains important to maintain investor confidence and stability in the markets in light of the crucial role they play in the UK economy. Tackling market abuse helps achieve this, and the FCA has stated that this remains a high priority. On average, the FCA receives reports of around 1,500 suspicious transactions a year.

10.1.1 The civil offence

The civil offence of market abuse was introduced so that market manipulators, who might otherwise have escaped punishment for the criminal offences referred to at (a) and (b) above, would be caught. It has, at least in theory, the following advantages over the criminal regime:

(a) it is wider in scope;
(b) it is easier to prove. The standard of proof in criminal cases is 'beyond all reasonable doubt'. This high standard means that it is very difficult to convict anyone of insider dealing, or of making misleading statements and/or manipulating the market. To date there have been few convictions for these offences. Market abuse, however, as a civil offence, has a lower standard of proof, namely 'on the balance of probabilities';
(c) it assesses behaviour according to its effect rather than the intention behind it (although there is an element of intention lurking in the detail of the regime);
(d) it can be committed by anyone – an individual or a company (contrast insider dealing, which can only be committed by an individual, see **11.7** below);
(e) a jury is not required to try the offence; and
(f) it is possible to settle a case of market abuse, unlike with a criminal offence, and the FCA has powers to offer leniency to wrongdoers, to encourage co-operation where more than one individual is involved.

10.1.2 The UK Market Abuse Regulation

The Market Abuse Regulation (EU) 596/2014 (MAR) came into force in the UK on 3 July 2016, as part of the EU's second generation set of rules regulating the financial markets (see **3.1** above). The introduction of new rules on market abuse was prompted by the fall-out from the financial crisis in 2007/08 and by a desire to see more effective and even enforcement of this offence across all Member States.

MAR, being an EU Regulation, had direct applicability in the UK; in other words no implementing UK legislation was required in order for it to have effect in English law. MAR is supplemented by delegated legislation at an EU level and by guidance (for example technical standards) prepared by ESMA at an EU level and by the FCA at a UK level. The FCA guidance forms Chapter 1 of the FCA Market Conduct Sourcebook (known as 'MAR Market Conduct'), which is part of the FCA Handbook and can be viewed under 'Business Standards' in the FCA Handbook section of the FCA's website.

With effect from 1 January 2021, MAR continues to have effect in the UK post-Brexit but with its statutory basis being under English law and in the form of UK MAR. The EU MAR delegated legislation has also been 'on-shored' into English law.

10.2 WHAT IS MARKET ABUSE?

Market abuse, in layman's terms, is certain behaviour, relating to certain investments which trade, or are seeking admission to trade, on certain markets, which is deemed unlawful. The offence punishes those who seek to abuse the market for their own benefit.

10.3 THE MAIN OFFENCES

UK MAR sets out three main offences which constitute market abuse. These are:

(a) insider dealing;
(b) unlawful disclosure of inside information; and
(c) market manipulation.

We will now consider each offence in turn.

10.4 INSIDER DEALING

Under UK MAR, Article 14, a person is prohibited from:

(a) engaging in insider dealing (Art 14(a));
(b) attempting to engage in insider dealing (Art 14(a));
(c) recommending that another person engage in insider dealing (Art 14(b)); or

(d) inducing another person to engage in insider dealing (Art 14(b)).

The FCA guidance contained in MAR 1.2.3G makes it clear that the person engaging in the behaviour in question does not need to have intended to commit market abuse.

10.4.1 What is insider dealing?

The context is provided by UK MAR, recital 23:

> The essential characteristic of insider dealing consists in an unfair advantage being obtained from inside information to the detriment of third parties who are unaware of such information and consequently the undermining of the integrity of financial markets and investor confidence. Consequently, the prohibition against insider dealing should apply where a person who is in possession of inside information takes unfair advantage of the benefit gained from that information by entering into market transactions ...

The definition of 'insider dealing' itself is set out in UK MAR, Article 8 and covers two different scenarios:

(a) where a person possesses inside information and uses that information by acquiring or disposing of, for its own account or for the account of a third party, directly or indirectly, financial instruments to which that information relates; and

(b) the use of inside information by cancelling or amending an order concerning a financial instrument to which the information relates where the order was placed before the person concerned possessed the inside information.

The first scenario would cover, for example, the situation where a director of a company is aware of a takeover offer which has not yet been announced, and buys shares in the company with the expectation that the share price will rise on the announcement of the offer.

The second would cover, for example, the situation where an employee had instructed her broker to sell the shares she owns in her company, but before the order is carried out she cancels the sale because she has learnt that the company has just won a major contract which is due to be publicly announced later that day and the share price is expected to rise significantly.

Remember this is a type of behaviour under the civil offence of market abuse and is quite separate from the criminal offence of insider dealing referred to in **Chapter 11**.

10.4.2 Inside information

The offence of insider dealing requires the possession of 'inside information'. This is defined in UK MAR, Article 7 and consists of four elements. It is information:

(a) of a precise nature;

(b) which has not been made public;

(c) which relates, directly or indirectly, to an issuer of a financial instrument or to the financial instrument itself; and

(d) if generally available, would be likely to have a significant effect on the price of the financial instrument or the price of related investments.

See **7.5.2.1–7.5.2.4** above for a full explanation of this definition.

10.4.3 People to whom the offence applies

Under UK MAR, Article 8(4), the offence of insider dealing applies to those people (natural and legal) who possess inside information as a result of:

(a) being a member of the board of directors of the company;

(b) being a shareholder in the company;

(c) having access to the information through the exercise of an employment, profession or duties;

(d) being involved in criminal activities; or

anyone else who knows or ought to know that it is inside information.

Under MAR 1.2.8G (see **10.4.7** below), the following factors may be taken into account in determining whether or not a person who possesses inside information ought to know that it is inside information for these purposes:

(1) if a normal and reasonable person in the position of the person who has inside information would know or should have known that the person from whom they received it is an insider; and

(2) if a normal and reasonable person in the position of the person who has inside information would know or should have known that it is inside information.

It is emphasised in MAR 1.2.9G (see **10.4.7** below) that the person concerned does not need to know that the information concerned actually is inside information.

10.4.4 Financial instrument

The offence of insider dealing relates to 'financial instruments'.

This term is defined in the same way as for the general obligation to disclose inside information under UK MAR, Article 17 (see **7.5.2.3** above). The definition is contained in UK MAR, Article 3(1)(1), which refers to those instruments specified in Part 1 of Sch 2 to the FSMA 2000 (Regulated Activities) Order 2001 (SI 2001/544), read together with Part 2. This includes 'transferable securities' which are defined in s 102A of the FSMA 2000 by reference to Article 2(1)(24) of MiFIR. For our purposes, put simply, financial instruments include shares of the type issued by listed companies, including ordinary shares.

10.4.5 Scope of the offence

As set out at **10.4.1** above, the offence covers the situation where the person themselves engages in or attempts insider dealing. It also extends to a person who recommends or induces another to do so. Further clarification is given in UK MAR, Article 8 as to what this entails.

It is where the person who possesses inside information recommends, on the basis of that information, that another person does any of the following:

(a) acquires or disposes of financial instruments to which that information relates, or induces that person to make such an acquisition or disposal (Art 8(2)(a));

(b) cancels or amends an order concerning a financial instrument to which that information relates, or induces that person to make such a cancellation or amendment (Art 8(2)(b)).

The use of the recommendations or inducements referred to in Article 8(2) of UK MAR amounts to insider dealing where the person using the recommendation or inducement knows or ought to know that it is based on inside information (UK MAR, Art 8(3)). Recital 26 to UK MAR explains that, in this respect, competent authorities should consider what a normal and reasonable person knows or should have known in the circumstances.

10.4.6 Legitimate behaviour

Where a person possesses inside information and then deals or attempts to deal in the financial instrument, it is presumed that they have used that information. This can be rebutted and does not apply to 'legitimate behaviours' (UK MAR, recital 24 and Article 8). UK MAR, Article 9 sets out certain types of 'legitimate behaviour' to avoid inadvertently prohibiting legitimate forms of financial activity where there is no effect of market abuse (UK MAR, recital 29). These types of legitimate behaviour include (Art 9):

(a) where the dealing is to satisfy an obligation which arose before the relevant person had inside information;

(b) where the inside information is the person's own intention to deal and they carry out that intention; and

(c) where a bidder in a takeover offer has obtained inside information in connection with that offer and uses it solely for the purposes of proceeding with the offer (as long as there is no undisclosed information at the point at which the shareholders accept the offer).

10.4.7 Guidance

Further guidance on what amounts to the offence of insider dealing is set out in Chapter 1 of the FCA Market Conduct Sourcebook (known as 'MAR Market Conduct'), which is part of the FCA Handbook and can be viewed under 'Business Standards' in the FCA Handbook section of the FCA's website. These provisions are referred to as 'MAR' and the relevant sections here are MAR 1.2 and 1.3. Obviously the scope for possible confusion with the UK Market Abuse Regulation when quoting provisions is all too evident and care should thus be taken.

10.5 UNLAWFUL DISCLOSURE OF INSIDE INFORMATION

Under UK MAR, Article 14(c), a person is prohibited from unlawfully disclosing inside information.

10.5.1 What is unlawful disclosure?

UK MAR, Article 10(1) explains that this arises where a person possesses inside information and discloses that information to any other person, except where the disclosure is made in the normal exercise of an employment, a profession or duties.

In addition, the onward disclosure of recommendations or inducements (for example to acquire or dispose of a financial instrument to which the inside information relates) amounts to unlawful disclosure of inside information where the person disclosing the recommendation or inducement knows or ought to know that it was based on inside information (UK MAR, Article 10(2)).

The FCA guidance contained in MAR 1.2.3G makes it clear that UK MAR does not require the person engaging in the behaviour in question to have intended to commit market abuse.

This would include, for example, a director telling a friend in the gym that her company was going to sell off a major division of the company before it was publicly announced.

10.5.2 Inside information

This offence requires the disclosure of 'inside information' or a recommendation or disclosure based on such information. See **10.4.2** above for an explanation of this definition.

10.5.3 People to whom the offence applies

Under UK MAR, Article 8(4), the offence of unlawful disclosure applies to those people (natural and legal) who possess inside information as a result of:

(a) being a member of the board of directors of the company;

(b) being a shareholder in the company;

(c) having access to the information through the exercise of an employment, profession or duties;

(d) being involved in criminal activities; or

anyone else who knows or ought to know that it is inside information.

Under MAR 1.2.8G, the following factors may be taken into account in determining whether or not a person who possesses inside information ought to know that it is inside information for these purposes:

(1) if a normal and reasonable person in the position of the person who has inside information would know or should have known that the person from whom they received it is an insider; and

(2) if a normal and reasonable person in the position of the person who has inside information would know or should have known that it is inside information.

It is emphasised in MAR 1.2.9G that the person concerned does not need to know that the information concerned actually is inside information.

10.5.4 In the normal exercise of an employment, profession or duties

As set out at **10.5.1** above, the offence does *not* cover the situation where the disclosure of inside information is in the normal exercise of an employment, a profession or duties.

The FCA has provided guidance in MAR 1.4.5G by setting out the factors to be taken into account in determining whether or not the disclosure was made by a person in the normal exercise of their employment, profession or duties. They are also to be taken as indications that the disclosure was in the normal exercise:

(a) whether the disclosure is permitted by FCA rules, the rules of a trading market (such as the Main Market), or the Takeover Code (see **20.5** below);

(b) whether the disclosure is accompanied by the imposition of confidentiality requirements on the person to whom the disclosure is made and is:

 (i) reasonable and is to enable a person to perform the proper functions of their employment, profession or duties;

 (ii) reasonable and is for the purposes of facilitating or seeking or giving advice about a transaction or takeover bid (for example, to a professional adviser);

 (iii) reasonable and is for the purpose of facilitating any commercial, financial or investment transaction (including prospective underwriters or placees of securities);

 (iv) reasonable and is for the purpose of obtaining a commitment or expression of support in relation to an offer which is subject to the Takeover Code; or

 (v) in fulfilment of a legal obligation, including to employee representatives or trade unions acting on their behalf.

It would therefore not amount to market abuse for a director(s) of a listed company to disclose inside information (such as an intended takeover bid) to their solicitors.

10.5.5 Market soundings

UK MAR, recital 32 explains that:

> Market soundings are interactions between a seller of financial instruments and one or more potential investors, prior to the announcement of a transaction, in order to gauge the interest of potential investors in a possible transaction and its pricing, size and structuring. ... They are a highly valuable tool to gauge the opinion of potential investors, enhance shareholder dialogue, ensure that deals run smoothly, and that the views of issuers, existing shareholders and potential new investors are aligned. They may be particularly beneficial when markets lack confidence or a relevant benchmark, or are volatile. Thus the ability to conduct market soundings is important for the proper functioning of financial markets and market soundings should not in themselves be regarded as market abuse.

An example of a market sounding would be where a listed company intends to issue more shares and key investors are contacted by an investment bank and given the full terms of the deal to obtain a financial commitment to participate in the transaction.

UK MAR, Article 11(4) therefore provides an exception to unlawful disclosure for these market soundings. The disclosure of inside information made in the course of a market sounding will be deemed to be made in the normal exercise of a person's employment, profession or duties where the disclosing market participant ('DMP') complies with certain specified conditions.

The rules surrounding this exception are very detailed and are found in UK MAR and in accompanying ESMA guidance, 'MAR guidelines – persons receiving market soundings' (available on the ESMA website). Broadly they cover:

- internal arrangements: eg establishing internal procedures for carrying out market soundings, limiting the number of employees who carry out soundings and ensuring they are adequately trained;
- pre-sounding arrangements: eg specifically to consider if the sounding will involve the disclosure of inside information;
- sounding procedures: eg get the recipient's consent to receiving inside information, inform them they cannot use it and must keep it confidential;
- record keeping: eg detailed records of each step to be kept for five years;
- ESMA guidance: eg the recipient of the information must itself decide if it has inside information.

10.5.6 Guidance

Further guidance on what behaviour might and might not amount to the offence of unlawful disclosure is set out by the FCA in MAR 1.4.

10.6 MARKET MANIPULATION

Under UK MAR, Article 15, a person is prohibited from:

(a) engaging in market manipulation; or

(b) attempting to engage in market manipulation.

The FCA guidance contained in MAR 1.2.3G makes it clear that the person engaging in the behaviour in question does not need to have intended to commit market abuse.

10.6.1 What is market manipulation?

UK MAR, Article 12 sets out the activities which may amount to market manipulation. There are four: manipulating transactions, manipulating devices, dissemination and misleading behaviour and distortion, and misleading information or inputs in relation to benchmarks.

Market transactions

This is entering into a transaction, placing an order to trade or any other behaviour which (other than for legitimate reasons, in conformity with an accepted market practice that has been established in accordance with UK MAR, Article 13) either:

(a) gives, or is likely to give, a false or misleading impression as to the supply of, or demand for, or as to the price of, a financial instrument (see **10.4.4**); or

(b) secures the prices of such an instrument at an abnormal or artificial level.

This offence is most likely to be committed by a market professional, such as a trader. Further guidance is provided in Annex 1(A) to UK MAR. This sets out a non-exhaustive list of indicators of manipulative behaviour relating to false or misleading signals and price securing. Further indicators are listed in the UK version of Delegated Regulation (EU) 2016/522. In addition, UK MAR, Article 12(2) gives some examples of behaviour which will be considered to be market manipulation. In practice, it will include, for example:

(a) *An abusive squeeze.* This is perhaps less interesting than it sounds. It describes a situation where a person corners the market and uses that position to distort the market (UK MAR, Article 12(2)(a)).

(b) *Price positioning.* This consists of entering into a transaction, or series of transactions, to position the price at a distorted level (that is, materially different to that which reflects the operation of usual market forces).

Manipulating devices

This is entering into a transaction, placing an order to trade or carrying out any other activity or behaviour that affects or is likely to affect the price of one or several financial instruments which employ fictitious devices or any other form of deception or contrivance. Again, this is most likely to be committed by a market professional, such as a trader. Further guidance is provided in Annex 1(B) to UK MAR. This sets out a non-exhaustive list of indicators of manipulative behaviour relating to the employment of a fictitious device or any other form of deception or contrivance. Further indicators are listed in Delegated Regulation (EU) 2016/522. In addition, UK MAR, Article 12(2) gives some examples of behaviour which will be considered to be market manipulation. An example of this type of behaviour is a trader who buys shares, then spreads misleading positive information about the shares to increase their price, before selling the shares at a profit (known as a 'pump and dump').

Dissemination and misleading behaviour and distortion

This is disseminating information through the media, including the internet, or by any other means, which gives, or is likely to give, false or misleading signals as to the supply of, demand for, or price of, a financial instrument (see **10.4.4**) or secures, or is likely to secure, the price of one or several financial instruments at an abnormal or artificial level, including the dissemination of rumours, where the person who made the dissemination knew, or ought to have known, that the information was false or misleading.

Posting false information on a website about a listed company's financial position would fall under this type of behaviour.

Misleading information or inputs in relation to benchmarks

This is transmitting false or misleading information or providing false or misleading inputs in relation to a benchmark where the person who made the transmission or provided the input knew or ought to have known that it was false or misleading, or any other behaviour which manipulates the calculation of a benchmark.

10.7 EXEMPTIONS

It is important to note that there are no defences once market abuse has been proven. Certain behaviour will fall outside the market abuse regime (see **10.4.6** above) and it will then of course not amount to market abuse. There are further exemptions included in UK MAR which take behaviour outside of the offences in UK MAR. These are quite technical and cover buybacks of the listed company's shares and stabilisation programmes carried out in accordance with UK MAR, Article 5. Also certain behaviour carried out by Member States in relation to monetary policy, public debt management and climate change policy (UK MAR, Article 6) is exempt from UK MAR.

10.8 SANCTIONS

If the FCA suspects that market abuse may have occurred, it can use its statutory powers (including under Part VIII of the FSMA 2000) to investigate the issue.

One of the biggest problems in proving market abuse is evidence. In an attempt to tackle this, the FCA requires the firms it regulates to record telephone conversations (on landlines and on company mobile phones) and other electronic communications (including e-mail, texts and instant messages) relating to client orders and the conclusion of transactions in the equity and other markets, and keep the records for six months. Although personal mobiles are exempt, authorised firms are expected to ensure that transactions are not made on personal phones.

Once market abuse has been proved, though, the FCA can:

(a) impose an unlimited fine on any person (including a company) (s 123(1)(a) and (2));
(b) as an alternative to (a), make a public statement censuring a person who has engaged in market abuse (s 123(3)). Clearly, the hope here is that 'naming and shaming' will serve as a deterrent;
(c) suspend *trading* in the listed company's shares (FSMA 2000, s 122I);
(d) temporarily ban an individual from buying or selling financial instruments (including shares) (FSMA 2000, s 123A(1));
(e) require the company, PDMRs and persons closely associated with PDMRs to provide any information the FCA reasonably requires for the protection of investors or the orderly operation of the financial markets (FSMA 2000, s 122A) and require the company to publish such information (FSMA 2000, s 122G);
(f) apply to the court for an injunction (s 381);
(g) require the person to pay back profits made, or losses avoided (s 383); or
(h) require the person to compensate any victims (s 384).

Details of the FCA's approach to the exercise of its enforcement powers are set out in the Enforcement Guide (EG) and the Decision, Procedure and Penalties Manual (DEPP) which form part of the FCA Handbook, available on the FCA's website.

The largest fine of £17 million for market abuse and for breaches of the former listing rules was imposed on Royal Dutch Shell in 2004. In 2013 the Upper Tribunal upheld a £8 million fine for market abuse on a Canadian company, Swift Trade Inc. The Tribunal said it was 'as serious a case as might be imagined, and there is nothing which could possibly be said by way of mitigation'. The company systematically and deliberately engaged in a form of manipulative trading activity known as 'layering' or 'spoofing' in relation to shares traded on the Stock Exchange. This is a method of trading whereby a person attempts to increase the price of shares in order to benefit from selling them at a high price and then attempts to decrease the price of the shares so that they can buy them again at a lower price.

In July 2022 the FCA imposed a public censure on Carillion plc, given that the firm was insolvent and in liquidation. Were it not for Carillion's financial circumstances, the FCA would have imposed a financial penalty of £37,910,000 for market manipulation and breaches of the former listing rules arising out of misleading positive statements made about the company's financial condition prior to its spectacular collapse in 2018. Three directors were also fined between £155,000 and £400,000, suspended until an appeal has been considered.

In March 2017 the FCA used its powers under the FSMA 2000, s 384 for the very first time. It ordered Tesco plc to pay an estimated £85 million plus interest in compensation for an overstatement of its expected profit announced in 2014 due to an accounting error. Those eligible to be compensated were the buyers of Tesco plc's shares in the period between the original misleading announcement and a corrective statement issued by Tesco plc three weeks later which resulted in an approximately 25% drop in the share price.

Details of current and recent investigations can be found on the FCA's website.

MAR is accompanied by a Directive on Criminal Sanctions for Market Abuse (2014/57/EU) (known as 'CSMAD') which sets out the minimum sanctions for breach of the market abuse offences in MAR. The UK Government decided to exercise its opt out under the Lisbon Treaty and therefore the Directive was not implemented in the UK before Brexit and does not form part of English law.

10.9 FUTURE DEVELOPMENTS

Financial Services and Markets Act 2023

This Act intends, amongst other things, to revoke EU financial services law that had been retained following Brexit and replace it with UK-sourced rules. The then UK Government's vision is for an open, green, and technologically advanced financial services sector that is globally competitive, with this Act being at its core. The Act will result in fundamental amendments to the FSMA 2000. It will also grant the FCA much wider powers to enable it to draw up legally binding rules which will be included in the FCA's Handbook (eg the UK Listing Rules, Prospectus Rules and Disclosure Guidance and Transparency Rules) rather than, as is currently the case, in legislation.

Laws which will be repealed include the UK version of MAR, the UK version of MiFIR and the related delegated legislation. It is unclear in what legislation the market abuse rules will appear after such repeal. There appears currently to be no intention to amend the substance of the current market abuse rules.

CHAPTER 11

INSIDER DEALING

11.1 INTRODUCTION

Part V of the Criminal Justice Act 1993 (CJA 1993) contains the insider dealing provisions. These provisions existed before the offence of market abuse came into force. As explained at **10.1** above, the criminal offence of insider dealing overlaps considerably with the civil offence of market abuse. The market abuse regime, however, does not affect the insider dealing regime. It is therefore possible to commit both the offences of insider dealing under the CJA 1993 and market abuse under UK MAR.

Lord Lane explained the reason for the insider dealing regime very effectively in layman's terms as follows: '... the clear intention to prevent, so far as possible, what amounts to cheating when those with inside knowledge use that knowledge to make a profit in their dealing with others' (*Attorney-General's Reference (No 1 of 1988)* [1989] 2 WLR 729).

As part of its ongoing get-tough strategy for market misconduct, the FCA has been using its criminal powers of prosecution for insider dealing with vigour. There have been at least 25 convictions for insider dealing, leading to prison sentences of up to four years, and further arrests have been made (see **11.6**).

11.2 THE OFFENCE

Section 52 of the CJA 1993 provides that the offence of insider dealing can be committed in three ways, namely, if an *individual who has information as an insider*:

(a) *deals* in price-affected securities, when in possession of *inside information* (s 52(1));

(b) *encourages another* to deal in price-affected securities, when in possession of *inside information* (s 52(2)(a)), or

(c) *discloses inside information* other than in the proper performance of their employment, office or profession (s 52(2)(b)).

Whichever way the offence is committed, there are two common requirements, namely, an individual as an 'insider' and 'inside information'.

11.2.1 Insider

Section 57(1) of the CJA 1993 defines what it is for a person to have information as an insider. This is where a person:

(a) has information which is *inside information*;

(b) has received that information *from an inside source*; and

(c) they *know* (a) and (b).

11.2.2 Inside information

Unlike the market abuse regime and the DTRs, which use the definition in UK MAR, Article 7, the insider dealing regime uses the definition of 'inside information' under s 56 of the CJA 1993. This is information which:

(a) relates to particular, rather than general, securities or companies;
(b) is specific or precise;
(c) has not been made public; and
(d) is price-sensitive (that is, would be likely to have a significant effect on the price of securities, such as shares, if it were made public).

This definition has been criticised because there is not much guidance about the meaning of the terms used. Until these words are defined, or their meaning falls to be decided by the courts, they must be given their ordinary dictionary meaning. It is not clear, for example, whether a rumour which turns out to be false would be 'specific or precise' (although common sense would suggest it would not).

11.2.2.1 Particular not general

This includes information which may affect a company's prospects (which may be about the sector in which the company operates rather than about the company itself).

11.2.2.2 Specific or precise

As discussed at **11.2.2** above, there is no definition of these terms.

11.2.2.3 Not made public

If information has been made public it is not inside information. Think back to Lord Lane's comments at **11.1** above; how can someone cheat if they are using freely available information? Section 58 provides some guidance as to when information has been made public. Information which a company provides to an RIS has been made public and therefore will not be inside information. Further s 58 provides that information made available only to a section of the public can also be treated as having been made public. It is difficult to see the logic in this. Surely it is unfair if, in order to make a profit, you use information I am unable to access? There is no guidance as to what constitutes a 'section' of the public.

11.2.2.4 Price-sensitive

There is no guidance on what amounts to a 'significant effect' on price, and so this has to be considered on a case-by-case basis.

11.2.3 From an inside source

Section 57(2) provides that a person has information from an inside source if they:

(a) are an inside source (that is, a director, employee or shareholder) of 'an issuer of securities' (for our purposes, a company (but not necessarily the company whose securities are the subject of insider dealing)); or
(b) have access to the information because of their employment, office or profession; or
(c) obtained the information from someone who obtained it by way of (a) or (b) above.

Persons falling within (a) and (b) are known as 'primary insiders'. Persons falling within (c) are known as 'secondary insiders', or 'tippees'. An example of a tippee is a director's relative, who overhears talk about an impending takeover bid and then invests in the target company.

11.3 THREE WAYS THE OFFENCE CAN BE COMMITTED

As explained at **11.2**, the offence can be committed in three different ways.

11.3.1 The dealing offence (s 52(1))

It is an offence to *deal* in price-affected *securities* on a *regulated market*, or by or through a *professional intermediary*.

11.3.1.1 Dealing

Section 55 of the CJA 1993 explains the meaning of 'dealing'. It includes:

(a) the acquisition, or disposal, of securities;
(b) any agreement to acquire securities (for example, entering into a share option agreement);
(c) any agreement to create securities (for example, subscribing for shares), whether as principal or agent; and
(d) procuring an acquisition or disposal of securities by any other person.

11.3.1.2 Securities

Securities are defined by s 54 of and Sch 2 to the CJA 1993. The definition is wide and includes shares, bonds, warrants and options.

11.3.1.3 Regulated market

Under powers granted by s 60 of the CJA 1993, this has been defined by the Insider Dealing (Securities and Regulated Markets) Order 1994 (SI 1994/187) as including both the Main Market and the AIM, as well as other, lesser-known UK markets, such as Aquis Stock Exchange. Dealing on a regulated market is referred to as an 'on-market' transaction. If you or I decide to buy shares in Marks and Spencer Group plc through the Stock Exchange, that is an on-market transaction. The dealing offence is concerned with on-market transactions.

11.3.1.4 Professional intermediary

A professional intermediary is a person who carries on a business of acquiring or disposing of securities, or who otherwise acts as a professional intermediary between persons taking part in any dealing in securities (s 59). A stockbroker acting in the normal course of business will be a professional intermediary, but lawyers and accountants acting in their normal course of business will not.

EXAMPLE

Imagine that B plc is considering making a takeover bid for X plc, a listed company. B's investment bank acquires some shares in X plc on B's behalf, as a preliminary stake-building exercise. The shares are purchased privately, directly from a shareholder in X plc. This is known as an 'off-market' transaction. Although this acquisition has not taken place on a regulated market, B plc made the deal through a professional intermediary, the merchant bank, and therefore the deal has the potential to be within the scope of the dealing offence.

11.3.2 The offence of encouraging another to deal (s 52(2)(a))

It is not necessary for the person who is encouraged to deal either:

(a) actually to deal; or
(b) to realise the securities are price-affected.

A simple statement such as 'I cannot tell you why, but now is a good time to buy shares in X plc' could be caught by s 52(2)(a).

11.3.3 The disclosing offence (s 52(2)(b))

This prohibits any individual from disclosing inside information to another person other than in the proper performance of the functions of their employment, office or profession.

EXAMPLE

Imagine that X plc, a listed company, is a weapons manufacturer. X plc is about to sign a lucrative deal with the Ministry of Defence. D, a director of X plc, knows about the deal. L is the company's lawyer. B is L's brother. Over a family dinner at which much wine is consumed, L mentions to B that this deal is pending. B, D and L all buy shares in X plc on the Stock Exchange before details of the deal have been made public. Who is guilty of an offence (subject to any defences)?

(a) D is guilty of insider dealing under s 52(1) (see **11.3.1**). She is an insider. She has inside information (she knows about the proposed takeover, which is specific information relating to X plc which has not been made public and is likely to have a significant effect on X plc's share price). D, presumably, knows that she is an insider with inside information. She received the information from an inside source (she has the information as a director of X plc). She has dealt in price-affected securities (the shares) on a regulated market (the Main Market).

(b) L is also guilty of insider dealing under s 52(1). He is in a similar position to D, although L is an insider because he has information through having access to it by virtue of his profession.

L is also guilty of an offence under s 52(2)(b) (see **11.3.3**) as he has disclosed the information to his brother, which is not in the proper performance of his profession.

If L encouraged his brother to buy shares in X plc, L is also be guilty of an offence under s 52(2)(a) (see **11.3.2**).

L is also guilty of serious professional misconduct and liable to be punished by the Solicitors Regulatory Authority (SRA) for breaches of the SRA Code of Conduct for Solicitors, such as breach of his duty of confidentiality.

(c) B may also be guilty of the dealing offence under s 52(1) (see **11.3.1**). Is he an insider? He is a tippee (see **11.2.3**). The source of the information is a primary insider (his brother, a lawyer) and B knows this. B has inside information. Does B know this? If B does, he will be guilty of the dealing offence.

11.4 TERRITORIAL SCOPE

11.4.1 Dealing

Section 62(1) of the CJA 1993 provides that a person is not guilty of the dealing offence unless:

(a) they were within the UK at the time of dealing;

(b) the market is a UK regulated market (such as the Main Market, or AIM); or

(c) the professional intermediary was within the UK at the time they are alleged to have committed the offence.

11.4.2 Encouraging or disclosing

Section 62(2) of the CJA 1993 provides that a person is not guilty of the encouraging or disclosing offence unless:

(a) they were within the UK at the time of the encouragement or disclosure; or

(b) the recipient of the encouragement or information was within the UK when they received that encouragement or information.

11.5 DEFENCES

11.5.1 General defences

Section 53 of the CJA 1993 provides defences to each of the three ways of committing the offence.

11.5.1.1 Dealing or encouraging

No offence will be committed if the defendant can prove that:

(a) they did not expect to gain an advantage. This is a difficult defence to run. The prosecution will have proved already that they were an insider and knew they had insider information;

(b) they believed the information had been (in the case of the dealing offence) or would be (in the case of the encouraging offence) disclosed widely enough to ensure no-one would be prejudiced; or

(c) they would have traded anyway, even if they did not have inside information. This could be used, for example, if they had to meet urgent financial commitments.

11.5.1.2 Disclosing

No offence will be committed if the defendant can prove that:

(a) they did not expect dealing to occur; or

(b) they did not expect profit to result.

Again, the defence set out at (b) is a difficult defence to run once the prosecution has proved the defendant was an insider who knew they had inside information.

11.5.2 Special defences

Schedule 1 to the CJA 1993 includes some special defences relating to market-makers, market information and price stabilisation.

11.5.2.1 Market-makers

A market-maker (see **2.5.2**) has a special defence to the dealing and encouraging offences (but not the disclosing offence) if they act in good faith in the course of their business as, or employment by, a market-maker.

11.5.2.2 Market information

There are special defences available to those who have inside information which qualifies as 'market information'. Market information is information consisting of any of the following facts:

(a) that securities of a particular kind have been, or are to be, acquired or disposed of, or that their acquisition is under consideration or the subject of negotiation;

(b) the number or price (or range of prices) of those securities;

(c) the identity of those involved, or likely to be involved, in any capacity in an acquisition or disposal; or

(d) the fact that securities of a particular kind have not been, or are not to be, acquired or disposed of.

There are two separate defences available. In each case, the defences are only available to an individual charged with dealing and/or encouraging. They are not available in relation to the disclosing offence. The defences are:

(a) The information which the individual had as an insider was *market information* and it was *reasonable* for a person in their position to have acted as they did, despite having that information as an insider at the time. Paragraph 2(2) of Sch 1 sets out a non-exhaustive list of factors to be taken into account in determining reasonableness (the content of information, the circumstances and the capacity in which the individual first had the information and the capacity in which they now act).

(b) The individual acted in connection with an acquisition or a disposal which was under consideration or the subject of negotiation (or in the course of a series of such acquisitions or disposals), and with a view to *facilitating the accomplishment* of the relevant transaction(s). The individual must also show that the information they had was *market information* arising directly out of their involvement in the transaction(s) in question. This is referred to as the 'facilitation defence'. Note that there is no reasonableness element for this defence.

It may help to consider an example of the 'market information' defence.

EXAMPLE

Imagine that X plc is considering making a takeover bid for Y plc, a listed company. The directors of X plc decide that, as a preliminary to the bid, X plc should purchase shares in Y plc on the Stock Exchange. X plc's directors instruct the company's stockbrokers to buy shares in Y plc. Are the directors guilty of insider dealing?

At the time of dealing the directors are insiders. They have inside information (namely, that X plc is about to make a bid for Y plc). The directors have that information from an inside source (in their capacity as directors). They will know that they have inside information from an inside source. The directors are dealing in price-affected securities (remember that the definition of dealing includes the situation where a person procures an acquisition of securities by another, here X plc (see **11.3.1.1**)) on a regulated market (the Main Market). It would seem that they are guilty of insider dealing under s 52(1).

Nonetheless, in these circumstances, the directors may be able to rely on the market information defence if they can show they acted to facilitate the accomplishment of the takeover of Y plc, and the information they had was solely market information arising directly out of their involvement in the takeover, and not any other confidential price-sensitive information.

11.5.2.3 Price stabilisation

There is a special defence for individuals engaged in price stabilisation operations within any price stabilisation rules made under s 144(1) of the FSMA 2000. Price stabilisation is market activity undertaken to support the price of shares offered on an IPO (see **Chapter 4**) and some secondary issues (see **Chapter 17**), as there is often a disproportionately large amount of selling at these times. The defence is available as the practice is justified on policy grounds (that it encourages equity finance and shores up confidence in the market).

11.6 SANCTIONS

The offence of insider dealing is punishable in the same way as the criminal offence of making a misleading statement or manipulating the market (under the FSMA 2000 – see **9.4** above), namely by imprisonment and/or a fine. On summary conviction, the maximum sentence is six months, and on conviction on indictment the maximum sentence is 10 years. This was raised from seven years on 1 November 2021.

Note that s 63(2) provides that no contract shall be void or unenforceable solely because an offence has been committed under s 52.

Insider dealing will also amount to a breach of a listed company's share dealing code and therefore usually a breach of the individual concerned's employment contract (see **7.8** above).

The FCA has responsibility for enforcing the insider dealing provisions of the CJA 1993, and has the power to launch criminal prosecutions in its own right without the need for permission from the Secretary of State of DBT or the Director of Public Prosecutions. A challenge to this power in an action brought by three individuals who were prosecuted for insider dealing failed in the High Court in December 2008.

In the first-ever criminal prosecution for insider dealing brought by the forerunner to the FCA, the FSA, in *R v McQuoid and Melbourne* in relation to TTP Communications plc, the two defendants, one a solicitor, were sentenced to eight months' imprisonment (one suspended for 12 months) in March 2009. In June 2010, Anjam Ahmad was sentenced to 10 months' imprisonment suspended for two years, 300 hours' community service and a £50,000 fine. Mr Ahmad was the first person to take advantage of new powers granted to the FCA under the Serious Organised Crime and Police Act 2005 allowing it to offer lower sentences or immunity from prosecution for co-operating witnesses.

One of the most egregious examples of insider dealing brought before the courts to date has been the case involving Christian Littlewood, a corporate financier, his wife Angie and her friend, juice-bar owner Helmy Sa'aid. They pleaded guilty to insider dealing in 2011. Littlewood was sentenced to three years and four months in prison, his wife to a 12-month suspended sentence, and Sa'aid was jailed for two years. In addition to the prison sentences, a confiscation order of £767,000 was subsequently made for each of Mr and Mrs Littlewood, failing payment of which an extra three years each would be added to their sentences. Mr Sa'aid was ordered to pay £640,000.

In February 2024 Mohammed Zina, a former analyst at Goldman Sachs, was sentenced to 22 months' imprisonment for six offences of insider dealing (and three of fraud). He came into inside information through potential mergers and acquisitions involving Goldman Sachs. He made a profit of just over £140,000 from trading on this information.

11.7 SCOPE OF THE OFFENCE

The offence of insider dealing is narrower in scope than the offence of market abuse (see **Chapter 10**). Unlike market abuse, only an individual can commit the offence of insider dealing; a company cannot (although an individual can commit the offence by requiring a company to deal). A company can, however, be convicted of aiding and abetting the offence. Anything done by an individual acting on behalf of a public sector body in pursuit of monetary policies, or policies with respect to exchange rates, the management of public debt or foreign reserves, cannot be the subject of an insider dealing offence.

As the offence is so narrow and subject to the criminal burden of proof and the vagaries of the jury system, it is difficult to convict anyone of it, and this explains the lack of prosecutions until 2008.

As one of the FSA's (the forerunner to the FCA) leading officials said in a speech on 22 May 2007 to leading financial institutions:

> Insider dealing cases are amongst the most difficult cases we are called upon to prove, they are time consuming and complex and we may not be able to establish all of the facts necessary to support an insider trading charge. Insider dealing may have been conducted by a number of defendants, involved multiple trades over a number of months and have been of a sophisticated nature. The trading may have been conducted through a number of accounts and attempts made to hide the distribution of proceeds. The investigation into such activities increasingly involves a number of foreign jurisdictions.
>
> It is rare to find a 'smoking gun' and often cases hinge on circumstantial evidence. It is quite common for insider traders to come up with alternative rationales for their trading strategies that can be difficult to disprove. In the consultative document preceding the legislation, the Government stated it would be inappropriate to impose criminal penalties if the individual did not realise that the information he had

> was inside information. This is something which can be very difficult to establish, for example in the face of a defendant who states that he was simply fortunate in the timing of his dealing.

For example in the Littlewoods case (see **11.6** above) the FSA amassed 1,700Gb of computerised material (described as a skyscraper sized pile of A4 paper), 43,000 hard-copy pages, and 10 years' worth of banking and trading records across 150 bank accounts and 18 trading accounts.

This was one of the reasons, of course, for the introduction of the market abuse regime. However, the FCA's keenness to use the criminal provisions seems to be bearing fruit.

CHAPTER 12

FINANCIAL PROMOTION

12.1 INTRODUCTION

As **Chapter 9** stated, the regulation of financial promotion is one of the key features of the FSMA 2000. The main restriction on financial promotion is in s 21 of the Act, but there are two other important sources which provide further detail about the financial promotion regime.

The first is the Financial Services and Markets Act 2000 (Financial Promotion) Order 2005 (SI 2005/1529) ('FPO 2005'), as amended.

The second is Chapter 8 of a regulatory guide, the Perimeter Guidance Manual ('PERG'), available in the FCA Handbook section of the FCA's website. The guidance is not legally binding, but may be persuasive.

The FCA's Conduct of Business Sourcebook ('COBS'), in particular Chapter 4, is also relevant, as it contains the rules for authorised persons on financial promotion.

The financial promotion regime is not confined to listed companies. The majority of the provisions referred to in this chapter are equally applicable to unlisted companies, other than the exemptions referred to in **12.9.2**, some of which apply to listed companies only.

12.2 SECTION 21 OF THE FSMA 2000

Section 21(1) provides that a person must not, in the course of business, communicate an invitation or inducement to engage in investment activity. This is referred to as the 's 21 restriction'; the criteria are explored in more detail at **12.7** below. Section 21(2) provides that s 21(1) does not apply if:

(a) the person making the communication is an authorised person; or

(b) the content of the communication *has been approved by* an authorised person.

Section 21(1) will also not apply if the communication is covered by an *exemption* (see **12.9**).

12.3 CONSEQUENCES OF BREACH

The consequences of a breach of s 21 of the FSMA 2000 are as follows:

(a) it is a criminal offence punishable by a fine and/or imprisonment (a maximum of six months on summary conviction; two years on conviction on indictment) (s 25);
(b) any agreement which results from a communication made in breach of s 21 may be unenforceable (s 30);
(c) any third party to the unenforceable agreement can sue for any loss incurred (s 30);
(d) there may be an order for an injunction or for restitution (ss 380, 382); and
(e) there may be an action for damages (s 150).

Standard Life Assurance Ltd was fined £2.45 million for failures resulting in the production of misleading marketing material for one of its investment funds.

In May 2024 the FCA brought charges against nine so-called online 'Finfluencers' for breaches of financial services law including issuing unauthorised financial promotions in breach of s 21 of the FSMA 2000. The nine are accused of using their instagram accounts to promote a complex financial product to their combined 4.5 million followers without the necessary authorisation.

The FCA can also take lesser action, such as requiring the amendment or withdrawal of a promotion with immediate effect, or censuring the wrongdoer.

12.4 WHAT IS A FINANCIAL PROMOTION?

Before we proceed, it would be helpful to identify what a financial promotion actually is. The term 'financial promotion' can be confusing. It is the name of an entire regime, yet the term is not actually referred to in the FSMA 2000, other than in the heading and side note to s 21. There is certainly no definition of the term. It does not mean much to the layman, or indeed to the lawyer who has not encountered it before. So what is a 'financial promotion'? Well, consider it as a generic term to refer to a communication covered by s 21. In very basic layman's terms, it is a communication that contains information which might entice someone to invest in a company, or do certain other activities in relation to investments in that company.

The key point to note at this stage is that what amounts to a financial promotion may not be immediately obvious. Of course, some financial promotions should set off alarm bells immediately. Take, for example, the company secretary who calls to inform you that the company is about to place a newspaper advertisement, 'Need extra cash? Invest in us – we are doing really well'. Hopefully, even the most inexperienced lawyer would consider that this might fall foul of s 21. However, consider a company which is planning to run a television advertising campaign to raise its profile. You happen to know that the company is preparing an IPO within the next month. The TV advertising campaign does not mention this at all. Would s 21 spring to mind? Would the company even consider bringing the existence of the campaign to the notice of its lawyers? Perhaps not, but it should, as in the context of the impending IPO, the advertisements might well fall within s 21.

Even advertising on the carrier bags used by sandwich shops for a spread-betting company has been held to be a financial promotion.

Its importance is reflected by the fact that every year in the UK hundreds of millions of pounds are spent by financial services companies across all media.

12.5 RELEVANCE IN PRACTICE

In practice, the rules relating to financial promotion mean that, if a client company is proposing to make a communication, the lawyer must check whether that communication will fall within s 21 of the FSMA 2000. If it does then this is not good, for the reasons set out at **12.3** above. The lawyer must advise the client that it needs to ensure that the communication falls outside s 21. The easiest way to do this is to instruct an authorised person (see **9.4.3**) to approve the communication before it is made (see **12.2** above). Sometimes it is not possible for an authorised person to approve the communication (see **12.9.1.1** below), and in such circumstances the lawyer must advise the client not to make the communication at all, or to change it to a form which can be approved. This approach is summarised by the flowchart in **Figure 12.1** below.

To put this into context, it is important for a lawyer advising a listed company to be alert to the types of communication that company might make, and to analyse whether these communications might fall within s 21. For example, if a company is raising funds, as considered in **Chapter 17**, then the company will publish a prospectus, perhaps a preliminary prospectus or a pathfinder document (see **6.9.3**), and a press announcement. If the company is effecting a takeover, as considered in **Chapters 20**, **21** and **22**, then the company may seek irrevocable undertakings and will make a r 2.5 announcement, circulate an offer document and announce levels of acceptance. The lawyers must advise as to whether these communications fall within the s 21 restriction or not, and the consequences of this. This advice will depend on the individual circumstances of the communication (which may affect, for example, whether an exemption applies).

Figure 12.1: Financial promotion flowchart

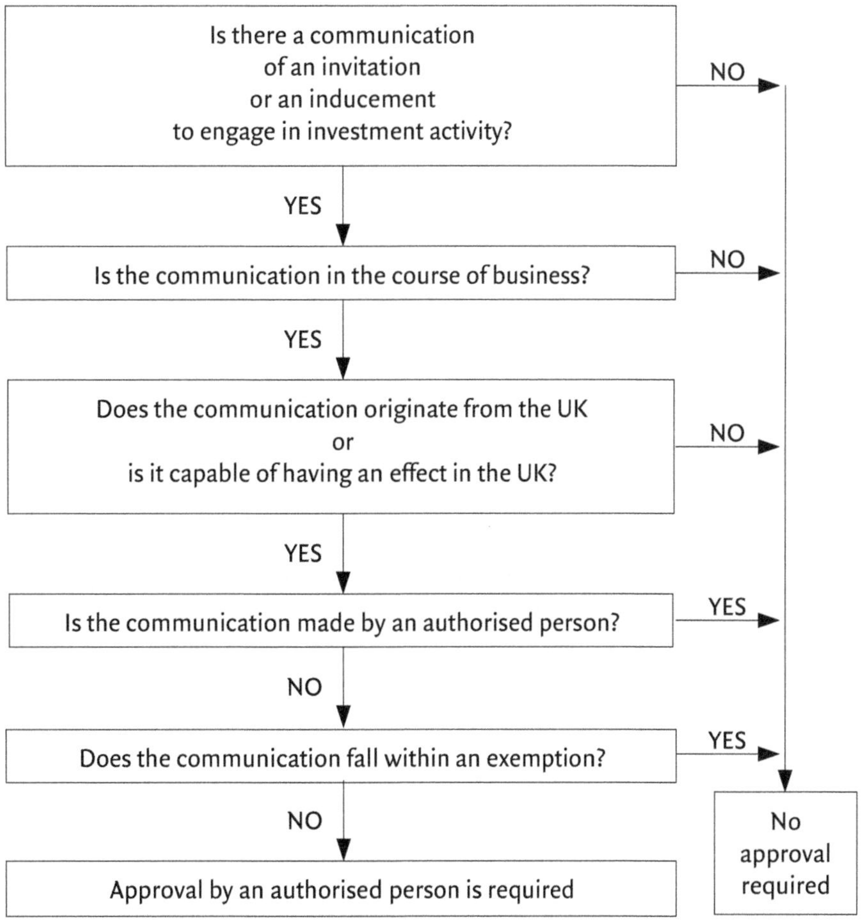

12.5.1 Example

Below is an extract from Foxton Group's announcement of its intention to float (ITF) announcement. This ITF is an announcement that is often used in IPOs as part of a strategy to raise the company's profile with a view to stimulating investors' interest in the offer of new shares. Note that it refers to the 'premium listing segment' under the former listing rules regime. At the time of writing we are still awaiting the first IPO of an ESCC company under the new listing rules.

Company Foxtons Group PLC

TIDM

Headline Intention to Float

Released 07:00 27-Aug-2013

Number 4547M07

NOT FOR RELEASE, DISTRIBUTION OR PUBLICATION, IN WHOLE OR IN PART, DIRECTLY OR INDIRECTLY, IN OR INTO THE UNITED STATES OF AMERICA (THE "UNITED STATES") (INCLUDING ITS TERRITORIES AND POSSESSIONS, ANY STATE OF THE UNITED STATES AND THE DISTRICT OF COLUMBIA), AUSTRALIA, CANADA, JAPAN OR SOUTH AFRICA OR ANY OTHER JURISDICTION WHERE IT IS UNLAWFUL TO DISTRIBUTE THIS ANNOUNCEMENT.

This announcement is not an offer of securities for sale in the United States or any other jurisdiction. This announcement is an advertisement and not a prospectus. Investors should not subscribe for or purchase any transferable securities referred to in this announcement except on the basis of information in the prospectus (the "Prospectus") intended to be published by Foxtons Group plc (the "Company" and, together with its subsidiaries, the "Group") in due course in connection with the proposed admission of its ordinary shares to the premium listing segment of the Official List of the Financial Conduct Authority and to trading on the main market for listed securities of the London Stock Exchange plc (the "London Stock Exchange"). Copies of the Prospectus will, following publication, be available for inspection from the Company's registered office: Building One, Chiswick Park, 566 Chiswick High Road, London W4 5BE.

For immediate release

27 August 2013

Foxtons Group plc

Announcement of intention to float on the London Stock Exchange

Foxtons Group plc today announces its intention to launch an initial public offering (the "Offer" or "IPO"). The Company intends to apply for admission of its ordinary shares (the "Shares") to the premium listing segment of the Official List of the Financial Conduct Authority and to trading on the main market for listed securities of the London Stock Exchange (together "Admission"). The Offer will comprise an offer of Shares to institutional investors.

Important Notice

The contents of this announcement, which has been prepared by and is the sole responsibility of the Company, have been approved by Credit Suisse and Numis solely for the purposes of section 21 of the Financial Services and Markets Act 2000 (as amended).

12.6 PURPOSE

The s 21 restriction on making financial promotions, like so many other statutory provisions in the field of corporate finance, is to protect investors. A financial promotion is basically a business communication which could encourage the recipient to take some action in relation to an investment. Section 21 controls how those communications are made and what they say, so that advantage is not taken of investors and potential investors.

12.7 THE DETAIL OF s 21

The following paragraphs consider some of the detail of the s 21 restriction and the exemptions from it. The FCA has provided a lot of guidance on the interpretation of the restriction and the main exemptions in PERG. This does not bind the courts, but it may be persuasive.

12.7.1 Person

'Person' includes a corporate entity such as a company.

12.7.2 Course of business

Section 21(4) of the FSMA 2000 gives HM Treasury the power to define this term, but to date it has not done so. This requirement excludes from the ambit of s 21 communications of a personal nature. So, if tonight in the pub I mention that I am going to buy a few shares in company X, and suggest that my friends do the same, my suggestion will not be caught by the s 21 restriction; the communication would not have a commercial nature. Further guidance is provided by PERG 8.5.

12.7.3 Communication

'Communication' means all communication, through whatever medium, so it includes oral and written communication as well as electronic communication (for example, a website announcement). 'Communicate' includes causing a communication to be made (FSMA 2000, s 21(13)). This means that if a company makes an announcement through, for example, financial PRs, and the announcement is in breach of s 21, then, subject to any exemptions which apply, not only the company but also the financial PRs would be responsible for the communication, and therefore caught by the s 21 restriction. PERG 8.6.3 sets out categories of persons whom the FCA does not consider will communicate or cause a communication to be made.

12.7.4 Invitation or inducement

Neither term is defined by the FSMA 2000. 'Invitation' will catch direct invitations to engage in investment activity, such as an invitation to buy shares. It can range from a polite request to an encouragement. A prospectus, together with an application form (see **Chapter 6**) would constitute an invitation to buy shares. 'Inducement' is thought to be wider. The Treasury stated that the term is intended to catch any communication which contains a degree of incitement to engage in an investment activity and that a communication of purely factual information would not amount to an inducement. It is unclear how wide this could be: what if a company embarks on a marketing campaign to raise its profile? It is possible that this could amount to an inducement if it contains any incitement to invest in that company. If the campaign involves putting the company's name onto a few umbrellas, then it would probably not amount to an inducement. PERG 8.4 provides further guidance.

12.7.5 Engaging in investment activity

Section 21(8) and (9) of the FSMA 2000, together with art 4 of and Sch 1 to the FPO 2005, define 'engaging in investment activity' as:

(a) entering into an agreement which constitutes a 'controlled activity' (such as buying, selling and underwriting shares; see Pt I of Sch 1 to the FPO 2005); and

(b) exercising any rights conferred by a 'controlled investment' (such as shares and bonds; see Pt II of Sch 1 to the FPO 2005) to buy, sell, underwrite or convert that investment.

This definition could affect how a company chooses to structure transactions. For example, while share sales constitute 'investment activity', asset sales do not.

12.8 TERRITORIAL SCOPE

The s 21 restriction will apply to any communication which is:

(a) made from the UK; or

(b) made from overseas, but is capable of having an effect in the UK (s 21(3)).

(However there are exemptions, under art 12 of the FPO 2005, for certain communications which are made to a recipient who receives the communication outside the UK, or which is directed only at persons outside the UK.)

Additional guidance is to be found in COBS 4.

12.9 EXEMPTIONS

As the s 21 restriction is so wide, to counterbalance this, the FPO 2005 contains over 65 exemptions from the restriction. Remember that while approval by an authorised person brings the communication outside the scope of s 21, it is not an exemption. If an exemption applies, there is no requirement for the communication to be approved by an authorised person.

The exemptions do contain some new terminology, however. The application of certain exemptions depends on the nature of the communication, in particular whether it is 'real time' or 'non real time' and, if real time, whether it is 'solicited' or 'unsolicited'. The meaning of these terms is explained at **12.9.1** below.

The s 21 restriction applies to both listed and unlisted companies. Nevertheless, there are some very useful exemptions which apply to listed companies only. The exemptions are detailed in, and in practice recourse must be made to, the relevant article of the FPO 2005 and PERG. However, the exemptions of particular use to listed companies are summarised at **12.9.2** below.

12.9.1 Terminology

In **12.9.1.1** and **12.9.1.2** below, references to 'art' are references to articles of the FPO 2005.

12.9.1.1 Real time and non-real time communications (art 7)

A real time communication is any communication made in the course of a personal visit, telephone conversation or other interactive dialogue. A non-real time communication is any communication which is not a real time communication. Examples include letters, e-mails and newspaper announcements. Article 7(5) contains a list of indicators that the communication is 'non-real time'.

The reason that the exemptions distinguish real time communications from non-real time communications is that the FCA considers that investors require more protection from real time communications (because people can get carried away in interactive dialogue and there is less opportunity for a cooling-off period). The exemptions which apply to real time communications therefore are narrower in scope than those exemptions which apply to non-real time communications. In fact, it is not possible for even an authorised person to approve real time communications, so care must be taken to ensure that any real time communication does fall within the scope of an exemption.

Further guidance on this issue is provided by PERG 8.10.

12.9.1.2 Solicited and unsolicited real time communications (art 8)

A solicited real time communication is a real time communication which has been initiated by the recipient, or which has been made in response to a request from the recipient. An unsolicited real time communication is a real time communication which is not a solicited communication.

12.9.2 Exemptions useful to listed companies

In **12.9.2.1** to **12.9.2.9** below, references to 'art' are references to articles of the FPO 2005.

12.9.2.1 Communications to shareholders and creditors (art 43)

The s 21 restriction does not apply to non-real time or solicited real time communications made by, or on behalf of, a company to, or directed at, its shareholders, provided that the communication does not relate to an investment (for example, shares) issued, or to be issued, outside the company's group. (However, any individual who sends such a communication, for example the chair, may be at risk of breaching s 19 of the FSMA 2000; see **9.4.**)

12.9.2.2 Group companies (art 45)

The s 21 restriction will not apply to any communication between a company and any of its group companies.

12.9.2.3 Annual report and accounts (art 59)

The s 21 restriction will not apply to the distribution by a company of its annual report and accounts, provided it meets certain criteria, such as not including any invitation or advice to persons to buy, sell, underwrite or subscribe for any investments.

12.9.2.4 Employee share schemes (art 60)

The s 21 restriction will not apply to any communications by the company, or its group companies or trustees, which are for the purpose of any employee share scheme (see **13.9**).

12.9.2.5 Sale of body corporate (art 62)

This is subject to certain conditions. The intention of this exemption seems to be to enable controlling shareholders of small companies to buy and sell those companies without being caught by the s 21 restriction. However, as drafted, the scope of this exemption is not clear. If read literally, this exemption would apply to takeovers of public companies, which many consider cannot have been intended. The Treasury recognised this issue and, during 2004, drafted proposals to narrow the exemption. It was expected that the exemption would be amended when the FPO 2005 replaced the previous Financial Promotion Order. However, surprisingly, no changes were made, and the Treasury has not clarified why it has not implemented its proposals.

12.9.2.6 Other communications by listed companies (art 69)

The s 21 restriction will not apply to some communications made by listed companies, provided that certain criteria are met.

12.9.2.7 Promotions included in listing particulars, etc (art 70)

The s 21 restriction will not apply to any non-real time communication in a prospectus or supplementary prospectus which has been approved in accordance with the UK Prospectus Regulation, or to any other document required or permitted to be published by the UK Listing Rules or the UK Prospectus Regulation (except an advertisement within the meaning of the UK Prospectus Regulation). This is because it is presumed that the FCA will provide sufficient protection to investors in these rules, so protection under the financial promotion regime is unnecessary.

The FCA considers that 'permitted' means something which is expressly permitted rather than simply not expressly prohibited (PERG 8.21.14G).

12.9.2.8 Material relating to prospectus for public offer of unlisted securities (art 71)

The s 21 restriction will not apply to any non-real time communication relating to a prospectus or supplementary prospectus, in the circumstances set out in art 71.

12.9.2.9 Investment professionals (art 19), certified high net worth individuals (art 48), high net worth companies (art 49) and certified and self-certified sophisticated investors (arts 50 and 50A)

Section 21 will not apply to communications made to the above-mentioned recipients. This can be useful to a company seeking to raise funds; by targeting these recipients only, the communication will be exempt from the s 21 restriction. There is the problem, of course, of how a company would know that the high net worth individuals and sophisticated investors it targets are certified.

Note that arts 48 and 50A apply only to communications relating to investments in *unlisted* companies.

12.10 CONCLUSION

Section 21 of the FSMA 2000 is very wide in its application. It covers most of the communications a listed company would make in its day-to-day corporate and trading activities. The exemptions, and the ability of authorised persons to approve non-real time communications, narrow the scope of the s 21 restriction. The exemptions are drafted with the rationale of s 21 in mind (see **12.6** above), namely investor protection. The more inexperienced the recipient, the more likely it is that the exemptions will not apply, and that s 21 will either prohibit the communication, or ensure that the communication is approved by an authorised person, in order to protect that recipient.

12.11 FUTURE DEVELOPMENTS

The UK Government and the FCA have become increasingly concerned at the risk for the public of promotions relating to new financial assets, such as cryptocurrencies, and the development of new high-risk financial investment products. Further concerns are the use of social media to promote these financial investments and the increasing ease by which the public can invest their money through online trading platforms (even via a smartphone). As a consequence, at the time of writing HM Treasury is consulting on changes to the financial promotions regime. These include:

(i) increasing regulation for the promotion of high-risk investments; and

(ii) bringing 'buy now pay later' services, such as Klarna, within s 21.

You can find information on the current status of these changes via the FCA's website. Changes to the existing financial promotion regime are expected in the coming months.

PART III

EQUITY FINANCE

CHAPTER 13

SHARES

13.1 INTRODUCTION

Shares are not unique to listed companies, or even to public companies. Most companies have limited liability. Most companies with limited liability have a share capital, and are limited by shares rather than by guarantee. So why dedicate a whole chapter of this book to shares? Well, any corporate finance lawyer needs to have a sound understanding of the basic law relating to share capital. **Chapter 1** established that the principal reason most companies choose to float is to take advantage of the opportunities afforded by the market to raise funds, both on an IPO (considered in **Chapters 4, 5** and **6**) and once listed (considered in **Chapter 17**). **Chapter 1** also set out the requirements that a company's share capital has to meet before the company can re-register as a public company. **Chapter 4** explained that the company's share capital has to meet further requirements before the company can seek an IPO. **Part IV** of this book also explains that listed companies often use their share capital as consideration when entering into various transactions, such as acquisitions or takeovers of other companies.

So listed companies are always making changes to their share capital. It is the lawyer's job to make sure they do so in a way permitted by law. **Chapters 13** to **16** explore the law relating to the share capital of a company, with particular focus on the law relating to listed companies.

13.2 WHAT IS A SHARE?

A share represents ownership of a company. A person who owns a share owns a bundle of rights in the company, such as the right to receive a dividend and, maybe, the right to vote. This person is referred to as a 'member', or 'shareholder', of that company. This book uses the term 'shareholder', but 'member' means exactly the same thing. The term 'investor' may be used to describe someone who has invested cash in return for shares in a company, but it could also be used to describe someone who has provided a loan to the company. In the former scenario, the investor will be a shareholder; in the latter, she will not.

13.3 SOME TERMS RELATING TO SHARE CAPITAL

13.3.1 Nominal value (also known as par value)

Shares must have a fixed nominal value (CA 2006, s 542). A company can have shares with a nominal value of 1p ('1p shares'), 10p ('10p shares') £1 ('£1 shares') – in fact, shares of any nominal value, although the nominal value should not be too high, as, under s 580 of the CA 2006, a company cannot issue a share at a discount to (that is, for any less than) its nominal value. This means, for example, that a company could not issue a £1 share for 80p. If it wanted to issue the share for 80p, the nominal value of that share would have to be equal to or less than 80p.

Note that the nominal value will usually bear no correlation to the current market value of the share (see **13.3.5**). Most shares will be sold at a premium (see **13.3.2**). A share with a nominal value of £1 (a £1 share) could be worth, say, £5 when sold on the market.

13.3.2 Premium

A premium is the difference between the nominal value of the share and the price paid for that share. For example, if I pay £5 for a share which has a nominal value of £1, I have paid £1 nominal value and a premium of £4.

13.3.3 Restrictions on share capital

Under the CA 2006 a company may restrict the number of shares that it can issue by including a provision in the company's articles of association.

Companies formed before 1 October 2009, before the relevant provisions of the CA 2006 came into force, had restrictions on the number of shares they could issue in their pre-CA 2006 memorandum of association (the authorised share capital). Under s 28 of the CA 2006 these provisions are automatically treated as restrictions in the articles with effect from 1 October 2009. The restrictions can be removed by passing an ordinary resolution or by adopting new articles by special resolution with no limit on the issue of shares or authorising the directors to issue shares in excess of the current limit.

Remember that there is a minimum authorised share capital requirement for a public company of at least £50,000 or its euro equivalent (see **1.9.2** and **1.9.3.2** above).

13.3.4 Issued share capital

This is the total nominal value of the shares a company has in issue, ie owned by shareholders.

Remember that there is a minimum issued share capital requirement of £50,000 for a public company which is trading (see **1.9.2.2** and **1.9.3.2** above).

13.3.5 Market value

The market value is the price that investors are willing to pay for a share on the market. It usually bears no correlation to the nominal value of the share (see **13.3.1**). By way of example, the ordinary shares in J Sainsbury plc, the supermarket chain, have a nominal value of 28.57p. On 13 October 2024, the closing market value on the Main Market was 271p. Market-makers (see **2.5.2**) will set a price at which they are willing to buy shares and a price at which they are willing to sell shares. The market value of shares which are quoted in the newspaper is, in fact, a middle price between these two prices.

13.3.6 Market capitalisation

Market capitalisation is one method of valuing a company. It represents the market value of the company's issued share capital. It is calculated as follows:

number of issued shares × current market value of each share

J Sainsbury plc had a market capitalisation of (ie was worth) £6.42 billion (2,368,990,000 issued shares × 271p) at the close of trading on 13 October 2024.

13.3.7 Fully, nil or part paid

A share is 'fully paid' when the shareholder has paid the company the nominal value of the share together with any premium payable on it. If the shareholder has paid nothing in this regard, the share is 'nil paid'. If the shareholder has made a payment towards this, but has not paid the full amount, the share is 'part paid'.

Remember that there are specific requirements as to the amount which must be paid up on any share if the company is a public company. Each share (other than a share allotted pursuant to an employee share scheme – see **13.9**) must be paid up at least as to one-quarter of its nominal value together with the whole of any premium paid on it (see **1.9.2.2** and **1.9.3.2** above).

13.4 WHAT BENEFITS DOES A SHARE HAVE?

The share has a number of benefits.

13.4.1 Limited liability

Any shareholder is liable to pay the company the amount due on the share. Once the share is fully paid, the shareholder (together with any person to whom the shareholder transfers that share) will have no further liability to the company. Even if the share is nil paid or part paid (see **13.3.7** above), the shareholder will have liability only up to the balance due on the share.

Why is this relevant? Well, imagine that Marks & Spencer Group plc goes bust tomorrow. I have 100 shares of 1p (nominal value) in the company, for which I paid £270. I am a humble lecturer (from the corporate lawyer's viewpoint) living on the breadline. Should I be worried? Might I have to stand behind the company's debt and help to satisfy all those unpaid suppliers of ladies underwear? No, because my shares limit my liability to the company and to any liquidator of the company. In paying the amount due on the shares, I discharged my liability in full. The only issues that may concern me are that I might have lost some or all of the £270 I paid for my shares (see **13.5.2.3**) and I have lost the potential for further capital growth.

13.4.2 Rights

A share will convey various rights on the shareholder. The rights may be set out in the company's memorandum of association (but this is rare), or in a special resolution, but usually they are set out in the company's articles of association, under the following headings (or similar):

(a) *Income rights.* This is the right to share in the profits of the company, through the right to a dividend.

(b) *The right to receive notice of, attend and vote at meetings.* The right which gives the shareholder the most power is the right to vote.

(c) *Capital rights.* This is the right to share in the capital of a company, on a winding up, after payment of the company's debts. This may be a right to be repaid the capital paid up on the shares (that is, the nominal value and any premium paid for the shares), or an additional right to share in any surplus assets once the amount paid up on all classes of shares has been repaid.

13.4.3 Capital growth

Many investors are attracted to shares because of the opportunity they afford for capital growth. A shareholder will buy shares on the Main Market at a certain price. The price of those shares is likely to change throughout the period the shareholder owns the shares. The shareholder's original investment will rise or fall in value. The shareholder therefore takes the risk of capital gains or losses. Investors hope, of course, that they will be able to weather any storms and sell when their investment has increased in value. The reality, of course, can be very different. Some will remember (and the author's wallet can testify to this) the dotcom 'boom and bust' in the late 1990s, when shareholders who bought shares in dotcom businesses early enough became millionaires overnight. Some of these shareholders had the good sense (or luck?) to sell some shares and bank the profit, but others lost considerable amounts when the dotcom bubble burst in 2000.

13.5 CLASSES OF SHARE

Often the company will want to create different types of share, with different rights attaching to each type. The company may, for example, be pre-IPO, and want to attract a venture capital company to invest, in return for shares. Usually, the venture capital company will be in a position to demand enhanced rights over the other ordinary shareholders. Alternatively, perhaps the company wants to reward its loyal employees for their commitment, or the original owners who built up the company, with some shares, but does not want to give them the power to vote, which ordinary shares would convey. The company will create a separate class of shares to issue to the venture capital company, or to its employees. Again, the company's articles will detail the rights attached to each class of share, using the headings set out at **13.4.2** above. The lawyer may well have to draft these rights, and they can be quite complex.

The common classes of shares are discussed below. Note, however, that it is impossible to list all the classes you are ever likely to encounter. That is another advantage of the share; there is an infinite number of permutations. Take care, however, not to presume anything from the name of the class of share; always check the articles for the specific rights, and any restrictions, which attach to a share.

13.5.1 Ordinary shares

Ordinary shares are the most common class of share. Usually listed companies will list their ordinary shares. They may, however, choose not to list other classes of share. Remember that if a company chooses to list a class of shares, it must list all the shares in that class (see **4.3.1.1** above). It is Marks & Spencer Group plc's ordinary shares of 1p that you or I are able to buy on the Main Market.

Typical rights attaching to ordinary shares are examined at **13.5.1.1** to **13.5.1.3** below.

13.5.1.1 Income rights

The holders of other classes of shares might be entitled to a preferential dividend payment before the ordinary shareholders (see **13.5.2.1** below), but usually any profits to be paid out over and above that preferential dividend will be paid entirely to the ordinary shareholders. Shares which carry this unlimited right to income are referred to as equity shares (to draw an analogy with a law firm, equity shareholders are like equity partners; they have an unlimited, but proportionate, right to share in profits). Note, however, that the company is not obliged to declare a dividend. It may not declare one if it has not had a profitable year and there are insufficient profits available for distribution (see **18.2.1**).

13.5.1.2 The right to receive notice of, attend and vote at meetings

The ordinary shareholders are usually entitled to receive notice of, attend and vote at company meetings. Occasionally, however, non-voting ordinary shares are created, for example to raise capital without diluting control of the company. Usually, other classes of share will not afford the right to vote save in very limited circumstances.

13.5.1.3 Capital rights

On a winding up of the company, the company's assets are used, first, in paying off the company's liabilities, then in repaying the capital (that is, the amount paid up) on all the classes of shares other than ordinary shares. Only then will the ordinary shareholders be repaid the amount paid up on their shares. However, if there are any surplus assets once all these payments have been made, they will usually be distributed between the ordinary shareholders.

13.5.2 Preference shares

A preference share is any share which has preferential rights over other classes of share, particular ordinary shares. A company may have more than one class of preference shares, for example it may have 'A' preference shares, with one set of rights, and 'B' preference shares, with another set of rights. Again, the company's articles will list the rights which attach to the shares.

Often, as stated in **13.5** above, preference shares are tailor-made for a particular scenario and with particular preference shareholders in mind. The bargaining position of these shareholders might dictate the rights which attach to the shares. If preference shares are being created as a 'freebie' reward, the company will have a free hand in drafting the rights. However, if the company is keen to bring on board a venture capital company, that venture capital company might well be demanding as to the share rights it obtains in return for its cash injection into the company.

Typical rights which may attach to preference shares are examined at **13.5.2.1** to **13.5.2.3** below.

13.5.2.1 Income rights

Preferential dividend

The holders of preference shares might be entitled to a fixed preferential dividend payment from distributable profits before the ordinary shareholders are entitled to their dividend (see **3.5.1.1** above). This is often expressed as a percentage of the nominal value of the share. For example, a '5% preference share' will entitle a preference shareholder, on the declaration of a dividend, to a fixed payment of 5% of the nominal value of their shareholding before any dividend is paid to ordinary shareholders. To continue the analogy with a law firm from **13.5.1.1** above, preference shareholders are like salaried partners; they have a limited right to share in profits.

If the company does not declare a dividend then, subject to any cumulative rights (see below), the shareholders are not entitled to a dividend payment.

Cumulative right to a dividend

Unless the articles expressly state to the contrary, all preference shares will be 'cumulative'. Usually the articles state expressly that preference shares are cumulative. This means that if the company does not declare a dividend, or if it declares a dividend so small that the preference shareholders do not receive their full dividend, then the dividend (or the shortfall, as the case may be) will be carried forward to the next year automatically; and if there is no dividend that year, it will be carried forward to the following year, and so on.

EXAMPLE

Imagine that X plc has an issued share capital of £100m, divided into 90 million ordinary shares of £1 each and 10 million cumulative 5% preference shares of £1 each. This means that in any year in which a dividend is declared, the first £500,000 (5% of £10 million, the nominal value of the shares) is payable to the preference shareholders. Any excess is payable to the ordinary shareholders. The table below shows the dividend payments over a five-year period.

Year	Total dividend	Preference dividend	Ordinary dividend	Preference entitlement carried forward to following year
1	£900,000	£500,000	£400,000	Nil
2	£400,000	£400,000	Nil	£100,000
3	£550,000	£550,000	Nil	£50,000
4	Nil	Nil	Nil	£550,000
5	£1,200,000	£1,050,000	£150,000	Nil

In year 3, although a total dividend of £550,000 is declared, the ordinary shareholders do not receive £50,000. Instead, that is also paid to the preference shareholders, to make up some (but not all) of the £100,000 arrears carried forward from year 2. The rest of the shortfall (£50,000) is not paid to the preference shareholders in year 4; no dividend at all was declared then. Instead, it, together with the arrears of £500,000 from year 4, is made up in year 5, and there is even some left for the ordinary shareholders this year.

Dividend on a winding up

When preference shares are cumulative, the articles should make clear whether any arrears of the preference dividend are payable to the preference shareholders on a winding up of the company. For example, in the example used above, if X plc was wound up in year 4, the articles should clarify whether the £550,000 arrears would be payable to the preference shareholders.

Participating preference shares

Participating preference shares have further rights to a dividend, not just a preferential right to a fixed amount before the ordinary shareholders. Participating preference shares can be cumulative, but they do not have to be. Take again the example above. You can see that once the preference shareholders have taken their 5% dividend, the remainder goes to the ordinary shareholders in their entirety. Take year 5. The remaining £150,000 is paid to the ordinary shareholders. If the preference shares had been participating preference shares, the preference shareholders would have had some right to part of this amount. In other words, they get a second bite at the dividend cherry. The articles will provide what that right is, but it could be, for example, that the ordinary shareholders also take a fixed percentage, then the balance is divided equally between the preference shareholders and the ordinary shareholders. Participating preference shares may also have further rights to capital (see **13.5.2.3** below).

13.5.2.2 The right to receive notice of, attend and vote at meetings

Usually, preference shares will give preference shareholders the right to receive notice of general meetings and to attend meetings. However, they will seldom give preference shareholders the right to vote, other than in relation to certain limited matters, such as on a resolution to wind up the company, or to vary the rights which attach to the preference shares.

13.5.2.3 Capital rights

Just because a preference shareholder has a preferential right to a dividend does not necessarily mean that they will have a preferential right on a return of capital, and vice versa. Often in practice, however, preference shareholders do have preferential rights as to capital. It may be that once the company has repaid its debts, the preference shareholders are repaid their capital before the ordinary shareholders. If there are any surplus assets remaining after even the ordinary shareholders have been repaid, then the preference shareholders may have some rights over the surplus, for example to divide it between themselves and the ordinary shareholders. In this case the preference shares would be participating preference shares. Unless there is an express provision to the contrary, however, this surplus will belong to the ordinary shareholders alone.

13.5.3 Redeemable shares

13.5.3.1 Creation

Under s 684 of the CA 2006, a company can issue shares which will, or may, be redeemed at the option of the company or the shareholder, if the company has in issue other shares which are not redeemable.

For a public company only, the company must be authorised to do this by its articles of association. A private company may include a provision in its articles excluding or restricting its ability to issue redeemable shares.

A company may find it useful to issue redeemable shares if, for example, a venture capital company wishes to invest in the company for a fixed period of time. Any lawyer drafting redeemable share rights should pay particular attention to s 685 of the CA 2006, which provides some guidelines as to the terms and manner of redemption which must be dealt with on creation of the shares.

13.5.3.2 Redemption

The general rule under s 687(2) of the CA 2006 is that redeemable shares can be redeemed only out of either:

(a) distributable profits of the company; or

(b) the proceeds of a fresh issue of shares made for the purpose of the redemption.

Any premium payable to redeemable shareholders on redemption must be paid out of distributable profits rather than capital (but see s 687(4) of the CA 2006, which provides that any premium payable in relation to redeemable shares which were issued at a premium may be made out of the proceeds of a fresh issue of shares, up to a certain amount). There is, however, an exception for private companies, which can redeem out of capital, subject to any restrictions in the articles of association and provided the company adopts the procedure in Chapter 5 of the CA 2006 to effect the redemption (s 687(1)). ***Business Law and Practice*** considers further the law relating to the redemption of redeemable shares.

13.5.3.3 The effect of redemption

Pursuant to s 688 of the CA 2006, the effect of redemption is that the shares are treated as cancelled. This means that the issued share capital of the company will be reduced by the nominal value of the shares redeemed.

13.5.4 Convertible shares

A company may issue convertible shares, which, as their name suggests, can be converted into ordinary shares. The conversion may be at a specified time, or may be triggered by the happening of some event (eg, an IPO). The attractions to a convertible shareholder of converting to ordinary shares may be the acquisition of voting rights, or the fact that the market value of the ordinary shares has risen above the conversion price of the convertible shares.

13.5.5 Bonus shares (also known as 'scrip' or 'scrip issues')

If its articles permit, a company can transfer profits to a fund called its 'capital redemption reserve' and use it to issue 'bonus' shares to the shareholders in proportion to their existing shareholdings. Since the issue may reduce the amount of money available for paying dividends, the term 'bonus' is not really appropriate. The correct term is 'capitalisation of reserves' (or 'capitalisation issue'), but the terms 'scrip', or 'scrip issues' are also used to describe such shares.

13.5.6 Subscriber shares

The memorandum will show the names of the people who agreed to own shares when the company was first registered. These people are called the subscribers, and the shares which were allotted to them on the company's registration are referred to as subscriber shares (see CA 2006, s 8(1)). Section 584 of the CA 2006 provides that in a public company the subscriber shares must be paid up in cash.

13.5.7 Summary

You will now appreciate that, usually, ordinary shares bear the greatest financial risk, because, unlike preference shares, typically they do not afford any prior right to a dividend or return of capital. It is because ordinary shareholders bear this risk that, generally, they also are afforded full voting rights. However, ordinary shares also carry the greatest potential for financial gain, because the rights they do afford in relation to income and capital tend to be unlimited, unlike preference shares, which often afford fixed rights to income and capital.

13.6 SHARES OR DEBT?

This book is concerned with equity finance. There is another book in the series which deals with debt finance (see ***Banking and Capital Markets***). **Chapter 18** of this book provides an overview of the difference between equity and debt finance.

Some classes of share, which are equity finance, can easily be confused with debt finance. Take, for example, a 5% cumulative redeemable preference share. It will yield a return (the 5% fixed dividend), like interest on a loan, and it is redeemable, so repayable, like a loan. However, a closer inspection reveals that preference shares are in fact equity finance, not debt finance, for the following reasons:

(a) The 5% return is a dividend, not interest. It will therefore have different tax consequences. It will not be a deductible expense in the calculation of the taxable profits of the company.

(b) There is no guaranteed right to a dividend. The company will pay a dividend only to the extent that distributable profits are available for that purpose. The cumulative nature of preference shares does not alter this fact, as it is a benefit only if there are distributable profits in the future which are sufficient to cover the arrears of the preference dividend (or if the preference shareholder is afforded a right to arrears on a winding up). Conversely, an investor would expect the company to guarantee interest payments on a loan.

(c) The fact that the shares are redeemable is not a guarantee that the shareholder will be repaid. The company can redeem the shares only out of distributable profits or a fresh issue of shares (unless it is a private company; see **13.5.3.2** above). If it cannot redeem the shares this way, the shareholder will not be repaid.

13.7 VARYING CLASS RIGHTS

13.7.1 Introduction

Section 630 of the CA 2006 provides that rights attaching to a class of shares, 'class rights', can be varied. This is good news for a company, as it provides a degree of flexibility, for example to reduce the amount of a preference dividend, or to create a new class of preference shares which rank ahead of an existing class of preference shares.

In both of these examples, however, there will be a class of shareholders who are worse off as a result of the variation of the rights of the existing preference shares, namely, the existing preference shareholders. As you might expect, the CA 2006 provides some protection for these shareholders in the procedures it prescribes for the variation of class rights. The Act provides different procedures, and the procedure the company must follow is dictated by whether the articles of association provide a variation procedure or not.

13.7.2 Class rights not defined in the articles of association

If the articles do not contain a procedure for variation, s 630(4) provides that class rights can be varied if:

(a) the holders of 75% in nominal value of the issued shares of the class of shares to be varied consent in writing to the variation; or

(b) a special resolution, passed at a separate general meeting of the class in question (known as a 'class meeting'), sanctions the variation (this means that 75% of those who attend the class meeting and vote in person or by proxy must vote in favour of the resolution).

While this affords protection to the holders of the shares whose rights are to be varied, in that a majority of them must agree to the variation, it does mean that the rights attached to the 25% minority of shares can be changed without their owners' consent.

Section 633 of the CA 2006 addresses this. It provides a procedure by which those shareholders who hold, in aggregate, not less than 15% of the issued shares of the class can (provided they did not consent to, or vote for, the variation) apply to the court within 21 days of the consent to, or vote for, the variation to have it cancelled. The court can then choose either to disallow (if satisfied the variation would unfairly prejudice the shareholders), or to confirm the variation. If a s 633 application is made, the variation has no effect until the court confirms it.

13.7.3 Class rights defined in the articles of association

If the articles contain a procedure for varying class rights, s 630(2) states that it is this procedure which should be followed, not the statutory procedure under s 630. The rationale behind this is that the class of shareholders need no extra statutory protection; they had notice of the articles when they became shareholders, and also have power to change the articles.

The articles can specify a procedure for varying class rights which sets a higher or, importantly, a lower standard than the statutory procedure.

The same right to apply to court to have the variation cancelled under s 633 (see **13.7.2**) applies to variations made in accordance with the articles' procedure.

13.8 REGISTRATION OF SHARE RIGHTS

A company must send details of share rights it has created or varied to the Registrar of Companies (that is, to Companies House). This obligation arises under ss 636–640 of the CA 2006.

13.9 EMPLOYEE SHARE SCHEMES

It was explained at **1.7.6** above that one of the benefits of listing is that companies can issue shares with an identifiable value to their employees to incentivise and reward them. Companies do this through schemes known as employee share schemes, which, if structured correctly, have the following tax benefits:

(a) for the company – the cost to the company is a deductible expense for corporation tax purposes;

(b) for the employee – the benefit is not normally subject to income tax or national insurance contributions (if all the criteria of the individual plan are met). The shares do have some tax consequences, however; capital gains tax will be charged when the employee disposes of the shares.

Note that share schemes do not usually create a separate class of share; in fact, this is specifically avoided, as it can mean that the scheme does not attract the beneficial tax treatment outlined above.

The law relating to share schemes is particularly specialised, and firms will often have a discrete team dedicated to advising solely in relation to such schemes. The corporate lawyer will, however, need to know about the existence of any share schemes, because they will be referred to in documents they draft, such as a prospectus (see **Chapter 6**) or an offer document (see **22.4.1**). A noddy guide to the four share schemes which are currently approved by the Revenue is provided at **13.9.1** to **13.9.4** below. It covers the basics but not much more.

The corporate lawyer should also appreciate the following points about employee share schemes:

(i) they are exempt from the application of s 551 of the CA 2006 (see **14.5.2**);

(ii) they do not trigger pre-emption rights under s 561 of the CA 2006, although they do entitle their holders to pre-emption rights (see **14.6.8.2**);

(iii) there is an exception for employee share scheme shares from the prohibition on financial assistance (see **16.5.3**);

(iv) shares allotted in pursuance of an employee share scheme are also excluded from the requirement, under s 586 of the CA 2006, that shares must be paid up to at least one quarter of their nominal value, together with the whole of any premium (see **13.3.7**); and

(v) generally a prospectus is not required where shares are offered by a listed company to existing or former directors or employees. Instead, a short document giving details of the company, the offer and the shares will suffice (see **6.4.1.5(h)** and **6.4.2.4(e)**).

13.9.1 Savings-related share option scheme or save as you earn (SAYE)

This scheme must be open to all employees. The company grants options to purchase shares in the company. At the time the option is granted, the price of the shares is fixed and the employees start to make regular monthly contributions to savings accounts. When an employee's account matures, the employee can use the proceeds to fund the exercise of the option.

13.9.2 Share incentive plan (SIP)

This scheme must also be open to all employees. There is a number of possible features. The company may:

(a) issue up to £3,600 worth of shares each year to an individual employee;

(b) allow an individual to purchase shares each year up to a value of the lower of £1,800, or 10% of salary; or

(c) issue up to two shares for each share purchased by an individual employee.

13.9.3 Approved company share option plan (CSOP)

This scheme can be made available to selected employees, and so is often used to reward senior executives. The company grants options to purchase shares in the company. As with the approved savings-related share option scheme (see **13.9.1** above), at the time of the option is created, the price for the shares is fixed. However, with this scheme there is no associated savings account; the employee must provide their own funds to exercise the option.

13.9.4 Enterprise management incentives (EMI)

This scheme can also be made available to selected employees, and, like the approved company share option plan (see **13.9.3** above), it is often used to reward key employees. The company grants options to purchase shares in the company. Again, at the time the option is created, the price for the shares is fixed. There is no associated savings account. A number of significant conditions attach to this scheme (for example, the scheme is only available to companies with gross assets not exceeding £30m and fewer than 250 employees).

CHAPTER 14

ISSUING SHARES

14.1 INTRODUCTION

Chapter 13 explored the concept of the share and the classes of share which may comprise a company's share capital. Once a listed company has created a class of share, it will want to use those shares to raise capital. This will involve issuing shares to shareholders, in return for consideration.

The legislation relating to the issue of shares is relatively easy to apply when the issuing company is a private company. However, the application of those rules to the issue of shares by a public company can be more complex, not because the legislation is fundamentally different (it is not), but because usually public companies have more complex share structures, so it is necessary to delve a little further into the detail of the legislation. In the case of the issue of shares by listed companies, there are other considerations in addition to the legislation to take into account, namely guidelines issued by the Investment Association, the Statement of Principles issued by the Pre-Emption Group and the requirements of the UK Listing Rules. This chapter considers share issues by a listed company.

In this chapter we shall be examining only those rules which apply to public companies.

14.2 TERMINOLOGY

Some terminology, which has the potential to be confusing, is explained below.

14.2.1 Issuing shares or transferring shares?

'Issuing' relates to the issue of a share from the company to a shareholder. It is different to 'transferring' or 'selling' a share, which is when a shareholder transfers a share to another person. On a share issue, the company is party to the transaction and receives money for the share. On a share transfer, the parties will be the shareholder selling the share and the shareholder buying the share, not the company, and so the selling shareholder receives the proceeds and not the company. This chapter considers only the issue of shares. **Chapter 19** considers the transfer of shares.

14.2.2 Allotted shares or issued shares?

When considering the subject of issuing shares, the terms 'allotted' and 'issued' arise frequently. Let us be clear from the outset what they mean and the distinction between them. In practice the terms are used interchangeably and, usually, it is entirely appropriate to do this. However, it is essential for the corporate finance lawyer to be aware of the specific meaning of terminology she uses when advising a client.

14.2.2.1 Allotted

Pursuant to s 558 of the CA 2006, shares are allotted when a person acquires the *unconditional right to be included* in the company's register of members in respect of those shares.

14.2.2.2 Issued

Although there is no statutory definition of the meaning of 'issued', case law suggests that shares are issued when the allottee's name *is registered* in the company's register of members in respect of those shares (*Ambrose Lake Tin and Copper Co, Re (Clarke's Case)* (1878) 8 Ch D 635, CA and *National Westminster Bank plc and Another v IRC and Barclays Bank plc* [1994] 2 BCLC 30, CA).

14.2.2.3 The distinction

The above explanations reveal the minute difference between the two terms. The distinction lies in whether the shareholder's name has been included in the register of members, with allotment preceding issue. Of course, the majority of companies ensure that the register of members is kept up to date. This will remove any distinction between the two terms, as one will equate to the other; as soon as a person has an unconditional right to be entered into the register of members in respect of certain shares, their name will be entered into the register of members in respect of those shares. At that stage, the shares will be both allotted and issued.

14.3 ISSUING SHARES: THREE VITAL QUESTIONS

Now that the terminology is clear, let us turn to the topic of issuing shares. There are three important questions which the lawyer must consider in relation to any issue of shares, namely (and in this order):

(a) Limit on the number of shares – does the company have a limit in its articles of association on the number of shares that it can issue?

(b) Authority to allot – do the directors have sufficient authority to allot the shares under s 551 of the CA 2006?

(c) Pre-emption rights – do the pre-emption rights under s 561 of the CA 2006 apply to the issue and, if so, does the company need to disapply them?

The detail of, and the potential action required by, these questions is considered at **14.4** to **14.6** below.

14.4 LIMIT ON NUMBER OF SHARES

The first question the lawyer must consider, then, on a share issue, is whether there is a provision in the company's articles of association which limits the number of shares the company can issue.

Companies formed after 1 October 2009 under the CA 2006 can place a limit in their articles on the number of shares which can be issued.

Companies formed before 1 October 2009, before the relevant provisions of the CA 2006 came into force, were required to have restrictions on the number of shares they could issue in their pre-CA 2006 memorandum of association (known as the 'authorised share capital'). Under s 28 of the CA 2006 these provisions are automatically treated as restrictions in the articles with effect from 1 October 2009.

If there is a limit in the articles and the proposed issue of shares will result in that limit being exceeded then that provision must either be removed or altered to permit the issue.

14.4.1 Checking articles and issued share capital

14.4.1.1 Locating the filings at Companies House

The lawyer should first locate and check the articles to see if there are any restrictions on the issue of shares. In a company formed before 1 October 2009 the lawyer should also check the memorandum of association (as the authorised share capital clause became a limit under the articles on that date).

The lawyer must check back through the records the company has filed at Companies House, to identify the current articles. If these contain a limit on the number of shares then the lawyer must also check the existing issued share capital to see if the new issue of shares will exceed this limit. The easiest way to find the existing issued share capital is to take the figures provided in the latest statement of capital, which will be included on the relevant form which must be filed at Companies House. For example, after the allotment of new shares, the company must file a return of allotment Form SH01 within one month, which form will include a statement of capital. The lawyer should then check that the figure on record at Companies House corresponds with the company secretary's records (see **14.4.1.2** below).

Once the lawyer has identified the current figures, and knows how many shares the company is proposing to issue, it should be easy to calculate whether the company needs to remove the limit.

EXAMPLES

X plc wants to issue 50,000 shares in return for cash consideration. It has a restriction in its articles limiting its issued share capital to £1m divided into 1 million ordinary shares of £1 each. Let us take a couple of scenarios and analyse whether X plc needs to remove the restriction.

(a) *Issued share capital is £1m*

It is easy to see that in this case, X plc must remove or increase the limit by £50,000 to £1.05 million.

(b) *Issued share capital is £500,000*

In this case, X plc can issue a further 500,000 shares; it does not need to remove the limit.

(c) *Issued share capital is £975,000*

X plc needs to remove the limit or increase it, but only by £25,000 to £1.025 million; as it is currently below the £1 million limit by 25,000 shares.

14.4.1.2 Ensuring filings are up to date

The lawyer should always check that the issued share capital figures on record at Companies House correspond with the company secretary's records. This is to make sure the company is up to date with its filings. If it is not, it will need to make late filings, otherwise this may lead to problems later on in the share issue.

14.4.2 Checking the guidelines

If the company is a listed company, the guidelines issued by the Investment Association and the Statement of Principles issued by the Pre-Emption Group have a bearing on the extent to which the company can issue new shares. It is preferable to check these guidelines and principles at this stage, to identify from the outset whether they will affect the proposed share issue. If they will, the company may decide not to proceed with the issue, and any preliminary steps, such as removing the limit in the articles on issued share capital. The provisions of the guidelines and principles are considered at **14.5.7** and **14.6.16** below.

14.4.3 Removing the limit on issued share capital

Let us assume that X plc wishes to issue 50,000 shares of £1 each. The records at Companies House reveal the following:

(a) Issued share capital is £1m, divided into 1 million shares of £1 each.

(b) The articles contain a restriction preventing the company from issuing shares which would take the issued share capital over £1 million, being one million shares of £1 each.

The company secretary has confirmed that the records at Companies House accord with their records and are up to date. The lawyer has checked, and the issue will be within the guidelines issued by the Investment Association and the Pre-Emption Group (see **14.5.7** and **14.6.16** below).

X plc instructs its lawyer to draft the documentation to remove the limit on its issued share capital in its articles to enable the 50,000 shares of £1 each to be issued. How can this be done?

14.4.3.1 Special resolution

Section 21 of the CA 2006 provides that the company can change its articles by special resolution of the shareholders.

The lawyer must now draft the special resolution. The shareholders must pass this resolution by way of a special resolution in general meeting. The written resolution procedure under s 288 of the CA 2006 is not available to a public company.

If the company is formed before 1 October 2009 and there is an existing limit (see **14.4**) then it can be removed in one of three ways:

(a) by passing an ordinary resolution to remove the limit; or

(b) by passing a special resolution to adopt new articles without a limit; or

(c) by passing a special resolution amending the articles authorising the directors to allot shares in excess of the limit.

Of course if there is no limit in the articles of association in the company concerned then this step can be dispensed with altogether.

14.4.3.2 Notifying Companies House

Under ss 29 and 30 of the CA 2006, a copy of the resolution and the amended articles must be sent to Companies House within 15 days of the date of the resolution (s 30(1)). Failure to comply with s 30 renders the company, and every officer who is in default, liable to a fine (s 30(2) and (3)).

14.4.4 The UK Listing Rules

The lawyer must also ensure that if the issuing company is a listed company it complies with the continuing obligations of the FCA in relation to communicating with its shareholders about the increase in issued share capital. These requirements are explained at 7.9 above. In particular, an ESCC-listed company must publish a circular giving information on the change of articles (if relevant) and on the issue of new securities, including the arrangements for the allotment. The circular does not require the approval of the FCA (UKLR 10.2.1R). UK Listing Rule 10.6.9R provides that it must include the following information relating to the new articles (if relevant):

(a) an explanation of the effect of the proposed amendments; and

(b) either the full terms of the proposed amendments or a statement that they will be available for inspection:

(i) from the date of the sending of the circular until the close of the relevant GM at a place in or near the City of London or such other place as the FCA may determine; and

(ii) at the place of the GM for at least 15 minutes before and during the meeting.

In addition, the circular must contain certain information relating to the directors' authority to allot the new securities (see **14.5.6** below) and the disapplication of pre-emption rights (see **14.6.15** below).

The company must file a copy of the resolution and circular with the FCA by uploading it at the NSM, and notify an RIS that it has done so (UKLR 6.4.1R, UKLR 6.4.2R and UKLR 6.4.3R). Any proposed alteration of an ESCC-listed company's capital structure must be notified to an RIS as soon as possible (UKLR 6.4.4R(1)).

The aim of the additional rules is, of course, to provide full protection for shareholders in the listed company and to ensure the markets have all the information on the company as quickly as possible.

14.5 AUTHORITY TO ALLOT

Once the company has removed any limit (if this is required) on the issue of shares in the articles, the second question the lawyer must consider is whether the directors have authority to allot the shares.

14.5.1 Section 551 of the CA 2006

Section 551 of the CA 2006 applies to public companies (and private companies with more than one class of share). It prohibits directors from allotting 'relevant securities' unless they are authorised to do so by:

(a) the company's articles of association; or

(b) ordinary resolution of the shareholders.

14.5.2 Shares

Section 551 applies to:

(a) the allotment of any type of share (ordinary and preference) (s 551(1)(a)) *other than–*

  (i) the subscriber shares (s 559), and

  (ii) shares allotted under an employee share scheme (see **13.9**) (s 549(2)(a)); and

(b) the grant of any right to subscribe for, or convert to, any type of share (s 551(1)(b)) *other than* under an employee share scheme (s 549(2)(b)).

The exceptions are clear; no s 551 authority is needed to issue the initial subscriber shares in a company (see **13.5.6**), or to issue employee share scheme shares.

Clearly, most shares fall outside the exceptions referred to at (a)(i) and (ii) above and so are caught by s 551(1)(a); s 551 authority is therefore needed before those shares can be allotted.

What is not so obvious, however, is the effect of s 551(1)(b). Basically, this brings more than just shares within the ambit of s 551. A few typical examples, which often are the source of some confusion as to *when* s 551 authority is required in respect of them, are considered below.

14.5.2.1 Convertible loan stock

Convertible loan stock is a class of debt security which carries the right to convert into shares.

Is it within s 551?

Yes, provided the stock does not convert to employee share scheme shares.

When is s 551 authority needed?

There are three possibilities. Is it:

(a) when the debt securities are allotted; or

(b) when the debt securities are converted into shares; or

(c) both (a) and (b)?

The answer is (a) – s 549(3). This is important; *at the time the debt securities are allotted* there must be sufficient s 551 authority to cover the ordinary shares into which the debt securities will convert.

14.5.2.2 Options

Is an option within s 551?

The grant of an option to subscribe for shares (other than employee share scheme shares) will fall within s 551.

When is s 551 authority needed?

Section 551 authority is required *at the time of the grant*, not at the time of the exercise, of the option.

14.5.2.3 Convertible preference shares

A convertible preference share is a share which carries the right to convert into ordinary shares.

Is it within s 551?

Yes. In fact, both parts of s 551 (see above) catch these shares. Section 551(1)(a) catches the initial allotment of preference shares. However, the preference shares also carry a right to convert into ordinary shares, and this right is caught by s 551(1)(b) (see **14.5.2.1** above).

When is s 551 authority needed?

Again, the question is whether s 551 authority is required:

(a) when the convertible preference shares are allotted; or

(b) when the shares are converted into ordinary shares; or

(c) both (a) and (b)?

The answer is (a). Note, however, that, on the basis of the analysis set out above, the s 551 authority will need to cover *both* of the shares comprised in this type of shares, namely, the convertible preference shares and the ordinary shares they will convert into. For example, if the company is issuing 50 preference shares, which carry the right to convert into 50 ordinary shares, *at the time the convertible preference shares are allotted* the directors require authority to allot both share 1 and share 2, so two separate s 551 authorities are required.

A flowchart summarising the application of s 551 is set out at **Figure 14.1** below.

Figure 14.1: Section 551 flowchart

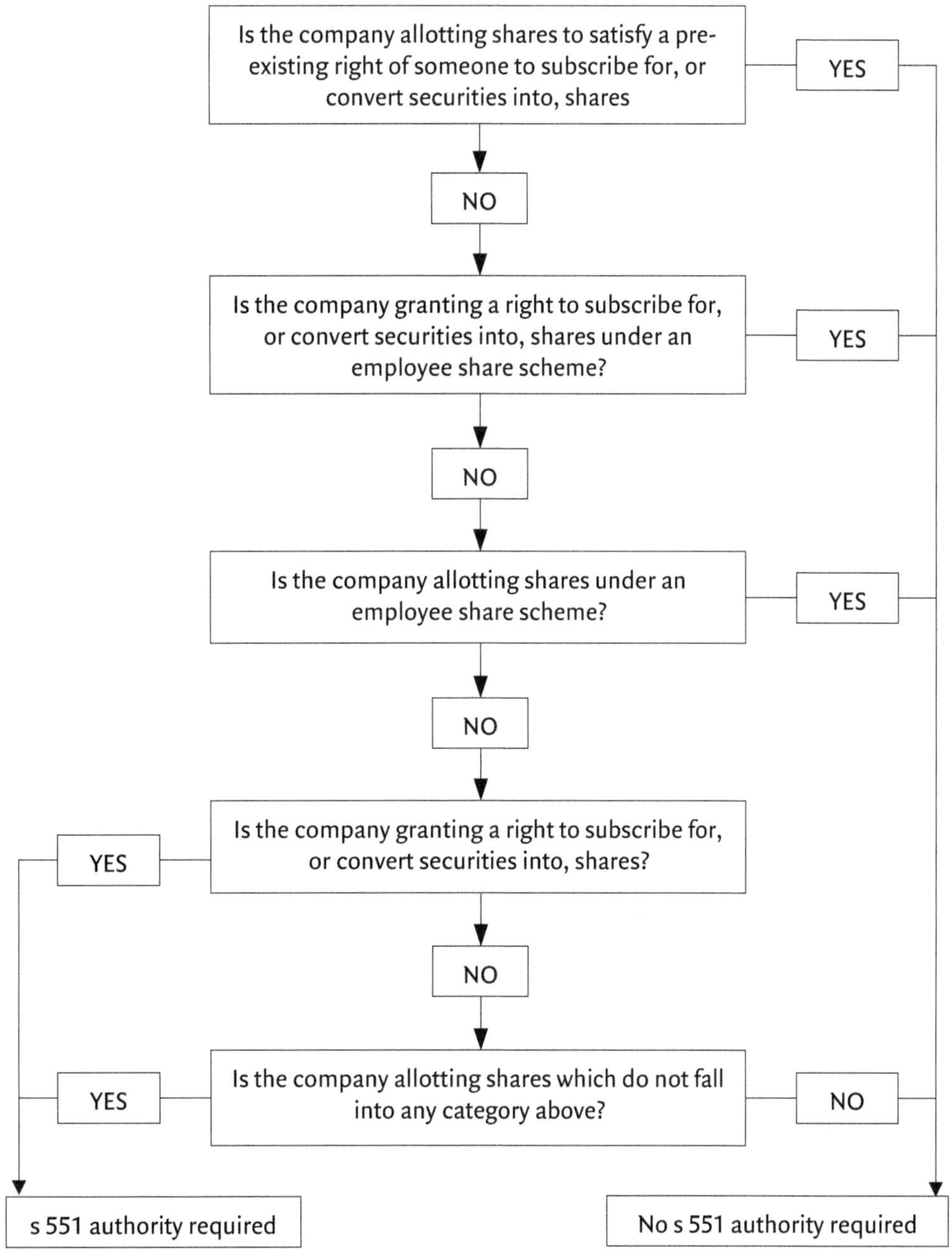

14.5.3 Checking the existing s 551 authority

We now know that it is necessary to examine carefully the nature of the securities to be issued, to determine whether s 551 authority is required. However, our example of X plc wishing to issue 50,000 ordinary shares (see **14.4.3** above) is relatively straightforward. The shares fall within s 551(1)(a). Section 551 authority is required. So now what? First the lawyer will need to check the existing s 551 authority, to see whether the directors already have authority to allot the 50,000 shares or whether a new s 551 authority is required.

As explained at **14.5.1**, any s 551 authority will be either in the articles of association, or in an ordinary resolution. The lawyer must check the articles and the records at Companies House to identify the most recent s 551 authority. The lawyer must then check this authority to identify two key features, namely:

(a) the date on which it expires; and

(b) the maximum amount of relevant securities which can be allotted under it.

If the expiry date has passed then the answer is obvious; a new s 551 authority is required for the new issue in its entirety.

If the expiry date has not passed, so the s 551 authority is still current, then the lawyer must identify how many shares have been issued pursuant to that authority. If the maximum amount of shares has been issued, or if the proposed issue would exceed that amount, then a new s 551 authority is required. If not, then the existing s 551 authority will suffice.

14.5.4 Obtaining a new s 551 authority

Section 551(8) provides that whether the original authority was given in the articles of association, or by ordinary resolution, it can be renewed by ordinary resolution. This is clearly a departure from the usual rule that changes to the articles require a special resolution. The lawyer will need to draft this resolution.

14.5.5 The resolution

Under s 551(2) of the CA 2006, the authority can be restricted to a specific allotment, or it can be drafted as a general power to allot. It may be made subject to conditions, or it can be unconditional. You can find an example of a resolution granting a s 551 authority in the notice of AGM attached to any listed company's annual report and accounts available via its website.

As **14.5.3** explained, s 551(3) provides that the authority must include two key pieces of information:

(a) the date on which it expires; and

(b) the maximum amount of shares which can be allotted under it.

The lawyer must bear this in mind, not only when checking any existing s 551 authority, but also when drafting a new s 551 authority. The two key pieces of information are considered at **14.5.5.1** and **14.5.5.2** below.

14.5.5.1 The expiry date

Under s 551(3)(b) of the CA 2006, the expiry date must not be more than five years from either:

(a) the date on which the company was incorporated (if the authority is contained in the articles of association); or

(b) the date of the resolution giving the authority.

Clearly (a) is relevant only in relation to drafting the original s 551 authority, and therefore it is (b) which applies in relation to drafting the majority of s 551 authorities. The authority can be for up to a fixed period of five years. In an abundance of caution, this is usually expressed in the resolution as being the fifth anniversary of the resolution less one day.

Note that, in practice, listed companies usually grant the directors a new s 551 authority each year, at the AGM, to comply with the Investment Association Share Capital Management Guidelines (see **14.5.7** below). Another safeguard in relation to the expiry date which can be drafted into a s 551 authority is to allow the directors to allot shares, even if the s 551 authority has expired, if they do so pursuant to an offer or agreement made by the company before the authority expired.

14.5.5.2 Maximum amount of relevant securities

The s 551 authority must state the maximum amount of shares which can be allotted under it. The amount is usually stated in terms of the maximum nominal amount (for example, £50,000), rather than the number of shares (for example, 50,000 shares of £1 each), so that if the company consolidates or subdivides its shares (for example, into shares of £2 or 10p), it will not need to amend the s 551 authority.

In relation to s 551(1)(b) (see **14.5.2** above), the maximum amount relates to the shares which will be issued on exercise of the right. If the issue were of 10 debt securities, for example, which will be converted to a maximum of 100 ordinary shares of £1 each, then the maximum amount would be £100.

When determining this maximum amount, if the company is a listed company, regard must be had to the Investment Association Share Capital Management Guidelines, which impose a limit on the amount. The provisions of the guidelines are considered at **14.5.7** below.

14.5.5.3 Notifying Companies House

Under s 555 of the CA 2006 the company must file with Companies House within one month a return of the allotment together with a statement of capital. These are contained in one Companies House form, Form SH01. Under s 554, directors must register an allotment as soon as practicable, but no later than two months after the allotment, otherwise an offence will have been committed.

The lawyer must also ensure that the s 551 ordinary resolution is filed at Companies House within 15 days of it being passed.

14.5.6 The UK Listing Rules

Again, if the company issuing the shares is a listed company then it must comply with the continuing obligations of the UK Listing Rules regarding communications with shareholders (see **7.9** above). In particular, UKLR 10.6.1R provides that when an ESCC-listed company sends out the s 551 resolution to its shareholders, the explanatory circular (which does not require approval by the FCA (UKLR 10.2.1R)) must include the following information:

(a) a statement of:
  - (i) the maximum amount of relevant securities which the directors will have authority to allot, and
  - (ii) the percentage which that amount represents of the total issued ordinary share capital as at the latest practicable date before publication of the circular;

(b) a statement by the directors as to whether they have any present intention of exercising the authority, and if so for what purpose; and

(c) a statement as to whether the authority will lapse.

The circular must also include information relating to any treasury shares held by the company.

The company must file a copy of the resolution and circular with the FCA by uploading them at the NSM, and notify an RIS that it has done so (UKLR 6.4.1R, UKLR 6.4.2R and UKLR 6.4.3R).

14.5.7 The Investment Association Share Capital Management Guidelines

The Investment Association has issued guidelines (see **Appendix 2**) which restrict the amount of share capital which can be included in a s 551, CA 2006 authority given by listed companies. The Investment Association Share Capital Management Guidelines provide that the maximum amount of relevant securities for which authority can be given is one-third of the issued ordinary share capital.

The Investment Association will accept an authority to allow the allotment of a further one-third of the issued share capital, provided that the additional authority is only used for fully pre-emptive rights issues and both the general and additional authorities expire at the next AGM (rather than up to five years for a general authority).

The permission for this additional one-third authority was introduced in 2008 in response to the frequency with which some listed companies, principally banks, were having to exceed the original one-third limit to raise sufficient funds from its shareholders to stave off possible insolvency during the financial crisis at that time.

EXAMPLES

Let us use X plc as an example. X plc is now a listed company and has an issued share capital of £1m.

(a) X plc wants to issue 50,000 shares of £1 each (not by way of rights issue). The sum equal to one-third of the issued ordinary share capital is £333,333. So it is fine to give the directors the s 551 authority for issuing the 50,000 shares.

(b) Imagine instead that X plc wants to issue 500,000 rather than 50,000 shares (not by way of rights issue). The issued share capital is still £1m. The sum equal to one-third of the issued ordinary share capital is £333,333. So the Investment Association Share Capital Management Guidelines would prevent X plc giving s 551 authority over the entire amount of shares X plc wants to issue, namely 500,000. It could issue only 333,333 shares.

(c) Imagine instead that X plc wants to issue 500,000 rather than 50,000 shares but this time fully pre-emptively by way of rights issue. The issued share capital is still £1m. The sum equal to two-thirds of the issued share capital is £666,666. As £500,000 is less than £666,666, the Investment Association Share Capital Management Guidelines would permit X plc to give s 551 authority to issue the number of shares it wants. This is only because the issue will be by way of fully pre-emptive rights issue. The further conditions mentioned above must also be satisfied.

This is why, as stated in **14.4.2** above, it is important to analyse the Investment Association Share Capital Management Guidelines upfront.

The Investment Association Share Capital Management Guidelines are non-statutory and designed to prevent the dilution of (principally institutional investors') shareholdings without the shareholders' prior approval. If the company considers that it has good reason to exceed the limit set out in the Guidelines, it can discuss this with the Investment Association in advance of any allotment.

14.5.8 Sanctions for breach of s 551

Breach of s 551 does not actually invalidate the share allotment (CA 2006, s 549(6)). However, s 549(4) and (5) provide that any director who knowingly and wilfully contravenes, or permits or authorises a contravention of, s 551 is liable to a fine.

14.5.9 Sanctions for breach of the UK Listing Rules

The sanctions for breach of the UK Listing Rules are as set out at **3.6** above.

14.6 PRE-EMPTION RIGHTS ON ALLOTMENT

Now that X plc has removed any limit in the articles on issuing the 50,000 shares, and the directors have authority to allot the 50,000 shares, what is preventing the company from allotting the shares? Well, there is one final question to consider: do the pre-emption rights under s 561 of the CA 2006 apply to the allotment and, if so, does the company need to disapply them?

(Remember not to confuse pre-emption rights on allotment of new shares with pre-emption rights on the transfer of existing shares. This chapter is considering the issue of new shares, not the transfer of existing shares, and therefore is concerned only with pre-emption rights on allotment.) Any pre-emption rights on transfer will be drafted into the company's articles of association or, if the company has issued any convertible securities, or warrants and options etc, the deeds or agreements setting out the terms of issue may also contain specific pre-emption rights on transfer.)

14.6.1 What is a pre-emption right on allotment?

A pre-emption right on allotment is a right of first refusal for existing shareholders on an issue of shares by a company. This means that when a company wants to issue shares, it must first offer those shares to the existing shareholders in proportion to their existing shareholdings.

14.6.2 Rationale

The right of pre-emption protects the shareholders against the dilution of their shareholdings. If each shareholder takes up the shares offered to them under the right of pre-emption, although the number of shares held by them will increase, their percentage shareholding will be preserved. Of course, the right helps the existing shareholder to preserve their percentage shareholding only if they can afford to buy the shares offered to them.

14.6.3 Where are pre-emption rights on allotment?

The main provisions relating to pre-emption on allotment are in the CA 2006 and the UK Listing Rules. A company's articles of association may also contain specific provisions relating to pre-emption on allotment. If a listed company has issued any convertible securities, or warrants and options etc, the deeds or agreements setting out the terms of issue may also contain specific pre-emption provisions on allotment.

14.6.4 Obstruction

We are about to consider the complex provisions relating to pre-emption rights. Bear in mind, while you are reading, that from the company's perspective (acting through its directors) pre-emption rights can be a pain. They may prevent, at least initially, the company from issuing shares to those to whom it would prefer to issue and compel the company to offer those shares to existing shareholders. We shall come back to this at **14.6.13** below.

14.6.5 Section 561 of the CA 2006

Section 561 of the CA 2006 provides statutory pre-emption rights on allotment. A company proposing to issue *equity securities* in return for *cash* must first offer the shares to holders of *ordinary shares* in proportion to the nominal value of their existing shareholdings.

Let us be very clear: this means that there are two types of securities we need to analyse:

(a) equity securities – that is, the shares the company is proposing to issue which might *trigger* pre-emption rights, so that those equity securities must be offered first to those people who have pre-emption rights; and

(b) ordinary shares – that is, the shares which *entitle* their owners to pre-emption rights, so that their owners are offered first refusal over an issue of equity securities.

These two types of securities are considered further at **14.6.6** and **14.6.8** below.

14.6.6 Equity securities

This term relates to the shares the company is proposing to issue. If the company is proposing to issue an equity security, it will trigger pre-emption rights under s 561. Section 560(1) of the CA 2006 defines 'equity securities'. It does so by reference to the term 'ordinary shares'.

Basically, equity securities are:

(a) any 'ordinary shares' in the company (see **14.6.8** below) *other than:*

  (i) a subscriber share (s 577) (see **13.5.6**),

  (ii) a bonus share (s 564),

(iii) shares held under an employees' share scheme (s 566), and
(iv) shares allotted *pursuant to* a right to subscribe (s 549(3)); and

(b) any *right to subscribe* for, or convert securities into, ordinary shares.

14.6.7 For cash

Section 565 provides that the pre-emption rights under s 561(1) will apply only if the issue of shares is *wholly* in return for cash. If the consideration for the issue is partly or wholly anything other than cash (for example, shares or land), the s 561 pre-emption rights on allotment will not apply. Section 583 of the CA 2006 defines a payment of cash to include cash or cheque.

14.6.8 Ordinary shares

This term relates to the shares that entitle their owners to benefit from pre-emption rights in the event that the company issues equity securities. Section 560(1) defines 'ordinary shares' as any shares *other than* a share which, in relation to both dividends and capital, carries a right to participate only up to a specified amount (the definition therefore includes shares such as an ordinary share and a participating preference share, and excludes, for example, non-participating preference shares – see **13.5.2.1**).

If you compare the definition of 'equity securities' (see **14.6.6**) with the definition of 'ordinary shares', you will notice several important distinctions between the two.

14.6.8.1 The right to subscribe for, or convert into, ordinary shares

This falls within the definition of equity securities but outside the definition of 'ordinary shares'. This means that while the issue of a right to subscribe for, or convert securities into, ordinary shares will *trigger* the pre-emption rights (see (a) and (b) below for more detail), those rights to subscribe or convert will not *entitle* their owners to pre-emption rights. Let us delve a little further into this by exploring the position regarding two different types of convertible security and whether they *trigger* pre-emption rights:

(a) *Convertible loan stock*. The loan stock will fall within para (b) of the definition of 'equity securities' at **14.6.6** above and the issue of convertible loan stock for cash will *trigger* s 561 pre-emption rights.

By 'triggering pre-emption rights' we are saying that the company must first offer the loan stock to existing shareholders *pro rata*. Why? the loan stock is convertible into shares, and if this conversion takes place it will dilute the existing shareholders' ownership if converted shares are held by outsiders.

(b) *Convertible preference shares*. The issue here is whether the convertible preference shares are participating or non-participating shares. If they are participating, they will be caught by the definition of 'equity securities' (para (a) at **14.6.6** above: they are 'ordinary shares' for these purposes) and will *trigger* s 561 pre-emption rights, assuming they are issued for cash. If they are non-participating, they will fall outside para (a) at **14.6.6** above (they are not 'ordinary shares'); however, they will be caught by para (b) at **14.6.6**. The issue of those shares will *trigger* the pre-emption rights, assuming they are issued wholly for cash.

14.6.8.2 Employee share scheme shares

Section 566 states that s 561 pre-emption rights do not apply to shares held under an employees' share scheme (see **14.6.5** above). This means that employee share scheme shares will not trigger the s 561 pre-emption provisions when they are issued, but, once issued, they will *entitle* their owners to pre-emption rights in the event that the company issues equity securities.

Employee share schemes are explored in more detail at **13.9**.

14.6.8.3 Bonus/subscriber shares

Sections 564 and 577 state that the allotment of bonus/subscriber shares will not trigger pre-emption rights, but holders of bonus and subscriber shares will be *entitled* to pre-emption rights provided they are ordinary shares and are not excluded because they carry only a limited right to participate in income and share capital.

14.6.9 How to consider pre-emption rights

When analysing whether s 561 will apply to a share issue, you need to separate your analysis of the securities the company is proposing to issue, which might *trigger* pre-emption rights, from your analysis of the securities which might *entitle* their holders to a pre-emption right on an issue of equity securities.

Now, two pieces of good news. The first is that the summary at **14.6.10** below, and the examples at **14.6.11** below, should simplify the application of s 561. The second is that, if the company decides to disapply the pre-emption rights, you will not need to apply s 561 at all (see **14.6.15** below) (although unfortunately you do need to be capable of applying s 561 to find out whether you need to disapply it in the first place).

14.6.10 Summary of statutory pre-emption rights on allotment

(a) Equity securities which *can trigger* pre-emption rights when they are issued (that is they must be offered pro rata to the existing shareholders):
   (i) ordinary shares;
   (ii) participating preference shares; and
   (iii) rights to subscribe for, or convert into, ordinary or participating preference shares.

(b) Securities which are not equity securities and *cannot trigger* pre-emption rights when they are issued:
   (i) non-participating preference shares;
   (ii) employee share scheme shares;
   (iii) any share issued for non-cash consideration;
   (iv) bonus shares; and
   (v) subscriber shares.

(c) 'Ordinary shares' which *entitle* their owners to pre-emption rights on an issue of equity securities (in other words, these shareholders will expect a pro rata offer of the equity securities being offered):
   (i) ordinary shares;
   (ii) participating preference shares;
   (iii) employee share scheme shares (if they are (i) or (ii) above);
   (iv) bonus shares (if they are (i) or (ii) above); and
   (v) subscriber shares (if they are (i) or (ii) above).

(d) Shares which *do not entitle* their owners to pre-emption rights on an issue of equity securities (in other words, these shareholders cannot expect a pro rata offer of the equity securities being offered):
   (i) non-participating preference shares;
   (ii) rights to subscribe for, or to convert into, ordinary or participating preference shares.

14.6.11 Examples

The following examples assume that there is not already in place a disapplication of the statutory pre-emption rights on allotment and that, unless otherwise stated, the consideration for the proposed issue is wholly cash.

EXAMPLE 1

A plc is proposing to issue ordinary shares. The company's existing share capital comprises ordinary and participating preference shares. The shares to be issued are equity securities and the proposed issue is for cash consideration. Therefore, unless a disapplication of s 561 is obtained, the directors must offer the shares first to the holders of the ordinary and the preference shares (both are 'ordinary shares') pro rata to their respective holdings.

EXAMPLE 2

B plc is seeking to acquire the entire issued share capital of Z plc and is offering Z's shareholders two B plc shares for each of their Z shares. Section 561 does not apply to the issue of B shares because the consideration for them is not cash. The consideration comprises the shares in Z.

EXAMPLE 3

C plc intends to issue ordinary shares. The existing capital structure comprises ordinary shares and convertible loan stock. This is an issue of equity securities but the new shares will be offered only to the holders of the ordinary shares. Convertible loan stock does not fall within the definition of 'ordinary shares' and so does not entitle its owners to pre-emption rights.

EXAMPLE 4

D plc intends to issue convertible loan stock. The existing capital structure comprises ordinary shares and non-participating preference shares. The issue of convertible loan stock does amount to an issue of equity securities. On this assumption, s 561 applies. Unless the section is disapplied the directors must offer the convertible loan stock first to the ordinary shareholders. The holders of the non-participating preference shares do not have statutory pre-emption rights as they are not the holders of 'ordinary shares'.

14.6.12 Pre-emption rights on allotment under the UK Listing Rules

As explained at **7.6.3** above, ESCC-listed companies only must, in addition to the statutory pre-emption rights, comply with pre-emption rights on allotment (UKLR 9.2.1R). The statutory rights under the CA 2006 apply to all companies registered in the UK, whether public or private. The UK Listing Rules rights apply just to ESCC-listed companies. These will usually be UK-registered, but they may also be registered overseas and so not subject to the CA 2006. On an issue of *equity securities for cash*, there is a continuing obligation on an ESCC-listed company to offer those shares first to the *existing equity shareholders* (of shares of that class, or of another class who are entitled to be offered them) in proportion to their existing holdings.

An issue of shares by an-ESCC listed company pursuant to the pre-emption rights set out in UKLR 9.2.1R is known as a 'rights issue' or an 'open offer'. **Chapter 17** considers these in more detail.

These rights of pre-emption on allotment under the UK Listing Rules reflect the statutory rights of shareholders of any company, listed or not, under ss 561 to 577 of the CA 2006, but the pre-emption rights on allotment under the UK Listing Rules are not identical. For example, UKLR 9.2.2R(2) provides that a company does not need to comply with the pre-emption rights in UKLR 9.2.1R in relation to equity shares which:

(a) represent fractional entitlements; or
(b) the directors think it is necessary or expedient to exclude from any offer due to legal problems under the laws of any territory or due to any regulatory body,

where there is a disapplication in a rights issue or an open offer, used solely in respect of the shares covered by (a) and (b) above, rather than generally for *all* shares.

In addition, UKLR 9.2.2R(3) and UKLR 9.2.2R(4) provide that the pre-emption rights under the UK Listing Rules will not apply if the company is selling treasury shares for cash to an employee share scheme, or if the company is an overseas company with an ESCC listing.

Section 561 makes no provision for fractional entitlements so, in practice, entitlements are rounded down. Further, in order to comply with s 561 without making an offer in jurisdictions outside the EEA with onerous requirements, companies must follow the procedure under s 562(3) of the CA 2006, known as the '*Gazette* route'.

These differences are easier to understand in the context of a rights issue. Their practical effect is considered at **17.7.6** below. Pre-emption rights under the CA 2006 can cause problems on a rights issue in a way that the pre-emption rights under the UK Listing Rules do not.

Note that there are no pre-emption rights on *transfer* in the UK Listing Rules. (Indeed, this would be contrary to the requirement that the shares of listed companies should be freely transferable – see **4.3.1.1**.)

14.6.13 What is the problem with pre-emption rights?

By now (perhaps with the help of a cold towel) you should be able to work out whether the proposed issue will trigger pre-emption rights either under the CA 2006, or under the UK Listing Rules. Let us consider the example of X plc again. X plc is proposing to issue 50,000 ordinary shares. These fall within limb 1 of the 'equity securities' test. The shares are to be issued wholly for cash. They will therefore *trigger* statutory pre-emption rights; they must first be offered to holders of relevant shares and relevant employee shares who are entitled to pre-emption rights.

Does this suit the company's purposes? Well usually no, not really. If pre-emption rights apply, the company must follow the detailed procedure set out in s 562 of the CA 2006, regarding the form the offer must take and the length of time for which it must remain open (14 days from the date the offer is made). Only once this period has expired, or the company has received a reply from each shareholder who benefits from the pre-emption rights, can it allot any shares which have not been taken up through pre-emption.

This usually inconveniences the company, so it will normally disapply the statutory pre-emption rights.

14.6.14 Disapplication of pre-emption rights under the CA 2006

The CA 2006 provides a number of ways in which a company can disapply s 561 when allotting equity securities for cash. Those under ss 567 and 569 are available only to private companies. We are not concerned with private companies, and so do not consider these methods any further.

Public companies can disapply pre-emption rights under ss 570 and 571 of the CA 2006. These sections provide that the company can disapply the s 561 pre-emption rights:

(a) specifically (see **14.6.14.1**); or

(b) generally (see **14.6.14.2**).

14.6.14.1 Specific disapplication (s 571)

A disapplication of pre-emption rights in relation to a specific allotment must be effected by a special resolution. However, this is not a popular method because of the requirements of s 571(5)–(7). This provides that before the resolution is proposed, the directors must recommend that the resolution be passed and circulate a written statement setting out:

(a) their reasons for making the recommendation;

(b) the amount of consideration for the shares; and

(c) the justification of that amount.

The statement must be circulated to the members before the general meeting to pass the special resolution. The directors risk up to 12 months' imprisonment or a fine if the statement contains anything which is materially misleading, false or deceptive (s 572).

14.6.14.2 General disapplication (s 570)

This is the most common method of disapplying pre-emption rights, and can be used where there is in place a general authorisation for the purposes of s 551 of the CA 2006. The disapplication can be effected either by special resolution, which is most common, or by a provision in the articles. Unlike under s 571, the directors are not required to make any recommendation in relation to the resolution (see **14.6.14.1**).

14.6.14.3 Duration

Whether the disapplication is specific or general, it will be effective only until the s 551 authority to which it relates expires (s 570(3)). This means that the disapplication cannot last more than five years. Whenever a new s 551 authority is obtained, a new s 570 or 571 disapplication should also be obtained.

14.6.14.4 Example

You can find an example of a s 570 disapplication and how it relates to the s 551 authority in the notice of AGM attached to any listed company's annual report and accounts available via its website.

14.6.14.5 Notifying Companies House

The company must file a copy of the s 570 (or 571) resolution at Companies House within 15 days of its being passed (s 29(1)(a) and s 30).

14.6.15 Disapplication of pre-emption rights under the UK Listing Rules

As explained at **7.6.3** above, the shareholders of an ESCC-listed company can also agree to dispense with their pre-emption rights under the UK Listing Rules. UK Listing Rule 9.2.2R(1) makes clear that a general disapplication by the shareholders of their statutory pre-emption rights in accordance with s 570 (or 571) of the CA 2006 will also dispense with the pre-emption rights under UKLR 9.2.1R. In practice, most public companies effect a general disapplication of the statutory pre-emption rights at each AGM, at the same time that they take any s 551 authority.

Again, if the company has an ESCC-listing, it will need to observe the continuing obligations of the UK Listing Rules relating to communications with shareholders. These obligations are considered at **7.9** above. UK Listing Rule 10.6.2R provides that a circular should accompany the s 570 or s 571 disapplication containing the following information (the circular does not require approval by the FCA – UKLR 10.2.1R):

(a) a statement of the maximum amount of equity securities that the disapplication will cover; and

(b) (in the case of a general disapplication in respect of equity securities for cash made otherwise than to existing shareholders in proportion to their existing shareholdings) the percentage which the amount generally disapplied represents of the total ordinary share capital in issue as at the latest practicable date before publication of the circular.

The company must file a copy of the resolution and circular with the FCA by uploading them to the NSM, and notify an RIS that it has done so (UKLR 6.4.1R, UKLR 6.4.2R and UKLR 6.4.3R).

14.6.16 The Pre-Emption Group's Statement of Principles

The institutional investors do not generally support issues of new shares by listed companies other than by way of a rights issue, because otherwise the issue will dilute a shareholder's shareholding, resulting in a smaller share of the company's profit (dividend) and a smaller percentage of voting rights. The Pre-Emption Group's members represent listed companies, investors and intermediaries. It was originally set up in 2005. In November 2022, the Group produced an updated 'Statement of Principles' to provide guidance to shareholders and companies on the disapplication of pre-emption rights. The Principles are supported by the PLSA and the Investment Association. They are set out in full at **Appendix 3**. They can also be viewed at the Pre-Emption Group's website (<www.pre-emptiongroup.org.uk>).

The Principles do not have the force of law but are stated to be a basis for discussion between companies and their investors. In practice, they reflect the position that the powerful institutional shareholders will take in relation to any s 570 disapplication. Paragraph 1 of Part 1 of the Statement makes clear that the Principles apply to equity issues for cash, other than on a pre-emptive basis, by UK and non-UK companies which have an ESCC listing on the Main Market. AIM companies are encouraged to comply too, although it is recognised that they may require a greater degree of flexibility. Paragraph 1 also makes clear that the Principles do *not* apply to issues of equity securities for cash if the issue is on a pre-emptive basis. The Principles therefore regulate placings, for example (see **17.9** below).

The Pre-Emption Group has stated that it will monitor the application of the Principles.

14.6.16.1 General disapplications

The Principles recognise that shareholders will consider some requests to disapply pre-emption rights as non-controversial. These are 'general' disapplications of pre-emption rights which do not exceed the size and duration set out in the Principles. A general disapplication is one sought by a company at an AGM other than for the purpose of an identified, proposed issue of ordinary shares (Part 2A, para 1). While the company needs to explain why the disapplication is required, and notify shareholders of the need for it in good time, shareholders are likely to agree in principle with such requests and will require less in-depth discussion about them.

The Principles set out the following guidance as to when a general disapplication is likely to be supported by the institutional shareholders:

(a) when the company is seeking authority to issue non-pre-emptively 10% or less of issued ordinary share capital in any one year (regardless of the purpose) (Part 2A, para 3); and

(b) when the company is seeking authority to issue non-pre-emptively no more than an additional 10% of issued ordinary share capital provided that the company intends to use it only in connection with an acquisition or specified capital investment which is announced together with the issue, or which has taken place in the preceding 12-month period (Part 2A, para 3).

In each of (a) and (b) above, the company may obtain an additional disapplication of no more than 2% of issued ordinary share capital but this can only be used for the purposes of making a 'follow-on offer'. This is designed to enable existing shareholders and retail investors to participate in a non-pre-emptive issue of new shares (placing) by the company. The requirements for a 'follow-on' offer are set out in Part 2B, para 3 and include the offer being made to existing shareholders who did not participate in the main non-pre-emptive offer (placing), for not more than £30,000 worth of shares per shareholder, where the price of the 'follow-on' offer does not exceed that for the main placing and the 'follow-on' offer is announced at the same time or as soon as reasonably practicable after the main placing is announced.

Companies that need to raise larger amounts of capital more frequently ('capital hungry companies') may seek additional disapplication of pre-emption rights, whether or not in connection with an acquisition or specified capital investment, if the reason for exceeding the level set out above is specifically highlighted at the time at which the request for the general disapplication is made (Part 2A, para 4).

(c) The price at which shares are proposed to be issued should be at a discount of no more than 5% (Part 2B, para 6).

A disapplication should not be granted for more than 15 months or until the next AGM, whichever is the shorter (Part 2A, para 5). Capital hungry companies may seek a disapplication for a longer period if the reason for the longer period is specifically highlighted at the time at which the request for the general disapplication is made (Part 2A, para 5).

The Pre-Emption Group has decided to assist companies by publishing template resolutions for the disapplication of pre-emption rights complying with the Principles. These can be found on its website. They comprise two separate resolutions and listed companies will therefore pass two separate special resolutions to make these disapplications.

14.6.16.2 Specific disapplications

In Part 3, the Principles recognise that some requests to disapply pre-emption rights might be non-general (ie 'specific') but nevertheless in the interests of the company and its shareholders. The Principles emphasise that the limits set out above are intended to ease the granting of authority to general requests to disapply pre-emption rights, not prohibit the granting of specific disapplications. Rather, any request for a specific disapplication should be considered by shareholders on a case by case basis.

The Principles set out examples of issues which are likely to be critical to shareholders in terms of voting on any specific disapplication, such as the strength of the business case, the size and stage of development of the company in the sector in which it operates and the extent to which the issue would dilute the value and voting control of existing shareholdings (Part 3, para 2).

14.6.16.3 The disapplication procedure

For both general and specific disapplications, the company must communicate with shareholders as soon as possible (Part 2B, para 1 and Part 3, para 2). Following the granting of a general disapplication, the company must make a post-transaction report in the format set out in Part 2B, para 10 of the Principles within one week of completion of the non-pre-emptive issue. The report should then be publicly announced through an RIS. The company should include this information in its next annual report. The report covers details such as the level of discount, the amount raised and how it was used (Part 2B, paras 10 and 11).

EXAMPLE

Let us apply the Statement of Principles to our example of X plc (see **14.5.7** above). The issued ordinary share capital at the date of the last published accounts was £1m. 10% of £1m is £100,000, so the disapplication required relating to the issue of 50,000 shares of £1 is 'general'. This would fall within the Principles and so these shares could be issued non-pre-emptively without seeking further shareholder approval than that already obtained at X plc's AGM.

14.6.17 Sanctions for breach of s 561

A breach of s 561 will not invalidate or cancel an allotment. However, s 563 of the CA 2006 provides that the company and any director who knowingly permitted the breach are jointly and severally liable to compensate any person to whom the shares should have been offered under the pre-emption rights.

14.6.18 Sanctions for breach of the UK Listing Rules

The sanctions for breach of the UK Listing Rules are as set out at **3.6** above.

14.7 ISSUING THE SHARES

Once the three questions listed at **14.3** above have been considered and the appropriate action taken, the company is in a position to issue the shares. However, the lawyer must check that the circumstances of the issue do not trigger any other legal problems. The areas to check are as follows.

14.7.1 Directors' duties

The directors must issue the shares in accordance with their statutory obligations under the CA 2006 and the remaining common law and fiduciary obligations. In particular, they must:

(a) act in a way they consider, in good faith, would be most likely to promote the success of the company for the benefit of the company as a whole (CA 2006, s 172); and

(b) act in accordance with the company's constitution and only exercise their powers for their proper purpose (CA 2006, s 171).

14.7.2 Financial assistance

There is a general prohibition on a public company providing financial help to anyone acquiring its shares. This can cause problems on a share issue, and the lawyer must analyse the terms of the issue carefully to identify any potential problems relating to financial assistance. **Chapter 16** considers this topic in detail.

14.7.3 Consideration

'Consideration' means the price paid for the shares. Generally, this does not have to be cash; a subscriber may pay cash, but may also pay in money's worth, such as with other shares (if the subscriber is a company) or other assets. However, where the issuer of shares is a public company, s 585(1) of the CA 2006 provides that it cannot accept consideration in the form of an undertaking:

(a) to do work; or

(b) to perform services.

In addition, a public company cannot allot shares as fully or partly paid up otherwise than in cash, if the consideration is or includes an undertaking which will, or may, be performed more than five years after the date of the allotment (s 587(1)). This is referred to as a 'long-term undertaking'.

14.7.4 Issuing shares at a discount

As explained at **13.3.1** above, s 580 of the CA 2006 provides that no company, public or private, listed or unlisted, can issue a share at a discount to its nominal value. The company can, of course, issue a share which is partly paid, but, as discussed at **13.3.7** above, in the case of a public company, each share (other than a share allotted pursuant to an employee share scheme – see **13.9**) must be paid up at least as to one-quarter of its nominal value together with the whole of any premium paid on it.

Finally, as **14.6.16** above explained, the Pre-Emption Group's Principles provide that a listed company should not issue any share under a s 570 or s 571 disapplication (on a non pre-emptive basis) at a discount of more than 5% of its market value. This restriction does not apply, however, if the pre-emption requirements of the UK Listing Rules are followed.

14.7.5 Valuation of non-cash consideration

Section 593(1) of the CA 2006 provides that if the consideration for the allotment is not cash ('non-cash consideration'), the consideration must be independently valued, and a report of the valuation must be given to the company and the subscriber. There are some exceptions to this rule, however, and one important exception relates to a 'share-for-share exchange', that is, when the consideration for the issue of shares by one company is shares in another company. In this case no valuation is required (s 594).

14.7.6 Class rights

The procedure required to vary rights which attach to a certain class of shares was examined at **13.7** above. The lawyer must examine the rights attaching to the shares the company proposes to issue, to check that the issue will not, in fact, vary any existing class rights (for example, if the shares to be issued are a new class which will rank above an existing class in terms of dividend rights). If they will vary class rights, the procedures detailed in **13.7** above will need to be followed.

14.7.7 The UK Prospectus Regulation

The lawyer must analyse the terms of the share issue to check whether a prospectus is required. **Chapter 17** considers this in relation to listed companies which are seeking to issue further shares.

14.7.8 Filing details of the issue

The company must notify the Registrar of any allotment of shares within one month of the allotment, by completing and delivering Form SH01 to Companies House. Note that the form must include a brief description of the consideration for which the shares were allotted. If the consideration was other than for cash, a simple description of the asset which comprises the consideration will suffice, such as '100 ordinary shares of £1 in Z Limited' if the consideration for the issue is shares. A statement of capital (contained in the form) must also be completed.

14.8 CONCLUSION

This chapter has shown that, while it is common for a company to issue shares, it can cause a few headaches for the lawyer. However, a methodical approach will ensure that all the required checks are made, and appropriate action taken. Do not forget, either, that while the lawyer should consider the three vital questions outlined at **14.3** above in relation to all issues of shares, not all issues will require action to be taken in relation to all three questions. For example, it may be that the company does not have a restriction in its articles on the number of shares it can issue, the directors already have authority to allot those shares, and the pre-emption rights have already been disapplied.

Also, the introduction to this chapter stated that it is not that the legislation which applies to listed companies is any more onerous than that applying to private companies, it is simply that the share capital of listed companies tends to be more complex. We have considered some of the more complex classes of securities that a listed company may have, such as convertible debt securities and convertible preference shares, in the context of whether an issue of such securities would require a s 551 authority, or trigger, or entitle recipients to, s 561 pre-emption rights on allotment. However, often listed companies will be issuing ordinary shares, like our example of X plc, where the process is much more straightforward because it is easier to determine whether the shares fall within the definitions in the CA 2006.

14.9 FUTURE DEVELOPMENTS

Financial Services and Markets Act 2023

This Act intends, amongst other things, to revoke EU financial services law that had been retained following Brexit and replace it with UK-sourced rules. The Act includes repeal of the UK version of the Prospectus Regulation and related delegated legislation.

A fundamental overhaul of the prospectus regime is expected in 2025. You will be able to follow this process via the FCA's website.

CHAPTER 15

DISCLOSURE OF INTERESTS IN SHARES

15.1 INTRODUCTION

People become shareholders of a company, public or private, in one of two ways. They either subscribe for shares which the company issues (see **Chapter 14**), or they buy shares from existing shareholders (see **Chapter 19**). In both cases, the new shareholder will identify themselves (or itself) to the company, so that the company can record the shareholder's details in its register of members and send out a share certificate.

This chapter considers the rules which require certain shareholders of public companies to disclose their interests in shares to the company, and why, despite the seemingly adequate process outlined above, a public company requires this extra protection.

15.2 NOMINEE SHAREHOLDERS

A 'nominee' shareholder is the registered owner of a share, but they hold that share on trust for the benefit of another person, the 'beneficial owner'. The nominee will hold the legal title to the share but will have no beneficial interest in that share. Usually the beneficial owner will require the nominee to execute a declaration of trust in respect of the share, in which the nominee will give various undertakings to the beneficial owner, such as:

(a) to account to the beneficial owner for dividends and other income received in respect of the share;

(b) to exercise rights attaching to the share, such as voting rights, as the beneficial owner directs; and

(c) to transfer the share as the beneficial owner directs.

For example, stockbrokers use companies to act as nominee shareholders, to manage the accounts of their clients more efficiently. We have also seen an example with the CREST system of holding shares in listed companies in electronic form (see **2.5.3.1**).

15.3 THE REGISTER OF MEMBERS

All companies must maintain a register of members, pursuant to s 113 of the CA 2006. However, s 126 of the CA 2006 prohibits a company from recording notice of any trust in the register of members. This means that the register will record details of the holder of the legal title only. It will not record any details of the holder of the beneficial title. In some cases, of course, this is one and the same person. If I buy a share in Marks and Spencer Group plc tomorrow, I will own both legal and beneficial title to it. However, anyone who buys shares through a nominee will remain off the register; it is the nominee's details which the register will record.

15.3.1 Advantages of s 126

The purpose of s 126 is to make the company's administration easier, because the company does not have to concern itself with matters of beneficial entitlement to shares. The company has no obligation to identify the beneficial owner, or to involve itself in the detail of what a nominee shareholder can or cannot do in relation to the shares. As far as the company is concerned, no one has an interest in the share other than the person entered in the register of members. This is so helpful to a company that it will often reiterate this provision in its articles of association.

15.3.2 Disadvantages of s 126

Section 126 does have its disadvantages. It means that the company is not aware of who has beneficial ownership of its shares. Why is this a problem? For private companies it does not tend to be problematic. Often in private companies the shareholders are a relatively small group of people who know each other.

However, with public companies whose shares are traded on the Stock Exchange this is not the case. There are many shareholders. Nominee shareholders can be useful to market abusers or insider dealers seeking to hide their true identities (see **Chapter 10** and **11**). The value of those companies whose shares are traded on the Stock Exchange means that they are often targets for a takeover offer (see **Chapters 20** to **23**). If the company is not aware of the beneficial ownership of its shares, what is to stop a potential bidder secretly building up a large shareholding in the target company by buying shares through a nominee? These shares would come in very useful when it comes to securing acceptance of the offer from target company shareholders.

For these reasons, there are rules which require the disclosure to the company of certain interests in shares. Some of them should be familiar, as we encountered them briefly in **Chapter 7** when we examined the continuing obligations of listed companies.

15.4 RULES REQUIRING THE DISCLOSURE OF SHARE INTERESTS

In implementing the Transparency Directive in the UK (see **3.1** and **3.5.3** above), Chapter 5 of the DTRs was introduced, requiring major shareholdings to be disclosed to the company. Chapter 5 is considered at **15.5** below.

Part 22 of the CA 2006 concerns a public company's right to investigate who has a beneficial interest in its shares. This is examined at **15.6** below.

There are certain other provisions under the DTRs and the Takeover Code which also require the disclosure of the beneficial ownership of a public company shares in particular circumstances. These requirements are discussed at **15.7**.

15.5 NOTIFICATION OF THE ACQUISITION OR DISPOSAL OF MAJOR SHAREHOLDINGS

The Transparency Directive requires rules to be in place in every EU Member State relating to the notification of the acquisition or disposal of major shareholdings in certain companies. The relevant provisions were introduced by Pt 43 of the CA 2006, which enacted new provisions in Pt VI of the FSMA 2000. Pursuant to these provisions the Transparency Rules were drawn up by the FCA. Chapter 5 of the DTRs contains the particular rules relating to the notification of major shareholdings. Chapter 5 applies to companies whose shares are admitted to trading on a *regulated* market (such as the Main Market). The rules therefore apply to the companies considered by this book. In addition, Chapter 5 of the DTRs applies to companies whose shares are admitted to trading on a *prescribed* market. This includes AIM. Chapter 5 is therefore the only part of the DTRs which extends beyond Main Market companies to include AIM-quoted companies. Chapter 5 requires a shareholder of such companies to disclose their shareholding to the company in certain circumstances. Paragraph **15.3.2** above explains why this protection extends only to certain public companies.

In looking at these rules for this book we shall only consider the position of a UK plc which has its shares admitted to the Official List and admitted to trading on the Main Market. We shall not be considering either AIM-quoted companies or non-UK companies. There is detailed guidance provided by the FCA on the application of the rules for all types of company in the FCA's Technical Notes.

15.5.1 Purpose

The purpose of Chapter 5 of the DTRs is to ensure that companies whose shares are traded on the Stock Exchange are made aware of the identity of the beneficial owners of their shares, and therefore who controls voting rights in the company. As explained in **15.3.2** above, this is particularly helpful in terms of assisting the company to expose insider dealing or market abuse and to defend against a possible unwanted takeover bid.

15.5.2 When the obligation arises

The obligation to disclose interests in shares is triggered when the percentage of voting rights a person holds either as a shareholder, or directly or indirectly through their holding of financial instruments, crosses certain thresholds, the lowest of which is 3% (DTR 5.1.2R). Although 3% may not seem like a major shareholding, it is worth remembering that companies whose shares are trading on the Stock Exchange are the biggest in the country. A 3% stake in Shell plc, one of the Stock Exchange's largest companies, is worth approximately £5 *billion* at the time of writing. So a shareholder with such a stake in the company has influence well beyond the apparently unimportant percentage, as so few shareholders will be able to reach this level.

15.5.3 The thresholds triggering disclosure

The applicable thresholds depend on two factors:

(a) whether the company is a UK company or a non-UK company; and

(b) the type of person holding voting rights in a company.

15.5.3.1 UK company

A person must notify a UK company if the percentage of voting rights they hold reaches, exceeds or falls below 3% and every whole percentage above 3% up to 100% (DTR 5.1.2R(1)).

It is important to note that a decrease as well as an increase in voting rights may be caught by the obligation to notify. Also, DTR 5.1.2R requires further changes, up or down, in the whole percentage figure of voting rights held by the person after an initial notification to be notified.

EXAMPLE

C buys 2% of listed UK company Z plc in January 2025. No obligation to notify arises (C has not reached 3%). In March 2025 C buys a further 1%. C must make a notification under DTR 5.2.1R as C now owns 3% of Z plc. C buys a further 2% in June 2025. C must make a further notification under DTR 5.1.2R as C now owns 5% and C's voting rights have changed by a whole percentage figure from 3% to 5%. In July 2025 C sells 1% of C's shares in Z plc. Again, as C's voting rights have changed by a whole percentage figure (from 5% to 4%), C must make another notification.

15.5.3.2 Specialist holders of voting rights

Certain institutional investors (such as an asset manager) need make a notification only at 5% and 10% and every whole percentage above 10% for certain types of share (DTR 5.1.5R).

15.5.3.3 Change in voting rights

Under DTR 5.6.1R, a listed company is obliged, at the end of each month during which there has been an increase or decrease in the number of its issued voting shares, to publish a statement of the new total number of voting rights in the company through an RIS. In addition, under DTR 5.6.1AR, a listed company must publish the same information after a transaction which produces a material change in its voting rights. This is defined in DTR 5.6.1BG as an increase or decrease of 1% or more. An increase can occur, for example, after a rights issue or an issue of shares under an employee share scheme. A decrease can occur, for example, after a buyback of shares by the company. The importance of this is that the percentage voting rights of a person who owns, say, 10 shares in a company with 100 issued shares (10%) changes if the number of issued shares in that company increases to 1,000 shares (now 1%) or decreases to 50 shares (now 20%) and that person does not buy or sell any shares.

Transparency Rule 5.1.2R(2) therefore obliges a person whose voting rights reach or cross one of the required thresholds by virtue of a change in the company's issued share capital, to make the necessary notification. This is a logical extension of the basic rule, for even though the person has not bought or sold any shares, their relative voting power (as shown in the example above) has now changed, and 3% is still 3% of the voting rights in the company even if it arose without any shares being bought or sold by the holder.

An example of an announcement made under DTR 5.6.1R is set out below.

Company	Rentokil Initial PLC
TIDM	RTO
Headline	Total Voting Rights
Released	17:30 21-Nov-2013
Number	6808T17

21 November 2013

Rentokil Initial plc
("the Company")
Total Voting Rights

In conformity with provision 5.6.1R of the Financial Conduct Authority ("FCA's") Disclosure and Transparency Rules the Company notified the market of the following:

As at 1 November 2013 the Company's issued share capital consisted of 1,817,498,329 ordinary shares of 1 pence each. The voting rights of these shares are identical with each share carrying the right to one vote per share. No shares are held in Treasury.

This total number of voting rights in the Company is 1,817,498,329 and this figure may be used by shareholders in the Company as the denominator for the calculations by which they will determine if they are required to notify their interest in, or a change to their interest in, the share capital of the Company under the Disclosure and Transparency Rules.

15.5.3.4 Percentage level

For the purposes of calculating whether any of the percentage thresholds in **15.5.3.1** and **15.5.3.2** has been reached, exceeded or fallen below, the percentage figure shall be rounded down to the next whole number (DTR 5.1.1R(6)): 3.5% therefore becomes 3% for the purposes of Chapter 5 of the DTRs; 14.99% becomes 14%; 6.07% becomes 6%, and so on. What this means is practice is that the notification obligation kicks in only when a whole percentage number changes. A person who buys more shares in a company, resulting in a change in voting rights from 3.2% to 3.9%, does not need to make a notification. Both figures are rounded down to the whole number 3% (that person will of course have made a notification on first crossing the 3% threshold). However, a person who sells shares, resulting in a drop in voting rights from 8.1% to 7.9%, must make a notification. The 8.1% is rounded down to 8% and 7.9% is rounded down to 7%. So although the sale represents a drop of only 0.2% in actual voting rights in the company, for the purposes of Chapter 5 it is a drop of whole percentage, thereby triggering a notification under DTR 5.1.2R.

15.5.3.5 Indirect holdings of voting rights

Under DTR 5.1.2R, for the purposes of calculating whether any of the percentage thresholds in **15.5.3.1** and **15.5.3.2** has been reached, exceeded or fallen below, a person must include any indirect holdings of voting rights (by virtue of the definition of 'shareholder' in the Glossary to the UKLR). Direct holdings, which we have considered up to now, are those in shares fully owned in the name of the person concerned. Indirect holdings are specified in DTR 5.2.1R. They cover scenarios where a third party has ownership of the shares but another person is entitled to acquire, exercise or dispose of the voting rights in certain circumstances. Three examples are set out below.

Controlled companies

Transparency Rule 5.2.1R(e) includes voting rights held by a company which another person controls. So, for example, if Mr T owned 2.5 % of the voting shares in A plc in his own name, no notification obligation would arise as he owns below 3% of the voting rights. If, though, a company, ACME Limited, owned 100% by Mr T, subsequently bought 1% of the shares in A plc then this indirect holding would be aggregated with Mr T's direct holding and take him to 3.5%, and therefore require him to make a notification under DTR 5.1.2R.

Proxies

Where the chair of a company is given proxy votes to exercise at their discretion at a general meeting then this too will amount to an indirect shareholding; and if totalling 3% or more of the voting rights, will also have to be notified (DTR 5.2.1R(h)).

Concert parties

Transparency Rule 5.2.1R(a) covers people who have an agreement to adopt a lasting common policy towards the directors of the company by the exercise of their joint voting rights. If such people hold 3% or more of the shares in a company then they must make a notification. This would catch people otherwise seeking to avoid the disclosure thresholds by clubbing together to acquire voting rights in a company, but with each holding of voting rights falling below the relevant threshold. For example, if G, H and J each own 2.5% of V plc's shares individually they have no notification obligation. However, if they had an agreement in accordance with DTR 5.2.1R(a) then the obligation would arise. This is particularly useful for a company in defending it against a surprise takeover bid. The rule seeks to ensure that the company is aware not only of a potential bidder's stake in the company (if it breaches 3%), but also of the group companies and the financial advisers of the bidder who may also be buying up shares.

15.5.3.6 Holdings of qualifying financial instruments

Under DTR 5.1.2R and DTR 5.3.1R, for the purposes of calculating whether any of the percentage thresholds in **15.5.3.1** and **15.5.3.2** has been reached, exceeded or fallen below, a person must consider not only direct holdings of voting rights and indirect holdings of voting rights (**15.5.3.5**), but also direct or indirect holdings in qualifying financial instruments which give the right to acquire shares with voting rights in the company. Transparency Rule 5.3.2R gives examples of such instruments, which could include convertible loan stock, options, etc.

15.5.4 Procedure for the making the notification

We now know what the disclosure obligation is and when it must be made. The question now arises as to how the holder of voting rights fulfils their obligation.

15.5.4.1 Who is notified and how?

The person must notify the company in which they hold the voting rights (DTR 5.1.2R and DTR 5.8.2(2)R). Furthermore, a copy of the notification must also be sent to the FCA (DTR 5.9.1 and 5.8.2(2) and the FCA's Technical Note UKLA/TN/543.3 Shareholder obligations).

In accordance with DTR 5.8.10R and DTR 5.9.1R, the notification must be made on Form TR1 (available on the FCA's website) and the copy sent to the FCA must be submitted electronically via the major shareholdings notification portal on its Electronic Submission System (ESS). The content of the Form TR1 can be seen in the example at **15.5.4.3** below.

15.5.4.2 Deadline for making the notification

The notification must be made by the relevant person to the company and the FCA within two trading days after the day when the person became aware, or should have become aware, of the acquisition or a disposal, or possibility of exercising voting rights (DTR 5.8.3R). This deadline is also triggered by the publication of a statement of a change in voting rights made under DTR 5.6.1R. The deadline for disclosure triggered by DTR 5.6.1AR is by the end of the next trading day after the material transaction. The FCA provides a link to a calendar of trading days through its website (DTR 5.8.9G). Basically, weekends and public holidays are excluded.

15.5.4.3 Content of the notification

The notification must include the information in DTR 5.8.1R for a notification of a direct or indirect holding of voting rights in shares, and DTR 5.8.2R sets out the required contents for a notification of voting rights in qualifying financial instruments. As explained at **15.5.4.1** above, a Form TR1 should be used. An example of a Form TR1 is set out below. Note that in the copy sent to the FCA only there must be an additional Annex containing contact details (DTR 5.9.1R).

Company French Connection Group PLC

TIDM FCCN

Headline Holding(s) in Company

Released 11:23 21-Nov-2013

Number 6278T11

TR-1: NOTIFICATION OF MAJOR INTEREST IN SHARES[i]	
1. Identity of the issuer or the underlying issuer of existing shares to which voting rights are attached:[ii]	French Connection Group
2 Reason for the notification (please tick the appropriate box or boxes):	
An acquisition or disposal of voting rights	X
An acquisition or disposal of qualifying financial instruments which may result in the acquisition of shares already issued to which voting rights are attached	
An acquisition or disposal of instruments with similar economic effect to qualifying financial instruments	
An event changing the breakdown of voting rights	
Other (please specify):	
3. Full name of person(s) subject to the notification obligation:[iii]	Schroders plc
4. Full name of shareholder(s) (if different from 3.):[iv]	
5. Date of the transaction and date on which the threshold is crossed or reached:[v]	30.10.13

6. Date on which issuer notified:	30.10.13
7. Threshold(s) that is/are crossed or reached:[vi, vii]	14% - 13%
8. Notified details:	

A: Voting rights attached to shares[viii, ix]

Class/type of shares	Situation previous to the triggering transaction		Resulting situation after the triggering transaction				
if possible using the ISIN CODE	Number of Shares	Number of Voting Rights	Number of shares	Number of voting rights		% of voting rights[x]	
			Direct	Direct[xi]	Indirect[xii]	Direct	Indirect
Ordinary GB0033764746	14,368,105	14,368,105	13,418,779	N/A	13,418,779	N/A	13.993%

B: Qualifying Financial Instruments

Resulting situation after the triggering transaction

Type of financial instrument	Expiration date[xiii]	Exercise/Conversion Period[xiv]	Number of voting rights that may be acquired if the instrument is exercised/converted	% of voting rights

C: Financial Instruments with similar economic effect to Qualifying Financial Instruments[xv, xvi]

Resulting situation after the triggering transaction

Type of financial instrument	Exercise price	Expiration date[xvii]	Exercise/ Conversion period[xviii]	Number of voting rights instrument refers to	% of voting rights[xix, xx]	
					Nominal	Delta

Total (A+B+C)

Number of voting rights	Percentage of voting rights
13,418,779	13.993%

9. Chain of controlled undertakings through which the voting rights and/or the financial instruments are effectively held, if applicable:[xxi]

Schroder Investment Management Limited	13,418,779 13.993%

Proxy Voting:

10. Name of the proxy holder:	
11. Number of voting rights proxy holder will cease to hold:	
12. Date on which proxy holder will cease to hold voting rights:	
13. Additional information:	The shares referred to in section 9 are held in portfolios managed by those firms on a discretionary basis for clients under investment management agreements. This disclosure has been calculated based on issue share capital amount 95,899,754
14. Contact name:	*[removed]*
15. Contact telephone number:	*[removed]*

15.5.5 The company's response to the notification

The notification made to the company concerned must be made public through an RIS by the end of the next trading day following receipt, in accordance with DTR 5.8.12R. The FCA provides a link to a calendar of trading days through its website (DTR 5.8.9G). The company must comply with DTR 6.3 when releasing the information. There is no set format for such an announcement, but if the Form TR1 is published the Annex must be removed (FCA's Technical Note UKLA/TN/543.1 Shareholder obligations).

15.5.6 Sanctions for breach

The FCA can impose the following sanctions for breaches of Chapter 5 of the DTRs:

(a) private or public censure;
(b) an unlimited fine;
(c) require the relevant information to be disclosed to it (FSMA 2000, s 89H); and
(d) may suspend or prohibit trading in the shares (FSMA 2000, s 89L).

For example, in August 2011 the FSA, the forerunner to the FCA, fined Sir Ken Morrison, the former Chair of Wm Morrison Supermarkets Plc, £210,000 for breaching DTR 5.8.3R for failure to notify the company of a drop in his voting rights below 6, 5, 4 and 3%.

15.6 THE COMPANY'S POWER TO INVESTIGATE BENEFICIAL OWNERSHIP

We have already established that direct and indirect major owners of shares (and certain financial instruments) in companies whose shares are trading on the Stock Exchange must disclose certain levels of voting rights to the company. Part 22 of the CA 2006 supplements Chapter 5 of the DTRs by allowing public companies (whether listed or not) to be proactive and investigate the beneficial ownership of its shares in certain circumstances either:

(a) on its own initiative, pursuant to s 793 of the CA 2006; or
(b) because a shareholder has compelled it to do so, under s 803 of the CA 2006.

This power reflects just how important it is considered to be that a public company, particularly one trading on the Stock Exchange, is able to identify the ultimate ownership of its shares. The aim is to enable the company to identify any shareholder who may have predatory intentions toward the company and may be considering or seeking to launch a takeover bid. This power has become all the more important due to the increasing use of nominee shareholder accounts in CREST (the dematerialised system for owning shares in listed companies – see **2.5.3.1**).

15.6.1 Section 793 notice

If a public company knows, or has reasonable cause to believe, that a person:

(a) is interested; or
(b) has been interested, at any time within the last three years,

in the company's shares, the company can serve a s 793 notice on that person, requesting them to confirm whether or not they do have such an interest, details of those interests and certain other relevant information. The notice may be served in writing or electronically. Section 793 details the specific information which the company can request, but it also includes, for example, details of any concert party arrangements (see **15.5.3.5** above). In fact, the company can request information which is not covered by the disclosure obligation; for example, even if the recipient of the notice has interests which are less than 3%, the recipient can still be requested to disclose their interests.

The s 793 notice must specify a reasonable time within which the recipient must respond. This is not defined. In practice, this seems to be interpreted as two days in an emergency situation (such as when the company suspects it is the target of an impending takeover bid), and five days in all other circumstances.

Of course, s 793 is particularly welcome when a company suspects it is about to be the target of an unwanted takeover bid. Imagine that the share price of X plc has been falling dramatically and that the press has speculated that now would be a good time for one of X plc's competitors to launch a takeover bid. The company secretary of X plc will send out s 793 notices in order to expose any prospective bidder. In the event that the bidder then makes the bid, the company secretary will continue to send out s 793 notices, to monitor the level of acceptances. Of course, the bidder should also comply with the disclosure obligations under Chapter 5 of the DTRs and notify the company whenever its shareholding increases by a percentage level.

In practice, while the company secretary will often draft the notice (as it is the company secretary who will have daily contact with the company's registrars), they will often consult the company's lawyers about the interpretation of aspects of the legislation, for example what the current practice is as to the minimum 'reasonable time' within which the company can demand a reply.

The CA 2006 does not specify a particular format for a s 793 notice.

15.6.2 Shareholders' s 803 requisition

Section 803 of the CA 2006 provides that shareholders who hold at least one-tenth of the company's paid-up voting share capital can requisition the company to use its powers under s 793. The requisition must:

(a) be in hard copy or electronic form;
(b) state that the company is requested to exercise its powers under s 793;
(c) give reasonable grounds for requiring the company to exercise its powers in that way;
(d) be authenticated; and
(d) be served in accordance with Pt 37 of the CA 2006.

Section 805 provides that the company must respond by carrying out the requested investigation and compiling a report of its findings, which it must make available at the company's registered office or at a place specified under regulations to be made in accordance with s 1136 of the CA 2006.

The company must act on the request within certain time limits set out in s 805. If it fails to do so, sanctions may be imposed (see **15.6.3.2**).

15.6.3 Sanctions

15.6.3.1 Criminal penalties

It is a criminal offence under s 795(2) of the CA 2006 to fail to comply with a s 793 notice, or knowingly or recklessly to make a false statement in reply. The offence is punishable with up to two years' imprisonment and/or a fine.

Fines can be imposed under s 798 of the CA 2006 for attempts to evade the restrictions placed under a s 794 order (see **15.6.3.2** below).

Fines can also be imposed for a failure to comply with a s 803 shareholder requisition, and for failing to meet various requirements relating to the obligation to provide a report under s 805 and allow access to it.

15.6.3.2 Imposing restrictions on shares

Section 794 of the CA 2006 allows the company to apply to court to have restrictions placed on shares covered by a s 793 notice where the recipient of the notice has failed to respond in time. Section 797 of the 2006 Act sets out the consequences of such an order if it is made:

(a) any transfer of the shares is void;
(b) no voting rights are exercisable in respect of the shares;
(c) the shareholder cannot benefit from any rights given by their shares to receive new shares in the company (such as a bonus or rights issue); and

(d) except on liquidation, no payment can be made of any sums due from the company on the shares, such as a dividend.

These restrictions are onerous, and are intended to prevent the person in breach of the s 793 notice from taking advantage of the breach, such as by launching a surprise takeover bid (the shares acquired could not be used to vote in favour of the bid) or by profiting from insider dealing or market abuse (the transfer is void). The company or any aggrieved person can apply to court for the removal of the restrictions under s 800 of the CA 2006. The court shall remove the restrictions only if it is satisfied that the relevant facts about the shares have been disclosed to the company and that no unfair advantage has accrued to anyone as a result of the breach of the disclosure obligation, or the shares are sold and the court approves the transfer.

15.6.3.3 Restrictions in articles of association

The articles of association of most publicly listed companies also set out restrictions that the company can itself impose on a person failing to give the information pursuant to a s 793 notice. Those restrictions will usually involve the shares being excluded from votes at general meetings of the company. See for example *Eclairs Group Ltd v JKX Oil & Gas Plc* [2014] EWCA Civ 640.

15.6.4 The register of share interests

Section 808 of the CA 2006 provides that the company must keep a separate register which records interests disclosed to it pursuant to a s 793 notice. The company must keep the register, and the public have the right to inspect this register under s 811 of the CA 2006.

Section 817 of the CA 2006 provides protection for anyone who has been entered into the register who does not consider they should be in that register. It can arise in the process of complying with the s 793 notice that a shareholder identifies another person as being interested in shares. Section 817 provides a process whereby that person can insist on being removed from the register, provided the information which has been supplied is incorrect.

15.7 OTHER REQUIREMENTS

There are further disclosure requirements under the DTRs and the UK Listing Rules. Both sets of rules apply only to listed companies.

15.7.1 Transactions by PDMRs and persons closely associated

As discussed in greater detail at **7.8** above, UK MAR, Article 19 requires PDMRs and persons closely associated (PCAs) to disclose to the company and to the FCA all transactions conducted on their own account in the shares of the company (or derivatives or any other financial instruments relating to those shares). This must be done promptly and no later than three working days after the transaction (UK MAR, Article 19(1)). The PDMR or PCA must include in the disclosure the information required by UK MAR, Article 19(6).

A listed company must then make that information public by notifying an RIS of the information it receives under UK MAR, Article 19(1) (UK MAR, Article 19(3)). The company must provide the information to the RIS within two working days of receipt of such a notification (UK MAR, Article 19(3)).

A template form for both notifications is annexed to UK Commission Implementing Regulation (EU) 2016/523 and contains the information required by UK MAR, Article 19(6).

An example of such a notification is set out below. They can be found on the RNS section of the Stock Exchange's website under the heading 'Director/PDMR shareholding'.

RNS Number: 8338K

Prudential PLC

26 September 2016

Notification and public disclosure of transactions by persons discharging managerial responsibilities and persons closely associated with them

<table>
<tr><td>1</td><td colspan="2">Details of the person discharging managerial responsibilities / person closely associated</td></tr>
<tr><td>(a)</td><td>Name</td><td>Tony Wilkey</td></tr>
<tr><td>2</td><td colspan="2">Reason for the notification</td></tr>
<tr><td>(a)</td><td>Position/status</td><td>Executive Director (PDMR)</td></tr>
<tr><td>(b)</td><td>Initial notification/Amendment</td><td>Initial notification</td></tr>
<tr><td>3</td><td colspan="2">Details of the issuer, emission allowance market participant, auction platform, auctioneer or auction monitor</td></tr>
<tr><td>(a)</td><td>Name</td><td>Prudential plc</td></tr>
<tr><td>(b)</td><td>LEI</td><td>5493001Z3ZE83NGK8Y12</td></tr>
<tr><td>4</td><td colspan="2">Details of the transaction(s): section to be repeated for (i) each type of instrument; (ii) each type of transaction; (iii) each date; and (iv) each place where transactions have been conducted</td></tr>
<tr><td>(a)</td><td>Description of the financial instrument, type of instrument
Identification code</td><td>Ordinary shares of 5 pence each
GB0007099541</td></tr>
<tr><td>(b)</td><td>Nature of the transactions</td><td>(i) Acquisition of shares for nil consideration following the release of an award under the PCA Long Term Incentive Plan
(ii) Sale of shares acquired following the release of an award under the PCA Long Term Incentive Plan</td></tr>
<tr><td>(c)</td><td>Price(s) and volume(s)</td><td>(i) Acquisition:<table><tr><td>Price(s)</td><td>Volume(s)</td></tr><tr><td>Nil</td><td>47,182</td></tr></table>(ii) Sale:<table><tr><td>Price(s)</td><td>Volume(s)</td></tr><tr><td>£14.0098</td><td>47,182</td></tr></table></td></tr>
<tr><td>(d)</td><td>Aggregated information
– Aggregated volume
– Price</td><td>
47,182
£14.0098</td></tr>
<tr><td>(e)</td><td>Date of the transactions</td><td>2016-09-23</td></tr>
<tr><td>(f)</td><td>Place of the transactions</td><td>London Stock Exchange</td></tr>
</table>

15.7.2 Directors' interests in shares

UK Listing Rule 6.6.6R(1) requires a statement, setting out the directors' holdings of shares in their ESCC-listed company, to be included in the annual report, together with any changes to this information over the past year.

15.7.3 UK MAR, Article 19

As explained at **7.8** above, PDMRs and persons closely associated (PCAs) are required to notify both the listed company and the FCA of every transaction conducted on their own account relating to shares (and other financial instruments) of that listed company.

15.7.4 Takeovers

15.7.4.1 Application of the Takeover Code

Chapter 20 explores this in more detail, but, broadly speaking, the Takeover Code applies during the offer period for a takeover of, for example, a UK plc listed on the Stock Exchange (see **22.3.4**). If the Takeover Code does apply, it applies to everyone participating in the takeover, such as the offeror (the bidder) and the offeree (the target company), and their directors and any advisers.

15.7.4.2 Nature of the Takeover Code

The Takeover Code has the force of law under the Takeover Directive which has been implemented in the UK. It exists to ensure that all takeovers are conducted fairly and in an orderly manner (see **Chapter 20**).

15.7.4.3 The obligations

Disclosure of issued shares (r 2.9)

The two main disclosure obligations are under r 8 of the Takeover Code (see below) and relate to the shareholdings at the announcement of the offer and subsequent dealings in shares during the offer period. However, as a precursor to those disclosure obligations, those companies whose securities will be subject to the disclosure obligations must notify the market, via an RIS, of the exact number of relevant securities which are in issue during the offer period and the classes of relevant securities it has in issue.

Rule 2.9 of the Takeover Code provides that:

(a) the target company must announce this as soon as possible after the commencement of the offer period (and in any event by 7.15 am on the next business day); and

(b) the bidder, or a publicly identified potential bidder, must announce this as soon as possible after any announcement of a firm intention to make an offer (and in any event by 7.15 am on the next business day) unless it has already stated that its offer will be, or is likely to be, solely in cash.

Relevant securities are defined as:

(a) voting shares in the target company;

(b) any other shares in the target company which are the subject of the offer;

(c) equity share capital in the target company and the bidder;

(d) securities of the bidder which carry substantially the same rights as any to be issued as consideration for the offer; and

(e) any securities in the target company and the bidder which are convertible into, or carry subscription rights over, any of the shares referred to at (a) to (c) above.

Disclosure of opening positions (r 8)

Rule 8 of the Takeover Code provides that an 'Opening Position Disclosure' must be made by:

(a) the offeror;

(b) the offeree company; and

(c) holders of 1% or more of the offeror's or offeree's shares.

This disclosure is an announcement containing details of (inter alia) interests in or rights to subscribe for relevant securities (see above). It must be made both to an RIS and electronically to the Takeover Panel no later than 12 noon, 10 business days following the start of the offer period or, for the offeror only, from the earlier of the announcement which first identifies the offeror and the time of the announcement of the offer.

The offeror and offeree must include the holdings of any concert parties (see below) in their disclosure.

This provision ensures that all parties to a takeover, the Takeover Panel and, ultimately, members of the public are aware of who could be an important player in deciding the outcome of the takeover. It will also highlight any shareholders who have a stake in both the offeror and the offeree.

Disclosure of subsequent dealings by the offeror or offeree (r 8)

Rule 8 of the Takeover Code provides in addition that, once the offer period has commenced:

(a) the offeror;

(b) the offeree company; and

(c) anyone 'acting in concert' with the offeror or offeree company,

must make a 'Dealing Disclosure', disclosing any dealings (as defined by the Takeover Code) in relevant securities (see above) to an RIS and the Takeover Panel no later than 12 noon on the business day following the date of the transaction.

People 'acting in concert' (also known as a 'concert party') are defined in the Takeover Code as persons who co-operate to obtain or consolidate control of a company or to frustrate its successful outcome. The term is intended to cover those who have an interest in the outcome of the offer. The Code gives the following examples of persons who typically will be concert parties:

(a) the offeree group companies or the offeror group companies (and their associated companies, being companies in which they have a shareholding of 20% or more);

(b) the offeree or offeror with any of its directors (and their close family and related trusts);

(c) the offeree or offeror group of companies and its pension funds;

(d) a fund manager of any investment company, unit trust or other person whose investments are managed by the fund manager on a discretionary basis;

(e) connected advisers of the offeree company and the offeror (and any members of the connected adviser's groups);

(f) directors of a company which is subject to an offer or where the directors have a bona fide belief that an offer is imminent.

Disclosure of subsequent dealings by 1%+ shareholders (r 8.3)

Rule 8.3 of the Takeover Code provides that if a person is interested or, as the result of any transaction, will be interested (directly or indirectly) in 1% or more of any class of relevant securities of an offeror or offeree, then they must make a Dealing Disclosure, disclosing their dealings in any relevant securities of that company, as well as the dealings of any other person through whom they derive their interest. The disclosure must be made by 3.30 pm on the business day following the date of the transaction (Note 2).

If disclosure is required under r 8.1 (offeror) or r 8.2 (offeree) or r 8.4 (concert party), then the same information does not also need to be disclosed under r 8.3.

The aim is therefore to ensure maximum transparency in share dealings by parties involved in a takeover. It is very important that the offeree company is aware of how big a stake the offeror has in it and when it changes.

Although r 8 applies only during the offer period, in Takeover Panel Statement 2011/3 (see **20.5.6.2** below), the Takeover Panel in one case extended the need for r 8 disclosures beyond the end of the offer period due to the special circumstances of that takeover.

15.7.4.4 Content of the notification

The 'Disclosure Forms' section of the Takeover Panel's website contains specimen Opening Position Disclosure and Dealing Disclosure forms which set out the format these r 8 notifications should take. Further information on the content can be found in Note 8 to r 8. A real-life example of a r 8.1 Opening Position Disclosure is set out below.

Company	News Corporation
TIDM	NCRA
Headline	Form 8 (OPD) NewsCorp/BSkyB
Released	11:56 29-June-2010
Number	4207O11

FORM 8 (OPD)

PUBLIC OPENING POSITION DISCLOSURE BY A PARTY TO AN OFFER

Rules 8.1 and 8.2 of the Takeover Code (the "Code")

1. KEY INFORMATION

(a) Identity of the party to the offer making the disclosure:	News Corporation
(b) Owner or controller of interests and short positions disclosed, if different from 1(a): *The naming of nominee or vehicle companies is insufficient*	
(c) Name of offeror/offeree in relation to whose relevant securities this form relates: *Use a separate form for each party to the offer*	British Sky Broadcasting Group Plc
(d) Is the party to the offer making the disclosure the offeror or the offeree?	OFFEROR
(e) Date position held:	28 June 2010
(f) Has the party previously disclosed, or is it today disclosing, under the Code in respect of any other party to this offer?	NO

2. POSITIONS OF THE PARTY TO THE OFFER MAKING THE DISCLOSURE

(a) Interests and short positions in the relevant securities of the offeror or offeree to which the disclosure relates

Class of relevant security:	**50p ordinary**			
	Interests		**Short positions**	
	Number	**%**	**Number**	**%**
(1) Relevant securities owned and/or controlled:	**686,021,700**	**39.1%**		
(2) Derivatives (other than options):				
(3) Options and agreements to purchase/ sell:				
TOTAL:	**686,021,700**	**39.1%**		

All interests and all short positions should be disclosed.

Details of any open derivative or option positions, or agreements to purchase or sell relevant securities, should be given on a Supplemental Form 8 (Open Positions).

Details of any securities borrowing and lending positions or financial collateral arrangements should be disclosed on a Supplemental Form 8 (SBL).

(b) **Rights to subscribe for new securities**

Class of relevant security in relation to which subscription right exists:	
Details, including nature of the rights concerned and relevant percentages:	

If there are positions or rights to subscribe to disclose in more than one class of relevant securities of the offeror or offeree named in 1(c), copy table 2(a) or (b) (as appropriate) for each additional class of relevant security.

(c) **Irrevocable commitments and letters of intent**

Details of any irrevocable commitments or letters of intent procured by the party to the offer making the disclosure or any person acting in concert with it (see Note 3 on Rule 2.11 of the Code):

3. POSITIONS OF PERSONS ACTING IN CONCERT WITH THE PARTY TO THE OFFER MAKING THE DISCLOSURE

Details of any interests, short positions and rights to subscribe of any person acting in concert with the party to the offer making the disclosure
J.P. Morgan Securities Ltd. has a non-exempt short position of 106,407 in British Sky Broadcasting Group Plc representing 0.006% of the 50p ordinary shares issued by British Sky Broadcasting Group Plc

If there are positions or rights to subscribe to disclose in more than one class of relevant securities of the offeror or offeree named in 1(c), copy table 3 for each additional class of relevant security.

Details of any open derivative or option positions, or agreements to purchase or sell relevant securities, should be given on a Supplemental Form 8 (Open Positions).

Details of any securities borrowing and lending positions or financial collateral arrangements should be disclosed on a Supplemental Form 8 (SBL).

4. OTHER INFORMATION

(a) **Indemnity and other dealing arrangements**

Details of any indemnity or option arrangement, or any agreement or understanding, formal or informal, relating to relevant securities which may be an inducement to deal or refrain from dealing entered into by the party to the offer making the disclosure or any person acting in concert with it: *If there are no such agreements, arrangements or understandings, state "none"*

(b) **Agreements, arrangements or understandings relating to options or derivatives**

Details of any agreement, arrangement or understanding, formal or informal, between the party to the offer making the disclosure, or any person acting in concert with it, and any other person relating to: **(i) the voting rights of any relevant securities under any option; or** **(ii) the voting rights or future acquisition or disposal of any relevant securities to which any derivative is referenced:** *If there are no such agreements, arrangements or understandings, state "none"*

(c) **Attachments**

Are any Supplemental Forms attached?

Supplemental Form 8 (Open Positions)	**NO**
Supplemental Form 8 (SBL)	**NO**

Date of disclosure:	**29 June 2010**

15.8 SUMMARY

The table below summarises the key notification obligations, relating to the disclosure of interests in shares, covered by this chapter. The table is intended to be an overview only, and recourse should be made to the text for the specific detail of the rules.

Rule	Notifier	Notifiee	Interest	Deadline
DTR 5.1.2R	Shareholder of public company	Company	Acquires 3% (or further increase beyond whole percentage point), or falls by a whole percentage point or below 3% (see **15.5.3** for detail)	2 trading days after they become aware of interest
DTR 5.8.12R	Listed company	RIS	Information received under DTR 5.1.2R	By end of trading day following the day the company receives the information
UK MAR, Article 19(1)	PDMRs of listed company (and persons closely associated)	Company and FCA	All transactions conducted on their own account relating to shares (and other financial instruments) of that listed company over €5,000 in a calendar year	3 working days after the date of the transaction
UK MAR, Article 19(3)	Listed company	RIS	Information received under UK MAR, Article 19(1)	2 working days after the date of the notification by the PDMR or PCA
Takeover Code Rule 2.9	Offeror and offeree company	RIS	Number of relevant securities in issue	By 9 am on the next business day after the start of the offer period (offeree) By 9 am on business day after announcement of firm intention to make offer (offeror)
Takeover Code Rule 8	Offeror, offeree company and those holding interests of 1%+	RIS and Takeover Panel	Opening Position Disclosure (interests in and rights to subscribe to relevant securities)	12 noon 10 business days after offer period starts (offeree/1+%) 12 noon 10 business days after earlier of date offeror first publicly identified or firm offer announcement (offeror)

Rule	Notifier	Notifiee	Interest	Deadline
Takeover Code Rule 8	Offeror, offeree company and concert parties	RIS and Takeover Panel	Dealing Disclosure (dealings in relevant securities)	12 noon on business day following date of transaction

15.9 FUTURE DEVELOPMENTS

Financial Services and Markets Act 2023

The Act intends, amongst other things, to revoke EU financial services law that had been retained following Brexit and replace it with UK-sourced rules. Laws which will be repealed include the UK version of MAR and the related delegated legislation. It is unclear in what form the market abuse rules will appear after such repeal. There appears to be no intention to amend the substance of the current market abuse rules.

You will be able to follow developments via the FCA's website.

CHAPTER 16

FINANCIAL ASSISTANCE

16.1 INTRODUCTION

So far, **Part III** of this book has considered the concept of shares: what they are; the different classes of share; the law relating to share issues; and how a company can find out who owns its shares. This chapter considers a potential problem which can arise on the *acquisition* of shares; the problem that, subject to certain exceptions, a public company cannot give 'financial assistance' for the purchase of its shares.

In its simplest form this means that if I want to buy shares in X plc, X plc cannot give me any financial help to buy those shares.

The rule itself is straightforward enough. So why is it described as a problem? In practice, financial assistance can arise in ways which are not easy to spot. In addition, the lawyer is often removed from the detail of the funding arrangements and is concentrating, instead, on the negotiation of the transaction. These two factors can conspire to make financial assistance an area that can inject an element of last-minute panic into a share acquisition that is otherwise running quite smoothly.

16.2 RATIONALE

To achieve a good understanding of the financial assistance rules, it can help to consider the rationale behind those rules. Why is financial assistance prohibited?

Let us consider a practical example of financial assistance. I am a financier and I want to buy a company. I lack significant funds. I find a company, X plc, which has substantial cash reserves and easily realisable assets (that is, they can be sold for cash readily). I agree to buy X plc for cash consideration. I am the buyer, and the shareholders of X plc are the sellers. I structure the transaction so that X plc uses its cash reserves, and cash realised from selling some of its assets, to advance me the cash I need to pay consideration to the shareholders of X plc. I then buy the company, but in effect X plc has funded the transaction.

The question is, who has lost out in this transaction? X plc's creditors. Their security is that X plc is cash-rich. This cash is now lining the pockets of the shareholders who sold shares in the company. It is no longer in X plc. X plc has misused its assets.

The prohibition on financial assistance would not permit the transaction described above. The reason? To protect creditors.

16.3 THE FINANCIAL ASSISTANCE PROHIBITION

Sections 678 and 679 of the CA 2006 contain the prohibitions on financial assistance. Section 678 prohibits the giving of financial assistance for the acquisition of shares in a public company. Section 679 prohibits the giving of financial assistance by a public company subsidiary for the acquisition of shares in its private holding company. Each section contains two prohibitions. The difference between them is:

(a) s 678(1) and s 679(1) apply to financial assistance given *before or at the same time as* the acquisition of shares; and

(b) s 678(3) and s 679(3) apply to financial assistance given *after* the acquisition of shares.

16.3.1 Financial assistance given before or at the same time as the acquisition of shares

We shall start by looking at s 678(1), which provides that:

(a) where a person is acquiring or *proposing to acquire* shares in a *public* company;

(b) it is not lawful for the company;

(c) or any of the company's *subsidiaries*;

(d) to give financial assistance;

(e) directly or indirectly;

(f) *for the purpose* of that acquisition;

(g) before or at the time the acquisition takes place.

The following points are of interest here:

(i) Section 678(1) only applies to the acquisition of shares in a *public* company (whether listed or not).

(ii) 'Proposing to acquire' means that there does not actually have to be an acquisition of shares for s 678(1) to apply; it is the fact that the person *intends* to acquire shares which is important.

(iii) The person giving the financial assistance (Assistor) does not necessarily have to be the company whose shares are being acquired (Target); if the Assistor is a subsidiary of Target, s 678(1) will apply even if it is a private company.

(iv) 'For the purpose' (see (f) above) means that this is a purpose-based, not a results-based, test. It is not sufficient simply that financial assistance results in the acquisition, or is somehow connected with the acquisition. The Assistor must have *intended* to facilitate the transaction by giving the assistance. It is vital, therefore, to identify why the Assistor has provided the assistance.

For the s 679(1) prohibition, the test is broadly the same as in (a)–(g) above, but in (a) substitute 'private' for 'public', and (b) and (c) will read 'it is not lawful for a public company that is a subsidiary of that company'.

16.3.2 Financial assistance given after the acquisition of shares

Once again we shall start by considering s 678(3), which provides that:

(a) where a person has acquired shares in a *public* company;

(b) and a *liability has been incurred* (by that, or *any other*, person) for the purpose of that acquisition;

(c) it is not lawful for the company;

(d) or any of the company's *subsidiaries*;

(e) to give financial assistance;

(f) directly or indirectly;

(g) *for the purpose of reducing or discharging the liability incurred.*

Again, note the following points:

(i) Section 683(2) provides that 'incurring a liability' includes a change in financial position (there is no indication that this change must be for the worse). The obvious example of this is someone borrowing money to fund an acquisition.

(ii) The liability does not have to have been incurred by the person acquiring the shares.

(iii) As with s 678(1), the Assistor does not have to be Target; if the Assistor is a subsidiary of Target, s 678(3) will apply even if it is a private company.

(iv) As with s 678(1), the words 'for the purpose' feature in s 678(3) too. This means that the financial assistance does not actually have to reduce or discharge the liability incurred, as long as it was *intended* to reduce or discharge that liability. As with s 678, it is vital to identify why the Assistor has provided the assistance.

(v) Section 683(2) provides that 'reducing or discharging the liability incurred' includes wholly or partly restoring a person's financial position to what it was before the acquisition.

For the s 679(3) prohibition, the test is broadly the same as in (a) to (g) above, but in (a) substitute 'private' for 'public', and (b) and (c) will read 'it is not lawful for a public company that is a subsidiary of that company'.

16.4 WHAT IS FINANCIAL ASSISTANCE?

Section 677 of the CA 2006 defines 'financial assistance' as:

(a) financial assistance given by way of gift (that is, where the Assistor transfers an asset of value for nil consideration);

(b) financial assistance given by way of:

  (i) guarantee, security, indemnity (subject to a limited exception); or

  (ii) release or waiver; or

(c) financial assistance given by way of loan (or certain other types of agreement such as credit); or

(d) any other financial assistance given by a company:

  (i) the net assets (defined by s 677(2) as the actual value of assets less liabilities) of which are thereby reduced to a material extent (this is not defined, but appears to be a de-minimis level), or

  (ii) which has no net assets.

You will note that the 'definition' of financial assistance actually uses the words 'financial assistance'. Section 677(1) therefore does not really define what financial assistance is, rather it gives examples of financial assistance.

Nethertheless, this definition makes clear that financial assistance is not limited to the more obvious situations, such as where the Assistor makes a gift or loan to the buyer to fund the acquisition of shares. Assistance of an indirect nature, such as when a bank gives a loan to the buyer to fund the acquisition, but the Assistor guarantees that loan or gives any type of security for it, will also constitute financial assistance. As mentioned in the introduction to this chapter at **16.1** above, these less obvious examples of financial assistance can cause problems for the corporate lawyer.

EXAMPLE

Imagine a typical day in practice. The chief executive of X plc calls you, its lawyer, to instruct you in relation to a share disposal. X plc is selling the entire issued share capital of its wholly-owned subsidiary, Target plc, to Buyer plc. The acquisition must be completed urgently. X plc needs the cash consideration from the sale by the end of the month (three days' time) or it will go bust.

> You download your firm's precedent agreement and launch yourself into a series of meetings, first with your client, X plc, to find out the detail of the transaction, then with Buyer plc and its lawyers, to thrash out a deal.
>
> Can you imagine how easy it is, in that first meeting with your client, for the client to say to you, 'We are selling all the shares in our subsidiary, Target plc. The buyer, Buyer plc, is paying a good price; it has secured a loan on really good terms from the bank', for you to make a note of this, then move on to more pressing areas of detail, such as the structure of the deal and the warranties X plc is prepared to give?
>
> Forty-eight hours later you have an agreement ready to sign. At that point, you receive a call from a colleague in your firm's banking department, who says she has just received a call from the assistant company secretary of Target plc, asking her to review the form of guarantee Target plc is giving to Buyer plc's bank.
>
> Suddenly you have a problem. Target plc cannot give Buyer's bank a guarantee, as this would be financial assistance and prohibited under s 677(1). The bank will not provide the loan to Buyer plc unless it receives the guarantee from Target plc it was promised. Without the bank loan, Buyer plc cannot purchase the shares in Target plc. Without the consideration, X plc will go bust. You have to explain this problem to X plc.
>
> How could this situation have been avoided? Well if, at that first meeting, you had probed a little more into the funding arrangements with Buyer plc's bank, you might have prompted the client to mention the bank guarantee. This is clear with hindsight, but can be very easy to miss in the rush to make a start on the acquisition agreement within the time constraints imposed.

16.5 WHAT IS NOT FINANCIAL ASSISTANCE?

The CA 2006 provides three categories of exceptions to the financial assistance prohibition. These exceptions are considered below.

16.5.1 The purpose exceptions

It was explained at **16.3.1** and **16.3.2** above that purpose and intention are important when considering the prohibition on financial assistance. It should come as no surprise, then, to find that one of the exceptions to the financial assistance prohibition is concerned with purpose.

Section 678(2) and s 679(2) provide that s 678(1) and s 679(1) respectively (that is, pre-acquisition financial assistance) do not prohibit the Assistor from giving financial assistance if:

(a) either:
  - (i) the Assistor's *principal purpose* is not to give the financial assistance for the purpose of the acquisition (principal purpose exception), *or*
  - (ii) the giving of the financial assistance for the purpose of the acquisition was only an incidental part of some *larger purpose* of the Assistor (larger purpose exception); *and*

(b) the Assistor gives the financial assistance in good faith in the interests of the Assistor.

Section 678(4) and s 679(4) provide principal purpose and larger purpose exceptions for financial assistance under s 678(3) and s 679(3) respectively too (that is, post-acquisition financial assistance), but the words 'the acquisition' (see (a)(i) and (ii) above) are replaced with 'reducing or discharging the liability which has been incurred'.

The 'principal purpose' and 'larger purpose' exceptions are somewhat vague, and it is difficult for the lawyer to be able to state definitively that they will apply. The decision in *Brady v Brady* [1989] AC 755 has made the application of the purpose exceptions even less clear.

16.5.1.1 *Brady v Brady*

In this case, an arrangement was made in good faith to divide a family company's assets into two new companies, so that the two brothers who ran the family company could go their separate ways. The arrangement involved the family company giving financial assistance, as Assistor. At first instance, it was held that while the arrangement was prohibited by the forerunner to s 678(1), it was saved by the larger purpose exception; the Assistor's giving of the assistance for the purpose of the acquisition was only an incidental part of the Assistor's *larger purpose*. The House of Lords, however, did not agree that the exception applied.

16.5.1.2 The principal purpose exception

In *Brady v Brady*, Lord Oliver explained that, for this exception to apply, there must be a principal and a secondary purpose behind the giving of the financial assistance. For example, if the principal purpose of the Assistor is to obtain an asset that it really wants, but the secondary purpose is to put the person who is willing to sell the asset in a position to acquire shares in the company, then, as long as the Assistor genuinely enters into the transaction in the belief that it is in the Assistor's best interests, the transaction will fall within the exception. There may be difficulties, however, in proving that the secondary purpose was not, in fact, the primary purpose.

16.5.1.3 The larger purpose exception

This exception covers transactions where the financial assistance is intended but it is incidental to the Assistor's 'larger purpose'. As outlined at **16.5.1.1** above, the House of Lords (now UK Supreme Court) has interpreted this exception very narrowly and, as such, it is not relied upon in practice.

16.5.2 Section 681: unconditional exceptions

Section 681(2) permits the following (which all involve removing value from the company) on the basis that they are not anything against which creditors require protection:

(a) (i) a dividend lawfully made – this would allow, for example, the Assistor to pay a pre-sale dividend to its shareholders before its shares are sold (this may have tax benefits, as it allows shareholders to take some of the value of the company as income not capital);

(ii) a distribution in a winding up;

(b) the allotment of bonus shares;

(c) a reduction of capital under Chapter 10 of Pt 17 of the CA 2006;

(d) a lawful redemption or purchase of own shares;

(e) schemes of arrangement made pursuant to a CA 2006, s 899 court order;

(f) anything done pursuant to an arrangement under s 110 of the Insolvency Act 1986 (this will cover a liquidator accepting shares as consideration for property sold in a winding up); and

(g) anything done pursuant to a voluntary arrangement made between the company and its creditors.

16.5.3 Section 682: conditional exceptions

Section 682(2) provides the following exceptions:

(a) the lending of money by money lending companies in the ordinary course of their business;

(b) where the financial assistance is given in good faith to fund an employee share scheme; and

(c) loans to bona fide employees (not directors) to allow them to buy shares in the company, or its holding company (no share scheme is required for the exception to apply).

The s 682(1) proviso

Section 682(1) adds an important proviso to the application of the s 682(2) exemptions where the Assistor is a public company. If the Assistor is a public company, it can rely on the s 682(2) exemptions only if the company has *net assets*:

(a) which are not thereby reduced; or

(b) to the extent those assets are thereby reduced, the assistance is provided out of distributable profits.

Note that net assets are defined as the *book value* of assets less liabilities (that is, their value for accounting purposes). This is different to the definition of net assets for the purposes of s 677(1) (see **16.4** above), where the definition is the *actual value* of net assets less liabilities. (Liabilities are defined by s 682(4)(b) and distributable profits by s 683(1).)

16.6 AVOIDING THE RESTRICTIONS

There is always the option of re-registering a public company as a private company, under s 97 of the CA 2006, so that the company is a private company at the time the financial assistance is given, and that financial assistance can then be given. This is, of course, a little extreme, and certainly would not be appropriate in the case of a listed company.

16.7 SANCTIONS

16.7.1 Criminal sanctions

Section 680 provides that breach of the prohibition on financial assistance is a criminal offence. The company is liable to a fine, and any officer in default is liable to a fine and/or imprisonment.

16.7.2 Consequences for the share acquisition

The acquisition will be void and unenforceable (*Brady v Brady*) unless the offending term can be severed from any acquisition agreement (*Carney v Herbert* [1985] AC 301).

If the provision of financial assistance breaches the directors' duty to act in good faith in the way most likely to promote the success of the company (CA 2006, s 172) and the breach has not been ratified by a shareholder resolution, the directors may have to compensate their company for any loss it has incurred.

Any third party who received the financial assistance may be required to account for any cash or assets received in breach of s 678 or s 679 (*Belmont Finance Corp Ltd v Williams Furniture Ltd (No 2)* [1980] 1 All ER 393).

16.8 CONCLUSION

The prohibition on financial assistance has the potential to cause serious problems with share acquisitions involving public companies.

The key is to consider the issue of financial assistance as soon as possible in any share acquisition transaction. This will involve asking questions about how the transaction is funded and, if necessary, making changes to the structure of the deal.

In June 2017 the Serious Fraud Office (SFO) announced charges against a listed bank, Barclays plc, and four of its former senior executives (John Varley, the CEO, Roger Jenkins, Head of Investment Banking and Investment Management for the Middle East, Thomas Kalaris, Head of the Wealth Management Division, and Richard Boath, Head of European Financial Institutions) including for unlawful financial assistance relating to a fund raising in 2008 during the UK's banking crisis which led to some High Street banks being rescued by the British Government. Barclays sought to avoid being taken over by the Government by obtaining billions of US$ from Qatari investors. The particular issue regarding financial assistance is that during this period Barclays made a loan of US$3 billion to the State of Qatar. One of the arguments advanced by the SFO was in effect that Barclays lent money to the Qataris who then used that money to buy shares in the company, an act which would have improved the appearance of Barclay's financial position. Both the company and the individuals concerned strongly reject the allegations. A trial started in Southwark Crown Court in January 2019. In April 2019 John Varley was acquitted. The remaining defendants were acquitted in February 2020 in a significant defeat for the SFO.

CHAPTER 17

EQUITY FINANCE

17.1 BACKGROUND

Part I of this book considered the IPO process, that is (for the purposes of this book) how a company can admit its shares to listing on the Official List and to trading on the Main Market.

As was seen at **4.4** above, a company seeking to float can do so in a number of different ways:

(a) a public offer (encompassing an offer for subscription and/or sale);

(b) a placing;

(c) an introduction; or

(d) an intermediaries offer.

These methods were considered in some detail in **Chapter 4**.

Chapter 1 explained that one of the advantages of an IPO is that, after it has taken place, a listed company can raise further finance through issuing new shares ('equity finance') in a way that an unlisted company cannot. This chapter explores the various methods by which a listed company can seek a listing for further share capital, in order to raise equity finance.

17.2 WHAT IS EQUITY FINANCE?

Equity finance involves a company using its equity, namely securities (and more specifically for our purposes, shares), in order to raise finance. An example of a company raising equity finance is when it issues new shares in return for cash, or in exchange for an asset.

As you will realise on reading this chapter, equity finance involves both:

(a) the issue of shares; and

(b) the admission of those shares to listing and to trading on the Main Market of the Stock Exchange.

It is the dual admissions of those shares which gives them their value. The issue and admissions of shares in a listed company in this way is often referred to as a 'secondary issue'. The 'primary issue' is when the company floats and its issued shares are listed for the first time. Subsequent issues of new shares, and the listing of those shares, are therefore 'secondary issues'. (Be aware that this terminology can be confusing, as sometimes the term 'primary issue' is used to describe any issue of shares by the company, and the term 'secondary issue' is used to refer to a sale (transfer) by a shareholder of existing shares. However, for the purposes of this book, the terminology is given the meanings outlined above: a 'primary issue' is an issue of shares by the company on an IPO; and a 'secondary issue' is any subsequent issue of shares by the company.)

When a company raises equity finance, then, the lawyer must be aware of, and be able to apply, not only the law which relates specifically to the raising of equity finance, but also the wider set of rules and regulations which apply to listed companies:

(a) generally;
(b) on the issue of shares; and
(c) on the admission of those shares to listing and trading.

This chapter looks at the law which relates specifically to the raising of equity finance. However, at **17.4** below there is a brief reminder of the other rules and regulations which relate to (a), (b) and (c) above, and an indication of where you can read about them in this book.

Note that for the period 1 January to 30 September 2024, companies listed on the Main Market raised just over £9 billion through secondary issues.

17.3 WHY A COMPANY NEEDS EQUITY FINANCE

There are numerous reasons why a company might want to raise equity finance. Just like us, it needs money. It may want to pay off debt, buy something, or just make its bank balance look a little healthier. It may be concerned about gearing (its ratio of debt to equity). By increasing the amount of share capital in issue, the company will improve its gearing ratio without having to repay any debt. This may enhance the company's ability to borrow in the future. The company will also have the option to use the cash proceeds from the rights issue to pay off debt, which will improve the company's gearing even more. **Chapter 18** considers the concept of gearing. It also considers briefly the concept of debt finance, and examines the issues a company will take into account in deciding whether to raise equity or debt finance.

Since the outbreak of the global financial crisis in 2007/08, many billions of pounds have been raised on the Stock Exchange by listed companies, initially by banks as they desperately scrambled to access whatever money they could to fend off their collapse as a result of the powerful shockwaves emanating from the global financial crisis. This included rights issues by the Royal Bank of Scotland Group plc and HSBC Holdings plc, which raised £12 billion in June 2008 and £12.5 billion in March 2009 respectively, to ensure they had sufficient capital. This was followed by the UK's largest ever rights issue by Lloyds Banking Group plc, which raised £13.5 billion in November 2009. The money was raised to prevent the company from having to sell more of its shares to the UK Government in return for further State insurance for its toxic debt. In 2009 and 2010, over £100 billion was raised on the Main Market through secondary issues. More recently, secondary issues were used by many listed companies to shore up their finances which were battered by the restrictions imposed during the Covid pandemic.

17.4 LISTED COMPANY RULES AND REGULATIONS

17.4.1 General rules

The general rules relating to listed companies are set out in **Part II** of this book. The general obligation of disclosure under UK MAR, Article 17 (see **7.5.1**) and the continuing obligations of the UK Listing Rules, relating to the disclosure of new issues (see **7.5.5** above) and communicating with shareholders in relation to new issues (see **7.9** above), are particularly relevant to any company seeking to raise equity finance. The lawyer must also be alert to any suggestion that the issue might fall foul of the rules relating to corporate governance (see

Chapter 8), misleading statements and market manipulation (see **Chapter 9**), market abuse (see **Chapter 10**) or insider dealing (see **Chapter 11**). Finally, the lawyer must ensure that the issue is not marketed in a way which would breach the financial promotion rules of the FSMA 2000 (see **Chapter 12**).

17.4.2 Issuing shares

Part III of this book considers the rules of the CA 2006, the UK Prospectus Regulation, the UK Listing Rules, the Takeover Code, and the Investment Association Share Capital Management Guidelines and the Pre-Emption Group's Statement of Principles which relate to the issue of shares. The following are particularly important, from the company's perspective, when raising equity finance.

17.4.2.1 The Companies Act 2006

Chapters 2 to 4 of Pt 17 of the CA 2006 are all relevant to the issue of shares (see **Chapter 14**). The 2006 Act also sets out the procedure which companies must follow if a share issue will vary the class rights of any existing shares. Again, this may be relevant in an equity finance transaction (see **13.7** above). Finally, the issue must be structured in a way which does not cause the company to fall foul of the prohibition on financial assistance (see **Chapter 16**).

17.4.2.2 The UK Listing Rules

UK Listing Rules 9.2.1R and 9.2.2R set out the pre-emption rights provisions which are relevant on an issue of shares for ESCC-listed companies only (see **14.6.12** above).

17.4.2.3 Guidelines and Principles

The Investment Association, acting as representative of many of the UK's institutional investors, imposes its own requirements relating to the issue of shares. These requirements do not have the force of law, but they are significant because listed companies do not want to get on the wrong side of their largest shareholders. **Chapter 14** considers the Investment Association Share Capital Management Guidelines (see **14.5.7**) and the Statement of Principles of the Pre-Emption Group (see **14.6.16**) which are relevant on an issue of shares. In addition, in November 2014 the Investment Association published its Transaction Guidelines, which include advice relating to secondary offerings. The Guidelines can be found at **Appendix 1**.

17.4.3 Admitting new shares to listing and trading

Part I of this book considered the admission of shares on an IPO. Many of the issues addressed by **Part I** are also relevant to the admission of shares on a secondary issue.

It was explained at **4.3.1.1** above that a company cannot choose to list only part of a class of shares. It must list all of the shares in a class. So, if a listed company proposes to issue more shares *of a class which is already listed*, it must seek admission to listing on the Official List and admission to trading on the Main Market in respect of those shares. As mentioned above, this is not only a requirement of the UK Listing Rules, it also makes the issues commercially attractive, as a listing gives the shares value.

In relation to the listing aspects of a secondary issue, the lawyer must be aware of the following rules and regulations:

(a) *The FSMA 2000.* Part VI of the FSMA 2000 sets out the rules relating to the listing of shares. Section 90 (compensation for loss) is particularly important. See **Chapter 6**.

(b) *The UK Prospectus Regulation and Prospectus Regulation Rules.* The requirement for a prospectus under Article 3 of the UK Prospectus Regulation (and s 85 of the FSMA 2000) is discussed at **17.5.1** below. The requirement for a prospectus on an IPO was considered in **Chapter 6**. The prospectus and accompanying documents must be submitted to the FCA as required by the UK Prospectus Regulation (see **5.3.6.1** and

5.3.6.2 above; but note that the submission date for a secondary issue is 10 working days before the prospectus is due to be approved, rather than the 20 working days required for an IPO).

It is worth remembering that approval of the prospectus is not a foregone conclusion. Prudential plc embarrassingly had to delay publication of its prospectus for what would have been a record £14.5 billion rights issue in May 2010 because the forerunner to the FCA, the FSA, needed clarification that Prudential's finances could withstand the takeover of the company (AIA) for which it was going to use the proceeds of the rights issue. Ultimately the rights issue was cancelled due to shareholder opposition.

(c) *The UK Listing Rules.* A formal application for admission of the shares to the Official List must be made to the FCA under the UK Listing Rules. This involves a process very similar to that set out at **5.3.6.3** to **5.3.6.5** above, in the context of an IPO, namely the submission of:

   (i) '48 hour' documents;

   (ii) 'on the day' documents (note the documents differ on a secondary issue to those required for an IPO; a Pricing Statement, rather than a Shareholder Statement signed by the sponsor, is required – see UKLR 20.4.4R); and

   (iii) certain information following admission.

   Where the requirements are the same as those for an IPO, see **5.3.6** for further detail. Any raising of equity finance will be made conditional upon admission to listing on the Official List. Admission will be effective when the FCA makes its Official List announcement (see **5.4.3.1**).

(d) *The Admission and Disclosure Standards.* A formal application for admission of the shares to the Main Market must be made to the Stock Exchange under the Admission and Disclosure Standards. Again, the process involved practically mirrors that required for the application for admission to trading set out in **5.3.7** in relation to an IPO, namely (under ADS 2) the submission of:

   (i) an application for admission to trading – Form 1 (note that for a secondary issue this is submitted with the other two-day documents, rather than 10 days in advance, as on an IPO);

   (ii) various two-day documents in electronic form;

   (iii) written confirmation of the number of securities to be allotted; and

   (iv) certain information following admission.

   Where the requirements are the same as those for an IPO, see **5.3.7** for further detail. Any raising of equity finance will be made conditional upon admission to trading on the Main Market. Again, admission will be effective when the Stock Exchange makes an announcement via a Regulatory Information Service (see **5.4.3.2**).

Note that, in the context of a rights issue, once the shares have been admitted to listing and trading nil paid, no further application is required to admit the shares fully paid (see **17.7.3.2** below).

17.5 EQUITY FINANCE DOCUMENTATION

The lawyer spends much of their time drafting, and therefore any lawyer will need to know what documentation is required on a secondary issue. Specific documentation required for each method of raising equity finance considered by this chapter is detailed at **17.7** to **17.11** below. However, the reason these documents are required is explained below.

17.5.1 Prospectus

As referred to at **6.4**, the effect of Article 3 of the UK Prospectus Regulation (PRR 1.2.1UK) [and s 85 of the FSMA 2000] is that if the company wishes to do either or both of the following:

(a) *offer* securities *to the public* in *the UK* (Art 3(1) of the UK Prospectus Regulation); or

(b) request *admission* of transferable securities *to trading* on a regulated market situated or operating *in the UK* (even if there is no offer to the public) (Art 3(3) of the UK Prospectus Regulation),

an FCA-approved prospectus is required. These rules apply equally to a secondary issue as they do to an IPO (see **6.4** above).

Article 1(4) (PRR 1.2.3UK) and Article 3(2) of the UK Prospectus Regulation and s 86(1)(e) of the FSMA 2000 set out various circumstances when an *offer to the public* will not require a prospectus. Article 1(5) of the UK Prospectus Regulation (PRR 1.2.4UK) sets out the circumstances when an *admission to trading* will not require a prospectus.

17.5.1.1 Full prospectus

Once the need for a prospectus has been established, there are two possibilities regarding the content of the prospectus. The first includes the full content as required in an IPO, as set out at **6.5.2** above, where the content requirements are prescribed by the annexes of the UK PR Regulation. For a secondary issue of ordinary shares the appropriate annexes will be Annex 1 (registration document for equity securities), Annex 11 (securities note for equity securities) and Annex 20 (pro forma financial information), so the level of disclosure required in any prospectus relating to a secondary issue of ordinary shares in this case is exactly the same as for a prospectus relating to an IPO of ordinary shares. The prospectus for Prudential plc's potentially record-breaking £14.5 billion rights issue (which was aborted for financial reasons and management incompetence in May 2010) ran to a record 940 pages, and if copies for each of its 71,700 shareholders were stacked up, the pile would have reached 3.5 miles high!

17.5.1.2 Simplified disclosure prospectus

The second possibility arises if the company falls within the UK Prospectus Regulation's simplified disclosure regime under Article 14 of the UK Prospectus Regulation (PRR 2.5.1UK).

This applies to any company whose shares have been admitted to trading on a UK regulated market continuously for at least the past 18 months and, for example, who issue further shares of the type that they have already admitted to trading.

The big advantage for the company is that it is able to produce an abbreviated prospectus containing less information, as set out in Annexes 3, 13 and 20 of the UK PR Regulation. This rule was introduced to recognise the reality that companies which are already listed on a regulated market publish huge amounts of information, and so investors (be they existing shareholders or new investors) will usually already be aware of its financial situation and the risks of investing in it and so need less information. One was used in Aston Martin Lagonda Global Holdings plc's £650 million rights issue and placing in September 2022.

A company eligible to use the simplified disclosure regime may still elect to produce a full prospectus instead. They may have to do this, for example, for regulatory approval of the prospectus overseas, eg an offer involving the US.

17.5.1.3 Supplementary prospectus

An approved supplementary prospectus (see **6.9.4**) will also be required if, for example, during a rights issue, there arises or is noted any significant new factor, material mistake or inaccuracy relating to the information included in the approved prospectus. This supplementary prospectus will trigger statutory withdrawal rights under Article 23(2) of the UK Prospectus Regulation (PRR 3.4.1UK).

17.5.1.4 Exemptions

The only difference is that exemptions, which may not apply in the context of an IPO (see **6.4**), may apply on a secondary issue, depending on its circumstances, with the effect that a prospectus is not required. Clearly, if the lawyer can structure a secondary issue so that no prospectus is required, this will save the company considerable time and expense. **Table 17.1** below analyses whether the exemptions are likely to apply to the key methods of raising money via a secondary issue (see **17.6**): a rights issue, open offer, placing, acquisition issue or vendor consideration placing. As you can see, it is likely that only a placing, acquisition issue or vendor consideration placing can be structured in a way which avoids the need to prepare a prospectus.

Table 17.1

Method of equity finance	Public offer under Art 3(1) [s 85(1)]?	Admission to trading under Art 3(3) [s 85(2)]?	Prospectus required?
Rights issue	Yes. Unlikely to benefit from any exemption. (As a pre-emptive offer made to all shareholders, is unlikely to benefit from the '150 persons' or 'only qualified investors' exemptions.)	Yes, however small rights issues may be structured so that '20%' exemption applies.	Yes.
Open offer	As for rights issue.	As for rights issue.	As for rights issue.
Placing	Yes ; however, likely to benefit from 'only qualified investors' or '150 persons' exemption.	Yes, however small placings may be structured so that '20%' exemption applies.	Yes, unless structured so that is exempt from the requirement for a prospectus.
Acquisition issue	May benefit from 'only qualified investors' or '150 persons' exemption, depending on target shareholder profile.	Yes, however small rights issues may be structured so that '20%' exemption applies.	Yes, unless structured so that is exempt from the requirement for a prospectus. (Where shares are issued in the context of a takeover, the publication of an 'exempted document' will suffice – see **22.4.4.2**.)
Vendor consideration placing	As for acquisition issue.	As for acquisition issue.	As for acquisition issue.

17.5.2 Circular

The DTRs require an ESCC-listed company to communicate to its shareholders by way of circular on a new issue (see **7.6.2** above). This may take the form of a notice of GM, and incorporate by reference information in any prospectus. The circular for an ESCC-listed company must conform with the requirements of UKLR 10.3 and 10.6 (see **7.9.3**).

In practice, often the requirement for the circular is met by the prospectus, which will contain all the information required to be in the circular. However, the prospectus also contains an offer of securities, which can cause problems with regard to very strict securities law in certain overseas jurisdictions. One solution is not to send the prospectus to such jurisdictions but a circular. If there are overseas shareholders therefore, the company may prepare both a prospectus and a separate circular. Also, if time is of the essence, the company may (with the permission of the FCA) send out a brief circular outlining the main reasons for the issue, together with a notice of GM, and then send out the prospectus once the document has been completed (as happened, for example, with Bradford and Bingley's £400 million rights issue in the summer of 2008).

17.5.3 RIS notification/press announcement

Any new issue of listed securities must be notified to an RIS under the specific disclosure requirements of the UK Listing Rules (see **7.5.7.2** above). This will usually take the form of a press announcement to announce the issue to the market. It will contain all material information about the issue, and any related acquisition. Further announcements will be required as the rights issue progresses.

17.5.4 Sale and purchase agreement

If the company is issuing shares as consideration for the acquisition of a non-cash asset, such as shares in another company, then a sale and purchase agreement (also referred to as an acquisition agreement, an S&P or an SPA) will be required for the transfer of that asset.

17.5.5 Underwriting agreement

The concept of underwriting in the context of an IPO was introduced at **4.2.7** above. It is also relevant on a secondary issue. In return for a fee, the underwriters will agree to take up any shares which are not subscribed for. The underwriting agreement will record the agreement between the company and the underwriter.

17.5.6 Placing agreement

If the chosen method of raising equity finance involves a placing of shares, a placing agreement will also be necessary (see **4.4.1.2** above).

17.6 METHODS OF RAISING EQUITY FINANCE

As **17.1** above explained, a company can float in a number of different ways. However, once listed, a company can bring securities to listing using a wider variety of methods.

The main methods by which a company can raise equity finance once it is listed are:

(a) a rights issue;
(b) an open offer;
(c) a placing;
(d) an acquisition issue; and
(e) a vendor consideration placing (UKLR 9.4.12R).

These methods are considered in detail at **17.7** to **17.11** below, and we examine why a company might choose one method rather than another. As with an IPO, however, more than one method may be combined, depending on the circumstances (such as the combined placing and open offer by Marshalls plc in April 2022 which raised £187 million). Specific documentation required for each method is also set out.

Note that some of the less common methods of raising equity finance are not discussed in detail in this chapter. Two of these, an offer (for subscription and/or sale) and an intermediaries offer, are considered in **Chapters 4** and **6**, albeit in the context of an IPO rather than a secondary issue.

UK Listing Rule 9.4 contains the rules relating to the methods by which secondary issues can be listed. These rules apply only to ESCC-listed companies.

17.7 RIGHTS ISSUE

17.7.1 What is a rights issue?

A rights issue was referred to at **14.6.12** above, when considering pre-emption rights. The Glossary to the UK Listing Rules defines a rights issue. Basically, it is:

(a) an offer to issue new shares or transfer existing shares (or other securities);

(b) to existing shareholders (or security holders) in proportion to their existing holdings;

(c) made by way of the issue of a renounceable letter;

(d) which may be traded 'nil paid' for a period before payment for the shares (or other securities) is due.

The aim is to raise money for the company by issuing new shares. For example, a company could offer to issue two shares to each shareholder for every one share that shareholder already holds (known as a '2-for-1' offer). There is no magic to this figure. The key calculation is how much money the company wishes to raise. It considers how many shares are in issue and then makes the offer accordingly, because of course all shareholders must be offered the right to buy the new shares. In May 2024 National Grid plc undertook a £7 billion '7 for 24' rights issue; shareholders were entitled to buy 7 new shares for every 24 existing shares held.

17.7.2 Price

The shares are usually allotted for cash, at a discount to the market price of the existing shares. Why is that? Well, if the company is going to raise finance, it requires shareholders to take up their rights under the rights issue and pay the cash consideration for the shares to the company. This means that the price for the shares must be better (that is, cheaper) than the price of buying shares on the open market. If it is not, the shareholders might choose to buy shares on the market instead, in which case they will pay the selling shareholder, not the company, for the shares.

A company sometimes makes what is known as a 'deep-discount rights issue', when it issues shares at a substantial discount to market value. Originally this was done so that the company did not have to pay for the issue to be underwritten (because no shareholder is likely to refuse to take up the rights) (see **17.7.5**), or because the company had an urgent need for the new money, although it is now the norm for even deeply discounted rights issues to be underwritten to protect against any unforeseen events that may affect the market. Issuing shares at a deep discount will make the issue more attractive to shareholders, so it can increase the chances of success of the rights issue, particularly in a weak market (which, in turn, can help to reduce any underwriting costs, as the company may be able to negotiate lower fees with the underwriter to reflect the reduced risk that shareholders will not take up the shares).

Note that as long as the price exceeds the nominal value of the share (CA 2006, s 580), there is no legal limit to the discount at which the company can sell the shares. As explained at **14.6.16**, the Pre-Emption Group's Statement of Principles does not apply if the company observes the pre-emption requirements of the UK Listing Rules. Before the financial crisis in 2007/08, the rule of thumb was that companies can usually discount by up to 50%, a typical discount being 15–20%, and a deep discount being 40–50%. More recently, a typical discount is 40% with a deep discount exceeding 50%. However, in these more uncertain times, some companies are so desperate for money that they have even exceeded the 50% threshold. Aston Martin Lagonda Global Holdings plc announced in April 2020 a deep discount rights issue of 86% to the market price of its shares. As with humans, so with companies – desperation is often eye-catching but never pretty.

One disadvantage of the discount applied to shares is that it tends to cause a drop in the market value of the shares for a period following the rights issue.

17.7.3 Structure

17.7.3.1 The PAL

The offer to shareholders of the right to buy new shares in the company is made by way of a renounceable letter, known as a provisional allotment letter (PAL). This does exactly what its name suggests: it provisionally allots to the shareholder her pro rata entitlement of shares. At this stage no money has changed hands. The company has given the shareholder a document which sets out her *right* to buy the new shares. The PAL will provide details of the rights issue, including the number of shares to which the shareholder is entitled and the price of those shares. The PAL is a temporary document of title, and as such it must comply with the requirements of UKLR 9.4.18R. (It is not a permanent document of title such as a share certificate, because so far the shareholder has not paid for the shares offered to them.)

On receiving the PAL, the shareholder then has a number of options. They can:

(a) take up the rights, by subscribing for the shares (see **17.7.3.2** below);

(b) renounce the rights and sell them on to a third party, nil paid (see **17.7.3.3** below);

(c) combine (a) and (b), by taking up some rights and renouncing the rest (**17.7.3.4** below); or

(d) do nothing (**17.7.3.5** below).

17.7.3.2 Taking up the rights to subscribe

Before the end of the offer period (as **17.7.4** below explains, the offer must be open for at least 14 days) the shareholder who holds the rights to subscribe, and who wishes to exercise them, must submit the consideration and the PAL to the company's receiving agents. (At the end of the offer period, this right will lapse.) This means that the shareholder will have bought the new shares and ensure her existing percentage shareholding is not diluted.

17.7.3.3 Renouncing the rights to subscribe

Rationale

As we have seen in **17.7.3.2** above, if the shareholder takes up the rights, she ensures that her existing percentage shareholding is not diluted. However, if the shareholder renounces the rights, her shareholding will be diluted, meaning a smaller share of the company's profits and a lower percentage share of the voting rights. So why would a shareholder renounce the right to subscribe for shares? As ever with listed companies, usually the motivation is financial.

EXAMPLE

Imagine that shares in X plc have a current market value of £2 each. X plc gives its shareholders the right to subscribe for more shares, in proportion to their existing shareholdings, for £1.60 per share (that is, at a discount of 20%). The right to subscribe has a value, therefore, of 40p per share. However, the fact that the market value in the shares is likely to drop (see **17.7.2** above) must be taken into account. Imagine that the market value drops to £1.95. If the shareholder renounces their rights and sells them for 35p each, they will have made a profit of 35p per share (less any dealing costs). If the shareholder has, say, 1,000 shares, they can make £350 with no capital outlay. They might consider that this makes diluting their shareholding worthwhile.

(Note, however, that the shareholder may incur an immediate capital gains tax charge if they sell their rights. If they exercised the rights, however, capital gains tax would arise only on a subsequent disposal of the shares.)

The shareholder wishing to renounce and sell rights should not find it too difficult to find a buyer for those rights, as the buyer will be able to buy shares from the shareholder at the market value, here £1.95. The buyer will pay £1.60 per share to the company under the rights issue, plus 35p per share to the shareholder for the right to subscribe. Of course, the risk to the buyer is that the market price drops further.

> **EXAMPLE**
>
> Imagine the market price of shares in X plc drops not to £1.95 but to £1.50. The buyer has already paid 35p per share to the selling shareholder for the right to subscribe and must pay an additional £1.60 to the company for shares they can buy in the market for £1.50. In this case, the buyer will probably cut their losses; while they cannot claim back the price they paid to the selling shareholder for the right to subscribe, they can avoid paying the remaining £1.60 to the company simply by not exercising the right and letting it lapse.

Nil paid dealings

So how does the shareholder renounce and trade her rights to subscribe? The PAL is negotiable, which means that it can be transferred by delivery (ie it can be bought and sold). As **17.7.4** below explains, the offer must be open for at least 14 days. 'Nil paid dealings' can take place during this 14-day period. This means that a shareholder can trade the rights to subscribe simply by signing the PAL and passing it on to someone else. These dealings are referred to as 'nil paid dealings' because trading takes place before any subscription monies have been paid for the shares represented by the PAL. The third party can then exercise the right to subscribe in the manner described at **17.7.3.2** above and will become the owner of the new shares mentioned in the PAL. It is on the admission of the shares to trading in nil paid form that the FCA will grant admission of the shares to the Official List. Once the shares are paid up, and the allotment becomes unconditional, there is no need for a further listing application (UKLR 9.5.3G).

17.7.3.4 Taking up some rights and renouncing the rest

Alternatively, the shareholder may choose to take up some rights (using the procedure outlined at **17.7.3.2**) and renounce the remainder (using the process outlined at **17.7.3.3**). This may be used where the shareholder has insufficient funds to buy the whole allocation or does not wish to take up all her rights. The proceeds received from trading some of the rights may help to finance the purchase of the balance of these rights (known as 'tail swallowing').

17.7.3.5 Doing nothing

Shareholders who do nothing are known as 'lazy shareholders'. Even lazy shareholders can benefit from a rights issue, because arrangements are made for the sale of any shares not taken up. Even if a shareholder does not take up the shares and does not trade the PAL, she may still receive a cash payment to the extent that the shares which were provisionally allotted to her are sold in the market for more than their subscription price. For ESCC-listed companies only, the proceeds must exceed £5 (UKLR 9.4.4R). (As explained in **17.7.3.3**, the nil paid rights have a value.)

17.7.4 Timing

The FCA does not allow shares in listed companies to be allotted provisionally on a conditional basis (UKLR 3.1.5G). This means that if any shareholder approvals are required in relation to the issue (such as to give the directors authority to allot – see **Chapter 14**), the PALs can be posted only after all necessary shareholder approvals have been obtained at the GM.

ESCC-listed company

Once the PALs are posted, UKLR 9.4.6R provides that the offer must remain open for at least 10 business days. Section 562(5) states that the offer must be open for 14 days. This section will only be relevant if s 561 is not disapplied. If s 561 does apply then the ESCC-listed company must still also comply with the 10 business days requirement under UKLR 9.4.6R.

This matters because this could be slightly longer than the 14-day period under s 562(5) (due to the definition of business day in the UK Listing Rules which excludes public holidays).

When calculating the 10 business days under UKLR 9.4.6R, the first business day will be the first day the rights issue offer is open for acceptance. This will be the day of the posting of the PAL. When calculating the 14 days under s 562(5), the first day is counted from the day of making the offer. This therefore starts from the day of posting the PAL.

Conclusion

The combination of the time required for the GM notice (14 clear days for a special resolution at a GM (and not an AGM) under the CA 2006 provisions assuming the conditions in s 307A of the CA 2006 – see **8.6.1** – are met), added to the subsequent minimum offer period of 14 days under the CA 2006/10 business days (under the UK Listing Rules for ESCC-listed companies), means that the rights issue will often take weeks to complete.

17.7.5 Underwriting

The role of underwriters on an IPO was explored at **4.2.7** above. The process of underwriting is equally relevant to a secondary issue. The underwriters (usually an investment bank or a broker) basically guarantee that the company will receive the equity finance it seeks, by agreeing to take up, at no less than the subscription price under the rights issue, any shares which are not taken up by shareholders and which cannot be sold in the market (including fractional entitlements if s 561 has been disapplied – see **17.7.6.1**). These shares are referred to as 'the rump'. As explained at **17.7.3.5**, any premium received over the subscription price must be given to the person to whom the shares were provisionally allotted.

The underwriters must buy any of the rump which is left (that is, which they have been unable to sell). These leftover shares are referred to as 'the stick'. The stick represents the underwriter's risk, and the underwriter will try to predict what the stick, and therefore the risk, will be, in calculating their commission (see **17.7.5.1** at (a) below). As with an IPO, it is common for a secondary issue to be sub-underwritten either in part, or in its entirety (see **4.2.7**).

Events in the second half of 2008, at the height of the financial crisis in the UK, demonstrated in stark terms both the need for underwriting arrangements and the risks involved for underwriters. HBOS plc sought to raise £4 billion via a rights issue. It was a disaster. Investors took up just 8.3% of the shares offered even though they were priced at a near 50% discount to its then market price. That level of support was one of the lowest ever recorded for a rights issue. This resulted in underwriters Morgan Stanley and Dresdner Kleinwort being left with the rump of almost £3.8 billion worth of shares. Ultimately, the underwriters and sub-underwriters had to pay almost £2.5 billion to buy the stock. Of course such failures are extremely rare and reflect the turmoil caused by the grave crisis in the financial markets and the collapse of the share price of banks listed on the Stock Exchange at that time.

17.7.5.1 The underwriting agreement

The underwriting arrangements will be recorded in an underwriting agreement, which typically includes the following:

(a) *Details about the commission payable.* Underwriting costs increase with the length of time for which the underwriter is 'on risk' to take up shares, because the longer the period, the less certain the underwriter can be about how the market in those shares will move. The higher the risk for the underwriter, the more the underwriter will charge for their services. With a rights issue, the underwriter is 'on risk' for a considerable period of time (see **17.7.4** above); therefore the underwriting costs can be high. Traditionally, a typical underwriting agreement might provide, for example, that the underwriter's fees will be 2% of the amount underwritten for the first 30 days of the rights issue, and a further commission of 0.125% of the aggregate amount raised in respect of any further period (although the amount and formula will vary depending on factors such as the amount of the rights issue and the amount of discount). However, in light of the financial crisis, underwriting fees soared to an average of 3.5%, which prompted an inquiry by the UK competition authorities. More recently, fees seem to have settled into the 2–3.25% range.

(b) *Conditions*. These will include the passing of any necessary resolutions at a GM and the admission of the shares to the Official List and the Main Market, nil paid (known as the 'admission condition'). In other words, the agreement is a conditional contract. If these conditions are not met, the underwriter can walk away from the agreement.

(c) *Representations and warranties from the company*. Breach of these may give rise to the right to terminate the agreement, in addition to damages.

(d) *Material adverse change (MAC) clause and force majeure clause*. These clauses will allow the underwriter to terminate the agreement in very limited circumstances. There has been greater attention paid to these clauses in light of the financial crisis. Underwriters are increasingly drafting termination rights more precisely rather than relying on generally-worded MAC clauses. It is also worth noting that a recent case, *Tandrin Aviation Holdings Ltd v Aero Toy Store* [2010] EWHC 40 (Comm), reiterated the accepted principle that extraordinary economic or financial difficulties do not fall within a generally-worded force majeure clause, and that explicit reference to such events must be made to discharge the parties from contractual liability.

As stated at **17.7.4**, the FCA does not allow shares in listed companies to be allotted provisionally on a conditional basis. This means that underwriters should not have any right to terminate their underwriting obligation once the nil paid rights have been admitted, because once this point is reached shareholders will begin trading in the rights. Companies must therefore ensure that their underwriting arrangements do not allow the underwriters to invoke withdrawal rights (see **6.9.4** and **17.5.1**) under any circumstances.

17.7.6 Pre-emption rights

A rights issue is a pre-emptive offer, that is, it is in accordance with the statutory pre-emption rights on allotment under s 561 of the CA 2006; the company is issuing *equity securities* (for our purposes, ordinary shares) to holders of *ordinary shares* in proportion to the nominal value of their existing shareholdings, in return for cash consideration (see **14.6.5**). This therefore accords with the rationale behind pre-emption rights, namely to allow existing voting shareholders to protect their proportionate share of the votes at the company's GM and of the profits paid by way of dividend.

As the issue is in accordance with s 561, there is no requirement to disapply s 561; however, the company must also comply with s 562 of the CA 2006, which sets out how to make the offer. In particular, the offer:

(a) must be in hard copy or electronic form (s 562(2));

(b) must state a period of not less than 14 days during which it can be accepted (s 562(5)) (see **17.7.4**); and

(c) such period begins:

   (i) for an offer made in hard copy, with the date on which the offer was sent or supplied; or

   (ii) for an offer made electronically, with the date on which the offer was sent.

However, having said that there is no *legal requirement* to disapply s 561 for a rights issue, *in practice* s 561 is often disapplied, for the reasons set out at **17.7.6.1** to **17.7.6.3** below. As explained at **14.6.15**, for this reason typically listed companies effect a general disapplication of the statutory pre-emption rights (that is, s 561) at each AGM. Remember, however, that any existing s 561 disapplication will relate to an existing s 551 authority (see **14.6.14.3**). If the rights issue requires a new s 551 authority (because the existing s 551 authority has expired in terms of time or number of shares) then the existing s 561 disapplication will be of no use. If this is the case, the company will need to pass a new s 561 disapplication specifically for the issue if the statutory procedure is not to be followed.

The differences outlined below should be familiar to you from **14.6.12**.

17.7.6.1 Fractional entitlements

If the company offered shareholders their exact proportional entitlements under a rights issue, the calculation may entitle some shareholders to fractions of shares. The CA 2006 is unclear as to how a company should deal with fractional entitlements, so, in practice, the company rounds down each shareholder's entitlement to the nearest whole share. The fractional entitlements which have not been offered have the potential to raise further finance, if the company can aggregate them and sell the aggregate. Unfortunately, the CA 2006 is not clear as to whether fractional entitlements are covered by s 561. Selling the aggregate might infringe the existing shareholders' pre-emption rights. However, if those pre-emption rights are disapplied, the company can sell the aggregate fractional entitlements. The company can take both the subscription price and any premium over the subscription price which it receives. This is subject to UKLR 9.4.4R for premium listed companies. If the fractional entitlement for that particular shareholder exceeds £5, the whole entitlement should go to the shareholder. However, this is unlikely to be an issue in practice due to the large number of shares in existence in most listed companies and because the shares are being offered at a (usually sizeable) discount.

EXAMPLE

The company has 500,000 shareholders. One of them, X, holds 302 shares. The company announces a '1 for 3' rights issue, that is 1 new share is offered for every 3 shares held. Strictly X is entitled to 100 shares plus two-thirds of a share (302 divided by 3).

However, as the CA 2006 is unclear as to whether fractional entitlements can be allocated, the company rounds down X's entitlement to 100 shares. This leaves two-thirds of a share unissued. A similar situation has arisen for most of the other 499,999 shareholders, so that, together with X's two-thirds of a share, there is an aggregate of, say, 200,000 shares unissued.

If s 561 applies to the issue, it is thought that selling these 200,000 shares to a third party may infringe the pre-emptive right of X (to their two-thirds of a share) and of each of the other existing shareholders (to their respective fractional entitlements), so the company cannot do anything with these shares.

However, if s 561 is disapplied, these shares can be sold to one or more third parties, raising further finance for the company. The company will take the subscription price for the 200,000 shares and can take any premium received.

17.7.6.2 Overseas shareholders

Certain jurisdictions, such as Japan, Canada and the USA, have very strict laws concerning the offering of securities. These laws mean that it can be so expensive and time-consuming to make an offer of securities in those jurisdictions that many companies prefer not to make an offer there. If the pre-emption rights have not been disapplied and the company has shareholders in those jurisdictions, the company has a problem. Section 562(3) of the CA 2006 does provide for this situation; it allows companies to make an offer to those overseas shareholders by way of a notice in the *Gazette* (known as the '*Gazette* route'). However, companies often prefer instead to disapply the pre-emption rights, and arrange for the entitlements of those shareholders to be aggregated and sold in the market, nil-paid. Any premium the company receives over the subscription price will then usually be given to those overseas shareholders. For ESCC-listed companies this will be done in accordance with UKLR 9.4.4R (subject to the company's right to retain amounts under £5 per shareholder if it wishes).

17.7.6.3 Convertible securities

If a company has issued securities and the terms of those securities state that they will entitle the holder to pre-emption rights, but under the CA 2006 the holder is not entitled to pre-emption rights (because the securities do not fall within the definition of 'ordinary shares': see **14.6.8** above), the company must disapply s 561. This will ensure that the company will be able to make the rights issue to those holders, in accordance with the terms of the securities.

EXAMPLE

The company has in issue convertible loan stock. The terms of the loan stock state that the holders of the stock are entitled to pre-emption rights on any rights issue. However, under s 561, convertible loan stock does not fall within the definition of ordinary shares (it is not a share), and so, under s 561 the loan stock does not entitle its holders to pre-emption rights. There is a conflict. It would be very difficult to change the terms of the stock, so instead s 561 is disapplied to resolve the conflict; and the rights issue is offered to the holders of the convertible loan stock.

17.7.6.4 Pre-emption rights under the UK Listing Rules for ESCC-listed companies

As **14.6.12** explained, the pre-emption rights under the UK Listing Rules for ESCC-listed companies are slightly more flexible than the pre-emption rights under the CA 2006, and they do not raise the problems listed at **17.7.6.1** and **17.7.6.2** above (although they do raise similar problems relating to convertible securities). When the company disapplies s 561, although this also disapplies the pre-emption rights under the UK Listing Rules (see UKLR 9.2.2R and **14.6.15**), the company will nevertheless still offer the rights pre-emptively (except to overseas shareholders and fractional entitlements) as envisaged by the UK Listing Rules. This removes the practical problems of the statutory pre-emption rights in relation to fractional entitlements and overseas shareholders, but keeps the IPCs happy.

17.7.6.5 The IPCs

If the statutory pre-emption rights are disapplied, does this mean that the Pre-emption Group will no longer support the issue? No. As explained at **14.6.16** above, para 1 of Part 1 of the Pre-Emption Group's Statement of Principles makes clear that the Principles do not apply to issues of equity securities on a pre-emptive basis. Paragraph 2 of Part 3 of the Pre-Emption Group's Statement of Principles (see **14.6.16**) states that the choice of financing options (that is, the method of raising equity finance) is one of the considerations relating to a request for a specific disapplication (see **14.6.16.2**). The Group notes that a wide variety of financing options are now available to companies, and if a non-pre-emptive issue of shares is the most appropriate means of raising capital, companies should explain why that is, and why other financing methods have been rejected.

17.7.7 Timetable

Table 17.2 below is an example of a basic rights issue timetable, assuming that a GM is required. Please note that in practice most documents are submitted to the FCA and to the Stock Exchange in draft form well before the required deadline. Similarly, applications may be made in advance of the date required by the regulatory rules. Remember also that the timetable will be dependent on the particular circumstances of the listed company involved (for example, the time period in the company's articles for receipt of documents sent in the post may vary from company to company). The timings may therefore vary from rights issue to rights issue.

Table 17.2

Date	Event
1.5 to 3 months (deadline is 10 working days) before impact day.	Submit draft prospectus and related draft documentation to FCA for approval under the UK Prospectus Regulation and Prospectus Regulation Rules.
Day before impact day	Board meeting to approve rights issue. Underwriting agreement signed and held in escrow.
Impact day	Press announcement released. Underwriting agreement released from escrow. Prospectus published, containing notice of GM. (PALs cannot be sent out until after GM.)
2 business days before D day (UKLR 20.4.2R)	Apply for admission of shares, nil paid, to the Official List and Main Market (by submitting '48 hour' documents to FCA under the UK Listing Rules, and 'two- day' documents to the Stock Exchange under the Admission and Disclosure Standards).
14 clear days after impact day (assuming a GM (and not an AGM) held) (s 307A and s 360, CA 2006)	GM to pass shareholder resolutions (eg grant directors authority to allot, disapply s 561, create a new class of shares, alter articles of association, and/ or approve any related acquisition). PALs sent out immediately after GM.
One business day after GM ('**D day**')	Submit 'on the day' documents to the FCA under the UK Listing Rules (UKLR 20.4.4R). Shares admitted to Official List and Main Market, nil paid. Statement made by FCA to an RIS and statement published by the Stock Exchange on its website. 'Admission condition' in underwriting agreement is satisfied. Nil paid dealings in shares begin. Sale of overseas shareholders' shares and fractional entitlements (if s 561 pre-emption rights disapplied).
10 business days (UKLR 9.4.6R) from posting of PALs if s 561 disapplied (ESCC listing); or 14 days (CA 2006, s 562(5)) and 10 business days (UKLR 9.4.6R) if s 561 not disapplied (ESCC listing) ('Close of offer')	End of nil paid dealing period. Deadline for acceptance and payment in full.
1 business day after close of offer	Dealings in shares commence, fully paid. Notify underwriters of acceptances. Underwriters try to sell rump.

Date	Event
2 business days after close of offer	Identify stick. Final confirmation of acceptances announced. Announce result of rights issue to RIS (for ESCC-listed companies) see **17.7.11** below.
Week after close of offer	Underwriters pay company consideration for the stick, if any. Company receives net proceeds of the issue and dispatches share certificates to shareholders/credits CREST accounts.

17.7.8 Advantages of a rights issue

A rights issue has the following advantages:

(a) *Price.* If the issue is in accordance with the pre-emption requirements of the UK Listing Rules, there is no limit on the level of discount at which the company can issue the shares (save that the shares must not be issued at a discount to their nominal value in breach of s 580 of the CA 2006).

(b) *The IPCs.* The IPCs are more likely to support this pre-emptive method of raising equity finance (see **17.7.6.5**).

17.7.9 Disadvantages of a rights issue

A rights issue has the following disadvantages:

(a) *Cost.* The costs of underwriting can be high.

(b) *Market value.* The shares issued under a rights issue are usually issued at a discount. This can cause the market value of the shares to fall.

(c) *Timing.* The offer period is 10 business days under UKLR 9.4.6R for ESCC-listed companies, which cannot run concurrently with the GM notice.

(d) *Pre-emption.* Even though the offer is on a pre-emptive basis, a s 561 disapplication is often required (see **17.7.6** above).

17.7.10 Is a rights issue appropriate?

When considering whether a rights issue is the most appropriate method to raise equity finance, the following questions will be useful:

(a) Is the company concerned about underwriting costs? If so, a rights issue may not be the best method.

(b) Does the company need to raise finance quickly? If so, a rights issue may not be the best method.

(c) Does the company need flexibility in the amount by which it can discount shares? If so, a rights issue has some advantage over the other methods of equity finance in this regard.

17.7.11 Documentation

The following documentation may be required for a rights issue:

(a) press announcement of rights issue on impact day and of the results of the issue, issued via an RIS and satisfying the need for an RIS notification (UKLR 9.4.5R for ESCC-listed companies);

(b) underwriting agreement;

(c) PAL;

(d) notice of GM;

(e) prospectus;

(f) perhaps, a separate circular (see **17.5.2**);

(g) documents required for admitting shares to listing and to trading (see **17.4.3**);

(h) if the rights issue involves CREST shareholders, additional documents to enable dealing in the rights; and

(i) *Gazette* notice (for overseas shareholders).

17.8 OPEN OFFER

17.8.1 What is an open offer?

The Glossary to the UK Listing Rules defines an open offer. Like a rights issue (see **17.7** above), an open offer is:

(a) an offer to issue new shares, or transfer existing shares (or other securities);

(b) to existing shareholders (or security holders) in proportion to their existing holdings.

Again, the offer is usually for cash. However, unlike a rights issue, the offer is not made by means of a PAL (see **17.7.3.1** above), but by an application form. The structure of the offer is considered at **17.8.3** below.

17.8.2 Price

The shares are offered at a discount, but the discount tends to be less than that for a rights issue (see **17.7.2** above). The default position is that an open offer for an ESCC-listed company cannot be priced at a discount of more than 10% of market value (UKLR 9.4.13R(1)). UK Listing Rule 9.4.13R(4) provides that this rule does not apply if:

(a) the company's shareholders have specifically approved the terms of the open offer at a discount of more than 10%; or

(b) the shares are being issued for cash consideration under a pre-existing general authority to disapply s 561 of the CA 2006.

Note that any shares issued under the exception at (b) above will render the disapplication 'specific' under the Pre-Emption Group's Statement of Principles, which advocate limiting any discount to 5%, unless the issue is in accordance with the pre-emption requirements of the UK Listing Rules (see **14.6.16**).

17.8.3 Structure

The company sends a personal application form to each shareholder. Unlike the PAL used in a rights issue, this form simply offers shares; it does not provisionally allot them. The shareholder can either take up the offer, or do nothing. No shareholder can assign or sell the benefit of the offer. There is no trading in rights. In addition, no arrangements are made for the sale of shares which shareholders do not take up. This is bad news for the 'lazy shareholder'; in contrast to a rights issue (see **17.7.3.5** above), if a shareholder does nothing in relation to the offer, they will receive nothing under the offer.

The traditional structure of an open offer gives shareholders less flexibility than on a rights issue (the shareholder cannot trade the rights nil paid, and the lazy shareholder receives nothing) and open offers tend to be cheaper for companies than rights issues. The IPCs have stated, informally and not through formal guidance, that if an issue represents more than 15–18% of a company's issued share capital, or if the discount is greater than 7.5%, this may cause them concern (if the issue does not otherwise protect shareholders adequately). In such circumstances, the IPCs prefer a rights issue to an open offer. In order to mitigate some of this criticism, it is possible to have so-called 'compensatory' open offers (eg Lloyds Banking Group plc open offer in May 2009) which are structured so that shareholders who do not take up their entitlement are compensated as on a rights issue by receiving any premium above the offer price when the rump is sold in the market by the underwriters. However, these are very rare indeed in practice.

17.8.4 Timing

UK Listing Rule 9.4.7R provides that the timetable for an open offer for an ESCC-listed company must be approved by the RIE on which the shares are traded. For our purposes this is the London Stock Exchange. UK Listing Rule 9.4.8R states that the offer period must be a minimum period of 10 business days from the date of posting the application forms. This mirrors the Stock Exchange's requirement in Admission and Disclosure Standards, Sch 3, para 7. The offer period is therefore the same for a rights issue.

In addition, and of more significance to timing, is the fact that, unlike with a rights issue, the application forms do not provisionally allot shares. This means that the problem with provisionally allotting shares on a conditional basis does not arise. Therefore, if a GM is required in order to obtain the consent of the shareholders in connection with the share issue (to increase the company's share capital and such like – see **Chapter 14**), the offer period can run concurrently with the GM notice. This means that, compared to a rights issue, the underwriting commission is less and the company will receive its cash sooner.

17.8.5 Advantages of an open offer

An open offer has the following advantages for the company:

(a) *Timing.* The offer period can run concurrently with the GM notice.

(b) *Cost.* For an ESCC-listed company the default position is that shares cannot be offered at a discount of more than 10%. Unless the offer is structured to fall within one of the exceptions to this, the open offer will be cheaper for the company (but see **17.8.6**(b) below).

17.8.6 Disadvantages of an open offer

An open offer has the following disadvantages for the company:

(a) *Pre-emption.* Even though the offer is on a pre-emptive basis, a s 561 disapplication is usually required, because the statutory pre-emption rights have the potential to cause problems (as they do on a rights issue; see **17.7.6**).

(b) *Flexibility.* For an ESCC-listed company the default position is that shares cannot be offered at a discount of more than 10%. Unless the offer is structured to fall within one of the exceptions to this, an open offer might be less attractive to shareholders than a rights issue.

(c) *The IPCs.* The IPCs prefer rights issues to open offers in certain circumstances (see **17.8.3**).

17.8.7 Documentation

The following documentation may be required for an open offer:

(a) press announcement/RIS notification;

(b) underwriting agreement;

(c) notice of GM;

(d) prospectus;

(e) perhaps, a separate circular (see **17.5.2**); and

(f) other documents required for admitting shares to listing and to trading (see **17.4.3**).

17.9 PLACING

A placing is one of the methods by which a company can float (see **4.4.2** above). It is also a method which can be used for a secondary issue.

17.9.1 What is a placing?

The formal definition of a placing is in the Glossary to the UK Listing Rules. Basically, a placing is:

(a) an offer by the company to issue new shares and/or an offer by existing shareholders to transfer existing unlisted shares (or other securities);

(b) to specified persons or clients of any financial adviser assisting in the placing;

(c) which does not involve an offer to the public or to existing holders of the company's securities.

Again, a placing is usually for cash. The key distinguishing feature is therefore that a placing involves a much smaller number of people than a rights issue or an open offer, and they are usually institutional investors.

17.9.2 Price

Paragraph 5 of Part 2B of the Pre-Emption Group's Statement of Principles (set out at **Appendix 3**) provides that a request for a discount of more than 5% of market value is not likely to be regarded as 'general' (see **14.6.16**).

UK Listing Rule 9.4.13R also provides that for an ESCC-listed company, a placing, as with an open offer, cannot be priced at a discount of more than 10% of market value unless it is structured to fall within either of the exceptions set out at UKLR 9.4.10R(4)(a) or (b) (see **17.8.2**).

17.9.3 Advantages of a placing

The advantage of a placing is its cost. The limitations on the discount that can be applied (see **17.9.2**) mean that a placing can be cheaper for the company than a rights issue. As soundings will be taken from the market as to likely demand and an acceptable price, underwriting fees, if any, are likely to be lower than on a rights issue.

17.9.4 Disadvantages of a placing

A placing is not a pre-emptive offer, so:

(a) a s 561 disapplication is required; and

(b) the Pre-Emption Group's Statement of Principles will restrict the number of shares which can be issued (see **14.6.16** above) (and the discount which can be applied – see **17.9.2**).

17.9.5 Documentation

The following documentation may be required for a placing:

(a) press announcement/RIS notification;

(b) placing agreement;

(c) underwriting agreement;

(d) prospectus, unless the placing is exempt (see **17.5.1**);

(e) if the placing is exempt, or possibly if overseas shareholders, a separate circular (see **17.5.2**); and

(f) other documents required for admitting shares to listing and to trading (see **17.4.3**).

17.9.6 Example

Metro Bank Holdings plc completed a placing in November 2023 which raised £150 million to strengthen the group's balance sheet as soon as possible due to forthcoming debt repayments.

17.10 ACQUISITION ISSUE

17.10.1 What is an acquisition issue?

An acquisition issue is also known as a 'share-for-share exchange', or a 'securities exchange offer'. It is:

(a) an issue of new shares by the company;

(b) to the seller(s) of an asset or assets (which includes shares);

(c) in consideration for the acquisition by the company of that asset or assets.

17.10.2 Structure

An acquisition issue does not involve marketing shares, as in the case of a rights issue, an open offer or a placing. Instead, it consists of the offer of shares as consideration for an acquisition.

> **EXAMPLE**
>
> Imagine that X plc wants to buy the entire issued share capital of another company, Y Ltd. The buyer is X plc. The sellers are all the shareholders of Y Ltd. The sellers will transfer the shares they hold in Y Ltd to X plc. X plc will then issue shares in itself to the shareholders of Y Ltd, as consideration. See **Figure 17.1** below.

Figure 17.1: Acquisition issue

Before the acquisition

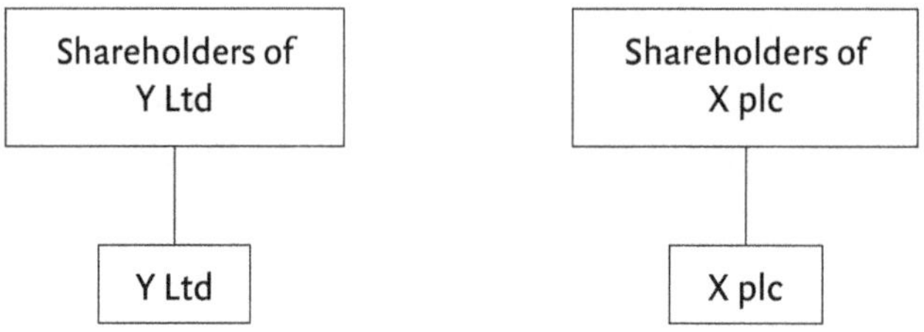

The acquisition

1. Shareholders in Y Ltd *transfer* all the shares in Y Ltd to X plc, so X plc becomes the sole shareholder of Y Ltd.
2. X plc *issues* shares in itself to the shareholders of Y Ltd, as consideration for the transfer, so the former shareholders of Y become additional shareholders of X plc.

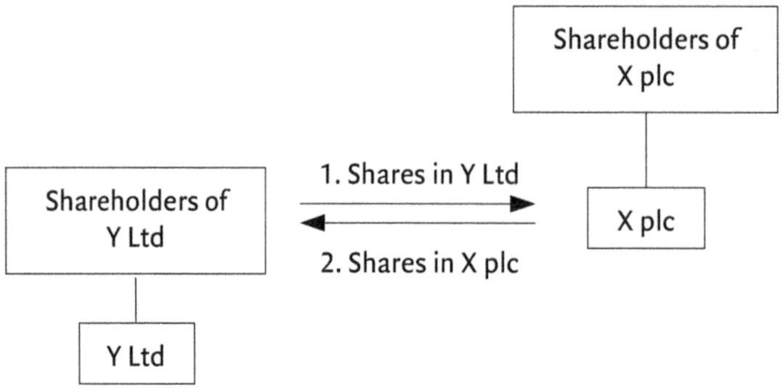

After the acquisition

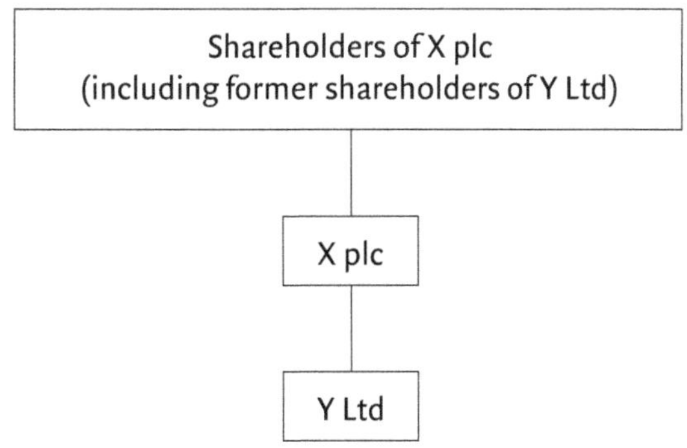

17.10.3 Advantages of an acquisition issue

An acquisition issue has the following advantages:

(a) *Timing.* There are no significant timetabling issues.

(b) *Cost.* An acquisition issue is inexpensive.

(c) *Pre-emption.* The issue is not for cash, so s 561 pre-emption rights are not triggered.

17.10.4 Disadvantages of an acquisition issue

An acquisition issue has the disadvantage that a valuation may be required under s 593 of the CA 2006 (see **14.7.5** above), if the asset to be acquired is anything other than shares.

17.10.5 Documentation

The following documentation may be required for an acquisition issue:

(a) press announcement/RIS notification;

(b) sale and purchase agreement;

(c) prospectus, unless the acquisition issue is exempt;

(d) circular; and

(e) other documents required for admitting shares to listing and to trading (see **17.4.3**).

17.11 VENDOR PLACING

17.11.1 What is a vendor placing?

A vendor placing (also known as a 'vendor consideration placing') is used in the context of an acquisition only. It is useful when:

(a) the company wants to make an acquisition; but

(b) the company does not have sufficient cash to buy the company or business; and

(c) the seller is not willing to accept non-cash consideration (so that an acquisition issue (see **17.10** above) is not appropriate).

Instead, the vendor placing is structured so that:

(a) there is an acquisition issue; then

(b) the company arranges for its investment bank to place the shares it has issued to the seller as consideration; then

(c) the company's investment bank gives the proceeds of the placing, in cash, to the seller.

So the listed company acquires the company or business it wants. The seller gets the cash it wants. In recent years these have become much less popular.

17.11.2 Price

UK Listing Rule 9.4.13R provides that, as with an open offer and a placing, a vendor placing for an ESCC-listed company cannot be priced at a discount of more than 10% of market value unless it is structured to fall within either of the exceptions set out at UKLR 9.4.13R(4)(a) and (b) (see **17.8.2**). The vendor placing is not an issue of shares for cash, so it will not fall within the exception at UKLR 9.4.13R(4)(b).

17.11.3 Advantages of a vendor placing

(a) *Cost*. The limitation on the discount that can be applied for an ESCC-listed company (see **17.11.2**) means that a vendor placing can have cost advantages for the company.

(b) *Pre-emption*. A vendor placing is not an issue for cash. The company issues the shares for non-cash consideration (it exchanges them for shares). The pre-emption rules do not apply, therefore, so no s 561 disapplication is required. However, the Investment Association has issued guidelines which provide that vendor placings:

(i) of over 10% of the company's issued equity share capital; or

(ii) at more than 5% discount,

must be placed on a basis which gives existing shareholders the right to 'claw back' their pro rata share of the issue. The claw-back is usually offered by way of an open offer (vendor placing with open offer), but it can also be made by way of rights issue (vendor consideration rights issue).

17.11.4 Disadvantages of a vendor placing

A valuation may be required under s 593 of the CA 2006 (see **14.7.5** above), if the asset to be acquired is anything other than shares.

17.11.5 Documentation

The following documentation may be required for a vendor placing:

(a) press announcement/RIS notification;

(b) sale and purchase agreement;

(c) placing agreement;

(d) underwriting agreement;

(e) prospectus, unless the vendor placing is exempt;

(f) circular; and

(g) other documents required for admitting shares to listing and to trading (see **17.4.3**).

17.12 FUTURE DEVELOPMENTS

Financial Services and Markets Act 2023

This Act intends, amongst other things, to revoke EU financial services law that had been retained following Brexit and replace it with UK-sourced rules. It will also grant the FCA much wider powers to enable it to draw up legally binding rules which will be included in the FCA's Handbook (eg the UK Listing Rules, Prospectus Rules and Disclosure Guidance and Transparency Rules) rather than, as is currently the case, in legislation. This will allow for greater flexibility in changing the rules in the future. Laws which will be repealed include the UK version of the Prospectus Directive, the UK version of MAR, the UK version of MiFIR and the related delegated legislation.

The regime governing the need for a prospectus will be fundamentally overhauled. Following repeal of the UK version of the Prospectus Regulation, the two tests for a prospectus under s 85 of the FSMA 2000 will be replaced by a prohibition on 'offers to the public' with a series of exemptions which are wider than currently is the law. Regarding secondary issues, there will be an exemption from the prohibition on making public offers where it is to existing shareholders. The 'admission to trading' test will be superseded by rules in the FCA's Handbook (new Prospectus Rules replacing the PRRs) governing the need for a prospectus. For example, it is expected that the exemption when a listed company increases its share capital by 20% or less in a year will be increased to 75%. The detailed content requirements for a prospectus will be drawn up by the FCA and included in its rules. The FCA will have the power to amend the rules setting out the procedure for approval of a prospectus and those who should take responsibility for it once it is published.

You will be able to follow developments via the FCA's website.

Please note that these amendments may result in significant changes to the content of this chapter.

CHAPTER 18

EQUITY FINANCE OR DEBT FINANCE?

18.1 INTRODUCTION

Chapter 17 considers that when a company needs finance to provide working capital, reduce borrowings, fund a specific acquisition, or, indeed, for any other reason, it may decide to raise equity finance. This involves the company issuing shares in return for cash or assets. Another book in the series, ***Banking and Capital Markets***, discusses another way in which a company may raise finance – debt finance. This involves the company using debt to obtain the cash or assets it requires.

The remainder of this chapter provides a brief overview as to why a company might choose to raise equity finance rather than debt finance, and vice versa. It then examines why most companies, regardless of their size, are financed by a combination of both debt and equity, and considers the key to the right combination.

18.2 INCOME

18.2.1 Equity finance

A company does not have to declare a dividend. If it does not, the shareholders will not receive any income from their investment. The company does not have to pay any interest to the shareholders. The shareholders do not have a *right* to income.

However, in the real world, any listed company will be aware that if it does not declare a dividend, it risks both losing the support of its shareholders and damaging its reputation as a good investment. It is not a good idea, therefore, for a company to perceive a dividend as something which it can withhold without good reason.

To the extent a company does declare a dividend, the shareholders will share in the profits of the company. For equity shareholders, this right is infinite (see **13.5.1.1**).

18.2.2 Debt finance

Lenders will negotiate a rate of interest with the company. The cost of debt to the company depends on the interest rate which a lender charges. The company will have to pay interest regardless of profits (unlike a dividend). Interest provides lenders with income from their investment (unlike a dividend, this income is finite).

The term 'leverage' is often used in this regard. Leverage is the opportunity to create profit by financing a business through debt which is entitled to a finite return. Imagine that you and nine of your friends own a company; you are its shareholders. You have no more cash to invest. If you finance the business solely through equity, you need to bring on board other shareholders who are willing and able to inject cash into the company in return for shares. All the profits of the company will now be shared not just between you and your nine friends, but between all the other shareholders too. Now imagine that you decided to finance the company solely through debt. Any profits which are surplus, once the interest on the debt has been paid, will be shared just between you and your nine friends.

18.3 CAPITAL

18.3.1 Equity finance

On a winding up of the company, the company repays its debts first, then it pays to the shareholders the nominal value of their shares, together with any premium they paid on those shares. The shareholders do not have a *right* to capital. This risk, that shareholders will lose their capital, is balanced by the opportunity, described at **18.2.1** above, to share in the profits of the company without limit, and the potential, described at **18.4** below, for capital growth.

18.3.2 Debt finance

Ultimately, the company must repay the capital to the lender. The holders of debt securities will be paid in priority to shareholders on a winding up.

18.4 CAPITAL GROWTH

18.4.1 Equity finance

There is scope for capital growth. The share value will reflect the success of the company. This can help a successful company to market shares.

18.4.2 Debt finance

There is no scope for capital growth. The lender has a right to be repaid only the capital sum, plus interest, no matter how well the company is performing.

18.5 TAXATION

18.5.1 Equity finance

Dividends are not a deductible expense in calculating the company's corporation taxation liability.

18.5.2 Debt finance

Interest payable on a loan is tax deductible.

18.6 RIGHTS

18.6.1 Equity finance

When a company issues shares, unless it issues such shares in proportion to the existing shareholders' shareholdings, the issue will dilute those shareholdings.

If the issue is of voting shares, the balance of power within the company could change. This may be a high price to pay for raising finance.

18.6.2 Debt finance

Debt finance will not affect the power structure of the company, nor afford the lender any right to vote in the company.

18.7 INVESTORS

The differences between debt and equity considered above mean that investors have different priorities, depending on how they intend to invest in a company.

The extent to which a potential investor will investigate a company before choosing to invest will differ, depending on whether the investor is seeking to invest by way of equity or debt.

18.7.1 Equity investors

Substantial equity investors include pension funds and other similar financial institutions. Potential equity investors will analyse not only the company's current financial position, but also how the company is placed in the long term, by considering the business sector in which the company operates, the company's expenditure on research and development for new products (R&D), and the company's future earning potential. This reflects the fact that once equity investors invest in a company, they pass the point of no return. They have no right to recover their cash, unless they can sell the shares. They risk losing all their capital.

18.7.2 Debt investors

Substantial debt investors include banks and finance houses. Potential lenders tend to confine their analysis to whether the company can service a loan (and any other loans taken out by the company which would rank ahead of, or equal with, the investor's loan) from current earnings.

This reflects the fact that lenders are entitled to be repaid their capital, and also that it is common for the lender to negotiate the right to monitor the financial position of the company through a series of tests known as 'financial covenants' (which relate to issues such as the net worth, cash flow and gearing (see **18.9.1** below) of the company).

18.8 THE PROBLEM

It should now be clear that equity finance and debt finance both bring advantages and disadvantages for a company.

With equity finance, there comes the significant risk for shareholders that they will lose capital. This risk usually means that it is impossible for a company to find enough shareholders with sufficient funds to enable it to finance itself solely through equity. Even if it could, a company would still be likely to use debt finance in order to achieve some leverage.

Why not finance the company entirely through debt, to achieve complete leverage, as in the example at **18.2.2** above? The company must repay debt on a regular basis, regardless of the profits the company has made. Imagine what happens if there is a downturn in business. Perhaps the company's major customer goes bust and cannot repay its debts to the company, or perhaps interest rates rise dramatically, or there is a world event which adversely impacts on trading (consider, for example, the restrictions brought in over 2020/21 as a result of the Covid pandemic resulting in the periodic total or near total closure of some businesses' operations). If a business is financed through too much debt, any of these events might mean that the company cannot generate enough cash to enable it to pay its debts as they fall due. (With equity, of course, the company would not have to declare a dividend.)

18.9 THE SOLUTION

The solution is for a company to achieve a proper balance between debt and equity finance. What is a 'proper balance'? The company needs:

(a) sufficient equity to provide a cushion against any unexpected problems with the business and/or cash flow; and

(b) sufficient debt to achieve appropriate leverage and an appropriate return to the equity shareholders.

18.9.1 Gearing

The ratio of a company's debt to equity is referred to as 'gearing'. The higher the proportion of debt, the higher the gearing will be.

Prospective investors in the company will be interested in the company's gearing. In particular, lenders will consider the company's gearing before they negotiate the terms of a loan. If the gearing is high, then, as considered above, there is a greater risk that unexpected problems with the business and/or cash flow will render the company unable to service its debt. This means that there is a higher risk of the company going bust. A lender will demand a higher interest rate, therefore, for a loan to a company which is highly geared.

18.9.2 Articles of association

A company seeking to raise equity finance must involve its shareholders in the decision at some point in the process (for example, to authorise the directors to allot shares). However, the decision whether a company should enter into a loan is usually reserved to the board.

A company's articles of association can protect shareholders in this regard. The articles can provide that while the ratio of debt to equity is at a certain level, the company can borrow without having to seek permission from the shareholders; but that once gearing reaches a certain level, the company will require the authorisation of the shareholders in order to borrow.

18.10 CONCLUSION

A public company must think carefully about whether it should use debt or equity to raise the finance it needs. The company needs to monitor its gearing carefully. Not only might a highly-geared company bear a greater risk of going bust, but prospective investors will also scrutinise a company's gearing before deciding whether to invest in the company. It is important, therefore, that the company gets it right.

There are, very rarely, periods of time when it is difficult for a listed company to raise money, by way either of debt or equity. The summer of 2007 was one such rare occasion. The so-called 'credit crunch' in the financial markets, brought on by the housing crisis in the US caused by excessive mortgage lending to the highest credit risk (so-called 'sub-prime' mortgages) and the subsequent problems of borrowers defaulting on repayments, led to banks across the world dramatically cutting back on their lending to one another. This in turn led to the supply of money for lending (including to companies) temporarily drying up. The ability of companies to raise money through equity finance was also affected by the uncertainty of the impact of the losses incurred by financial institutions.

PART IV

LISTED COMPANY TRANSACTIONS

CHAPTER 19

SIGNIFICANT AND RELATED PARTY TRANSACTIONS

19.1 INTRODUCTION

Chapters 7 and 8 of the UK Listing Rules regulate certain transactions undertaken by ESCC-listed companies. Chapter 7 considers the size of the transaction in relation to the listed company. The larger the transaction, the greater the risk for the listed company and its shareholders who have invested their money in it and so, as we shall see, the level of protection for the shareholders increases according to the size of the transaction. Chapter 7 transactions principally involve acquisitions and disposals by the listed company (ie mergers and acquisitions).

Chapter 8, however, considers transactions between the listed company and parties closely related to it, such as a director of the company. Chapter 8 therefore seeks to regulate transactions not based on their size but on who the listed company enters them with. The aim is to ensure that shareholders of the listed company are fully informed of these 'related party' transactions so they can be better aware of the risks of a conflict of interest arising when terms were agreed with the listed company. Chapter 8 also applies to acquisitions and disposals by the listed company but also catches a wider range of additional transactions than Chapter 7.

We will now consider the main issues which arise under the UKLR when a listed company enters into a UKLR Chapter 7 significant transaction or a UKLR Chapter 8 related party transaction. **Chapters 20** to **23** discuss the additional rules relating to takeovers and mergers which might apply to the same acquisition or disposal being considered in this chapter.

19.2 OTHER CONSIDERATIONS ON AN ACQUISITION TRANSACTION

As we will see, a transaction often refers to an acquisition or disposal of assets or a business. The basic issues which a listed company must consider when it is proposing to enter into such a transaction are no different to those an unlisted company would consider. They are:

(a) Structure – purchasing/selling assets or shares?

(b) Consideration – cash or non-cash?

(c) Finance – existing cash, equity or debt?

(d) Due diligence – how much?

(e) Contractual protection – warranties and indemnities?

The Legal Practice Guide, ***Acquisitions*** explores these basic issues.

However, if a listed company is involved in the transaction, the approach of the company to these issues may differ in the following ways:

(a) *Consideration.* As **Chapter 17** explained, if the buyer is a listed company, it has the option of using its shares as consideration.

(b) *Finance.* Even if the seller does not want shares in the buyer as consideration, if the buyer is a listed company it can choose from a variety of methods (not available to an unlisted company) to raise equity finance (see **Chapter 17**).

(c) *Due diligence.* If the target company is a listed company, there will be information about it in the public domain, which will assist the due diligence process.

(d) *Contractual protection.* If the target company is a listed company and its shares are widely held by members of the public or institutions, they, as sellers, will not provide much (if any) contractual protection to any buyer. (Would you be willing to vouch for anything Vodafone Group plc might warrant about its business in a sale and purchase agreement, just because you own a few ordinary shares?)

As well as having a different approach to the basic issues of a transaction, a listed company will also have some additional considerations. These are examined at **19.3** below.

19.3 OTHER LISTED COMPANY CONSIDERATIONS ON AN ACQUISITION TRANSACTION

Most of the additional considerations for listed companies should be familiar to you already, as they have been explained in the preceding chapters of this book. A summary of the main issues follows.

19.3.1 Consideration

If the company is:

(a) issuing shares as consideration, or

(b) using equity finance to raise cash to use as consideration

for the acquisition, then the rules and regulations considered in **Chapter 17** will be relevant.

19.3.2 The continuing obligation of disclosure

The general obligation of a listed company, under UK MAR, Article 17(1), to disclose major new developments in its sphere of activity if the information is not already public knowledge and may lead to substantial movement in its share price, is discussed in **Chapter 7**. This obligation will require companies to disclose significant acquisitions and disposals. An exception to this rule – that a company does not need to disclose information about matters in the course of negotiation, unless there is a breach of confidence during those negotiations – is examined at **7.5.2.9** above. These rules are relevant during an acquisition or disposal, to make sure the company discloses the transaction, through an RIS, in a timely manner as soon as UK MAR requires.

19.3.3 The disclosure of interests in shares

Chapter 15 considers the obligation of a listed company:

(a) under DTR 5.8.12R, to disclose to the public the information it acquires under Chapter 5 of the DTRs (see **15.5.5**);

(b) under UK MAR, Article 19, to disclose to the public certain transactions by PDMRs and persons closely associated (see **15.7.1**); and

(c) under the Takeover Code, to disclose its interest in shares to the public once its shareholdings exceed a certain level (see **15.7.4**).

These requirements can be particularly relevant in the context of acquisitions or disposals of shares.

19.3.4 Misleading statements, misleading impressions, market abuse and insider dealing

Chapters 9, **10** and **11** consider the civil offence of market abuse and the criminal offences of misleading statements, misleading impressions and insider dealing. These offences can be relevant on an acquisition or a disposal. The acquisition or disposal of shares by a listed company has the potential to increase that company's value. There is scope for the company's directors, and others, to abuse their inside knowledge that the transaction will take place, by investing in shares which will increase in value once the transaction becomes public knowledge.

19.3.5 Financial regulation

As **Chapter 9** explains, anyone who carries out regulated activities in the process of the transaction must be either authorised, or (less likely) exempt.

19.3.6 Financial promotion

Any communication which persuades someone to do something in relation to an investment must comply with the rules of the FSMA 2000 relating to financial promotion. This is discussed in more detail in **Chapter 12**.

19.3.7 Financial assistance

Chapter 16 explains that the lawyer must always check the structure of any share acquisition, to make sure that it does not give rise to financial assistance problems. There may be further scope for such problems if the consideration also involves shares (that is, the consideration is the issue of shares, or the consideration has been raised through equity finance).

19.3.8 The classification of transactions

The remainder of this chapter examines:

(a) how transactions (including acquisitions and disposals) by ESCC-listed companies are classified under the UK Listing Rules; and

(b) the consequences for the ESCC-listed company of that classification.

19.4 THE CLASSIFICATION OF TRANSACTIONS

19.4.1 What is a 'transaction' under the UK Listing Rules?

The term 'transaction' is defined differently in Chapter 7 and in Chapter 8.

UK Listing Rule 7.1.6R defines 'transaction' for Chapter 7. It includes all agreements entered into by a listed company or any of its subsidiaries. On the face of it, this seems to catch an awful lot of what the listed company would do in its day-to-day activities. However, the rule goes on to exclude a whole series of transactions:

(a) a transaction in the ordinary course of business (this is defined in UKLR 7.1.8R to 9R and includes regular trading activities by the listed company, eg a listed biotech company agreeing to sell its vaccine to a health service, a listed car manufacturer agreeing to buy glass for its windscreens or a listed software company agreeing to license its technology will not fall within Chapter 7. However, a listed airline agreeing to buy a fleet of new aircraft from Airbus or Boeing is not something the airline does ordinarily and this would fall within Chapter 7);

(b) an issue of shares, or a transaction to raise finance, which does not involve the acquisition or disposal of any fixed asset of the listed company or subsidiary (eg a rights issue or placing undertaken by the listed company where the money raised from shareholders will not be used to buy a new business but, for example, instead to repay existing debt will not fall within Chapter 7);

(c) a transaction between a listed company and its wholly-owned subsidiary, or between the listed company's wholly-owned subsidiaries (that is, intra-group transactions will not fall within Chapter 7); and

(d) certain other arrangements or transactions set out in UKLR 7.1.6R(2)(d)–(g) including where there is a 'break fee' in a contract the listed company has entered into or where a listed company buys back its own shares from its shareholders will not fall within Chapter 7.

A 'transaction' does, however, also include the grant of certain options to purchase shares in the listed company.

UK Listing Rule 7.1.7G provides general guidance as to the FCA's intention regarding the Chapter 7 regime. It states that it is intended to cover transactions that are outside the ordinary course of a company's business and may change a shareholder's (or other investor's, eg a bondholder's) economic interest in the listed company's assets or liabilities. This clarifies that the regime is focused on the potential impact of the transaction on the financial position of the company and investors in it.

Specific transactions

So, what does a Chapter 7 'transaction' mean in practice? Well, broadly speaking, it means where the listed company acquires or disposes of assets or shares. This usually arises when a listed company buys another company or a business or sells one of its own companies or businesses. This is far and away the most common transaction which gives rise to the application of Chapter 7. For example in March 2024 Vodafone Group plc sold its subsidiary company, Vodafone Italy, for £6.8 billion to a Swiss company. In April 2024 Icatha Energy plc acquired an Italian company, ENI SpA, owning UK oil and gas assets, for £750 million. In October 2023 easyJet plc bought 157 new Airbus aircraft in a deal worth £ billions (acquisition of assets outside easyjet plc's ordinary course of business). All these transactions fell within what is now Chapter 7.

In addition to the acquisition and disposal of a company or a business, Chapter 7 can also result in joint ventures by the listed company being classified as significant transactions. For example, in May 2024 British Land plc sold its 50% share in Meadowhall Shopping Centre in Sheffield to its Norwegian joint venture partner.

Chapter 7 also covers two further types of transaction but these are highly unlikely to arise in practice. The first is the giving of an 'exceptional' indemnity by the listed company. An indemnity is a contractual undertaking by one party to pay another party if an agreed event giving rise to the indemnity occurs. There is no need for the other party to establish that they have suffered loss. UK Listing Rule 7.1.6R(2)(e), UKLR 7.4.1R and UKLR 7.4.2G define the circumstances in which these indemnities amount to transactions for the purposes of Chapter 7.

The second covers certain issues of shares by a major subsidiary undertaking of the listed company. UK Listing Rule 7.1.6R(f) and UKLR 7.4.3R provide that if these would dilute thelisted company's percentage shareholding in that subsidiary and its economic effect is equivalent to the sale of 25% or more of the value of the listed company's group, then the share issue by the subsidiary will be a transaction under Chapter 7.

19.4.2 The classification regime

Chapter 7 of the UK Listing Rules contains rules relating to the classification of transactions. The rules in Chapter 7 divide transactions into two different categories: significant transactions and reverse takeovers, according to the size of the transaction when compared with the size of the listed company. This comparison is made using three calculations referred to as the 'class tests', set out at UKLR 7 Annex 1 (see **19.4.3**). Each calculation results in a percentage figure and is referred to as a 'percentage ratio'. The percentage ratios determine whether the transaction is classified as a significant transaction or a reverse takeover (see **19.4.5.1**, **19.4.6.1** and **19.4.7.1**).

Why is this classification necessary? As ever, it is to protect shareholders. The purpose of classifying a transaction is so that the UK Listing Rules can determine the extent to which the transaction needs to be regulated, in order to protect the interests of shareholders. Chapter 7 regulates transactions on the basis of size. If a transaction is classified as a 'significant transaction', ie it is of a significant size compared to the size of the listed company, it means that the company must follow certain procedural requirements before it can complete the transaction. If, however, a transaction is classified as a 'reverse takeover', this means that the company must follow much stricter procedural requirements (for example the company must seek its shareholders' approval of the transaction). This reflects the practical reality that the bigger the transaction (say, the acquisition of a new company), the greater the risk to the purchasing listed company and its shareholders.

19.4.3 The class tests

If the thought of taking figures and applying percentage ratio tests to them brings unwelcome flashbacks of school and makes you break out in a cold sweat, do not worry. The company's financial advisers and its reporting accountants will actually apply the tests to the relevant figures. However, the lawyer must be aware of and understand the need for, and the principles behind, the class tests. In particular, the lawyer must make sure that the company considers these class tests at an early stage in the transaction in light of the implications for timing, certainty and cost which the results of these class tests may bring.

So, the first stage is to apply all of the relevant class tests. The class tests, set out in UKLR 7 Annex 1, are as follows:

(a) Gross assets test (para 2R)

$$\frac{\text{Gross assets which are the subject of the transaction}}{\text{Gross assets of the listed company}} \times 100 = ?\%$$

(b) Consideration test (para 4R)

$$\frac{\text{Consideration for the transaction}}{\text{Aggregate market value of the listed company's ordinary shares}} \times 100 = ?\%$$

(c) Gross capital test* (para 6R)

$$\frac{\text{Gross capital of the company or business being acquired}}{\text{Gross capital of the listed company}} \times 100 = ?\%$$

*This test is to be performed only for the acquisition of a company or business and not for a disposal (para 6R(2)).

UK Listing Rules 7 Annex 1 provides further guidance on the application of the class tests, including defining the terms used, such as 'gross assets'.

The 'listed company' referred to in the class tests is the ESCC-listed company that is party to the transaction and which you are advising. If both parties to the transaction, that is, buyer and seller, are ESCC-listed companies, then the transaction will need to be classified twice, once from the buyer's perspective, where the buyer's details will be the 'listed company' referred to above (which will establish the formalities the buyer needs to comply with to make the acquisition), and once from the seller's perspective, where the seller will be the 'listed company' referred to above (this will establish the formalities the seller needs to comply with to make the disposal).

Note that in share sales the sellers are the *shareholders* rather than the company itself, so, even if the target is a listed company, the transaction will need to be classified from one perspective (the listed company buyer's) only.

There are modified rules for classifying a joint venture involving a listed company (eg it must be classified twice – once for the disposal into the new joint venture company and again for the acquisition of an interest in the joint venture company (UKLR 7.2.9R)) and for certain specialist listed companies: property companies (UKLR 7.2.3R–7.2.5R) and mineral companies, such as oil and gas exploration companies (UKLR 7.2.6R–7.2.8R).

UK Listing Rule 7 Annex 1, para 9G provides that the FCA can modify the class tests, to substitute other relevant indicators of size, in the event that they produce an anomalous result, or if the calculation is inappropriate to the activities of the listed company.

UK Listing Rule 7.2.11R provides that, for the purposes of the calculations, the transaction must be aggregated with certain other transactions (broadly those involving the same parties, the acquisition or disposal of shares in the same company, or which, taken together, result in a substantial involvement in a new business activity) which took place in the preceding 12 months. The aim is to ensure that a series of transactions over a relatively short space of time, which cumulatively may have the same risks for the listed company and its shareholders as one big transaction, are subjected to the same regulatory protection. The FCA also has discretion to aggregate in other circumstances (UKLR 7.2.14G).

In practice, typically the consideration test proves to be the key test.

19.4.4 The classification of transactions

Ordinarily two class tests will be applied for a disposal, and all three on an acquisition (see **19.4.3**). This will produce either two or three separate percentage ratios. These figures determine the class of the transaction. There are two classes of transaction regulated under Chapter 7 of the UKLR, namely:

(a) significant transaction; and
(b) reverse takeovers.

As mentioned at **19.4.2** above, the purpose of classifying a transaction is to determine the level of procedural safeguards which the UKLR will impose to protect the shareholders. Let us now consider:

(a) the percentage ratios required to amount to a significant transaction or a reverse takeover;
(b) the requirements of Chapter 7 of the UKLR in relation to those two classes of transaction.

19.4.5 Significant transaction

19.4.5.1 Percentage ratios

If *any* of the percentage ratios is 25% or more, the transaction will be classified as a significant transaction (UKLR 7.1.3R). For example, imagine that X plc, a listed company, is acquiring Y Ltd. The gross assets of X plc are £100m. The gross assets of Y Ltd are £30m. The percentage ratio resulting from the profits class test is 30% (30/100 × 100%). The transaction is a significant transaction under Chapter 7.

Therefore where *all* the percentage ratios fall *below* 25%, it will not be a significant transaction and no additional requirements arise under Chapter 7 for the listed company.

19.4.5.2 Chapter 7 requirements

UK Listing Rule 7.3.1R provides that the listed company must notify an RIS as soon as possible after the terms of any significant transaction are agreed. This will usually be on exchange of contracts. The notification (which takes the form of a press announcement) must contain the information prescribed by UKLR 7.3.1R(2) and (3). Most of this is set out in UKLR 7 Annex 2. It includes information relating to the transaction (such as details of the transaction including the name of the other party) and an explanation of the reasons for entering into the transaction. Detailed financial information and other pro forma information is also required. The purpose of this announcement is therefore to ensure that shareholders of the company, and the wider market, are fully informed about the transaction and are able to assess the impact of what is, financially, a very large transaction for the listed company.

This requirement for an announcement for a significant transaction represents a very considerable relaxation of the rules in place before the UKLR came into force on 29 July 2024. Previously a listed company needed to obtain prior shareholder approval for the transaction and prepare a detailed circular to be sent to its shareholders. The removal of these requirements is certainly not without controversy as shareholder protection is being substantially diminished.

Tate & Lyle plc announced a significant transaction (the £1.4 billion acquisition of CP Kelco) in June 2024 under the old listing rules. The planned shareholders' meeting ultimately did not, with FCA approval, need to be held as the transaction had not completed before the new UK Listing Rules came into force.

If, after the original announcement has been made, the listed company later:

(a) becomes aware that there has been a significant change which affects any matter in the original announcement; or
(b) becomes aware that a material new matter has arisen which the company would have been required to mention in the original announcement if it had arisen at the time it was preparing that announcement; or
(c) has agreed a material change to the terms of the transaction,

the listed company must make a supplementary announcement through an RIS without delay (UKLR 7.3.11R). This ensures that the shareholders and the market have the most accurate information about the transaction.

19.4.6 Reverse takeover

19.4.6.1 Definition

Under UKLR 7.1.4R, if:

(a) a listed company, one of its subsidiaries or a new holding company of it acquires:
   (i) a business,
   (ii) a company, or
   (iii) assets; *and*
(b) either:
   (i) *any* percentage ratio is 100% or more, *or*
   (ii) the transaction will result in:
      – a fundamental change in the business, or
      – a change in board or voting control of the listed company,

then the transaction will be a reverse takeover (UKLR 7.1.4R). What this means, in layman's terms, is that the listed company is acquiring a company which is either bigger than it is (on the basis of the class tests explained above), or will, in any event, cause fundamental changes to the listed company's business, or the balance of power at either board or shareholder level. In other words, it is a particularly important transaction for the listed company resulting in fundamental change to it.

In practice, reverse takeovers can be a useful way for an unlisted company to list shares when it might otherwise not meet the criteria of the UKLR that were considered in **Chapters 4, 5** and **6.** In effect, the unlisted company 'reverses into' a listed company.

> **EXAMPLE**
>
> Imagine that X plc, our listed company, has fallen on hard times. A large private company, Z Ltd, is doing very well. The shareholders of Z Ltd negotiate a deal, whereby they will sell Z Ltd to X plc in return for an issue of shares in X plc. The shareholders in Z Ltd will become shareholders in X plc, a listed company. The original shareholders of X plc hope that the acquisition by X plc of the successful company, Z Ltd, might help X plc back on its feet.

Figure 19.1 below shows the reverse takeover process in simplified form, using the details in the example above.

Figure 19.1: Reverse takeover

Before the reverse

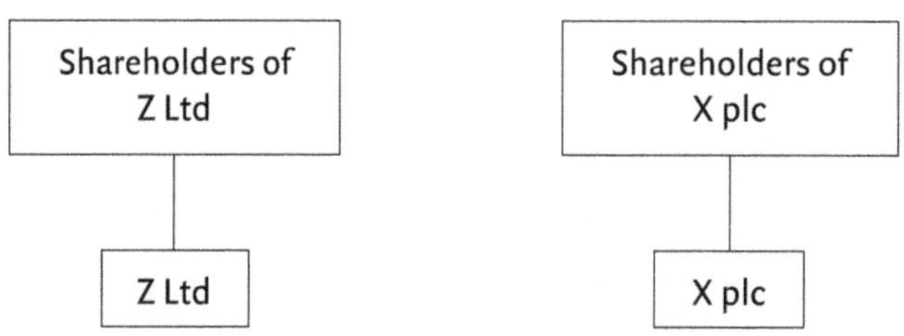

The reverse

1. Shareholders in Z Ltd *transfer* shares in Z Ltd to X plc
2. X plc *issues* shares in itself to the shareholders of Z Ltd, as consideration for the transfer.

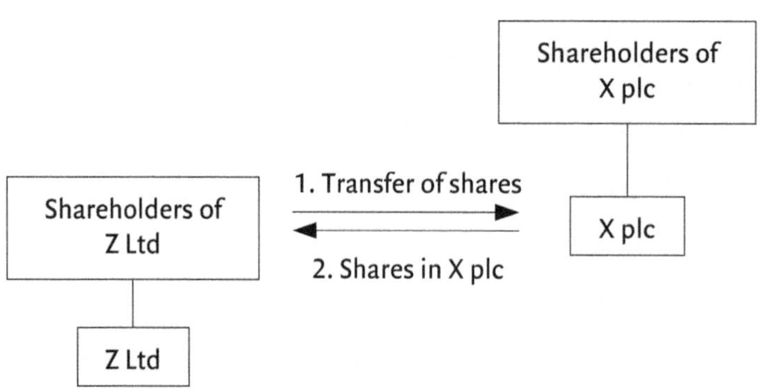

End result

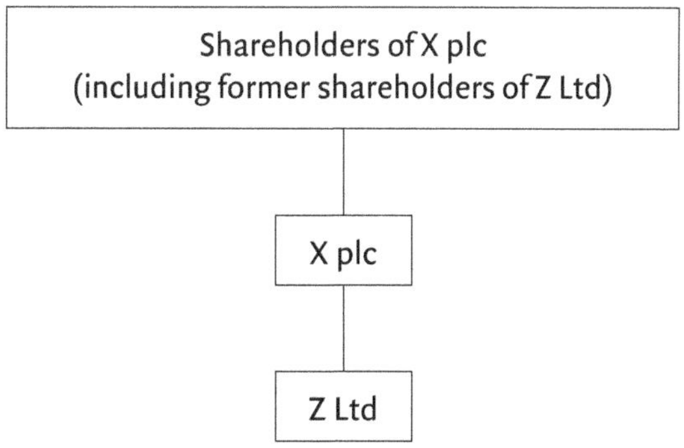

19.4.6.2 Chapter 7 requirements

UK Listing Rule 7.5.1R provides that the listed company must:

(a) make a significant transaction announcement under UKLR 7.3 (see **19.4.6.2** above), although with less information from Annex 2 (UKLR 7.5.1R(1));

(b) send a circular, approved by the FCA, and containing the information prescribed by UKLR 10, to shareholders (see **19.6.1** below) (UKLR 7.5.1R(2));

(c) obtain its shareholders' approval of the transaction (by ordinary resolution in general meeting before completing the transaction – the notice of the GM will be sent out with the circular referred to at (b) above) (UKLR 7.5.1.R(2)); and

(d) if the agreement is to be entered into before shareholder approval is obtained, ensure that completion of the transaction is conditional on shareholder approval being obtained (UKLR 7.5.1R(3)).

If, after obtaining shareholder approval but before completion of the reverse takeover, there is a material change to the terms of the transaction (for example a change in the consideration payable of 10% or more), the listed company must make a new announcement in accordance with UKLR 7.5.1R (UKLR 7.5.3R). If after the publication of a circular there is a material change to the information contained in it, the listed company must notify the FCA and send its shareholders a supplementary circular (UKLR 7.5.5R).

UK Listing Rule 7.5.8G provides that the FCA may cancel the listing of the company's shares after a reverse takeover. If this happened, the company would then have to reapply for the listing of its shares (UKLR 7.5.9R) and satisfy the relevant conditions for listing. The FCA must be contacted as early as possible before a reverse takeover has been agreed to discuss whether a cancellation of the listed company's listing is appropriate (UKLR 7.5.10R).

This reflects the possibility that a listed company is, in effect, being used as a 'Trojan horse' by the unlisted company's shareholders to gain a listing on the Main Market. As we saw in **Chapter 4**, the directors and the company are normally scrutinised intensely before a company can float on the Stock Exchange. To prevent this process being circumvented by a reverse takeover, the company under new ownership may have to reapply for listing of the company's shares.

The circumstances when a cancellation of a listed company's shares after a reverse takeover will not generally be necessary are set out in UKLR 7.5.12G–UKLR 7.5.14G. They include where a listed company buys another listed company and both companies have an ESCC listing. So, for example, where one listed trading company takes over another much larger listed trading company, the original company's listing may continue without interruption. In this case the concerns raised in the previous paragraph do not apply as both companies are ESCC-listed and have already been through the same intense vetting process before joining the Stock Exchange.

19.4.6.3 The sponsor's role

A listed company must appoint a sponsor if the transaction is a reverse takeover requiring the submission of a circular to the FCA for approval (UKLR 4.2.1R(3)).

19.4.6.4 Shell companies

Reverse takeovers also arise with companies listed on the Main Market and defined under UKLR 13.1.3R as a 'shell company'. They are also commonly known as a Special Purpose Acquisition Company or SPAC. These are companies specifically formed with the purpose of raising funds from investors through an IPO of their shares, with those funds then used to acquire an operating business or company already in existence. The acquisition constitutes a reverse takeover as it represents a fundamental change to the shell company's business. However these transactions are subject to different rules under UKLR Chapter 13 rather than those in Chapter 7 as outlined above.

19.5 RELATED PARTY TRANSACTIONS

While Chapter 7 of the UKLR sets out the rules relating to the classification of transactions on the basis of the *size* of the transaction compared to the size of the listed company, Chapter 8 of the UKLR is dedicated to related party transactions. Related party transactions are classified by the *nature* of the relationship between the parties to the transaction, one of which will be the ESCC-listed company or one of its subsidiaries.

The rationale behind the related party classification is the same as that behind the Chapter 7 significant transaction classification: the protection of investors. Related party transactions are subject to certain safeguards which are designed to prevent those who have considerable power over a listed company from taking advantage of their position.

19.5.1 What is a related party transaction?

A related party transaction is defined by UKLR 8.1.7R as:

(a) a transaction (other than a transaction in the ordinary course of business) between a listed company (or any of its subsidiary undertakings) and a related party;

(b) an arrangement (other than an arrangement in the ordinary course of business) pursuant to which a listed company and a related party each invests in, or provides finance to, another undertaking or asset; or

(c) any other similar transaction or arrangement (other than a transaction or arrangement in the ordinary course of business) between a listed company and any other person, the purpose and effect of which is to benefit a related party.

If the transaction falls within the above definition, it will be a related party transaction, regardless of the size of the transaction. However, the transaction does still need to be classified by size, using the Chapter 7 classification system. This is because it is only if the related party transaction reaches a certain size that the requirements under Chapter 8 will have to be met by the company (see **19.6.2** below).

19.5.2 Who is a related party?

A 'related party' means a substantial shareholder, director or shadow director, a person exercising significant influence and any of their associates (UKLR 8.1.11R).

19.5.2.1 Substantial shareholder

This is defined in UKLR 8.1.12R and refers to anyone who is entitled to exercise, or control the exercise of, 20% or more of the votes able to be cast on all or substantially all matters at a general meeting of either the listed company, or any other company in the listed company's group (but see **19.5.4.1** below in relation to insignificant subsidiaries). Therefore a transaction between the listed company and one of its shareholders who owns 20% or more of the company's shares will amount to a related party transaction.

There are exemptions in UKLR 8.1.14R for certain shareholders who hold 20% or more in certain circumstances, for instance investment banks conducting trades on behalf of a group of clients.

19.5.2.2 Director or shadow director

This refers to anyone who is (or, at any time in the 12 months before the transaction, was) a director or shadow director of the listed company, or of any other company in the listed company's group (but see **19.5.4.1** below in relation to insignificant subsidiaries). The UK Listing Rules define 'shadow director' as anyone who falls within the definition of a director in s 417(1) of the FSMA 2000. This covers anyone in accordance with whose directions or instructions the directors of the company are accustomed to act. There is, however, some protection for the likes of lawyers; a person will not be a shadow director just because the directors act in accordance with advice they provide in a professional capacity.

A related party transaction most usually arises in these circumstances when there is a transaction between the listed company and one of its existing directors.

19.5.2.3 Person exercising significant influence

This is defined in the Glossary to the UKLR as a person who exercises significant influence over the company. This category of person is included to ensure that parties who are not a director or a substantial shareholder of the listed company, but can still hold sway over it, are brought within the restrictions of Chapter 8 to ensure that they are fully effective.

19.5.2.4 Associate

This means anyone who, at the time of the transaction, was an associate of the substantial shareholder, director, shadow director, or person exercising significant influence, referred to at **19.5.2.1** to **19.5.2.3** above. 'Associate' is defined in the Glossary to the UKLR as follows:

- In relation to a director, substantial shareholder, or person exercising significant influence, who is an individual:
  - (1) that individual's spouse, civil partner or child (together 'the individual's family');
  - (2) the trustees (acting as such) of any trust of which the individual or any of the individual's family is a beneficiary or discretionary object (other than a trust which is either an occupational pension scheme or an employees' share scheme which does not, in either case, have the effect of conferring benefits on persons all or most of whom are related parties);
  - (3) any company in whose equity securities the individual or any member or members (taken together) of the individual's family or the individual and any such member or members (taken together) are directly or indirectly interested (or have a conditional or contingent entitlement to become interested) so that they are (or would on the fulfilment of the condition or the occurrence of the contingency be) able:
    - (a) to exercise or control the exercise of 30% or more of the votes able to be cast at general meetings on all, or substantially all, matters; or
    - (b) to appoint or remove directors holding a majority of voting rights at board meetings on all, or substantially all, matters;
  - (4) any limited partnership or limited liability partnership in which the individual or any member or members (taken together) of the individual's family are directly or indirectly interested (or have a conditional or contingent entitlement to become interested) so that they hold or control or would on the fulfilment of the condition or the occurrence of the contingency be able to hold or control:

(a) a voting interest greater than 30% in the partnership; or

(b) at least 30% of the partnership.

For the purpose of paragraph (3), if more than one director of the listed company, its parent undertaking or any of its subsidiary undertakings is interested in the equity securities of another company, then the interests of those directors and their associates will be aggregated when determining whether that company is an associate of the director.

- In relation to a substantial shareholder, or person exercising significant influence, which is a company:
  (1) any other company which is its subsidiary undertaking or parent undertaking or fellow subsidiary undertaking of the parent undertaking;
  (2) any company whose directors are accustomed to act in accordance with the substantial shareholder's, or person exercising significant influence's directions or instructions;
  (3) any company in the capital of which the substantial shareholder, or person exercising significant influence and any other company under (1) or (2) taken together, is (or would on the fulfilment of a condition or the occurrence of a contingency be) interested in the manner described in (3) above.

As you can see, the definition is not particularly user-friendly. It may help to consider an example of who is an associate:

EXAMPLE

Mr A is a non-executive director (NED) of X plc, a fashion retailer. He also owns 30% of Y Ltd, a marketing company. X plc decides to acquire the business (ie all of the assets) of Y Ltd, to provide an in-house marketing facility for its business.

Y Ltd is an associate of Mr A. This is because Mr A is a director of X plc, and an individual. Y Ltd is caught by para (3) of the appropriate part of the definition; it is a company in whose equity securities Mr A is directly interested and in which he can exercise 30% of the votes.

As a result of Y Ltd's being an associate of a director of X plc, Y Ltd is also a related party of X plc. The acquisition by X plc of the business of Y Ltd is not a transaction in the ordinary course of business (retailers do not buy marketing businesses on a day-to-day basis). The acquisition therefore is a related party transaction for X plc. There is a risk that Mr A could abuse his position as a director of X plc, for example in negotiating the price, and so the shareholders of X plc will be afforded extra protection under Chapter 8 of the UKLR.

19.5.3 Chapter 8 requirements

Subject to the exceptions referred to at **19.5.4** below, UKLR 8.2.1R provides that if an ESCC-listed company enters into a related party transaction where any percentage ratio is 5% or more, the listed company must:

(a) obtain the approval of its board of directors for the transaction before it is entered into (UKLR 8.2.1R(1));

(b) ensure that any director who is the related party (or associate of any director is) or who is the director of a related party does not take part in the board's consderation of the transaction and does not vote on the relevant board resolution to approve the transaction (UKLR 8.2.1R(2));

(c) before entering into the transaction, obtain written confirmation from a sponsor that the terms of the proposed related party transaction are fair and reasonable as far as the shareholders of the listed company are concerned (UKLR 8.2.1R(3));

(d) notify an RIS as soon as possible after the terms of the transaction or arrangement are agreed (UKLR 8.2.1R(4)).

The notification (which takes the form of a press announcement) must contain the information prescribed by UKLR 8.2.2R and UKLR 8.2.3R. It includes details of the related party transaction (such as the name of the related party and a description of the transaction), and details of the related party's interest in the transaction. The board must state that the related party transaction is fair and reasonable as far as the shareholders of the listed company are concerned and provide the name of the sponsor providing the written confirmation. As with a significant transaction, the purpose of this announcement is to ensure that shareholders of the company, and the wider market, are fully informed about the transaction, and if needs be allowing, for example, an institutional shareholder to liaise with the listed company.

The requirement for just an announcement for a related party transaction represents a very considerable relaxation of the rules in place before the UKLR came into force on 29 July 2024. Previously a listed company needed to obtain prior shareholder approval for the transaction and prepare a detailed circular to be sent to its shareholders. The removal of these shareholder protections is of course not without controversy or indeed risk.

Under UKLR 8.2.5R, if there is a material change to the terms of the transaction after the announcement has been given but before completion of the transaction, the company must repeat the requirements set out in UKLR 8.2.1R and UKLR 8.2.2R. For example, this would cover an increase of 10% or more in the consideration payable (UKLR 8.2.6G). If there has been a material change (for the purposes of making an informed assessment of the financial situation or prospects of the company) of any other type, a supplementary announcement must be made containing details of the change (UKLR 8.2.8R).

19.5.4 Exceptions

The related party transaction rules referred to at **19.5.3** above will not apply if all of the percentage ratios fall below 5% (UKLR 8.2.1R). Furthermore they will not apply in the circumstances set out in UKLR 8 Annex 1R:

(a) If the transaction was agreed before the person became a related party (Annex 1R, para 1).

(b) To any issue of new securities to a related party pursuant to a pre-emptive offering (ie a rights issue or open offer but *not* a placing) or pursuant to the exercise of conversion or subscription rights attaching to listed securities (Annex 1R, para 2).

The rationale behind this exception is that the shareholders have been protected by other means.

(c) To various awards made pursuant to an employees' share scheme (Annex 1R, para 3).

(d) To a grant of credit (including a loan or guaranteeing a loan) in certain circumstances, eg to a related party on normal commercial terms.

(e) To the grant of an indemnity to a director of a listed company or any of its subsidiaries, if the terms of the indemnity are in accordance with those specifically permitted under the CA 2006 (Annex 1R, para 5).

(f) To the underwriting by a related party of share issues by the listed company or any of its subsidiaries, provided the consideration to be paid to the underwriter:

  (a) is no more than the usual commercial underwriting consideration; and

  (b) is the same as will be paid to any other underwriters (Annex 1R, para 6).

(g) If the related party is a related party only through being a substantial shareholder, director or shadow director of an insignificant subsidiary of the listed company (or the associate of any such person). An insignificant subsidiary is a subsidiary which has:

  (a) contributed less than 10% of the profits, and

  (b) represented less than 10% of the assets of,

the listed company for each of the three financial years preceding the date of the transaction for which accounts have been published (or for each financial year for which accounts have been published, if the insignificant subsidiary has been part of the group for less than three years).

Note that this exception will not apply in certain circumstances, such as if the insignificant subsidiary has been part of the group for less than one year, or if the insignificant subsidiary itself is party to the transaction and the ratio of consideration to market capitalisation is more than 10% (Annex 1R, para 8).

19.5.5 The sponsor's role

Under UKLR 8.1.4G, a listed company that is proposing to enter into a related party transaction requiring the listed company to make an announcement under UKLR 8.2.1R(4) must appoint a sponsor to give the written confirmation required by UKLR 8.2.1R(3) (see **19.5.3** above).

19.5.6 Sanctions

In April 2012, the FSA, the forerunner to the FCA, imposed the first ever fine for a breach of the former listing rules relating to related party transactions. It fined Exillon Energy plc £292,950 for failing to identify certain payments made to its Chair as related party transactions, and breaching the procedural requirements as a result.

19.5.7 The Companies Act 2006

The UK Listing Rules operate alongside the statutory provisions of the CA 2006. In the event of a related party transaction, the following sections of the CA 2006 may also be relevant.

19.5.7.1 Sections 177 and 182 of the CA 2006

These sections require directors to declare their interests in a transaction.

19.5.7.2 Section 190 of the CA 2006

This section requires shareholder approval of substantial property transactions between directors (but not substantial shareholders) and the company.

19.5.8 The memorandum and articles

The company's memorandum and articles may also contain provisions regulating transactions between the company and its directors.

19.6 THE REVERSE TAKEOVER CIRCULAR

As explained in **Chapter 7**, the circular is a means by which a company communicates with its shareholders, particularly where the company requires the shareholders to approve a transaction. The circular should provide enough information to shareholders to allow them to make an informed decision whether to vote for or against the transaction. The circular will also contain the notice of GM, convening the meeting at which the shareholders will vote on the transaction.

Chapter 10 of the UK Listing Rules prescribes the content of a circular. UK Listing Rule 10.3 sets out the content requirements for circulars generally (see **7.9.3**); specific content requirements for specific types of circular are then prescribed by other Chapter 10 UK Listing Rules. For example, UKLR 10.4 and UKLR 10 Annexes 1 and 2 set out the specific requirements, over and above the general UKLR 10.3 requirements, for a reverse takeover circular.

Just as the UK Prospectus Regulation allows information to be incorporated by reference into a prospectus (see **6.5.2.2** above), so UKLR 10.1.3R allows information in a prospectus, or other published document filed with the FCA, to be incorporated into a circular.

It was explained at **7.9.4** above that the FCA categorises circulars either as requiring approval prior to being sent out to the listed company's shareholders, or as not requiring prior approval. The reverse takeover circular requires FCA approval.

Once a circular has been finalised and approved, the company must forward a copy of the circular with the FCA by uploading it to the NSM (UKLR.6.4.1R) (see **7.5.7.1**).

Note that the preparation of the circular can be very time-consuming and costly in light of the information required to be included, and may also delay the timing of the transaction to which it relates (see **19.7** below).

19.6.1 Content

As explained at **19.6**, UKLR 10.3 sets out the general requirements, and UKLR 10.4 and UKLR 10 Annexes 1 and 2 the specific requirements for a reverse takeover circular. UK Listing Rule 10 Annex 2 cross-refers to Annex 1 of the UK PR Regulation. This aligns the content requirements of a circular with some of the content requirements for a prospectus (see **6.5.2**). Some of the information in UKLR 10 Annex 2 must be provided not only for the listed company buyer or seller, but also for the company the subject of the transaction. The requirements of the rules referred to above include the following:

(a) *General disclosure*. The circular must provide a clear and adequate explanation of the reverse takeover, giving due prominence to its essential characteristics, benefits and risks; it must state why the shareholder is being asked to vote and contain all information necessary to allow the shareholders to make a properly informed decision (UKLR 10.3.1R(1)–(3)). The content of the announcement to the RIS under UKLR 7.5.1R must be included (UKLR 10.4.1R(1)).

(b) *Recommendation* (UKLR 10.3.1R(5)). A recommendation to shareholders from the directors as to how they should exercise their votes for each resolution, and a statement from the directors as to whether they consider the proposal to be in the shareholders' best interests.

(c) *The directors' responsibility statement* (UKLR 10.4.1R(6)). A statement by the directors, in the form set out at UKLR 10.4.1R(6), that they take personal responsibility for the circular.

(d) *Financial information* (UKLR 10 Annexes 1 and 2). The detailed financial information required by UKLR 10 Annex 1 and information about any significant change since the last published accounts, in respect of the listed company, any other company in the listed company's group and the target company.

(e) *Litigation* (UKLR 10 Annex 2.1R). See **6.5.2.1** above. For both the listed company and the target company.

(f) *Risk factors* (UKLR 10 Annex 2.1R). For both the listed company and the target company.

(g) *Material contracts* (UKLR 10 Annex 2.1R). See **6.5.2.1** above. For both the listed company and the target company.

19.6.2 The sponsor's role

The listed company must appoint a sponsor when a reverse takeover circular is required (UKLR 4.2.1R(3)). The sponsor has various obligations under the UK Listing Rules relating to a 'sponsor service', the definition of which includes a company preparing a reverse takeover circular. The obligations include the following:

(a) The sponsor owes a general duty of skill and care, honesty and integrity and must take reasonable steps to ensure that the company understands its obligations under the UK Listing Rules (UKLR 24.2.6R to 24.2.8R).

(b) UK Listing Rule 24.3.10R provides that, before the sponsor submits the reverse takeover circular to the FCA for approval, it must be of the opinion, having made due and careful enquiry, that:

 (i) the company has satisfied all requirements of the UK Listing Rules relevant to the production of a reverse takeover circular; and

 (ii) the transaction will not have an adverse impact on the company's ability to comply with the UK Listing Rules, UK MAR or the Transparency Rules.

 The requirement at (ii) above is particularly onerous from the sponsor's point of view.

(c) UK Listing Rule 24.3.11R sets out further tasks for the sponsor, including:

 (i) submitting to the FCA a Sponsor's Declaration for the Production of a Circular (on the day the circular is to be approved, but before such approval has been given); and

 (ii) ensuring that all matters known to it, which, in its reasonable opinion, should be taken into account by the FCA in considering the transaction, have been disclosed with sufficient prominence in the documentation or otherwise in writing to the FCA.

The pro forma Sponsor's Declaration for the Production of a Circular is available from the Knowledge Base section of the FCA's website.

19.6.3 Verification

The verification process in the context of an IPO is explained at **5.3.5** and **6.8** above. Verification is also required in relation to other documents published by listed companies, such as circulars, to protect directors against claims from shareholders on the basis set out at **6.7** above.

19.7 THE REVERSE TAKEOVER TIMETABLE

The requirements of Chapter 8 of the UK Listing Rules can have a significant effect on the transaction timetable where a reverse takeover is involved.

The skeleton timetable below provides a basic overview of how the requirements for listed companies undertaking a reverse takeover impact an acquisition timetable compared to an acquisition carried out by an unlisted company. The listed company requirements are italicised.

(a) Sign heads of agreement.

 This document will include legally binding provisions. It will contain important provisions about confidentiality and exclusivity.

(b) Sign the *(conditional)* agreement.

 As the transaction is a reverse takeover, the agreement must be conditional upon shareholder approval.

(c) *Make an announcement.*

 As the transaction is a reverse takeover, the company must make an announcement through an RIS.

(d) *Post the circular and the GM notice.*

 As the transaction is a reverse takeover, a circular is required (which must be prepared, verified and approved by the FCA before it is sent out).

(e) *Hold a GM.*

As the transaction is a reverse takeover, shareholder approval is required at a general meeting held after the proper notice period has expired.

(f) Completion.

Company/business finally bought/sold.

Note that there are several steps in between steps (b) and (f) for a listed company. Usually an unlisted company can sign and complete a sale and purchase agreement simultaneously.

19.8 CONCLUSION

The UK Listing Rules regulate the process by which an ESCC-listed company can make acquisitions and disposals. Depending on the size of the transaction and the relationship between the parties to the transaction, the UK Listing Rules can require a company to notify an RIS of the transaction and, for reverse takeovers, circulate an explanatory circular and obtain shareholder approval of the transaction. These requirements can impact significantly on the timing and cost of the transaction, but reflect the pervasive aim of the regulation of listed companies: to protect investors where this is most needed.

CHAPTER 20

TAKEOVERS: REGULATION

20.1 INTRODUCTION

Chapters 21 and **22** consider the detail of a takeover offer (also known as a 'takeover bid'). The purpose of this chapter is to introduce the regulation which will be relevant to any lawyer who advises on such an offer.

20.2 THE PANEL

The Panel on Takeovers and Mergers (the 'Panel') was established in 1968 as a non-statutory body with the support of the Bank of England. Since then it has supervised the regulatory aspects of takeovers. It has statutory powers to regulate takeovers under Chapter 1 of Pt 28 of the CA 2006. Since the end of the Brexit transition period, the Panel no longer operates within the EU framework as set out in the EU Takeovers Directive.

20.2.1 What does the Panel do?

The Panel is an independent body with two roles:

(a) *Rule-making.* The Panel issues and administers the Takeover Code, the rulebook relating to takeovers (see **20.4** below).

(a) *Judicial.* The Panel supervises and regulates takeovers and other matters dealt with in the Takeover Code.

20.2.2 Who is on the Panel?

The Panel comprises a maximum of 36 members. It self-appoints a Chair, up to two Deputy Chairs and a maximum of 20 other members. Certain financial institutions and professional bodies such as the ABI, the CBI and the PLSA appoint the 12 remaining members.

20.2.3 The Panel Executive

The full Panel itself meets rarely. Instead the Panel Executive carries out the day-to-day work of the Panel, monitoring takeovers and interpreting, consulting on and giving rulings on the Takeover Code. The Panel Executive is headed by the Director General, typically an investment banker seconded to the Panel, and is staffed not only by employees, but also by secondees, including accountants, brokers, investment bankers and, significantly, corporate lawyers. In practice, the term 'Panel Executive' is rarely used; if a lawyer is consulting the Panel Executive, they will invariably refer to this as 'consulting the Panel'. Further information about the Panel Executive is contained in para 5 of the Introduction to the Takeover Code and is available on the Panel's website.

20.2.4 The Panel Committees

The Panel operates principally through the following committees.

20.2.4.1 The Code Committee

The Code Committee, comprising up to 12 members appointed by the Panel, carries out the rule-making role of the Panel (see **20.4**). This Committee is responsible for reviewing and amending the Takeover Code. Typically, the Committee will announce a period of public consultation before amending the Code. The Public Consultation Papers ('PCPs') are published on the Panel's website. Paragraph 4(b) of the Introduction to the Takeover Code provides further detail on the Code Committee.

20.2.4.2 The Hearings Committee

The Hearings Committee carries out the judicial role of the Panel (see **20.2.1**). The Committee reviews the Panel Executive's rulings, and also hears any disciplinary proceedings (which the Panel Executive instigates – see **20.4.7.4**), relating to breaches of the Takeover Code. Usually the secretary to the Hearings Committee is a senior lawyer (such as a partner in a law firm). Paragraphs 4(c) and 7 of the Introduction to the Takeover Code provide further detail on the Hearings Committee.

There is a right to appeal to the Takeover Appeal Board in relation to a decision of the Hearings Committee (Introduction to the Takeover Code, para 8). The Takeover Appeal Board is a separate organisation from the Panel. Further information can be found at www.thetakeoverappealboard.org.uk.

Paragraph 4(d) of the Introduction to the Takeover Code ensures that membership of the Committees are kept separate: a member of the Code Committee (see **20.2.4.1**) cannot be or become a member of the Hearings Committee or the Takeover Appeal Board.

20.2.4.3 The Nomination Committee

The Nomination Committee monitors the size, composition and balance of the Panel. It will therefore doubtless be aware of the fact that there are only seven women on the full Panel of 32 at the time of writing, and that the Panel Executive is led by a man and two male deputies.

20.2.5 The nature of the Panel

Originally, the Panel was a wholly non-statutory body. In cases such as *R v Panel on Takeovers and Mergers, ex p Datafin plc and Another (Norton Opax plc and Another intervening)* [1987] 1 All ER 564 and *R v Panel on Takeovers and Mergers, ex p Guinness plc* [1989] 1 All ER 509, the courts marvelled at the unique nature of the Panel, which in practice had enormous power as a regulator of some of the largest, most expensive transactions in the financial industry, despite its lack of actual statutory powers. For example, when Guinness breached r 11 of the Takeover Code during its offer for Distillers, the Panel had the power to force Guinness to pay a considerable sum to the former Distillers shareholders, despite its non-statutory footing at the time (see the article in **Chapter 21**).

However, on 20 May 2006, the implementation of the EU Takeovers Directive in the UK placed the exercise of the Panel's powers on a statutory footing in relation to takeover offers to which the Takeovers Directive applied. This was extended on 20 April 2007 to include other takeovers covered by the Takeover Code but outside the Takeovers Directive. From the end of the Brexit transition period on 31 December 2020, the Panel retained its statutory control of takeovers in the UK but under UK law.

20.3 PART 28 OF THE COMPANIES ACT 2006

This is the legal basis for the Panel exercising certain statutory powers in relation to public company takeovers in the UK. Section 942 of the CA 2006 grants the Panel the power to do anything it thinks is necessary or expedient to carry out its functions.

Section 943 of the CA 2006 gives the Takeover Code a statutory basis (formerly it operated without statutory backing, as an informal set of rules which in practice all listed companies observed). The Panel must make rules governing certain matters set out in Sch 1C to the CA 2006 (which are now in the Takeover Code) and it has also been given the power to make rules for takeover bids and other transactions which have an effect on the ownership or control of companies.

The CA 2006 has also given the Panel statutory powers of investigation and the right to impose sanctions for breaches of the Takeover Code (see **20.4.7**).

20.4 THE TAKEOVER CODE

The main source of regulation of takeovers is called the Takeover Code on Takeovers and Mergers. This is often referred to as the 'Takeover Code', or the 'City Code'. This book refers to it as the Takeover Code. It may be viewed in full on the Panel's website. (It is also known, in practice, as the 'Blue Book', not for any particularly titillating content but with unquestionable accuracy in describing the colour of the original hard-copy book containing the Takeover Code.)

20.4.1 When does the Takeover Code apply?

The application of the Takeover Code is set out in para 3 of the Introduction to the Takeover Code. It applies to offers (see **20.4.1.2**) for certain companies (see **20.4.1.1**).

20.4.1.1 Companies within the Takeover Code

The Takeover Code will apply if the offeree company falls into any of the following categories:

1. Intro section 3(a)(i)

- **a public company**, or **UK Societas**
- with its registered office in the UK, the Channel Islands or the Isle of Man
- whose securities are admitted to trading:
  - (i) on a UK regulated market (such as the Main Market, which is the focus of this book); or
  - (ii) on a UK multilateral trading facility (such as AIM); or
  - (iii) on any stock exchange in the Channel Islands or the Isle of Man

2. Intro section 3(a)(ii)

- **any other public company**, or **UK Societas** (including **unlisted public companies**) which
  - (i) has its registered office in the UK, the Channel Islands or the Isle of Man; and
  - (ii) in the Panel's opinion, has its place of central management and control in the UK, the Channel Islands or the Isle of Man
- or a **private company** but only if it has during the last 10 years:
  - (i) had its securities admitted to trading on a UK regulated market or UK MTF or on any stock exchange in the Channel Islands or the Isle of Man; or
  - (ii) advertised dealings for a six-month continuous period; or
  - (iii) has filed a prospectus; or
  - (iv) had securities subject to a CA 2006, s 693(3) marketing arrangement); and
  - (v) has its registered office in the UK, the Channel Islands or the Isle of Man, and

(vi) in the Panel's opinion, has its place of central management and control in the UK, the Channel Islands or the Isle of Man

20.4.1.2 Offers within the Takeover Code

The Takeover Code applies to 'offers' for those companies mentioned at **20.4.1.1** above. 'Offer' is defined to include those transactions set out in para 3(b) of the Introduction to the Takeover Code. These are principally 'takeover bids and merger transactions however effected, including by means of statutory merger or scheme of arrangement'. (The Takeover Code does extend to less common and more technical transactions as well, but these are beyond the scope of this book.) Usually such a transaction will involve the offeror seeking control of the offeree company. Section 943(7) of the CA 2006 defines takeover bids by reference to para 20 of Sch 1C to the CA 2006. This states that 'a "takeover bid" means a public offer made to the holders of the securities of a company to acquire some or all of those securities, whether mandatory or voluntary, which follows or has as its objective the acquisition of control of that company ...'. 'Control' is defined in the Takeover Code as 30% or more of the voting rights in the offeree company. This book concentrates on the most common situation in practice, of an offeror seeking to gain 100% control of the offeree company.

It is worth noting that sometimes it can be difficult to pin down whether a transaction is a 'takeover' or a 'merger'. A merger denotes a union of equals, but frequently the term is used in practice when a takeover (one company taking ownership of another) is occurring. This use of 'merger' is usually done for PR reasons to give the impression that the offeree company is not being swallowed up by the offeror. Ultimately this has no impact on the application of the Takeover Code as it covers both situations.

The Takeover Code even applies to transactions which are in contemplation but not yet announced. For example, there are strict rules governing secrecy in r 2 of the Takeover Code (see **21.3**) and dealing in shares (r 4, see **21.8.10.1**) which apply even if a takeover offer has not yet been firmly decided upon.

Note also that the Takeover Code will apply regardless of how the takeover is carried out. For example, it applies to a takeover effected by way of a general offer or by way of a scheme of arrangement – see **21.12**.

20.4.1.3 The offeror/bidder

There are no rules in the Takeover Code regarding the status or nature of the offeror making the offer. The offeror may be any company, listed or unlisted, public or private, UK or foreign registered. It could be a partnership or limited liability partnership, UK or foreign registered. It could even be an individual or group of individuals. As mentioned in **20.4.1.1** above, it is the status of the *offeree company* which is important. In practice, the offeror may also be referred to as the 'bidder'.

20.4.2 To whom does the Takeover Code apply?

Paragraph 3(f) of the Introduction to the Takeover Code confirms that the Code applies to everyone who is involved in a transaction to which it applies. This includes not only the offeror and the offeree company, but also the directors of the offeror and the offeree company, and their respective professional advisers. The lawyers advising on the transaction, therefore, will be subject to the Takeover Code.

20.4.3 The purpose of the Takeover Code

The Introduction to the Takeover Code explains, in para 2, that its purpose is to:

(a) ensure fair and equal treatment of all shareholders in an offeree company in relation to takeovers;

(b) provide an orderly framework within which takeovers are conducted; and

(c) promote the integrity of the financial markets.

Importantly, the Takeover Code is *not* concerned with the commercial advantages or disadvantages of a takeover. For example, whether the offer price fairly reflects the offeree company's true value. These are matters for the directors and shareholders of the offeree company to decide upon. The Takeover Code's purpose is not to facilitate or impede takeovers, and also is not concerned with other regulatory issues, such as competition policy, which are subject to their own sets of rules and regulatory bodies (see **20.6**).

20.4.4 The nature of the Takeover Code

As discussed at **20.3** above, s 943 of the CA 2006 gives statutory effect to the Takeover Code.

The Takeover Code comprises six general principles (see **20.4.5**), 38 rules which are based on, and develop, these principles, and nine Appendices. The rules must be read in conjunction not only with the general principles but also with the accompanying notes, which give practical guidance on the applicability of the rules.

The six general principles are taken directly from the Takeovers Directive and are essentially statements of standards of commercial behaviour.

The Takeover Code is an interesting creature from the common law lawyer's perspective, as, under para 2(b) of the Introduction, it is the *spirit*, and not just the letter, of both the general principles and the rules which is to be applied. This means that the Panel Executive may be willing to modify or relax the wording of the rules, on a case-by-case basis, if this is consistent with the underlying purpose of the rules. This, of course, is a significant departure from normal practice and clearly affects how the lawyer must advise in relation to the Takeover Code (see **20.4.6** below).

20.4.5 The general principles

The general principles are the key to understanding the spirit of the Takeover Code. They are the cornerstone of the Code, and they may apply in situations which the rules of the Takeover Code do not cover expressly. The six general principles are set out below, together with (the author's) summaries to help reinforce the essence of each principle:

1. All holders of the securities of an offeree company of the same class must be afforded equivalent treatment; moreover, if a person acquires control of a company, the other holders of securities must be protected.
   Summary: shareholders should be treated equally and fairly.
2. The holders of the securities of an offeree company must have sufficient time and information to enable them to reach a properly informed decision on the bid; where it advises the holders of securities, the board of the offeree company must give its views on the effects of implementation of the bid on employment, conditions of employment and the locations of the company's places of business.
   Summary: sufficient information should be made available to shareholders in a timely fashion, to enable them to decide whether to accept or reject the offer.
3. The board of an offeree company must act in the interests of the company as a whole and must not deny the holders of securities the opportunity to decide on the merits of the bid.
   Summary: Directors have duties of fairness in relation to takeovers.
4. False markets must not be created in the securities of the offeree company, of the offeror company or of any other company concerned by the bid in such a way that the rise or fall of the prices of the securities becomes artificial and the normal functioning of the markets is distorted.
   Summary: Parties should not commit market abuse, etc.

5. An offeror must announce a bid only after ensuring that they can fulfil in full any cash consideration, if such is offered, and after taking all reasonable measures to secure the implementation of any other type of consideration.
   Summary: The bidder must be in a position to pay for the offeree company's shares.
6. An offeree company must not be hindered in the conduct of its affairs for longer than is reasonable by a bid for its securities.
   Summary: The offer timetable should not drag on.

The practical effect of these general principles is considered in **Chapters 21** and **22**.

20.4.6 The Takeover Code in practice

If there is any doubt as to how the Takeover Code might apply in a certain situation, the parties and their advisers should consult the Panel Executive, who will provide a ruling on the issue. In fact, para 6(b) of the Introduction to the Takeover Code states expressly that legal advice is not an appropriate alternative to obtaining a ruling from the Panel Executive. Does this mean that the lawyer does not need to know anything about the Takeover Code? Far from it. In fact, the lawyer plays a pivotal part in the interpretation of the Code.

First, the lawyer will be involved in trying to identify a 'third way', in circumstances where the company will struggle to comply with the letter of the Takeover Code, but there is a possibility of an alternative approach which would not compromise the spirit of the Takeover Code. The Panel Executive is likely to be much more receptive to a company which approaches it in the hope of modifying the interpretation of a rule if the company has a well thought-out suggestion for such modification. Obviously the lawyer's knowledge and experience, of previous occasions when the Panel Executive has been willing to modify the interpretation of rules of the Takeover Code, will assist in this role.

The second role of the lawyer in relation to the Takeover Code is that, together with certain of the company's other advisers, they will have regular contact with the Panel Executive during the takeover process.

20.4.6.1 Practice Statements

The Panel Executive publishes Practice Statements, which it posts, in date order, on its website. These statements provide informal guidance on how the Panel Executive interprets and applies the Takeover Code in certain circumstances. The Practice Statements do not form part of the Takeover Code, and so are not binding and no substitute for consulting the Panel Executive.

20.4.6.2 Panel Statements

The Panel also publishes Panel Statements on its website in date order. These statements record decisions taken by the Panel in relation to real-life takeovers, including enforcement decisions.

20.4.6.3 Panel Bulletins

Panel Bulletins are published by the Panel Executive from time to time to remind practitioners and market participants of the operation of specific provisions of the Takeover Code in the light of issues of which the Executive becomes aware. Panel Bulletins do not entail any changes to the interpretation or application of the Code.

20.4.7 Enforcement of the Takeover Code

The Takeover Code has the force of law in relation to all takeovers to which it applies.

20.4.7.1 Monitoring powers

The Panel has powers to monitor the progress of a takeover. Those dealing with the Panel must do so in an open and cooperative way, and disclose all relevant information (subject to legal professional privilege) (Introduction to the Takeover Code, para 9(a)). The Panel also has the power to require documents and information from persons dealing with the Panel (CA 2006, s 947 and Introduction to the Takeover Code, para 9(b)).

20.4.7.2 Enforcement powers of the Panel

Anyone reporting a breach to the Panel must do so promptly, otherwise the Panel may exercise its discretion to disregard the complaint (Introduction to the Takeover Code, para 10(a)).

Once it is certain that the Code has been breached, the Panel has several powers of enforcement, set out below.

Compliance rulings

The Panel has the power to make a compliance ruling, either to prevent a breach of the Code (if there is a reasonable likelihood of a breach of the Takeover Code or a Panel ruling) or, if the breach has already occurred, to ensure the breach is remedied (Introduction to the Takeover Code, para 10(b)).

Compensation rulings

The Panel has a limited power to make a compensation ruling to order a party to compensate any offeree company shareholders who have suffered financially as a result of a breach of the Code (Introduction to the Takeover Code, para 10(c)). The Panel can exercise this power only in relation to breaches of those rules which deal with the offer consideration (namely rr 6, 9, 11, 14, 15, 16.1 and 35.3). The effect of a compensation ruling is to put the shareholders into the position they would have been had the breach not occurred. The Panel can also order that simple or compound interest be paid to the shareholders.

Enforcement by the courts

The Panel can ask the courts to enforce the Takeover Code (CA 2006, s 955 and Introduction to the Takeover Code, para 10(d)). The Panel has stated that it will exercise this power only as a last resort, or in urgent cases.

Bid documentation rules

For offers made for a company that has voting shares admitted to trading on a UK regulated market (such as the Main Market of the LSE), there is a criminal offence under s 953 of the CA 2006 for non-compliance with the 'bid documentation rules'. These are defined in the Introduction to the Takeover Code, para 10(e), and set out in Appendix 6.

The bid documentation rules relate to the content requirements of the main takeover document, known as the offer document (see **22.4.1**) (the 'offer document rules'), and any defence documents (see **22.4.2**) (the 'response document rules'). In the event that the documents do not comply with the rules, a criminal offence is committed (in the case of a breach of the offer document rules) not only by the offeror but also by any director, officer or member of the offeror who caused the document to be published, and (in the case of a breach of the response document rules) by any director or officer of the offeree company if they knew, or were reckless as to whether, the document did not comply with the Takeover Code, and failed to take all reasonable steps to ensure compliance. The offence is punishable by a fine. The offence applies only to takeovers of companies listed on the Official List and trading on the Main Market (so not to schemes of arrangement or to offers for unlisted companies, or companies listed on AIM).

In certain circumstances, disciplinary action may be taken (see **20.4.7.4**).

20.4.7.3 Enforcement powers of the FCA

Under the Introduction to the Takeover Code, para 11, the Panel can request the FCA to take enforcement action against any person authorised by the FSMA 2000 who contravenes the Takeover Code or a ruling of the Panel. The definition of 'authorised person' is considered at **9.4.3**. In practice, this will cover the stockbroker (see **21.5.3**) and the financial adviser (see **21.5.1**) acting for the company in relation to the takeover. The stockbroker and financial adviser will not continue to act unless the takeover complies with the Takeover Code, as otherwise they risk the sanctions listed below. Note that the FCA can also take enforcement action against an 'approved person', for example a director of an authorised firm.

The FCA can take the following enforcement action in the event of a breach of the Takeover Code:

(a) public censure;
(b) fine;
(c) the removal of authorisation under the FSMA 2000;
(d) injunction; and
(e) order for restitution.

Note also the requirement, referred to at **20.4.7.4(e)** below, that the rules of the FCA prohibit a person authorised by the FSMA 2000 from acting for any offender.

20.4.7.4 Disciplinary powers

Paragraph 11 of the Introduction to the Code allows the Panel Executive to deal with a matter on its own where the offender agrees to the facts and the action to be taken. It also outlines the power of the Panel Executive to institute disciplinary proceedings before the Hearings Committee (see **20.2.4.2**). If the Committee finds that there has been a breach of the Takeover Code, it can impose the following sanctions:

(a) private reprimand;
(b) public statement of censure;
(c) suspension or withdrawal of, or the imposition of conditions on, any exemption, approval or other special status the Panel has granted;
(d) reporting the offender's conduct to another regulatory body such as DBT, the Stock Exchange or the FCA; or
(e) publishing a Panel Statement indicating that the offender is unlikely to comply with the Takeover Code. This can trigger other requirements of the FCA and certain professional bodies which oblige their members, in certain circumstances, not to act for the offender in a transaction to which the Takeover Code applies. This in effect means the party is 'cold shouldered' by financial institutions and is unable to be involved in takeover activity in the UK.

There is an example of (b) in Panel Statement 2010/14, available on the Panel's website. The Panel publicly criticises the US food company Kraft for a breach of r 19.1 of the Takeover Code (see **22.4.5.1** below). Kraft made pledges during an £11.7 billion bid for Cadbury that it would keep open a particular factory if it won control of Cadbury. It did take over Cadbury and promptly announced the closure of the factory. It demonstrated a shocking disregard for the spirit of the rules, as well as a brutal change in fortunes for employees of a company whose original Quaker owners went to great lengths to improve the living and working conditions of its workers. The impact of Kraft's decision has been dramatic, with a review of certain provisions of the Takeover Code instituted by the Panel which resulted in a new version of the Takeover Code being issued.

An extremely rare example of (e) was imposed on Brian Myerson, an investor and AIM company director, in 2010 when he was banned from takeover activity for three years for serious breaches of the Takeover Code.

The Panel Executive has set out, in the 'compliance' section of its website, the issues it will take into account when considering whether to take disciplinary action.

20.5 OTHER RULES AND REGULATIONS

Chapter 17, which considers the methods of raising equity finance, and **Chapter 19**, which considers listed company acquisitions and disposals, explain that the specific subject matter of those chapters cannot be considered in a vacuum; most of the rules and regulations examined in this book are relevant to the specific areas of law those chapters consider. The same can be said of takeovers. In addition to the Takeover Code, takeovers are subject to other rules and regulations, all of which are considered in this book. They are summarised below.

20.5.1 Consideration

If the company is:

(a) issuing shares as consideration, or

(b) using equity finance to raise cash to use as consideration,

for the acquisition, then the rules and regulations considered in **17.4** above will be relevant.

20.5.2 Acquiring shares

A takeover is, after all, just an acquisition of shares. This means that all the rules and regulations summarised at **19.3** above are relevant, including rules under the CA 2006, the UK Listing Rules, the DTRs, FSMA 2000 and UK MAR.

20.5.3 Merger control

The takeover of a UK company can give rise to merger control issues in the UK under the EA 2002, or in the EU under the EC Merger Regulation. **Chapter 23** considers this issue further.

20.5.4 Sector-specific regulatory controls

Certain sectors have their own specific regulatory provisions. Examples include the defence, travel and broadcasting industries. The lawyer may need to take advice from their client as to the sector-specific regulations which may apply to any takeover transaction.

20.5.5 Compulsory acquisition of minority shareholdings

The provisions of ss 974 to 991 of the CA 2006, which are important in the context of a takeover, are discussed at **22.7** below.

20.6 REGULATORY BODIES

The rules and regulations which may apply to a takeover, and which are considered in this chapter, mean that the following regulatory bodies may become involved in a takeover bid:

(a) The Panel, which administers the Takeover Code (see **20.2** above).

(b) The FCA, which has powers of enforcement in relation to the Takeover Code (see **20.4.7.3** above).

(c) The FCA (acting in its capacity as markets regulator). If the offeror is listed and is issuing new shares as consideration, or to raise cash consideration, those shares must be admitted to listing on the Official List by the FCA. Also, if the acquisition is a reverse transaction, the FCA will need to approve the reverse takeover circular (see **19.6** above).

(d) The Stock Exchange. If the offeror is listed and is issuing new shares as consideration, or to raise cash consideration, those shares must be admitted to trading on the Main Market by the Stock Exchange.

(e) The CMA and the European Commission. If the takeover raises competition issues, these bodies may become involved (see **Chapter 23**).

(f) Sector-specific regulatory bodies. This will depend on the sector in which the parties to the takeover specialise. For example, the Civil Aviation Authority is likely to be involved in the takeover of an airline company, to check the company holds an ATOL licence.

(g) The UK Government. It can exercise its powers under the National Security and Investment Act 2021 to intervene in takeovers that could harm UK national security, particularly in areas of the economy such as defence, advanced robotics, synthetic biology, energy and others (see **Chapter 23**).

CHAPTER 21

TAKEOVERS: PREPARATION

21.1 INTRODUCTION

Chapter 20 introduces the concept of a takeover and considers the rules and regulations which the lawyer will need to apply in relation to a takeover. In particular, it explains that the Takeover Code contains the key rules relating to takeovers, and that the unique nature of the Code means that the lawyer will need to consult the Panel Executive (referred to in this chapter as 'the Panel') to determine how the Takeover Code might apply in the circumstances of a particular takeover.

It is very exciting to be instructed in relation to a takeover. Of all the listed company issues considered in this book, it is the takeover which arrests the attention not only of your client, but also, once announced, of shareholders, your colleagues, the press and the general public.

Chapter 22 considers the takeover process once the bid has been announced. However, the lawyer's work begins long before that. This chapter considers the work which the lawyer undertakes prior to the announcement of a takeover bid.

Note that, as explained in **Chapter 20**, in practice the terms 'offer' and 'bid' are used interchangeably, as are the terms 'offeror' and 'bidder', and 'offeree' and 'target'. The Takeover Code uses the terms 'offer', 'offeror' and 'offeree'.

21.2 RECOMMENDED OR HOSTILE?

Rule 1 of the Takeover Code provides that the offeror must make the offer first to the directors (or advisers) of the offeree company. The most significant factor which will determine the nature of the offeror's preparation is whether the takeover is intended to be recommended or hostile. They could not be more different.

21.2.1 The recommended offer

If the directors of the offeree company consider that the offer is in the best interests of the company's shareholders, employees and (if the company's solvency is in issue) creditors, they must recommend the offeree's shareholders to accept the offer. The offer is described as 'recommended'. Remember, it is the shareholders of the offeree company who own it and who ultimately will determine the success of the offer, in other words, whether to sell their shares to the offeror or not.

Bear in mind that a takeover often results in a change in management. The directors of the offeree company risk losing their jobs, or being relocated, if the takeover goes ahead. The culture of the business may change. However, the directors of the offeree company must not allow personal considerations to influence the exercise of their duties to the company when considering whether to recommend the offer.

With a recommended offer, both the offeror and the offeree company have a common aim in ensuring the takeover goes ahead. A recommended offer to acquire all the securities in a company is the most straightforward form of takeover. The boards of directors of both companies will act consensually to try to achieve that takeover. It has the best chance of success, and it can be completed in the shortest period of time.

21.2.2 The hostile offer

If, having been approached under r 1 by the offeror, the board of the offeree company advises its shareholders not to accept the offer, it is described as a 'hostile' offer. The offeror and the offeree company have diametrically opposed aims. The offeror wants the takeover to be successful, while the offeree company will do everything in its power to ensure the offer fails so that it maintains its independence. For both sides there is much at stake. For the offeror, the takeover could be central to the company's strategy of expansion. The shareholders of the offeree company, who ultimately decide whether to accept the offer, need to balance the fact that their board is advising them to reject the offer against the claims of the offeror about how attractive the offer is, in terms of the consideration they will receive in exchange for their shares in the offeree company. The stakes are raised still further by the offer being played out in the public arena, with hard-won reputations on the line.

Of the 40 offers completed under the Takeover Code in the year to 31 March 2021, three were originally hostile and 35 were recommended. The remaining two were r 9 mandatory bids (see **21.8.10.3** below).

21.2.3 The effect on preparation

If the offeror has an existing relationship with the offeree company, it may know in advance whether the offeree company will recommend the offer or not. If so, the offeror can prepare accordingly. However, if the offeror does not have an existing relationship with the offeree company, it has a choice: it can either approach the offeree company with a view to negotiating a recommended offer (and consider whether it is prepared to 'go hostile' in the event the offeree company decides not to recommend an offer), or it can launch a surprise hostile offer for the offeree company without discussing this first with the offeree company.

Whether the offer is intended to be recommended or hostile, the offeror must also plan for the possibility that another offeror may make a rival offer for the offeree company.

21.3 THE NEED FOR SECRECY

Rule 2.1(a) of the Takeover Code provides that all persons with confidential information on an offer, particularly price-sensitive information, must treat that information as secret until the offer is announced to the public under r 2.4 or r 2.7 (see **22.3**). In practice, this means that the lawyer must advise their client company, together with all advisers who are instructed to work on the transaction, of the importance of secrecy and security (r 2.1(b)). The number of people to whom confidential information is given should be kept to a minimum. Anyone who receives confidential information can pass it on only if it is necessary to do so, and they must ensure that they inform the recipient of any information of the need for secrecy in relation to that information. For the lawyer, this translates into ensuring that:

(a) the team working on the transaction is no larger than it needs to be;

(b) each member of the team is aware of the secrecy obligation;

(c) due diligence (see **21.6**) is carried out discreetly;

(d) documents relating to the takeover are kept confidential (for example, not left lying around on the printer); and

(e) the transaction and each of the parties to the transaction are referred to by way of code name rather than their actual names. The code names should not be too obvious. The client may already have code names which it used while carrying out its initial research into the offeree company as a potential target. To take a facile example (although in real life the code names do tend to be facile), imagine a takeover of a company which has an American chair. The transaction might be code-named 'Project Baseball', the offeror code-named 'Bat' and the offeree company code-named 'Ball'. This means that, in all conversations, meetings, telephone calls, documentation and such like, the code names will be used rather than the real names. The documentation will then be amended, to replace the code names with the real names, just before it is published. All very MI5!

To the layman (and, indeed, to a trainee who has not come across the concept before) this can all seem a little dramatic. It can also result in rather awkward situations for the lawyers. There will be a distinct buzz of activity around the offices of the team of lawyers who are working on a takeover. This can draw inquisitive comments from colleagues, regarding what the team is working on. The effect of r 2.1 is that those colleagues must be rebuffed in as polite a manner as you can manage. This can be particularly difficult for any trainee working on the takeover, who will not be able to discuss the transaction even with more senior lawyers who enquire what the trainee is doing. These measures, however, are vital. A leak can have disastrous consequences for the bid (see **22.3.3.2** and **22.3.3.3** below). While the secrecy obligation can be frustrating for the lawyer, consider just how much more embarrassing it would be if a leak was traced back to them.

The Panel reiterated the importance of r 2.1 in Practice Statement 2008/20 (updated in 2019), and expresses its support for the FCA's attempts to tackle the problem of misuse of inside information in takeovers.

21.4 AN EXAMPLE

Obviously, the work involved for a lawyer advising on a takeover depends on whether they are advising the offeror or the offeree company. This book examines the takeover principally from the point of view of the offeror. To make sense of what **Chapter 20** and **Chapter 21** have covered so far, let us consider an example.

21.4.1 The facts

Imagine that we advise X plc, a company whose shares are admitted to listing on the Official List and to trading on the Main Market, which is seeking to make an offer for the entire issued ordinary share capital of Y plc, also a company whose shares are admitted to listing on the Official List and to trading on the Main Market. The share price of X plc is looking healthy. Y plc, however, has had some bad press lately. It has been underperforming compared to its main rivals (which include X plc) and its share price is at an all-time low. The press have been speculating about whether Y plc is ripe for a takeover.

21.4.2 The analysis

The transaction is a takeover which is subject to the provisions of the Takeover Code. X plc is seeking to acquire 100% of the shares in a UK company whose securities are admitted to trading on a regulated market (ie the Main Market) (see **20.5.1.1** above), Y plc. X plc is the offeror. Y plc is the offeree company.

Note that the fact that X plc, the offeror, is a listed company is, in fact, irrelevant in terms of the application of the Takeover Code, where it is the identity of the offeree company which is important. It is, however, relevant in terms of applying the class tests and other continuing obligations imposed on listed companies, and in terms of the ability of X plc to offer shares as consideration, or raise cash consideration through the issue of shares.

For the purposes of the application of the Takeover Code, it is worth remembering (see **20.5.1.1**) that Y plc need not be listed. The takeover of *any* public company will fall under the Takeover Code.

21.4.3 Code names

The company secretary of X plc has decided that the code name for the transaction is Project Gotham. The code name of X plc is Batman. The code name of Y plc is Robin.

21.4.4 The parties

The main parties involved in Project Gotham will be as follows:

(a) The offeror, Batman.

(b) The offeree company, Robin.

(c) The board of Batman.

(d) The board of Robin.

(e) The shareholders of Batman. The shareholders of Batman may need to be involved for two reasons:

  (i) if the transaction is a reverse takeover, Batman will require shareholder approval before it can complete the acquisition (see **Chapter 19**); and

  (ii) if Batman decides to issue Batman shares to Robin's shareholders as consideration, the shareholders may need to increase Batman's authorised share capital and/or give the directors authority to allot the consideration shares under s 551 of the CA 2006. Batman shareholders would not need to disapply s 561 of the CA 2006 in these circumstances, as the shares are to be issued for non-cash consideration (see **14.6.7**, which sets out the position under the CA 2006).

(f) The shareholders of the offeree, Robin. The shareholders of Robin own the shares which Batman wants to acquire. The fate of the takeover rests on whether they decide to accept the offer or not. Ultimately, they are the most important people in the takeover.

(g) The advisers to both Batman and Robin. See **21.5** below.

21.5 APPOINTING A TEAM OF ADVISERS

As with an IPO, a takeover involves not only lawyers, but a wider team of advisers, who must all work together seamlessly to advise either the offeror or the offeree on all aspects of the transaction.

21.5.1 Financial advisers

Rule 3 of the Takeover Code provides that the offeree must have an independent financial adviser. In practice, the offeror will also have an independent financial adviser. An investment bank will usually adopt the role of financial adviser. In relation to advising the offeror, it will use its experience of other transactions, and its knowledge of the regulatory environment and the Takeover Code, to:

(a) plan and coordinate the takeover (although increasingly the lawyers are leading coordination of the documentation);

(b) advise the board in relation to tactics, such as:

  (i) when to make the offer,

   - (ii) the level of consideration to be offered (including when to raise the level in the event that the offer is not well received),
   - (iii) the type of consideration to be offered (if equity finance is required to raise cash consideration, the financial advisers will advise on the method of equity finance to be used);

(c) be the offeror's principal point of contact with the Panel, to discuss any provisions of the Takeover Code which are causing concern;

(d) issue and approve the offer documentation under s 21 of the FSMA 2000 (unless an exemption applies);

(e) underwrite any cash offer or cash alternative;

(f) report on profit forecasts and quantified benefits statements (r 28.1(a)); and

(g) advise in relation to any information published during the offer (r 19.1, note 1) (see **22.4.5.1**).

21.5.2 Lawyers

The offeror will require lawyers as, of course, will the offeree. However, the financial adviser of the offeror may also be advised, separately from the offeror, by a further team of lawyers.

The lawyers will advise in relation to the rules and regulations considered in **Chapter 20**. They will also be involved in speaking to the Panel in relation to the interpretation of the Takeover Code, and in drafting and, increasingly, coordinating the documentation for the takeover.

21.5.3 Stockbrokers

The investment bank acting as financial adviser will often take on the role of stockbroker. The stockbrokers play an important part in deciding tactics. They are able to do this because of the unique relationship they have with shareholders. Stockbrokers have day-to-day contact with key representatives of institutional shareholders. Remember that institutional shareholders have large stakes in public companies. Usually, therefore, the stockbrokers will have the 'inside track' on the appetite of the offeree company shareholders, and the market, for the offer. This is particularly important in a hostile bid, where the offeror will have to convince offeree company shareholders to accept the offer even though the offeree company board has advised them not to.

The stockbrokers will use this knowledge to:

(a) monitor market purchases and rumour;

(b) advise the offeror on the likely reaction of:
   - (i) its shareholders (see **21.4.4**) to the proposed acquisition, and
   - (ii) the offeree company's shareholders to the nature and amount of consideration to be offered; and

(c) arrange meetings with the offeree company's principal shareholders, before the offer is announced, to explain the basic terms of the offer and to see if those shareholders will commit irrevocably to accept the offer once it is made (see **21.10** below).

21.5.4 Accountants

The accountants will gather the financial information which must be included in the takeover documentation. They will also give comfort to the board in relation to financial information in the takeover documentation, and report on any profit forecast or merger benefits statement (or working capital or indebtedness statement in any prospectus or equivalent document).

21.5.5 Financial public relations consultants

The role of the public relations adviser is to liaise with the press to secure good coverage of the offer, and to ensure that the key messages in connection with the bid are published accurately.

The highly regarded 'Lex' column of the *Financial Times* (unfortunately subscription only) will comment on high-profile takeovers, as will the business editors of other national daily newspapers, websites and TV channels (and no doubt they will feature on Instagram and TikTok too). The offeror, particularly on a hostile takeover, will hope that the media comment favourably on the offer, so that they might persuade offeree company shareholders to accept the offer.

21.5.6 Registrars or receiving bankers

The registrars or receiving bankers (often the same institution) will receive the forms of acceptance from the shareholders of the offeree company who want to accept the takeover offer. They will monitor the level of acceptances to determine whether the critical level necessary to allow the offer to be declared unconditional as to acceptances has been reached (see **22.4.7.1** below). If a meeting of the shareholders of the offeror is required (see **21.4.4** above), the registrars or receiving bankers will also receive and monitor the return of proxies for that meeting. Appendix 4 to the Takeover Code sets out a code of practice for receiving agents.

21.5.7 Printers

The role of the printers on a takeover is not unlike that on an IPO (see **4.2.11**). The takeover documentation will be created by word processor at the outset of the transaction, but ultimately the final version will be professionally printed. Once each document is substantially in final draft form, therefore, it will be taken to print, and thereafter each draft will be printed (referred to as 'proof printing'). The printers need to process the documentation quickly, accurately and securely.

Note that under r 30.2 of the Takeover Code, takeover documents will be considered sent if either they are sent in hard copy or electronic form or published on a website. If a document is sent in electronic form or published on a website, the recipient has the right to ask for a hard copy version under r 30.3 of the Takeover Code.

21.6 DUE DILIGENCE

21.6.1 The requirement for due diligence

The effect of General Principle 5 (see **20.4.5** above) and r 2.7(a) of the Takeover Code is that an offeror should announce a takeover offer only after the most careful and responsible consideration, when it has every reason to believe that it can and will implement the offer. This means that the offeror must undertake some careful planning and investigation before it announces an offer.

21.6.2 What is 'due diligence'?

The concept of due diligence in the context of an IPO was explained at **5.3.4** above. The concept is not so different on a takeover. While due diligence on an IPO involves investigating the company seeking to float, and collating comprehensive information about the company which can then be used in the prospectus, due diligence on a takeover seeks to investigate the offeree company (and, in certain circumstances, such as if shares in the offeror are to be issued as consideration, the offeror) so that this information can be used in the offer document (**22.4.1**). However, the effect of the secrecy obligation outlined at **21.3** above, means that the due diligence exercise is more limited on a takeover than on an IPO.

21.6.3 The purpose of due diligence

Due diligence is used to discharge the offeror's obligations under General Principle 5 and r 2.7(a) of the Takeover Code (see **22.3.3.1**). For example, the Panel will not look too kindly on an offeror who announces an offer, only to discover that it does not have enough cash to fund it.

The information the offeror will require includes the following:

(a) Is the offeree company really an attractive acquisition?
 (i) How has it been performing lately?
 (ii) What are its main assets and liabilities?
 (iii) Where is it located?
 (iv) What do its latest report and accounts reveal?

(b) Can the offeror successfully integrate the offeree company into its business? What costs savings could be made after the takeover?

(c) How should the offer be structured?
 (i) Might the offeree company be willing to recommend the offer?
 (ii) If not, is the offeror willing to proceed on a hostile basis?
 (iii) Should the offeror offer cash or shares as consideration?
 (iv) If offering shares, does the offeror have sufficient unissued authorised share capital, and do the directors have sufficient authority to allot those shares?
 (v) If not, will the offeror's shareholders be willing to pass the necessary resolution(s)?
 (vi) Will the offer constitute a reverse takeover? If so, will the offeror's shareholders be willing to approve it?
 (vii) Are there any issues which might affect the timing of the offer; for example, should the offeror company wait until the offeree company's next annual report or accounts are published?

(d) What are the chances of success?
 (i) Who are the main shareholders of the offeree company, whom the offeror would need to persuade to accept the offer?
 (ii) How many offeree company shareholders might be willing to provide irrevocable undertakings? (See **21.10** below.)
 (iii) How many shares does the offeror hold which it can vote in favour of the bid? (See **21.8** below.)
 (iv) Is anyone else interested in the offeree company: might there be a more attractive competing bid?
 (v) Are there any competition or regulatory issues which could jeopardise the bid? (See **Chapter 23**.)

21.6.4 The due diligence process

21.6.4.1 If the offer is recommended

The offeror will undertake some initial due diligence itself, using publicly available information, before it approaches the offeree company. If the offeree company is receptive to the offer, it will then assist the offeror with its due diligence exercise and provide the information the offeror requires. However, the offeree company must be careful. Rule 21.3 requires any information provided to an offeror, whether publicly identified or not, to be provided to a competing offeror (should one arise). While the original offeror might have been welcomed by the offeree, the competing offeror may be unwanted, and sensitive information on the offeree, given to the original offeror, will have to be revealed to this new, unwelcome suitor.

21.6.4.2 If the offer is hostile

If the offer is hostile, the offeror will not receive the help from the offeree company which is outlined above. However, as noted at **21.6.4.1**, if the offeree company has provided information to any competing offeror, then r 21.3 of the Takeover Code provides that the offeree company must provide the same information on request to all other offerors or potential offerors. In practice, however, it is probable that a hostile offeror will want to launch a 'surprise' offer on the offeree company, so it will not avail itself of its rights under r 21.3 until its hostile offer has been announced, by which time it should already have completed its due diligence exercise, in order to comply with General Principle 5 and r 2.7(a) of the Takeover Code (see **22.4.5.4**).

21.6.5 Publicly available information

The following information about the offeree company should already be in the public domain:

(a) articles of association (Companies House);

(b) details of directors (Companies House, annual report and accounts (on offeree's website), RIS disclosures, the offeree's register of directors);

(c) details of shareholders and share capital (Companies House, annual report and accounts, RIS disclosures (eg under DTR 5 and UK MAR), the offeree's register of members);

(d) financial information (annual report and accounts). Section 415 of the CA 2006 provides that a company must prepare a directors' report as part of its annual report and accounts, which contains the information required by Chapter 5 of Part 15 of the CA 2006. The report must contain a business review (CA 2006, s 417), which must contain a fair review of the company's business and a description of the principal risks and uncertainties facing the company. The review should be a balanced and comprehensive review of the development and performance of the business of the company during the financial year and the position of the company's business at the end of that year;

(e) the directors' remuneration report (see **8.4.3.1**);

(f) any published prospectus (on offeree's website or the NSM (see **7.5.7.1** above)); and

(g) any analyst research (available from investment banks).

Plenty of other information will be available on the company's website, in trade magazines, and possibly in the newspapers.

Section 992 of the CA 2006 requires additional information to be disclosed in the directors' report for companies whose voting shares are admitted to trading on a UK regulated market (ie the Main Market but not AIM). Although the requirements are not limited to companies which are the subject of a takeover offer, the effect of the additional disclosure is to ensure that more information on the share structure of the company, including any share transfer or voting restrictions which might be triggered on a takeover, becomes public information.

21.7 FINANCING THE OFFER

The offeror must know, before announcing a takeover offer, how it will finance that offer. This is not only a practical consideration; it is a requirement of General Principle 5 and r 2.7(a) of the Takeover Code.

The choices available to the offeror are as follows.

21.7.1 Cash consideration

21.7.1.1 Debt finance

The offeror could obtain a loan to fund the takeover. However, as **Chapter 18** explained, this will affect the company's gearing and so may not be desirable. It will also depend on the prevailing bank interest rates and the prevailing economic climate. Currently, of course, debt finance is very difficult to come by.

21.7.1.2 Equity finance

The offeror could obtain the funds from its existing shareholders, using one of the methods described at **17.7** to **17.9** above. This depends on the existing shareholders being willing to subscribe to a fresh issue of shares.

21.7.2 Paper consideration

21.7.2.1 Debt finance

The company could offer loan notes to the shareholders of the offeree company rather than cash.

21.7.2.2 Equity finance

The company can offer shares (often referred to as 'paper') as consideration rather than cash. This is discussed at **17.10** above.

21.7.3 The option to take cash or shares

It is relatively common for an offeror to offer the offeree company's shareholders the option to take either cash or shares in the offeror in return for their shares in the offeree company. This sounds complicated, but in fact the method by which a company does this should be familiar to you already. This can be achieved through a vendor placing, described at **17.11** above. The offeror will actually issue only shares as consideration, but the issue will be on the basis that, for those shareholders in the offeree company who want to take up the cash alternative, the offeror will have those shares placed, and the shareholders will receive the cash proceeds of that placing.

The idea behind this is to make the offer as appealing as possible to the offeree shareholders who decide the success of the offer. Some shareholders may be more likely to accept the offer if they receive cold, hard cash rather than shares in the offeror. Other shareholders may prefer to receive shares rather than cash, for tax reasons.

In some offers, the offeror may offer the offeree shareholders *both* cash and shares. This may be accompanied by a 'mix and match' election, where the shareholders can choose to vary the split of cash and shares being offered. Say that X plc offered offeree shareholders three shares in X plc and £1 in cash for every one share in the offeree. The offeror may allow the offeree shareholders to take four shares in X plc and 50p in cash, or any other combination, so long as the total value paid for each offeree share remains the same.

21.8 STAKEBUILDING

21.8.1 What is stakebuilding?

Stakebuilding is the strategic purchase of shares in the offeree company by the offeror, in the period before the announcement of an offer, and during the offer period (see **22.3.4**).

21.8.2 The purpose of stakebuilding

The key to the success of the offer depends on reaching a minimum threshold of just over 50% of the voting rights in the offeree company. Once that level is reached, the offeror controls the offeree company. Of course the offeror often wants 100% control, but just over 50% is the minimum required (Takeover Code, r 10). If the offeror buys shares in the offeree it reduces the number of shares required to reach the level necessary to complete the offer and successfully take over the offeree company.

21.8.3 Advantages of stakebuilding

The advantages of stakebuilding are as follows:

(a) Rule 10 of the Takeover Code provides that the offer can be declared unconditional as to acceptances (see **22.4.7.1**) once the offeror holds over 50% of the voting rights in the offeree company. In other words, the offeror has won control of the offeree. Imagine, then, that an offeror already has a stake of 25% in the offeree company. The offeror would only need to persuade the owners of just over 25% of the offeree company shares to accept the offer in order to be able to declare the offer unconditional as to acceptances.

(b) The offeror can acquire shares at the market price before the offer is announced. Once the offer is announced the price of the shares in the offeree will rise, often substantially, to reflect the fact that the offeror wants to buy all the shares and they have therefore become more valuable.

(c) The offeror does not need to alert the offeree to the acquisition if it acquires the shares before it announces the offer and it acquires fewer than 3% of the shares (remember that the disclosure of interest obligations under Chapter 5 of the DTRs would require disclosure of the offeror's interest once that interest reached 3% (see **Chapter 15**)) – but see **21.8.4(e)** below.

(d) If the offeror has a substantial shareholding by the time it announces the offer, other shareholders may be more inclined to accept the offer.

21.8.4 Disadvantages of stakebuilding

The disadvantages of stakebuilding are as follows:

(a) The offeror will own the shares even if the offer fails. The offeror will usually want all or nothing – total control of the offeree company, not just to be a minority shareholder.

(b) If anyone finds out about the strategic purchase (and this is likely given the requirement for the company to pass on to an RIS information it receives under Chapter 5 of the DTRs – see **Chapter 15**), market rumour about a possible takeover may raise the market price of the offeree company's shares. As the consideration for a takeover offer is usually at a premium to the market price, this may make the offeror's intended offer price less attractive.

(c) The increase in price and/or rumour referred to at (b) above may trigger an announcement under r 2.2 (see **22.3**), thereby removing any element of surprise.

(d) Purchases prior to the publication of the offer document do not count towards the 90% compulsory acquisition threshold (see **22.7.2** below).

(e) The purchase may dictate the level or nature of the consideration the offeror must pay pursuant to the offer, under r 6 and r 11 (see **21.8.10.4**), or trigger a mandatory offer under r 9 (see **21.8.10.3**).

21.8.5 Rules and regulations relating to stakebuilding

Some of the rules relating to stakebuilding are considered at **21.8.6** to **21.8.11** below. **Table 21.1**, at **21.9** below, summarises the various stakebuilding thresholds.

The lawyer must be familiar with these rules in order to advise an offeror client whether there are any reasons why it cannot build a stake in the offeree company, or whether it is restricted in building its stake in any particular way. (Note also that the provisions of any standstill letter (see **21.13.4**) will also affect the offeror's ability to build a stake in the offeree company.)

21.8.6 Insider dealing

The fact that the offeror is buying shares in the offeree company at a time when the takeover bid is not public knowledge might suggest that the directors of the offeror are guilty of insider dealing (by requiring the offeror to buy shares; remember that the offeror, as a company, cannot commit the offence – see **11.7**). However, as **11.5.2.2** above explains, in fact the directors may be able to make use of the 'market information' defence.

21.8.7 Market abuse

Again, you could be forgiven for thinking that the offeror's stakebuilding exercise might fall foul of the market abuse regime under UK MAR (see **Chapter 10**). However, UK MAR, Article 9(5) provides protection which is similar to the defence that exists for insider dealing. This provides that an offeror should not be prevented by the market abuse regime from acquiring shares in a potential target with a view to pursuing a takeover offer, simply because the offeror knew that it would be making an offer.

21.8.8 The UK Listing Rules

If the offeror seeks to acquire a large stake, consideration must be given to how the acquisition of the stake might be classified under the UK Listing Rules, and to related requirements of the UK Listing Rules (see **Chapter 19**).

21.8.9 Disclosure requirements

Stakebuilding can trigger the disclosure requirements under Chapter 5 of the DTRs and (during the offer period – see **22.3.4**) the Takeover Code, as set out in **Chapter 15**.

21.8.10 The Takeover Code

The following rules of the Takeover Code may affect any attempt to acquire a stake in an offeree company.

21.8.10.1 Rule 4.1: prohibited dealings

Rule 4.1(a) prevents anyone other than the offeror from building a stake in the offeree where they have confidential price-sensitive information about an intended offer, until the offer, or approach, is announced. Note 1 on r 4 also prohibits the offeror, and 'other persons', from dealing before an announcement if the offeree company has given the offeror confidential price-sensitive information in the course of offer negotiations.

To prevent a would-be stake builder avoiding this rule simply by asking someone else to buy the stake on their behalf, r 4.1(b) prohibits anyone who has confidential price-sensitive information about an intended offer from recommending to another person to buy offeree company shares.

21.8.10.2 Rule 5.1: acquiring 30% or more

Subject to exceptions, this rule prevents the offeror (or anyone acting in concert with it – see **22.6.1.2**) acquiring any interest in offeree company shares (see **21.8.10.5**), which, when aggregated with the offeree company shares in which it is already interested, would carry 30% or more of the voting rights in the offeree company. Paragraph 5 of the definition of 'interests in securities' and the preamble to r 5 confirm that irrevocable undertakings count towards the 30% threshold for the purpose of r 5.1 (see **21.10**).

The Takeover Code considers that a 30% shareholding represents 'control' of a company (see 'Definitions' section of the Takeover Code). The aim of r 5.1 is to prevent a person gaining control of an offeree company without making a full takeover bid for that company, governed by the Takeover Code with all its protection for offeree company shareholders.

Rule 5.2 sets out the exceptions to r 5.1 referred to above. This rule provides that r 5.1 does not apply to an acquisition of an interest in shares:

(a) from a single shareholder, when it is the only acquisition within a 7-day period (r 5.2(a)). (Note that the offeror cannot then make any further acquisitions, other than pursuant to the exceptions below (r 5.3), and details of the acquisition must be disclosed (r 5.4));

(b) immediately before (and conditional upon) the r 2.7 announcement (see **22.3.3.1**) of a firm intention to make a *recommended* offer (r 5.2(b));

(c) after a r 2.7 announcement (see **22.3.3.1**) of a firm intention to make a bid (not subject to a pre-condition), and:
   (i) the offeree company board has agreed to the acquisition,
   (ii) the offeree company board has recommended the offer, or a competing offer,
   (iii) Day 21 of the offer, or a competing offer, has passed (at least 21 days after publishing the offer document; see **22.5.2**) and the offer, or competing offer, has been cleared on competition grounds (see **Chapter 23**), or
   (iv) the offer is unconditional in all respects (see **22.4.7**) (r 5.2(c));

(d) by way of acceptance of the bid (r 5.2(d)); or

(e) which is permitted by Note 11 on r 9.1 or Note 5 on the Dispensations from r 9 (r 5.2(e)).

In the context of a *hostile* offer (see **21.2.2**) these exceptions tend to prevent the offeror from building a stake of more than 29.9% until after Day 21 (see **22.5.2**).

21.8.10.3 Rule 9: mandatory offer

Rule 5.1 of the Takeover Code provides that a person can acquire an interest in shares carrying between 30% and 50% of the voting rights in the offeree company only if the acquisition falls within an exception to that rule. What happens if one of the exceptions to r 5.1 applies and the potential offeror does acquire such an interest? The answer is that r 9 will apply, and for the offeror the consequences of this can be serious.

Rule 9 provides that if:

(a) a person acquires an interest in shares (see **21.8.10.5**) in a company which results in that person holding 30% or more of the voting rights of that company; or

(b) a person already interested in shares carrying between 30% and 50% of the voting rights in a company for someone in concert with that person acquires an interest in any other voting shares of that company;

that person must make an offer to acquire all the equity share capital and all other transferable voting capital of that company on the terms set out in r 9.

If r 9 applies, therefore, not only is the potential offeror forced to make a takeover offer, but they cannot even choose the terms of that offer. The terms imposed by r 9 are not favourable to the offeror. Consideration must be cash, or there must be at least a cash alternative. The consideration must be at a level which is equal to the highest price paid by the offeror (or any person acting in concert with the offeror – see **22.6.1.2**) for any interest in shares of that class in the 12 months preceding the announcement of the offer (r 9.5(a)). If the offeror acquires shares above the offer price during the course of the r 9 offer, then it must increase its offer to the highest price it has paid for the shares (r 9.5(b)). The only conditions which can be attached to the offer are that over 50% of the offeree company shareholders must vote in favour of the offer, and that the offer will lapse if referred on competition grounds. It is explained at **22.4.7** why relying on just these conditions is not ideal. However, as set out in the extract from the regulatory announcement below, sometimes an offeror is happy to follow this route.

The reason for r 9 is that same as that for r 5; if r 9 is triggered, the offeror has acquired 'control', that is 30%, of the offeree company, and so must make a full takeover offer for the company, governed by the Takeover Code.

Note that, in contrast to r 5; irrevocable undertakings do not count towards the 30% threshold for the purposes of r 9 (see **21.10** below).

Below you can see an example of what the mandatory offer means in practice. In this case the owner of Frasers Group plc, Mike Ashley, and his now historical takeover of the Newcastle United football club.

Company	St James Holdings Limited
Headline	Offer for Newcastle United
Released	14:12 23-May-07
Number	1114X

For immediate release

NOT FOR RELEASE, PUBLICATION OR DISTRIBUTION IN, INTO OR FROM AUSTRALIA, CANADA, JAPAN OR THE UNITED STATES

Cash Offer
by
St James Holdings Limited
for
Newcastle United PLC

Summary

- St James Holdings Limited (SJHL) (a company formed at the direction of Mike Ashley) announces that it has today acquired 55,342,223 Newcastle United Shares, representing approximately 41.6 per cent. of the issued share capital of Newcastle United, from Wynyard (Guernsey) Limited, Cameron Hall Developments Limited and Cameron Hall Developments Limited Executive Pension Scheme (the ultimate beneficial owners of each of which are all members of Sir John Hall's family) at a price of 100 pence for each Newcastle United Share.
- SJHL is a UK private limited company which is wholly-owned by Mike Ashley and which has been incorporated for the specific purpose of acquiring Newcastle United Shares and making the Offer.
- In accordance with the provisions of Rule 9 of the City Code, SJHL also announces the terms of a cash offer to be made for all of the issued and to be issued share capital of Newcastle United which is not already owned by SJHL. SJHL intends to seek a recommendation of the Offer from the board of Newcastle United.
- The Offer will, when formally made, be conditional only upon the receipt of acceptances in respect of Newcastle United Shares which, together with the Newcastle United Shares acquired or agreed to be acquired before or during the Offer, will result in SJHL holding Newcastle United Shares carrying more than 50 per cent. of the voting rights in Newcastle United.
- The Offer will be **100 pence in cash for each Newcastle United Share**, valuing the entire issued share capital of Newcastle United at £133.1 million
- The Offer represents:
  - — a premium of approximately 19 per cent. to the Closing Price of 84 pence for each Newcastle United Share on 22 May 2007; and
  - — a premium of approximately 50 per cent. to the average Closing Price of 66.9 pence for each Newcastle United Share in the three month period up to and including 22 May 2007,

  22 May 2007 being the last business day prior to the announcement of the acquisition.

Another example arose in 2018 when the Walt Disney Company had to make a r 9 offer for the British broadcaster, Sky plc, when it acquired a number of businesses owned by Fox, including Fox's 39% shareholding in Sky plc.

21.8.10.4 Rule 11 and rule 6: consideration

The offeror cannot consider stakebuilding in isolation from the takeover offer itself. The acquisition of a stake may dictate the level (in the case of r 6), or the nature (in the case of r 11) of the consideration the offeror must pay for shares in the offeree company pursuant to the takeover offer. The rationale for these rules is General Principle 1, which provides that shareholders should be treated similarly.

> **EXAMPLE**
>
> Imagine that A plc, seeking to make a takeover bid for Y plc, acquires a stake in Y plc from Shareholder 1 on Monday at £2.00 per share. A plc then announces a takeover offer on Tuesday for the entire issued ordinary share capital of Y plc at a price of £1.95 per share. Shareholder 1 has clearly been given an advantage over the other shareholders. What if A plc had announced a takeover offer on Tuesday for the entire issued ordinary share capital of Y plc where the consideration was shares in A plc? Again, Shareholder 1 has received special treatment. The effect of r 6 and r 11 is to prevent an offeror breaching General Principle 1.

Rule 11

Rule 11.1: cash consideration

The consideration the offeror might offer to the offeree's shareholders is examined at **21.7** above. However, r 11.1 provides that in certain circumstances the offeror *must* offer cash consideration (or a cash alternative).

If:

(a) the offeror (or any concert party) purchased interests in shares in the offeree company, of a class which is now under offer, during the offer period or within 12 months prior to the start of the offer period, and:

  (i) the purchase was *for cash*, and

  (ii) the shares carry 10% or more of the voting rights currently exercisable at a meeting of that class; or

(b) the offeror (or any concert party) purchased interests in voting or non-voting shares in the offeree company, of a class which is now under offer, during the offer period, and the purchase was *for cash*; or

(c) the Panel considers that cash consideration is required in order to give effect to General Principle 1,

then, unless the Panel otherwise agrees, the offer for that class of shares must be in cash, or accompanied by a cash alternative (see **21.7.3**), at not less than the highest price paid by the offeror (or any concert party) for those shares.

Note that the words 'for cash' are very widely defined. Note 5 on r 11 provides that they actually include the situation where the offeror acquired interests in shares in exchange for *securities*, provided the seller of the offeree shares (or the other party to the transaction giving rise to the interest, if the interest is not the sale of the share itself) is not subject to selling restrictions, such as being required to hold the securities received in exchange for the interest in the offeree shares until the offer has lapsed, or the offer consideration has been published to accepting shareholders. If the offer falls within this meaning of 'for cash' then, unless the offeror or its concert parties arranged the immediate placing of those shares, it must also comply with the provisions of r 11.2 (see below).

> **EXAMPLE**
>
> Imagine that A plc intends to make an offer for the entire issued ordinary share capital of Y plc, offering two A plc shares as consideration for each Y plc share. A plc's lawyers will advise that A plc needs to consider whether it has purchased Y plc shares in the past. A plc provides information about its previous purchases of Y plc shares. It acquired a 4% stake at £3 per share 11 months ago, and a 6% stake at £4 per share 8 months ago. The lawyer must advise A plc that the consideration under the offer cannot be two A plc shares as consideration for each Y plc share, as A plc intended. It must be £4.00 per share, in cash, or at least include a cash alternative.

Rule 11.2: paper consideration

Rule 11.2 provides that if:

(a) the offeror (or any concert party) purchased interests in shares in the offeree company, of a class which is now under offer, during the offer period or within three months prior to the start of the offer period; and

(b) the purchase was *in exchange for securities*; and

(c) the shares carry 10% or more of the voting rights currently exercisable at a meeting of that class,

then those securities must be offered to all other holders of shares of that class. As detailed above, an obligation will also arise, under r 11.1, to make an offer in cash, or to provide a cash alternative, unless the exchange falls outside the wide definition of 'for cash' in Note 5 on r 11.1 (because there are some selling restrictions on the seller of the offeree company shares, or, in the case of an interest in offeree company shares, the other party to the transaction giving rise to the interest).

Rule 6: minimum consideration

Rule 6.1

Rule 6.1 provides that, unless the Panel otherwise consents, if:

(a) an offeror (or a person acting in concert with the offeror) (see **22.6.1.2** for the meaning of 'in concert');

(b) has acquired an interest in the offeree company shares (see **21.8.10.5**);

(c) within three months before the beginning of an offer period (see **22.3.4** for the meaning of 'offer period');

(d) or during the period (if any) between the commencement of the offer period and a r 2.7 announcement (see **22.3.4** below);

then the offer to shareholders of the same class must be on the same, or better, terms.

Let us consider the example of A plc bidding for Y plc, referred to above. The effect of r 6 is that A plc will not be able to fix the offer price at £1.95 per share. Instead, A plc must offer the Y plc shareholders at least £2.00 per share under the takeover offer.

Note that the Panel has discretion to extend the three-month period if it considers it is necessary to give effect to General Principle 1 (r 6.1(c)).

Rule 6.2

While r 6.1 covers acquisitions the offeror makes *before* the offer period, r 6.2 covers acquisitions the offeror makes *during* the offer period. Rule 6.2 provides that, if:

(a) an offeror (or a person acting in concert with the offeror);

(b) has acquired an interest in the offeree company shares (see **21.8.10.5**) above the offer price;

(c) after a r 2.7 announcement (see **22.3.3.1**) has been made but before the offer closes for acceptance,

then the offeror must increase its offer to equal the highest price it has paid for the interest in those shares, and, immediately after the purchase, it must announce that the revised offer will be made.

Note that while the example below involves cash consideration, neither r 6.1 nor r 6.2 requires the offer to be in cash. However, any paper consideration offered must, as at the date the offer is announced, have a value equal to the highest price the offeror has paid for the relevant prior purchase of offeree shares. (Note, however, that if r 9 or r 11 also apply, the offer does have to be in cash (or accompanied by a cash alternative); see **21.8.10.3** and below.)

> **EXAMPLE**
>
> Imagine that A plc, having been advised that the offer price must be £2.00, pursuant to r 6.1, announces an offer for Y plc at a price of £2.00 per share on Tuesday. On Wednesday, A acquires some Y shares from Shareholder 2 at a price of £2.00 per share. On Thursday, A acquires some Y shares from Shareholder 3 at £2.05 per share. In breach of General Principle 1, Shareholder 2 has been treated differently from Shareholder 3. A plc must make an announcement, immediately after it acquires the shares from Shareholder 3, that a revised offer will be made in accordance with r 6.2.

Overlap between rules 11 and 6

Note that there is clearly the potential for overlap between r 6 and r 11, as both may apply where the offeror has purchased offeree shares *for cash*. Rules 6.1 and 6.2 provide that, in such a case, usually compliance with r 11 will be regarded as sufficient to satisfy the requirements of r 6.

21.8.10.5 Derivatives and options

In relation to disclosure and stakebuilding, the Takeover Code applies to dealings in derivatives referenced to shares and options over shares, as well as actual shares themselves. These terms are explained below. The effect of this is that the acquisition of 'interests in shares', and not just actual shares, are taken into account for the purposes of rr 5, 6, 9 and 11. In relation to r 4, the definition of 'dealing' includes the taking, granting, acquisition and disposal of an option over securities and a derivative referenced to securities, so if the rule applies, no interests in shares can be acquired.

Derivative

This term is defined in the Takeover Code. Broadly, it is a financial product whose value depends on the performance of an underlying security. An example of a derivative is a contract for differences ('CFD') under which the holder of the CFD benefits from a change in the price of a company's securities from the reference price agreed at the time the CFD is entered into.

Option

An option is the right to buy or sell a share at a fixed price within a particular time-frame.

Interests in shares

This term is defined in the Takeover Code (under 'interests in securities'). It includes:

(a) ownership of shares (para 1, definition of 'interests in securities');

(b) the right to exercise or direct, or having general control of, the voting rights attached to shares (para 2, definition of 'interests in securities');

(c) the right, option, or obligation to acquire shares (para 3, definition of 'interests in securities');

(d) being party to certain derivatives in relation to shares (para 4, definition of 'interests in securities'); and

(e) for the purposes of r 5 only (see **21.8.10.2**), irrevocable commitments (see **21.10**) in relation to shares (para 5, definition of 'interests in securities').

21.9 STAKEBUILDING THRESHOLDS

As the rules relating to stakebuilding are complex, **Table 21.1** below sets out a summary of the significant thresholds, and the consequences for the stakebuilder of acquiring certain stakes.

Table 21.1: Stakebuilding thresholds and consequences

Voting rights in target	Consequences for the stakebuilder
Any amount	Must disclose if issued with a notice under s 793 of CA 2006 (see **15.6**). If within three months prior to, or during, the offer period, any offer must not be on less favourable terms (r 6) (see **21.8.10.4**). If in exchange for cash, during the offer period, and these shares are now under offer, offer must be in cash, or accompanied by a cash alternative (r 11.1) (see **21.8.10.4**). Disclose dealings during an offer period (r 8.1) (see **15.7.4.3**).
1%	Must make Opening Position Disclosure and disclose dealings during an offer period (Dealing Disclosure) (r 8) (see **15.7.4.3**).
3%	Disclose interests to the offeree company (DTR 5 – see **15.5**) and disclose subsequent movements through another percentage point level, or if the interest falls below 3%.
10% or more in exchange for cash in the 12 months prior to an offer period and during the offer period	If shares are voting shares, offer must be in cash, or accompanied by a cash alternative (r 11.1) (see **21.8.10.4**).
10% or more, in exchange for securities, in the 3 months prior to an offer period and during the offer period	Must offer those securities (r 11.2). May also need to make a cash offer, or provide a cash alternative under r 11.1 (see **21.8.10.4**).
25% + 1	Power to block special resolutions. May give rise to a notification requirement under the National Security and Investment Act 2021 (see **Chapter 23**).
30%	May be prohibited from dealing (r 5) (see **21.8.10.2**). May have to make mandatory bid for the offeree (r 9) (see **21.8.10.3**).
50%	Power to block ordinary resolutions.
More than 50%	Power to pass ordinary resolutions. Offer capable of becoming unconditional as to acceptances (r 10) (see **22.4.7.1**). Takeover Code generally no longer applicable. A subsidiary as defined in CA 2006, s 1159.
75%	Power to pass special resolutions.
90% (applies to each class separately)	May be forced to buy the shares of offeree minority shareholders under s 983 of CA 2006 (see **22.7.3**).
90% of shares subject to the offer (applies to each class separately)	Power to purchase minority shareholdings under s 979 of CA 2006 (see **22.7.2**)

21.10 IRREVOCABLE UNDERTAKINGS

How a potential offeror can acquire interests in shares in order to secure some votes in favour of the takeover offer is considered at **21.8** above. As you will appreciate, the restrictions set out at **21.8.6** to **21.8.10** above mean that it is not easy for the potential offeror to do this. In practice, stakebuilding is usually restricted to an acquisition from a single shareholder, or made immediately before the announcement of a recommended offer (see **21.8.10.2**), so that it falls within the exceptions in the Takeover Code.

A more widely used technique, which also enables the potential offeror to improve the chances of success of the takeover offer, is the irrevocable undertaking (also known as an 'irrevocable commitment' or 'lock-up'). This is where the potential offeror obtains undertakings from certain offeree company shareholders (often major shareholders and directors who hold shares), in advance of the announcement of the offer and with the consent of the Panel (r 4.3), that they will accept the offer if it is made (and, sometimes also that they will vote in favour of any resolution that the offeree company may require to progress the offer).

While with stakebuilding the potential offeror knows that certain shares will vote in favour of the offer (because they own interests in those shares), with irrevocable undertakings the potential offeror knows that certain shares will vote in favour of the offer because they have irrevocable undertakings from the shareholders which confirm that they will vote in favour.

Irrevocable undertakings fall into two categories:

(a) Hard irrevocables, which remain binding even if a higher offer is made for the offeree.

(b) Soft irrevocables, which will fall away to allow the shareholder to accept a higher offer which is made (typically one which is at least 10% higher than of the value of the offer to which the irrevocable relates).

The consideration for providing an irrevocable is the promise of the potential offeror to make the offer. As a safeguard against the irrevocable being held void for lack of consideration, the lawyer should ensure that any irrevocable is entered into by way of deed (see **21.10.4**).

If the offeror (or any associate of the offeror – as defined by the Takeover Code) obtains an irrevocable undertaking during an offer period (see **22.3.4**), it must disclose this through an RIS. The details it must disclose are set out in Note 5 on r 8 of the Takeover Code.

The effect of irrevocables on certain other public company issues is considered below.

21.10.1 Stakebuilding

Paragraph 5 of the definition of 'interests in securities' (which also covers 'interests in shares') and the preamble to r 5 confirm that, while irrevocable undertakings will not count towards the 30% shareholding threshold for the purposes of r 9 (see **21.8.10.3** above), they will count towards the 30% threshold for r 5 (see **21.8.10.2** above). Rule 5, therefore, acts as a cap on the level of undertakings the offeror can obtain. If one of the exceptions to r 5 applies, an offeror can obtain irrevocable undertakings over 30% or more of the offeree shares without triggering the r 9 mandatory bid provisions.

Is an irrevocable undertaking an 'interest in shares' for the purposes of rr 5, 6, 9 and 11? The effect of para 9(b) of Note 9 on the definition of 'interests in securities' is that the receipt of an undertaking falls outside the para 3 'right to acquire' category of interests (see **21.8.10.5(c)**). However, if the undertaking allows the offeror general control of the voting rights attached to the shares, the offeror will be treated as interested in those shares under para 2 of the definition of 'interests in securities' (see **21.8.10.5(b)**).

21.10.2 Financial promotion

Seeking an irrevocable undertaking may be capable of comprising an inducement or invitation to enter into investment activity. This means that any communication the company makes in order to persuade someone to provide such an undertaking will constitute a financial promotion under s 21 of the FSMA 2000 (see **Chapter 12**). Therefore the company must ensure that the communication either falls within an exemption (for example, because it is made to a professional investor under art 19 of the FPO 2005, or is a communication in relation to the sale of a body corporate under art 62 of the FPO 2005 – if takeovers do fall within this exemption), or that the communication is made by or authorised by an authorised person.

21.10.3 Insider dealing and market abuse

Giving an irrevocable undertaking may also amount to insider dealing (see **Chapter 11**); however, usually the market information defence (see **11.5.2.2**) will apply, unless the person providing the undertaking has confidential price-sensitive information other than simply knowledge that a takeover is proposed. Similarly, the provision of an irrevocable undertaking can amount to market abuse, but is likely to fall outside the regime under UK MAR, Article 11(2).

21.10.4 Squeeze-out provisions

Shares which are the subject of irrevocable undertakings are not considered to be shares already held by the bidder. Therefore they are 'shares to which the offer relates' and count towards the 90% threshold (see **22.7**) provided that they are entered into by way of deed, or for no consideration, for consideration of negligible value or for no consideration other than the promise of the potential offeror to make the offer (CA 2006, s 975(2)).

21.10.5 Acting in concert

A person who provides an irrevocable undertaking usually is not treated as acting in concert with the offeror or offeree company (Note 9 on the definition of 'acting in concert'). However, if the undertaking allows the offeror or the offeree company to exercise voting rights, or allows the person providing the undertaking to acquire shares, then the Panel should be consulted before the undertaking is given. In its Practice Statement 2008/22, the Panel has advised that where an undertaking on how to vote is given with an irrevocable commitment, it will not normally be acting in concert, provided it is limited to the duration of the offer at the latest and is limited to matters which relate to ensuring that the offer is successful.

21.11 NON-BINDING INDICATIONS OF INTENTION TO ACCEPT

Some shareholders, as a matter of policy, will not provide irrevocable undertakings. Sometimes, however, those shareholders will provide non-binding indications of their intention to accept the offer (also known as 'letters of intent'). While these indications are not legally binding, they can provide further reassurance to the potential offeror that the offer will be successful.

If the offeror (or any associate of the offeror – as defined by the Takeover Code) obtains a letter of intent during the offer period (see **22.3.4**) then, as with an irrevocable undertaking (see **21.10**), it must disclose this through an RIS under r 8.4(a) of the Takeover Code.

21.12 GENERAL OFFER OR SCHEME OF ARRANGEMENT?

The bidder must decide how to structure the takeover. A takeover can be effected by:

(a) a general offer; or

(b) a scheme of arrangement under Pt 26 of the CA 2006.

21.12.1 General offer

This involves the offeror (or the investment bank, on behalf of the offeror) making an offer to acquire shares in the offeree for consideration. As set out at **21.7**, the consideration can take several forms, such as cash, loan notes, shares or other securities. Sometimes the offer gives the offeree shareholders a choice of consideration, such as cash or shares (and under r 9 and, in certain circumstances, r 11.1, the offeror must provide a cash alternative – see **21.8.10** above). The shareholder accepts the offer by returning a form of acceptance (see **22.4.2**).

This structure is suitable for use with both recommended and hostile offers. This book, and in particular **Chapter 22**, focuses on this structure. Rothermere Continuation Ltd's £2.69 billion recommended takeover of Daily Mail and General Trust plc in December 2021 was conducted by way of an offer.

21.12.2 Scheme of arrangement

An alternative way of structuring a recommended takeover is by a scheme of arrangement pursuant to Pt 26 of the CA 2006. They are currently very much in favour as an alternative to a recommended takeover by way of general offer. Typically more than two-thirds of the takeovers currently announced are structured as a scheme of arrangement. Some of the largest recommended takeovers in the last few years were proposed as schemes of arrangement.

The £78.4 billion takeover of the UK brewer, SABMiller plc, by the Belgian company, Anheuser-Busch InBev SA/NV, which completed in October 2016, was effected by a scheme of arrangement. This was the largest ever takeover in the UK to date.

21.12.2.1 What is a scheme of arrangement?

A scheme of arrangement is a court-sanctioned arrangement between a company and its shareholders or creditors. It is a statutory procedure governed by Pt 26 (ss 896 to 901) of the CA 2006. Section 895 of the CA 2006 does not limit the subject matter of the arrangement (although the court's approval must be obtained). There is, therefore, considerable scope for using a scheme (for example, to effect a reorganisation or return or capital). While the section was not drafted with the takeover in mind, it has also come to be used as a way of effecting a takeover.

There is just one form of scheme for takeovers, namely a transfer scheme. A transfer scheme involves the transfer of the existing offeree shares to the offeror, in exchange for the payment of consideration by the offeror to the offeree shareholders. There used to be a second type of scheme, known as a cancellation scheme, but these are no longer legal for takeovers (CA 2006, s 641(2A)).

In theory, the consideration offered by the offeror to the offeree shareholders under a scheme can take any form, as with a general offer. However, given the longer overall timetable of a scheme, underwritten cash offers can prove too expensive.

As the scheme is arranged by, and so requires the cooperation of, the offeree, a scheme is suitable only for a recommended takeover.

Sections 896 to 899 of the CA 2006 set out the following main requirements for a scheme:

(a) *Members' meeting (s 896(1))*. The court will (after an application to the Companies Court by the company) convene a meeting of the offeree shareholders (or the offeree company shareholders of the relevant class, as appropriate). At this meeting, the scheme must be approved by (s 899(1)):
   (i) a majority in number;
   (ii) representing 75% in value of the offeree company shareholders, or class of offeree company shareholders, voting at the meeting (in person or by proxy).

The resolution to approve the scheme must be by way of a poll in order to calculate whether the test referred to at (ii) above has been satisfied. Neither the offeror, nor any shareholder connected with the offeror, can vote. This means the offeror cannot increase its chances of success by stakebuilding and/or obtaining irrevocable undertakings.

(b) *Explanatory statement (s 897(1) and (2)).* The offeree company must send an explanatory statement to its shareholders together with the notice of meeting. The statement should explain the effect of the scheme, and set out any material interests of directors and the effect of the scheme on those interests. The statement must be fair and, as far as possible, give all information reasonably necessary to enable the offeree shareholders to make an informed decision how to vote.

(c) *Court approval (s 899).* The scheme must obtain not only the approval of the offeree company shareholders, referred to at (a) above, but also the approval of the court. The court considers four matters when deciding whether to sanction the scheme, that:

(i) the provisions of the CA 2006 have been complied with;

(ii) the class of shareholders who could attend the meeting was fairly represented and there was a majority acting bona fide and not coercing the minority;

(iii) an intelligent, honest member of the class concerned acting in their own interests might reasonably approve the scheme; and

(iv) there was no 'blot' on the scheme. (*Re TDG plc* [2008] EWHC 2334 (Ch))

A copy of the court order must be filed at Companies House. The scheme takes effect on delivery of the order to Companies House or, if the court orders, on its registration by Companies House. The scheme will then bind the offeree company, its shareholders and the offeror (who will have agreed to be bound by it).

21.12.2.2 The Takeover Code

Paragraph 3(b) of the Introduction to the Takeover Code confirms that the Takeover Code governs a scheme of arrangement. Typically certain modifications to the Code will be required for a scheme (for example, as the scheme requires the involvement of the court, it may not be possible to adhere strictly to the timetable requirements set out in the Takeover Code). Appendix 7 to the Takeover Code sets out the modifications to the Takeover Code which apply as a result of the takeover being effected by way of a scheme. It also lists those provisions of the Takeover Code which do not apply to a scheme.

21.12.2.3 Advantages of a scheme

A scheme has the following advantages over a general offer:

(a) A scheme requires a smaller percentage of offeree shareholder support (see **21.12.2.1(a)**), in order to obtain 100% control of the offeree company, than a general offer (where the offeror must acquire not less than 90% in value of the shares to which the offer relates – see **22.7.2.1**).

(b) Once the requisite majority of shareholders has approved the scheme, all shareholders are bound by it (with a general offer the offeror must compulsorily acquire the remaining 10% under s 979 of the CA 2006.

(c) Usually a scheme is quicker than a general offer in reaching the stage where all offeree company shareholders are bound. In the case of a general offer, the compulsory acquisition procedure can increase the timetable considerably. (However, overall, a scheme tends to take longer to effect – see **21.12.2.4(c)**.)

(d) A scheme is not deemed to be an offer to the public for the purposes of Article 3(1) of the UK Prospectus Regulation [s 85(1) of the FSMA 2000] (but nevertheless a prospectus will be required if the offeror shares will be admitted to trading and none of the exemptions to Article 3(3) of the UK Prospectus Regulation [s 85(2)] apply).

21.12.2.4 Disadvantages of a scheme

(a) A scheme cannot be used with a hostile offer (the application to court is made by the offeree company).

(b) It is more difficult to revise a scheme than a general offer, given the requirement for court approval.

(c) The requirement for court approval, filed at Companies House, means it can takes longer to effect the takeover than with a general offer (but see **21.12.2.3(c)**).

(d) There is more time for a competing bidder to intervene (unlike a general offer, a scheme cannot be declared unconditional on Day 21 – see **22.5.2**).

(e) Stakebuilding and irrevocable undertakings will not increase the offeror's chances of success (see **21.12.2.1(a)**).

(f) The offeree company controls the timing and implementation of the scheme (this may be a disadvantage from the offeror's perspective).

(g) A scheme involves greater costs (but see **21.2.2.3(e)**).

21.13 DEAL PROTECTION

If the offer is recommended, then the lawyer will be involved in drafting various documents to try to ensure that the takeover completes, and to protect their client's interest in the event that it does not. The documents are as follows:

(a) heads of agreement;

(b) exclusivity agreement;

(c) confidentiality agreement;

(d) standstill agreement; and

(e) (in rare cases) break fee letter.

The exclusivity, confidentiality and standstill agreements are often incorporated into one agreement. Brief details of the documents are set out at **21.13.1** to **21.13.5** below.

21.13.1 Heads of agreement

This agreement is also referred to as heads of terms, a letter of intent or a memorandum of understanding. It is not legally binding, but aims to record the parties' agreement in relation to certain fundamental issues at an early stage in negotiations. Key issues which it addresses include:

(a) the parties;

(b) the shares which are to be acquired;

(c) consideration;

(d) the extent of the due diligence exercise;

(e) major terms and conditions;

(f) timing; and

(g) choice of law and jurisdiction.

21.13.2 Exclusivity agreement

This agreement is also referred to as a lock-out agreement. Its aim is to prevent a party negotiating with a third party for a certain period. In *Walford v Miles* [1992] 2 WLR 174, it was held that while this type of agreement is enforceable, an agreement which seeks to force a party to negotiate (a 'lock-in' agreement) would not be enforceable. This means the effect of an exclusivity is persuasive only; it will encourage (but not compel) a party to persevere with negotiations rather than start negotiations with another third party who may appear offering a better deal (as the agreement will prevent such negotiations within a certain time).

21.13.3 Confidentiality agreement

This agreement will set out the terms to govern the passing of confidential information from one party to another. It will provide what happens to the information if the deal falls through (usually that the information and any copies must be returned, but sometimes that it must be destroyed), and what will happen in the event of a breach of the agreement.

21.13.4 Standstill letter

A standstill agreement aims to prevent a recommended offeror from being able to launch a hostile offer. It will provide that the potential offeror will not buy any shares in the offeree for a specified period without the offeree's consent.

21.13.5 Break fee letter

The exclusivity, confidentiality and standstill arrangements referred to above are often recorded in a single agreement. Also known as an inducement fee, a break fee is a sum paid by one party to another on the occurrence of a specified event leading to the deal falling through, such as the directors of the offeree company failing to recommend the offer, or the offeree company shareholders failing to pass any necessary resolutions. An example of this is shown in the September 2008 £12.5 billion takeover of British Energy Group plc, listed on the Stock Exchange, by EDF. Each party agreed to pay a break fee of £50 million to the other. British Energy's fee was payable in two instalments. The first instalment of £20 million was payable if the directors did not unanimously recommend acceptance of EDF's offer, or withdrew their recommendations or recommended a competing offer. The second instalment of £30 million would have been payable if a competing offer was successful. Although no fee needed to be paid in the British Energy/EDF takeover, one example where it did was a failed takeover (not under the Takeover Code) by Prudential (listed on the Main Market) for AIG in Asia. Prudential's withdrawal of its bid resulted in its having to pay £153 million under its break fee.

The lawyer must be aware of the law relating to directors' statutory, common law and equitable duties, the financial assistance provisions of s 678 of the CA 2006 (see **Chapter 16**) and r 21.2 of the Takeover Code when drafting a break fee arrangement. Guidance on the application of r 21.2 to break fees can be found both in the notes on r 21.2 and in Practice Statement 2008/23. Details of any break fee must also be provided in the r 2.5 announcement of the offer (see **22.3.3.1(g)**).

Break fees used to be an integral part of a recommended takeover. However, following the review of the Takeover Code in light of the Cadbury takeover (see **20.5.7.4** above), they were generally prohibited with effect from 19 September 2011. There were concerns that break fees were acting as a disincentive to boards of offeree companies to recommend possible competing offers, this being contrary to the spirit of GP 3 and r 21. It was thought that break fees could have been causing a competing offeror to have been put off from making an offer by the cost of the break fee payable by the offeree company.

Rule 21.2(a) of The Takeover Code prohibits 'offer-related arrangements' between the offeree (and persons acting in concert) and the offeror during the offer period or when an offer is reasonably in contemplation. The prohibited arrangements are defined in r 21.2(b) and include arrangements having a similar effect to break fees. Rule 21.2(b) also excludes certain arrangements from the prohibition, including those relating to confidentiality and the non-solicitation of employees, customers or suppliers. In a couple of cases, though, a break fee can still be used despite the general prohibition. The most relevant for our purposes is in the context of a hostile offer when subsequently a preferred competing offeror also makes an offer which the offeree board then accepts (such an offeror is known as a 'white knight'). A break fee can be entered into by the white knight and the offeree, provided it does not exceed 1% of the value of the offer and other conditions are met (Note 1 to r 21.2). It is important to note that the offeree board's decisions to enter into a break fee (if permitted) and also which competing offer to recommend, if any, are still subject to their overriding duties as directors under the CA 2006 and other legal controls such as those on financial assistance.

CHAPTER 22

THE TAKEOVER PROCESS

22.1 INTRODUCTION

Chapter 20 considered the rules and regulations which can apply to a takeover. **Chapter 21** explained that a substantial part of the lawyer's work on a takeover is undertaken before the offer is announced, to ensure that, once announced, the offer will run smoothly. This chapter looks at what happens after that.

22.2 TIMETABLE

Table 22.1 below sets out a typical timetable for a takeover offer. Note that the events which typically relate to hostile bids only are italicised. This chapter explains in more detail what happens at each stage, but it is useful to consider the timetable at the outset, as it provides an overview of the process.

The Takeover Code sets out the timetable of the offer by reference to the date on which the offeror publishes the offer document. Under r 31.4 there are a number of situations which might alter this timetable, including:

(a) a rival offer is launched (Note 1 on r 31.3 provides that, usually, the timetable of the original offer will default to that of the later offer);

(b) if the board of the offeree company consents to an extension; and

(c) no official authorisation or regulatory clearance decision (eg from a competition authority) has been reached by 5pm on Day 37 (the Panel will usually grant permission to freeze the timetable until the decision is announced) (r 31.4(a) and (b)).

Note also that the offer must include a 'long-stop date' on which the offer will end. For the circumstances when this is relevant, see **22.4.7.4** below.

22.3 ANNOUNCING THE OFFER

The lawyers will have worked extremely hard to plan the bid. The culmination of this work is when the offer is ready to announce. This is an exciting time, but again the lawyers need to make sure that the announcement is made pursuant to the provisions of the Takeover Code.

22.3.1 Timing

Chapter 21 explained that a considerable amount of the work required to plan a takeover happens behind closed doors. How does an offeror know when to open those doors and announce the bid?

Table 22.1: Timetable for a takeover offer

Date	Event	Rule
Before the announcement	Due diligence by offeror Approach offeree board Draft documents Obtain any irrevocable undertakings Build stake in offeree company Possibly make r 2.4 announcement (if so, the offer period will begin)	1 and 2.2 to 2.8
D – 28 (Announcement day)	Announce the offer under r 2.7 (earliest date) (if no prior r 2.4 announcement, the offer period will begin)	2.2 to 2.8
DAY 0	**Offeror publishes, displays, sends and announces offer document (and forms of acceptance) (normally within 28 days of r 2.7 announcement)** **Market purchases now count towards CA 2006, s 979**	24.1 and 30
D + 14	*Offeree dispatches, displays and announces first defence document if offer is hostile (latest date)*	25.1
D + 21	Earliest date on which the offer can be declared unconditional (ie offeror wins control) or the offeror wishes to end the offer (due to insufficient acceptances)	31.2(a)
By 8am, the business day after Day 21	Announce acceptance levels Announce any extension of the offer	17.1
D + 32	If offer suspended (see Day +37) timetable resumes here if authorisation/regulatory clearance condition satisfied	31.4(b)
D + 37 (by 5pm)	Timetable suspended if authorisation/regulatory clearance outstanding	31.4(a)
D + 39	*Latest date for offeree to release any material new information*	31.8
D + 46	*Latest date for offeror to improve offer*	32.1(c)
D + 53 (by 5pm)	*Latest date for a potential competing offeror to either announce the competing offer under r 2.7 or confirm it won't make an offer under r 2.8*	2.6(d) and (e)
By midnight, D + 60	Latest date for offeror to fulfil all conditions including acceptance condition (ie wins control) and declare the offer 'unconditional'	31.1(a)
D + 74 (assuming offer declared unconditional on D + 60)	Earliest date offer can close Latest date to post consideration to offeree shareholders	31.2(b) 31.9

Rule 1(a) provides that, when the offeror is ready to announce the bid, it must first put forward the offer to the offeree board or its advisers. Rule 2.2 then provides that where the offeror has notified the board of the offeree company of a firm intention to make an offer, this triggers the requirement for an announcement. The announcement must be made via an RIS (r 30.1). Note that a 'firm intention' excludes mere expressions of interest by a possible offeror. The obligation to announce arises only when, in accordance with r 2.7, the offeror has every reason to believe it can proceed with the offer. Financing must therefore be in place before this can be achieved. Subject to UK MAR, Article 17(4) (see **7.5.2.9**), an announcement will also be required pursuant to the general obligation under UK MAR, Article 17(1) (see **7.5.1**). In practice, the announcement required by r 2.2 will satisfy both obligations.

If everything goes to plan, the offeror will notify the offeree company board and then the offer will be announced under r 2.7 once it has been put together. In these circumstances, it is the offeree company's obligation to make the announcement (r 2.3(c)). In a hostile bid (see **21.2.2**), typically the offeror will seek to keep the amount of time, between putting the offer to the board and releasing the press announcement, to a bare minimum, and will telephone the offeree company's Chair just minutes before releasing the r 2.7 press announcement. This ensures that the offeree company is as ill-prepared as possible to deal with the takeover offer (and the offeree company's lawyers will have to get up to speed with the details of the offer from a standing start).

The obligation to announce the offer under r 2.2 can also arise in other circumstances, namely:

(a) there is an acquisition which gives rise to a r 9 mandatory bid (see **21.8.10.3** above);

(b) if the offeror has approached the board (but has not notified the offeree company board of a firm intention to make the offer) and the offeree company is then the subject of rumour and speculation, or there is an 'untoward' movement in its share price (the Panel will interpret 'untoward') (this is dealt with further in r 2.4 – see **22.3.3.2**);

(c) if the offeror has not even approached the board, but the offeree company is the subject of rumour and speculation, or there is an untoward movement in its share price, and there are reasonable grounds for concluding that it is the potential offeror's actions which have led to the situation (this is dealt with further in r 2.4 – see **22.3.3.2**);

(d) negotiations are about to be extended beyond the parties and their immediate advisers (see **21.3** above); or

(e) the offeree company is seeking a buyer for an interest or interests in 30% or more of its voting shares and there is either rumour and speculation, or an 'untoward' movement (as determined by the Panel) in the share price, or the number of potential purchasers approached is about to exceed a very restricted number.

You will note that rumour and speculation can lead to the need for the offer to be announced. This explains why secrecy is paramount in the preparation of any bid (see **21.3**), as the offeror will want to avoid having to announce its intentions before it is ready.

Note 1 on r 2.2 provides that parties should consult the Panel if they are in doubt as to whether an announcement is required. It is common for the Panel to be consulted in relation to (d) above in particular, as parties may wish to seek irrevocable undertakings (see **21.10**) or non-binding indications of intention to accept (see **21.11**) without triggering an obligation to announce the offer.

The Panel has reprimanded publicly financial advisers who have decided that no announcement is necessary without first consulting the Panel (see, for example, Panel Statement 2004/9, criticising Nabarro Wells & Co, financial adviser to Transcomm plc, which became the subject of a bid by British Telecommunications plc). However, if it is obvious that an announcement is required, the parties should not use consultation as a delaying tactic (see Panel Statement 2008/20).

22.3.2 Responsibility

Who is responsible for making the announcement in the circumstances listed at (a) to (e) above? Rule 2.3 of the Takeover Code provides that if the announcement is required before the offeror has approached the offeree company (which most likely will arise under r 2.2(c) due to rumour and speculation), or a r 9 obligation has arisen (see (a) above), responsibility for making the announcement lies with the offeror. If the announcement is required after the offeror has approached the offeree company, then responsibility lies with the offeree company. However, Panel Statement 2008/20 provides that if the offeror's approach has been rejected before the announcement is required, usually responsibility for making the announcement will revert back to the offeror.

22.3.3 Method

Rule 2.2 requires that an announcement should be made. To what type of announcement does this refer? There are two options:

(a) the announcement of a firm intention to make an offer (r 2.7); and
(b) the announcement of a possible offer (r 2.4).

22.3.3.1 The announcement of a firm intention to make an offer

The ideal scenario is that the announcement triggered by r 2.2 will be of a firm intention to make an offer. This is often referred to as the 'Rule 2.7 announcement', or the 'press announcement'. The potential offeror can make this announcement only after the most careful and responsible consideration, and only if it has every reason to believe that it can, and will continue to be able to, implement the offer (r 2.7(a)). It must also be certain that it can fulfil any cash consideration, and has taken all reasonable measures to secure the implementation of any other type of consideration (General Principle 5); in other words, it must have decided what consideration it will offer, and its financing arrangements must be in place. If it has any doubts, it must make a r 2.4 announcement rather than a r 2.7 announcement (see **22.3.3.2** below).

The r 2.7 announcement is a key document. Typically, it is the first public document to contain details of the offer. It is vital, therefore, that it contains the right message. As well as complying with r 2.7, there are certain conventions as to the matters which the announcement will address.

Content

Rule 2.7 sets out the content requirements of the announcement. The main requirements include:

(a) the terms of the offer;
(b) the identity of the offeror;
(c) the conditions or pre-conditions of the offer (including details of any circumstances where the offeror cannot invoke the conditions or pre-conditions);
(d) details of any dealing arrangements involving the offeror or concert parties for relevant securities (as defined by the Takeover Code; see **15.7.4.3**);
(e) details of any relevant securities of the offeree company in which the offeror or any person acting in concert with it has an interest or in respect of which it has a right to subscribe;
(f) details of any irrevocable undertakings (see **21.10** above);
(g) details of any offer-related arrangements under r 21.2 (see **21.13.5** above);
(h) a list of documents which must be published on a website under r 26.2 and the website address, and the website on which the r 2.7 announcement will be published; and
(i) if the offer is for cash, or includes an element of cash, confirmation by the offeror's financial adviser that the offeror's resources are sufficient to make the offer (known as the 'cash confirmation').

Publication

Rule 30.1 governs the publication of any r 2.7 announcement. The announcement must be published via an RIS. If the announcement is submitted outside normal business hours, it must also be distributed to at least two newswire services in the UK.

Rule 2.11 sets out what must be done following the publication under r 30.1. The offeree company must send a copy of the announcement (or a circular summarising the terms and conditions of the offer, together with a r 8 summary – see **15.7.4.3**) promptly to its shareholders, persons with information rights under s 146 of the CA 2006 and the Panel (r 2.11(b)(i) and (c)). In practice, the offeree company tends to send the announcement itself rather than a circular, so will arrange for a glossy version of it to be published for this purpose. This can be sent in hardcopy form, electronically or published on a website (r 30.2).

The offeror and offeree company must also make the announcement (or circular) available to their respective employee representatives (or, if there are none, to their employees) and to the trustees of its pension scheme (r 2.11(b)(ii)). If the company has chosen to distribute a circular rather than the announcement itself, nevertheless the announcement must be made readily and promptly available to them (and the circular must include a website address on which the announcement will be posted, such as the offeror or offeree company's website) (Note 1 on r 2.11).

Where necessary, the offeror or offeree company, as the case may be, should explain the implications of the announcement and, for an offeree company, the fact that contact information may be provided to the offeror (to enable it to send information) (r 2.11(c)).

If there has been no r 2.4 announcement then the publication of the r 2.7 announcement will start the offer period and the offeree company must make the disclosure required by r 2.9 (details of all classes of relevant securities issued by the offeree company). The offeror must also do this unless the offer is wholly for cash (see **15.7.4.3**).

Effect

Once the offeror has made a r 2.7 announcement, r 2.7(b) provides that it must proceed with the offer (unless the offer is stated to be subject to a pre-condition which, in accordance with the provisions of r 13.5, has not been met, or is subject to a condition which could be invoked if the offer were made). In other words, once the r 2.7 announcement is made, usually there is no going back. The only way an offer can be withdrawn is with the consent of the Panel, if a competing offeror subsequently announces a firm intention to make a higher offer. Panel Statements 2007/25, 2007/23 and 2007/13 give an example of how strictly this rule is applied in practice. An offeror's attempt to withdraw its offer for Freeport plc was rejected by the Panel, which ordered an offer to be made. However, in October 2007, the Panel did allow the offeror for Telent plc the right to withdraw its offer. This was due to exceptional intervention by the Government in the offeree to protect Telent plc's pension fund. Ultimately, the offeror proceeded with the offer.

22.3.3.2 The announcement of a possible offer

If the potential offeror must issue an announcement under r 2.2 but is not in a position to issue a r 2.7 announcement then, as a temporary measure, it, or the offeree company, may issue what is known as a 'possible offer announcement' under r 2.4.

Content

An extract from a possible offer announcement is set out below. As you can see, the announcement will contain limited information, such as a potential offeree company announcing that talks are in progress with a potential offeror, or a potential offeror announcing that it is considering making an offer for a potential offeree company. Crucially any announcement of a possible offer by the offeree company must usually include the identity of the potential offeror under r 2.4(a). This is important, because usually it will trigger a deadline by which the offeror must announce a r 2.7 firm announcement (see 'Effect' below). The announcement should also include the deadline required by r 2.6(a) (see 'Effect' below) and a summary of the provisions of r 8 (see **15.7.4.3**).

Company	HBOS PLC
TIDM	HBOS
Headline	HBOS in Talks with LLoyds TSB
Released	13:25 17-Sep-08
Number	6588D13

In the light of market speculation, the Board of HBOS plc confirms that it is in advanced talks with Lloyds TSB Group plc which may or may not lead to an offer being made for HBOS.

A further announcement will be made when appropriate.

Publication

A r 2.4 announcement must be published under r 30.1 in exactly the same way as a r 2.7 announcement (see **22.3.3.1**).

As the r 2.4 announcement will start the offer period (see **22.3.4**), the offeree company must also:

(a) send the announcement to its shareholders, persons with information rights under s 146 of the CA 2006 and the Panel under r 2.11(a); and

(b) make the disclosure required by r 2.9 (see **15.7.4.3**). (The offeror must also do this unless the offer is wholly for cash.)

Effect

A typical example of when a holding announcement is required is if there has been a leak which breaches the secrecy requirement under r 2.1, and which starts rumours that trigger the requirement for an announcement under r 2.2.

Even though the leak may have occurred at a very early stage in planning the offer, once the potential offeror or offeree has made a r 2.4 announcement, in which the potential offeror is identified as required, then subject to an extension being granted by the Panel, the potential offeror has 28 days to 'put up or shut up'. This means that the potential offeror has 28 days from the announcement within which it must make either a r 2.7 announcement (ie that it definitely will proceed with an offer for the offeree company), or a statement under r 2.8 that it does not intend to make an offer (r 2.6(a)). This can leave an under-prepared offeror with little choice but to make a r 2.8 statement. This again can help to protect an offeree company from unwanted hostile offers as the potential offeror may not be ready or able to launch a takeover (including arranging the finance) within the 28 days. An example of a 'put up or shut up' notice is set out below.

Company	Sportingbet PLC
TIDM	SBT
Headline	Statement re approach by William Hill and GVC
Released	11:17 01-Oct-2012
Number	5849N11

Statement by the Board of Sportingbet regarding the approach by William Hill plc ('William Hill') and GVC Holdings plc ('GVC')

Sportingbet notes the recent press speculation regarding the approach by William Hill and GVC. The Board of Sportingbet confirms that it has received an indicative offer from William Hill and GVC of 52.5 pence comprising of 45 pence in cash from William Hill and 7.5 pence in shares in GVC. The Board of Sportingbet has responded that this indicative offer significantly undervalues the business and its future prospects.

> This announcement is made without the consent of the potential offerors. There can be no certainty that an offer will be made nor as to the terms on which any offer might be made.
>
> A further announcement will be made in due course.
>
> In accordance with Rule 2.6(a) of the City Code on Takeovers and Mergers (the 'Code'), William Hill and GVC are required, by not later than 5.00 p.m. on 16 October 2012, to either announce a firm intention to make an offer for Sportingbet in accordance with Rule 2.7 of the Code or announce that they do not intend to make an offer, in which case the announcement will be treated as a statement to which Rule 2.8 of the Code applies. This deadline can be extended with the consent of the Panel in accordance with Rule 2.6(c) of the Code.
>
> A copy of this announcement will be available at www.sportingbetplc.com. The content of the website referred to in this announcement is not incorporated into and does not form part of this announcement.

The offeree board can approach the Panel to ask it to extend this 28-day period, and will normally grant this in accordance with r 2.6(c). The usual reason for requesting an extension in these circumstances will be when the offeree board needs more time to negotiate a possible recommended offer with the potential offeror.

22.3.3.3 Statement of intention not to make an offer

The effect of a r 2.8 statement is that the potential offeror (or any concert party) must 'down tools'. It will not be able to:

(a) make another offer for the offeree company;

(b) acquire any interest in shares in the offeree company which would trigger a r 9 mandatory bid (see **21.8.10.3** above);

(c) acquire any interest in, or procure an irrevocable undertaking (see **21.10**) in respect of, shares in the offeree company which, when aggregated with the shares of other concert parties, would carry 30% or more of the voting rights in the offeree company;

(d) make any statement which raises or confirms the possibility that an offer might be made for the offeree company;

(e) take any steps to prepare a possible offer for the offeree company where knowledge of the possible offer might extend beyond the offeror and its immediate advisers; or

(f) purchase, agree to purchase, or make any statement which raises or confirms the possibility that it is interested in purchasing assets which are significant in relation to the offeree company;

for six months from the date of the r 2.8 statement, unless:

(i) it has the consent of the Panel;

(ii) the board of the offeree company agrees to the statement being set aside; or

(iii) another offeror makes an r 2.7 announcement for the offeree; or

(iv) the offeree announces a 'Rule 9 waiver' under Note 1 on Dispensations from Rule 9 or a reverse takeover; or

(v) there is a material change of circumstances; or

(vi) an event has occurred which the potential offeror specified in the r 2.8 statement as an event which would enable the statement to be set aside.

These requirements are onerous (in fact, they mirror those which apply under r 35.1 to a failed bid (see **22.6.1.1**), albeit for a shorter period). Practice Statement 2014/28 provides guidance on when the Panel will grant consent to an approach before the expiry of the six-month period.

Much can happen to the fortunes of a potential offeror and offeree company during this six-month period, and of course the potential offeror can no longer launch a surprise offer, so a r 2.8 statement can mean the end of any takeover offer plans. Now it may be clearer why so much care is taken to ensure that the r 2.1 secrecy obligation (see **21.3**) is not breached.

Rule 2.8 will apply to any statement to the effect that the company does not intend to make an offer. The lawyer should advise the board not to make such a statement, simply with a view to keeping its intentions secret, if in fact it does intend to make an offer (and, in particular, warn about the severe implications of r 2.8 before the board members give interviews to the media).

An extract of a r 2.8 statement follows.

Company	Coms PLC
TIDM	
	COMS
Headline	Statement re Possible Offer
Released	14:18 03-Sep-2013
Number	1342N14

COMS PLC

("Coms" or the "Company")

Statement Regarding a Possible Offer

3 September 2013

The Board of Coms plc (the "Board") notes the recent share price movement in the shares of Pinnacle Technology Group plc ("Pinnacle") and confirms that it is considering a possible corporate transaction with Pinnacle that could result in an offer by Coms for the entire issued and to be issued ordinary share capital of Pinnacle being made. In the event that an indicative offer is made, it is the current expectation of the Board that any such indicative offer would be at or around 21p per Pinnacle share.

This is an announcement falling under Rule 2.4 of the City Code on Takeovers and Mergers (the "Code"). It does not represent a firm intention to make an offer under Rule 2.7 of the Code. Discussions are at a very preliminary stage and accordingly, there can be no certainty that any transaction or offer for Pinnacle will ultimately be forthcoming.

In accordance with Rule 2.6(a) of the Code, Coms must, by not later than 5.00pm on 30 September 2013, either announce a firm intention to make an offer for the Company in accordance with Rule 2.7 of the Code or announce that it does not intend to make an offer, in which case the announcement will be treated as a statement to which Rule 2.8 of the Code applies. This deadline will only be extended with the consent of the Takeover Panel in accordance with Rule 2.6(c) of the Code.

A further announcement will be made when appropriate.

22.3.4 The offer period

The offer period will begin:

(a) when the offeror makes either a r 2.7 announcement of a firm intention to make an offer (see **22.3.3.1**), or a r 2.4 announcement of a possible offer (see **22.3.3.2**); or

(b) when a company announces that shares carrying 30% or more of the voting rights in the company are for sale, or that the board is seeking potential offerors.

When an offer begins, the offeree company and, unless the offer is wholly for cash, the offeror, must make the disclosure required by r 2.9 (see **15.7.4.3**).

The offer period will end:

(a) on Day 21 (a minimum of 21 days from the date the offeror publishes the offer document – see **22.5.2**); or

(b) if later, the date the offer becomes or is declared unconditional (see **22.5.3**); or

(c) all announced offers have been withdrawn or lapsed (see **22.4.7** and **22.5.7**) or all potential offerors have made r 2.8 statements (see **22.3.3.3**).

The Disclosure Table on the Panel's website lists all the companies which are currently in an offer period and offerors and potential offerors.

22.4 THE OFFER

22.4.1 The offer document

The offer document is the principal document that the lawyer must draft in relation to a takeover offer.

22.4.1.1 Nature

The offer document is addressed to the offeree shareholders. It makes the formal contractual offer to acquire their shares in the offeree. It will constitute a financial promotion under s 21 of the FSMA 2000 (see **Chapter 12**) and will therefore have to be approved by a financial adviser who is an authorised person (see **12.2**).

22.4.1.2 Timing

While the offer period can begin with either a r 2.4 or a r 2.7 announcement, the offer timetable will start to run with effect from the r 2.7 announcement. Rule 24.1(a) provides that the offeror normally has 28 days from the date of the r 2.7 announcement in which to send the offer document to shareholders and persons with information rights under s 146 of the CA 2006. In practice, however, it is unlikely that the offeror will want to leave 28 days between making the announcement and sending the offer document. This is because the offeror will want the offeree company shareholders to be reading its offer document, not that of any other offeror who announces a rival offer and sends an offer document during this 28-day period. However, the offeror may only publish an offer document within the 14 days following announcement of its firm intention to make an offer with the consent of the board of the offeree company (r 24.1(a)).

In the timetable at **Table 22.1**, the day the offer document is sent is referred to as 'D day', and other dates in the offer timetable are calculated from this day.

22.4.1.3 Publication

Before it is published the document must be sent in electronic form to the Panel (r 30.5). In Response Statement 2005/5 the Code Committee confirmed that it will continue to be acceptable where, under the direction of a financial adviser, the document is sent to the Panel at the same time it is sent to the offeree shareholders.

The offer document is then published. The Takeover Code requires the offeror to:

(a) send the offer document to the offeree company shareholders and persons with information rights under s 146 of the CA 2006 (r 24.1(a));

(b) publish the offer document on a website, in accordance with r 26.1, on the date it sends the document to offeree company shareholders (r 24.1(c)(i));

(c) announce to an RIS, in accordance with r 30.1, that it has displayed the document, and where (r 24.1(c)(ii));

(d) make the document readily available to its employee representatives, and if there are none, to its employees (the offeree company must also do this) and to the trustees of the offeree's pension scheme (r 24.1(b)); and

(e) send the document in electronic form to the advisers of the other parties to the offer (r 30.5(a)).

Note that under r 30.2 a document, announcement or other information (including the offer document) is deemed sent to a person under the Takeover Code if it is sent in hard copy or electronic form to them or it is published on a website provided a notification of website publication is sent to that person. This applies to both the offeror and the offeree. There are a number of exceptions to this:

(a) The Note on r 30.2 states that only hard copy versions are acceptable for acceptance forms (see **22.4.3**), withdrawal forms (see **22.5.5.1**), proxy forms and other forms required in the offer.

(b) Rule 30.3(a) allows persons sent documents electronically or by website publication to request that the documents be sent to them in hard copy.

(c) Certain rules, such as r 30.5(a), expressly state the method of communication, in that case electronic. Website publication alone would therefore not be sufficient.

However, when an offeror or offeree sends the document, announcement or information, it must put a copy on its website under r 26.1 by midday of the next business day (subject to certain exemptions in Note 7). The document must be in a 'read-only' format to prevent alterations being made (Note 3).

Note 4 on r 26 extends the obligation to putting documents on a website accessible to shareholders outside the UK unless there is an objectively good reason not to.

22.4.1.4 Content

Rule 24 (and, for a recommended offer, also r 25) sets out the detailed content requirements of the offer document. Typically, it will include the following:

(a) a section (sometimes in the form of a letter from the Chair of the offeror), which explains the rationale of the offer and urges the offeree shareholders to accept it;

(b) a letter from the Chair of the offeree company (under r 25.2 of the Takeover Code), which recommends the offer to the offeree shareholders (if the offer is recommended: if not, see **22.4.2** below);

(c) a formal letter from the offeror making the offer and setting out the principal terms and other important information;

(d) a detailed appendix setting out the full terms and conditions of the offer;

(e) a detailed appendix setting out the information relating to the offeror which is required by r 24 of the Takeover Code and, if the offer is recommended, the information relating to the offeree company which is required by r 25 of the Takeover Code; and

(f) information about how the offeree company shareholders can accept the offer.

An example of the front page of an offer document is set out below.

> **THIS DOCUMENT IS IMPORTANT AND REQUIRES YOUR IMMEDIATE ATTENTION. If you are in any doubt as to the action you should take, you are recommended to seek your own personal financial advice immediately from your stockbroker, bank manager, solicitor, accountant or other independent professional adviser duly authorised under the Financial Services and Markets Act 2000 if you are resident in the UK or, if not, from another appropriately authorised independent financial adviser.**
>
> If you have sold or otherwise transferred all of your Amstrad Shares, please forward this document, together with the Form of Acceptance, at once to the purchaser or transferee or to the stockbroker, bank or other agent through whom the sale or transfer was effected, for onward transmission to the purchaser or transferee. However, these documents should not be forwarded or transmitted in or into any jurisdiction in which such act would constitute a violation of the relevant laws of such jurisdiction. If you have sold or otherwise transferred only part of your holding of Amstrad Shares, you should retain these documents and consult the stockbroker, bank or other agent through whom the sale or transfer was effected.
>
> **The distribution of this document into jurisdictions other than the United Kingdom may be restricted by the laws of those jurisdictions and therefore any person into whose possession this document comes should inform themselves about, and observe, any such restrictions. Failure to comply with any such restrictions may constitute a violation of the securities law of any such jurisdiction.**

Recommended Cash Offer
by Sky Digital Supplies Limited
a wholly-owned subsidiary of
British Sky Broadcasting Group plc
for Amstrad plc

Your attention is drawn to the letter of recommendation from the Chairman of Amstrad, set out on pages 3 to 7 of this document, which explains why the Amstrad Directors are unanimously recommending acceptance of the Offer.

The procedure for acceptance of the Offer is set out on pages 15 to 18 of this document and in the Form of Acceptance. If you hold Amstrad Shares in certificated form, to accept the Offer, the Form of Acceptance should be completed, signed and returned in accordance with the instructions printed on it as soon as possible and, in any event, so as to be received by Capita Registrars no later than 3:00 p.m. on 21 August 2007. If you hold Amstrad Shares in uncertificated form, to accept the Offer, you should comply with the procedure for acceptances set out on pages 16 to 18 of this document and ensure that an electronic acceptance is made which settles no later than 3:00 p.m. on 21 August 2007. If you are a CREST sponsored member, you must refer to your CREST sponsor as only your CREST sponsor will be able to send the necessary TTE instruction to CRESTCo.

Merrill Lynch is acting exclusively as financial adviser to Sky and Sky Digital Supplies and no one else in connection with the Offer and the matters referred to in this document. Merrill Lynch will not be responsible to any person other than Sky and Sky Digital Supplies for providing the protections afforded to customers of Merrill Lynch, nor for providing advice in relation to the Offer or any other matters referred to in this document.

Rothschild is acting exclusively for Amstrad and no one else in connection with the Offer and the matters referred to in this document. Rothschild will not be responsible to any person other than Amstrad for providing the protections afforded to customers of Rothschild, nor for providing advice in relation to the Offer or any other matters referred to in this document.

The Loan Notes will not be listed on any stock exchange and have not been, and will not be, registered under the United States Securities Act of 1933, as amended, or under any relevant securities laws of any state of the United States and the relevant clearances have not been, and will not be, obtained from the regulatory authority of any province or territory of Canada. In addition, no prospectus in relation to the Loan Notes has been, or will be, lodged with or registered by the Australian Securities and Investments Commission and no steps have been, nor will be, taken to enable the Loan Notes to be offered in compliance with the applicable securities laws of Japan, New Zealand or any other country or jurisdiction outside the United Kingdom. The Loan Notes will not be offered, sold, resold, delivered or distributed, directly or indirectly, in or into the United States, Canada, Australia, New Zealand or Japan or any other jurisdiction if to do so would constitute a violation of the relevant laws in such jurisdiction.

Reproduced by kind permission of Sky plc.

22.4.2 The defence document

22.4.2.1 Nature

If the offer is recommended, the views of the board of the offeree company will usually be included in the offer document. However, if the offer is hostile, the offer document will have been prepared by the offeror only. Rule 25.1(a) requires the board of the offeree company to communicate with its shareholders and persons with information rights under s 146 of the CA 2006 by way of circular, which is often referred to as a 'defence document'.

Once the defence document has been sent, the offeror will usually send a further document, to respond to the arguments raised in the defence document and draw the attention of the offeree company shareholders once more to the merits of the offer. The offeree may then send a further defence document to the offeree shareholders in response to the offeror's latest claims, and so on.

22.4.2.2 Timing

Rule 25.1(a) provides that the offeree company board must publish a circular containing its opinion on the offer within 14 days following publication of the offer document. For lawyers advising a company which is the subject of a surprise hostile offer, this will involve some swift drafting and several late nights.

22.4.2.3 Publication

The defence document is also a public document. The Takeover Code requires the offeree company to:

(a) send the defence document to its shareholders (and persons with information rights under s 146 of the CA 2006 (r 25.1(a));

(b) publish the defence document on a website in accordance with r 26.1, promptly following publication (r 25.1(c)(i));

(c) announce to an RIS, in accordance with r 30.1, that it has published the document (r 25.1(c)(ii));

(d) make the document readily available to its employee representatives, and if there are none, to its employees and to the trustees of its pension scheme (r 25.1(b)); and

(e) send the document to the Panel and to the advisers to all other parties to the offer electronically (r 30.5(b)).

As mentioned at **22.4.1.3** above, Note 4 on r 26 extends the obligation in relation to putting documents on a website accessible to shareholders outside the UK.

22.4.2.4 Content

The content of the defence document is prescribed by r 25.2 to r 25.9. The information the offeree company must set out includes:

(a) the substance of the advice it has received from its r 3 advisers (see **21.5.1**);

(b) the board's reasons for forming its opinions and its views on:

 (i) the effects of the offer on the offeree company's interests (including, specifically, employment); and

 (ii) the offeror's strategic plans for the offeree company and their likely repercussions on employment and the locations of the offeree company's place of business; and

(c) an opinion from its employee representatives and a separate opinion from the trustees of its pension scheme on the effects of the offer on employment on the pension scheme respectively (provided the representatives and pension trustees provide the opinion in good time) (r 25.9).

The defence document will seek to make clear to the offeree company shareholders that the offeror's offer is poor (for example, it undervalues the offeree company, or the premium offered is too low) and will advise the offeree company shareholders to reject the offeror's offer. As acceptance of the offer involves offeree company shareholders relinquishing their offeree company shares to the offeror, the defence document tends to focus on the benefits to the shareholder of keeping their shares. However, it must be careful not to make a profit forecast unless it is willing to report on that forecast (see **22.4.5.1**). If the consideration for the offer is shares in the offeror (a securities exchange offer), the defence document may also attack the worth of the offeror, further fanning the flames of the hostile bid.

22.4.3 The forms of acceptance

The offeree company shareholder must complete a form of acceptance and return it to the offeror's registrars in order to accept the offer. These forms are of crucial importance, and the lawyer will make sure that they are as clear and straightforward as possible. They must be sent in hard copy (Note to r 30.2).

22.4.4 Other documentation

As you will now be aware, the lawyer cannot consider the takeover in isolation from the other rules relating to listed companies. While the main documents relating to the takeover itself are the r 2.7 announcement and the documents considered at **22.4.1** to **22.4.3** above, the following circumstances will also call for further documentation.

22.4.4.1 Significant transaction/reverse takeover

The takeover is an acquisition of shares, and if the offeror is an ESCC-listed company then the acquisition must be classified under the UK Listing Rules Chapter 7 and the offeror must comply with the requirements which attach to that classification (see **Chapter 19**). It is likely that a large takeover will constitute a significant transaction. This means that the offeror must make a detailed announcement. If it is, for example, a particularly large transaction in relation to the offeror, it may amount to a reverse takeover, requiring the company to make a detailed announcement, send a circular to its own shareholders (that is, the offeror's shareholders) and obtain the prior consent of those shareholders to the takeover by ordinary resolution and possibly re-apply to the Stock Exchange for admission to the Official List.

22.4.4.2 Securities exchange offer

If the offeror is offering shares as consideration then, if that class of shares is listed (which is likely, as a listing gives shares an identifiable value), the consideration shares will also need to be listed. This means that the offeror must prepare a marketing document.

The rule is that a prospectus will be required for a takeover unless the exemption in connection with takeovers applies. This exemption, referred to at **6.4.1.5(f)** and **6.4.2.4(c)** above, is that a prospectus is not required if the takeover involves a share-for-share exchange (that is, the consideration for the takeover is shares) and a document is made available containing information describing the transaction and its impact on the company ('exempted document').

If an exempted document is used, then there is no obligation to produce a supplementary prospectus, so it has the advantage that it will not raise the potential problem of withdrawal rights outlined at **22.5.5**.

The prospectus (or exempted document) will be published as a separate document, but is usually sent out to shareholders at the same time as the offer document. Much of the information which would normally be included in the offer document will be contained in the prospectus (or exempted document).

Finally, it is possible that the offeror will need the consent of its own shareholders to authorise the directors to allot shares under s 551 of the CA 2006. Remember that no disapplication of s 561 is required if the issue is for non-cash consideration. (See **Chapter 14**.)

22.4.4.3 Resulting extra documentation

As a result of either of the circumstances discussed at **22.4.4.1** and **22.4.4.2** above, the offeror might need to produce:

(a) a circular (which contains in the case of a reverse takeover the UKLR Chapter 10 information and, if appropriate, information relating to any required increase in share capital and/or the s 551 authority, and the notice of the GM which convenes the meeting where the shareholders of the offeror can vote on these issues); and

(b) a prospectus, or 'exempted document'.

There will also be various r 17.1 press announcements (for example, of the level of acceptances (see **22.5.3**), or notifying an extension to the bid) during the course of the offer.

22.4.5 Standard of information

The Takeover Code sets high standards for any information provided to shareholders and persons with information rights under s 146 of the CA 2006 during an offer. As noted at **22.4.1.4**, the specific requirements regarding this information are contained in rr 24 and 25. However, the Takeover Code also sets out the following general rules about the nature and quality of that information.

22.4.5.1 Rule 19.1: accuracy of information

Rule 19.1 provides that:

(a) any document or advertisement issued, or statement made, during the course of an offer must be prepared with the highest standard of care and accuracy; and

(b) the information given must be adequately and fairly presented.

Again, the lawyers will use the verification process to help to protect the board in this regard.

The notes on r 19.1 provide valuable drafting guidance to the lawyer. They advocate the use of unambiguous language, citing sources for any material facts stated (typically this is done in a 'sources and bases' section in the document), and warn against using quotations out of context.

Note 1 on r 19.1 highlights certain areas of particular sensitivity, including profit forecasts, on which comment should be avoided. A profit forecast is any statement which puts a floor under, or a ceiling on, the expected profits for a certain period (for example, 'don't accept the bid as we are going to be much more profitable next year in any event'). As is the case with an IPO (see **6.5.2.1**), any profit forecast made during the course of a takeover must be reported on (r 28). Typically, a forecast will not be made unless it has already been decided that the benefit of making a forecast outweighs the work necessary to report on that forecast. This may be the case, for example, if the offer falls late in the financial year, and the most recent published accounts appear a little dated. Even then, as recognised by Note 1, it should not be the subject of media comment.

The Panel considers that the financial adviser is responsible for ensuring that its client complies with this rule (see **21.5.1(g)**). This can lead to something of a strain in relationships between the financial adviser, who needs to advise caution in making media statements, and the financial public relations consultants (see **21.5.5**), who want to deliver powerful messages to the media.

Rule 19.6 explains that where the offeror makes a statement of intention of action it intends to take or not in any document, announcement or other information (a 'post-offer intention statement') then it is committed to that course of action for 12 months unless it first consults with the Panel. This rule was introduced as direct result of the Kraft/Cadbury takeover (see **20.4.7.4**).

22.4.5.2 Rule 19.2: the responsibility statement

Rule 19.2 makes clear that it is the directors who must ensure that these standards are met. Each document issued to shareholders and persons with information rights under s 146 of the CA 2006, or advertisement published in connection with an offer, must contain what is referred to as a 'responsibility statement' from the directors of the offeror and/or, where appropriate, the offeree. The information that must be included in the statement is provided by r 19.2. Typically, the statement is drafted as follows:

> The directors of [the company], whose names appear on page [ ], accept responsibility for the information contained in this [document/advertisement]. To the best of the knowledge and belief of the directors (who have taken all reasonable care to ensure that such is the case) the information contained in this document is in accordance with the facts and does not omit anything likely to affect the import of such information.

In a recommended bid, the offer document will include a responsibility statement from the directors of the offeror in relation to the information provided about the offer and about the offeror. However, it will also include a responsibility statement from the directors of the offeree company in respect of the information it includes about the offeree.

In a hostile offer, the directors of the offeree company will not usually have provided the offeror with any of the information which is included in the offer document. The offer document will include a responsibility statement from the directors of the offeror only. However, any defence documents circulated by the offeree company must include a responsibility statement from the directors of the offeree company (see **22.4.2** above).

The wording of the responsibility statement should be familiar. As explained at **6.5.2.1** above, Annexes of the UK PR Regulation require a similar responsibility statement in a prospectus. You will remember that the purpose of the IPO verification process is to make sure that the directors are in a position to make this statement. The position on a takeover is no different. The junior lawyer will be involved in the process of ensuring that each statement in the offer document is properly verified, and will produce a verification note. The verification process is discussed in more detail at **5.3.5** above.

22.4.5.3 Rule 19.3: unacceptable statements

Rule 19.3 provides that the parties to the offer and their advisers must take care not to issue statements which, while not factually incorrect, may mislead shareholders and the market, or which may create uncertainty. In particular, the offeror should not make a statement which hints that it may improve the offer or that it may make a change to the structure, conditionality or the non-financial terms of its offer, without committing itself to doing so and specifying the improvement. To see an example of a breach of r 19.3 (by Universe Bidco Limited), see Panel Statement 2010/17.

22.4.5.4 Rule 20: equality of information

Rule 20.1

Rule 20.1 develops General Principle 1 (see **20.5.5**). It provides that information about companies involved in an offer must be made equally available to all offeree company shareholders as nearly as possible at the same time and in the same manner.

Rule 20.2 provides guidance in relation to meetings the board may have with shareholders, analysts, brokers or other investment professionals prior to the announcement of the offer, and during the offer itself. It provides that the directors must not disclose, in the case of a meeting prior to the announcement of the offer, any material new information or significant new opinions that will not be in the r 2.7 announcement and, in the case of a meeting during the offer period, any material new information or significant new opinions at all. A profit forecast is capable of falling within r 20.2.

Of course, the board is very keen to enthuse the audience at such meetings with just the type of statements that r 20.2 seeks to prevent. The financial adviser or corporate broker of the party convening any such meeting must be present at the meeting and has the happy task of providing written confirmation to the Panel, by midday the following day, that the restrictions were complied with. The lawyers tend not to attend these meetings: the risk of soaring blood pressure is too high.

Rule 21.3

Rule 21.3 seeks to level the playing field for any competing offeror. It provides that the offeree, on request, must provide the same information to each offeror or genuine potential offeror, no matter how unwelcome that offeror's offer is.

The problem which r 21.3 can cause to an offeree company is illustrated well by the takeover of Midland Bank plc in 1992. Midland had provided information to its preferred offeror, HSBC Holdings Ltd (HSBC) (a subsidiary of the Hong Kong and Shanghai Banking Corporation). Lloyds Bank plc, a high street rival, then stated that it was also 'considering' making an offer for Midland. A pre-condition of Lloyds' offer was the receipt by Lloyds of all the information that Midland had provided to HSBC. Midland objected, on the grounds that it was not fair to oblige it to give commercially sensitive information to one of its arch rivals. Lloyds argued that, without the information, it would not be able to progress its offer and so the shareholders of Midland would lose out on an offer from Lloyds. The Panel upheld Lloyds' request. It saw no reason to modify or relax r 21.3. Lloyds was a genuine potential offeror, and it was in the best interests of Midland shareholders that Midland provide the information to Lloyds. It follows that an offeree company should exercise caution when revealing information, even to a preferred offeror.

Two practical points are worthy of note here. First, the potential offeror must specify the information it requires from the offeree company; it cannot simply ask the offeree company to provide everything which it gave to the preferred offeror. Secondly, r 21.3 is usually of use only once the rival bid is public. As many hostile bids are launched as surprise attacks, and all the preparation and due diligence is undertaken in secret, the usefulness of r 21.3 is limited.

Note also that r 21.3 extends to site visits and meetings with the offeree's management. So, if one bidder has met the offeree's directors, the competing offeror should, if it requests this, be given equivalent access.

22.4.5.5 Rule 23: sufficiency of information

Rule 23 relates to the documents which the offeror and the offeree company prepare during an offer. The rule embodies General Principle 2 of the Takeover Code (see **20.5.5** above) and provides that the offeree shareholders must be given sufficient information and advice, in a timely manner, to enable them to reach a properly informed decision as to the merits or demerits of the offer, and that no relevant information should be withheld from those shareholders.

Rule 27.1 sets out specific matters which must be updated, including irrevocable undertakings and letters of intent, interests and dealings in shares and changes to directors' service contracts.

22.4.5.6 Bid documentation rules

As detailed at **20.4.7.2**, the failure to comply with the bid documentation rules in Appendix 6 to the Takeover Code is a criminal offence punishable by a fine.

22.4.6 Consideration

In certain circumstances the Takeover Code will dictate the level and type of consideration which must be offered (see **21.8.10.4** above).

22.4.7 Conditions of the offer

The offeror will make the offer subject to certain conditions. The r 2.7 announcement and the offer document will set out the detailed terms of these conditions. If the conditions are not fulfilled, the offer will lapse, unless the offeror can waive the conditions.

There will always be a condition as to the number of offeree company shares which the offeror must acquire in order for the offer to succeed (the 'acceptance condition'; see **22.4.7.1** below), but usually there will be other conditions too. The Takeover Code regulates the conditions which the offeror can impose. Rule 13 provides that the offer must not normally be subject to conditions which depend solely on subjective judgements by the directors of the offeror or of the offeree, or the fulfilment of which is in their hands.

The most common conditions which may be attached to an offer are set out at **22.4.7.1** to **22.4.7.7** below. Note, however, that if the offeror seeks to rely on the non-fulfilment of a condition as justification for lapsing the offer, and invoke that condition, it must consult the Panel (r 13.5(a)). In particular, it must satisfy the Panel that the issue in question could not have been discovered through the due diligence exercise carried out before the offer was announced (see Practice Statement No 5) and that the issue is genuinely material to the offeror (r 13.5(a)). The exception to this rule is if the offer will lapse because any of the conditions referred to at **22.4.7.1**, **22.4.7.4** or, in practice, **22.4.7.2** below are not fulfilled.

Usually, the offeror will reserve the right to waive conditions (other than those set out at **22.4.7.2** and **22.4.7.3** below, which, in practice, must be fulfilled), and the acceptance condition cannot be waived in its entirety; see **22.4.7.1**). This means that the offeror can choose to declare an offer unconditional despite certain conditions not being fulfilled, if it so chooses.

Rule 12 of the Takeover Code requires an offeror to set a 'long-stop date' for an offer. This is aimed at avoiding the risk of a timetable becoming open-ended if the offer timetable can be suspended (under r 31.4) pending the satisfaction or waiver of one or more conditions relating to an official authorisation or regulatory clearance. The long-stop date is the latest date by which, in the event of a suspension of the offer timetable, the acceptance condition will be required to be satisfied, and all conditions relating to an official authorisation or regulatory clearance will be required to be either satisfied or waived.

22.4.7.1 Acceptance

This is a key condition which must reflect r 10 of the Takeover Code. Rule 10 provides that the offeror must have acquired, or agreed to acquire, shares carrying over 50% of the voting rights in the offeree company. Once the offeror has acquired such shares it can declare the offer 'unconditional as to acceptances'. In other words, it has won legal control of the offeree company.

However, in practice, the offer condition is usually drafted so that it will be fulfilled only if the offeror acquires 90% of the shares to which the offer relates. This is to enable the offeror to acquire the remaining 10% of shares by invoking s 979 of the CA 2006 (see **22.7** below). Typically the offeror will not want to be left with troublesome minority shareholders whom it is not entitled to buy out.

Usually the condition will specify that the offeror can waive the condition at a level of acceptances below 90% (but not 50% or below as this would breach the minimum acceptance requirement of r 10).

As explained at **22.5.5.1**, until the offer is declared unconditional, shareholders who have already accepted the offer can withdraw their acceptances. However, once the offer is declared unconditional as to acceptances, such shareholders are bound by their acceptances.

22.4.7.2 Admission of consideration shares to listing and trading

If the offeror is issuing shares of a class which is already listed as consideration then, as explained at **17.4.3** above, in order to:

(a) comply with the requirements of the UK Listing Rules; and

(b) give value to the shares,

these shares must be admitted to listing on the Official List and to trading on the Main Market.

In this case a condition will be included which states that the offer will become wholly unconditional only once the consideration shares are effectively admitted to listing and to trading. In April 2011, the City of London Law Society agreed standard wording for this condition with the FCA. It may be found on the Society's website at www.citysolicitors.org.

A similar condition is also required if the offeror is issuing shares in order to raise cash consideration for the offer (see r 13.4).

22.4.7.3 Offeror shareholder approval

If the takeover is a reverse takeover then the UK Listing Rules require the transaction to be approved by the offeror shareholders (see **Chapter 19**). In addition, the offeror shareholders may need to authorise the increase of share capital and the issue of shares (if the offeror is offering its shares as consideration). Again, if the offeror is issuing shares to raise cash consideration, then it will need to include a condition regarding any required shareholder approval, relating to issues such as increasing the share capital, issuing the shares and/or disapplying pre-emption rights (r 13.4).

It is usual for the offer to be conditional upon the passing at a GM of the offeror of all resolutions that are necessary to implement the offer.

22.4.7.4 Merger control clearance

An offeror will usually make the offer conditional on a decision being made that there will be no reference to the CMA (see **23.4.3**), or, in the case of a takeover which falls within the scope of the EC Merger Regulation, that there will no reference to the European Commission (see **23.3**). Rule 31.4(a) of the Takeover Code provides that if one or more offer conditions relating to 'an official authorisation or regulatory clearance' (which includes there being no reference to merger control authorities such as the CMA or the European Commission) has not been satisfied or waived by 5pm on Day 37, the Panel will normally suspend the offer timetable either at the request (jointly) of the offeror and offeree company, or at the request of either party. The suspended offer timetable will resume on the date on which the last condition relating to merger control is satisfied or waived, which will then normally become Day 32.

Rule 12 of the Takeover Code requires an offeror to set a 'long-stop date' for an offer. This is aimed at avoiding the risk of a timetable becoming open-ended if the offer timetable can be suspended (under r 31.4) pending the satisfaction or waiver of one or more conditions relating to an official authorisation or regulatory clearance. The long-stop date is the latest date by which, in the event of a suspension of the offer timetable, the acceptance condition will be required to be satisfied, and all conditions relating to a reference to the CMA or the European Commission will be required to be either satisfied or waived. The specific date must be included in the r 2.7 announcement and in the offer document.

22.4.7.5 Authorisations

This condition states that all authorisations for carrying on the business of the offeree company and other offeree group companies are in full force and effect.

22.4.7.6 Material litigation

This condition provides that no material litigation or arbitration proceedings have been instituted or threatened against the offeree group.

22.4.7.7 Material adverse change

This condition (the 'MAC condition') states that there are no material adverse changes in the offeree company's financial or trading position, other than those which the offeree has already disclosed. In 2001, the Panel refused to allow an offeror, WPP, to invoke its MAC condition on the basis that a material adverse change had taken place in the prospects of the offeree company, Tempus, after the announcement of WPP's offer on 10 September 2001 and, in particular, following the terrorist attacks in the US on 11 September 2001. The Panel stated that a change in economic, industrial or political circumstances will not normally justify the withdrawal of an announced offer.

22.4.8 Frustrating action

This is relevant only in connection with a hostile bid. If an offeree company receives an unwelcome takeover offer, the directors may be tempted to frustrate the offer by taking some action which will make the offeree company more difficult to acquire, or less attractive to the offeror. Rule 21 expands General Principle 3 of the Takeover Code (see **20.5.5** above) by providing that directors of an offeree company cannot undertake frustrating action without the approval of the offeree company shareholders. Remember that an offer which may be unwelcome from the offeree company board's point of view may be very welcome from the offeree company shareholders' perspective. Account must also be taken of the offeree company's directors' statutory duties.

A non-exhaustive list of frustrating actions is set out in r 21.1(b). It includes:

(a) the issue of, or granting of options over, unissued shares;

(b) the sale, disposal or acquisition of assets; and

(c) the entering into of contracts other than in the ordinary course of business (such as amending a director's service contract to improve their terms without justification).

22.4.9 Poison pills

A poison pill is a general term used to describe defensive measures a company may take even before a bid is imminent (when the Takeover Code rules on frustrating action described at **22.4.8** do not apply). An example of a poison pill is drafting change of control clauses into key agreements (for example, Marks & Spencer Group plc inserting a clause into its contracts with suppliers of all socks and underwear that such contracts would terminate if anyone made a takeover offer for Marks & Spencer Group plc, thus leaving an offeror potentially with a much less valuable offeree company). These are common in the UK, but in practice do not tend to pose too much of a deterrent to a hostile offeror (who may have its own contacts with whom to contract, or indeed have good relations with the party subject to the change of control clause in any event).

When considering whether to adopt a poison pill, the board must take care not to breach its fiduciary duty to the company. *Criterion Properties plc v Stratford Properties UK plc and Others* [2004] UKHL 28 provides some guidance on this issue. In that case, Criterion Properties plc ('Criterion') had entered into a joint venture agreement with Stratford Properties UK plc ('Oaktree') under which Oaktree had a put option, namely the option to require Criterion to purchase Oaktree's shares, in the event that there was a change of control of Criterion, or if two named directors left the Criterion board. The purchase price was so high that it guaranteed Oaktree a minimum return of 25% pa on the investment. Obviously, the effect of the change of control clause was to deter any potential offeror from making an offer for Criterion. Criterion applied to the court to set aside the agreement.

The House of Lords found that the case turned on whether the Criterion directors had authority to enter into the contract. If the directors had actual or apparent authority, the agreement would be valid. If they did not, the court discussed whether the directors had ostensible authority. The court noted that this issue raised a question of considerable public importance, namely whether the directors of a public company have the power to authorise the signing of a poison pill agreement intended to deter third parties from making offers to purchase the company's shares and, in particular, whether they had authority to do so when the deterrent consisted of divesting of some of the company's assets.

Unfortunately, the court of first instance and the Court of Appeal had not considered the issue of authority, and so the House of Lords could not resolve the issue further; however, the case contains some useful commentary on poison pills.

22.4.9.1 Breakthrough provisions

Article 11 of the EU Takeovers Directive (see **20.3**) sets out what it refers to as 'breakthrough provisions'. These provisions provide that, on a takeover, the offeror can override some poison pills in certain circumstances. Article 11 specifies the types of poison pill which can be overridden. It includes restrictions on transferring shares which are contained in the company's articles or contracts, and restrictions on voting rights.

However, the breakthrough provisions proved so controversial that art 12 of the Directive permits Member States to opt out of art 11. In the event that a Member State does opt out, however, the Directive provides that companies must be able to opt back into (and, if required subsequently, back out of) the breakthrough provisions if they so choose.

Whilst still in the EU, the UK Government opted out of art 11. It preferred to leave to shareholders the decision on whether to have enforceable poison pills. Under s 966 of the CA 2006 (which still applies post-Brexit) a UK company must opt into (and, if required, then opt to back out of) the breakthrough procedures.

In order to opt in, the company must, under s 966(1) of the CA 2006, pass a special resolution, and fulfil the following conditions:

(a) the company must have voting shares admitted to trading on a UK regulated market (see **20.3.1**) (s 966(2));

(b) the company's articles of association must not contain (s 966(3)):

    (i) any of the restrictions on share transfer or voting rights which are listed in art 11 (or if they do, they must fall away in the same circumstances as they would under the breakthrough provisions); or

    (ii) any other provisions that would be incompatible with art 11 of the Directive; and

(c) no shares conferring special rights in the company can be held by a Government minister, their nominees or any company they directly or indirectly own or control (s 966(4)).

Under s 970(1) and (2) of the CA 2006 the company must notify the Panel of any special resolution passed to opt in to (or subsequently opt out of) the breakthrough provisions, within 15 days after the passing of that resolution. Section 968 sets out the consequences of opting in, and in particular which poison pills will be invalid.

22.5 ACCEPTING THE OFFER

Once the offer documents and any defence documents have been published, the fate of the offer will be determined by whether the offeree shareholders choose to accept it.

22.5.1 Method of acceptance

The offeree company shareholders accept the offer by completing the forms of acceptance (referred to at **22.4.3**) and returning them to the company's registrars, who will then count the votes (as explained at **21.5.6**).

22.5.2 Day 21

Most forms of acceptance will urge shareholders to vote by a specified time and date, known as Day 21. Rule 31.2(a) provides that the offer must be open for a minimum of 21 days from the date the offeror publishes the offer document. The offeror will be keen to complete the takeover as soon as possible, and therefore Day 21 is usually the first day on which the offer can be declared unconditional, ie successful, but it can be a longer period. Most offers continue beyond Day 21, but the offeror could use the acceptance condition to lapse the offer at this date if it no longer wished to proceed by publishing an 'acceptance condition invocation notice' in accordance with r 31.6.

Institutional shareholders may delay casting their votes, to see if anything happens to change their decision to vote for or against the offer (such as a rival offeror announcing a better offer, or a dramatic change in market conditions).

22.5.3 Announcing the level of acceptances

Rule 17.1 provides that the offeror must announce the level of acceptances by 8am on the business day after Day 21.

If the bid is recommended, the offeror will expect to be able to declare the offer unconditional on Day 21. However, if the offer is hostile, the offeror is unlikely to have received the required level of acceptances (see **22.4.7.1** above), as shareholders may wait to see if the offeror will improve the offer, or whether another rival offer will be made.

The level of acceptances must also be announced, under r 17.1, every seventh day after Day 21 and after any extension or revision of the offer (see **22.5.4**).

22.5.4 Continuing and revising the offer

If the conditions of the offer, including the condition as to acceptances, have not been met by Day 21, the offeror can withdraw the offer. Rule 31.6 provides that the offeror is not obliged to continue the offer provided it has published an 'acceptance condition invocation notice' in accordance with r 31.6. However, usually the offeror will continue the offer in the hope that it will eventually receive a sufficient level of acceptances. The offeror may also improve the terms of the offer. Typically the offeror will announce the extension or revision of the offer at the same time that it announces the level of acceptances.

If the offeror does decide to revise its offer, it must do as it did with the original offer (see **22.4.1.3**), namely:

(a) send a revised offer document to the offeree company shareholders and persons with information rights under s 146 of the CA 2006. This must comply with the content requirements of r 24, and also with r 27, which provides that any documents sent to shareholders after the offer document must contain details of any material changes to the documents published previously during the offer period (or state that there are no such changes) (r 32.1(a));

(b) publish the revised offer document on a website, in accordance with r 26.1, on the date it publishes the document to offeree company shareholders (r 32.1(a));

(c) announce to an RIS, in accordance with r 30.1, that it has published the document on the website (r 32.1(a));

(d) make the document available to its employee representatives, and if there are none, to its employees and to the trustees of its pension scheme (the offeree company must also do this) (r 32.1(b)); and

(e) send the document to the Panel and to the advisers to all other parties to the offer electronically (r 30.5(b)).

As mentioned at **22.4.1.3** above, Note 4 on r 26 extends the obligation in relation to putting documents on a website accessible to shareholders outside the UK unless there is an objectively good reason not to.

Rule 32.1(c) provides that the revised offer must be open for at least 14 days following the publishing of the revised document. The effect of this requirement, together with the final day rule, referred to at **22.5.7** below, is that the offer cannot normally be revised after the 46th day following the publishing of the announcement of the original offer document.

Rule 32.3 provides that any shareholder who accepted the original offer is entitled to receive the revised consideration.

In the event of a revised offer in a hostile offer, the offeree company must do as it did with the defence document (see **22.4.2.3**), namely:

(a) send a circular to its shareholders and persons with information rights under s 146 of the CA 2006 setting out its views on the revised offer, as required by r 25.1(a), drawn up in accordance with rr 25 and 27 (see **22.5.4(a)**) (r 32.6(a)). The offeree company must append to the circular an opinion from its employee representatives on the effects of the offer on employment (provided the representatives provide the opinion in good time) (r 32.6(b));

(b) publish the circular on a website, in accordance with r 26.1, on the date it sends the document to offeree company shareholders (r 32.6(a));

(c) announce to an RIS, in accordance with r 30.1, that it has published the circular on the website (r 32.6(a));

(d) make the circular available to its employee representatives, and if there are none, to its employees and to the trustees of its pension scheme (r 32.6(a)); and

(e) send the document to the Panel and to the advisers to all other parties to the offer electronically (r 30.5(b)).

Again, Note 4 on r 26 extends the obligation in relation to putting documents on a website accessible to shareholders outside the UK unless there is an objectively good reason not to.

22.5.5 The right of withdrawal

22.5.5.1 Withdrawal rights under the Takeover Code

Under r 34.1, a shareholder who has accepted the offer can change their mind and withdraw that acceptance at any time until the time that the acceptance condition is satisfied.

This is why so much importance is attached to the offer becoming unconditional; once this has happened, shareholders who have accepted the offer are bound by this acceptance, and cannot withdraw.

In a hostile offer, the offeree company will send withdrawal forms to its shareholders to encourage them to take advantage of these rights.

22.5.5.2 Withdrawal rights under the UK Prospectus Regulation

We have just noted that, under the Takeover Code, usually withdrawal rights cease to be available after an offer has become or has been declared unconditional. As explained at **6.9.4** above, however, Article 23(2) of the UK Prospectus Regulation provides that investors have the right to withdraw their acceptances during the two days following publication of any supplementary prospectus. So what happens if a takeover is made by way of share-for-share exchange, and a supplementary prospectus is required? Can withdrawal rights arise under the UK Prospectus Regulation after the offer has become or has been declared unconditional, meaning that the offeror's acceptance level could drop below 50%? Neither the UK Prospectus Regulation nor the Takeover Code is clear on this point. The Panel has addressed this issue in Panel Statement 2005/29. It states that it has received legal advice that the provisions can be interpreted as meaning that the period for withdrawal by an acceptor of an offer ends once the offer has become or has been declared wholly unconditional and the relevant securities have been unconditionally allotted (that is, wholly unconditional bids, where the unconditional allotments of securities have been made, could not be reopened through the exercise of withdrawal rights).

However, it is important to note that this is based on the law preceding the UK Prospectus Regulation. It is not clear if the position would be the same today.

Until the courts ultimately decide this matter, practically it is prudent for the offeror to either:

(i) make the offer by way of an exempted document rather than a prospectus; or

(ii) take steps to avoid becoming or being declared unconditional as to acceptances when a two-day withdrawal period is running, or when there is a possibility that a supplementary prospectus may be required (possibly by organising matters so that the offer becomes wholly unconditional at the same time the offer becomes or is declared unconditional as to acceptances, which is already common practice); and/or

(iii) include an extra condition to the offer which it can invoke should the exercise of withdrawal rights under the UK Prospectus Regulation result in acceptance levels dropping below 50% after the offer has become or been declared unconditional as to acceptances.

22.5.6 Day 39

Rule 31.9 provides that the offeree company should not, without the consent of the Panel, announce any material new information after the 39th day following the publication of the initial offer document. If any relevant competition authority has not given its decision by this time, the Panel will usually grant permission to extend the deadline until the second day after the decision is announced.

22.5.7 Day 60: the unconditional date

For reasons of the offeree's stability (and the advisers' sanity), the takeover process is not allowed to continue indefinitely. Rule 31.1 provides that, except with the consent of the Panel, the offer will lapse if the offeror cannot declare the offer unconditional (ie has not satisfied or waived all conditions to the offer) by midnight on the 60th day after the initial offer document was published. The circumstances when the Panel will grant consent to an extension of this period are set out in r 31.3. For example, if a competing offeror launches a bid for the offeree company, the timetables for both offers will be co-ordinated and run from the publication of the competing offeror's offer document, which will inevitably lead to an extension of Day 60 for the original offer.

Under r 31.5, an offeror can bring forward the unconditional date by making an 'acceleration statement' (provided it meets the conditions for making such a statement as set out in that rule).

22.5.8 Day 74: earliest date the offer can close

Rule 31.2(b) provides that, after the offer has become or been declared unconditional, it must still remain open for further acceptances for at least 14 days after the current closing date. As explained at **22.5.7**, the unconditional date will tend to be Day 60, and so, if this is the case, the earliest date the offer can close will be Day 74.

Rule 31.2(d) provides that if the offer remains open for acceptances beyond Day 70, the offeror must give at least 14 days' written notice to all offeree company shareholders who have not accepted the offer.

In practice, typically the offeror keeps the offer open until further notice, and then runs the offer in parallel to the compulsory acquisition procedure (see **22.7**).

22.6 SUCCESS OR FAILURE?

22.6.1 The failed offer

22.6.1.1 The 12-month restriction

If the offeror withdraws the offer, or the offer lapses, r 35.1 of the Takeover Code provides that, without the consent of the Panel, neither the offeror nor any concert parties (see **22.6.1.2**) can:

(a) make another offer for the offeree company;
(b) acquire any interest in shares in the offeree which would trigger a r 9 mandatory bid (see **21.8.10.3** above);
(c) acquire any interest in, or procure an irrevocable undertaking (see **21.10**) in respect of, shares in the offeree company which, when aggregated with the shares of other concert parties, would carry 30% or more of the voting rights in the offeree company;
(d) make any statement which raises or confirms the possibility that an offer might be made for the offeree company;
(e) take any steps to prepare a possible offer for the offeree company where knowledge of the possible offer might extend beyond the offeror and its immediate advisers; or
(f) purchase, agree to purchase, or make any statement which raises or confirms the possibility that it is interested in purchasing assets which are significant in relation to the offeree company,

for at least 12 months from the date the offer is withdrawn or lapses. The rationale for this rule is to promote certainty in the market and avoid companies becoming embroiled in an endless takeover battle (as reflected in General Principle 6). Note that the requirements to 'down tools' mirror those that apply following a r 2.8 statement (see **22.3.3.3**), albeit for a longer period.

The note to r 35.1 of the Takeover Code sets out the usual circumstances when the Panel will waive the 12-month restriction imposed by r 35.1 These include:

(a) if the offeror wants to announce a new offer which is recommended;
(b) if the offeror wants to announce a new offer to compete with another offer;
(c) if there has been a material change of circumstances.

Practice Statement 2014/28 provides guidance on when the Panel will grant consent to an approach before the expiry of the 12-month period.

22.6.1.2 Acting in concert

The Takeover Code defines 'persons acting in concert' as persons:

> who, pursuant to an agreement or understanding (whether formal or informal), co-operate to obtain or consolidate control of a company or to frustrate the successful outcome of an offer for a company.

Affiliated persons (such as a majority shareholder; see Note 2 to the definition) are deemed to be acting in concert with each other.

Certain persons, such as directors and other companies in the same group, are presumed to be acting in concert unless the contrary is established.

22.6.1.3 Restrictions on dealings

If an offer has lapsed which was one of two or more competing offers, then, until the other competing offer(s) have also lapsed, or become wholly unconditional, r 35.4 prevents the failed offeror from acquiring any interest in shares of the offeree company on terms more favourable than under its lapsed offer.

22.6.2 The successful bid

Once the offer is declared unconditional, the offeror can breathe a sigh of relief: the takeover has been successful. However, r 31.2(b) of the Takeover Code provides that the offer must still remain open for acceptance for not less than 14 days. This affords offeree company shareholders, who did not accept the offer before the offer was declared unconditional as to acceptances, an opportunity to accept the offer once the offeror has acquired control of the offeree.

Ideally, an offeror will want to acquire 100% of the offeree company's shares, to avoid being left to cope with unfriendly minority shareholders (see **22.7.1**). If the offeror has received acceptances in respect of at least 90% of the shares to which the offer relates, it can compel the other offeree company shareholders to sell their shares to the offeror using the compulsory acquisition procedure under s 979 of the CA 2006 (see **22.7** below). However, if the offeror cannot invoke the compulsory acquisition procedure, it must abide with the minority shareholders who rejected the offer. After six months following the closure of the original offer, however, the offeror may be able to buy the shares of this minority by offering them more favourable terms than those of the original offer.

22.7 BUYING OUT MINORITY SHAREHOLDERS

22.7.1 The problem with minority shareholders

The typical offeror will not want to become the majority shareholder of the offeree company alongside minority shareholders who did not accept the offer. Minority shareholders can be problematic for various reasons, including their ability to disrupt GMs and create bad publicity for the company. The presence of a minority can also prevent the company from carrying out its day to day business effectively (for example, the minority may be able to block special resolutions if they hold more than 25% of the company's shares, or prevent a GM from being held on short notice if they hold more than 5%).

The minority shareholders, too, may be less than happy to find themselves holding a minority stake in a company which is controlled by the offeror. In particular, if the offeror decides to take the company private after the takeover, the minority may struggle to find a market for their shares in order to exit from the company.

For the reasons outlined above, once the majority of shareholders have accepted the offer, ss 979 and 983 of the CA 2006 give a statutory right respectively:

(a) to the offeror, to buy out the minority shareholders, and so acquire 100% of the offeree company (referred to as a 'squeeze-out' right); and

(b) to each minority shareholder who has refused the takeover offer, to require the offeror to purchase their shares (referred to as a 'sell-out' right).

22.7.2 The right of the offeror to buy out minority shareholders ('squeeze-out')

22.7.2.1 The conditions

Two conditions must be satisfied before the offeror can invoke the compulsory acquisition provisions:

(a) the takeover offer condition; and

(b) the 90% squeeze-out threshold condition.

The takeover offer condition

There must be a 'takeover offer', which is defined by s 974 of the CA 2006 as:

(a) an offer to acquire all the shares in the offeree company (or, where there is more than one class of shares, all the shares of one or more classes) other than the offeree company shares already held by the offeror, or contracted to be acquired by it; and

(b) where the terms of the offer are the same in relation to all the shares to which the offer relates.

Note that, in relation to overseas shareholders, under s 978 of the CA 2006 the offer can constitute a 'takeover offer' for the purposes of the CA 2006 even if the offer is not communicated to an overseas shareholder, provided:

(a) the shareholder does not have a registered UK address;

(b) the offer is not made to the shareholder in order to avoid contravening the law of an overseas territory; and

(c) the offer is either:

   (i) published in the *Gazette*; or

   (ii) available for inspection at, or can be obtained from, a place in the UK, or a website, and notice of this is published in the *Gazette*.

The 90% squeeze-out threshold condition

Under s 979 of the CA 2006 the offeror must have acquired or unconditionally contracted to acquire, by virtue of acceptances of the offer, not less than 90% in value of all the shares *to which the offer relates* and, where the shares to which the offer relates are voting shares, not less than 90% of the voting rights carried by those shares (or, if the offer is for more than one class of share, not less than 90% in value and, where voting shares, not less than 90% of voting rights, for any of the classes to which the offer relates). Note that under s 974(2) of the CA 2006 any shares acquired by the offeror or its concert parties *before* the offer document was published do not count towards the 90% threshold, but any shares acquired *after* the document was published will count towards the threshold (CA 2006, s 979(8)–(10)).

For example, if the offeror already owned 25% of the offeree company's shares before the offer document was published, the offer relates to only 75% of the offeree company's share capital. The offeror must, therefore, secure acceptances in respect of 90% (in both value and voting rights) of this 75%.

Under s 975(2) of the CA 2006, shares which are the subject of irrevocable undertakings (see **21.10**) as at the date of the offer (which is the date the offer document is published) do count towards the 90% threshold. Shares which the offeror's concert parties hold or have contracted to acquire as at the date of the offer (CA 2006, s 975(4)) do not count towards the 90% threshold.

Section 986(9) of the CA 2006 provides that the offeror can apply to the court for an order which allows it to serve a squeeze-out notice (see **22.7.2.2**) even though it has not acquired the 90% threshold, if it can prove that:

(a) after reasonable enquiry the offeror has been unable to trace one or more of the persons holding shares to which the offer relates;

(b) if account were taken of the shares of these missing persons, the 90% threshold would be reached; and

(c) the consideration offered is fair and reasonable.

However, the court will make such an order only if it considers it just and equitable to do so, having regard to the number of shareholders who have been traced but who have rejected the offer.

22.7.2.2 The squeeze-out notice

Provided the offeror has acquired or unconditionally contracted to acquire 90% of the shares to which the offer relates and 90% of the voting rights before the expiry of three months after the last day on which the offer can be accepted, the offeror can give notice to those offeree company shareholders who did not accept the offer that it wishes to acquire their shares by the deadline just mentioned.

The squeeze-out notice under s 981 of the CA 2006 entitles, and also obliges, the offeror to acquire the offeree company shareholder's shares on the same terms as those of the takeover offer. For example, if the offer gave shareholders a choice of paper or cash consideration, the same choice must be given to shareholders who did not accept the offer. However, there are some exceptions, for example for certain overseas shareholders. Also, where a cash alternative was due to be provided by a third party who can no longer provide it (eg, through a vendor placing), the offeror must pay a cash equivalent to the offeree shareholder.

The notice must make clear:

(a) that the shareholder must make their choice of consideration known to the offeror, in writing, within six weeks of the notice; and
(b) the default consideration that the shareholder will receive if they do not make their choice known to the offeror.

The offeror must copy the first notice (they are usually distributed in the order they appear on the register of members) to the board of offeree company, together with a statutory declaration that the conditions referred to at **22.7.2.1** above have been satisfied.

22.7.2.3 The acquisition

Six weeks after serving the notice (CA 2006, s 981(6) and (7)) the offeror must send to the offeree:

(a) a copy of all the squeeze-out notices;
(b) a stock transfer form executed by a person the offeror nominates on behalf of the shareholder; and
(c) the consideration for the shares.

The offeree will then:

(a) register the offeror as the holder of the shares to which the s 979 notice relates (s 981(7)); and
(b) hold the consideration on trust for the relevant shareholders (s 981(9)).

Section 982(4) and (5) provide what should happen on the rare occurrence that a shareholder cannot be traced.

22.7.2.4 Preventing the acquisition

Section 986(1) of the CA 2006 provides that any shareholder who receives a s 979 notice can apply to the court, within six weeks of the date on which the notice was given, for an order preventing the acquisition or allowing the acquisition on such terms as the court thinks fit (ie on different terms). However, the courts are unlikely to be willing to investigate the merits of an offer which has already been endorsed by at least 90% of shareholders, unless there is a compelling reason to do so.

22.7.3 The right of minority shareholders to be bought out ('sell-out')

Section 983 of the CA 2006 provides a mechanism whereby an offeree company shareholder who has refused the takeover offer may be able to 'sell out', that is, force the offeror to purchase their shares.

22.7.3.1 The conditions

Two conditions must be satisfied before an offeree company shareholder can require the offeror to take their shares:

(a) the takeover offer condition; and
(b) the 90% sell-out threshold condition.

The takeover offer condition

This condition is the same as for squeeze out (see **22.7.2.1**).

The 90% sell-out threshold condition

A shareholder can compel the offeror to buy their shares only when the offeror has obtained an interest in 90% in value carrying 90% of the voting rights of *all the shares in the offeree company* (or the class of shares to which the shares of the minority shareholder belong). Note that the 90% sell-out threshold is different to the 90% squeeze-out threshold (see **22.7.2.1**). For squeeze-out purposes, only shares *to which the offer relates* are included. For sell-out, *all shares* in the offeree are included. Shares held by the offeror before the offer document was published will count, therefore, towards the 90% sell-out threshold but not towards the 90% squeeze-out threshold (as they would not be shares to which the offer relates). Irrevocable undertakings and shares held by any associate of the offeror also count towards the sell-out threshold.

The effect of this difference is that the offeror may meet the 90% sell-out threshold before it meets the 90% squeeze-out threshold.

EXAMPLE

Imagine that the offeror acquired a 25% stake in the offeree before it published the offer document. For squeeze-out, the offeror must acquire 90% of the remaining 75%, which will be triggered once the offeror has acquired an aggregate of 92.5% (90% x 75% + the existing 25%). For sell-out, the offeror must acquire only 90%, and the 25% already acquired will count towards this.

22.7.3.2 The sell-out notice

The average shareholder of an offeree company is unlikely to be aware of their sell-out rights. Therefore, within one month of reaching the 90% threshold, the offeror must notify those shareholders who have not accepted the offer of their sell-out rights (under CA 2006, s 984(3)). If the sell-out notice is served before the end of the offer period, it must state that the offer is still open for acceptance.

The offeror must specify the period within which the shareholder can take up their sell-out rights. Under the CA 2006 procedure, they must be exercised within three months from the last date on which the offer could be accepted or, if later, the date on which the offeror serves the sell-out notice.

Of course, if (as is usual) the offeror has already served a squeeze-out notice to acquire the minority shareholders' shares, the offeror does not need to notify the shareholders of their sell-out rights. For this reason, sell-out notices are not common.

If the minority shareholder exercises their sell-out rights, the offeror must acquire those shares on terms which are the same as the terms of the takeover offer, or on such other terms as may be agreed. If the offer included a choice of consideration, the position is similar to that under squeeze-out: if the chosen consideration is not available, the shareholder will receive the cash equivalent. The court has an overriding jurisdiction, on the application of either the shareholder or the offeror, to determine the terms on which the shares will be acquired.

22.7.3.3 The notice from the shareholder

The shareholder must give the offeror written notice of their desire to sell out. If there is a choice of consideration under the offer, the shareholder must state their choice of consideration.

CHAPTER 23

TAKEOVERS: MERGER CONTROL

23.1 INTRODUCTION

It is difficult to define exactly what constitutes a merger, and from a legal perspective the distinction between a takeover and a merger is not particularly important. It follows that the law relating to *merger* control can, in fact, apply to a *takeover*.

Why would the competition authorities be concerned with a takeover? Imagine that a supermarket chain, with a 40% market share, decides to make an offer for the entire issued share capital of one of its rivals, which also has a 40% market share. If the takeover is successful, the result will be a supermarket chain with a substantial share of the market. It will have considerable bargaining power and is likely to be able to source produce on very competitive terms. It is possible that other, smaller supermarket chains might be squeezed out of the market, and that others who wanted to break into the market would not be able to do so. The probable result of all of this is that consumers on their weekly shop will have less choice and may have to pay more. This is why the competition authorities will keep a close eye on any takeover offer.

Practically, the corporate lawyer will enlist the help of their colleagues who specialise in competition law, who will then advise in relation to any merger control issues relevant to the takeover. However, this means that the corporate lawyer must be aware of the merger control rules to know when they should consult such colleagues; and, as always, the corporate lawyer will need to know enough about the process to follow discussions at meetings and to understand the impact it may have on the takeover offer. This chapter aims to introduce the corporate lawyer to the basics of merger control.

A takeover in the UK will typically fall within the UK national competition regime (if at all). In addition, it is possible that the takeover may fall under the jurisdiction of the EU competition regime, if there is sufficient impact within the EU.

23.2 MERGER CONTROL PROVISIONS IN THE TAKEOVER CODE

23.2.1 Rule 12.1

Rule 12.1(ii) of the Takeover Code provides that it must be a term of the takeover offer that the offer will not proceed, will lapse or will be withdrawn on a specific date (a 'long-stop date') if, with the consent of the Panel, a condition or pre-condition relating to an official authorisation or regulatory clearance has not been satisfied or waived. The will include the situation where:

(a) the offer is referred to the CMA for investigation under the Enterprise Act 2002 (EA 2002) (see **23.4**); or

(b) the offer gives rise to a concentration with a Community dimension within the scope of the EU Merger Regulation (see **23.4**), and the European Commission commences Phase II proceedings under art 6(1)(c) of the EU Merger Regulation (see **23.4.6**).

The rationale for this is due to the fact that the investigation by the relevant competition authorities will usually take a substantial period of time. It would be unreasonable to leave the offeree company subject to the uncertainty of a bid, possibly for many months, which may or may not be permitted once the authorities reach a decision.

23.2.2 Rule 31.4

If one or more conditions relating to an official authorisation or regulatory clearance (which will include the offer not being referred to the CMA or the European Commission not initiating proceedings in relation to it) has not been satisfied or waived by 5pm on Day 37, the Panel will normally suspend the offer timetable:

(i) at the joint request of the offeror and the offeree company; or

(ii) at the request of either the offeror or the offeree company,

provided that at least one of the outstanding conditions relates to a material official authorisation or regulatory clearance (as defined in the Takeover Code).

A suspended offer timetable will resume on the date on which the last condition relating to a relevant official authorisation or regulatory clearance is satisfied or waived, which will normally be Day 32.

23.3 UK MERGER CONTROL

The EA 2002 governs merger control in the UK. The merger control provisions of the EA 2002 will apply to a takeover if:

(a) it is a *relevant merger situation*; and

(b) it results, or may be expected to result, in a *substantial lessening of competition*.

23.3.1 Relevant merger situation

A takeover will constitute a 'relevant merger situation' if:

(a) two or more enterprises cease to be distinct;

(c) the time limit for a reference to the CMA has not yet expired; and

(d) either:

  (i) the turnover test, or

  (ii) the share of supply test,

  is fulfilled.

Let us now consider each criterion in turn.

23.3.1.1 Two or more enterprises cease to be distinct

Enterprise

Section 129(1) of the EA 2002 provides that an 'enterprise' is the activities, or part of the activities, of a business. 'Business' in this context includes an undertaking carried on for gain or reward, or in the course of which goods or services are supplied otherwise than free of charge.

At least one of the enterprises must be carried on in the UK (or by, or under the control of, a body corporate which is incorporated in the UK).

Ceasing to be distinct

Enterprises cease to be distinct under s 26 of the EA 2002 if they are brought under common ownership or control. An offeror will acquire 'control' for these purposes if:

(a) it can materially influence the policy of the offeree ('influential control');

(b) it can control the policy of the offeree ('de facto control'); or

(c) it has a controlling interest (that is, more than 50% of the voting rights) in the offeree ('legal control').

The CMA has produced guidelines to assist in the determination of (a) and (b). BSkyB Group plc's 17.8% acquisition in ITV plc in 2006 was held to amount to 'influential control' by the forerunner to the CMA, the Competition Commission. This was because, in practice, it would enable BSkyB to block special resolutions (due to average ITV shareholder turnout), BSkyB was the only significant industry shareholder and it could get board representation due to its shareholding. It was ordered in 2008 to cut its shareholding to 7.5%. BSkyB's appeals against the decision to the Competition Appeal Tribunal and to the Court of Appeal failed.

23.3.1.2 The time limit for a reference has not expired

Section 24 of the EA 2002 provides that the takeover must either:

(a) not have completed; or

(b) have completed less than four months ago (unless the takeover completed without a public announcement, and the CMA was not notified, in which case the four-month period will start from the time the takeover comes to the attention of the CMA).

23.3.1.3 The turnover test and the share of supply test

To qualify for investigation the takeover must satisfy at least one of the following tests:

Turnover test

This test (EA 2002, s 28(1)) will be fulfilled if the value of the UK turnover of the *offeree* exceeds £70m.

Share of supply test

This test (EA 2002, s 23) will be fulfilled if:

(a) after the takeover, the offeror will supply, or be supplied with, at least 25% of a defined class of goods or services which are supplied in the UK (or a substantial part of it (see below)); or

(b) if this was already the case before the takeover, then after the takeover the offeror acquires an even greater share of the market.

EXAMPLE

If X plc, which controls 20% of the market for the supply of cars, makes a bid for Y plc, another car manufacturer with a market share of 10%, this would fulfil the market share test, because after the takeover X plc would own at least 25% of the UK car market. Even if X plc owned 25% of the car market before the takeover, the takeover of Y plc would still qualify for a reference as it would increase further X plc's market share.

Note that the example above assumes that the car market is a distinct market. In practice it can be difficult for lawyers to predict what is a distinct market. Ultimately, the CMA has the discretion to determine what the criteria are for determining the market. For example, it may consider the number of units sold, the value of goods sold, or the number of employees engaged in the manufacture or supply of the goods.

In a case (decided under the Fair Trading Act 1973, the predecessor of the EA 2002) involving bus companies in the north of England, the House of Lords held that South Yorkshire, which amounts to 1.65% of the area of the UK and which contained 3.2% of the population, was a substantial part of the UK for the purposes of the EA 2002 (*South Yorkshire Transport Ltd and Another v Monopolies and Mergers Commission and Another* [1993] 1 All ER 289).

Note that an alternative test applies to 'relevant enterprises' mentioned above. In this case, the share of supply test will also be fulfilled if the 'relevant entrerprise' has a pre-existing share of at least 25% of the defined market *before* the takeover.

23.3.2 A substantial lessening of competition

The EA 2002 does not define this term, which is referred to in practice as an 'SLC'. However, the explanatory notes to the EA 2002 state the following:

> Similar language is used in the legislation controlling mergers in a number of other major jurisdictions including the US, Canada, Australia and New Zealand. The concept is an economic one, best understood by reference to the question of whether a merger will increase or facilitate the exercise of market power (whether unilateral or through co-ordinated behaviour), leading to reduced output, higher prices, less innovation or lower quality of choice. A number of matters may be potentially relevant to the assessment of whether a merger will result in a substantial lessening of competition. These matters include, but are not limited to:
>
> - market shares and concentration
> - extent of effective competition before and after the merger
> - efficiency and financial performance of firms in the market
> - barriers to entry and expansion in the relevant market
> - availability of substitute products and the scope for supply – or demand – substitution
> - extent of change and innovation in a market
> - whether in the absence of the merger one of the firms would fail and, if so, whether its failure would cause the assets of that firm to exit the market, and
> - the conduct of customers or of suppliers to those in the market.

The CMA has produced Merger Assessment Guidelines (CMA129) in which guidance is given as to what is an SLC and when it might arise.

23.3.3 The competition authorities

The EA 2002 is administered by the following authorities:

23.3.3.1 The Competition and Markets Authority (CMA)

The CMA is a statutory body established by the Enterprise and Regulatory Reform Act 2013 (ERRA 2013) which is independent of the Government. It replaced the previous UK competition authorities, the Office for Fair Trading (OFT) and the Competition Commission, on 1 April 2014. It has the primary duty to seek to promote competition both within and outside the UK for the benefit of consumers (s 25 of the ERRA 2013). The CMA's role encompasses two possible phases.

Phase 1

The initial stage is Phase 1, during which the CMA has 40 days to conduct an initial merger control investigation. If the CMA decides that:

(a) the takeover constitutes a relevant merger situation (see **23.3.1** above); and

(b) the takeover has resulted, or may be expected to result, in an SLC within any UK market(s) for goods or services (see **23.3.2** above), s 33(1) of the EA 2002 provides that it must refer the case for a Phase 2 investigation (see below). In *OFT v IBA Health Limited* [2004] EWCA Civ 142, concerning the takeover by iSoft plc of Torex plc, the Court of Appeal clarified the meaning of 'or may be expected to result'.

The Court ruled that the relevant test is whether the CMA believes that a takeover may be expected to result in an SLC. The CMA's belief must be more than a mere suspicion, and must be reasonable and objectively justified. If the CMA believes the probability of the takeover resulting in an SLC is over 50%, it should refer. If it believes the probability is less than 50%, but more than fanciful, the CMA has discretion as to whether to refer.

As stated at **23.2.1** above, if the CMA does refer for a Phase 2 investigation a takeover which is subject to the Takeover Code, the takeover must lapse.

Phase 2

Phase 2 decisions will be taken by an inquiry group of at least three people, selected from the independent experts appointed to the CMA's panel by the Secretary of State for DBT.

In doing so, under ss 35 and 36 of the EA 2002 they must decide:

(a) whether the takeover has resulted, or will result, in an anti-competitive outcome. Note that this involves deciding whether it is more likely than not that the takeover has resulted, or will result, in a substantial lessening of competition. In contrast, in Phase 1 the CMA only had to reasonably believe that there had been, or might be, an SLC; and
(b) (if there is, or will be, an anti-competitive outcome) what remedies are appropriate.

The CMA has the power to require attendance of witnesses and production of documents. It must take into account any representations made to it by those with a substantial interest in the subject matter of the reference.

Within 24 weeks from the date of the reference, the CMA must consider the reference and make its decisions. In exceptional circumstances the 24-week period can be extended by up to a further eight weeks. It will then publish a report on its assessment of the takeover, the remedies it recommends and the reasons for its decisions. The report will be made available on the CMA's website.

A guidance note, 'Guidance on jurisdiction and procedure', which sets out how the CMA will assess cases in both phases, is also available on its website.

An example of a Phase 2 investigation arose in September 2018 with Sainsbury's plc and Walmart Inc's planned merger of the Sainsbury's and Asda supermarket businesses. In April 2019 the CMA announced that the merger would be blocked over fears that it would raise prices for consumers and lead to longer checkout queues.

23.3.3.2 The Secretary of State for Business and Trade

The Secretary of State's power to intervene in merger control decisions under the EA 2002 is limited to mergers involving exceptional public interest issues. In such cases, the Secretary of State can decide, first, whether to refer the merger to the CMA and, secondly, whether to follow the CMA's decision.

In the first use of this power under the EA 2002, the Secretary of State intervened in relation to BSkyB Group plc's acquisition of 17.9% of the shares of ITV plc. The forerunner to the CMA, the Competition Commission subsequently held the purchase to be anti-competitive and ordered the sale of just over 10% of the shareholding. This decision was subsequently upheld by the Court of Appeal.

23.3.3.3 The National Security and Investment Act 2021

The Secretary of State for DBT has powers under the National Security and Investment Act (NSIA) 2021 to intervene in acquisitions (including takeovers) to protect national security in the UK. These powers apply, for example, where there is the acquisition of votes or shares exceeding a threshold of 25% or 50%, or reaching at least 75%.

The NSIA 2021 sets out a mandatory notification system requiring prospective offerors in 17 sensitive sectors of the UK economy to seek authorisation and obtain approval from the Secretary of State for DBT before completing their acquisition. These sectors include civil nuclear, defence, quantum technologies, robotics and synthetic biology. A voluntary notification system supplements the mandatory system. On acceptance of a mandatory notification, there is a review period (30 working days) in which the Secretary of State may clear the notifiable acquisition, or initiate a full national security assessment (30–75 working days). Voluntary notifications are encouraged from parties who consider that their transaction may raise national security concerns.

In addition, the Secretary of State for DBT has power to 'call in' any transaction falling within the NISA 2021 (whether or not it was notified) where there is a reasonable suspicion that it could give rise to a risk to national security.

The Secretary of State can impose conditions on the acquisition, or indeed prohibit or unwind it. The NSIA 2021 does not define national security but the factors that will be taken into account when deciding whether to exercise the call-in power are set out in a statutory statement made under s 3 of the NSIA 2021.

Breaches of the NSIA 2021 render the acquisition voidable, and persons involved commit a criminal offence with a maximum fine of £10 million or 5% of worldwide turnover.

In September 2024 the Secretary of State for DBT published the required annual report under the NISA 2021 covering the period 1 April 2023 to 31 March 2024. 960 mandatory and 120 voluntary notifications were made, with many being in the defence, artificial intelligence and data storage sectors.

23.3.4 Notification

23.3.4.1 Clearance

Unlike the EU merger control process, outlined at **23.4.4** below, under the EA 2002 there is no obligation on the parties to notify a merger or proposed merger to the CMA. However, most parties to a takeover choose to notify the CMA in advance in order to seek formal confirmation that it will not be referred for a Phase 2 investigation. This is referred to as a 'clearance'. The takeover process is expensive in terms of both time and money, and the parties will want to be certain that they are not going to make such an investment only for the CMA to block the takeover at a later stage in the process.

The parties to a takeover can seek clearance by pre-notification by a statutory merger notice once the takeover has been announced. The parties file a merger notice which answers questions about the takeover and which markets it may affect.

23.3.4.2 Informal advice

As an alternative to the offeror seeking clearance, the CMA will consider applications for informal advice on competition and jurisdictional issues arising out of a prospective merger situation that has not yet been made public. This procedure is only available to confidential transactions where there is a good faith intention to proceed, and where the CMA's duty to refer for a Phase 2 investigation is a genuine issue. Details of this guidance are available from the CMA website.

23.3.5 Undertakings

If the CMA concludes that, having considered the two issues referred to at **23.3.3.1** above, it is under an obligation to make a reference for a Phase 2 investigation, the parties may be able to provide certain undertakings with the effect that the takeover will not result in an SLC and so no reference is necessary. A good example of the use of undertakings was in the bid in 2003 by the supermarket chain Morrison for Safeway, which was cleared when Morrison provided an undertaking (referred to as a 'divestment undertaking') that it would sell 53 Safeway stores.

Note that the provision of undertakings can have an impact on the takeover timetable (see **Table 22.1** above), so any party seeking to provide such undertakings must keep the Panel informed and seek any necessary extensions to the timetable.

23.3.6 The lawyer's role

The competition lawyer's role will include the following:

(a) giving preliminary advice on the likelihood of the takeover being referred to the CMA;
(b) co-ordinating other advisers who may be needed to formulate arguments in favour of the offeror, such as economists and, perhaps, political consultants;
(c) preparing submissions on behalf of the offeror, and representing the offeror at hearings before the CMA; and
(d) negotiating undertakings to ensure the takeover falls outside the scope of the EA 2002.

23.4 EU MERGER CONTROL

On 1 May 2004 the Regulation on the control of concentrations between undertakings (EU Council Regulation 139/2004) (the 'EU Merger Regulation') came into force.

The EU Merger Regulation will apply if the takeover constitutes a *concentration* with a *Community dimension*. If the takeover fulfils these criteria then, subject to limited exceptions (see **23.4.7** below), the Regulation will apply to the exclusion of any national competition law rules and the takeover will fall within the exclusive jurisdiction of the European Commission. This is intended to relieve the burden on the parties to the takeover, by reducing the number of regulatory authorities to which they are subject. For this reason the Regulation is often referred to as 'the one-stop shop'.

If the takeover does not fulfil these criteria, then it falls outside the scope of the EU Merger Regulation, but it may still be caught by domestic merger control rules (see **23.3**).

23.4.1 Concentration

Article 3 of the EU Merger Regulation provides that a concentration can arise on:

(a) the merger of two or more independent undertakings;
(b) the acquisition of direct or indirect control of the whole or part of an undertaking or undertakings; or
(c) some joint ventures.

This definition reflects the fact that the EU Merger Regulation is drafted to catch more than simply takeovers. It is category (b) which may bring a takeover within the EU Merger Regulation. Note, however, that (b) can also catch acquisitions which do not constitute a takeover, for example the acquisition of assets.

'Control' in the context of the EU Merger Regulation is wider than the definition of 'control' in the Takeover Code. In this context, 'control' means more than just voting control. It includes, for example, where one party can exercise 'decisive influence' (art 3). An 18% shareholding was considered insufficient to confer control (EDF/AEM/Edison Case COMP/M.3729), whereas in Aker Maritime/Kvaerner Case COMP/M.2117 a 26.7% share constituted control for the purposes of the EU Merger Regulation.

23.4.2 Community dimension

Article 1 provides that a concentration will have a Community dimension if, subject to the two-thirds rule (see **23.4.3** below), it fulfils certain turnover criteria. There are two alternative sets of criteria, namely:

(a) the aggregate *worldwide* turnover of *all* parties exceeds z5,000m (approx £4,250m); and

(b) the aggregate *Community-wide* turnover of *at least two* of the parties exceeds z250m (approx £215m);

or

(a) the aggregate *worldwide* turnover of *all* parties exceeds z2,500m (approx £2,125m);

(b) the aggregate *Community-wide* turnover of *at least two* of the parties exceeds z100m (approx £85m); and

(c) in at least three Member States:

  (i) the aggregate *national* turnover of *all* the parties exceeds z100m (approx £85m), and

  (ii) the aggregate *national* turnover of *at least two* of the parties exceeds z25m (approx £21m).

Even if the takeover does not have a Community dimension, art 4, para 5 of the EU Merger Regulation provides that, if the takeover is capable of being reviewed under the national competition laws of at least three Member States, the parties can request the European Commission to take jurisdiction over the offer instead of the national authorities.

23.4.3 The two-thirds rule

A concentration will not have a Community dimension if each of the parties achieves more than two-thirds of its Community-wide turnover within the same Member State. This means, practically, that if the main impact of the takeover is within one Member State, it will not have a Community dimension. It could, of course, still be caught by the national competition rules of that Member State.

Practically, when calculating whether a takeover falls within the jurisdiction of the Commission, it is helpful to check whether the two-thirds rule applies *before* applying the 'Community dimension' test referred to at **23.4.2** above. If the two-thirds rule applies then there is no need to apply the 'Community dimension' test; the Commission will not have jurisdiction.

23.4.4 Notification

If the takeover constitutes a concentration with a Community dimension then the EU Merger Regulation provides that the parties must notify the European Commission before completion. The takeover cannot complete until the European Commission clears it. The notification should answer the Commission's questionnaire, Form CO, which requires considerable information about the parties and the transaction. Form CO is annexed to Regulation 802/2004/EC (as amended by the Implementing Regulation 1269/2013), which implemented the EU Merger Regulation.

23.4.5 Phase I

Article 10 provides that the Commission has 25 working days from the date of notification to decide that it:

(a) does not have jurisdiction because the offer does not fall within the scope of the EU Merger Regulation;

(b) will clear the offer (because it does not create or strengthen a dominant position in any relevant Community market);

(c) will allow the offer to proceed, subject to conditions (for example, the parties agreeing to dispose of part of the business);

(d) will investigate the offer further (because it has serious doubts whether it creates or strengthen a dominant position in any relevant Community market); or

(e) will refer the offer back to a Member State under art 9 (because the offer threatens to affect significantly competition in a distinct market within that Member State; see **23.4.7**).

This period of 25 days is referred to as Phase I. Phase I can be extended to 35 working days in certain circumstances, such as where remedies are offered, or where a Member State makes a request for an art 9 reference (see **23.4.7** below).

If the Commission decides (d) above, and commences a Phase II investigation, or decides (e) above, and there is then a Phase 2 CMA reference, the takeover offer will lapse under r 12.1 of the Takeover Code (see **23.2.1.1(b)**).

23.4.6 Phase II

If, at the end of Phase I, the Commission decides to investigate the offer further (option (d) above), that period of investigation is referred to as Phase II. As explained at **23.2.1**, if the European Commission initiates Phase II proceedings, the offer period will end. Phase II can last up to 90 working days. It can be extended by 20 working days at the request of the parties or the Commission (if the parties so consent). Phase II will automatically be extended by 15 working days where the parties offer remedies after the 54th day of the Phase II investigation.

At the end of Phase II, the Commission can:

(a) clear the takeover; or

(b) allow the takeover to proceed subject to certain conditions; or

(c) block the takeover.

An example of (c) above was seen in March 2017 when the Commission blocked Deutsche Boerse's £25 billion takeover of the London Stock Exchange Group plc which owns the LSE. It said that the merged entity would create a de facto monopoly in certain financial markets. The Commission would have approved the takeover if the LSE Group plc had sold its majority stake in a bond trading platform. It, however, refused to do so.

23.4.7 Exceptions

As **23.4** explains, the EU Merger Regulation is intended to be a 'one-stop shop' and applies to the exclusion of any national competition laws. However, a Member State can intervene to request repatriation of a case if it can demonstrate to the Commission that a reference back to the national authorities is necessary:

(a) to protect legitimate interests (such as national security) (art 21); or

(b) because the takeover threatens to affect significantly competition in a distinct market within that Member State (art 9).

For an example of (a), Spain imposed conditions on E.ON's and Enel and Acciona's bids for Endesa, the Spanish energy company, even though the European Commission had cleared both bids, arguing that it was necessary to protect Spain's national interests. The ECJ ruled that Spain had broken EU law by not withdrawing conditions on E.ON's bid (*Commission v Spain* (E.ON/Endesa) (Case C-196/07)). Separately, Poland launched infringement proceedings against the European Commission claiming that it had failed to take account of its interests in clearing the Unicredito/HVB merger (Case COMP/M.3894).

PART V

AIM

CHAPTER 24

AIM

24.1 BACKGROUND TO THIS CHAPTER

The focus of Parts I to IV of this book is the company which has its shares admitted to listing on the Official List and admitted to trading on the Main Market. However, in recent years much of the IPO activity in the UK has been on the Alternative Investment Market (AIM). As a result, it would be impossible to practise corporate law in today's climate without at least a basic understanding of AIM, how it compares to the Main Market, and the perceived advantages and disadvantages of an admission to AIM. This chapter seeks to help provide that basic understanding.

24.2 AN INTRODUCTION TO AIM

In 1995 the Stock Exchange established the AIM as its international market for smaller and growing companies. The Stock Exchange states that its objective 'was to offer smaller and companies – from any country and any industry sector – the chance to raise capital on a market with a pragmatic and appropriate approach to regulation. With this in mind, AIM was designed to be a highly flexible public market offering many unique attributes both for companies and investors'.

AIM has proved a great success. In fact, until recently it was the most successful growth market in the world. Since its launch in 1995, almost 4,000 companies have joined the market, raising more than £130 billion between them. As at 31 May 2024, approximately 720 companies were trading on AIM, with a total market capitalisation in excess of £100 billion. The market's appeal is not limited to the UK. The popularity of AIM with overseas companies rose sharply before the onset of the global financial crisis. In 2001, 16 overseas companies joined AIM; this rose to 124 in 2006 alone, but fewer international companies are now joining, reflecting on-going economic uncertainty in certain parts of the world; although there were still some 150 overseas companies trading on AIM as at 31 May 2024.

That said, AIM has been under pressure for a few years now. In the year to April 2024, 76 companies de-listed or left the market. Some went insolvent, a couple transferred to the Main Market, but for the majority it seems that the costs of being on AIM (Stock Exchange and professional advisers' fees, estimated at an average of £500,000 for the IPO and £200,000 each following year) and the tighter regulatory controls outweighed the benefits of being on AIM. In addition, valuations of companies on UK stock markets are low, reflecting their unpopularity in recent years. Since the global financial crisis in 2007, AIM now hosts almost 60% fewer companies. How long this trend will continue remains to be seen, but the cumulative effect of Brexit, the Covid pandemic, and economic and political instability in the

UK from 2016–2023 have certainly not helped. In addition, there have in recent years been a series of financial scandals involving AIM companies, such as Burford Capital, Patisserie Valerie, Eddie Stobart and even the owner of 5-a-side football pitches, Goal Soccer Centres, leading one institutional investor to call the market 'a cesspit ... guaranteed to rip the public off' and 'probably the worst market in the western world due to its low standards and low scrutiny'.

Typically it is the smaller UK companies who list on AIM, particularly natural resources, technology and fast-growing companies. Some AIM companies are household names, such as ASOS, Fevertree Drinks and boohoo.

AIM is regulated by the Stock Exchange. The UK Listing Rules do not apply to AIM companies (see **3.5.2**). Instead, AIM companies are governed by a set of rules helpfully titled the 'AIM Rules', and they apply equally to companies incorporated in the UK and overseas. The AIM Rules are drafted with smaller companies in mind; they do not contain much legal or technical jargon, and this allows them to be applied flexibly and comprehensively. The AIM Rules comprise two parts. Part One contains the rules, while Part Two contains guidance notes (available from the AIM section of the Stock Exchange website). The latest version of the AIM Rules is from 1 January 2021.

24.3 WHY AIM?

The advantages of listing, set out at **1.7** above, apply equally to AIM as they do to the Main Market. As, typically, it is the smaller, emerging companies who join AIM, the accessible market, easy access to capital and acquisition opportunities and employee incentives AIM offers are a particular draw.

So why join AIM rather than the Main Market? This decision has become much more difficult for companies since the introduction of the UK Listing Rules in July 2024 and the ESCC listing category. The ESCC category of the Main Market remains a more regulated market than AIM, but following substantial deregulation, it is in some areas less regulated than AIM.

In addition to the benefits referred to above, the following aspects of AIM can render it more attractive than an ESCC listing on the Main Market, particularly for smaller companies:

(a) AIM is easier to access:
   (i) it has reduced eligibility requirements (see **24.4**); and
   (ii) the role of the 'Nomad' (see **24.4.1**) means the admission process is more straightforward.

(b) AIM has a more relaxed regulatory regime. In particular:
   (i) there are reduced disclosure requirements;
   (ii) the brevity of the AIM Rules means that the day-to-day regulatory work required for an AIM company costs less than that for an ESCC-listed Main Market company; and
   (iii) the requirement for a prospectus is confined to circumstances where there is a public offer; Article 3(3) of the UK Prospectus Regulation and s 85(2) of the FSMA 2000 do not apply to AIM companies (see **24.5.1**).

(c) AIM offers tax advantages for investors which the Main Market does not.

24.4 ELIGIBILITY CRITERIA

The minimum requirements for admission to AIM are different from those of the Main Market (set out at **4.3.1.2** and **4.3.1.3** above). For example, unlike an ESCC category listing on the Main Market, there are no requirements in respect of market capitalisation or the number of shares in public hands.

In order to seek admission to AIM, a company must comply with the following minimum requirements:

(a) *Incorporation*. The company must be legally established under the laws of its place of incorporation and be able to offer shares to the public. (For UK companies this means being a public company – CA 2006, s 755.)

(b) *Transferability*. Shares admitted to AIM must be freely transferable (AIM Rules, r 32).

(c) *Whole class to be listed*. All issued shares of the same class must be admitted (AIM Rules, r 33).

(d) *Electronic settlement*. All shares admitted must be eligible for electronic settlement (AIM Rules, r 36).

(e) *Accounts*. The company (if it is incorporated in an EEA country) must have published accounts which conform with International Accounting Standards (ie IFRS) (AIM Rules, r 19).

(f) *Nominated adviser*. A nominated adviser (known as a 'Nomad') (AIM Rules, r 1) and broker must be appointed and retained at all times (AIM Rules, r 35) (see **24.4.1**).

In the event that the company's main activity is a business that has been generating revenue and/or been independent for less than two years prior to its admission to AIM, it is subject to a condition that all directors (and their families) and employees who hold an interest in the company and certain substantial shareholders must agree not to dispose of their interests for at least one year following admission to AIM (AIM Rules, r 7).

24.4.1 The Nomad

One of the most significant differences between the Main Market and AIM is the role of the nominated adviser (or 'Nomad'). The Stock Exchange attributes the success of AIM largely to the role of the Nomad, which is to guide a company first through the admission process and then through its life as a publicly quoted company. Rule 1 of the AIM Rules requires every AIM company to retain a Nomad at all times. The Stock Exchange will suspend trading in the securities of any AIM company which ceases to have a Nomad, and cancel their admission if a replacement Nomad is not appointed within one month.

24.4.1.1 Duties and responsibilities

Under r 39 of the AIM Rules the Nomad must comply with a separate set of rules, the AIM Rules for Nominated Advisers (the 'Nomad Rules', available in the AIM section of the Stock Exchange website). These separate rules for Nomads were introduced on 20 February 2007 and strengthen the regulatory regime for AIM-quoted companies.

The Nomad owes its responsibilities solely to the Stock Exchange.

The Nomad must:

(a) ensure that the company is suitable for admission to AIM; and

(b) advise and guide the company through the admission process and, once quoted on AIM, on its on-going responsibilities; and

(c) most importantly, confirm to the Stock Exchange that any admission document or prospectus (see **24.5**) complies with the requirements of Sch 2 to the AIM Rules.

Schedule 3 to the AIM Rules for the Nominated Adviser sets out more detailed responsibilities which the Nomad must perform. These are split into three categories: Admission Responsibilities; Ongoing Responsibilities; and Engagement Responsibilities. Only the first two are relevant to a Nomad acting for a new applicant to AIM. A list of Nomads is available on the AIM section of the Stock Exchange website.

These various Responsibilities are presented as a group of overriding principles accompanied by supporting 'actions'. The Nomad must comply with the principles in all cases. The 'actions' provide examples of how the principles translate into practice.

For example, principle AR1 requires the Nomad to gain a sound understanding of the company and its business before admission to AIM. One of the listed actions states that usually this requires the Nomad to visit the material places of operation of the company and to meet the directors. This ensures a business trip to Qatar, Kazakhstan, China or Wigan, depending on the company concerned.

There are two points to note about these actions. First, they are not an exhaustive list of actions the Nomad should take and, secondly, although the Stock Exchange usually will expect all the actions listed to be taken, a Nomad can take alternative action if it feels it is better suited to achieving the principle. The Stock Exchange's AIM Regulation team has started to produce a periodic publication, somewhat uninspiringly called 'Inside AIM' (available on the Stock Exchange's website), to offer guidance on the AIM Rules and the market, particularly to Nomads.

24.4.1.2 Admission Responsibilities

In preparation for admission of the new applicant company to AIM the Nomad is obliged, in addition to AR1 mentioned at **24.4.1.1** above, to assess the suitability of the board of directors (individually and collectively), oversee the due diligence procedure leading up to flotation, satisfy itself that the admission document complies with Sch 2 to the AIM Rules, and ensure that procedures are in place for the new company and its directors to comply with the AIM Rules.

24.4.1.3 Ongoing Responsibilities

Once the company has been admitted to AIM, the Nomad must consult regularly with the company, review announcements before they are released to the market, monitor trading in the company's shares, particularly when there is unpublished, price-sensitive information in existence, and advise on any changes to the board of directors to the company and their impact.

On 7 December 2018, the Stock Exchange publicly censured and fined Bushveld Minerals Limited a record £700,000 for breaches of the AIM Rules, including r 11 and r 31 for failing to seek the advice of its Nomad, and for failing to release price-sensitive information. In May 2014 an AIM company was privately censured and fined £90,000 for breaches of the AIM Rules, including ignoring the advice of its Nomad and failing to provide the Nomad with full information on a related party transaction.

24.4.2 The broker

An AIM company must retain a broker at all times (AIM Rules, r 35). If there is no registered market maker (see **2.5.2**), the broker must use its best endeavours to find a matching business. Any member firm of the Stock Exchange can act as broker, subject to any required authorisation by any other regulator. A list of member firms is available on the AIM section of the Stock Exchange website, together with a separate list of brokers which AIM companies have appointed.

24.5 THE MARKETING DOCUMENT

When a company applies for admission to AIM, or is raising further equity finance on AIM then, subject to exemptions (see **24.5.1.1**), the company must produce a prospectus or an admission document.

24.5.1 Prospectus or admission document?

Chapter 6 sets out in detail when a company is required to publish a prospectus pursuant to the UK Prospectus Regulation and s 85 of the FSMA 2000. As stated at **3.5.1** above, the UK Prospectus Regulation applies to AIM companies as well as to Main Market companies. A prospectus is required when a company either:

(a) offers transferable securities to the public in the UK (Art 3(1) of the UK Prospectus Regulation and s 85(1)); or

(b) requests admission of transferable securities to trading on a regulated market situated or operating in the UK (Art 3(3) of the UK Prospectus Regulation and s 85(2)).

The AIM is a UK Multilateral Trading Facility (MTF) and it is regulated by the LSE. A UK MTF is not a 'UK regulated market' for the purposes of Art 3(3) of the UK Prospectus Regulation and s 85(2), and Article 3(3) of the UK Prospectus Regulation and s 85(2) do not apply to an AIM company or a company seeking admission to AIM. Nevertheless, if an AIM company, or a company seeking admission to AIM, is offering transferable securities to the public in the UK then, subject to any applicable exemptions, a prospectus is required under Article 3(1) of the UK Prospectus Regulation and s 85(1). If a prospectus is required on admission to AIM, this prospectus will serve as the admission document (Guidance note to Schedule 2 to the AIM Rules).

However, as a company seeks admission to AIM because of its more flexible and pragmatic regulation, typically AIM companies will seek to structure any public offer to fall within one of the exemptions set out in Article 1(4) of the UK Prospectus Regulation.

If a prospectus is not required, the company must instead produce an admission document in accordance with the AIM Rules, which require less content than a prospectus under the UK Prospectus Regulation (see **24.5.3**). An admission document does not require approval by the FCA.

24.5.1.1 Exemptions to the requirement to produce a prospectus

The exemptions to Article 3(1) of the UK Prospectus Regulation and s 85(1) are set out at **6.4.1.4** above. The most common exemptions relied upon by AIM companies are those set out at **6.4.1.4(a)** (offers to qualified investors), **6.4.1.4(b)** (offers to fewer than 150 persons who are not qualified investors), **6.4.1.4(c)** (offers involving significant investment by each investor), **6.4.1.4(h)** (small offers) and **6.4.1.4(e)** (offers in conjunction with takeovers by way of share for share exchange).

If any of the exemptions to Article 3(1) of the UK Prospectus Regulation and s 85(1) apply, a prospectus will not be required (remember that Article 3(3) of the UK Prospectus Regulation and s 85(2) are not relevant in relation to AIM as it is not a UK regulated market). In practice, any sizeable rights issue or open offer to raise further finance will tend to be to more than 150 persons in the UK (as is the case with the Main Market), and therefore in these circumstances it will be necessary to draft a prospectus and have it approved by the FCA.

24.5.2 Responsibility

The directors take overall responsibility for a prospectus or admission document (although a third party may take responsibility for a specific part of the document). The directors are responsible for ensuring compliance with the AIM Rules.

24.5.3 Content requirements

24.5.3.1 Prospectus

The content requirements of a prospectus are as set out in the UK PR Regulation (see **6.5**).

24.5.3.2 Admission document

The Stock Exchange has carved out certain requirements of the UK PR Regulation in relation to the content requirements of an admission document. The carve-outs reflect the nature of AIM and the companies admitted to it.

The content requirements are set out in Sch 2 to the AIM Rules.

24.6 CONTINUING OBLIGATIONS

24.6.1 The general obligation of disclosure

As stated at **3.5.3**, the Disclosure Rules do not apply to AIM companies. The AIM Rules set out continuing obligations of AIM companies. The primary obligation is a general duty of disclosure, set out in r 11. This provides that every AIM company must announce, without delay, any new developments which:

(a) are not public knowledge; and
(b) concern a change in its financial condition, its sphere of activity, performance of its business, or its expectation of its performance; and
(c) if made public, would be likely to cause a substantial movement in the price of its securities.

This includes but is not limited to information which a reasonable investor would be likely to use as the basis for her investment decisions. The company must make the announcement through an RIS. Rule 10 of the AIM Rules requires that the company must take reasonable care to ensure that any information it notifies is not misleading, false or deceptive, and does not omit anything likely to affect the import of such information.

It is important to note that the r 11 obligation is in addition to the UK MAR, Article 17 obligation to disclose inside information (see **7.5.1** above), as explicitly stated in the Guidance to r 11 in the AIM Rules. Whilst there is a significant overlap between the two rules, they are not identical and so an AIM company must ensure that it complies with both rules. Remember that the FCA enforces UK MAR whereas the LSE enforces the AIM Rules.

24.6.2 Specific disclosure obligations

In addition to the general obligation to disclose price-sensitive information, there are specific obligations of disclosure in relation to the following:

(a) substantial transactions (AIM Rules, r 12 – see **24.6.2.1** below);
(b) related party transactions (AIM Rules, r 13 – see **24.6.2.2** below);
(c) reverse takeovers (AIM Rules, r 14 – see **24.6.2.3** below);
(d) any disposal resulting in a fundamental change of business (AIM Rules, r 15 – see **24.6.2.4** below);
(e) changes to significant shareholders (DTR 5 and AIM Rules, r 17 – see **24.6.2.5** below);
(f) changes in directors, directors' details, Nomad or broker (AIM Rules, r 17);
(g) any material change in the company's actual trading performance or financial condition and between any profit forecast or estimate included in the company's admission document, or which is otherwise in the public domain (AIM Rules, r 17);
(h) other matters set out in r 17 of the AIM Rules, including any change to the accounting reference date, registered office address or legal name;
(i) details of the directors' remuneration in the audited annual report (AIM Rules, r 19); and
(j) an AIM company must also disclose certain key information on its website, including its current constitutional documents, the number of AIM securities in issue and details of a

recognised corporate governance code that the company applies, how it complies with it, where it departs from it and why (AIM Rules, r 26).

24.6.2.1 Substantial transactions

An AIM company must disclose details of any substantial transactions. A transaction is substantial if it exceeds 10% of any class test contained in Sch 3 to the AIM Rules (which are similar to the class tests set out in UKLR 7 Annex 1; see **19.4**).

Schedule 3 sets out a comparison between the size of the transaction and the company itself in respect of the following:

(a) gross assets;
(b) profits;
(c) turnover;
(d) consideration to market capitalisation; and
(e) gross capital (in acquisitions of a company or business).

If a transaction is revenue in nature and occurring in the ordinary course of the business of the company, or if it has undertaken to raise finance that does not involve a change in the fixed assets of the company, it will not constitute a substantial transaction.

If the transaction exceeds 10% of any of the Sch 3 class tests, and so constitutes a substantial transaction, an announcement must be made pursuant to Sch 3, which must include the prescribed information set out in Sch 4. However, there is no requirement for shareholder approval, or for a circular (unless required under another AIM rule). Directors of AIM companies often cite this as a reason for choosing AIM over the Main Market.

24.6.2.2 Related party transaction

If the transaction is with a related party (as defined by the AIM Rules) and exceeds 5% in any of the Sch 3 class tests referred to at **24.6.2.1** above, an announcement containing prescribed information as set out in Sch 4 to the AIM Rules is required. The announcement must include a statement that the directors (excluding any director involved directly in the transaction) having consulted with the company's Nomad, consider that the terms of the transaction are fair and reasonable.

Where the class test exceeds 0.25%, the company must include details of any related party transaction in the company's annual audited accounts (see **24.6.3**).

In November 2021, the Exchange censured and fined Sensyne Health plc £580,000 for failing to maintain effective controls to enable compliance with the AIM Rules (r 31), and for failing to comply with r 13 in respect of bonus payments made to its CEO and CFO respectively. The company failed to consult adequately with a nomad or make the necessary disclosures in relation to these related party transactions.

24.6.2.3 Reverse takeover

A transaction (or transactions) over a 12-month period which either:

(a) exceeds 100% of any of the class tests sets out in Sch 3 to the AIM Rules (see **24.6.2.1**); or
(b) results in a fundamental change to the AIM company's business, board or voting control (or, in the case of an investing company (as defined by the AIM Rules), departs substantially from the investing strategy set out in its prospectus or admission document),

constitutes a reverse takeover under r 14 of the AIM Rules.

The company must:

(a) obtain shareholder approval (by ordinary resolution) for any reverse takeover (and any agreement relating to a reverse takeover must be conditional upon such approval);

(b) prepare a prospectus or admission document, which must describe the circumstances and details of the transaction and convene the shareholders' general meeting to approve the transaction; and

(c) make an announcement of the reverse takeover via an RIS without delay, disclosing the information specified by Sch 4 to the AIM Rules.

Trading in the company's securities will be cancelled. The enlarged entity must seek admission in the same manner as any other AIM company which is seeking admission for the first time.

24.6.2.4 Disposal resulting in a fundamental change of business

Any disposal which, when aggregated with any other disposal or disposals over the previous 12 months, exceeds 75% in any of the class tests set out in Sch 3 to the AIM Rules (see **24.6.2.1** above), is a disposal which results in a fundamental change of business ('DFCB') (AIM Rules, r 15).

A DFCB must be conditional on shareholder approval (by ordinary resolution). A circular containing the information specified in Sch 4 to the AIM Rules (and r 13 insofar as the disposal is to a related party) and a notice of GM will also be required. Where the proposed disposal will divest the company of all, or substantially all, of its trading business activities, the circular must state the company's investing strategy going forward.

The Company must notify an RIS of the DFCB without delay, disclosing the information specified by Sch 4 to the AIM Rules. If the transaction involves a related party, the information required by r 13 of the AIM Rules must also be disclosed.

The company must make the acquisition (or acquisitions) constituting a reverse takeover under r 14 of the AIM Rules within 12 months of receiving the consent of its shareholders.

24.6.2.5 Changes to significant shareholders

Under r 17 of the AIM Rules, any changes of 1% or more in the holdings of 'significant shareholders' must be notified to an RIS as soon as possible. A significant shareholder is one who holds at least 3% of the AIM company's issued share capital.

In addition, DTR 5 applies to AIM companies incorporated under the Companies Act or who have their principal place of business in the UK (see **15.6**).

Generally compliance with DTR 5 will satisfy r 17 of the AIM Rules, but the Stock Exchange has pointed out that whereas DTR 5 requires the disclosure to be made as soon as possible on receipt of a notification and by no later than the end of the third trading day following notification (DTR 5.8.12R), under r 17 it must be made without delay, which is a stricter standard.

24.6.3 Financial information

The AIM Rules supplement the financial obligations in the CA 2006 with more specific obligations.

The AIM Rules require companies incorporated in the UK or in an EEA country to publish annual accounts in accordance with International Accounting Standards (ie IFRS). The company must send the accounts to shareholders within six months of the end of the financial year to which they relate (AIM Rules, r 19). The accounts must disclose any transaction with a related party (see **24.6.2.2**), whether or not previously disclosed under the AIM Rules, where any of the class tests in Sch 3 to the AIM Rules exceed 0.25%, and specify the identity of the related party and the consideration for the transaction.

The AIM Rules also require listed companies to prepare interim reports in respect of the first six months of the company's financial period. The company must publish the interim reports within three months of the end of this half-year period and must notify an RIS that they have been published (AIM Rules, r 18).

In addition, although not mandatory, it is best practice for an AIM company to include a statement in its annual report which discloses the extent to which it has complied with the principles set out in the UK CGC (see **24.7**).

24.6.4 Share dealing policy

Rule 21 of the AIM Rules requires that an AIM company must have in place from admission a reasonable and effective dealing policy setting out the requirements and procedures for directors' and applicable employees' dealings in any of its securities. At a minimum, an AIM company's dealing policy must set out the following:

- the AIM company's close periods during which directors and applicable employees cannot deal;
- when a director or applicable employee must obtain clearance to deal in the AIM securities of the AIM company;
- an appropriate person(s) within the AIM company to grant clearance requests;
- procedures for obtaining clearance for dealing;
- the appropriate timeframe for a director or applicable employee to deal once they have received clearance;
- how the AIM company will assess whether clearance to deal may be given; and
- procedures on how the AIM company will notify deals required to be made public under UK MAR.

24.7 CORPORATE GOVERNANCE

The UK CGC does not apply to AIM companies, although they are encouraged to comply with it. In April 2018, the Quoted Company Alliance ('QCA') published the latest version of its Corporate Governance Code for small and mid-sized quoted companies which applies to AIM companies. The guidelines are available to order from the QCA website. AIM companies have a choice as to which corporate governance code to follow. In practice, just under a half of AIM companies follow the QCA and the remainder the UK CGC (to the extent that it is practicable) or other codes, eg foreign corporate governance codes.

The AIM Rules, r 26 requires the company to put details on its website of a 'recognised' corporate governance code the company applies, how it complies with it, where it departs from it and why. This information must be updated annually.

APPENDICES

APPENDIX 1

The Investment Association Transaction Guidelines

Note: The Guidelines dated November 2014 are reproduced below by kind permission of the Investment Association. Please check the Institutional Voting Information Service (IVIS) website of The Investment Association (see <www.ivis.co.uk>) for any updates.

THE
INVESTMENT
ASSOCIATION

TRANSACTION GUIDELINES

November 2014
(Updated for the purpose of rebranding on 3rd June 2015)

Registered office: The Investment Association
65 Kingsway, London, WC2B 6TD
The Investment Association is a company limited
by guarantee registered in England and
Wales. Registered number 04343737.

Following the merger of ABI Investment Affairs with the IMA on 30th June, 2014, the enlarged Investment Management Association (IMA), which was renamed The Investment Association in January 2015, has assumed responsibility for guidance previously issued by the ABI.

This guidance sets out the expectations and views of The Investment Association's members as institutional investors on various aspects of equity capital market transactions. These views build on the key recommendations published in the ABI's 'Encouraging Equity Investment' Report, July 2013, and 'Improving Corporate Governance and Shareholder Engagement', July 2013.

The guidance below is structured under the three headings of "Initial Public Offerings" (IPOs), "Secondary Offerings", and "Corporate Governance during Corporate Transactions".

1. INITIAL PUBLIC OFFERINGS (IPOs)

1.1 Syndicate Size

Syndicates provide the required access and distribution to an investor base, which will ultimately make up a stable shareholder register for a company undergoing an IPO. Maintaining a balance between achieving depth of distribution to a wide range of investors and avoiding duplication of investor opinion from across and within the various categories is essential to an efficient IPO process.

1.1.1 The Investment Association believes that, as a rule of thumb, no more than three book-runners should be appointed for large transactions (i.e. above £250m excluding any over-allotment option). Below this issue size, there should generally be no more than two book-runners.

1.1.2 Issuers should ensure that any additional members of the syndicate are included based on their sector expertise or distributional reach.

1.1.3 We discourage the inclusion of syndicate members who are present solely on the basis of past or future services to the issuer or vendors. Nonetheless, we acknowledge that vendors and/or companies may occasionally need to appoint more banks to the syndicate due to on-going relationships. In these instances, companies should clearly specify the roles and responsibilities of each syndicate member, including those with entirely passive roles in relation to the transaction.

1.1.4 Issuers, with the assistance of independent advisers if appropriate, should scrutinise the allocations carefully, to ensure that shares are being distributed to those most likely to be long-term shareholders.

1.1.5 We encourage issuers and vendors to consider including a retail tranche when listing in the Premium segment.

1.2 Fees

IPO fees in the UK vary widely depending on a number of factors, including size of issue; size of company; identity of vendor; complexity of the transaction; likely breadth of distribution;

and desirability of mandate. There remains amongst new investors at the IPO a significant concern with the overall level of fees.

1.2.1 There should be, as a matter of good practice, greater disclosure in the prospectus of all the fees paid for an IPO, including the maximum incentive fee, if any. This should include a breakdown of fees as a percentage of the size of the offering, and those fees that are independent of size, such as, but not limited to, independent advisers', lawyers' and accountants' fees. Syndicate members' individual fees should also be disclosed.

1.2.2 The final determination and payment of incentive fees in an IPO should be made either at the release of the first quarterly results of the issuer as a listed company or three months after listing (whichever of the two events occurs later). The amount paid should be disclosed to the market at the time of award.

1.2.3 The following criteria should be taken into consideration when awarding the incentive fee:

- the stability of the share price in the newly listed environment;
- the allocation of the shares of the issuer to a predominantly long-term shareholder base, as evidenced by the stability of the share register in the aftermarket;
- the extent and quality of the syndicate research both during and after the IPO, in the eyes of the investor; and
- the continuity of research coverage post IPO.

1.2.4 A mechanism should be established for investors to give input into the allocation of the incentive fee, but on an anonymous basis.

1.3 Prospectus

Market views on prospectuses include that they:

- are too detailed to be understood by retail investors;
- contain too many generic or boiler plate risk factors that obscure the most important risks and opportunities; and
- are too time consuming to fully consider, given the short time between the Pathfinder prospectus being issued and investors' meetings with management as part of the roadshow, resulting in some investors feeling ill-prepared for the company meeting.

1.3.1 We are strongly supportive of the UKLA's aim to reduce the amount of generic information in the prospectus. We encourage issuers, their Sponsors and lawyers to work with the UKLA to provide a document that is more succinct in providing the important information relevant to an investment decision.

1.4 Sponsor Regime

The Sponsor regime is fundamental to ensuring the effectiveness of the Premium equity market by:

- considering whether an issuer is suitable for admission and that admittance will not be detrimental to investors' interests;

- ensuring that issuers seeking a Premium listing understand the regulatory framework that they operate in; and
- providing the UKLA with assurance that the relevant rules have been complied with and that the issuer has established appropriate procedures and therefore meets the UKLA's eligibility criteria.

1.4.1 The Investment Association's members as institutional investors therefore expect:

- clarity on the role of the Sponsor in an IPO process so that the appointment is clear to market participants and distinguishable from the role of the lead book-runner(s);
- Sponsors to consider including an institutional 'stamp of approval' in relation to the suitability of the company for listing;
- any potential conflicts of interest that may arise if a Sponsor is also one of the lead distributors of an IPO, and so may be conflicted if there are any contentious issues with the company, to be managed and mitigated; and
- the Key Adviser for issuers who seek a flotation on the High Growth Segment of the Main Market should already be an approved Sponsor under the UK Listing Rules.

1.5 Role of the Independent Adviser

In recent years, there has been an increase in the use of independent advisers ("IAs"). IAs are typically appointed by management teams or vendors who have limited, or less frequent experience of equity capital markets, or require extra resources to help them through the process.

Investors typically have limited contact with the IAs as part of the IPO process. However, they value the importance of a well-run syndicate and proper flow of information.

1.5.1 IAs should ensure that a syndicate is well managed; that the right information and advice is provided both to and by the issuer; and that the syndicate and issuer's interests are protected.

2. SECONDARY OFFERINGS

2.1 Underwriting Capacity and Fees and Discounts

There is sufficient primary and sub-underwriting capacity in the UK market. However, capacity from traditional sub-underwriters in the UK has fallen. Most parties agree that the split of risk and the reward for taking such risk between primary and sub-underwriters could be improved. Greater transparency and unbundling of fees will lead to greater reconciliation of risk with reward.

2.1.1 Companies should use deep discounts in rights issues in order to reduce the level of underwriting fees paid to both primary underwriters and sub-underwriters. They are also encouraged to reduce primary underwriting fees where possible, by getting firm undertakings from sub-underwriters before announcing the transaction.

2.1.2 The gross spread for rights issues and open offers should be unbundled, so that the amounts for advice, including document preparation, primary underwriting and sub-underwriting are shown separately. These unbundled fees should be fully disclosed in the offering documents, along with disclosure of other rights issue related fees including, but not limited to, lawyers, accountants and independent advisers.

2.1.3 Investors would like to see disaggregated disclosure as a matter of best practice, despite there being no legal requirement for the disclosure of disaggregated fees.

2.1.4 Tendering for both primary and sub-underwriting should be pursued only if the unbundling of fees does not lead to a lowering of the overall fee levels.

2.1.5 We encourage both the buy-side and the sell-side to develop standard sub-underwriting agreements. This will help make the sub-underwriting process more efficient, particularly if institutions are engaged ahead of announcement, which in turn should result in a reduction in overall fees.

2.1.6 The aggregate fees charged, and the discounts to the mid-market price at the time of agreeing the placing, should be disclosed in the pricing announcement for non-pre-emptive placings.

2.2 Timetables

There are two parts to a timetable for pre-emptive issue:

i. Private: before the transaction is publicly announced
ii. Public: the period after announcement in which any general meeting and the offering will take place

2.2.1 Efforts should be made to shorten a pre-emptive timetable even further by examining ways to eliminate the physical distribution of documents and reducing the time needed by custodians to enact their clients' instructions to exercise.

2.2.2 We encourage the UKLA to investigate the feasibility of introducing a fast-track review process for time critical offerings. Issuers should expect to pay higher fees for any extra resources needed for the UKLA to provide this service.

3. CORPORATE GOVERNANCE DURING CORPORATE TRANSACTIONS

The Investment Association believes that non-executive directors are crucial to good governance; we are recommending structural measures to ensure that non-executives can maintain and assert independence during corporate transactions.

3.1 Corporate Transactions and Independence

In the context of a transaction, it is particularly important that non-executives are able to exercise their function of independent challenge effectively. Independence is more than the nature of the non-executive's connections with the company and extends to avoiding circumstances (which may involve a deficiency in internal structures and procedures) which may undermine, or appear to undermine, the ability of non-executive directors to act independently.

3.1.1 Non-executive directors should be given sufficient time and information to give proper consideration to the merits of the transaction in question, as well as the opportunity to provide their views to shareholders when they are first made insiders. This will help to balance the need for the provision of sufficient information to shareholder with the desire to maintain secrecy before announcements and avoid false markets.

3.1.2 Executive directors should inform the appropriate non-executive director of the proposed transaction when an approach is received from a possible bidder or management first actively considers a transaction in respect of which a shareholder approval is to be sought.

3.1.3 The non-executive directors should be provided with a narrative description of discussions between the company and the transaction counterparty and this narrative should be disclosed in summary form in the circular to shareholders.

3.1.4 Non-executive directors should be given direct access to financial and legal advisers to the company on a transaction in order to ensure that information can be rapidly obtained and understood.

3.1.5 We encourage the practice for non-executives, both regularly and in specific circumstances, to have discussions without the executives present. When considering a transaction, the non-executives' group should confirm to the Chairman, prior to publication of any circular or recommendation to shareholders, that they are satisfied they have received sufficient time and information.

3.1.6 Non-executive directors should consider whether it is appropriate to seek separate, independent advice on the merits of the proposed transaction. In these instances, the adviser should be paid on a fixed fee (as opposed to a 'success' or 'incentive') basis.

3.2 Independent Committees

Where a company is subject to a management buy-out or similar transaction, or engaging in a transaction with a controller or a group of controllers, or where a conflict may otherwise arise, a special independent committee comprising only un-conflicted directors should always be formed to consider the transaction.

3.2.1 The committee should always take independent financial and legal advice. It is not acceptable for a 'Chinese Wall' to be established within the existing advisers to the company.

3.2.2 Independent committees formed to consider a transaction should ensure their mandate is clear and is disclosed in any circular to shareholders or annual report, as is currently required. The mandate should normally extend to considering the terms of the transaction and whether the transaction itself (as opposed to the other courses of action) is in the best interests of the company and shareholders as a whole.

Last Updated: November 2014

Enquiries to:
Markets Team
ivis@theinvestmentassociation.org
020 7831 0898

APPENDIX 2

The Investment Association Share Capital Management Guidelines

Note: The Guidelines dated July 2016 are reproduced below by kind permission of the Investment Association. Please check the Institutional Voting Information Service (IVIS) website of The Investment Association (see <www.ivis.co.uk>) for any updates.

THE
INVESTMENT
ASSOCIATION

SHARE CAPITAL MANAGEMENT GUIDELINES

July 2016

Registered office: The Investment Association
Camomile Court, 23 Camomile Street, London
EC3A 7LL
The Investment Association is a company limited
by guarantee registered in England and
Wales. Registered number 04343737.

Following the merger of ABI Investment Affairs with the IMA on 30th June, 2014, the enlarged Investment Management Association (IMA), which was renamed The Investment Association in January 2015, has assumed responsibility for guidance previously issued by the ABI.

This guidance sets out the expectations of The Investment Association's members as institutional investors on various aspects of share capital management. It applies to companies whose shares are admitted to the premium segment of the Official List of the UK Listing Authority.

Companies whose shares are admitted to the standard segment of the Official List, to trading on AIM, or to the High Growth Segment of the London Stock Exchange's Main Market, are encouraged to adopt this guidance.

1 Directors' Power to Allot Shares

This sets out the expectations of Investment Association members where companies seek shareholder authorisation for the general allotment of new shares and any disapplication of pre-emption rights.

The ABI guidelines on directors' powers to allot shares were last revised in January 2009 following a recommendation by the Rights Issues Review Group to the Chancellor that the ceiling on allotments of shares should be increased from one-third to two-thirds of the issuer's share capital. This has generally functioned well.

1.1 Section 551 – General Power to Allot

1.1.1 Members will regard as routine an authority to allot up to two-thirds of the existing issued share capital. Any amount in excess of one-third of existing issued shares should be applied to fully pre-emptive rights issues only.

1.1.2 This routine authority is acceptable as appropriate protections against shareholder dilution are provided both by pre-emption rights and the requirement that shareholders of premium listed companies in the UK have a vote on all major transactions – under Listing Rule 10.5, a listed company must, in relation to a Class 1 transaction send an explanatory circular to its shareholders and obtain their prior approval in a general meeting for the transaction / ensure that any agreement effecting the transaction is conditional on that approval being obtained.

1.1.3 The authority should be approved by ordinary resolution and be for the period until the next Annual General Meeting.

1.1.4 In calculating existing issued share capital, any shares held in Treasury should be excluded.

1.2 Section 570 – General Power to Disapply Pre-emption Rights

1.2.1 The terms of a special resolution to disapply pre-emption rights should comply with the provisions of the Pre-emption Group's current Statement of Principles.

1.2.2 The Investment Association notes that the Pre-emption Group has provided template resolutions for the disapplication of pre-emption rights. The template provides for two separate resolutions, which relate to:

a) Disapplication of pre-emption rights on up to five per cent of the issued share capital to be used on an unrestricted basis; and

b) The second resolution, to be put forward by companies when appropriate, requests the disapplication of pre-emption rights for an additional five per cent in cases when boards consider the use to be for the purposes of an acquisition or specified capital investment in accordance with the Statement of Principles.

1.2.3 Investment Association members' are supportive of this update and expect that any company seeking a disapplication of pre-emption rights which in aggregate is equal to 10% of the issued capital to follow the model resolutions.

1.2.4 Investment Association members have asked the Institutional Voting Information Service (IVIS), the IA's corporate governance research service, to take the following approach for companies seeking a disapplication of pre-emption rights which in aggregate is equal to 10% of the issued share capital:

a) From **1 August 2016,** IVIS will amber top any company which does not provide two separate resolutions as set out in the template.

b) From **1 January 2017,** IVIS will red top any company which does not provide two separate resolutions as set out in the template.

2 Own Share Purchase

Institutional investors are supportive of companies' efforts to return surplus funds to shareholders. Dividend payments remain the preferred method for regular distributions to shareholders. However, the following guidelines are provided for companies who decide that share repurchases are in the best interests of their shareholders.

2.1 Authority to Repurchase Own Shares

2.1.1 Companies should seek authority to purchase their own shares whether on market or off market by special resolution and not simply an ordinary resolution as is allowed by Sections 694 and 701 of the Companies Act 2006.

2.1.2 A general authority to purchase shares should be renewed annually.

2.1.3 Shareholders expect that a general authority for a company to purchase its own shares will be exercised only if it is in the best interests of shareholders generally and normally only if it would result in an increase in earnings per share or, in the case of property companies and investment trusts, if it would result in an increase in asset value per share for the remaining shareholders. Where this is not expected, the benefits should be explained clearly.

2.1.4 Companies should disclose in their next Annual Report the justification for any own share purchases made in the previous year, including an explanation of why this method of returning capital to shareholders was decided upon. In this context, companies should discuss the effect share buybacks have on earnings per share (EPS), total shareholder return (TSR) and net asset value (NAV) per share. EPS and TSR targets under both short and long-term incentive schemes should take account of the effect of share buybacks. Market conditions should be carefully considered and an average price paid should be disclosed. The effect on the holdings of major shareholders might also merit discussion in the Annual Report.

2.2 Amount

2.2.1 A general authority to purchase up to 10% of the existing issued Ordinary share capital is unlikely to cause concern.

2.2.2 The Institutional Voting Information Service (IVIS) will note a general authority to purchase more than 10% (but less than 15%) of the existing issued ordinary share capital. A repurchase of more than 15% is not permitted under the Listing Rules, unless carried out by a tender offer.

2.2.3 In calculating existing issued share capital, any shares held in Treasury should be excluded.

2.2.4 Whilst the Companies Act now allows companies to hold more than 10% of their shares in Treasury, the Investment Association's preference is for companies not to hold more than 10% in Treasury.

2.3 Price

2.3.1 Investment Association members consider as appropriate the requirement of the Listing Rules that (unless a tender offer is made to all shareholders) purchases of less than 15% of the issued share capital pursuant to a general authority should be at a price which does not exceed the higher of:

a) 5% above the average market value of the company's shares for the five business days before the purchase is made; and

b) the higher of the price of the last independent trade and the highest current independent bid on the market where the purchase is carried out.

2.3.2 Members discourage share buybacks that are done off-market unless there is transparency on terms and pricing.

2.4 Dealings by Companies in Derivatives over their Own Shares

2.4.1 Investors are concerned about unusual structures and transactions that relate to returns of capital where there might be unusual risks.

a) The boards of companies contemplating returns of capital through contingent dealings in their own shares, or in derivatives referenced to their shares, should explain these clearly to shareholders and demonstrate the expected benefits to, and safeguards for, shareholders.

b) Prior authority for any such dealings should be sought and approved via a specific special resolution and the amount should be counted within the general authority limit.

c) Companies should report in due course on the effectiveness and benefits of any such dealings in their next Annual Report.

3 Scrip Dividends

3.1.1 Investment Association members are concerned about the dilutive effects of scrip dividend issues. Consequently, they normally prefer that shares offered in lieu of dividends are sourced from shares purchased in the market (Dividend Reinvestment Plans or "DRIPs"), rather than primary issuance.

3.1.2 However, in some circumstances, shareholders may be offered an option of taking newly issued shares in lieu of a dividend.

3.1.3 Any authority to offer a scrip dividend using new shares should be renewed at least every three years.

3.1.4 Shares to the value of the cash dividend forgone should be allocated at the average of the middle market quotations on the London Stock Exchange, as derived from the Daily Official List, for the five business days beginning on the ex-dividend date.

3.1.5 Arrangements whereby a scrip dividend offer is cancelled are only acceptable if a clear rationale and explanation to shareholders is provided.

4 Issuance of Shares by Investment Trusts

4.1.1 New shares should not be issued below net asset value (NAV).

4.1.2 Treasury shares should only be re-issued at a discount which is lower than the weighted average discount at which all shares held in Treasury have been repurchased.

4.1.3 Boards should always explain why they believe it is in the interest of shareholders to hold shares in Treasury for potential re-issue at a discount rather than to cancel them at the time of re-purchase.

Last Updated: July 2016

Enquiries to:
IVIS Team
ivis@theinvestmentassociation.org
020 7831 0898

APPENDIX 3

Pre-emption Group: Disapplying Pre-emption Rights: A Statement of Principles 2022

DISAPPLYING PRE-EMPTION RIGHTS

A STATEMENT OF PRINCIPLES

2022

OVERARCHING PRINCIPLES

1 Pre-emption rights are a cornerstone of UK company law and provide shareholders with protection against inappropriate dilution of their investments. They are enshrined in law by the Companies Act 2006, which provides that they may be disapplied by a special resolution of shareholders at a general meeting of the company.

2 In addition to the statutory pre-emption provisions applying to UK incorporated companies, a company with a premium listing on the Official List of the Financial Conduct Authority that is incorporated outside the UK is required by the UK Listing Rules to ensure that its constitution provides for rights of pre-emption for shareholders that are at least equivalent to those statutory rights that apply to UK incorporated companies.

3 Whilst not undermining the importance of pre-emption rights, a degree of flexibility is appropriate in circumstances where issuance of equity securities on a non-pre-emptive basis would be in the interests of companies and their owners.

4 The principles set out in this paper aim to provide clarity on the circumstances in which such flexibility might be appropriate and the factors to be taken into account:

when companies propose, and when shareholders consider, a general disapplication of pre-emption rights (as defined in Part 2A);

when companies consider making use of a general disapplication of pre-emption rights to issue equity securities non-pre-emptively; and

when companies propose, and when shareholders consider, a specific disapplication of pre-emption rights (as defined in Part 3).

5 Companies, investors and voting advisory services all have an important role to play in ensuring the effective and flexible application of this guidance.

- Companies should, where possible, signal an intention to undertake a non-pre-emptive issue at the earliest opportunity and to establish a dialogue with the company's shareholders. They should also keep shareholders informed of issues related to an application to disapply their pre-emption rights.
- Shareholders should, where possible, engage with companies to help them understand the specific factors that might inform their view on a proposed disapplication of pre-emption rights by the company. They should review the case made by a company on its merits and decide on each case individually using their usual investment criteria.

Pre-Emption Group

- Where a shareholder intends to abstain on or vote against a resolution to disapply pre-emption rights, it is best practice to explain to the company in advance the reasons for the decision.
- While companies should, where possible, consult their main shareholders in a timely manner, advisory services should also be prepared to receive representations from companies. In such circumstances the advisory services should explain any recommendations made in light of the reasons provided. This should involve setting out the pros and cons of the proposal so that the ultimate decision maker can take an informed view.

6 The Pre-Emption Group will, on an annual basis, monitor the development of practice in relation to disapplying pre-emption rights and the issuance of equity securities pursuant to such disapplications. It expects that this Statement of Principles will inform the way in which all interested parties participate in this process. The Pre-Emption Group will not express a view on or otherwise intervene in specific cases.

7 These principles are supported by the Pensions and Lifetime Savings Association and the Investment Association as representatives of owners and investment managers.

Pre-Emption Group

PART 1: APPLICATION OF THE PRINCIPLES

1 The principles set out here relate to issues of equity securities for cash other than on a pre-emptive basis (i.e. other than pro rata to existing shareholders) by all companies (wherever incorporated) with shares admitted to the Premium Listing segment of the Official List of the Financial Conduct Authority and to trading on the Main Market for listed securities of the London Stock Exchange. Companies with shares admitted to the Standard Listing segment of the Official List of the Financial Conduct Authority, to the High Growth segment of the Main Market of the London Stock Exchange, or to trading on AIM, are also encouraged to adopt these principles.

2 The principles apply to all issues of equity securities that are undertaken to raise cash for the issuer or its subsidiaries, irrespective of the legal form of the transaction. For example, a "cashbox" transaction may be structured as an issuance of equity securities for non-cash consideration falling outside the scope of statutory pre-emption.[1] Nonetheless, such a transaction should be regarded, for the purposes of these principles, as being an issuance of equity securities for cash subject to the limits herein.

3 A "vendor placing" is to be distinguished from a "cashbox" transaction for the purposes of these principles.[2] A "vendor placing" is outside the scope of the principles set out in Parts 2A, 2B and 3, but shareholders will nonetheless expect a right of clawback in respect of any vendor placing that represents greater than 10% of ordinary share capital or that is undertaken at a discount[3] of greater than 5%.

4 For the purposes of these principles:

- the sale of treasury shares for cash by a company should be regarded as equivalent to an issuance of new shares by that company; and
- shares held by a company in treasury should not be regarded as forming part of the issued share capital of that company.

5 Companies that do not comply with these principles are likely to find that their shareholders are less inclined to approve subsequent requests for a general disapplication. This applies to compliance with both the letter of these principles (for example, the percentage limits on dilution and discount) and their spirit (for example, the determination as to whether the use of proceeds of a non-pre-emptive issuance of equity securities falls within the meaning of "specified capital investment").

[1] A "cash box" structure refers to a method of raising cash from the issue of equity securities for non-cash consideration through the acquisition of a special purpose vehicle whose principal asset is cash.
[2] A vendor placing is a marketing of equity securities that is allotted non-pre-emptively in consideration of the transfer to the issuer or its subsidiaries of a business or asset (other than a company whose principal asset is cash).
[3] Definition of discount in Appendix.

Pre-Emption Group

PART 2A: REQUESTING A GENERAL DISAPPLICATION OF PRE-EMPTION RIGHTS

1 A general disapplication of pre-emption rights is one sought by a company at an Annual General Meeting[4] other than for the purpose of an identified, proposed issuance of equity securities.

2 A request for a general disapplication is likely to be supported where it meets the criteria as to size and duration set out in paragraphs 3 and 4 of this Part 2A. While the fact that a request meets those criteria does not reduce the importance of effective dialogue and timely notification, such a request is less likely to need in-depth discussion and shareholders will be more inclined in principle to support it.

3 Size criteria - the company may seek authority by special resolution to issue non-pre-emptively for cash equity securities representing:

- no more than 10% of issued ordinary share capital in any one year, whether or not in connection with an acquisition or specified capital investment[5] (with a further authority of no more than 2% to be used only for the purposes of making a follow-on offer of a kind contemplated by paragraph 3 of Section 2B below); and
- no more than an additional 10% of issued ordinary share capital provided that, in the circular for the Annual General Meeting at which such additional authority is to be sought, the company confirms that it intends to use it only in connection with an acquisition or a specified capital investment which is announced contemporaneously with the issue, or which has taken place in the preceding 12 month period and is disclosed in the announcement of the issue (with a further authority for no more than 2% to be used only for the purposes of making a follow-on offer of a kind contemplated by paragraph 3 of Section 2B below).

4 Companies that need to raise larger amounts of capital more frequently ('capital hungry companies') may seek additional disapplication authority, for use whether or not in connection with an acquisition or specified capital investment, if the reason for exceeding the level set out above is specifically highlighted at the time at which the request for a general disapplication is made.

Companies seeking admission to the Official List of the Financial Conduct Authority that wish to be considered a 'capital hungry company' for these purposes and to make use of this approach should disclose that fact in their IPO prospectus. Such companies may choose to put in place a disapplication on this basis prior to IPO, with clear disclosure given to investors in the IPO prospectus.

5 Duration criteria - the disapplication of pre-emption rights should last no more than 15 months or until the next Annual General Meeting, whichever is the shorter period.

Capital hungry companies may seek disapplication authority for a longer period if the reason for the longer period is specifically highlighted at the time at which the request for a general disapplication is made (or, where relevant, disclosed in the issuer's IPO prospectus). Capital hungry companies seeking admission to the Official List of the Financial Conduct Authority may choose to put in place a disapplication on this basis prior to IPO, with clear disclosure given to investors in the IPO prospectus.

---

[4] Or at a general meeting other than an Annual General Meeting, where that general meeting is convened to consider a proposed transaction that will alter the company's share capital in a way that means it is appropriate to refresh the disapplication, provided that a general disapplication was granted by shareholders at the preceding Annual General Meeting.
[5] Definition in Appendix.

Pre-Emption Group

6 Proposals for approvals above the levels set out in paragraph 3 above should be considered by shareholders on a case-by-case basis and the considerations set out in Part 3 in the context of specific disapplications will be relevant. Shareholders will generally not support such a request without a sufficiently strong business case. Thus, a request for a general disapplication of pre-emption rights by a company that is not a growth company in excess of the size criteria set out in paragraph 3 above should be made only when the company is in a position to justify this approach by providing relevant information. Where this is not possible, a general meeting should instead be convened at the time an identified, proposed issuance is contemplated.

Pre-Emption Group

PART 2B: ISSUING EQUITY SECURITIES PURSUANT TO A GENERAL DISAPPLICATION

1 A company issuing equity securities non-pre-emptively for cash pursuant to a general disapplication of pre-emption rights should:

- prior to announcement of the issue, consult with its major shareholders to the extent reasonably practicable and permitted by law;
- give due consideration to the involvement, in the placing and / or in a follow-on issue as described in paragraph 3 of this Part 2B, of retail investors and existing investors not allocated shares as part of the soft pre-emptive process referred to below ;
- provide an explanation of the background to and reasons for the offer and the proposed use of proceeds, including details of any acquisition or specified capital investment;
- as far as practicable, make the issue on a soft pre-emptive basis;
- involve company management in the process of allocating the shares issued; and
- after completion of the issue, make a post-transaction report as described in paragraph 10 of this Part 2B.

2 A company issuing equity securities non-pre-emptively for cash pursuant to a general disapplication of pre-emption rights should give due consideration to whether retail investors and existing investors not allocated shares as part of the soft pre-emptive process should be enabled to take part in the placing. Where this is proportionate in the context of the issue, it may be appropriate to include retail investors through a retail investor platform; alternatively, or in addition, the issuer may choose to make a follow-on offer as described in paragraph 3 of this Part 2B. Details of how due consideration was given to the interests of retail investors and existing investors not allocated shares as part of the soft pre-emptive process should be included in the post-transaction report.

3 The expected features of any follow-on offer are set out below:

- **Qualifying shareholders:** The offer should be made to shareholders as at a record date prior to announcement of the placing, excluding any shareholder allocated shares in that placing. The company may exclude from the offer shareholders resident in jurisdictions where onerous requirements would otherwise apply, and may include holders of other equity securities where the directors consider it necessary or appropriate to do so.
- **Individual monetary cap:** Qualifying shareholders should be entitled to subscribe for shares up to a monetary cap to be determined by the issuer of not more than £30,000 per ultimate beneficial owner. The company should be able to make any arrangements which its directors consider necessary or appropriate to deal with fractional entitlements.
- **Size:** The number of shares issued in any follow-on offer should not exceed 20% of those issued in the placing. The offer may be made for 'up to' a specified number of shares, with fewer shares issued if applications are not received.
- **Price:** The issue price of shares in any follow-on offer should be equal to, or less than, the offer price in the placing.
- **Timing:** The company should announce any follow-on offer when, or as soon as reasonably practicable after, it announces the placing. In determining when to launch

Pre-Emption Group

any follow-on offer the company should ensure that both the price requirement above and the discount limit in LR 9.5.10R can be met.

- **Offer period:** The company should ensure that any follow-on offer is open for a period sufficient to allow qualifying shareholders to become aware of the offer and to reach an investment decision.

4 Other than in the case of instruments, such as contingent convertible bonds, issued by financial institutions for regulatory capital purposes, the initial conversion price of an instrument convertible into shares issued non-pre-emptively pursuant to a general disapplication of pre-emption rights should not be lower than the market price of the underlying shares at pricing of the instrument.

5 An issuance of equity securities may contain both a pre-emptive and non-pre-emptive element (a "combination issue"). The non-pre-emptive element of a combination issue should either fall within the criteria specified in this Part 2B or should be approved by a specific disapplication by special resolution. This includes a combination issue comprising a placing of equity securities with a partial clawback offer to existing shareholders, where only the firm element that is not subject to clawback need comply with these principles. Further, in the case of a combination issue where there is a substantial clawback element, provided that the firm element is priced at no greater discount than the element that is subject to clawback, that firm element need not comply with the 5% discount limit specified in paragraph 6 of this Part 2B.

6 When issuing equity securities non-pre-emptively, companies should aim to ensure that they are raising capital on the best possible terms in order to avoid unnecessary dilution of existing shareholders. This is particularly the case where the proposed issue is made in circumstances where the share price may reasonably be expected to rise as a result of the proposed equity issue, any related transaction or any other contemporaneous transaction or matter of which the directors are aware. Any discount[6] at which equity is issued for cash will be of concern, but companies should, other than in exceptional circumstances, seek to restrict the discount to a maximum of 5%, including expenses as set out in the Appendix to these guidelines. Companies will be expected to disclose any discount at which equity is issued in the announcement of the pricing of the relevant issue as well as in the post-transaction report described in paragraph 10 of this Part 2B. Companies' attention is drawn to the guidance on calculation of discounts for these purposes in the Appendix to these guidelines.

7 In the case of an investment trust or similar listed closed ended fund company, if there would be no resulting value dilution, for example if an investment trust were to issue shares at a premium to the underlying net asset value per share,[7] this would not normally raise any concerns.

8 Companies should also have regard to any adverse impact on the share price of any earlier announcement, which may create the potential for a significant loss or transfer of value, in deciding whether to proceed with an issue in such circumstances.

---

[6] Definition of discount in Appendix.

[7] In relation to premium listed investment trusts, shareholders note the protection from dilution afforded by Listing Rule 15.4.11 in this regard.

Pre-Emption Group

9 Companies sometimes find it desirable to seek a "backstop" underwriting commitment prior to carrying out a bookbuilt equity issue, particularly in the context of acquisition financing. It may be impossible or uneconomic for a company to procure a backstop underwriting commitment at a discount of less than 5%. Provided that it is not expected at execution of the underwriting agreement that the underwriter(s) will acquire equity securities pursuant to its commitment, an underwriting at a discount of greater than 5% will not typically be regarded as problematic from the perspective of these principles.

10 A company issuing equity securities non pre-emptively for cash pursuant to a general disapplication of pre-emption rights should make a post-transaction report in the format set out below within one week of completion of the issue. The report should be publicly announced through a regulatory information service and submitted to the Pre-Emption Group for inclusion in its Pre-Emption Database.

Name of issuer	
Transaction details	*To include:* • *offer size, including the percentage of issued share capital that it represents; and* • *settlement date*
Use of proceeds	*Use of proceeds of the offer, including details of any acquisition or specified capital investment*
Quantum of proceeds	*To include details of the gross proceeds and net proceeds raised by the offer*
Discount	*Discount issue price represented to market price*
Allocations	*To include:* • *whether the shares were allocated on a soft pre-emptive basis,* • *details of any allocations made other than on a soft pre-emptive basis; and* • *the role played by management in the allocation process*

Pre-Emption Group

Consultation	*Confirmation of appropriate consultation of major shareholders carried out prior to launch, to extent reasonably practicable and permitted by law*
Retail investors	*How due consideration was given to the interests and involvement of retail investors and existing investors not allocated shares as part of the soft pre-emptive process and an explanation of the approach taken*

11 The next annual report published by a company following a non-pre-emptive issue of equity securities pursuant to a general disapplication of pre-emption rights should also include the information included in the post-transaction report published in the week following the issue.

Pre-Emption Group

PART 3: REQUESTING A SPECIFIC DISAPPLICATION OF PRE-EMPTION RIGHTS

1 A specific disapplication of pre-emption rights is one sought by a company for the purpose of an identified, proposed issuance of equity securities. It is neither possible nor desirable to define all the circumstances in which shareholders might be willing to agree to such a proposed disapplication of pre-emption rights. Such proposals should be considered by shareholders on a case-by-case basis.

2 It is particularly important that there is early and effective dialogue between the company and its shareholders, and that the company is able to communicate to shareholders the information they need in order to reach an informed decision. Set out below is a (non-exhaustive) list of some general considerations that, in the majority of cases, are likely to be critical to shareholders' voting decisions in response to a request for a specific disapplication of pre-emption rights.

- **The strength of the business case.** In order to make a reasoned assessment shareholders need to receive a clear explanation of the purpose to which the capital raised will be put, the benefits to be gained and how the financing or proposed future financing fits in with the life-cycle and financial needs of the company.
- **The size and stage of development of the company and the sector within which it operates.** Different companies have different financing needs. For example, shareholders might be expected to be more sympathetic to a request from a small company with high growth potential than one from a larger, more established company.
- **The stewardship and governance of the company.** If the company has a track record of generating shareholder value, clear planning and good communications, this may give shareholders additional confidence in its judgement.
- **Financing options.** A wide variety of financing options are available to companies. Companies should explain why a non-pre-emptive issue of equity securities is the most appropriate means of raising capital, and why other financing methods have been rejected.
- **The level of dilution of value and control for existing shareholders.** Companies should aim to ensure that they are raising capital on the best possible terms in order to avoid unnecessary dilution of existing shareholders, particularly where the proposed issue is in the context of a possible rise in the share price. Any discount at which equity is issued for cash other than to existing shareholders will be a concern.
- **The proposed process following approval.** Companies should make clear the process they would follow if approval for a non-pre-emptive issue were to be granted, for example how dialogue with shareholders would be carried out in the period leading up to the announcement of an issue.
- **Contingency plans.** Companies should explain what contingency plans they have in place in case the request is not granted, and the implications of such a decision.

3 Companies should, where possible, signal the possibility of their intention to request a specific disapplication of pre-emption rights at the earliest opportunity. In some cases it may be appropriate for companies to consult a small number of major shareholders before making any announcement. Companies and shareholders should be mindful of the possible legal and regulatory issues in doing this.

Pre-Emption Group

CONTACT DETAILS

More details of the Pre-Emption Group and its activities can be found at:

www.pre-emptiongroup.org.uk

To contact the Pre-Emption Group please e-mail:

secretary@pre-emptiongroup.org.uk

or write to:

David Styles
Secretary, Pre-Emption Group
Financial Reporting Council
8th Floor
125 London Wall
London EC2Y 5AS

Pre-Emption Group

APPENDIX

DEFINITIONS

Acquisitions and Specified Capital Investments

The greater freedom to execute non-pre-emptive issues of equity securities in connection with an acquisition or specified capital investment pursuant to paragraph 3 of Part 2A is intended to allow companies the opportunity to finance expansion opportunities as and when they arise.

In the context of paragraph 3 of Part 2A, specified capital investment means one or more specific capital investment related uses for the proceeds of an issuance of equity securities, in respect of which sufficient information regarding the effect of the transaction on the listed company, the assets the subject of the transaction and (where appropriate) the profits attributable to them is made available to shareholders to enable them to reach an assessment of the potential return.

Items that are regarded as operating expenditure rather than capital expenditure will not typically be regarded as falling within the term “specified capital investment”. In situations where there is doubt as to whether the use of proceeds of a particular issuance falls within the meaning of the term “specified capital investment”, companies should, where possible, consult with their main shareholders in advance of agreeing to undertake the issuance.

While it is acknowledged that companies may occasionally raise equity finance in good faith for the purpose of a specific, identified acquisition or capital investment that subsequently fails to materialise for reasons outside the company’s control, the issuance of equity securities representing in excess of 10% of issued share capital in any one year in order to build a “war chest”, i.e. to fund unspecified or speculative opportunities, will be regarded as contrary to these principles.

Clawback

Clawback, as it is referred to in paragraph 5 of Part 2B, is the right of existing shareholders to subscribe for their pro rata share of an issue at the offer price. This differs from a full rights entitlement, since it is non-renounceable and therefore does not permit the shareholder to sell this entitlement to another investor.

Discounts

In general terms, the "discount" (paragraphs 5 to 11 of Part 2B and paragraph 2 of Part 3) is defined as the aggregate of:

(a) the amount by which the offering price differs from the market price, and

(b) expenses directly attributable to the making of the issue (including, without limitation, underwriting commissions, sub-underwriting fees, brokerage fees, corporate finance fees, performance or incentive fees, professional advisers’ fees and roadshow and other marketing costs, in each case to the extent borne by the company).

Where any item of expense is unknown at the time of an issuance of equity securities, the company shall include a reasonable estimate of the relevant item for the purpose of calculating and disclosing discount. Where the amount of any performance or incentive fee is undetermined at the time of an issuance of equity securities, for the purpose of calculating and disclosing discount, the company should assume that the maximum amount will be paid.

The reference market price for the calculation of discount will depend on the manner in which an issue of equity securities is executed.

Pre-Emption Group

- In the case of an equity issue priced during London market hours, the middle market, on-screen, intra-day quotation at the time the company agrees the issue price is likely to be the most appropriate benchmark for measuring discount.
- In the case of an equity issue priced outside London market hours, the middle market quotation derived from the latest available daily official list of the London Stock Exchange (SEDOL) is likely to be the most appropriate benchmark for measuring discount.
- In the case of an equity issue priced outside London market hours by a company with shares or depositary receipts also admitted to trading on a market outside London, provided liquidity in that market is sufficient, it may be appropriate to use an on-screen, intra-day, middle market quotation from that market at the time the company agrees the issue price as a benchmark for measuring discount.

In each case, the reference market price and the time at which it was calculated should be stated in pricing announcements.

APPENDIX 4

Websites

The following websites are referred to in this book:

BBC News	www.bbc.co.uk/news
The Chartered Governance Institute UK and Ireland	www.cgi.org.uk
City of London Law Society	www.citysolicitors.org
Competition and Markets Authority	www.gov.uk/government/organisations/competition-and-markets-authority
DBT	www.gov.uk/government/organisations/department-for-business-and-trade
Euroclear UK & Ireland	www.euroclear.com
European Commission	www.ec.europa.eu/index_en.htm
European Securities Markets Authority (ESMA)	www.esma.europa.eu
FCA	www.fca.org.uk
FCA Handbook	www.handbook.fca.org.uk
Financial Reporting Council	www.frc.org.uk
Hermes	www.hermes-investment.com
Institutional Voting Information Service	www.ivis.co.uk
London Stock Exchange	www.londonstockexchange.com
National Storage Mechanism (NSM)	www.fca.org.uk
Quoted Companies Alliance	www.theqca.com
Sky News	news.sky.com
Takeover Appeal Board	www.thetakeoverappealboard.org.uk
Takeover Panel	www.thetakeoverpanel.org.uk

The following websites may also be of interest:

ABI	www.abi.org.uk
CBI	www.cbi.org.uk
Companies House	www.companieshouse.gov.uk
European Union	www.europa.eu
HM Treasury	www.gov.uk/government/organisations/hm-treasury
Institute of Directors	www.iod.com
Investment Association	www.theia.org
NASDAQ	www.nasdaq.com
New York Stock Exchange	www.nyse.com

PIRC	www.pirc.co.uk
PLSA	www.plsa.co.uk
RNS (Regulatory News Service)	www.londonstockexchange.com

Bibliography

The Prospectus Regulation Rules, the UK Listing Rules and the Disclosure Guidance and Transparency Rules (Financial Conduct Authority)

The City Code on Takeovers and Mergers (The Panel on Takeovers and Mergers)

Practical Law Company (online)

LexisLibrary (online)

Westlaw (online)

Index